PHILOSOPHY
OF RELIGION

Jones and Bartlett Series in Philosophy
Robert Ginsberg, General Editor

A. J. Ayer, 1994 reissue with new introduction
by Thomas Magnell, Drew University
Metaphysics and Common Sense

Francis J. Beckwith,
University of Nevada, Las Vegas, Editor
*Do the Right Thing: A Philosophical Dialogue
on the Moral and Social Issues of Our Time*

Anne H. Bishop and John R. Scudder, Jr.,
Lynchburg College
Nursing Ethics: Therapeutic Caring Pr esence

Peter Caws, The George Washington University
Ethics from Experience

Joseph P. DeMarco, Cleveland State University
Moral Theory: A Contemporar y Overview

Bernard Gert et al., Dartmouth College
Morality and the New Genetics

Michael Gorr, Illinois State University, and
Sterling Harwood, San Jose State University,
Editors
Crime and Punishment: Philosophic Explorations

Joram Graf Haber,
Bergen Community College, Interviewer
Ethics in the 90's, a 26-part Video Series

Sterling Harwood,
San Jose State University, Editor
*Business as Ethical and Business as Usual:
Text, Readings, and Cases*

John Heil, Davidson College
First Order Logic: A Concise Introduction

Gary Jason, San Diego State University
Introduction to Logic

Brendan Minogue, Youngstown State University
Bioethics: A Committee Approach

Marilyn Moriarty, Hollins College
Writing Science through Critical Thinking

Linus Pauling, and Ikeda Daisaku,
Richard L. Gage, Translator and Editor
A Lifelong Quest for Peace, A Dialogue

Louis P. Pojman,
The University of Mississippi, and
Francis Beckwith,
University of Nevada Las Vegas, Editors
The Abortion Controversy: A Reader

Louis P. Pojman,
The University of Mississippi
*Life and Death: Grappling with the
Moral Dilemmas of Our Time*

Louis P. Pojman,
The University of Mississippi, Editor
Life and Death: A Reader in Moral Pr oblems

Louis P. Pojman,
The University of Mississippi, Editor
*Environmental Ethics:
Readings in Theor y and Application*

Holmes Rolston III,
Colorado State University, Editor
Biology, Ethics, and the Origins of Life

Melville Stewart, Bethel College
*Philosophy of Religion: An Anthology of
Contemporary Views*

Dabney Townsend,
The University of Texas at Arlington, Editor
*Aesthetics: Classic Readings fr om the
Western Tradition*

Robert M. Veatch,
Georgetown University, Editor
Cross-Cultural Perspectives in Medical Ethics

Robert M. Veatch,
Georgetown University, Editor
Medical Ethics, Second Edition

D.P. Verene, Emory University, Editor
*Sexual Love and Western Morality, A Philo-
sophical Anthology, Second Edition*

PHILOSOPHY OF RELIGION

An Anthology of Contemporary Views

Melville Y. Stewart, Editor

Department of Philosophy
Bethel College
St. Paul, Minnesota

Jones and Bartlett Publishers
Sudbury, Massachusetts

Boston   London   Singapore

Editorial, Sales, and Customer Service Offices

Jones and Bartlett Publishers
40 Tall Pine Drive
Sudbury, MA 01776
508-443-5000
800-832-0034

Jones and Bartlett Publishers International
Barb House, Barb Mews
London W6 7PA
UK

Libary of Congress Cataloging-in-Publication Data

Philosophy of religion : an anthology of contemporary views / Melville
 Y. Stewart, editor.
        p.   cm. — (Jones and Bartlett series in philosophy)
     Includes bibliographical references and index.
     ISBN 0-86720-512-1
     1. Religion—Philosophy.   2. Christianity—Philosophy.
  I. Stewart, Melville Y.   II. Series.
BL51.P533   1996
210--dc20   96-3682
                                                                    CIP

Acquisitions Editors: Arthur C. Bartlett and Nancy E. Bartlett
Production Coordinator: Marilyn E. Rash
Senior Manufacturing Buyer: Dana L. Cerrito
Cover Design: Hannus Design Associates
Printing and Binding: Edwards Brothers, Inc.
Cover Printing: John P. Pow Company

Printed in the United States of America
00 99 98 97 96   10 9 8 7 6 5 4 3 2 1

In loving memory of my father and mother
Charles and Nellie Stewart

Table of Contents

Table of Illustrations

Preface

This volume is a collection of recent essays in philosophy of religion representing the analytic and continental traditions of the west. A total of thirty-five authors from varying Christian traditions, and several from the atheistic orientation have contributed a total of forty-two essays nearly half of which have not appeared in other anthologies. In many cases, the most recent essay by an author has been selected, but always with the purpose of giving central focus to the topic under inquiry. All of the standard topics in contemporary philosophy of religion are included.

The editor wishes to thank the authors and publishers of the essays for allowing me to include them in this collection, and for the many encouragements extended in process of putting this volume together.

Many thanks to Arthur and Nancy Bartlett, and other editorial staff at Jones and Bartlett, particularly to Marilyn Rash, Production Editor of Jones and Bartlett, for the many helpful suggestions that led to significant improvements in the overall appearance of the manuscript. From the very beginning the goal of the editor and publisher has been to produce a quality user-friendly introduction to contemporary philosophy of religion literature.

Marion Larson in the Department of Literature at Bethel College, was kind enough to read the Introduction and make recommendations in respect to style and literary form. Linda Zagzebski of Loyola Marymount University made helpful comments on the content of the Introduction. My colleague Paul Reasoner recommended that I include a section on religious pluralism.

The cover picture was supplied by the people at Hubble Telescope Laboratory in Maryland. The picture, which the *Minneapolis Star and Tribune* called, "Birthplace of the Stars," was taken April 1, 1995, of stars being formed in the Eagle Nebula, 7,000 light years away in the constellation Serpens. The pillar-like images are columns of gas and dust that gave birth to new stars. The picture was constructed from three images taken in the light from different kinds of atoms. The illustrative pictures that provide a pictorial introduction to some issue in each section, were provided by the Minneapolis Institute of Arts. Kristine Douglas, Coordinator, Reproductions and Permissions, helped in the selection and provided valuable counsel.

The anthology is a good match for most contemporary introductions to philosophy of religion, such as Oxford University's *Reason & Religious Belief*, by Michael Peterson, William Hasker, Bruce Reichenbach, and David Basinger, but more particularly for *An Introduction to Contemporary Philosophy of Religion* by Philip Quinn and Charles Taliaferro, because the latter's primary focus is contemporary.

There is a wide spectrum as to the degree of difficulty in the readings. Many can be used for an introductory course in philosophy of religion on the undergraduate level. But the following are included to challenge the more advanced student: "Modal Versions of the Ontological Argument," William Rowe; "Some Emendations of Gödels Ontological Proof," C. Anthony Anderson; "The Free Will Defense," Alvin Plantinga; "Middle Knowledge," William Hasker; "Bayes, Hume, and Miracles," John Earman. The latter essays are flagged by an asterisk in the Contents.

I am delighted that the manuscript has reached this final form. That is largely because of the generous support of Bethel College for providing secretarial staff to ensure deadlines were met. Special thanks are due to Janine McFarland who spent many hours typing the manuscript, notwithstanding a painful wrist condition, and to Jaci Prior who spent many hours to bring the project to its final form. Thanks too to Jennifer Juntunen for proof-reading so many pages.

Melville Y. Stewart
Bethel College

Introduction

Contemporary western philosophy divides into two traditions, the analytic and continental. The former is the dominant tradition in the English-speaking world. Both traditions are represented in contemporary philosophy of religion discussions, and their respective agendas are usually reflective of the tradition. Continental philosophers typically do not give much attention to arguments for the existence of God, but keen interest is taken in hermeneutics and religious experience. By contrast, analytic philosophers of religion have endlessly scrutinized arguments for God's existence, and concepts relating to religious beliefs. Debates have raged over the attributes of God, particularly the omni-attributes.

The collection contained in this volume has been arranged under main headings listed in most introductions to philosophy of religion courses in the west. Brief summaries are contextualized in order to provide a historical flow of ideas and arguments.

I. Faith and Reason

Perhaps the most pivotal issue that presses itself upon us as we begin our journey into the philosophy of religion domain is the problem of the relationship between faith and reason. It is variously couched as the relationship between faith and science, between the Church and the Academy, between Jerusalem and Athens. How we view other parts of the philosophy of religion puzzle and piece them together will, in significant measure, depend upon the way we formulate concepts relating to this topic and conclusions we draw. Quite predictably, the fideist will likely find little if any interest at all in arguments for the existence of God, however carefully and convincingly drawn. Those who craft word and argument in the analytic temper, however cogent, will likely leave fideists high and dry. But disdain for, even adamant opposition to the rival tradition and its achievements can also be found among those with an analytic bent.

Historically, four positions have been distinguished relative to the relationship between faith and reason. They include: (1) reason alone (religious rationalism, René Descartes); (2) faith alone (fideism, Søren Kierkegaard); (3) reason prior to faith (Thomas Aquinas); (4) faith as the precondition to knowledge (Augustine, Anselm). Yet a fifth position might be distinguished, which places no priority on either, but sees them as complements and as always belonging together. The focus of this first section is on contemporary discussions of the faith/reason issue— discussions which (1) work to bring reason closer to faith, (2) examine the fideism of Søren Kierkegaard, and (3) consider current editions of foundationalism and evidentialism.

We begin with the rationalist systematic theologian, Wolfhart Pannenberg and his selection from *Basic Questions in Theology*, partly because of his awareness of and interest in the interplay of reason and faith, and because his emphasis on many accounts justifies including him under the rationalist banner. Noteworthy is the fact that his account of reason is tempered by an awareness of the "absolute presuppositional nature of reason," and augmented by an effort to eschatologically contextualize it. Adding this dimension gives faith a directive role regarding the future from which reason derives a fuller value and meaning. Moreover, the future, to which faith is directed, makes faith and reason compatible not antithetic. For Pannenberg, faith assists reason by making reason fully "transparent to itself in its (reason's) reflections." His conclusion to the matter is, faith can find confirmation as "the criterion for the rationality of reason," by reason of its "orientation toward a final, eschatological future." From a compatibility of faith and reason, where the latter finds eschatological justification, we turn to its typically paired opposite, the incompatibilist fideism of Søren Kierkegaard.

The selection of essays on Kierkegaard includes Robert Merrihew Adams' critical apprisal and two favorable readings. The first selection, by Robert Adams, offers a careful analysis of three arguments of Kierkegaard, the approximation argument, the postponement argument, and the passion argument. His conclusion in the rough is, Kierkegaard's position has "more logical structure than one might at first think," and this fact may make it more difficult for Kierkegaard to avoid objective justification than he imagined.

Marilyn Piety is concerned with Kierkegaard's views on the nature of human rationality in the context of the relation between "competing interpretations of existence." She contends that Kierkegaard's view of rationality has advantages over the more traditional dispassionate way of construing reason. Reason, she contends, is *not* "disinterested" and "dispassionate." Moreover, his account presents a fuller picture of reason because he sees it as "positive incorporation of what we essentially are, subjects situated in and passionately engaged with the flux which constitutes our temporal existence." His focus allows us to "justify the weight" we seem "compelled" by our nature to "attribute to our subjective experience."

The final essay on Kierkegaard is Stephen Evans' discussion of the relevance of historical evidence to Kierkegaard's position. He contends that there is no way of isolating the Christian faith from "the risks of historical criticism." Historical criticism is embodied in "faith-commitments," and this may open the door for Christians to argue that the historical beliefs "that are part of their faith are reasonable enough when viewed in the right context," that is, the context of a faith that is grounded in a "first-hand encounter with Jesus Christ."

Three essays focus on foundationalism and evidentialism. Alvin Plantinga has captured center stage in epistemology with his recent two-volume work on warrant. His Reformed epistemology is fleshed out in terms of warrant rather than justification, and is taken in a non-deontological direction in "Justification and Theism." Plantinga argues that from a theistic perspective, a belief has positive epistemic status just in case the human cognitive capacity that produced it is not dysfunctional, and the capacity in question operates in an appropriate environment.

Nicholas Wolterstorff raises the question, "Can Belief in God Be Rational if it Has No Foundations?" His central concern is with the evidentialist challenge to theistic belief, and more particularly whether the challenge itself is tenable. According to Wolterstorff, rationality only grants *prima facie* justification, and the lack of it leads only to *prima facie* "impermissibility." He examines the evidentialist challenge of John Locke in the course of his inquiry and finds his case unconvincing.

Philip Quinn takes a hard look at Plantinga's Reformed epistemology, and judges that he has failed to make good his claim that the modern foundationalist's criterion for proper basicality is self-referentially incoherent. He argues that if there are such things as properly basic beliefs, that such beliefs could probably seldom if ever serve as properly basic beliefs for contemporary theists who think critically and carefully about their religious beliefs and commitments.

The topic of faith and reason takes a different turn with Frederick Ferré's examination of the place of doubt regarding technology. Though such doubt may have its place, it need not lead to a "despair of all technology." He concludes, that "by combining Christian love with persistent Christian intelligence, it may be possible to look toward a modified technological future with chastened Christian hope."

II. Arguments for the Existence of God

Of all the questions facing the human species, none is more central or more urgently in need of an answer than the question, Does God exist? Are there convincing and cogent arguments? Is there such a thing as a proof for God's existence? If one were to conclude there were no valid arguments for God's existence, what does this entail? Arguments for God's existence are the stock and trade of natural theology. While some think it inappropriate to embark on this task for one reason or another, others have thought that they can establish his existence in such a way as to end all further dispute.

Those who see this effort as part of their craft do not agree as to which sorts of arguments are worth exploring. Aquinas thought that the ontological argument wasn't worth the effort, and Richard Swinburne agrees. Others, like Plantinga, have thought that they were close to finding a convincing form of it. Anselm of Canterbury devised at least one; some think that he has two or more variations on this line. The first is his non-modal version which runs roughly as follows:

Premise 1: God is that being than which nothing greater can be conceived.
Premise 2: We understand the meaning of the first premise.
Premise 3: We can distinguish between something existing in the mind alone, and something existing in the mind and reality.
Premise 4: That which exists in the mind and in reality also is greater than that which exists in the mind alone.
Premise 5: Assume that that than which nothing greater can be conceived exists in the mind alone

But then I can conceive of something that is greater than that than which nothing greater can be conceived, namely that which exists in the mind and in reality also, which is an absurdity.

Conclusion: Therefore, that than which nothing greater can be conceived exists not only in the mind but in reality also. Therefore, God exists.

The argument is ontological because it begins with a premise that defines the nature of the being of God as "that than which nothing greater can be conceived." That also makes it *a priori*. Scholars have contended that Anselm has another version which has a modal twist. The hypothesis involves the assumption that that than which nothing greater can be conceived, exists only contingently. The hypothesis in question is reduced to an absurdity by a procedure similar to the one employed in the former version, by the move, that one can conceive of a greater than that than which nothing greater can be conceived, namely, a being which exists necessarily, which is greater than a being which exists only contingently. Therefore, that being than which nothing greater can be conceived, doesn't exist contingently, but necessarily.

About five hundred years later, René Descartes gives the argument a new twist; existence is viewed as a predicate thus,

Premise 1: God has all perfections.
Premise 2: Existence is a perfection.
Conclusion: Therefore, God exists.

Various objections have been raised, some of which have been answered, others, at least some judge, have never been resolved. Plantinga has fashioned a modal version in his, *The Nature of Necessity,* and others have tried their hand at it. The first paper by William Rowe critically examines Anselm's, Plantinga's, and Gödel's modal versions of the argument. While Rowe acknowledges that Plantinga might have shown the argument doesn't contain "grossly fallacious reasoning" or an "obviously false premise," he contends that it is very difficult to establish the truth of the premises.

C. Anthony Anderson, in "Some Emendations of Gödel's Ontological Proof," revises Gödel's proof so as to make it immune to an objection raised by J. Howard Sobel, that the axioms invoked lead to "modal collapse," because "it follows from them (the axioms) that every proposition which is true at all is necessary." He is satisfied with having rescued at least the essentials of Gödel's proof.

Aquinas and Swinburne and others judge that the ontological argument is a misguided effort right from the start, and so isn't worth pursuing. Attention is given instead to the *a posteriori* arguments, beginning with the cosmological proof. An oversimplified version of it runs as follows:

Premise 1: Everything has a cause.
Premise 2: Everything that has a cause has an ultimate cause.
Conclusion: The ultimate cause exists, and that is what we mean by God.

The argument has three variant forms in the writings of Thomas Aquinas, in his famous "Five Ways," the cosmological-causal argument, the cosmological-motion argument, and the cosmological-contingency argument. Our first reading is by William Rowe, "An Examination of the Cosmological Argument."

The argument is divided into two stages, that which attempts to prove the existence of a self-existent being, and that which seeks to prove that the self-existent being is the God of Christian theism. After he introduces the principle of sufficient reason (the idea that there must be an explanation of the existence of any being or of any positive fact), he then examines four objections to the argument. He concludes that the argument doesn't succeed because the first stage doesn't go through.

Richard Swinburne examines eight objections to the argument from design found in David Hume's *Enquiry* and *The Dialogues*, and finds none of them make the argument dysfunctional. For him, the force of the argument pivots on the central analogy drawn between the order produced by humans and the order of the Universe.

Three essays on religious experience are included: the first focuses on the argument from religious experience, the other two are at least indirectly related. Gary Gutting contends that his modified version of the argument from experience establishes the existence of a good and powerful being who is concerned about the creature, and this provides justification for the "central core of the belief." Thus he is convinced that he has established the validity of religious belief. But he acknowledges that we need more than this because we have only "minimal reliable accounts of his nature and relation to us," and so he develops three criteria in terms of which we can test the reliability of religious experience: "they must be repeatable; they must be experienced by man in diverse places and cultures; they must issue forth in morally better lives."

Merold Westphal gives religious experience a continental gloss. For him, religious experience is definable as "self-transcendence." For models of this self-transcendence, we are not to look at the transcendence of intentionality, or in "contemplative or ecstatic self-forgetfulness," because these leave the self at the center. While they have an important role in authentic religion, failure to transcend them is "self-deception and ultimately idolatrous." There is only one way for self-transcendence, and that is when one places limits on the will in the ethical and encounters the other. But "Even here the form of true religion may assist self-deception about the presence of its substance" in terms of "self-transcendence" and "self-deception." He contends that religious experience cannot "provide any evidence for truth as objectivity until it has passed the test of truth as subjectivity."

William Alston compares the epistemology of Christian religious experience with the epistemology of perceptual experience and shows that though the latter has more stringent requirements, there are good reasons for this difference. Whereas the criteria for valid perceptual experience include verifiability and predictability, God's being wholly other may preclude these criteria from applying to religious experience.

Two essays deal with the issue of the value and need for proofs. Stephen Davis offers a clarification as to what a proof is, and argues that though believers do not need to define proofs to support faith, there might be aspects of such an exercise that would be good for those who entertain belief in the existence of God to go through.

J. Wesley Robbins questions whether William Alston and Alvin Plantinga have "succeeded in showing that there is something unreasonable about the exclusion of certain theistic manifestation propositions from the class of propositions that do not need proof." His contention is they have failed. He introduces a contrast to show that the account that Plantinga and Alston give of the evidentialist objection to belief in God is not the only one available.

III. Problems of Evil and Strategies of Defense

According to Augustine, there are two basic problems relating to evil, its origin and its justification. Attention here is mainly on the latter, principally because much of the contemporary discussion focuses on the issue of justification, designed as a response to a charge initially presented in a paper written by J. L. Mackie, "Evil and Omnipotence." It is Mackie's contention that the theist faces a logical problem relating to beliefs pivotal to the Christian faith. Those beliefs include the following:

1. God exists.
2. God is omnipotent, omniscient, and omnibenevolent.
3. Evil exists.

Actually, the set of beliefs in question were not found to have this deficiency, but if another belief—he lists two that are equivalent to what is proposed in (4)—is added, namely,

4. The God described in (2) would not allow any evil.

then we have what he called a "logical problem;" that is, the beliefs in question are inconsistent. This inconsistency strategy has been challenged in various ways by different defenses which are really consistency strategies. That is, propositions A and B can be shown to be consistent, if they are logically compatible with another proposition, Q. Each of the defensive strategies are specifications of a Q such that A and B are viewed as compatible with Q. Keith Yandell, in "The Greater Good Defense," offers a "parent" defense, in terms of which God is viewed as allowing evil so that goods may result. Simply expressed, the Q for Yandell is the greater good defense. That is, an omniscient, omnipotent and omnibenevolent God is viewed as allowing evil for a greater good.

John Hick, in his earlier work, *Evil and the God of Love,* formulates the classic account of the soul-making defense, which accounts for evil on the ground that souls are thereby enhanced and experience spiritual and moral growth. For Hick, the Q is the greater good of soul-making.

Alvin Plantinga takes the free will defense of Augustine and gives it new life in terms of possible worlds and transworld depravity. He contends that there is no logical inconsistency because the modal free will defense shows that the possibility of evil is compatible with the existence of an omniscient, omnipotent and omnibenevolent God. The free will defense specification is Plantinga's Q.

Yet another defensive line is taken by Louis Dupré relating to mystery. Dupré contends that modern efforts at theodicy are misguided because they work with a rationalist conception of God, a conception that on his account is alien to a living faith. In its place, he proposes a closer, more intimate relationship between the finite creature and infinite Being. On this model there is more autonomy and responsibility for the creature, and opportunities for the Creator to suffer and work redemptively in behalf of the creature.

Wearied, if not discouraged by the welter of consistency strategies of theists, atheists have turned instead to the probabilistic line. William Alston focuses on this strategy in terms of the human cognitive condition, and contributes to criticism of the argument "based on a low estimate of human cognitive capacities in a certain application." His focus is upon the formulation of the argument by William Rowe. He concludes that the inductive argument is "in no better shape than its lamented deductive cousin."

James Sennett offers a defense against William Rowe's inductive argument from evil, based on a contention that a key assumption in Rowe's argument—"that the goods we know of offer us good inductive grounds to make certain inferences about the goods there are—is not justified." His conclusion is that the sampling involved in Rowe's argument is not a "relevant inductive sample."

IV. The Attributes of God

I wonder if philosophers of religion have not given more attention to the attributes of God than theologians, at least in the contemporary period. Often the agenda has been set by discussions of the attributes relating to the problem of evil, namely, the omni-attributes of omnipotence, omniscience and omnibenevolence. Our readings are on the first two only, and the attribute of divine eternity.

Omnipotence has enlisted the interest of mathematicians and philosophers alike. How is omnipotence to be defined? Can God create a rock that he cannot lift? How one answers the latter question turns on whether God has the property in question necessarily or only contingently. In the reading by George Mavrodes, he applies the Thomistic view of God's omnipotence to the paradox of the stone, arguing that since the paradox entails doing something contradictory it can be resolved because the task is a "pseudo-task."

Peter Geach distinguishes the notion of "omnipotence" (the ability to do anything) from the notion of "almightiness" (God's power over all things) and argues that the latter is a Biblical concept but the former is not. He considers four versions of omnipotence and finds each deficient and suggests that almightiness is less problematic.

William Hasker, in this selection from his book, *God, Time and Knowledge*, examines the doctrine of middle knowledge as it was formulated in the sixteenth century and examines some of the arguments that were advanced. He then brings the reader up to date with Plantinga's account as it unfolds in his free will defense. Several objections are reviewed, one of which leads Hasker to reject the doctrine.

In the selection by William Alston on divine foreknowledge, he focuses on the "crucial distinction between a 'libertarian' and a 'compatibilist' understanding of terms like 'within one's power.'" He then goes on to argue that if we focus on efforts to "show that it is within no one's power to do other than one does," then it is important to take note of the variant ways of parsing 'within one's power,' and then it is going to be important to understand the sense the expression has in a given context.

In what has become the *locus classicus* in recent literature on the subject, Eleonore Stump's and Norman Kretzmann's "Eternity," defends a Boethian view of God's eternity. On this view, God's eternity transcends time in such a way that there are two different modes of existence: the divine order, with temporal categories such as "before" and "after," and where temporally indexed propositions cannot be paired up with correspondingly temporally indexed states of affairs, and the order of metricated time. They express their Boethianism this way: "there is no past or future, no earlier or later within its life; that is, the events constituting its life cannot be ordered sequentially from the standpoint of eternity. But in addition, no temporal entity or event can be earlier or later than or past or future with respect to the whole life of an eternal entity." Stump and Kretzmann analyze implications of their account, examine reasons for considering it incoherent, and sample the results of bringing it to bear on issues of philosophy of religion.

In the fifth chapter of his book, *God, Eternity, and the Nature of Time,* Alan Padgett develops and defends the doctrine of God's relative timelessness. He then anticipates objections and advances the view that God is the Lord of time

V. Miracles

A contemporary Humean adversary of theism, Michael Martin, in the seventh chapter of his book, *Atheism,* examines the argument from miracles to the existence of God. While he acknowledges that there are no *a priori* reasons for discounting miracles, he thinks that there are *a posteriori* obstacles that have to be removed before the theist can claim that miracles have taken place in either a straightforward sense or indirectly. Moreover, he argues that even if one were to grant that miracles occurred in a direct or indirect sense, this doesn't automatically mean that these occurrences count as inductive evidence for the truth of theism.

Four essays were selected on the affirmative side. Richard Swinburne vigorously takes issue with Hume in our selection. His first consideration is whether there could be evidence that a natural law had been violated. His second concern is whether one can establish that a violation of this sort is a result of divine agency. The condition of the first inquiry requires that "there be good reason to believe" that there is an exception to what we have reason to believe is a law of nature. We must also have reason to think that the event in question is not repeatable given the circumstances that obtained with the original event, or we would have to consider formulating a law.

He argues that in order for an exception to natural law to be miraculous, it would have to be the work of a divine agent. As for what kind of evidence one would need to believe that a divine being had intervened in our world, he says that would require "sufficient circumstantial evidence." On his account, answer to prayer would satisfy the necessary conditions.

Richard Purtill continues the critique of Hume begun by Swinburne, and argues that a two-stage case for miracles can be made: the first is an argument for the general possibilities of miracles, and the second is an argument for the actuality of miracles. Comparing the laws of nature to the laws of a nation, Purtill argues that a miracle is analogous to an exception to the law of the land—for example, President Ford's pardoning of Richard Nixon after Watergate.

Regarding the question of whether we have evidence that a miracle ever took place, Purtill looks at various reports of miracles and sets up limiting criteria—for example, (1) miracles must not be "fairy-tale" like, (2) "the miraculous (must be) interwoven with the primary story (of the religion);" (3) there must be independent evidence for the religion in question. Purtill then examines the miracles of Christ in the light of these criteria and concludes that it is very likely that the miracles in question are genuine. If we already have reason to believe in a God who is active in human affairs, we should expect miracles; but if we do not have such independent reason to believe in God, we will be far less likely to believe in divine interventions.

If one construes miracles as "violations," George Mavrodes argues that a law of nature must specify some kind of possibility. But we must have here a sense of possibility for which the ancient rule of logic—from being to possibility is a valid inference—does not hold. He draws upon statute law as a helpful example, and observes that such laws are not "destroyed by violation." By analogy, laws of nature specify what is "naturally possible," but they admit of exceptions without invalidating the laws in question; hence Humean miracles are a "genuine possibility."

In his article, "Bayes, Hume, and Miracles," John Earman critically analyzes recent Bayesian formulations of Hume's argument against miracles. The Bayesian analysis is viewed as clarifying the structure and substance of Hume's argument, but falls short of lending support to Hume's "various claims," one of which is no testimony could ever establish that a miracle had happened. Contrarywise, Earman contends that the analysis brings to light conditions under which one might reasonably reject "the more interesting of Hume's claims."

VI. Death and Immortality

All humans sooner or later in their journey in life come to grips with the inevitability of death. For most persons, if not for all, the question whether there is life after death is unavoidable. The ancient Greek philosopher, Plato, held that there is a soul, and that the soul is immortal because it cannot be destroyed. Some have seriously questioned whether the notion of life after death can make sense, and whether there is evidence for an afterlife. The Christian theistic hope extends beyond the notion of immortality to the idea that persons who follow the Christian message have hope in a resurrection.

Bertrand Russell outlines some of the major objections to the idea of life after death. He argues that it is not reasonable to believe that our personality and memories will survive the destruction of our bodies. He claims that the inclination to believe in immortality comes from emotional factors, notably the fear of death.

In defense of Christian theistic belief, Bruce Reichenbach in this selection from his book, *Is Man the Phoenix*, offers an analysis of dualism, the idea that persons are body and spirit, and concludes that there are no compelling arguments in support of this view. He opts instead for monism, and acknowledges that though survival is not possible at death, life after death is possible through a recreation of the person by God.

In the article, "The Possibility of Resurrection," Peter van Inwagen argues that the Christian doctrine of the resurrection of the body is possible. In a future life, we will be able to recognize each other because we will have the same bodies and because we will be able to communicate with each other. First, he argues against the notion of a reconstituted body, that God collects the atoms of a person's body at death and reassembles them in heaven—what he calls the "Aristotelian" view. He then sets forth a hypothesis that preserves essential bodily continuity.

In the selection taken from Richard Swinburne's book, *The Evolution of the Soul*, he argues that the soul "will function" only if it is connected with a functioning brain, otherwise not. But he holds out for the possibility that at some future time, an omnipotent God might "reassemble" the brain and thereby provide conditions for a reviving of the soul.

VII. Religious Pluralism

There are many rival religious options. Is any one set of religious beliefs of any one of the religious orientations true? Is there more truth in one religion than another? Might it be the case that there is only one way to God? If so, which religion is the right path? Are there objective criteria available by which a person can come to terms with these sorts of questions?

There are at least three models of religious pluralism: *exclusivism*, which claims that the core beliefs of a particular religion are true, and that salvation is unique to the religion in question. Many Christian theists, for example, have held the view that outside the church there is no salvation (*salus extra ecclesiam non est*).

The second is *inclusivism*, which is the view that no single core of religious beliefs are true, and salvation may be found in other religions.

The third model is *pluralism*, the view entertained by those in company with John Hick. They reject the idea that God uniquely revealed himself in one religion. Rather he has revealed himself equally in all religions.

Is there a way one can decide the matter? Is it possible that one religion more closely approximates the truth about God than any other? What sort of criteria might there be for arriving at truth in matters relating to religious belief, such that one might have some assurance that the religious orientation one is in is the true one?

John Hick wants to approach the problems of religious pluralism through the claims of the different traditions to offer salvation— generically, the transformation of human existence from self-centeredness to Reality-centeredness. He thinks that this approach will lead to a recognition of the great world religions as "spheres of salvation." The different truth claims, according to Hick, are merely different religious perceptions of "one ultimate divine Reality." There are recognizable differences on matters relating to "origin and destiny," but these are not important to salvation.

In his paper, "Plantinga, Pluralism and Justified Religious Belief," David Basinger takes Plantinga's"nonevidentialism" to be saying that neither formed beliefs nor one's "belief-forming mechanism" need the support of propositional evidence. However, in response to the competing options pluralism presents, Basinger urges that "the knowledgeable theist" will see the value of such evidence; nevertheless she will be able to hold "formed beliefs" as "properly basic."

In the final paper, "Thinking About Theocentric Christology," S. Mark Heim observes that Paul Knitter's book, *No Other Name?*, is a careful argument for the movement in contemporary theology toward "theocentric Christology." In such an approach, the focus shifts from Christ as the guide to God, to God as the key for theological interpretation of Christ. The "exclusivist" character of the Christian faith—its Christocentrism— can then be overcome, without diminishing its authenticity or power. He analyzes and critiques Knitter's exposition of theocentrism in Christology under two main headings. First, questions are raised about the coherence and meaning of "theocentrism" in theology. In particular, what are the character and provenance of that knowledge of God to which we may refer in relativizing other religious norms? Second, Knitter's argument that "theocentric Christology" has a solid basis in scripture and Christian tradition is examined and found to be convincing.

One prevailing objective of this anthology is that the readings included on the various topics will stimulate further discussion and that they will help promote dialogue among those of disparate religious orientations, so that ultimately, meaning and truth regarding religious belief might be advanced, with the hope that knowing the truth will make persons free.

PART I

FAITH AND REASON

1

Faith and Reason

Wolfhart Pannenberg
(Translator George H. Kehm)

Wolfhart Pannenberg is professor of systematic theology on the Protestant Faculty at the University of Munich and director of the Institute for Fundamental Theology and Ecumenics, and is author of: *Jesus—God and Man; Ethics; Basic Questions in Theology* (2 volumes); *The Apostles' Creed in the Light of Today's Questions; Theology and the Philosophy of Science; Anthropology in Theological Perspective.*

For Pannenberg, faith is directed toward that future from which reason derives. Faith is directed at this future, and because this future is not alien to reason, it cannot stand in opposition to reason. Rather, faith can assist reason by making reason fully transparent to itself in its reflections. Finally, faith can confirm itself as the criterion for the rationality of reason just by its orientation toward a final, eschatological future.

This is a lecture delivered before the theological faculty in Marburg on July 6, 1965, and in Hamburg on June 6, 1966. The introduction has been revised for publication. *

The relationship between faith and reason has been a problem since the beginning of Christian theology. On the one hand, theology is itself a process of thought, and one must hope that it is pursued in a rational manner. On the other hand, however, "reason," as commonly understood, can scarcely have the last word in theology without violating the exaltedness of the reality of God and his revelation above all human conceptualization. It was not by accident that the structure of the relationship between faith and reason in history has been charged with tensions. The Christian faith manifestly cannot withdraw from every kind of cooperation with rational thought. Some such cooperation is implied in the commissioning of the Christian message to all men, with the task of preaching the message convincingly as the truth which is universally binding. Yet, the Christian faith cannot thereby simply dissolve into what, in a variety of very different accentuations since the Greek beginning of our philosophical tradition, has at some given time been called "reason." Explicit reflection upon the togetherness and cooperation of faith and reason that takes place in all Christian thought must begin with the clarification of the tension that exists here. This point holds even if this relationship should be understood as a unity-in-tension [*Spannungseinheit*] and not as simply an opposition. Even someone who is concerned about the overarching unity of faith and reason will be unable to ignore the difference which is always breaking out anew between them, stemming from the duality of the spiritual roots not only of Christian theology but of our traditions generally insofar as they go back to Israel and Christianity, on the one hand, and Greek antiquity, on the other.

For Christians, the perfect unity of faith and reason has been promised for the eschaton only (I Cor. 13:12f.). Nevertheless, Christian eschatology does not mean simply that one should keep watch for a still-outstanding future and thereby become alienated from the present. On the contrary, the Christian understanding of the eschaton turns one's view back to the present, insofar as the present is also experienced as determined by the coming reign of God. In this sense, should not even the tension between the Greek and the Israelitic heritages belonging to our history which has been expressed again and again as the tension between faith and reason be considered in the light of their eschatological unity, so that this would be determinative for our thought already in the present? Is it perhaps the case that even the tension between faith and reason is possible only on the presupposition of a unity which encompasses both, namely, the presupposition of the unity of truth?

Concern about what it is that first makes possible a preliminary unity of faith and reason has a special urgency today. For the tension between faith and reason has sharpened into an opposition in the modern period and, despite all attempts to reconcile them, has finally snapped in many quarters and changed into a disconnected juxtaposition.

Harsh opposition between faith and reason had already appeared, of course, in the ancient and medieval churches. In the history of theology, Tertullian, Peter Damian, and Luther especially went down as opponents of reason. Nevertheless, all three made use of reason despite their sharp judgments upon reason and philosophy. The same Tertullian who asked what Athens had to do with Jerusalem, or the Academy with the church, and who wanted to affirm nothing that went beyond faith,[1] admitted Stoic thought into theology in a very risky way, for example, by conceiving God and the soul as special kinds of bodies.[2] Peter Damian, who damned philosophy as an invention of the devil, at the same used a dialectical-philosophical path to refute attacks on the omnipotence of

God, and formulated the principle that philosophy should serve theology as a maid.[3] Finally, Luther could certainly term reason a "monster," "the source of all evil," and "the blind whore of the Devil."[4] He never tired of stressing that the gospel is "against all reason." However, the same Luther not only esteemed reason as the highest court of appeal in the natural, worldly realm, but also affirmed the cooperation in the realm of theology of a reason illuminated by faith and the Holy Spirit. Lastly, at Worms, Luther appealed not only to Scripture but also to the clear evidence of reason [*ratio evidens*] as the judges of his case.[5]

The relative opposition of faith and reason which was occasionally—by no means predominantly—championed in the ancient and medieval churches, was marked by the tension between free, rational insight and obligation to an authoritative norm.

Wherein lies the real reason for the fact that Christian doctrine can never be transformed completely and without remainder into rational insights, but rather must always be assigned to the custody of an authoritative norm such as Scripture or the teaching office of the church? Augustine traced this state of affairs back to the fact that the genuine truths of faith deal with historical facts.[6] The ancients were convinced that there can be no science of the historical in the strict sense because science always deals with the universal, whereas historical accounts have to do with events which are always particular and occur only once. To the extent that historical knowledge does not rest upon eyewitness testimony or at least on interrogation of eyewitnesses, it is referred to the credibility, the authority, of a tradition. For this reason, then, genuine truths of faith cannot be fully transparent to reason, but must always be believed.[7] Thus, the reference of the Christian message to the historical and the necessity of belief on the basis of authority belong together, for Augustine. To be sure, this faith does not consist only in accepting what the authority says, but therein it takes the "step from the visible to the invisible, from the visible or verifiable authority of the witnesses, such as the church, to the invisible matter which the witnesses report."[8] Correspondingly, however, the eyewitnesses of the history of Christ must also have already made the step from the visible man to his invisible deity, and it is in this that faith consists. Luther placed the greatest emphasis on this aspect of the Augustinian concept of faith when he repeatedly stressed, appealing to Hebrews 2:1, that faith, in contrast to reason, is a certitude about that which man does not see. On this connection, Luther gives the phrase "what man does not see" the sense of "that which is future." "And while reason is wont to concern itself with the things that are present, faith apprehends the things that are not present and, contrary to reason, regards them as being present."[9] Luther, it is well known, set faith as trust in the invisible in sharp contrast to mere belief on the basis of authority, the *notitia historiae* ["historical knowledge"]. The two aspects of the Augustinian concept of faith separate here. However, this does not happen in such a way that Luther allows acceptance of the veracity of the history simply to be dropped as inconsequential. Therefore, he characteristically uses the formulation that one must look *not only* upon the history but also upon its "fruit."[10] This *"not only—but also"* [*non solum— sed etiam*] is often overlooked today when people appeal to Luther's criticisms of "historical faith." His criticism is by no means aimed at making the subjectivity of religious experience, in Wilhelm Herrmann's sense, or the existential decision of faith independent of belief on the basis of authority. On the contrary, Luther said: ". . . So it comes to the point that if one should forget that history [*illam historiam*], the foundation of faith would be done away with."[11] Thus, Luther argued for his stress on fruit, the significance of the history "for me," completely within the jurisdictional limits of belief on the basis of authority. For this reason, the opposition between faith and reason still remained for him, too, the foundation of statements about the relationship of faith and reason.

In the modern period, the situation with respect to the problem of the relationship of faith and reason has shifted because of the fact that the initiative has gone over to the side of reason. It is no longer a question of whether the authority of the Christian source of revelation, viz., Scripture, can be accepted by reason without contradiction. In the modern period the question is instead whether reason, after it has shown that belief on the basis of authority is irrational, can still allow any room at all for the Christian faith. A philosopher like Hume could put the Christian faith on record precisely for its (true or alleged) character as a belief based on authority precisely in order thereby to expose its absurdity. Thus, he states: "Our most holy religion is founded on faith, not on reason, and it is a sure method of exposing it to put it to such a trial as it is by no means fitted to endure,"[12] that is to say, by searching for rational grounds for its assertions. This reference to the irrationality of Christianity is pure derision, since Hume was convinced that Christianity is committed to the affirmation of miracles, the irrationality of which he had demonstrated. For him, therefore, faith is itself a continuing miracle in the person of the believer: "And whoever is moved by *faith* to assent to it, is conscious of a continued miracle in his own person, which subverts all the principles of his understanding, and gives him a determination to believe what is most contrary to custom and experience."[13]

In the face of this modern attack upon the meaningfulness of the Christian faith, theology cannot retreat to the standpoint of authority. The difference between the modern and the medieval situations consists in the fact that the authority of the Christian tradition (be it of the church and its dogmas, or of Holy Scripture) can scarcely be viewed any longer as unproblematically authoritative. As long as the mere authority of Scripture can guarantee the truth of its contents, theology can only demand that reason simply submit to it. In the realm of modern thought, however, where even historical questions are settled not by appeals to authorities but by the new science of historical criticism, persistence in maintaining the authoritative character of faith in contrast to reason takes on a new aspect. This insistence upon an authority that is no longer generally convincing as an authority takes on the character of an external coercion, and an individual's acceptance of such a claim becomes an arbitrary decision—quite the opposite of what it was earlier, when the acceptance of an authority was grounded in insight into its credibility.[14] If the authority is no longer intelligible as such, and if it no longer convinces our reason of its legitimacy, then all external maintenance of its claim is in vain. For in that case, no matter how much one may emphasize a prior authority, the believer turns himself into the ultimate ground of faith, as Hume incisively showed. For if an asserted authority is no longer able to prove itself convincing to our reason, then its acceptance can come about only by a sacrifice of the intellect and *ergo* as a work of man.

For this reason, the understanding of the kerygma has rightly been joined to faith. The obedience of faith in relation to the kerygma would be an illusory self-salvation by man if it were not motivated by understanding; if it did not mean being won over by the truth of the message. In any case, the question of the truth of the Christian message will not permit of being narrowed down to the theme of self-understanding, but must also be carried out in the realm of the understanding of the world, too, since self-understanding and understanding of the world are always correlative. Therefore the question of the truth of the Christian message involves not only ethical but also theoretical knowledge.

In the modern period, it is true, especially since Kant and Schleiermacher, the attempt has been made to overcome the hopeless opposition between authority and reason by contrasting theoretical reason with religious and ethical *experience*, instead of with an *authority* that had become unintelligible. The authority of the Christian doctrinal tradition was accepted only to the extent that it proved to be an expression of or was confirmed by religious and ethical experience. Nevertheless, the old opposition between reason and faith based on authority continued to exist. The decisive theme was the autonomy of religious experience—sometimes determined more as feeling, sometimes related more to conscience—over against theoretical reason. However, the assertion of the independence of religious and ethical experience from theoretical reason is problematical in the extreme, since religious and ethical contents are always mediated by theoretical consciousness. An independence here is at most only partial. In addition, this assertion locates the critical debate between faith and reason solely within the area of self-understanding. The universal validity of a special religious province within the human spirit is what needs to be proven. And beyond this, the peculiar appropriateness of Christian doctrine to this religious disposition must be shown if there is to be any basis for acknowledging the preeminence of

Christianity over other religions. If such proofs are not forthcoming, the appeal to experience can draw upon only the experience of the individual and thereby transform the Christian faith completely into a phenomenon of subjectivity, claiming no universal obligatoriness. So understood, however, the appeal to experience once again allows faith to become a work of self-salvation, or—judged externally—the expression of a neurosis, an "uneasiness toward culture." A religious subjectivity of such a sort has found a place in our society only because the understanding of man in positivistic science overlooks this aspect of man, and therefore leaves it vacant for occupation by subjective tastes which nevertheless remain without any universally binding power.

Thus, the task of a rational account of the truth of faith has acquired an ever more acute urgency in the modern period. The appeal to the authority of Scripture and to a proclamation grounded in this is no longer sufficient to establish the legitimacy of faith. And the appeal to religious-ethical experience or to the individual's decision, taken by themselves, can only lead to a subjectivism which is not only non-obligatory for one's fellow-men, but also destroys the essence of faith, since faith is not a work of man but remains faith only as a work of God in man.[15]

If, however, theology admits the necessity of rational accountability for the Christian faith, the problem we found formulated by Hume immediately arises: Is not modern reason so fashioned that it leaves absolutely no room for Christian faith other than a subjectivity which lacks any intersubjective binding force? Is not any attempt at a rational accounting of the Christian faith foredoomed to vain compromises?

The recent history of theology provides an abundance of material for such a pessimistic conjecture. However, instead of taking an inventory of the theological compromises that have been made with "the" modern reason and its understanding of the world, I want instead to ask whether there really is such a thing as "the" reason, which is so monolithic in form that theology can only be dashed to pieces against it. Are there really compelling reasons to concede to Hume and his positivistic followers the pathos of speaking in the name of "the" reason absolutely? Is it necessary to acknowledge as the *non plus ultra* of historical reason a certain kind of historical positivism that allows the uniqueness of events to be lost on the basis of a postulated homogeneity of all events? Theology could still have the task of inspecting more minutely such sorts of absolute claims put forth in the name of reason. Only in this way will it be possible to obtain a critical concept of reason and knowledge that will for the first time make it possible to give a rational account of the truth of the Christian message and thereby would itself already be a step on the way to such an account.

Upon closer inspection, "reason" is by no means a uniformly determined entity. For this reason, even the relationship between faith and reason has been presented in very different ways, each according to what has been understood as reason. Naturally, the same applies to the understanding of faith, too. We have already spoken about that. Regarding the ambiguity in the understanding of reason, I will limit myself to three typical forms. We will examine *a priori* reason; the so-called receiving reason [*vernehmende Vernunft*]; and historical reason.

(1) The reason [*ratio*] of which Luther spoke was the Aristotelian-Thomistic understanding of reason. Characteristic of this understanding of reason is the distinction between coordination of reason [*ratio*] and intellect [*intellectus*]. According to Thomas, reason and intellect are related to each other as movement and rest.[16] The intellect lives in serene contemplation of the truth. Reason, on the other hand, moves from one representation [*Vorstellung*] to another in its ranging about [*discursus*] in order to lay hold of the one truth that binds all truths together. The intellect does not need to engage in such discursive thought. It intuitively sees that which the reason can attain only as the result of its *discursus*.

According to Thomas, human knowledge is not yet of a perfectly intellectual sort. In contrast to angels, we are not able to have an unmediated view of the true essences of things. This is implied in the fact that the human soul is bound to the body so that all its knowledge must derive from sense impressions and not from immediate comprehension of the substance [*substantia*] of things. For this reason we need ratiocination [*ratiocinari*], discursive reasoning. But the process of ratiocination would not be possible without a firm starting point. This starting point is given in the fact that we at least possess general principles that are immediately evident. This "intuition of the principles" ["*intellectus principiorum*"] constitutes the point of departure for the activity of reason in theoretical knowing. The "practical" reason proceeds in a perfectly analogous way, its judgments likewise resting upon a knowledge of principles which, in this case, have their seat in the conscience. As the theoretical principles of the intellect are applied by the reason to sense impressions, so the practical principles of the *synderesis* are applied by the conscience to individual acts.[17]

We have here a form of aprioristic conception of reason, for all knowledge occurs as an application to the data of experience of principles already contained in the intellect. It could now be shown that this aprioristic understanding of reason goes back to Augustine and was formulated by him in contrast to Plato, as by Thomas in contrast to Aristotle, in order to avoid a confusion of the human spirit with God. However, we will limit ourselves to the relationship between reason, so conceived, and faith.

It is clear that the activity of reason conceived as the application of given principles to sense impressions cannot be open to something that is not congruous with these principles. Luther's sharp judgments upon reason are to be understood in the light of this insight. The contents of the Christian faith could not be derived from these *a priori* principles. In relation to Aristotelian reason, therefore, these contents had to be regarded as suprarational and supranatural, i.e., situated beyond the natural range of reason. Thomas Aquinas had in fact related faith and reason to each other in this way. The supranatural truths of faith must step into the place of natural principles of knowledge, the light of faith in place of the light of nature, in order that the knowledge of faith may occur.[18] In a similar sense, the young Luther also accepted an illumination of the intellect by the supernatural truths of faith,[19] and later could still praise reason illuminated by faith as much as he disparaged natural reason.[20] As an Ockhamist, Luther felt the opposition of Christian faith to natural reason more sharply than Thomas Aquinas. Nevertheless, their common involvement with the Aristotelian conception of reason cannot be overlooked.

Luther's evaluation of reason easily lends itself to being carried over to the Kantian understanding of reason. For Kant, too, rational activity is thought of as the application of *a priori* principles to the material of experience.[21] Thus, in relation to the Kantian aprioristic concept of reason, Luther's placing of the knowledge of faith in opposition to reason is still actual today. It would then have to be said, in any case, that to accord with Luther's sense, the Kantian reason would have to have new principles established in it by faith. In contrast to this, the usual theological Kantianisms of both rationalistic and supranaturalistic mintage, with their confinement to practical reason, to the ethical, can precisely not appeal to Luther.

In any case, the history of the relationship between philosophy and theology clearly shows that this illumination of the reason which Luther had in mind cannot result from an infusion of supernatural principles. The truths of faith imposed as supernatural principles are always felt, by a reason that understands itself as knowing by means of principles, to be nothing but fetters that have to be struck off, and not as the fulfillment of the essence of reason (which is what illumination really meant in Platonic thought).

(2) Thus, we have to ask whether another understanding of reason is possible which would open up a more meaningful relationship between faith and reason. In philosophical thought since Hamann, Herder, and Jacobi, the idea of "reception"[22] which lies in the word "reason" [*Vernunft*] has been set forth in opposition to the Kantian aprioristic form of reason. Thus, for example, Herder said that reason is no "innate automaton" but that the word "reason" [*Vernunft*] points to something's having been apprehended [*etwas Vernommenes*].[23] Today, the formula "receiving reason" has been renewed by Wilhelm Kamlah above all, in opposition to the self-mastering reason of the modern age which is bent on the domination of what is present at hand.[24] For Kamlah, the model of receiving reason is Platonic insight, which receives the pre-existing forms of true being through a sudden illumination. Receiving reason means in this case the reception of that which is, in contrast to the creative character of

modern reason. Now such a "receptive" reason seems to be related to faith, as Jacobi already believed. Would it not also receive a supernatural revelation as such, instead of dissolving it by criticism? If one looks into the matter more closely, however, it becomes apparent that this receiving reason is oriented toward something entirely different from the Christian faith, at any rate. What it receives is, in accord with Platonic intuition, just what the Parmenidean "mind" [nous] received, namely, that which always is. Faith, on the other hand, is directed toward something future, or toward him who promises and guarantees something future. The future played no role in the Greek understanding of receiving reason, as Gerhard Krüger pointed out, because the historicness of thought and of truth had not been discovered.[25] The historicness of truth, however, is not something first achieved in modern times, but already constituted a fundamental conviction of Israelitic thought. Hans von Soden showed this in his Marburg chancellor's address of 1927.[26] For the Israelite, as indeed for the Greek, truth was characterized by constancy and the reliability based on this. But the Israelite did not search for this reliable reality behind sense appearances, as if it were an imperturbable, timelessly present reality. Rather, for the Israelite, what is reliable and true is that which the future will bring forth,[27] namely that which will prove itself to be reliable. Obviously, the final future is of decisive importance in this view. To this extent, the Israelitic understanding of truth is, at least implicitly, fundamentally eschatological. And because the truth is futural, it therefore cannot be comprehended by the sort of reason (nous, as in Parmenides) that is directed toward what is contemporaneously present. Rather, it can only be grasped by faith, which trusts in him who will in the future prove himself truly reliable.

In the history of theology, receiving reason, in the Greek sense of a perception of what always is, has repeatedly obstructed understanding of the historical truth of the promising God, on which faith depends. As opposed to this, faith which, according to Hebrews 2:1, is oriented toward future things permits the question of historicness to be posed to reason as well. For if the truly constant being first comes to light in the future, then such historicness of truth must also have an influence upon reason, at least to the extent that every unhistorical self-understanding of reason and of the truth toward which it is oriented could be condemned to defeat.

(3) A historical reason is by no means a mere theoretical postulate. Rather, the discovery of the historic character of reason designates the main direction in which the understanding of reason has been deepened since Kant.

A point of departure for this development already existed in Kant, insofar as the "productive power of the imagination," creative fantasy, constituted the genuinely vital core of his concept of reason, since the gathering together of the manifoldness of experience into a unified representation, the synthesis, is an achievement of the imagination. Kant believed that knowledge won in this way "in its beginning, indeed, may be crude and confused, and is therefore in need of analysis—still, synthesis is that by which alone the elements of our cognitions are collected and united into a certain content."[28]   To be sure, Kant failed to take note of the creative profuseness of the activity of imagination, which is always bringing forth something new, for the creative imagination was concerned only to educe the forms of an *a priori* reason. But should not precisely the creative imagination break out of a closed system of that sort in that it may hit upon something quite different?

That has in fact happened, and was accomplished, indeed, by means of the discovery of the reflective structure of thought that was worked out along the way that led from Fichte to Hegel. Every insight is but a stage on the way to new insight. Since thought knows not only the object known, but also knows its knowledge of its object in that it constantly reflects upon itself, it never fails to run up against the limits of its knowledge in comparison with that which this knowledge claims to know. Thus, through the movement of reflection, imagination is called upon to bring forth ever new syntheses. What appeared in Kant as a rigid, permanently fixed structure of reason was dissolved by means of the principle of reflection into a process which continually moves forward from one stage to another. Such a process of reflection determined the systematic structure of Fichte's science of knowledge and Hegel's phenomenology and logic. But Hegel still conceived this process of reflection as a progression that from the very outset was undertaken of necessity. Therefore, in his philosophy, reflection fulfilled itself by becoming absolute in the Notion [*Begriff*]. Hegel did not see that every advance to a new synthesis in his own thought had in fact the character of an irreducible achievement of imagination, in the Kantian sense of an imagination that productively generates syntheses. This reflection of ours about the nature of the Hegelian process of thought demolishes its claim of having brought this process to completion in the Notion. What remains is an open process of a reflective movement of thought in which thought continually circles back on itself, and by its own movement runs up against the difference it thereby recognizes between itself and its object. This process reaches new stages by ever new syntheses which, like all earlier ones, arise as an output of the productive imagination. With the downfall of the Hegelian claim to a definitive ending of the path of reflection in the Notion, the historical movement of reason, which thrusts us into the open, has been uncovered.

The investigation of this historical life of reason was the theme of Wilhelm Dilthey.

Not the acceptance of a frozen *a priori* regarding our cognitive powers, but only a history of development which starts out from the totality of our nature, can answer the questions with which we have to deal in philosophy.[29]

It is true that Dilthey neglected the reflective nature of "historical reason."[30] For this reason, his analyses strike us as somewhat superficial in comparison with Hegel. But by his investigation of the category of "meaning," Dilthey worked out the peculiar openness of the historical mind. The category of meaning in Dilthey steps into the place occupied by the Hegelian Notion. Whereas reason allegedly reaches its culmination in the Notion, the total meaning of life is always only provisionally accessible. Every individual experience has its meaning only in connection with life as a whole. This is true for the individual person as well as for a people or the human race. A meaningful whole can only be seen in retrospect,[31] however, and thus always in a merely provisional way because history is never already finished. Dilthey once said:

> One would have to wait for the end of a life and, in the hour of death, survey the whole and ascertain the relation between the whole and its parts. One would have to wait for the end of history to have all the material necessary to determine its meaning.[32]

Dilthey resignedly drew from this insight—since no one stands at the end of history—the conclusion that all assertions of meaning are relative. Nevertheless, one must draw the opposite conclusion: every assertion of meaning rests upon a fore-conception of the final future, in the light of which the true meaning of every individual event first becomes expressible in a valid way. Heidegger drew this conclusion with respect to individual human existence when he spoke, in *Being and Time,* of human existence attaining its wholeness and thereby itself in anticipating its own death. But the anticipation of a final future cannot be limited to the individual human being because this one attains his significance again only as a member of a whole, a society, ultimately the whole human race—an aspect which Heidegger, unfortunately, leaves bracketed out. But not even the individual human being can attain wholeness for himself by anticipating his own death because every human life remains a fragment at death, and just for this reason cannot win its wholeness from death. The fore-conception of a final future which alone yields the true meaning of all individual events must therefore be, on the one hand, something that points beyond the death of the individual, and on the other hand, something that embraces the totality of the human race, indeed, of all reality. Only from such a fore-conception of a final future, and thus of the still unfinished wholeness of reality, is it possible to assign to an individual event or being—be it present or past—its definitive meaning by saying what it is. Thus, when someone names a thing and says, "This is a rose," or "This is a dog," he always does so from the standpoint of an implicit fore-conception of the final future, and of the totality of reality that will first be constituted by the final future. For every individual has its definitive meaning only within this whole.

Reflection upon the historical nature of reason has led us into the horizon of eschatology. Faith is not the only thing that has a relationship to the future in that as trust it anticipates something future and unseen. Rather, a fore-conception of the future is constitutive for reason, too, conceived in its historic openness, because it is only an eschatologically (because temporally) constituted whole that yields the definitive meaning of everything individual, which we ascribe to things and events as a matter of course by saying what this is or that is. The creative character of the productive imagination seems to draw its vitality from this fore-conception. Conversely, the eschatological structure of reason opens up room for faith's talk about an eschatological future of the individual, the human race, and the world as a whole. Such talk cannot any longer be cast aside as contrary to reason.

The question about the relationship of faith to reason must be presented differently in relation to historical reason, of which we last spoke, than in relation to the aprioristic views of reason in the Aristotelian or Kantian traditions. The antithesis between faith and reason that was meaningful there cannot be mechanically transported over to the historical understanding of reason. One cannot say that this reason, in contrast to faith, has to do only with what is visible. One cannot say without qualification that reason, in contrast to faith or conscience, is concerned only with denomination. Both these statements would signify an abridgment of reason, provided that every idea or every spontaneous flash of the imagination derives from that tacitly presupposed, anticipated totally to which Heidegger points when he speaks about the words of language coming from a "pealing of silence."

A difference between faith and reason remains, nevertheless. Faith is explicitly directed toward that eschatological future and consummation which reason anticipates while at the same time keeping behind it when it says what those things are whose essences it names. Reason is indeed not confined to such naming of present things. As a movement of reflection, it returns to its absolute presupposition, which has been shown to us to be the anticipation of a final future constituting the wholeness of reality. But reason is always concerned with present things in the first instance. For this reason, it can happen that it might forget its own implicit presupposition and understand itself on the basis of the present things with which it is involved.

The Christian faith, by contrast, is directed toward that future from which reason derives. To ask about the reason for this would take us beyond the limits of this essay, because this ground of faith is God who by his promise points to the future that he himself is, namely, the future of his reign. Faith is directed to this future which constitutes reality as a whole and thereby brings everything individual to its essential perfection. However, because this future is not alien to reason, but is rather its origin from which it implicitly always derives, faith cannot stand in opposition to reason. Much more does it remind reason of its own absolute presupposition by speaking about the eschatological future and its pre-appearance in the history of the resurrection of Jesus, from which faith derives. In this way, faith can assist reason to become fully transparent to itself in its reflections. This would be reason enough—even if there were others available—for theology not to abandon as obsolete its talk about the eschatological future. For it would thereby surrender precisely the positive reference of faith to the essence of reason. Faith can confirm itself as the criterion for the rationality of reason just by its orientation toward a final, eschatological future.

Endnotes

*Reprinted from *Basic Questions in Theology*, Vol.. II, by Wolfhart Pannenberg, copyright © 1971 Fortress Press. Used by permission of Augsburg Fortress.

1 Tertullian *De praescriptione haereticorum* 7 [see *ANF* 3, p. 246].

2 *Ad Praxean* 7 [see *ANF* 3, pp. 601f.].

3 *MPL* 145, 603D.

4 Cf. *LW* 40, p. 175 [= *WA* 18, p. 164, 11. 25f.]; *A Commentary on St. Paul's Epistle to the Galatians* (based on the lectures of 1531, published in 1535; London: James Clarke & Co., 1953), p. 224 [= *WA* 40/I, p. 365, 11. 18f.]. On this matter see also Bernard Lohse, *Ratio und Fides: Eine Untersuchung über die ratio in der Theologie Luthers* (Göttingen, 1958), pp. 72f.; and Paul Althaus, *The Theology of Martin Luther*, trans. Robert C. Schultz (Philadelphia: Fortress Press, 1960), pp. 64ff.

5 Lohse, *Ratio und Fides*, pp. 112f.; cf. pp. 98ff.

6 *On True Religion* 25, 46; in *Augustine: Earlier Writings*, trans. J. H. S. Burleigh, Library of Christian Classics 6 (Philadelphia: Westminster Press, 1963), p. 247.

7 Augustine *On True Religion* 10. 20; in *Augustine: Earlier Writings*, p. 235. On this point cf. Ephraem Hendrikx, "Augustins Verhältnis zur Mystik," in *Zum Augustingespräch der Gegenwart*, ed. Carl Andresen (Cologne, 1962), pp. 271-346, esp. pp. 321ff. See also the following additional references in Augustine: *De 83 quaest.*, q. 48 (*MPL*, Augustine 6, col. 50); and *On the Usefulness of Belief* 11. 25 (in *Augustine: Earlier Writings*, pp. 311f. [= *MPL*, Augustine 8, col. 120BC]).

8 R. Lorenz, "Gnade und Erkenntnis bei Augustine," *Zeitschrift für Kirchengeschichte* 76 (1964): 21-78. Augustine judges differently in *On the Trinity* 15, 21 (*NPNF*, First Series, 3: 221); cf. Lorenz, "Gnade und Erkenntnis bei Augustine," p. 36.

9 *LW* 2, p. 267 [= *WA* 42, p. 452, ll. 22ff.: *Ratio praesentibus soleat niti, fides absentia complectitur, et ea contra rationem praesentia esse judicat*]. On this point, see Lohse, *Ratio und Fides*, p. 103. On the beginnings of this idea in Luther, see Lohse, pp. 38ff., and also Reinhard Schwarz, *Fides, Spes und Caritas beim jungen Luther* (Berlin, 1962), pp. 15ff., 50ff.

10 "Not only the agony, but also the love which suffered for us" ["*non solum die marter, sed etiam die lieb, quod pro nobis patitur*" (*WA* 37, pp. 22f.) — translation mine — TR.]. On this, see Gerhard Ebeling, *Evangelische Evangelienauslegung: Eine Untersuchung zu Luthers Hermeneutik* (Darmstadt, ²1962), pp. 232f., 412ff.

11 *WA* 29, p. 657, 11. 3f. [translation mine — TR.].

12 David Hume, *An Enquiry Concerning Human Understanding* (Chicago: Open Court Pub. Co., 1912), p. 137.

13 Ibid., p. 138 (italics in original).

14 Thus, Augustine stated: "No one believes anything unless he has first thought that it is to be believed: (*NPNF*, First Series, 5: 499 [*Nullus quippe credit aliquid, nisi prius cogitaverit esse credendum (On the Predestination of the Saints* 2.5)]). Cf. Lorenz, "Gnade und Erkenntnis bei Augustine," pp. 28, 31.

15 There has been much talk these days about the death of God. It is supposed that theology must adapt itself to the soil of the modern consciousness for which God is no longer a self-evident presupposition. This does not exclude, however, the possibility of a justification of God-talk. To this extent, the catchword "death of God" is misleading. The truth in it must be taken seriously by theology, however. Every theological statement must prove itself on the field of reason, and can no longer be argued on the basis of unquestioned presuppositions of faith.

16*Summa Theologiae*, pt. I, quest. 79, art. 8 [in *Basic Writings of St. Thomas Aquinas*, ed. Anton C. Pegis (New York: Random House, 1945), p. 759].

17 [The term "conscience" here stands for Aquinas' *conscientia*, which designates the act of applying moral principles to particular acts, in contrast to *synderesis* which is the seat of knowledge of the primary principles of morals (cf. *Summa Theologiae*, pt. I, quest. 79, arts. 12-13). Thus, our ordinary usage of the term "conscience" to designate some kind of inherent moral arbiter in man is closer to *synderesis* than to "conscience" as used in the sentence above. — TR.]

18 *Summa Theologiae*, pt. I, quest, 12, art. 5 [in *Basic Writings of St. Thomas Aquinas*, pp. 98f.].

19 Cf. Lohse, *Ratio und Fides*, pp. 38ff., on the positive evaluation of *intellectus* in Luther's lectures on the Psalms. Lohse, however, does not go into the connection between this and the scholastic determination of the relationship between intellect and reason and with the understanding of the knowledge of faith as supernatural illumination of the intellect by the truths of faith.

20 Ibid., pp. 98ff.

21 Kant, as is well known, reversed the relationship between reason and intellect in this connection. The intellect [*Verstand*] is now taken as subordinate to the power of reason [*Vernunft*], which is taken as the higher cognitive power.

22 [*Des Vernehmens* — interpreted from its roots, *ver-* (= "away from") and *nehmen* (= "take" or "receive") — TR.]

23 Herder, *Ideen zur Philosophie der Geschichte der Menschheit*, reissue of 1st ed. (Berlin, 1965), vol. I, bk. 4, chap. 4.

24 Wilhelm Kamlah, *Der Mensch in der Profanität: Versuch einer Kritik der profanen durch vernehemende Vernunft* (Stuttgart, 1949).

25 Gerhard Krüger, *Grundfragen der Philosophie: Geschichte, Wahrheit, Wissenschaft* (Frankfurt on the Main, 1958), pp. 87f.

26 *Was ist Wahrheit? Vom geschichtlichen Begriff der Wahrheit*, Marburger akademische Reden 46 (Marburg, 1927).

27 Ibid., p. 15.

28 *Critique of Pure Reason*, trans. J. M. D. Meikeljohn (London: George Bell and Sons, 1884), p. 63.

29 Wilhelm Dilthey, *Gesammelte Schriften* (Leipzig and Stuttgart, 1927; 1948), I: xviii.

30 Ibid., 7:191f.
31 W. Dilthey, *Pattern and Meaning in History*, ed. H. P. Rickman (London: Allen and Unwin, 1961), p. 100 [= *Gesammelte Schriften*, 7:74].
32 *Ibid.*, p. 106 [= *Gesammelte Schriften*, 7:233].

Study Questions

1.   What are the five options relative to the faith/reason issue?

2.   Which of the five options listed in answer to question (1) best characterizes Wolfhart Pannenberg's position? Why?

3.   What does Pannenberg mean by "the absolute presuppositional nature of reason"?

4.   How does Pannenberg's attempt to eschatologically contextualize reason bring faith into the picture?

5.   What are the advantages you see in Pannenberg's compatibilist position regarding faith and reason?

2

Kierkegaard's Arguments Against Objective Reasoning in Religion

Robert Merrihew Adams

Robert Merrihew Adams is professor of philosophy at Yale University, and author of *Virtue Ethics*. He examines three arguments offered by Kierkegaard supportive of his fideism—the Approximation Argument, Postponement Argument, and Passion Argument—and judges the first is a bad argument, and the other two work with a notion of religiousness he does not accept. *

It is sometimes held that there is something in the nature of religious faith itself that renders it useless or undesirable to reason objectively in support of such faith, even if the reasoning should happen to have considerable plausibility. Søren Kierkegaard's *Concluding Unscientific Postscript* is probably the document most commonly cited as representative of this view. In the present essay I shall discuss three arguments for the view. I call them the Approximation Argument, the Postponement Argument, and the Passion Argument; and I suggest they can all be found in the *Postscript*. I shall try to show that the Approximation Argument is a bad argument. The other two will not be so easily disposed of, however. I believe they show that Kierkegaard's conclusion, or something like it, does indeed follow from a certain conception of religiousness—a conception which has some appeal, although for reasons which I shall briefly suggest, I am not prepared to accept it.

Kierkegaard uses the word "objective" and its cognates in several senses, most of which need not concern us here. We are interested in the sense in which he uses it when he says, "it is precisely a misunderstanding to seek an objective assurance," and when he speaks of "an objective uncertainty held fast in the appropriation-process of the most passionate inwardness" (pp. 41, 182).[1] Let us say that a piece of reasoning, R, is *objective reasoning* just in case every (or almost every) intelligent, fair-minded, and sufficiently informed person would regard R as showing or tending to show (in the circumstances in which R is used, and to the extent claimed in R) that R's conclusion is true or probably true. Uses of "objective" and "objectively" in other contexts can be understood from their relation to this one; for example, an objective uncertainty is a proposition which cannot be shown by objective reasoning to be certainly true.

I. The Approximation Argument

"Is it possible to base an eternal happiness upon historical knowledge?" is one of the central questions in the *Postscript,* and in the *Philosophical Fragments* to which it is a "postscript." Part of Kierkegaard's answer to the question is that it is not possible to base an eternal happiness on objective reasoning about historical facts.

> For nothing is more readily evident than that the greatest attainable certainty with respect to anything historical is merely an approximation. And an approximation, when viewed as a basis for an eternal happiness, is wholly inadequate, since the incommensurability makes a result impossible. (p. 25)

Kierkegaard maintains that it is possible, however, to base an eternal happiness on a belief in historical facts that is independent of objective evidence for them, and that that is what one must do in order to be a Christian. This is the Approximation Argument for the proposition that Christian faith cannot be based on objective reasoning. (It is assumed that some belief about historical facts is an essential part of Christian faith, so that if religious faith cannot be based on objective historical reasoning, then Christian faith cannot be based on objective reasoning at all.) Let us examine the argument in detail.

Its first premise is Kierkegaard's claim that the greatest attainable certainty with respect to anything historical is merely an approximation. I take him to mean that historical evidence, objectively considered, never completely excludes the possibility of error. "It goes without saying, he claims, "that it is impossible in the case of historical problems to reach an objective decision so certain that no doubt could disturb it" (p. 41). For Kierkegaard's purposes it does not matter how small the possibility of error is, so long as it is finitely small (that is, so long as it is not literally infinitesimal). He insists (p. 31) that his Approximation Argument makes no appeal to the supposition that the objective evidence for Christian historical beliefs is weaker than the objective evidence for any other historical belief. The argument turns on a claim about *all* historical evidence. The probability of error in our belief that there was an American Civil War in the nineteenth century, for instance, might be as small as

10(1/2,000,000); that would be a large enough chance of error for Kierkegaard's argument.

It might be disputed, but let us assume for the sake of argument that there is some such finitely small probability of error in the objective grounds for all historical beliefs, as Kierkegaard held. This need not keep us from saying that we "know," and it is "certain," that there was an American Civil War. For such an absurdly small possibility of error is as good as no possibility of error at all, "for all practical intents and purposes," as we might say. Such a possibility of error is too small to be worth worrying about.

But would it be too small to be worth worrying about if we had an infinite passionate interest in the question about the Civil War? If we have an infinite passionate interest in something, there is no limit to how important it is to us. (The nature of such an interest will be discussed more fully in section 3 below.) Kierkegaard maintains that in relation to an infinite passionate interest no possibility of error is too small to be worth worrying about. "In relation to an eternal happiness, and an infinite passionate interest in its behalf (in which latter alone the former can exist), an iota is of importance, of infinite importance . . ." (p. 28). This is the basis for the second premise of the Approximation Argument, which is Kierkegaard's claim that "an approximation, when viewed as a basis for an eternal happiness, is wholly inadequate" (p. 25). "An approximation is essentially incommensurable with an infinite personal interest in an eternal happiness" (p. 26).

At this point in the argument it is important to have some understanding of Kierkegaard's conception of faith, and the way in which he thinks faith excludes doubt. Faith must be decisive; in fact it seems to consist in a sort of decision-making. "The conclusion of belief is not so much a conclusion as a resolution, and it is for this reason that belief excludes doubt." The decision of faith is a decision to disregard the possibility of error—to act on what is believed, without hedging one's bets to take account of any possibility of error.

To disregard the possibility of error is not to be unaware of it, or fail to consider it, or lack anxiety about it. Kierkegaard insists that the believer must be keenly *aware* of the risk of error. "If I wish to preserve myself in faith I must constantly be intent upon holding fast the objective uncertainty, so as to remain out upon the deep, over seventy thousand fathoms of water, still preserving my faith" (p. 182).

For Kierkegaard, then, to ask whether faith in a historical fact can be based on objective reasoning is to ask whether objective reasoning can justify one in disregarding the possibility of error which (he thinks) historical evidence always leaves. Here another aspect of Kierkegaard's conception of faith plays its part in the argument. He thinks that in all genuine religious faith the believer is *infinitely* interested in the object of his faith. And he thinks it follows that objective reasoning cannot justify him in disregarding *any* possibility of error about the object of faith, and therefore cannot lead him all the way to religious faith where a historical fact is concerned. The farthest it could lead him is to the conclusion that *if* he had only a certain finite (though very great) interest in the matter, the possibility of error would be too small to be worth worrying about and he would be justified in disregarding it. But faith disregards a possibility of error that *is* worth worrying about, since an infinite interest is involved. Thus faith requires a "leap" beyond the evidence, a leap that cannot be justified by objective reasoning (cf. p. 90).

There is something right in what Kierkegaard is saying here, but his Approximation Argument is a bad argument. He is right in holding that grounds of doubt which may be insignificant for most practical purposes can be extremely troubling for the intensity of a religious concern, and that it may require great decisiveness, or something like courage, to overcome them religiously. But he is mistaken in holding that objective reasoning could not justify one in disregarding any possibility of error about something in which one is infinitely interested.

The mistake, I believe, lies in his overlooking the fact that there are at least two different reasons one might have for disregarding a possibility of error. The first is that the possibility is too small to be worth worrying about. The second is that the risk of not disregarding the possibility of error would be greater than the risk of disregarding it. Of these two reasons only the first is ruled out by the infinite passionate interest.

I will illustrate this point with two examples, one secular and one religious. A certain woman has a very great (though not infinite) interest in her husband's love for her. She rightly judges that the objective evidence available to her renders it 99.9 percent probable that he loves her truly. The intensity of her interest is sufficient to cause her some anxiety over the remaining 1/1,000 chance that he loves her not; for her this chance is not too small to be worth worrying about. (Kierkegaard uses a similar example to support his Approximation Argument; see p. 511.) But she (very reasonably) wants to *disregard* the risk of error, in the sense of not hedging her bets, if he does love her. This desire is at least as strong as her desire not to be deceived if he does not love her. Objective reasoning should therefore suffice to bring her to the conclusion that she ought to disregard the risk of error, since by not disregarding it she would run 999 times as great risk of frustrating one of these desires.

Or suppose you are trying to base your eternal happiness on your relation to Jesus, and therefore have an infinite passionate interest in the question whether he declared Peter and his episcopal successors to be infallible in matters of religious doctrine. You want to be committed to whichever is the true belief on this question, disregarding any possibility of error in it. And suppose, just for the sake of argument, that objective historical evidence renders it 99 percent probable that Jesus did declare

Peter and his successors to be infallible—or 99 percent probable that he did not—for our present discussion it does not matter which. The one percent chance of error is enough to make you *anxious*, in view of your infinite interest. But objective reasoning leads to the conclusion that you ought to commit yourself to the more probable opinion, *disregarding* the risk of error, if your strongest desire in the matter is to be so committed to the true opinion. For the only other way to satisfy this desire would be to commit yourself to the less probable opinion, disregarding the risk of error in it. The first way will be successful if and only if the more probable opinion is true, and the second way if and only if the less probable opinion is true. Surely it is prudent to do what gives you a 99 percent chance of satisfying your strong desire, in preference to what gives you only a one percent chance of satisfying it.

In this argument your strong desire to be committed to the true opinion is presupposed. The reasonableness of this desire may depend on a belief for which no probability can be established by purely historical reasoning, such as the belief that Jesus is God. But any difficulties arising from this point are distinct from those urged in the Approximation Argument, which itself presupposes the infinite passionate interest in the historical question.

There is some resemblance between my arguments in these examples and Pascal's famous Wager argument. But whereas Pascal's argument turns on weighing an infinite interest against a finite one, mine turn on weighing a large chance of success against a small one. An argument closer to Pascal's will be discussed in section 4 below.

The reader may well have noticed in the foregoing discussion some unclarity about what sort of justification is being demanded and given for religious beliefs about historical facts. There are at least two different types of question about a proposition which I might try to settle by objective reasoning: (1) Is it probable that the proposition is true? (2) In view of the evidence which I have for and against the proposition, and my interest in the matter, is it prudent for me to have faith in the truth of the proposition, disregarding the possibility of error? Correspondingly, we may distinguish two ways in which a belief can be *based on* objective reasoning. The proposition believed may be the conclusion of a piece of objective reasoning, and accepted because it is that. We may say that such a belief is *objectively probable.* Or one might hold a belief or maintain a religious faith because of a piece of objective reasoning whose conclusion is that it would be prudent, morally right, or otherwise desirable for one to hold that belief or faith. In this latter case let us say that the belief is *objectively advantageous.* It is clear that historical beliefs can be objectively probable; and in the Approximation Argument, Kierkegaard does not deny Christian historical beliefs can be objectively probable. His thesis is, in effect, that in view of an infinite passionate interest in their subject matter, they cannot be objectively advantageous, and therefore cannot be fully justified objectively, even if they are objectively probable. It is this thesis that I have attempted to refute. I have not been discussing the question whether Christian historical beliefs are objectively probable.

2. The Postponement Argument

Postponement Argument The trouble with objective historical reasoning, according to the Approximation Argument, is that it cannot yield complete certainty. But that is not Kierkegaard's only complaint against it as a basis for religious faith. He also objects that objective historical inquiry is never completely finished, so that one who seeks to base his faith on it postpones his religious commitment forever. In the process of historical research "new difficulties arise and are overcome, and new difficulties again arise. Each generation inherits from its predecessor the illusion that the method is quite impeccable, but the learned scholars have not yet succeeded . . . and so forth. . . . The infinite personal passionate interest of the subject . . . vanishes more and more, because the decision is postponed, and postponed as following directly upon the result of the learned inquiry" (p. 28). As soon as we take "an historical document" as "our standard for the determination of Christian truth," we are "involved in a parenthesis whose conclusion is everlastingly prospective" (p. 28)—that is, we are involved in a religious digression which keeps religious commitment forever in the future.

Kierkegaard has such fears about allowing religious faith to rest on *any* empirical reasoning. The danger of postponement of commitment arises not only from the uncertainties of historical scholarship, but also in connection with the design argument for God's existence. In the *Philosophical Fragments* Kierkegaard notes some objections to the attempt to prove God's existence from evidence of "the wisdom in nature, the goodness, the wisdom in the governance of the world," and then says, "even if I began I would never finish, and would in addition have to live constantly in suspense, lest something so terrible should suddenly happen that my bit of proof would be demolished." What we have before us is a quite general sort of objection to the treatment of religious beliefs as empirically testable. On this point many analytical philosophers seem to agree with Kierkegaard. Much discussion in recent analytical philosophy of religion has proceeded from the supposition that religious beliefs are not empirically testable. I think it is far from obvious that that supposition is correct; and it is interesting to consider arguments that may be advanced to support it.

Kierkegaard's statements suggest an argument that I call the Postponement Argument. Its first premise is that one cannot have an authentic religious faith without being totally committed to it. In order to be totally committed to a belief, in the relevant sense, one must be determined not to abandon the belief under any circumstances that one recognizes as epistemically possible.

The second premise is that one cannot yet be totally committed to any belief which one bases on an inquiry in which one recognizes any possibility of a future need to revise the results. Total commitment to any belief so based will necessarily be postponed. I believe that this premise, suitably interpreted, is true. Consider the position of someone who regards himself as committed to a belief on the basis of objective evidence, but who recognizes some possibility that future discoveries will destroy the objective justification of the belief. We must ask how he is disposed to react in the event, however unlikely, that the objective basis of his belief is overthrown. Is he prepared to abandon the belief in that event? If so, he is not totally committed to the belief in the relevant sense. But if he is determined to cling to his belief even if its objective justification is taken away, then he is not basing the belief on the objective justification—or at least he is not basing it solely on the justification.

The conclusion to be drawn from these two premises is that authentic religious faith cannot be based on an inquiry in which one recognizes any possibility of a future need to revise the results. We ought to note that this conclusion embodies two important restrictions on the scope of the argument.

In the first place, we are not given an argument that authentic religious faith cannot have an objective justification that is subject to possible future revision. What we are given is an argument that the authentic believer's holding of his religious belief cannot *depend* entirely on such a justification.

In the second place, this conclusion applies only to those who *recognize* some epistemic possibility that the objective results which appear to support their belief may be overturned. I think it would be unreasonable to require, as part of total commitment, a determination with regard to one's response to circumstances that one does not recognize as possible at all. It may be, however, that one does not recognize such a possibility when one ought to.

Kierkegaard needs one further premise in order to arrive at the conclusion that authentic religious faith cannot without error be based on any objective empirical reasoning. This third premise is that in every objective empirical inquiry there is always, objectively considered, some epistemic possibility that the results of the inquiry will need to be revised in view of new evidence or new reasoning. I believe Kierkegaard makes this assumption; he certainly makes it with regard to historical inquiry. From this premise it follows that one is in error if in any objective empirical inquiry one does not recognize any possibility of a future need to revise the results. But if one does recognize such a possibility, then according to the conclusion already reached in the Postponement Argument, one cannot base an authentic religious faith on the inquiry.

Some philosophers might attack the third premise of this argument; and certainly it is controversial. But I am more inclined to criticize the first premise. There is undoubtedly something plausible about the claim that authentic religious faith must involve a commitment so complete that the believer is resolved not to abandon his belief under any circumstances that he regards as epistemically possible. If you are willing to abandon your ostensibly religious beliefs for the sake of objective inquiry, mightn't we justly say that objective inquiry is your real religion, the thing to which you are most deeply committed?

There is also something plausible to be said on the other side, however. It has commonly been thought to be an important part of religious ethics that one ought to be humble, teachable, open to correction, new inspiration, and growth of insight, even (and perhaps especially) in important religious beliefs. That view would have to be discarded if we were to concede to Kierkegaard that the heart of commitment in religion is an unconditional determination not to change in one's important religious beliefs. In fact I think there is something radically wrong with this conception of religious commitment. Faith ought not to be thought of as unconditional devotion to a belief. For in the first place the object of religious devotion is not a belief or attitude of one's own but God. And in the second place it may be doubted that religious devotion to God can or should be completely unconditional. God's love for sinners is sometimes said to be completely unconditional not being based on any excellence or merit of theirs. But religious devotion to God is generally thought to be based on His goodness and love. It is the part of the strong, not the weak, to love unconditionally. And in relation to God we are weak.

3. The Passion Argument

In Kierkegaard's statements of the Approximation Argument and the Postponement Argument it is assumed that a system of religious beliefs might be objectively probable. It is only for the sake of argument, however, that Kierkegaard allows this assumption. He really holds that religious faith, by its very nature, needs objective *im*probability. "Anything that is almost probable, or probable, or extremely and emphatically probable, is something [one] can almost know, or as good as know, or extremely and emphatically almost *know*—but it is impossible to *believe*" (p. 189). Nor will Kierkegaard countenance the suggestion that religion ought to go beyond belief to some almost-knowledge based on probability. "Faith is the highest passion in a man. There are perhaps many in every generation who do not even reach it, but no one gets further." It would be a betrayal of religion to try to go beyond faith. The suggestion that faith might be replaced by "probabilities and guarantees" is for the believer "a temptation to be resisted with all his strength" (p. 15). The attempt to establish religious beliefs on a foundation of objective probability is therefore no service to religion, but inimical to religion's true interests. The approximation to certainty which might be afforded by objective probability is rejected, not only for the reasons given in the Approximation Argument and Postponement Argument, but also from a deeper motive, "since on the contrary it behooves us to get rid of introductory guarantees of security, proofs from consequences, and the whole mob of public pawnbrokers and guarantors, so as to permit the absurd to stand out in all its clarity—in order that the individual may believe if he wills it; I merely say that it must be strenuous in the highest degree so to believe" (p. 190).

As this last quotation indicates, Kierkegaard thinks that religious belief ought to be based on a strenuous exertion of the will—a passionate striving. His reasons for thinking that objective probability is religiously undesirable have to do with the place of passion in religion, and constitute what I call the Passion Argument. The first premise of the argument is that the most essential and the most valuable feature of religiousness is passion, indeed an infinite passion, a passion of the greatest possible intensity. The second premise is that an infinite passion requires objective improbability. And the conclusion therefore is that that which is most essential and most valuable in religiousness requires objective improbability.

My discussion of this argument will have three parts. (a) First I will try to clarify, very briefly, what it is that is supposed to be objectively improbable. (b) Then we will consider Kierkegaard's reasons for holding that infinite passion requires objective improbability. In so doing we will also gain a clearer understanding of what a Kierkegaardian infinite passion is. (c) Finally I will discuss the first premise of the argument— although issues will arise at that point which I do not pretend to be able to settle by argument.

(a) What are the beliefs whose improbability is needed by religious passion? Kierkegaard will hardly be satisfied with the improbability of just any one belief; it must surely be at least an important belief. On the other hand it would clearly be preposterous to suppose that every belief involved in Christianity must be objectively improbable. (Consider, for example, the belief that the man Jesus did indeed live.) I think that what is demanded in the Passion Argument is the objective improbability of at least one belief which must be true if the goal sought by the religious passion is to be attained.

(b) We can find in the *Postscript* suggestions of several reasons for thinking that an infinite passion needs objective improbability. The two that seem to me most interesting have to do with (i) the risks accepted and (ii) the costs paid in pursuance of a passionate interest.

(i) One reason that Kierkegaard has for valuing objective improbability is that it increases the *risk* attaching to the religious life, and risk is so essential for the expression of religious passion that "without risk there is no faith" (p. 182). About the nature of an eternal happiness, the goal of religious striving, Kierkegaard says "there is nothing to be said . . . except that it is the good which is attained by venturing everything absolutely" (p. 382).

> But what then does it mean to venture? A venture is the precise correlative of an uncertainty; when the certainty is there the venture becomes impossible. . . . If what I hope to gain by venturing is itself certain, I do not risk or venture, but make an exchange. . . . No, if I am in truth resolved to venture, in truth resolved to strive for the attainment of the highest good, the uncertainty must be there, and I must have room to move, so to speak. But the largest space I can obtain, where there is room for the most vehement gesture of the passion that embraces the infinite, is uncertainty of knowledge with respect to an eternal happiness, or the certain knowledge that the choice is in the finite sense a piece of madness: now there is room, now you can venture! (pp. 380-82)

How is it that objective improbability provides the largest space for the most vehement gesture of infinite passion? Consider two cases: (A) You plunge into a raging torrent to rescue from drowning someone you love, who is crying for help. (B) You plunge into a raging torrent in a desperate attempt to rescue someone you love, who appears to be unconscious and *may* already have drowned. In both cases you manifest a passionate interest in saving the person, risking your own life in order to do so. But I think Kierkegaard would say there is more passion in the second case than in the first. For in the second case you risk your life in what is, objectively considered, a smaller chance that you will be able to save your loved one. A greater passion is required for a more desperate attempt.

A similar assessment may be made of the following pair of cases. (A') You stake everything on your faith in the truth of Christianity, knowing that it is objectively 99 percent probable that Christianity is true. (B') You stake everything on your faith in the truth of Christianity, knowing that the truth of Christianity is, objectively, possible but so improbable that its probability is, say, as small as $10(1/2,000,000)$. There is passion in both cases, but Kierkegaard will say that there is more passion in the second case than in the first. For to venture the same stake (namely, everything) on a much smaller chance of success shows greater passion.

Acceptance of risk can thus be seen as a *measure* of the intensity of passion. I believe this provides us with one way of understanding what Kierkegaard means when he calls religious passion "infinite." An *infinite* passionate interest in x is an interest so strong that it leads one to make the greatest possible sacrifices in order to obtain x, on the smallest possible chance of success. The infinity of the passion is shown in that there is no sacrifice so great one will not make it, and no chance of success so small one will not act on it. A passion which is infinite in this sense requires, by its very nature, a situation of maximum risk for its expression .

It will doubtless be objected that this argument involves a misunderstanding of what a passionate interest is. Such an interest is a disposition. In order to have a great passionate interest it is not necessary actually to make a great sacrifice with a small chance of success; all that is necessary is to have such an intense interest that one *would* do so if an appropriate occasion should arise. It is therefore a mistake to say that there *is* more passion in case (B) than in case (A), or in (B′) than in (A′). More passion is *shown* in (B) than in (A), and in (B′) than in (A′); but an equal passion may exist in cases in which there is no occasion to show it.

This objection may well be correct as regards what we normally mean by "passionate interest." But that is not decisive for the argument. The crucial question is what part dispositions, possibly unactualized, ought to play in religious devotion. And here we must have a digression about the position of the *Postscript* on this question—a position that is complex at best and is not obviously consistent.

In the first place I do not think that Kierkegaard would be prepared to think of passion, or a passionate interest, as primarily a disposition that might remain unactualized. He seems to conceive of passion chiefly as an intensity in which one actually does and feels. "Passion is momentary" (p. 178), although capable of continual repetition. And what is momentary in such a way that it must be repeated rather than protracted is presumably an occurrence rather than a disposition. It agrees with this conception of passion that Kierkegaard idealizes a life of "persistent striving," and says that the religious task is to "exercise" the God-relationship and to give "existential expression to the religious choice (pp. 110, 364, 367).

All of this supports the view that what Kierkegaard means by "an infinite passionate interest" is a pattern of actual decision-making, in which one continually exercises and expresses one's religiousness by making the greatest possible sacrifices on the smallest possible chance of success. In order to actualize such a pattern of life one needs chances of success that are as small as possible. That is the room that is required for "the most vehement gesture" of infinite passion.

But on the other hand Kierkegaard does allow a dispositional element in the religious life, and even precisely in the making of the greatest possible sacrifices. We might suppose that if we are to make the greatest possible sacrifices in our religious devotion, we must do so by abandoning all worldly interests and devoting all our time and attention to religion. That is what monasticism attempts to do, as Kierkegaard sees it; and (in the *Postscript*, at any rate) he rejects the attempt, contrary to what our argument to this point would have led us to expect of him. He holds that

"resignation" (pp. 353, 367) or "renunciation" (pp. 362, 386) of *all* finite
ends is precisely the first thing that religiousness requires; but he means a
renunciation that is compatible with pursuing and enjoying finite ends (pp.
362-71). This renunciation is the practice of a sort of detachment;
Kierkegaard uses the image of a dentist loosening the soft tissues around a
tooth, while it is still in place, in preparation for pulling it (p. 367). It is
partly a matter of not treating finite things with a desperate seriousness,
but with a certain coolness or humor, even while one pursues them (pp. 368,
370).

This coolness is not just a disposition. But the renunciation also has a
dispositional aspect. "Now if for any individual an eternal happiness is
his highest good, this will mean that all finite satisfactions are
volitionally relegated to the status of what may have to be renounced in
favor of an eternal happiness" (p. 350). The volitional relegation is not a
disposition but an act of choice. The object of this choice, however, appears
to be a dispositional state—the state of being such that one *would* forgo
any finite satisfaction *if* it were religiously necessary or advantageous to
do so.

It seems clear that Kierkegaard, in the *Postscript*, is willing to admit
a dispositional element at one point in the religious venture, but not at
another. It is enough in most cases, he thinks, if one is *prepared* to cease for
the sake of religion from pursuing some finite end; but it is not enough that
one *would* hold to one's belief in the face of objective improbability. The
belief must actually be improbable, although the pursuit of the finite need
not actually cease. What is not clear is a reason for this disparity. The
following hypothesis, admittedly somewhat speculative as interpretation of the text, is the best explanation I can offer.

The admission of a dispositional element in the religious renunciation
of the finite is something to which Kierkegaard seems to be driven by the
view that there is no alternative to it except idolatry. For suppose one
actually ceases from all worldly pursuits and enters a monastery. In the
monastery one would pursue a number of particular ends (such as getting up
in the middle of the night to say the offices) which, although religious in
a way ("churchy," one might say), are still finite. The absolute *telos* or
end of religion is no more to be identified with them than with the ends
pursued by an alderman (pp. 362-71). To pretend otherwise would be to
make an idolatrous identification of the absolute end with some finite end.
An existing person cannot have sacrificed everything by actually having
ceased from pursuing *all* finite ends. For as long as he lives and acts he is
pursuing some finite end. Therefore his renouncing *everything* finite must
be at least partly dispositional.

Kierkegaard does not seem happy with this position. He regards it as
of the utmost importance that the religious passion should come to
expression. The problem of finding an adequate expression for a passion for
an infinite end, in the face of the fact that in every concrete action one will

be pursuing some finite end, is treated in the *Postscript* as the central problem of religion (see especially pp. 386-468). If the sacrifice of everything finite must remain largely dispositional, then perhaps it is all the more important to Kierkegaard that the smallness of the chance for which it is sacrificed should be fully actual, so that the infinity of the religious passion may be measured by an actuality in at least one aspect of the religious venture.

(ii) According to Kierkegaard, as I have argued, the intensity of a passion is measured in part by the smallness of the chances of success that one acts on. It can also be measured in part by its costliness—that is, by how much one gives up or suffers in acting on those chances. This second measure can also be made the basis of an argument for the claim that an infinite passion requires objective improbability. For the objective improbability of a religious belief, if recognized, increases the costliness of holding it. The risk involved in staking everything on an objectively improbable belief gives rise to an anxiety and mental suffering whose acceptance is itself a sacrifice. It seems to follow that if one is not staking everything on a belief one sees to be objectively improbable, one's passion is not infinite in Kierkegaard's sense, since one's sacrifice could be greater if one did adhere to an improbable belief.

Kierkegaard uses an argument similar to this. For God to give us objective knowledge of Himself, eliminating paradox from it, would be "to lower the price of the God-relationship."

> And even if God could be imagined willing, no man with passion in his heart could desire it. To a maiden genuinely in love it could never occur that she had bought her happiness too dear, but rather that she had not bought it dear enough. And just as the passion of the infinite was itself the truth, so in the case of the highest value it holds true that the price is the value, that a low price means a poor value. . . . (p. 207)

Kierkegaard here appears to hold, first, that an increase in the objective probability of religious belief would reduce its costliness, and second, that the value of a religious life is measured by its cost. I take it his reason for the second of these claims is that passion is the most valuable thing in a religious life and passion is measured by its cost. If we grant Kierkegaard the requisite conception of an infinite passion, we seem once again to have a plausible argument for the view that objective improbability is required for such a passion.

(c) We must therefore consider whether infinite passion, as Kierkegaard conceives of it, ought to be part of the religious ideal of life. Such a passion is a striving, or pattern of decision-making, in which, with the greatest possible intensity of feeling, one continually makes the greatest possible sacrifices on the smallest possible chance of success. This seems to me an impossible ideal. I doubt that any human being could have a passion of this sort, because I doubt that one could make a sacrifice so great that a greater could not be made, or have a (nonzero) chance of success so small that a smaller could not be had.

But even if Kierkegaard's ideal is impossible, one might want to try to approximate it. Intensity of passion might still be measured by the greatness of sacrifices made and the smallness of chances of success acted on, even if we cannot hope for a greatest possible or a smallest possible here. And it could be claimed that the most essential and valuable thing in religiousness is a passion that is very intense (though it cannot be infinite) by this standard—the more intense the better. This claim will not support an argument that objective improbability is absolutely required for religious passion. For a passion could presumably be very intense, involving great sacrifices and risks of some other sort, without an objectively improbable belief. But it could still be argued that objectively improbable religious beliefs enhance the value of the religious life by increasing its sacrifices and diminishing its chances of success, whereas objective probability detracts from the value of religious passion by diminishing its intensity.

The most crucial question about the Passion Argument, then, is whether maximization of sacrifice and risk are so valuable in religion as to make objective improbability a desirable characteristic of religious beliefs. Certainly much religious thought and feeling places a very high value on sacrifice and on passionate intensity. But the doctrine that it is desirable to increase without limit or to the highest possible degree (if there is one) the cost and risk of a religious life is less plausible (to say the least) than the view that *some* degree of cost and risk may add to the value of a religious life. The former doctrine would set the religious interest at enmity with all other interests, or at least with the best of them. Kierkegaard is surely right in thinking that it would be impossible to live without pursuing some finite ends. But even so it would be possible to exchange the pursuit of better finite ends for the pursuit of worse ones— for example, by exchanging the pursuit of truth, beauty, and satisfying personal relationships for the self-flagellating pursuit of pain. And a way of life would be the costlier for requiring such an exchange. Kierkegaard does not, in the *Postscript*, demand it. But the presuppositions of his Passion Argument seem to imply that such a sacrifice would be religiously desirable. Such a conception of religion is demonic. In a tolerable religious ethics some way must be found to conceive of the religious interest as inclusive rather than exclusive of the best of other interests—including, I think, the interest in having well-grounded beliefs.

4. Pascal's Wager and Kierkegaard's Leap

Ironically, Kierkegaard's views about religious passion suggest a way in which his religious beliefs could be based on objective reasoning—not on reasoning which would show them to be objectively probable, but on reasoning which shows them to be objectively advantageous. Consider the situation of a person whom Kierkegaard would regard as a genuine Christian believer. What would such a person want most of all? He would want above all else to attain the truth through Christianity. That is, he would desire both that Christianity be true and that he himself be related to it as a genuine believer. He would desire that state of affairs (which we may call S) so ardently that he would be willing to sacrifice everything else to obtain it, given only the smallest possible chance of success.

We can therefore construct the following argument, which has an obvious analogy to Pascal's Wager. Let us assume that there is, objectively, some chance, however small, that Christianity is true. This is an assumption which Kierkegaard accepts (p. 31), and I think it is plausible. There are two possibilities, then: either Christianity is true, or it is false. (Others might object to so stark a disjunction, but Kierkegaard will not.) If Christianity is false it is impossible for anyone to obtain S, since S includes the truth of Christianity. It is only if Christianity is true that anything one does will help one or hinder one in obtaining S. And if Christianity is true, one will obtain S just in case one becomes a genuine Christian believer. It seems obvious that one would increase one's chances of becoming a genuine Christian believer by becoming one now (if one can), even if the truth of Christian beliefs is now objectively uncertain or improbable. Hence it would seem to be advantageous for anyone who can to become a genuine Christian believer now, if he wants S so much that he would be willing to sacrifice everything else for the smallest possible chance of obtaining S. Indeed I believe that the argument I have given for this conclusion is a piece of objective reasoning, and that Christian belief is therefore *objectively* advantageous for anyone who wants S as much as a Kierkegaardian genuine Christian must want it.

Of course this argument does not tend at all to show that it is objectively probable that Christianity is true. It only gives a practical, prudential reason for believing, to someone who has a certain desire. Nor does the argument do anything to prove that such an absolutely overriding desire for S is reasonable. It does show, however, that just as Søren's position has more logical structure than one might at first think, it is more difficult than he probably realized for him to get away entirely from objective justification.

Endnotes

1 Søren Kierkegaard, *Concluding Unscientific Postscript*, translated by David F. Swenson; introduction, notes, and completion of translation by Walter Lowrie

(Princeton: Princeton University Press, 1941). Page references in parentheses in the body of the present paper are to this work.

Study Questions

1.   What flaws does Robert Adams see in the Approximation, Postponement and Passion Arguments of Søren Kierkegaard?

2.   Of the three critical responses of Adams, which one do you see as counting most decisively against Søren Kierkegaard's position, and why?

3.   What is the "logical structure" that Robert Adams sees in Søren Kierkegaard's position?

4.   How does Robert Adams interpret Søren Kierkegaard's view of "passionate interest?"

5.   Why do you think that Robert Adams claims that Kierkegaard's "leap of faith" is analogous to Pascal's Wager? Which of the two analogues do you think is superior?

3

Kierkegaard on Rationality

Marilyn Gaye Piety

Marilyn Gaye Piety of Yale University, is Visiting Scholar at the Department of Søren Kierkegaard Research of the University of Copenhagen.

This paper is concerned with Kierkegaard's views on the nature of human rationality in the specific context of the relation between competing interpretations of existence. Contemporary dialogue has reached the point where it appears movement between such interpretations can only be understood as rational, if it is seen as a natural or evolutionary development and not as the result of a choice. This paper provides a sketch of a theory of rationality which enables us to make sense of the impression that we do, at least occasionally, choose between competing interpretations of existence and that we make such choices for what we believe are good, or even compelling reasons.*

The idea has been advanced that human behavior, or more specifically, choice, can only be understood as rational within a particular conceptual framework. Proponents of this view contend that any possible system of justification must be understood as relative to a particular framework or system of values and hence that it is not possible to make rational choices *between* frameworks. Charles Taylor argues, on the other hand, that movement between frameworks can be rational. He bases this argument, however, on the claim that such movement is a natural or evolutionary development and not the result of a *choice*.[1] The contemporary debate on this issue has reached the point where it appears we must consider *either* that it is not possible to choose rationally between frameworks, *or* that there is rational movement between frameworks, but that this movement is not the result of a choice.

Taylor contends that the transition from one framework to another is effected through what he refers to as "error reducing moves."[2] That is, he asserts that insofar as a given framework may involve certain incoherences, and insofar as an individual may be motivated to reduce these incoherences, his effort to do this may actually eventuate in the

49

production of, or transition to, a new framework. He asserts that the situation of Luther with respect to traditional Catholicism could be understood as exemplifying a movement of this sort.

Taylor argues, however, that such a transition from one framework to another is not the result of an appeal to some criterion that is *independent* of the two frameworks in question, but rather that it is the natural result of the desire of the individual for a more coherent scheme for interpreting his existence. Taylor does not see the individual as *choosing* between competing systems of interpretation, but rather as developing new systems through an effort to reduce the incoherences or errors inherent in the old systems. Thus, while many theorists are disposed to see the movement from one framework to another as fundamentally irrational, Taylor sees it as rational. Taylor is in agreement with the former group, however, in that he is not willing to allow that there are any criteria independent of the two frameworks in question, such that an appeal to these criteria would justify, or show to be rational, the *choice* of one over another.

It would appear that the *impasse* at which the contemporary debate on the nature of human rationality has arrived is the result of the tendency of philosophers, despite their efforts to the contrary, to cling to the old Enlightenment view of disinterested and dispassionate reasoning as the paradigm of that rationality. I shall argue that Kierkegaard provides us with a picture of an *interested* and *impassioned* reason which enables us to see how it is possible for the transition from one framework to another to be *both* rational *and* the result of a choice and that insofar as it does this, it represents a more "reasonable" picture of reason than the one that has been traditionally offered by metaphysics.

I

The view that choice can only be understood as rational relative to a particular conceptual framework is precisely the one that provides the foundation for Alasdair MacIntyre's charge in *After Virtue*[3] that Kierkegaard considers moral commitment to be "the expression of a criterionless choice,"[4] or a choice between "incompatible and incommensurable moral premises, a choice for which no rational justification can be given." MacIntyre refers to this position as Kierkegaard's "discovery" and identifies it as his primary contribution to the history of moral or ethical philosophy; a contribution which MacIntyre claims marks the beginning of the "distinctively modern standpoint" on the nature of moral debate. MacIntyre is undoubtedly correct in his identification of the distinctively modern standpoint on such debates. He is not correct, however, as will become clear in the pages which follow, in his ascription of this view to Kierkegaard.

Kierkegaard's frameworks may be designated "aesthetic," "ethical," "religious" and "paradoxically religious" or "Christian."[5] That is, Kierkegaard's individual views existence from within one or the other of these alternative schemes of interpretation. The aesthetic individual, for example, views existence as defined aesthetically. He interprets the value of the phenomena of his existence—including his own actions—as derivative of, or reducible to, their aesthetic significance. Thus an aesthete values actions not insofar as they exemplify morally uplifting principles, but rather insofar as they are immediately compelling, interesting, or sensuously gratifying.

The difficulty, as MacIntyre so forcefully pointed out, is that different frameworks represent significantly different systems of values, hence what may serve as a criterion for choice within an ethical framework will very likely not enjoy the same status within an aesthetic framework.[6] The moral superiority of an ethical over an aesthetic interpretation of existence cannot serve, for an aesthete, as a criterion for choosing it over his present interpretation, because such "superiority" is not considered by an aesthete to be of any positive value. This situation is, of course, mirrored by that of the ethicist; hence one might conclude from this, as indeed MacIntyre does conclude, that such a choice between frameworks as Kierkegaard has B recommending to A in *Either-Or*, cannot be a rational one.

MacIntyre focuses upon the transition from an aesthetic to an ethical view of existence. It is clear, however, from Kierkegaard's own description of this transition, that MacIntyre has not properly understood Kierkegaard's position. The aesthetic stage of existence is also referred to by Kierkegaard as the stage of immediacy. To be an aesthete, for Kierkegaard, means to have an understanding of existence which interprets it in terms of what appears, in an immediate sense, to be true about it. Such an individual has his consciousness, according to Kierkegaard—and in particular his consciousness of suffering—in the dialectic of fortune and misfortune.[7] Thus Kierkegaard argues that misfortune or suffering is, for this individual,

> like a narrow pass on the way; now the immediate individual is in it, but his view of life must essentially always tell him that the difficulty will soon cease to hinder because it is a foreign element. If it does not cease, he despairs, by which his immediacy ceases to function, and the transition to another understanding of existence is rendered possible.[8]

What happens to the aesthete is that, in his despair, it seems to him as if there is a discrepancy between his suffering—insofar as it is persistent—and the interpretation of existence in which suffering is viewed as having merely accidental significance. Thus the aesthete, using the persistence of his suffering as a criterion for choosing between a view of existence in which suffering is considered merely accidental and a view in which it is seen as essential, may reject the aesthetic interpretation in favor of an ethical one. Such an individual adopts an ethical framework, not because it promises to *alleviate* his suffering, but because it provides an interpretation of his existence which sees suffering as something essential to that existence, and thus provides a more adequate—or one might even say more rational—account of his subjective experience.

It may be that there are other criteria, or other aspects of subjective experience apart from suffering, that could serve as criteria for choosing between competing interpretations of existence on Kierkegaard's view. Suffering is, however, the criterion which Kierkegaard himself chooses to focus upon when examining the nature of the transition from one stage of existence to another in the *Postscript*[9] and it will become apparent, in the pages which follow, that this criterion alone is enough to expose the erroneous nature of MacIntyre's interpretation of Kierkegaard and his subsequent charge that Kierkegaard was an irrationalist.

II

Insofar as one framework or interpretation of existence may be spoken of as more adequate than another—that is, insofar as it may be spoken of as providing a more satisfactory account of the nature of the subjective experience of a particular individual—it is entirely reasonable to consider that it is more rational.[10] What is likely less clear, however, is precisely *how* the individual comes to consider that one interpretation is more adequate than another. In this instance we are concerned specifically with how it is that the individual comes to consider that the persistence of suffering is too great for the aesthetic interpretation of existence to be plausible, for it appears that it would be entirely possible for an individual to persist in suffering while *simultaneously* persisting in the belief that the suffering was indeed accidental and that in the next moment, with a change of fortune, it would stop.

Objectively, there is no incoherence in the idea that an aesthetic individual may experience persistent suffering. The accidental may indeed be persistent. The aesthetic interpretation of existence is not contradicted by the occurrence of what is, within this framework, the improbable persistence of suffering. Such statements of probability or improbability as a given framework expresses

> cannot be strictly contradicted by any event [e.g., the persistence of suffering] however improbably this event may appear in its light. The contradiction must be established by a *personal* [my italics] act of appraisal.[11]

The question is: Whence arises this "personal act of appraisal"; or when and how does the individual come to consider the persistence of his suffering to be too great and hence too improbable, within the aesthetic framework, for that interpretation of existence to be correct?

It is at this point that Kierkegaard's views concerning the role of passion in human reason come into play. It is widely recognized by Kierkegaard scholars that, as Heinrich Schmidinger expresses it: "*Subjektives Engagement ist...immer mit Leidenschaft und Pathos verbunden.*"[12] It has also been observed, however, that Kierkegaard considers passion to be opposed to reflection,[13] hence it is often believed that subjective engagement, according to Kierkegaard, is purely emotional, or devoid of any intellectual component.

This view is the result of a failure to appreciate that the intellectual dimension of human experience is not reducible, for Kierkegaard, to reflection. Reflection is indeed dispassionate or disinterested, according to Kierkegaard.[14] He also speaks of "abstract" or "systematic" thought as disinterested.[15] This would appear, however, to be a rather abbreviated or short hand way of emphasizing that the object of such thought is not the self, for he states elsewhere that all knowledge "is interested,"[16] whether the object of interest is something outside the knower, as is the case in metaphysics, or whether it is the knower himself, as is the case in ethics and religion.

Kierkegaard often equates passion and interest.[17] It is thus reasonable to assume that, if knowledge is interested, then it is also passionate, or involves passion at some level. But if knowledge involves passion, then it would appear that passion is not essentially opposed to reason, but rather plays an important part in the activity of the knower as such. If this is the case, then the passionate nature of subjective engagement does not preclude the possibility that such engagement could be rational. Hence the "personal act of appraisal" in question is not a merely arbitrary, capricious or emotional reaction to a phenomenon or particular set of phenomena; it is the result of a rational assessment of this phenomenon, or these phenomena, where the reason in question is of a passionate or interested sort.

The difficulty is that very few scholars appreciate the way in which passion informs reason, on Kierkegaard's view. In order to throw some light on this issue I shall depart for a moment from the examination of Kierkegaard's texts and turn instead to the consideration of the views of a more contemporary philosopher on this same issue. Michael Polanyi, whose views on probability I quoted above, is concerned in his book *Personal Knowledge* with how it is that apparently objectively meaningless probability statements become subjectively meaningful guides for interpreting reality.[18] Polanyi maintains that there is an area of extremely low probability—i.e., what we would refer to in everyday speech as an area of high improbability—that we find generally unacceptable. The occurrence of an event that is associated with this level of improbability leads us, he argues, to reject the interpretation of existence within which this event is considered so improbable and to search for a new interpretation where events such as the one in question are considered more probable. Polanyi goes on to point out, however, that any attempt to *formalize* the precise degree of improbability that we find unacceptable and which, when connected to a particular phenomenon within a given theory or interpretation of existence, would lead us to reject that view as false "is likely to go too far unless it acknowledges in advance *that it* [i.e., the formalization] *must remain within a framework of personal* [i.e., impassioned subjective] *judgement.*"[19]

The metaphysical tradition has led us to believe that such impassioned subjective judgement is vastly inferior—if indeed it has any claim to legitimacy at all—to dispassionate objective judgement. In a situation such as the one described above, however, a purely dispassionate or objective perspective would lead to no judgement at all, but rather to a sort of skeptical *epoche*. That is, viewed purely objectively, the occurrence of a highly improbable event says nothing about the truth or falsity of the framework within which it is viewed as improbable; it neither supports it, nor discredits it, so it fails to provide us with a foundation—i.e., an *objective* foundation—for any judgement whatsoever concerning the status of the framework.

It is clear, though, that not only do we often make such judgements, we appear to be *compelled* to make them simply by virtue of the kind of creatures we are. The difficulty is that there appear to be no fixed guidelines in relation to these judgements. But to say that there are no *fixed* guidelines is not to say that there are no guidelines at all. Passion, which has traditionally been considered to be in essential opposition to reason, permeates our understanding—or attempts to understand—our situation at such points and it is this passion, according to Kierkegaard, which serves as a guide to the judgements we make in these situations.

III

The metaphysical tradition has been reluctant to appreciate the way in which passion informs our understanding of ourselves and the phenomena of our experience, hence it is to Polanyi, a chemist turned philosopher—i.e., a metaphysical interloper—that we must turn for the explicitly formulated observation that some of the most meaningful of our assertions in science are only possible as the result of a collaboration of reason and passion and that these assertions will thus always and necessarily "have a passionate quality attached to them."[20]

Passion is admittedly not an easy concept to elucidate. Some effort at elucidation is necessary, however, because it is precisely passion that, according to Kierkegaard, informs the understanding of an individual in such a way that extra-framework criteria, or reasons for choosing between competing interpretations of existence, may come to exist for him.

A *positive* account of the meaning of 'passion' is difficult, if not impossible, to provide. An impression of this meaning may be provided, however, if the expression is understood to be contrasted with such expressions as 'dispassion' or 'disinterestedness.' Polanyi claims that passion is to be found in our "personal *participation*"[21] with the phenomenon whose probability is in question. Such participation might be understood to exemplify an essentially interested, as opposed to disinterested, relation to this phenomenon. It is just such an *interested* stance which Kierkegaard believes is *appropriate* with respect to the subjective phenomenon of suffering[22] That is, Kierkegaard maintains that we have an essential interest in determining or choosing the proper interpretation of existence. Our eternal blessedness, or eternal damnation is, according to Kierkegaard, ultimately dependent upon this choice. But if we do not take such an interested stance in relation to the phenomena of our subjective experience, then it will never be possible for us to choose between various interpretations of existence[23]—and, in particular, to choose the *correct* one—for the criteria for such choices can only exist for the *interested* observer. It is for this reason that Kierkegaard argues in the *Postscript* that Christianity has "nothing whatever to do with the systematic zeal of the personally *indifferent* [my italics] individual," but assumes rather "an infinite personal passionate *interest* [my italics]" on the part of the individual as *"conditio sine qua non."*[24]

Thus it becomes clear that the discernment of a discrepancy between the aesthetic interpretation of existence, which sees suffering as accidental, and the persistence of the suffering which the individual experiences, is the result of an impassioned or subjective judgement on the part of that individual. The greater the degree of passion with which the consciousness of the individual is informed, the less high the degree of the improbability of the suffering need be, in order for the individual to seize upon that improbability as grounds for rejecting the interpretation of existence within which the particular account of suffering is contained.[25]

Picture the aesthete who experiences persistent suffering, but does not despair—i.e., he does not judge that his subjective experience discredits the interpretation of existence which views it as improbable. What distinguishes such an individual from one who does despair? It would appear that the individual who does not despair, fails to do so because he considers the phenomena of his existence—or of his subjective experience—objectively, which is to say, dispassionately; while the individual who does despair, does so precisely because he considers these same phenomena subjectively or passionately.

It is one thing, however, to observe that a choice between competing interpretations of existence is only possible if one takes a passionate or interested stance relative to the phenomena of one's subjective experience, and another to argue that such a stance justifies rather than merely explains this choice. Passion, for Kierkegaard, is the very essence of human existence. It is well known that Kierkegaard proposes that subjectivity is truth,[26] but it is not so well known that he also proposes that subjectivity is passion.[27] To be dispassionate, or insufficiently passionate, for Kierkegaard, is to be indifferent to existence, and this, in turn, amounts to being insufficiently human. It is for this reason that Kierkegaard considers the choice of an ethical over an aesthetic interpretation of existence to be justified, rather than merely explicable. That is, a passionate perspective relative to the phenomena of one's subjective experience is the only sort of perspective that is in keeping, on Kierkegaard's view, with the essence of the individual. A dispassionate perspective would not cohere with that essence.

Thus passion emerges as the catalyst of the exchange of one perspective of existence for another. That is, passion breaks down the apparent coherence or descriptive adequacy of a particular interpretation of existence. Unless the consciousness of the individual is informed with a sufficient degree of passion, the persistence of his or her suffering cannot serve as a criterion for rejecting the aesthetic in favor of the ethical interpretation of existence.

It is, of course, possible to be *too* passionate. If the consciousness of the individual is informed with too much passion, the resultant interpretation of existence may cross over into the pathological. Such a phenomenon is actually addressed by Kierkegaard and referred to by him in the *Postscript* as subjective madness (*subjective Galskab*).[28] It is important to note, however, that it is not possible to formalize the precise degree of passion which is sufficient to break down the aesthetic interpretation of existence so that the choice of another interpretation becomes possible, and yet not so great as to qualify the individual as pathological. It is precisely this resistance of passion, or of an understanding which is informed with passion, to such formalization that serves as a stumbling block to metaphysics. But this is simply our situation as human beings and part of the task of philosophy is to help us to achieve a more profound understanding of that situation.

IV

I have restricted my explication of the nature of the transition from one stage of existence to another to the transition from the aesthetic to the ethical stage. I have done this because this was the transition that MacIntyre examined and which he used in an effort to support his charge that Kierkegaard was an irrationalist. It should be clear now that Kierkegaard's own interpretation of the nature of this transition will not support MacIntyre's charge. Opponents of the view I am propounding might argue, however, that while it appears possible to consider the choice between any of the non-Christian interpretations as rational, the same thing cannot be said concerning the choice to adopt a Christian framework. It is tempting to interpret Kierkegaard such that it appears the transition to the Christian stage of existence is the result of a choice for which there can be no criterion.

We can see, however, from the quotation below, that there is a criterion for choosing the Christian interpretation; this criterion is precisely the phenomenon of the consciousness of sin. That is, Kierkegaard contends that

> Christianity is only related to the consciousness of sin. Any other attempt to become a Christian for any other reason is quite literally lunacy; and that is how it should be.[29]

Just as the ethical interpretation of existence provided a more adequate account of human suffering to the aesthete whose consciousness was informed with a sufficient degree of passion, so does the Christian interpretation provide a more adequate account of the subjective experience of the individual whose consciousness is informed with an even greater degree of passion .

Such passion arises, again, from an *interested* stance toward the question of which of the possible interpretations of existence is correct. The more extreme the interpretation presented to the individual, the more passionate as opposed to dispassionate—must his or her self examination be. That is, when an individual is presented with an interpretation of existence such as that offered by Christianity, an interpretation which makes his or her *eternal blessedness* or *eternal damnation* dependent upon its acceptance, then the proper response is not a casual concern as to the truth of this interpretation, but rather a deep and impassioned introspection in which the individual repeatedly asks himself: "Could this be the real nature of my existence?" "Does this interpretation of my existence make the most sense—i.e., more sense than any other interpretation—of my subjective experience?"[30]

V

With this we have a simple model of Kierkegaard's theory concerning the nature of human rationality. We must distinguish, however, what is essential to Kierkegaard's position as he understood it, and what is essential for the purposes of defending Kierkegaard against the charge of irrationalism as that charge was leveled against him by MacIntyre. It is important to appreciate that Kierkegaard's own understanding of the position described above involved a foundation of religious belief which is separable from the position itself. Kierkegaard would no more consider the persistence of an individual who has the good luck not to suffer in an aesthetic interpretation to be justified than we would consider the racism of an ignorant person to be justified. That is, just as we would consider that an ignorant person *should* know better than to be racist, Kierkegaard would consider that a fortunate person *should* know better than to persist in an aesthetic interpretation of existence.

Existence, for Kierkegaard, is characterized by sin and part of the way in which sin manifests itself is in the inability of the individual to sustain emotional equilibrium in the face of misfortune or adversity. It is this inability which accounts for the suffering in question. The difficulty is that this inability itself stems from an excessive attachment to worldly pleasure or comfort.[31] As long as the existence of an individual is characterized by such attachment, suffering is still present in it, *in potentia*. Hence, while suffering justifies the choice of an ethical over an aesthetic interpretation of existence, on Kierkegaard's view, the absence of suffering does not have the same significance. The absence of suffering does not justify the endorsement of an aesthetic view of existence because suffering is always present in the existence of an individual *in potentia*, so to speak, in the form of sin. Any individual who is sufficiently reflective to appreciate the tenuous nature of happiness on the aesthetic interpretation, would find his or her existence, no matter how "fortunate," characterized by an anxiety or fear of potential adversity which would itself constitute a kind of suffering. The only way to avoid such anxiety, on Kierkegaard's view, would be to avoid reflection.

We may argue that different levels of reflection are natural for different sorts of people and that it is even possible for certain individuals to live lives almost entirely devoid of reflection. Kierkegaard's religious convictions compel him to assume, however, that the activity of reflection is universally human and that whatever differences there may be in the degree of reflection which characterize various individuals, even the least reflective individual can only avoid recognizing the tenuous nature of happiness on the aesthetic view of existence by *willfully refusing* to reflect upon the significance of this view. And this willful refusal, on Kierkegaard's view, constitutes, in turn, a flight from the acknowledgement of oneself as sinful.

It is not necessary, however, that one share Kierkegaard's religious views in order to appreciate the force of his claim concerning the possibility of extra-framework criteria for choosing between competing interpretations of existence. If this were necessary, then the charge of irrationalism could still be leveled against him. That is, the support for his position would ultimately rest upon a foundation of dogma that could not itself be chosen for any reason, for it would only be relative to this foundation that reasons for such choices could exist.

One of the most important aspects of Kierkegaard's position is that experience is distinguished from the various interpretations which may be supplied to it. The medium of experience, according to Kierkegaard, is *actuality*, while the medium of such interpretations is *ideality*. That is, the interpretations represent clusters of concepts (hence the origin of the appellation "conceptual framework") and the medium of concepts is abstract, in contrast to the medium of experience, which is concrete.[32]

We can keep the view that subjective experience, insofar as it is actual, may be distinguished from a particular conceptual framework or ideal interpretation that is supplied to it and the claim that this experience can provide criteria for choosing between such frameworks, without having to accept the view that experience, properly defined, will always incline one toward a *particular* interpretation of existence. This is what one might refer to as the theoretical skeleton of Kierkegaard's view of rationality as it appears when stripped of the religious assumptions which gave the view its more specific definition in Kierkegaard's works.[33]

Taylor's contention that the transition from one interpretation of existence to another is effected through a move of error reduction is consistent with much of what Kierkegaard says concerning such transitions. On Kierkegaard's view, one rejects the aesthetic framework in favor of an ethical one precisely because a passionate interpretation of the persistence of one's suffering leads one to consider that there is an error in the aesthetic framework—the "error" in question being the view that suffering is of merely accidental significance or the result of misfortune. The difference between Taylor and Kierkegaard is that on Kierkegaard's account, the errors are not inconsistencies *within* a particular framework— for as we have seen, the persistence of suffering is not, objectively, inconsistent with the interpretation of existence which views such persistence as improbable—but are errors relative to the individual's subjective or impassioned *experience*.

One could express Kierkegaard's views in secular terms by substituting for "guilt consciousness" or "[t]he anguished conscience" what Taylor has identified as a "need for meaning."[34] Taylor contends that individuals are faced today with the problem of attempting to imbue their existence with some significance that goes beyond the expression and fulfillment—or lack thereof—of their daily needs.

Thus if one is more comfortable with the expression 'need for meaning' than with Kierkegaard's overtly religious expression like 'guilt consciousness,' an individual could be understood as adopting a particular framework because he perceived that that framework promised to imbue his existence with the meaning of which he felt a lack. In this way an ethical interpretation of existence could be seen as supplying meaning to the suffering of an individual that the aesthetic interpretation was unable to supply.[35]

Concluding Comments

It should now be clear that the charge of irrationalism leveled against Kierkegaard by MacIntyre is based upon a misunderstanding of the relation between the aesthetic and the ethical interpretations of existence on Kierkegaard's view. Not only is Kierkegaard's philosophy not irrationalist in the way in which MacIntyre and others have claimed, his conception of the nature of human rationality is one which can be of great help in relation to the contemporary debate on the nature of human rationality. The view that "rational" decisions need not always be the result of purely objective or dispassionate speculation and that hence emotional or non-rational phenomena may serve as criteria for such choices is clearly one which would be of use to contemporary theorists.

Kierkegaard's interpretation of human rationality provides us with a positive alternative to the traditional conception of reason as disinterested and dispassionate. But it is not *simply* an alternative to this more traditional conception. It is an alternative with an *advantage*. That is, it provides us with a way to get beyond the *impasse* at which the contemporary debate on the issue has arrived, by reminding us that there are some areas of inquiry where "an objective indifference can...learn nothing at all,"[36] or as Nagel expressed it in *The View From Nowhere*, where "the truth is not to be found by traveling as far away from one's personal perspective as possible,"[37] and hence where being "rational" means taking a passionate or interested stance in relation to the phenomena in question.

Kierkegaard's view of rationality possesses a further advantage over the traditional view in that it provides us with a more descriptively adequate account of our understanding of ourselves and of the phenomena of our subjective experience. That is, it does not preclude the possibility that our movement from one interpretation of existence to another may take place as a natural or evolutionary development rather than as the result of a choice, but it also allows us to make sense of the experience, that we at least occasionally have, that we *choose* to adopt a particular interpretation of existence, that there are good *reasons* for adopting this interpretation and that we choose to adopt it *for* those reasons and not simply as a matter of pure caprice.

What we have in Kierkegaard's picture of the role of passion in reason is a more "reasonable" picture of reason than the one that has been offered to us by the metaphysical tradition. It is a picture of reason that involves a positive incorporation of what we essentially are, subjects situated in and passionately engaged with the flux which constitutes our temporal existence. Finally, it is a picture that allows us to justify rationally the weight that we seem *compelled*, simply by virtue of the kind of creatures we are, to attribute to our subjective experience.

McGill University

Endnotes

1 Charles Taylor, "Inescapable Frameworks," in *Sources of the Self* (Cambridge: Harvard University Press, 1989), pp. 3-24.

2 See note 1 above.

3 Alasdair MacIntyre, *After Virtue* (Notre Dame, Indiana: University of Notre Dame Press, 1984), pp. 36-62.

4 This and all subsequent quotations of MacIntyre are taken from page 38 of *After Virtue*.

5 There is some disagreement among Kierkegaard scholars as to the precise number of stages or interpretations of existence that are to be found in Kierkegaard's works. There is general agreement, however, that there are at least the four stages listed here, although there may be perhaps more than these four.

6 It is possible that the status of certain choices as rational will remain constant across frameworks. Candidates for such constancy, however, would most likely be very mundane or innocuous sorts of choices (e.g., the choice of an aspirin to alleviate headache pain).

7 *Concluding Unscientific Postcript*, translated by David F. Swenson and Walter Lowrie (Princeton: Princeton University Press, 1941), p.388/*Søren Kierkegaards Samlede Vaerker*, edited by A. B. Drachman, J. L. Heiberg and H. O. Lang (Copenhagen: Gyldendal, 1901-06), Vol. VII, pp. 376-77.

8 *Postscript*, p. 388/*Samlede Værker*, Vol. VII, p. 377.

9 See notes 7 and 8.

10 The failure of many philosophers to appreciate this point is very likely the result of what Thomas Nagel has pointed out is an "ambiguity in the idea of the rational." That is, Nagel observes that "'[r]ational' may mean either rationally required or rationally acceptable" (*The View From Nowhere* [New York: Oxford University Press, 1986], p. 200).

11 Michael Polanyi, *Personal Knowledge* (Chicago: University of Chicago Press 1958), p. 24.

12 Heinrich Schmidinger, *Das Problem des Interesses und die Philosophie Sören Kierkegaards* (Freiberg/München: Verlag Karl Alber, 1983), p. 218.

13 Marold Westphal, *Kierkegaard's Critique of Religion and Society* (Macon, Georgia: Mercer University Press, 1987), p. 46.

14 *Philosophical Fragments; Johannes Climacus*, edited and translated by Howard and Edna H. Hong (Princeton: Princeton University Press, 1985), p. 170/*Søren Kierkegaards Papirer*, edited by P. A. Heiberg, V. Kuhr, E. Torsting and N. Thulstrup (Copenhagen: Glydendal, 1968-78), Vol. IV B 1, p. 149.

15 *Postscript*, p. 278/*Samlede Værker*, Vol. VII, p. 296; Søren Kierkegaard's Journals and Papers, translated by Howard V. and Edna H. Hong (Bloomington: Indiana University Press, 1967-78), Vol. 5 5621/*Papirer*, Vol. IV B 1, p. 149.

16 *Journals and Papers*, Vol. 2 2283/*Papirer*, Vol. IV C 99; *Journals and Papers*, Vol. 1 891/*Papirer*, Vol. IV B 13: 18.

17 See Schmidinger, op. cit., p. 254.

18 The purpose of Polanyi's claim that probability statements are objectively meaningless is to point out that such statements are essentially ambiguous.

Probability statements relating to the behavior of electrons, for example, convey to the researcher that electron *may* or *may not* be found in a particular spot at a particular time. Since this is something of which the scientist is undoubtedly already aware, even without the aid of the probability statement, Polanyi suggests that this ambiguity may lead one to conclude that probability statements do not *really* say anything. He argues, however, that there is "some meaning in assigning a numerical value to the probability of our finding an electron at a certain place on a particular occasion" (p. 21), but this meaning, he goes on to argue is to be found in our personal participation in the event to which the probability statement refers" (p. 21).

[19] Ibid., p. 29. The "passionate" or "impassioned" quality of our judgments, statements or assertions is the theme of the section of *Personal Knowledge* entitled "The Nature of Assertions" (pp. 27-30).

[20] Op. cit., p. 27.

[21] Ibid., p. 24.

[22] For a comprehensive treatment of the significance of the concept of interest in Kierkegaard's philosophy, see: Heinrich M. Schmidinger, op. cit.

[23] One might argue that a completely arbitrary choice would still be possible. This is not Kierkegaard's position, however. Kierkegaard believes that we inherit an aesthetic interpretation of existence simply by being human and that we will never adopt any other perspective without a specific reason for doing so; and such a reason cannot arise, on his view, unless we take an interested stance toward the phenomena of our subjective experience.

[24] *Postscript*, p. 19/*Samlede Værker*, Vol. VII, p. 6.

[25] This situation is perhaps best illustrated by referring to the example of little children. Young children have not yet learned to view their situations dispassionately (and, in general, the younger the children, the more this is true of them), hence their judgments are often informed with a very high degree of passion. Children thus often seize upon even the slightest improbability as grounds for rejecting either the event with which the improbability is associated, or the framework within which the event in question is viewed as improbable. Children playing a game, for example, often refuse to accept that the same person can win even twice in a row. When faced with such a phenomenon they will often attempt either to show that the child in question has not actually won (i.e., that his evaluation of his situation was not correct) or that he cheated.

[26] *Postscript*, pp. 169-244/*Samlede Værker*, Vol. VII, pp. 157-211.

[27] *Postscript*, p. 117/*Samlede Værker*, Vol. VII, p. 106.

[28] *Postscript*, p. 175/*Samlede Værker*, Vol. VII, p. 163.

[29] *Journals and Papers*, Vol. 1 492/*Papirer*, Vol. IX A 414. The translation above is from a book called *The Diary of Søren Kierkegaard*, edited by Peter P. Rhode (Secaucus, NJ: Citadel Press, 1960), p. 150, and not from the Hong and Hong translation of Kierkegaard's *Journals and Papers*. The Hong translation is not substantially different. I have chosen the former translation, however, because I believe it is a little more readable.

[30] This is one of the reasons that Kierkegaard had so little patience with organized Christianity, or, more specifically, with the Lutheran church in Denmark. That is, the version of Christianity offered to Danes by the Danish church was so denatured that the impassioned consciousness would reject it and hence the

possibility of the individual's coming to believe the truth of Christianity would be precluded. *See Postscript*, pp. 323-43/*Samlede Vaerker*, Vol. VII, pp. 312-33.

[31] The expression 'worldly' should not be equated with 'material.' 'Worldly' is a much broader determination which encompasses all human pleasures, including intellectual and emotional ones, conceived independently of any religious significance they might have.

[32] It is important to acknowledge, however, that the conceptual framework to which an individual subscribes helps to define his experience. This point was clearly not lost on Kierkegaard, as is demonstrated by his observation that "the true conception of despair is indispensable for conscious despair" (*The Sickness Unto Death*, translated by Howard V. and Edna H. Hong [Princeton: Princeton University Press, 1980], p. 47/*Samlede Værker*, Vol. XI, p. 160). An individual's experience must still, according to Kierkegaard, be assumed to be substantially independent of the remark which helps to define it, or else it cannot have the role in transition from one framework to another that it is described by him as having. This putative independence is strengthened by Nagel's claim that "we don't ascribe such states [e.g., suffering] only to creatures who have mental concepts: we ascribe them to children and animals, and believe that we ourselves would have experiences even if we didn't have the language" (op. cit., p. 23).

[33] This move should not be disturbing to anyone who shares Kierkegaard's religious convictions because saying that experience, properly defined, will not necessarily incline one toward a particular interpretation of existence does not make it so. If Kierkegaard is correct, then, of course, all roads will lead to Rome, so to speak (i.e., all experience, properly defined, will incline one toward a particular interpretation of existence). This is not, however, a matter for philosophers, but is rather between each individual and his or her own experience. That is, it is a matter for each individual as such, and this, according to Kierkegaard, is exactly as it should be.

[34] See note 1 above. Such a substitution does not entail that a "need for meaning" is equivalent to "guilt consciousness," but merely that they are criteria of the same kind. That is, both expressions are qualifications of subjective experience, although their content may be quite different.

[35] One could not conclude from this, however, that the ethical interpretation is *objectively* more meaningful than the aesthetic interpretation. A foundation of something on the order of Kierkegaard's religious convictions is necessary to sustain that sort of claim. It is enough, however, that one interpretation of existence is *subjectively* more meaningful than another in order for the choice of that interpretation to be viewed as a rational one for the individual in question.

[36] *Postscript*, p. 51/*Samlede Værker*, Vol. VII, p. 39.

[37] Op. cit., p. 27.

Study Questions

1. What are the advantages Marilyn Piety sees in Kierkegaard's view of the nature of human rationality over the more dispassionate way of construing it (reason)? Do you agree with her contention?

2.   Of the two approaches to Kierkegaard, which do you prefer, Adams or Piety? Why?

3.   What does Piety mean when she says that Kierkegaard has appreciated the way in which "passion informs our understanding of ourselves"?

4.   How would you compare and contrast Adams' analysis of Kierkegaard's view of passion with Piety's interpretation?

5.   In what way(s) does Piety construe Kierkegaard's rationality? Do you agree with her reading of Kierkegaard?

4

The Relevance of Historical Evidence for Christian Faith: A Critique of a Kierkegaardian View

C. Stephen Evans

C. Stephen Evans is professor of philosophy at Calvin College, and is author of *Subjectivity & Religious Belief.*

If we assume that Christian faith involves a propositional component whose content is historical, then the question arises as to whether Christian faith must be based on historical evidence, at least in part. One of Kierkegaard's pseudonyms, Johannes Climacus, argues in *Philosophical Fragments* that though faith does indeed have such an historical component, it does not depend on evidence, but rather on a first-hand experience of Jesus for which historical records serve only as an occasion. I argue that Climacus' account is coherent, and that on such a view historical evidence is not sufficient for faith for anyone. However, in contrast to Climacus, I argue that evidence might still be valuable and even necessary for some people. The resulting danger that the decision about faith might become a question for scholarship is best met, not by insulating faith from historical scholarship, but by recognizing the ability of faith to supply a context in which the evidence available is sufficient.*

While no one would wish to identify Christian faith with propositional belief, traditional Christians hold that Christian faith does involve, include, or presuppose certain propositional beliefs. Among these beliefs some are historical in character. For example, traditional Christians believe that Jesus suffered under Pontius Pilate, was crucified, buried, and rose again from the dead, and they also hold that these beliefs are central components of their faith.

I have already said that faith cannot simply be identified with these beliefs, or any set of propositional beliefs. Faith is a trusting commitment which transforms a person and leads to eternal life. For the Christian this faith consists in or is made possible by a relationship to an historical person, Jesus of Nazareth, but one could hardly be consciously related to a person about whom one had no beliefs at all. So the traditional view that faith involves historical belief is plausible.

That view, however, raises a number of weighty problems concerning the relationship of faith to history. One of the most important concerns the relation of faith to historical evidence. If faith includes historical beliefs, then it seems plausible that faith would not be reasonable unless it were reasonable to hold the historical beliefs in question. Ordinarily, historical beliefs are held on the basis of historical evidence of various types. Is it the case, then, that people should only seek to develop and maintain Christian faith if there is sufficient historical evidence to make the historical beliefs that are a component of that faith reasonable?

1. Faith and History in Philosophical Fragments

This question is explored at some length by Johannes Climacus, the pseudonymous character Søren Kierkegaard created to be the author of *Philosophical Fragments*. (In what follows I shall defer to Kierkegaard's wish to cite the pseudonymous authors when referring to his pseudonymous works.) In this work Climacus presents what he terms a thought-experiment. He first describes what he terms the "Socratic" view of "the Truth," a term which is here close to the religious concept of salvation. On the Socratic view, each person has the Truth within already, and a relationship to the divine can thereby be presupposed in every person. He then asks whether any alternative to such a view can be imagined, and proceeds to "invent," with clear ironical and humorous touches, a view that suspiciously resembles Christianity, according to which the Truth must be brought to the individual by a god who becomes a human being in order to make it possible for the individual to receive the Truth. A relationship to the divine is thus made possible by the god's historical appearance.

I shall assume that Climacus' thought-experiment is presented in order to illuminate the nature of Christian faith, as Climacus himself clearly says at the conclusion of the book, and that the significant features of this experiment are to be taken as features of Christian faith as well. When this assumption is made, Climacus' thoughts on the relationship between faith and historical evidence are quite unusual when compared with most Christian thinkers, and their oddity stems from what appears to be an internal tension.

On the one hand, Climacus wants to maintain there is an essential difference between Christianity and Greek modes of thought, a difference which depends on the historical component of Christianity. Climacus could say with respect to Christianity what Johannes de Silentio says about faith in *Fear and Trembling:* Either Christianity is something essentially different from what Socrates could have come up with, or else Christianity does not exist, "precisely because it has always existed."[1] In such a case, Christianity as a unique phenomenon would not exist because it would simply be a specific version of a generic human religiosity. Climacus locates the essential distinguishing feature of Christianity in the historical entrance of the God into history. A real alternative to Socratic "immanence" (a Kierkegaardian term for any view that regards the Truth as something human beings possess or can attain using only their own unaided natural powers) requires that we deny that the Truth is in us, even in the form of a potentiality for recognizing the Truth.[2] The Truth as well as the capacity to recognize the Truth must be brought to us by a God who enters history. So any attempt to replace the Jesus of history with a mythical figure whose real significance lies in the existential meaning of the narrative, or in the content of the teaching must be rejected.[3] The objectivity of the historical is required in order to get "the God outside yourself."[4]

This emphasis on history is, however, coupled with a depreciation of historical knowledge as in any way necessary or sufficient for becoming a disciple. Climacus seems to make historical knowledge virtually irrelevant to faith:

> Even if the contemporary generation had not left anything behind except these words, "We have believed that in such and such a year the god appeared in the humble form of a servant, lived and taught among us, and then died"—this is more than enough. The contemporary generation would have done what is needful, for this little announcement, this world-historical *nota bene,* is enough to become an occasion for someone who comes later, and the most prolix report can never in all eternity become more for the person who comes later.[5]

The unusual nature of Climacus' ideas is now clear. More commonly, those who have held that the incarnation was a genuinely historical event in something like the traditional sense, however varied that sense may be, have also held that it was important to have good historical evidence for that event. Those who believe we do not have such evidence, but still wish to affirm a faith in Christ as the divine lord, have tended to reinterpret the incarnation as a symbol whose power does not rest on its objective historicity.

The question I wish to pose is whether the conjunction of the claim that the historical is essential with the claim that historical evidence is unimportant makes sense. If not, the question of which to modify would still be open. Both traditional Christians as well as those more liberal Christians still engaged in the quest for the historical Jesus would argue that what must go is the cavalier dismissal of historical evidence. These groups have been suspicious of Kierkegaard for what they perceive as his irrationalism. Many contemporary theologians, on the other hand, convinced that making faith dependent on historical evidence is a recipe for disaster, would argue that what must go is the assumption that faith must be grounded in factual historical events.

2. Reasons for Making Faith Independent of Historical Evidence

I believe that Climacus has strong reasons for wishing to avoid both of these recommendations. Whether those reasons are ultimately decisive, and indeed whether there is really a coherent alternative to the revisions his critics would urge upon him remains to be determined. There are several reasons why he wishes to avoid making faith dependent on historical evidence. I shall discuss two of those reasons briefly at this point, postponing a look at the third and final reason until later.

The first reason is that if faith were dependent on historical evidence, it would violate a commitment to a kind of egalitarian principle of justice to which Climacus is committed. Climacus believes that the attainment of the Truth must somehow be equally available to people of every generation. "Would the god allow the power of time to decide whom he would grant his favor, or would it not be worthy of the god to make the reconciliation equally difficult for every human being at every time and in every place."[6] If faith were dependent on historical evidence, then it would be very difficult to satisfy this principle, since it would appear that eyewitnesses or those with greater access to the historical records would have an advantage.

Actually, it is not easy to see how this egalitarianism could be satisfied by a faith with historical, propositional content, even if that faith is not based on historical evidence, since it would be difficult for those people who have not even heard of the events to have any beliefs about them, even if they do not need historical evidence to believe them. Perhaps, Climacus can find a way to surmount this problem, however. He might assume that God somehow supplies people with the content of what they must believe, either in this life or after death.[7] Alternatively, the principle of equality might be restricted to those who have had a fair chance to hear of the historical events in question. Perhaps it is only their salvation that depends on attaining the right kind of historical faith, and those in a different situation are not measured by the same standard. If so, then one can see how the claim that faith does not rest on historical evidence introduces a greater measure of equality within the group of people who have heard the news. In any case, Climacus has other reasons for not allowing faith to depend on historical evidence.

A second reason is what might be called the incommensurability between authentic religious commitment and matters of intellectual evidence. This theme, which is more developed in *Postscript* than in *Fragments,* focuses on the character of Christian faith, which has about it an absoluteness and finality.[8] A person of faith is someone who is willing to risk her life and stake everything on what she believes. The evidence for an historical event can never be more than probable and tentative, subject to revision in light of new findings. Climacus thinks that if faith were based on evidence, it would necessarily share in this tentativeness. He wants to see faith as a life-transforming passion but does not see how such a passion could be engendered by calculation of evidential probabilities. Hence he does not wish to see faith as something that depends on evidence whose quality necessarily fluctuates as new discoveries are made and further inquiry is carried out.

3. Why Historicity Matters

On the other hand, Climacus wishes to resist giving up the objective historicity of the incarnation because it is the actual historicity of the incarnation that makes possible a revelation that can confront and correct my deep-rooted assumptions about God and myself. If I am indeed sinful, and if those deeply rooted assumptions are wrong, then the possibility of such a revelation is not to be dismissed in a cavalier way. The incarnation makes Christianity what is termed in *Postscript* a religion of "transcendence." Transcendence is important here not only for its possible value as a corrective and challenge to my individual errors and pride; it also represents the foundation of any genuinely human social order.

The established social order constantly attempts to deify itself; that is the secret of Christendom, which is merely the attempt to employ Christianity to do what human societies always do. To foil this human attempt at self-deification, epitomized in the Hegelian political philosophy, we need a God who is truly transcendent, so that the established order can be seen in its relativity, and the possibility of critical dissent be kept open. Despite Kierkegaard's own political conservatism, there is a radical element to his social and political thought, an element that is tied to transcendence. Without a transcendent God in time, who speaks to us from "outside" our innate religious consciousness, we humans will manufacture God in our own image, and we will do so to buttress the status quo. Any attempt to substitute for the historical incarnation a "myth" or "story" or "symbol" whose factual truth is unimportant inevitably transforms Christianity into a "Socratic" view that assumes that our religious consciousness does possess the Truth.

Despite these reasons for holding both to the historicity of the incarnation and the irrelevance of historical evidence, Climacus' view is problematic. Is it possible to believe that Jesus Christ lived and died for me as the Son of God, and be indifferent to critical questions about the factuality of my beliefs? Suppose, to push things to the extreme, that it could be shown that there was no first-hand evidence at all, and that overwhelmingly powerful evidence appeared that the New Testament was concocted in the fourth century. In such a situation would a person not naturally doubt whether Jesus had lived at all, and accordingly doubt whether or not he was indeed divine?

One could at this point retreat to the view that the object of faith is simply that the god has appeared somewhere, sometime. However, the content of faith would in that case seem distressingly vague, a blank canvas that will have little power to jolt and overturn our current Socratic ideas. Does such a vague historical claim really differ much from a Socratic myth? M. J. Ferreira puts the point by noting that genuine historical events have identity conditions if we are meaningfully to refer to them.[9] If we want to say that something occurred in history that is the foundation of our faith, but how it occurred can be left to the historians as unimportant, the question arises as to whether what occurred can be completely divorced from how it occurred. Ferreira claims that we need at least some information about an event in order to identify the event. Think, for example, of Moses. Moses is the individual who confronted Pharaoh, led Israel out of Egypt, inscribed the ten commandments, and so on. Some or much of this information may be inaccurate, but if we had no reliable information about Moses whatsoever, then it is hard to see how we could have any true beliefs about Moses, because we could not use the symbol "Moses" to successfully pick out an historical figure. In the same way, it would appear that to speak meaningfully about Jesus as the historical incarnation of God, we need some accurate historical information about Jesus. And if it is important for our information to be historically accurate, how can we avoid a concern for the quality of the historical evidence?

4. Faith as Epistemologically Basic

Climacus' answer to this problem lies in a view of faith which sees faith as epistemologically basic, in something like Alvin Plantinga's sense of the term.[10] A basic belief is one that is not held on the basis of any other beliefs or any evidence that is propositional in character. Basic beliefs are therefore not held on the basis of any inference or argument, though they may have what Plantinga calls a ground in the circumstances or experiences that evoke them. Plantinga holds that some beliefs are *properly* basic; that is, in certain circumstances certain persons may hold these beliefs without violating any intellectual duty or evidencing any epistemic fault or defect. Though this is controversial, I believe that

Climacus thinks that Christian faith is not only basic, but properly basic for the believer.

Climacus says that faith is a passion that is the result of a first-hand encounter between the individual and the incarnate God.[11] Historical records function as the occasion for this encounter, but what matters is the encounter itself, in which God grants the individual "the condition" of faith. "*By means of* the contemporary's report (the occasion), the person who comes later believes by virtue of the condition he himself receives from the god."[12] Thus, the encounter is itself the ground of faith, which is therefore not based on evidence in the sense that it is not based on arguments or inferences from any propositions whose probability must be evaluated. No amount of historical evidence is sufficient to guarantee that this encounter will occur or that faith will be its outcome, and no specific amount of historical evidence is necessary in order for the encounter to occur or faith to ensue. Climacus insists that the encounter is one that can as easily lead to offense as to faith.

He supports his claims here with two thought experiments. One can easily imagine a person who has all the evidence one could want of an historical sort, but who has not thereby been transformed through a meeting with God incarnate.[13] One can also imagine someone with very slender historical knowledge whose life has nevertheless been transformed by a meeting with God which that scant information made possible.[14] Implicit in all this, I believe, is the Christian conviction of the living Christ. Jesus is no mere dead historical figure, but a living person who can still be experienced by individuals.

So on my reading Climacus' answer to Ferreira is to steadfastly maintain that objectivity in the content of one's beliefs is compatible with subjectivity in the grounds. It is undeniable, I think, that to meaningfully believe in Jesus as God one must have some true historical beliefs about Jesus. But why must those beliefs be based on evidence? Why couldn't the beliefs be themselves produced as part of the outcome of the encounter?

To successfully refer to Jesus of Nazareth, some of my beliefs about Jesus must be true, but it seems possible that a person might believe in the historical record because of her faith in Jesus, rather than having faith in Jesus on the basis of the historical record. Of course if the beliefs are false, then they are false, and the person is mistaken, but that risk is unavoidable, and Climacus does not think one should try to avoid it. Nor does the fact that the belief in question is not based on evidence mean that the belief is arbitrary or groundless, since it is *grounded* in the first-person encounter with Jesus.[15] What is required is that this encounter be an experience of Jesus in which true knowledge is given. The situation is analogous to a case of ordinary sense perception in which I come to believe that there is a flower before me because I directly perceive the flower. In such a case I do not normally regard the existence of the flower as something that I infer or conclude on the basis of evidence.

One objection to Climacus' attempt to rest so much on an experience of Jesus as God is that such an experience necessarily rests on a host of background assumptions. Surely a person cannot simply directly come to perceive Jesus as forgiving them, commanding them to do something, or inviting them to faith in the pages of the gospels unless the gospels are indeed an accurate representation of Jesus, which provide a reliable means for becoming aware of Jesus at work in one's life. In a similar way, ordinary sense perception also depends on the truth of various background assumptions. For example, I could not perceive that there is a flower in front of me if the light was not normal, if my eyesight was not functioning normally and so on. To know that there is a flower in front of me these other things must be true. Similarly, to know that the historical person Jesus, whom I learn about through historical records, is God speaking to me, certain other things must be true as well. So, in both cases, it may be argued, my belief still rests on other evidence, namely the evidence I have for these background beliefs.

This kind of objection rests on a confusion of levels.[16] We should distinguish between *having* a ground for a belief and *knowing* that one has a ground for a belief, between being justified and knowing that one is justified. For my belief that there is a flower before me to be properly grounded, it is necessary that the light be of a certain sort, that my eyesight be functioning normally, and so on, but it is not necessary for me to know these things, or to have evidence that they are so. It is sufficient that they are true. To know *that* my belief is properly grounded I may need to know such things, but that is another matter. In a similar manner, in order to have a properly grounded belief that Jesus is God, it must be the case that Jesus reveals himself in certain ways. But it is not necessary for the individual to know these other things, or have evidence for them, though that may be necessary for the individual to know that her belief is properly grounded.

I conclude that Climacus' position is philosophically defensible, in the sense that there is nothing incoherent in the notion of an historical belief which is grounded in an experience, rather than historical evidence. Whether that is in fact how Christian faith is produced is another matter, of course. To decide that one must decide whether Jesus is indeed God and whether experiences of Jesus of the appropriate sort are possible.

5. The Relevance of Historical Evidence for Faith

To revert to the language of the "thought-experiment," Climacus is probably right in saying that the "scrap of paper" with the words "we have believed that the god appeared among us" could be "more than enough" to be an occasion for faith, should God choose to use that scrap of paper as an occasion to reveal himself. And he is clearly right in saying that no amount of evidence will necessarily produce faith in someone. So strong, historical evidence is neither sufficient nor necessary for faith. Nevertheless, it is difficult to accept the further conclusion he seems to draw, namely that evidence is simply irrelevant to faith.

My worry can be expressed as follows: Certainly God could use a scrap of paper to produce faith. Perhaps he often does produce faith in ways that make evidence irrelevant. But is this always or even normally the case? Since my belief in Jesus is a belief with historical content, it cannot be isolated from my other historical beliefs. Unless God produced my belief by over-riding my normal thought-processes, it is hard to see how I could regard massive evidence that Jesus never existed, or never said any of the things attributed to him, as utterly irrelevant to my faith. Even a belief which is "properly basic" and grounded in direct perceptual experience is subject to being overridden by contrary evidence. My perceptual belief that there is a live flower in front of me may be overridden, for example, by strong evidence that the object in question is plastic. Similarly, even though I believe that Jesus has revealed himself to me, is it not possible that I am mistaken, and is not the liveness of that possibility affected by the quality of the evidence I have for Jesus' historical reality?

I believe that the basic worry Climacus has about admitting the relevance of historical evidence for faith is that he does not want the question of faith to be a scholarly question. He does not want to leave the ordinary person who is deciding whether to be a Christian or not in the clutches of the historical scholars, with their endless debates and never-decided controversies. After all, the individual who must decide whether or not to become a Christian is making a decision about how her life should be lived. She does not have the luxury of waiting for the scholars to reach agreement, which will never happen in any case. I sympathize with Climacus' worry on this point, but I believe that this concern can be met without the drastic claim that historical evidence is irrelevant for faith. The actual situation with regard to historical evidence seems to be this. For orthodox Christians, the historical accounts of Jesus' life are regarded as reasonably accurate at least, plenty sufficient for faith, and the evidence for this conclusion is regarded as adequate. For others, the account is much less accurate, and the evidence accordingly less powerful. In extreme cases, skepticism extends to almost all the details of Jesus' life. However, all parties would agree that in reality there is far more evidence than Climacus' "scrap of paper." How much more is a matter of dispute.

Now why is it that the evidence seems adequate to one party and inadequate to the other? Doubtless each side will have its own preferred explanation. Perhaps skeptics will say that wish fulfillment is at work in the believer. Perhaps believers will follow Climacus and say that their own encounter with Jesus is the deciding factor. What I wish to maintain is that it is possible for the believer to follow Climacus in saying this without claiming that historical evidence is irrelevant. That is, it is possible for a believer to claim that it is significant that we have as much evidence as we have, and even to admit that some people would not find faith to be possible if they did not have evidence of reasonable, even if not decisive quality, while still properly believing that the decision is not in the end one which scholarship can settle. Though the evidence by itself would never be sufficient to produce faith in anyone, it is possible that evidence of a certain type might be necessary for faith for some people, though not everyone, since not everyone will have the reflective bent or cognitive capacities to appreciate the force of various possible problems. Faith in this case does not make evidence unimportant or irrelevant; it makes it possible properly to appreciate and assess the evidence, at least so as to be able to know that one's beliefs have not been vanquished by various "defeaters."

To go back to the level distinction we employed earlier, for some people, those of a certain reflective bent, being justified in believing may be linked to believing that they are justified. They want to know that they are justified, and if they lack such knowledge, their faith may be troubled by crippling doubts. Or, more modestly and more plausibly, I think, they at least need to rule out the possibility that their beliefs can be shown to be false. They may need this because they have encountered people who claim to be able to show that their beliefs are false. Such a believer who is troubled by doubt might admit the relevance of historical argument, while still holding to the Climacus-inspired view that what is finally decisive in settling the argument is his own first-hand experience of Jesus.

Such a person is not necessarily thrown back into the clutches of the scholars, even though he may not ignore the work of the scholars altogether. To avoid the specter of an unending scholarly inquiry which never leads to commitment either way, he may only need to believe that there is enough evidence to make the truth of his beliefs possible, and it is hard to see how that weak conclusion could be threatened by scholarship. What the believer must hold is that the evidence is good enough for one whose belief has the ground of a first-person encounter, or perhaps even that the evidence is seen in a different light for one who has had such an encounter. In the latter case the encounter could be understood as transforming the individual, giving her the proper perspective from which to view the evidence, or even as giving her the capacities she needs to appreciate its force.[17] It may be important to have evidence, but the evidence does not need to be of the type that would convince any "sane, rational person," but rather be such as to appear adequate to a person of faith. A view such as this one seems to me to make more sense of the way committed believers actually respond to disturbing historical evidence.

The usual stance is not dismissal of the evidence as irrelevant, but confidence that the contrary evidence will not be decisive.

6. Evidence for a Paradox: Making the Improbable Probable

Climacus has one further reason for treating historical evidence as insignificant, which might be called the "capital crime" argument. Just as a capital offense "absorbs all lesser crimes," so the paradoxicalness of the incarnation makes minor historical problems insignificant.[18] The idea is that the incarnation, being a paradox, is so improbable as to appear absurd. The viability of belief in such a paradox cannot be affected by petty details of the historical records, such as divergencies and contradictions of various witnesses. Its antecedent probability is so low that it cannot be made meaningfully lower; nor could resolving such problems make the probability meaningfully higher. Climacus goes so far as to argue that to try to make the incarnation probable is to falsify its character. The paradox is by definition the improbable, and one could make it probable only by making it into what it is not.[19]

These arguments are strikingly reminiscent of Hume's famous critical attack on miracles. In *An Enquiry Concerning Human Understanding* Hume argues that it could never be reasonable to believe that a miracle has occurred, because a miracle, which is by definition an exception to the laws of nature, is necessarily as improbable an event as can be imagined, since the laws of nature describe what normally happens and therefore what one can reasonably expect to occur. Even the best and strongest evidence for a miracle imaginable would only serve to balance and could never overcome this strong *a priori* improbability.[20]

It is worth inquiring, both for Climacus and Hume, what concept of probability and what assumptions about probability seem to underlie the arguments. The term "probability" is used in both objective and subjective senses. Objectively, to say that an event is probable is to say that it is objectively likely to occur. Thus the probability of a certain outcome when cards are dealt or dice are rolled can be calculated with some precision. We often say that an event is probable, however, when we know nothing about the objective probabilities of the matter. In these cases we mean that it seems likely to us that the event will occur. For example, I may think it is probable that I will receive an exceptionally large raise in salary next year, even though I have no statistical data on which to base such a claim. It is simply rooted in my belief that my work will be recognized and rewarded by the proper authorities. Such a claim is more an expression of my expectancies than it is a statement about statistical frequencies in the objective world, and such a probability claim is no stronger than the subjective beliefs on which it is based.

Hume's argument appears at first glance to be rooted in objective probability, since it is the infrequency with which laws of nature are violated which makes a miracle improbable. Critics have pointed out, however, that if this is Hume's argument, then it seems to rest on a shallow understanding of how the probability of historical events is estimated. The probability of an historical event cannot be estimated simply from the frequency with which an event of that type occurs, since history is replete with unique events. A French emperor may invade Russia only once in all human history. In estimating the probability of an event, we rely therefore not only on the frequency of the type of event in question but our total knowledge of the situation, including our knowledge of the intentions and characters of whatever historical agents are involved. To think otherwise is to confuse history with dice-rolling or coin-tossing.

Believers in miracles regard miracles as the work of God, who is regarded as a personal agent. To assess the probability of a miracle, therefore, one must do more than consider how frequently they occur. One must consider whether there is a God, whether he is the sort of being who could be expected to do miracles from time to time, in what circumstances this could be expected to occur, and so on. If I believe in a personal God, and believe that God has the ability to intervene in nature, and that he is a being who has good reasons to intervene in nature in certain circumstances, then I will estimate the probability of a miracle in those circumstances much more highly than does Hume. Anyone who judges miracles extremely improbable, as does Hume, bases the judgment not merely on objective statistical data, but on a variety of beliefs about other matters. Of course it is possible that Hume or others who judge miracles extremely improbable have objectively powerful evidence that God does not exist, or that God is not the kind of being who performs miracles, but it seems more likely to me that Hume is actually simply expressing his beliefs about these matters, and the judgment of probability made is therefore of the subjective kind. It seems or appears likely to Hume that miracles do not occur, but of course miracles may not appear nearly so improbable to someone else who holds different convictions about God. Anyone who actually believes that a miracle has occurred will of course believe that the objective probability of that miracle is 1.

I believe that the concept of probability that underlies Climacus' argument is also subjective. Climacus says that the believer must firmly hold to the notion that the incarnation is a paradox and is therefore improbable. However, since the believer thinks the incarnation has actually occurred, he cannot believe that the objective probability of the event is low, since the objective probability of an event that has occurred is 1. The meaning must be that the believer understands the event as one that will *appear* improbable to someone who holds certain beliefs. For example, someone such as Hume who believes that miraculous events are in general improbable, will certainly make the same judgment about the idea of a divine incarnation. Anyone who is inclined to think that only events that can be rationally understood can occur, and who also cannot understand how God could become a human being will think the event improbable. Anyone who is inclined to believe that genuinely unselfish love does not exist will find the idea of God suffering on behalf of human beings similarly improbable. All of this implies that the improbability of the incarnation must be seen as relative to the perspective from which it is viewed.

This conclusion corresponds perfectly with Climacus' own contention that the paradoxicalness of the paradox is a function of sin, which creates the "absolute qualitative distance" between God and human beings.[21] If, however, the improbability of the paradox is a function of the subjective perspective from which it is viewed, why is the idea of viewing the paradox as probable wrong-headed, as Climacus plainly says? Why is it that the perspective of sinful human beings gains a kind of authority here as the defining perspective? Why shouldn't the believer assert that it is probable to *her*?

The answer surely lies in the fact that Christianity assumes that human beings are in fact sinners. This perspective is in fact the perspective that every human being occupies, at least prior to faith. And since the transition from sin to faith is not, for Climacus, a one-time event, but a transition that must continually be renewed, it remains necessary for the believer to define the content of her faith polemically, as that which necessarily is in opposition to the thinking of sinful human beings. The believer is not offended but the believer is the person who has confronted and continues to confront the possibility of offense. If faith loses its provocative character, and no longer confronts our natural patterns of thinking as a rebuke, it has indeed essentially altered its character. Nevertheless, there is a sense in which the incarnation is no longer improbable to the believer, simply because it is for her something that has occurred. It is improbable only in the sense that she knows it appears unlikely or improbable to our sinfully corrupted patterns of thought. The event remains improbable in that it was not something we expected to occur.

Does the subjective improbability of the paradox imply that the quality of the historical evidence is no concern? It might appear so for the unbeliever, since the event will appear to him to be massively improbable. Whether this is so depends on how pervasive the corrupting effects of sin are on the intellect. However, I believe that the claim that evidence is of no value whatsoever to the unbeliever is not strictly implied by the requirements of Climacus' hypothetical version of Christianity. The hypothesis requires that people be construed as sinful enough so that they cannot arrive at the Truth apart from an encounter with God in which they receive the condition. It is not obvious to me that one aspect of this process of giving the condition could not consist in giving the individual evidence that the God-man is indeed God. Of course the individual's sinfulness may give him a strong tendency to dismiss this evidence, because the fact in question appears so improbable to him. But it seems possible that strong evidence might challenge this presumption of improbability. So long as we are careful to insist that the evidence alone could not produce faith in the individual, then this seems compatible with Climacus' view. No reversion to a Socratic view has occurred.

It also seems possible for evidence to have some value to the believer. Climacus' view to the contrary is surely rooted in his claim that the faith which is the result of the first-person encounter with God does not rest on such evidence. If such a faith is sufficient to overturn the subjective improbability of the event, it will surely not be troubled by flaws in the historical record.

This is essentially the same argument we examined in the previous section and is subject to the same reservations that I expressed there. Perhaps it is true that it is the experience of meeting Jesus that is decisive in altering the natural judgment that God would not become a human being. Thus the experience may be the decisive ground of faith, and the inconclusiveness of scholarly debate may be insignificant to the believer. However, this is compatible with claiming that it is important that there be evidence, at least for some people who are troubled by doubts of a certain kind. The evidence may not be of such a nature as to convince unbelievers, but it may be the kind of evidence that is seen as sufficient when seen through the right eyes.

After all, it is surely possible for someone to doubt whether the experience of Jesus which is the ground of faith is veridical. If we have some reasons to think that Jesus really existed, and really is divine, and has a certain character, and so on, such information could be helpful in resolving such doubts. If I have an experience of someone who appears to be Mother Teresa, I will be much more likely to believe the experience is veridical if I have background information about the reality of Mother Teresa, and about her character, than would be the case if I had never heard of Mother Teresa. Thus the traditional arguments for the reliability of the gospels, and the testimony provided in the gospels for the claim that Jesus is divine, including the miracles, Jesus' own claims to be divine, the profundity of Jesus' teaching, and especially the resurrection, could be of significance to a believer. They are not sufficient to produce faith, and perhaps not strictly necessary, but they may well be part of what one might call the normal process by which faith comes into being, and they may also have value in confirming faith that is present, helping to relieve doubts and allay various objections.

7. Traditional Apologetic Arguments

There is little doubt, I think, that the claims I am making run strongly contrary to the intentions of Climacus, who simply can see no value in traditional apologetics. It is instructive to look at Climacus' treatment of what is traditionally cited as evidence. Climacus admits that the god must make his presence known in the world in some way, though he says that every "accommodation for the sake of comprehensibility" is of no value to the person who does not receive the condition, and is therefore "elicited from him [the god] only under constraint and against his will."[22] I do not see why this should be so.

As Climacus himself says, it surely makes no sense to suppose that the god is literally indistinguishable from any other human being, and that there is no sign which points to his divinity. Of course the gospels meet this requirement in the case of Jesus by presenting him as an authoritative teacher, a worker of miracles, and someone who himself claims to be divine. If the god wills to reveal himself, and if this requires some sign or evidence of his divinity, then it is hard to see why the god should grant such signs only "under constraint and against his will." Even if we grant Climacus the claim that such signs will only be of value to people of faith, though I have given reason to question that claim, it does not follow that the signs are insignificant for those people who do indeed have faith.

Climacus says that miracles cannot help much, as a miracle does not exist immediately, but "is only for faith." It is not clear just what this means. The statement could be read as saying that an event becomes a miracle by my belief that it is. However, this claim is absurd on its face, and in any case directly contradicts a principle Climacus firmly holds, namely that the apprehension of something cannot alter the nature of what is apprehended.[23] If he means that miracles will only be believed by those who have faith, this is possible, though not obvious, but that does not mean that the miracles lack evidential value for those who do possess faith.

Surely Climacus is right when he says that miracles and other evidence do not lead automatically to faith, and that they can indeed lead to offense. If the gospels are accurate, many contemporaries of Jesus observed him perform miracles without becoming disciples, and in fact seem to have been offended by him. However, this does not imply that the miracles are of no value to those people who did possess faith. Certainly, the traditional Christian view is that the "signs" Jesus did are valuable in this way. For example, Peter's first sermon on the day of Pentecost appeals to the "mighty works, signs and wonders" which God had done among the people through Jesus.[24] So far as I can tell, Climacus' deviation from this traditional Christian view and complete denigration of historical evidence is unwarranted, even given the basic correctness of his own view of faith and its genesis in the individual.

There is therefore no way to completely insulate Christian faith from the risks of historical criticism. On the other hand, an understanding of the way such historical judgments themselves embody faith-commitments may make it possible for Christians to argue that the historical beliefs that are part of their faith are reasonable enough when viewed in the right context, that context being a faith which is grounded, not in historical evidence, but in a first-hand encounter with Jesus Christ.[25]

St. Olaf College

Endnotes

[1] Søren Kierkegaard, *Fear and Trembling,* translated and edited by Howard and Edna Hong, Princeton University Press (Princeton: 1983), p. 55.

[2] *Philosophical Fragments,* translated and edited by Howard and Edna Hong, Princeton University Press (Princeton: 1985), pp. 13-14.

[3] See *Philosophical Fragments,* p. 109.

[4] See Søren Kierkegaard, *Concluding Unscientific Postscript,* translated by David Swenson and Walter Lowrie, Princeton University Press (Princeton: 1968), pp. 498 and 507-08, for passages that develop this theme of having God outside of one's religious consciousness.

[5] *Philosophical Fragments,* p. 104.

[6] *Philosophical Fragments,* p. 106.

[7] Kierkegaard says something like this in *Christian Discourses,* translated by Walter Lowrie, Princeton University Press (Princeton: 1971), pp. 248-49.

[8] See, for example, pp. 509-12 in *Concluding Unscientific Postscript.*

[9] M. J. Ferreira, "The Faith/History Problem and Kierkegaard's *A Priori* 'Proof,'" *Religious Studies* 23 (1987), pp. 337-45.

[10] See Alvin Plantinga, "Reason and Belief in God," in *Faith and Rationality,* edited by Alvin Plantinga and Nicholas Wolterstorff, University of Notre Dame Press (Notre Dame, Indiana: 1983), pp. 46-47, for an account of what it is for a belief to be basic.

[11] See *Philosophical Fragments,* p. 103, where Climacus says that "only the person who personally receives the condition from the god...believes."

[12] *Philosophical Fragments,* p. 104.

[13] *Philosophical Fragments,* pp. 59-60.

[14] *Philosophical Fragments,* p. 60.

[15] I do not wish to deny here that in a wide enough sense of "evidence" this encounter which I describe as the ground could itself be viewed as evidence. In saying it is not evidence I mean first that it is not a propositional belief which has any logical relations to faith, and secondly that it does not form the basis for any process of inference by which the individual arrives at faith.

[16] The following remarks are inspired by some points made with respect to religious experience by William Alston, in an unpublished paper "The Place of Experience in the Grounds of Religious Belief," delivered at a conference on "The

Future of God" at Gordon College in May of 1989. I do not wish to claim that Alston would endorse this use of his point.

[17] See my "The Epistemological Significance of Transformative Religious Experience," in *Faith and Philosophy*.

[18] *Philosophical Fragments*, p. 104.

[19] *Philosophical Fragments*, p. 94n.

[20] See David Hume, *An Enquiry Concerning Human Understanding*, Hackett Publishing Company (Indianapolis, Indiana: 1977), pp. 72-90, particularly pp. 76-77.

[21] See *Philosophical Fragments*, pp. 46-47.

[22] *Philosophical Fragments*, p. 56.

[23] See the discussion of the necessity of the past in the "Interlude," in *Philosophical Fragments*, pp. 79-80.

[24] See Acts 2:22.

[25] The author wishes to thank N.E.H. for a fellowship that made the writing of this paper possible.

Study Questions

1.   In what ways does C. Stephen Evans bring historical evidence to bear on Kierkegaard's position?

2.   How important do you think the historical is to the theist's position?

3.   What are the two standard readings of paradox? Which reading does Evans attribute to Kierkegaard?

4.   How important is historical evidence of faith for Kierkegaard?

5.   How does a "first-hand experience of Jesus Christ" figure in Johanness Climacus' argument?

5

Justification and Theism

Alvin Plantinga

Alvin Plantinga is John A. O'Brien Professor of Philosophy and Director of the Center for Philosophy of Religion at the University of Notre Dame, and the author of *God and Other Minds, God, Freedom and Evil, The Nature of Necessity, Does God Have a Nature?, Warrant: The Current Debate*, and *Warrant and Proper Function*. The question is: How should a theist think of justification or positive epistemic status?

The answer I suggest is: a belief **B** has positive epistemic status for **S** only if **S**'s faculties are functioning properly (i.e., functioning in the way God intended them to) in producing **B**, and only if **S**'s cognitive environment is sufficiently similar to the one for which her faculties are designed; and under those conditions the more firmly **S** is inclined to accept **B**, the more positive epistemic status it has for her. I conclude by making some qualifications and applications and examining some objections.*

According to an ancient and honorable tradition, knowledge is *justified true belief*. But what is this "justification"? Theologians of the Protestant Reformation (however things may stand with their contemporary epigoni) had a clear conception of justification; justification, they held, is by faith. Contemporary epistemologists, sadly enough, do not thus speak with a single voice. They don't often subject the concept in question—the concept of epistemic justification—to explicit scrutiny; while there are many discussions of the conditions under which a person is justified in believing a proposition, there are few in which the principle topic is the *nature* of justification. But when they do discuss it, they display a notable lack of unanimity. Some claim that justification is by *epistemic dutifulness*, others that it is by *coherence,* and still others that it is by *reliability.*[1] The differences among these views are enormous; this is by no means a case of variations on the same theme. Indeed, disagreement is so deep and radical it is sometimes hard to be sure the various disputants are discussing approximately the same issue. Now what should a Christian, or more broadly, a theist, make of this situation? How should such a person react to this baffling welter of conflict, this babble or Babel of confusion? In what follows I shall try to get a clearer look at epistemic justification and allied conceptions. In particular, I propose to examine this topic from an explicitly Christian, or more broadly, theistic point of view: how shall we think of epistemic justification from a theistic perspective?   What can Christianity or theism contribute to our understanding of epistemic justification?

But here we need a preliminary word as to what it is, more exactly, I mean to be talking about. How shall we initially locate epistemic justification? First, such terms as "justification" and "justified" are, as Roderick Chisholm[2] suggests, terms of epistemic appraisal; to say that a proposition is *justified* for a person is to say that his believing or accepting it (here I shall not distinguish these two) has *positive epistemic status* for him. What we appraise here are a person's *beliefs:* more exactly, his *believings.* Someone's belief that there is such a person as God may be thus appraised, as well as her belief that human life evolved from unicellular life by way of the mechanisms suggested by contemporary evolutionary theory, and the less spectacular beliefs of everyday life. We may speak of a person's beliefs as *warranted,* or *justified,* or *rational,* or *reasonable,* contrasting them with beliefs that are unwarranted, unjustified, irrational, or unreasonable. The evidentialist objector to theistic belief, for example, argues that those who believe in God without evidence are unjustified in so doing, and are accordingly somehow unreasonable—guilty of an intellectual or cognitive impropriety, perhaps, or, alternatively and less censoriously, victims of some sort of intellectual dysfunction. Secondly, epistemic justification or positive epistemic status clearly comes in degrees: at any rate some of my beliefs have more by way of positive epistemic status for me than others.

And thirdly, among the fundamental concepts of epistemology, naturally enough, we find the concept of knowledge. It is widely agreed that true belief, while necessary for knowledge, is not sufficient for it. What more is required? It is widely agreed, again, that whatever exactly this further element may be, it is either epistemic justification or something intimately connected with it. Now it would be convenient just to *baptize* that quantity as 'justification', thus taking that term as a proper name of the element, whatever exactly it is, enough of which (Gettier problems, perhaps, aside) distinguishes knowledge from mere true belief. The term 'justification', however, has a deontological ring; it is redolent of duty and permission, obligation and rights. Furthermore, according to the long and distinguished tradition of Cartesian internalism (represented at its contemporary best by Roderick Chisholm's work[3]), aptness for epistemic duty fulfillment is indeed what distinguishes true belief from knowledge; using this term as a mere proper name of what distinguishes true belief from knowledge, therefore, can be confusing. Accordingly, I shall borrow Chisholm's term 'positive epistemic status' as my official name of the quantity in question—the quantity enough of which distinguishes mere true belief from knowledge. (Of course we cannot initially assume that positive epistemic status is a *single* or *simple* property; perhaps it is an amalgam of several others.) Initially, then, and to a first approximation, we can identify justification or positive epistemic status as a normative (possibly complex) property that comes in degrees, and which is such that enough of it (ignoring Gettier problems for the moment) is what distinguishes true belief from knowledge.

I. Positive Epistemic Status and Theism

Now how shall we think of positive epistemic status, or, indeed, the whole human cognitive enterprise, from a Christian or theistic point of view? What bearing does theism have on the human cognitive enterprise? What features of theism bear on this topic? The central point, I think, is this: according to the theistic way of looking at the matter, we human beings, like ropes and linear accelerators, have been designed; we have been designed and created by God. We have been created by God; furthermore, according to Christian and Jewish versions of theism, we have been created by him *in his own image;* in certain crucial respects we resemble him. Now God is an actor, an agent, a creator: one who chooses certain ends and takes action to accomplish them. God is therefore a *practical* being. But he is also an *intellectual* or *intellecting* being. He has knowledge; indeed, he has the maximal degree of knowledge. He holds beliefs (even if his way of holding a belief is different from ours); and because he is omniscient, he believes every truth and holds only true beliefs. He therefore has the sort of grasp of concepts, properties and propositions necessary for holding beliefs; and since he believes every true proposition, he has a grasp of every property and proposition.[4]

In setting out to create human beings in his image, then, God set out to create them in such a way that they could reflect something of his capacity to grasp concepts and hold beliefs. Furthermore, as the whole of the Christian tradition suggests, his aim was to create them in such a way that they can reflect something of his capacity for holding *true* beliefs, for attaining *knowledge.* This has been the nearly unanimous consensus of the Christian tradition; but it is worth noting that it is not inevitable. God's aim in creating us with the complicated, highly articulated establishment of faculties we do in fact display *could* have been something quite different; in creating us with these faculties he could have been aiming us, not at truth, but at something of some other sort—survival, for example, or a capacity to appreciate art, poetry, beauty in nature,[5] or an ability to stand in certain relationships with each other and with him. But the great bulk of the tradition has seen our imaging God in terms (among other things) of knowledge: knowledge of ourselves, of God himself, and of the world in which he has placed us; and here I shall take for granted this traditional understanding of the *imago dei*.

God has therefore created us with cognitive faculties designed to enable us to achieve true beliefs with respect to a wide variety of propositions—propositions about our immediate environment, about our own interior lives, about the thoughts and experiences of other persons, about our universe at large, about right and wrong, about the whole realm of abstracta—numbers, properties, propositions, states of affairs, possible worlds and their like, about modality—what is necessary and possible—and about himself. These faculties work in such a way that under the appropriate circumstances we form the appropriate belief. More exactly, the appropriate belief *is formed in us*; in the typical case we do not *decide* to hold or form the belief in question, but simply find ourselves with it. Upon considering an instance of *modus ponens*, I find myself believing its corresponding conditional; upon being appeared to in the familiar way, I find myself holding the belief that there is a large tree before me; upon being asked what I had for breakfast, I reflect for a moment and then find myself with the belief that what I had was eggs on toast. In these and other cases I do not *decide* what to believe; I don't total up the evidence (I'm being appeared to redly; on most occasions when thus appeared to I am in the presence of something red; so most probably in this case I am) and make a decision as to what seems best supported; I simply find myself believing. Of course in *some* cases I may go through such a procedure. For example, I may try to assess the alleged evidence in favor of the theory that human life evolved by means of the mechanisms of random genetic mutation and natural selection from unicellular life (which itself arose by substantially similar random mechanical processes from nonliving material); I may try to determine whether the evidence is in fact compelling or, more modestly, such as to make the theory plausible. Then I may go through a procedure of that sort. Even in this sort of case I still don't really *decide* anything: I simply call the relevant evidence to mind, try in some way to weight it up, and find myself with the appropriate belief. But in more typical and less theoretical cases of belief formation nothing like this is involved.

Experience, obviously enough, plays a crucial role in belief formation. Here it is important to see, I think, that two rather different sorts of experience are involved. In a typical perceptual case there is sensuous experience: I look out at my back yard and am appeared to greenly, perhaps. But in many cases of belief formation, there is present another sort of experiential component as well. Consider a memory belief, for example. Here there may be a sort of sensuous imagery present—I may be appeared to in a certain indistinct fleeting sort of way in trying to recall what I had for breakfast, for example. But this sort of sensuous imagery is in a way (as Wittgenstein never tired of telling us) inessential, variable from person to person, and perhaps in the case of some persons altogether absent. What seems less variable is a different kind of experience not easy to characterize: it is a matter, not so much of sensuous imagery, as of feeling impelled, or inclined, or moved towards a certain belief—in the case in question, the belief that what I had for breakfast was eggs on toast. (Perhaps it could be better put by saying that the belief in question has a sort of experienced attractiveness about it, a sort of drawing power.) Consider an *a priori* belief: **if all men are mortal and Socrates is a man, then Socrates is mortal.** Such a belief is not, as the denomination *a priori* mistakenly suggests, formed *prior to* or in the absence of experience; it is rather formed *in response to experience*. Thinking of the corresponding conditional of **modus ponens** feels different from thinking of, say, the corresponding conditional of **affirming the consequent**; thinking of 2+1=3 feels different from thinking of 2+1=4; and this difference in experience is crucially connected with our accepting the one and rejecting the other. Again, when I entertain or think of an example of **modus ponens**, there is both sensuous imagery—Descartes' clarity and distinctness, the luminous brightness of which Locke spoke; but there is also the feeling of being impelled to believe or accept the proposition; there is a sort of inevitability about it. (As I said, this isn't easy to describe.) Of course experience plays a different role here from the role it plays in the formation of perceptual beliefs; it plays a still different role in the formation of moral beliefs, beliefs about our own mental lives, beliefs about the mental lives of other persons, beliefs we form on the basis of inductive evidence, and so on. What we need here is a full and appropriately subtle and sensitive description of the role of experience in the formation of these various types of beliefs; that project will have to await another occasion, as one says when one really has no idea how to accomplish the project.

God has therefore created us with an astonishingly complex and subtle establishment of cognitive faculties. These faculties produce beliefs on an enormously wide variety of topics—our everyday external environment, the thoughts of others, our own internal life (someone's internal musings and soliloquies can occupy an entire novel), the past, mathematics, science, right and wrong, our relationships to God, what is necessary and possible, and a host of other topics. They work with great subtlety to produce beliefs of many different degrees of strength ranging from the merest inclination to believe to absolute dead certainty. Our beliefs and the strength with which we hold them, furthermore, are delicately responsive to changes in experience—to what people tell us, to perceptual experience, to what we read, to further reflection, and so on.

Now: how shall we think of positive epistemic status from this point of view? Here is a natural first approximation: a belief has positive epistemic status for a person only if his faculties are **working properly,** working the way they ought to work, working the way they were designed to work (working the way God designed them to work), in producing and sustaining the belief in question. I therefore suggest that a necessary condition of positive epistemic status is that one's cognitive equipment, one's belief forming and belief sustaining apparatus, be free of cognitive malfunction. It must be functioning in the way it was designed to function by the being who designed and created us. Initially, then, let us say that a belief has positive epistemic status, for me, to the degree that my faculties are functioning properly in producing and sustaining that belief; and my faculties are working properly if they are working in the way they were designed to work by God.

The first thing to see here is that this condition—that of one's cognitive equipment functioning properly—is not the same thing as one's cognitive equipment functioning *normally*, or in normal conditions—not, at any rate, if we take the term 'normally' in a broadly statistical sense. If I give way to wishful thinking, forming the belief that I will soon be awarded a Nobel Prize for literature, then my cognitive faculties are not working properly even though wishful thinking may be widespread among human beings. Your belief's being produced by your faculties working normally or in normal conditions—i.e., the sorts of conditions that obtain for the most part—must be distinguished from their working *properly*. It may be (and in fact is) the case that it is not at all abnormal for a person to form a belief out of pride, jealousy, lust, contrariness, desire for fame, wishful thinking, or self-aggrandizement; nevertheless when I form a belief in this way my cognitive equipment is not functioning properly. It is not functioning the way it ought to.

I shall have more to say about the notion of proper functioning below. For the moment, let us provisionally entertain the idea that the one necessary condition of a belief's having positive epistemic status for me is that the relevant portion of my noetic equipment involved in its formation and sustenance be functioning properly. It is easy to see, however, that this cannot be the whole story. Suppose you are suddenly and without your knowledge transported to an environment wholly different from earth; you awake on a planet near Alpha Centauri. There conditions are quite different; elephants, we may suppose, are invisible to human beings, but emit a sort of radiation unknown on earth, a sort of radiation that causes human beings to form the belief that a trumpet is sounding nearby. An Alpha Centaurian elephant wanders by; you are subjected to the radiation, and form the belief that a trumpet is sounding nearby. There is nothing wrong with your cognitive faculties; but this belief has little by way of positive epistemic status for you. Nor is the problem merely that the belief is false; even if we can add that a trumpet really is sounding nearby (in a soundproof telephone booth, perhaps, so that it isn't audible to you), your belief will have little by way of positive epistemic status for you. To vary the example, imagine that the radiation emitted causes human beings to form the belief, not that a trumpet is sounding, but that there is a large gray object in the neighborhood. Again, an elephant wanders by: while seeing nothing of any particular interest, you suddenly find yourself with the belief that there is a large gray object nearby. A bit perplexed at this discovery, you examine your surroundings more closely: you still see no large gray object. Your faculties are displaying no malfunction and you are not being epistemically careless or slovenly; nevertheless you don't know that there is a large gray object nearby. That belief has little by way of positive epistemic status for you.

The reason is that your cognitive faculties and the environment in which you find yourself are not properly attuned. The problem is not with your cognitive faculties; they are in good working order. The problem is with the environment. In approximately the same way, your automobile might be in perfect working order, despite the fact that it will not run well at the top of Pike's Peak, or under water, or on the moon. We must therefore add another component to positive epistemic status: your faculties must be in good working order, and the environment must be appropriate for your particular repertoire of epistemic powers. (Perhaps there are creatures native to the planet in question who are much like human beings, but whose cognitive powers differ from ours in such a way that Alpha Centaurian elephants are not invisible to them.)

It is tempting to suggest that positive epistemic status *just is* proper functioning (in an appropriate environment), so that one has warrant for a given belief to the degree that one's faculties are functioning properly (in producing and sustaining that belief) in an environment appropriate for one's cognitive equipment: the better one's faculties are functioning, the more positive epistemic status. But it is easy to see that this cannot be correct. Couldn't it happen that my cognitive faculties are working properly (in an appropriate environment) in producing and sustaining a certain belief in me, while nonetheless that belief has very little by way of positive epistemic status for me? Say that a pair of beliefs are (for want of a better term) *productively equivalent* if they are produced by faculties functioning properly to the same degree and in environments of equal appropriateness. Then couldn't it be that a pair of my beliefs should be productively equivalent while nonetheless one of them has more by way of positive epistemic status—even a great deal more—than the other? Obviously enough, that could be; as a matter of fact it is plausible to think that is the case. *Modus ponens* has more by way of positive epistemic status for me than does the memory belief, now rather dim and indistinct, that forty years ago I owned a second hand 16 gauge shotgun and a red bicycle with balloon tires; but both, I take it, are produced by cognitive faculties functioning properly in a congenial environment. Although both epistemic justification and **being properly produced** come in degrees, there seems to be no discernible functional relationship between them: but then we can't see positive epistemic status as simply a matter of a belief's being produced by faculties working properly in an appropriate environment. We still have no real answer to the question **what is positive**

epistemic status?; that particular frog is still grinning residually up from the bottom of the mug.

Fortunately there is an easy response. Not only does the first belief, the belief in the corresponding conditional of *modus ponens,* have more by way of positive epistemic status for me than the second; it is also one I accept much more firmly. It seems much more obviously true; I have a much stronger inclination or impulse to accept that proposition than to accept the other. When my cognitive establishment is working properly, the strength of the impulse towards believing a given proposition will be proportional to the degree it has of positive epistemic status—or if the relationship isn't one of straightforward proportionality, the appropriate functional relationship will hold between positive epistemic status and this impulse. So when my faculties are functioning properly, a belief has positive epistemic status to the degree that I find myself inclined to accept it; and this (again, if my faculties are functioning properly and I do not interfere or intervene) will be the degree to which I *do* accept it.

As I see it then, positive epistemic status accrues to a belief **B** for a person **S** only if **S**'s cognitive environment is appropriate for his cognitive faculties and only if these faculties are functioning properly in producing this belief in him; and under these conditions the degree of positive epistemic status enjoyed by **B** is proportional to the strength of his inclination to accept **B**. To state the same claim a bit differently: a belief **B** has positive epistemic status for **S** if and only if that belief is produced in **S** by his epistemic faculties working properly (in an appropriate environment); and **B** has more positive epistemic status than **B*** for **S** iff (1) **B** has positive epistemic status for **S** and (2) either **B*** does not or else **S** is more strongly inclined to believe **B** than **B***.

II. Eight Objections, Qualifications, or Applications

So far, of course, what I have said is merely programmatic, just a picture. Much more needs to be said by way of qualification, development, articulation. Let me therefore respond to some objections, make some qualifications and additions, and mention some topics for further study.

(1) Aren't such ideas as that of **working properly** and related notions such as **cognitive dysfunction** deeply problematic? What is it for a natural organism—a tree, for example, or a horse—to be in good working order, to be functioning properly? Isn't "working properly" relative to our aims and interests? A cow is functioning properly when she gives the appropriate kind and amount of milk; a garden patch is as it ought to be when it displays a luxuriant preponderance of the sorts of vegetation we propose to promote. But here it seems patent that what constitutes proper functioning depends upon our aims and interests. So far as nature herself goes, isn't a fish decomposing in a hill of corn functioning just as properly, just as

excellently, as one happily swimming about chasing minnows? But then what could be meant by speaking of "proper functioning" with respect to our cognitive faculties? A chunk of reality—an organism, a part of an organism, an ecosystem, a garden patch—"functions properly" only with respect to a sort of grid *we* impose on nature—a grid that incorporates *our* aims and desires.

Reply: from a *theistic* point of view, of course, there is no problem here. The idea of my faculties functioning properly is no more problematic than, say, that of a Boeing 747's working properly. Something we have constructed—a heating system, a rope, a linear accelerator—is functioning properly when it is functioning in the way in which it was designed to function. But according to theism, human beings, like ropes, linear accelerators and ocean liners, have been designed; they have been designed and created by God. Our faculties are working properly, then, when they are working in the way they were designed to work by the being who designed and created us and them. Of course there may be considerable room for disagreement and considerable difficulty in determining just how our faculties have in fact been designed to function, and consequent disagreement as to whether they are functioning properly in a given situation. There is disease, disorder, dysfunction, malfunction of the mind as well as of the body. This can range from the extreme case of Descartes' lunatics (who thought their heads were made of glass or that they themselves were gourds) to cases where it isn't clear whether or not cognitive dysfunction is present at all. I stubbornly cling to my theory, long after wiser heads have given it up as a bad job: is this a matter of cognitive dysfunction brought about by excessive pride or desire for recognition on my part? Or is it a perfectly natural and proper display of the sort of cognitive inertia built into our cognitive faculties (in order, perhaps, that we may not be blown about by every wind of doctrine)? Or a display of some other part of our cognitive design whose operation guarantees that new and unfamiliar ideas will persist long enough to get a real run for their money? Or what? So there may be great difficulty in discerning, in a particular instance, whether my faculties are or are not functioning properly; but from a theistic point of view there is no trouble in principle with the very *idea* of proper function.

But can a nontheist also make use of this notion of working properly? Is the idea of proper functioning tightly tied to the idea of design and construction in such a way that one can use it in the way I suggest only if one is prepared to agree that human beings have been designed? This is a topic I shall have to leave for another occasion;[6] here let me say just this much. This notion of proper functioning is, I think, more problematic from a nontheistic perspective—more problematic, but by no means hopeless. Can't anyone, theist or not, see that a horse, let's say, suffering from a disease, is displaying a pathological condition? Can't anyone see that an injured bird has a wing that isn't working properly? The notions of proper function and allied notions (sickness, dysfunction, disorder, malfunction and the like) are ones we all or nearly all have and use. If in fact this notion is ultimately inexplicable or unacceptable from a nontheistic point of view, then there lurks in the neighborhood a powerful theistic argument—one that will be attractive to all those whose inclination to accept and employ the notion of proper function is stronger than their inclinations to reject theism.

(2) Roderick Chisholm[7] sees fulfillment of epistemic duty as crucial to positive epistemic status; in fact he analyzes or explains positive epistemic status in terms of aptness for fulfillment of epistemic duty. Must we go with him, at least far enough to hold that a belief has positive epistemic status for me only if I am appropriately discharging my epistemic duty in forming and holding that belief in the way I do form and hold it? This is a difficult question. No doubt there *are* epistemic duties, duties to the truth, duties we have as cognitive beings; but the question is whether a necessary condition of my knowing a proposition is my violating or flouting no such duties in forming the belief in question. I am inclined to doubt that there is an element of this kind in positive epistemic status. It seems that that belief may constitute knowledge even if I am flouting an intellectual duty in the process of forming and holding it. Suppose I am thoroughly jaundiced and relish thinking the worst about you. I know that I suffer from this aberration, and ought to combat it, but do nothing whatever to correct it, taking a malicious pleasure in it. I barely overhear someone make a derogatory comment about you; I can barely make out his words, and, were it not for my ill will, I would not have heard them correctly. (Others thought he said your thought was deep and rigorous; because of my ill will I correctly heard him as saying that your thought is weak and frivolous.) In this case perhaps I am not doing my cognitive duty in forming the belief in question; I am flouting my duty to try to rid myself of my inclination to form malicious beliefs about you, and it is only because I am not doing my duty that I do form the belief in question. Yet surely it seems to have positive epistemic status for me.

Consider another kind of example. Suppose I am convinced by a distinguished epistemologist that (like everyone else) I have a duty to do my best to try to bring it about that for every proposition I consider, I believe that proposition if and only if it is true. Suppose he also convinces me that on most of the occasions when we form ordinary perceptual beliefs, these beliefs are false. I therefore undergo a strenuous, difficult regimen enabling me, at considerable cost in terms of effort and energy, to inhibit my ordinary belief-forming impulses so that I am able to withhold most ordinary perceptual beliefs. Now suppose I hear a siren: I take a quick look and am appeared to in the familiar way in which one is appeared to upon perceiving a large red fire truck. The thought that I must withhold the natural belief here flashes through my mind. I have been finding the regimen burdensome, however, and say to myself: "This is entirely too much trouble; I am sick and tired of doing my epistemic duty." I let nature take its course, forming the belief that what I see is a large red fire truck. Then (assuming that my beliefs do in fact induce in me a duty to try to inhibit the natural belief) I am forming a belief in a way that is contrary to duty; but don't I nonetheless know that there is a red fire truck there? I think so. I am therefore inclined to think that I could know a proposition even if I came to believe it in a way that is contrary to my epistemic duty. The matter is delicate and unclear, however, and complicated by its involvement with difficult questions about the degree to which my beliefs are under my voluntary control. I am inclined to think that fulfillment of epistemic duty, while of course an estimable condition, is neither necessary nor sufficient for positive epistemic status; but the relationship between positive epistemic status and epistemic duty fulfillment remains obscure to me.

(3) If a belief is to have positive epistemic status for me, then my faculties must be functioning properly in producing the *degree* of belief with which I hold **A**, as well as the belief that **A** itself. I am driving down a freeway in Washington D.C.; as I roar by, I catch a quick glimpse of what seems to be a camel in the median strip; if my faculties are functioning properly, I may believe that I saw a camel, but I won't believe it very firmly—not nearly as firmly, for example, as that I am driving a car. If, due to cognitive malfunction (I am struck by a sudden burst of radiation from a Pentagon experiment gone awry) I do believe the former as firmly as the latter, it will have little by way of positive epistemic status for me.[8]

(4) When my epistemic faculties are functioning properly, I will often form one belief *on the evidential basis of* another. The notion of proper function does not apply, of course, only to basic beliefs, that is, beliefs not formed on the evidential basis of other beliefs; my faculties are also such that under the right conditions I will believe one proposition on the basis of some other beliefs I already hold. I may know that either George or Sam is in the office; you inform me that Sam is not there; I then believe that George is in the office on the basis of these other two beliefs. And of course if my faculties are functioning properly, I won't believe a proposition on the evidential basis of just *any* proposition. I won't, for example, believe a proposition on the evidential basis of itself (and perhaps this is not even possible). I won't believe that Homer wrote the Illiad on the evidential basis of my belief that the population of China exceeds that of Japan. Nor will I believe that Feike can swim on the basis of the proposition that 99 out of 100 Frisians cannot swim and Feike is a Frisian. Proper functioning here involves believing a proposition on the basis of *the right kind* of proposition.

(5) A very important notion here is the idea of *specifications,* o r *design plan.* We take it that when human beings (and other creatures) function properly, they function *in a particular way.* That is, they not only

function in such a way as to fulfill their purpose (in the way in which it is the purpose of the heart to pump blood), but they function to fulfill that purpose in just one of an indefinitely large number of possible ways. Our cognitive faculties have been designed, no doubt, with reliability in mind; they have been designed in such a way as to produce beliefs that are for the most part true. But they are not designed to produce true beliefs in just any old way. There is a proper way for them to work; we can suppose there is something like a set of plans for us and our faculties. A house is designed to produce shelter—but not in just any old way. There will be plans specifying the length and pitch of the rafters, what kind of shingles are to be applied, the kind and quantity of insulation to be used, and the like. Something similar holds in the case of us and our faculties; we have been designed in accordance with a specific set of plans. Better (since this analogy is insufficiently dynamic) we have been designed in accordance with a set of specifications, in the way in which there are specifications for, for example, the 1983 **GMC** van. According to these specifications (here I am just guessing), after a cold start the engine runs at 1500 **RPM** until the engine temperature reaches 140 degrees **F**; it then throttles back to 750 **RPM**. In the same sort of way, our cognitive faculties are designed to function in a certain specific way—a way that may include development and change over time. It is for this reason that it is possible for a belief to be produced by a belief producing process that is *accidentally* reliable. This notion of specifications or design plan is also the source of counterexamples to the reliabilist claim that a belief has positive epistemic status if it is produced by a reliable belief producing mechanism.[9]

(6) We do have the idea of our cognitive faculties working properly in an appropriate environment and we also have the idea of positive epistemic status as what accrues to a belief for someone whose epistemic faculties are thus functioning properly. Still, there are cases in which our faculties are functioning perfectly properly, but where their working in that way does not seem to lead to truth—indeed, it may lead away from it. Perhaps you remember a painful experience as less painful than it was. (Some say, it is thus with childbirth.) Or perhaps you continue to believe in your friend's honesty after evidence and objective judgment would have dictated a reluctant change of mind. Perhaps your belief that you will recover from a dread disease is stronger than the statistics justify. In all of these cases, your faculties may be functioning just as they ought to, but nonetheless their functioning in that way does not obviously seem to lead to truth.

The answer here is simplicity itself: what confers positive epistemic status is one's cognitive faculties working properly or working as designed to work *insofar as that segment of design is aimed at producing **true** beliefs*. Not all aspects of the design of our cognitive faculties need be aimed at the production of truth; some might be such as to conduce to survival, or relief from suffering, or the possibility of loyalty, and the like. But someone whose holding a certain belief is a result of an aspect of our cognitive design that is aimed not at truth but at something else won't properly be said to know the proposition in question, even if it turns out to be true. (Unless, perhaps, the same design would conduce both to truth and to the other state of affairs aimed at.)

(7a) Consider Richard Swinburne's "Principle of Credulity": "So generally, . . . I suggest that it is a principle of rationality that (in the absence of special considerations) if it seems (epistemically) to a subject that x is present, then probably x is present; what one seems to perceive is probably so. How things seem to be is good grounds for a belief about how things are."[10] This principle figures into his theistic argument from religious experience: "From this it would follow that, in the absence of special considerations, all religious experiences ought to be taken by their subjects as genuine, and hence as substantial grounds for belief in the apparent object—God, or Mary, or Ultimate Reality or Poseidon."(254). Swinburne understands this "principle of rationality" in such a way that it relates *propositions:* the idea is that on any proposition of the form S **seems (to himself) to be experiencing a thing that is F,** the corresponding proposition of the form S **is experiencing a thing that is F** is more probable than not: "If it seems epistemically to S that x is present, then that is good reason for S to believe that it is so, in the absence of special considerations. . . . And it is good reason too for anyone else to believe that x is present. For if e is evidence for h, this is a relation which holds quite independently of who knows about e" (p. 260).

To understand Swinburne's thought here we must briefly consider how he thinks of probability. He accepts a version of the logical theory of probability developed by Jeffrey, Keynes and Carnap; Swinburne, himself develops a version of this theory in *An Introduction to Confirmation Theory*[11] On this theory for any pair of propositions [A, B] there is an objective, logical probability relation between them: the probability of A conditional on B $(P(A/B))$. This relation is *objective* in that it does not depend in any way upon what anyone (any human being, anyway) knows or believes; it is *logical* in that if $P(A/B)$ is n, then it is necessary (true in every possible world) that $P(A/B)$ is n. (Of course logical probability conforms to the Calculus of Probability.) Carnap spoke of the probabilistic relation between a pair of propositions as *partial entailment;* we may think of the logical probability of A on B as the degree to which B entails A, with entailment *simpliciter* as the limiting case. We could also think of the logical probability of A on B as follows: imagine the possible worlds as uniformly distributed throughout a logical space: then $P(A/B)$ is the ratio between the volume of the space occupied by worlds in which both A and B hold to the volume of the space occupied by worlds in which B holds. And Swinburne's suggestion, as we have seen, is that on any proposition of the form S **seems (to himself) to be experiencing a thing that** is **F**, the corresponding proposition of the form **S is experiencing a thing that is F** is more probable (logically probable) than not.

I find this dubious. First there are notorious difficulties with the very notion of probability thought of this way. (I'll mention one a couple of paragraphs further down.) But second, even if we embrace a logical theory of probability of this kind we are still likely to have grave problems here. Why suppose that on the proposition **It seems to Paul that Zeus is present** it is more probable than not (probability taken as logical probability) that Zeus really is present? Here we are not to rely on our having discovered that as a matter of fact most of what most people think is true; what we must consider is the probability of Zeus's presence on the proposition **it seems to Sam that Zeus is present** *alone*, apart from any background knowledge or beliefs we might have. (Alternatively, this is the case where our background information "consists of nothing but tautologies", as it is sometimes put.) But if all we have for background information is tautologies (and other necessary truths) why think a thing like that? Wouldn't it be just as likely that Sam was mistaken, the victim of a Cartesian demon, or an Alpha Centaurian scientist, or any number of things we can't even think of? What would be a reason for thinking this? That in most possible worlds, most pairs of such propositions are such that the second number is true if the first is? But is there any reason to think that? (That is, is there any reason apart from *theism* to think that; if theism is true, then perhaps most beliefs in most possible worlds are indeed true, if only because God does most of the believing.)

But there is a quite different way in which we might think of this principle. Suppose we think of it from the perspective of the idea that positive epistemic status is a matter of the proper function of our epistemic faculties. It is of course true that when our faculties are functioning properly, then for the most part we do indeed believe what seems to us to be true. This isn't inevitable: consider the Russell paradoxes, where we wind up rejecting what seems true (and what still seems true even after we see where it leads). A madman, furthermore, might find himself regularly believing what didn't seem to him true; and an incautious reader of Kant, intent upon accentuating his free and rational autonomy might undertake a regimen at the conclusion of which he was able to reject what he finds himself inclined by nature to believe. But all else being equal, we ordinarily believe what seems to us to be true, and what seems to us true (when our faculties are functioning properly in a suitable environment) will have more by way of positive epistemic status for us than what does not. The explanation, I suggest, is not that **p** is logically probable on the proposition **p seems to Paul to be true;** the explanation is much simpler: it is the fact that when my faculties are functioning properly, the degree of positive epistemic status a proposition has for me just is (modulo a constant of proportionality) the degree to which I am inclined to believe that proposition.

(7b) Similar comments apply to Swinburne's "Principle of Testimony": "the principle that (in the absence of special considerations) the experiences of others are probably as they report them" (272). Here again Swinburne apparently understands this principle in terms of his understanding of probability: the proposition **Sam's experience is F** is more probable than not, in the logical sense, on the proposition **Sam testifies that his experience is F**. But this seems dubious: is there any reason to think that in most possible worlds in which Sam claims to have a headache, he really does have a headache? Or that the volume of 'logical space' occupied by worlds in which Sam testifies that he has a headache and in fact does, is more than half of the volume of worlds in which Sam testifies that he does? What could be the basis of such a claim? Swinburne's suggestion is that if we do not accept principles of this sort, we shall land in the "morass of skepticism." But we can avoid that morass without accepting these implausible claims about logical probability. Thomas Reid[12] speaks of "Credulity"—the tendency we display to believe what we are told by others. This tendency is of course subject to modification by experience: we learn to trust some people on some topics and distrust others on others; we learn never to form a judgment about a marital altercation until we have spoken to both parties; we learn that people's judgment can be skewed by pride, selfishness, desire to exalt oneself at the expense of one's fellows, love, lust and much else. Nonetheless there is this tendency, and under the right circumstances when you tell me **p** (that your name is 'Paul', for example) then (if **p** is true, and I believe **p** sufficiently firmly and my faculties are functioning properly in the formation of this belief) I know **p**. And here we need not try to account for this fact in terms of the logical probability of one proposition on another; we can note instead that (1) when our faculties are functioning properly, we are typically inclined to believe what we are told and (2) if we believe what is true and what we are are sufficiently strongly inclined to believe, then if our faculties are functioning properly (and the cognitive environment is congenial) what we believe is something we know.

(7c) Finally, consider Swinburne's claim that *simplicity is* a prime determinant of *a priori* or intrinsic probability, at least for explanatory theories: "Prior probability depends on simplicity, fit with background knowledge, and scope. A theory is simple in so far as it postulates few mathematically simple laws holding between entities of an intelligible kind. . . . I am saying merely that a theory which postulates entities of an intelligible kind, as opposed to other entities, will have a greater prior probability, and so, *other things being equal,* will be more likely to be true. . . . For large scale theories the crucial determinant of prior probability is simplicity (52-53)." Here Swinburne is speaking of *prior* probability, not *a priori* or intrinsic probability: "the prior probability of a theory is the probability before we consider the detailed evidence of observation cited in its support" (52). The prior probability of a theory also depends on its fit with our background knowledge. But if we consider the *a priori* or *intrinsic* probability of the theory, then fit with background information drops outs, so that we are left with content (or 'scope', as Swinburne calls it in *the Existence of God*) and simplicity as the determinants of intrinsic probability; and of these two, it is simplicity that is the more important: ". . . sometimes it is convenient to let *e* be all observational evidence and let *k* be mere 'tautological evidence'. In the latter case the prior probability **P***(h/k)* will depend mainly on the simplicity of *h* (as well as to a lesser extent on its narrowness of scope)" (p. 65).

Now I believe there are real problems here. The chief problem, it seems to me, is with the very notion of intrinsic, logical probability. On the theory in question, as we have seen, for any pair of propositions there is an objective, logical probability between them. As a special case of this relation we have intrinsic probability: the probability of a proposition conditional on nothing but necessary truths. Take such a contingent proposition as **Paul Zwier owns an orange shirt;** on this view, there is such a thing as the probability of that proposition conditional on the proposition 7+5=12. And the problem here is substantially twofold. In the first place there is no reason, so far as I can see, to think that contingent propositions *do* in general have an intrinsic logical probability; and if they do, there seems to be no way to determine, even within very broad limits, what it might be.

But second and more important: there are many large classes of propositions such that there seems to be no way in which intrinsic probability can be distributed over their members in a way that accords both with the calculus of probability and with intuition. Consider, for example, a countably infinite set of **S** of propositions that are mutually exclusive in pairs and such that necessarily, exactly one of them is true: **S** might be, for example, the set of propositions such that for each natural number **n** (including 0), **S** contains the proposition **there exist exactly n flying donkeys.** Given nothing but necessary truths, none of these propositions should be more likely to be true than any others; if there is such a thing as a logical probability on nothing but necessary truths, one number should be as probable as another to be the number of flying donkeys. But the members of this countably infinite set can have the same probability only if each has probability 0. That means, however, that the proposition **there are no flying donkeys** has intrinsic probability 0; hence its denial—**there are some flying donkeys**—has an intrinsic probability of 1. Further, according to the Probability Calculus, if a proposition has an intrinsic probability of 1, then its probability on any evidence is also 1; hence no matter what our evidence, the probability on our evidence that there are flying donkeys is 1. Still further, it is easy to see that (under these assumptions) for any number **n**, the probability that there are at least **n** flying donkeys also has an intrinsic probability of 1[13] and hence a probability of 1 on any evidence. And of course this result is not limited to flying donkeys; for any kind of object such that for any number **n** it is possible that there be **n** objects of that kind—witches, demons, Siberian Cheeshounds—the probability that there are at least **n** of them (for any **n**) is 1 on any evidence whatever.[14]

The only way to avoid this unsavory result is to suppose that intrinsic probabilities are distributed in accordance with some series that converges to 0: for example, **there are no flying donkeys** has an intrinsic probability of 1/2, **there is just one flying donkey** gets 1/4, and so on. But then we are committed to the idea that some numbers are vastly more likely (conditional on necessary truths alone) than others to be the number of flying donkeys. In fact we are committed to the view that for any number **n** you please, there will be a pair of natural numbers **m** and **m*** such that **m*** is **n** times more likely (conditional on necessary truths alone) to be the number of donkeys than **m**. And this seems just as counterintuitive as the suggestion that for any number **n** you pick, the probability (on any evidence) that there are at least **n** flying donkeys is 1.

It therefore seems to me unlikely that such propositions have intrinsic probability at all; but similar arguments can be brought to bear on many other classes of propositions. Accordingly, I think the whole idea of intrinsic probability is at best dubious. But even if there is such a thing, why should we suppose that *simpler* propositions, all else being equal, have more of it than complex propositions? Is there some *a priori* reason to suppose that reality prefers simplicity? Where would this notion come from? Swinburne, again, believes that if we don't accept some such principle as this, we shall fall into that skeptical bog: if we don't accept some such principle, we will have no reason for preferring simple to complex hypotheses, but in many contexts all that our favored hypotheses have going for them (as compared to others that fit the same data just as well) is simplicity.

But suppose we look at the matter from the point of view of the present conception of positive epistemic status. Despite the real problems in saying just what simplicity is (and in saying in any sort of systematic way when one theory is simpler than another) there clearly is such a thing as simplicity, and it clearly does contribute to the positive epistemic status a theory or explanation has for us. But why think of this in terms of the problematic notion of intrinsic logical probability? Why not note instead that when our faculties are functioning properly, we do opt for simple theories as opposed to complex ones (all else being equal); we can therefore see the greater positive epistemic status of simple theories (again, all else being equal) as resulting from the fact that when our faculties are functioning properly, we are more strongly inclined to accept simple theories than complex ones.

(8)   There are presently three main views as to the nature of positive epistemic status: Chisholmian Internalism, Coherentism, and

Reliabilism. The present conception of positive epistemic status as a matter of degree of inclination towards belief when epistemic faculties are functioning properly—the conception that seems to me to go most naturally with theism—provides a revealing perspective from which, as it seems to me, we can see that none of these three views is really viable. For each we can easily see that the proposed necessary and sufficient condition for positive epistemic status is not in fact sufficient (and in some cases not necessary either) and not sufficient just because a belief could meet the condition in question but still have little by way of positive epistemic status because of cognitive pathology, failure to function properly. I don't have the space here to go into the matter with the proper thoroughness[15]; I shall say just the following.

First, the Chisholmian Internalist (or at any rate its most distinguished exemplar) sees positive epistemic status as a matter of aptness for epistemic duty fulfillment. Chisholm begins by introducing an undefined technical locution: 'p is more reasonable than q for S at t; here the values for **p** and **q** will be such states of affairs as **believing that all men are mortal and withholding the belief that all men are mortal**—that is, believing neither the proposition in question nor its denial. Given 'is more reasonable than' as an undefined locution, he goes on to define a battery of "terms of epistemic appraisal" as he calls them: 'certain', 'beyond reasonable doubt', 'evident', 'acceptable', and so on. A proposition **A** is beyond reasonable doubt for a person at a time **t**, for example, if it is more reasonable for him to accept that proposition then than to withhold it; **A** has some presumption in its favor for him at **t** just if accepting it then is more reasonable than accepting its negation. Now Chisholm introduces "is more reasonable than" as an undefined locution; but of course he intends it to have a sense, and to have a sense reasonably close to the sense it has in English. In *Foundations of Knowing,* his most recent full dress presentation of his epistemology, he says that "Epistemic reasonability could be understood in terms of the general requirement to try to have the largest possible set of logically independent beliefs that is such that the true beliefs outnumber the false beliefs. The principles of epistemic preferability are the principles one should follow if one is to fulfill this requirement."[16] In his earlier *Theory of Knowledge* Chisholm is a bit more explicit about intellectual requirements: "We may assume," he says,

> that every person is subject to a purely intellectual requirement: that of trying his best to bring it about that for any proposition p he considers, he accepts p if and only if p is true;[17]

and he adds that

> One might say that this is the person's responsibility qua intellectual being . . . One way, then, of re-expressing the locution 'p is more reasonable than q for S at t' is to say this: 'S is so situated at t that his

intellectual requirement, his responsibility as an intellectual being, is better fulfilled by p than by q'.

Reasonability, therefore, is a *normative* concept; more precisely, it pertains to requirement, duty, or obligation. And Chisholm's central claim here is that a certain epistemic requirement, or responsibility, or duty, or obligation lies at the basis of such epistemic notions as evidence, justification, positive epistemic status, and knowledge itself. To say, for example, that a proposition **p** is *acceptable* for a person at a time is to say that he is so situated, then, that it is not the case that he can better fulfill his epistemic duty by withholding than by accepting **p**; to say that **p** is *beyond reasonable doubt* for him is to say that he is so situated, then, that he can better fulfill his intellectual responsibility by accepting **p** than by withholding it. The basic idea is that our epistemic duty or requirement is to try to achieve and maintain a certain condition—call it 'epistemic excellence'—which may be hard to specify in detail, but consists fundamentally in standing in an appropriate relation to truth. A proposition has positive epistemic status for me, in certain circumstances, to the extent that I can fulfill my epistemic duty by accepting it in those circumstances. This duty or obligation or requirement, furthermore, is one of trying to bring about a certain state of affairs. My requirement is not to *succeed* in achieving and maintaining intellectual excellence; my requirement is only to try to do so. Presumably the reason is that it may not be within my power to succeed. Perhaps I don't know how to achieve intellectual excellence; or perhaps I do know how but simply can't do it. So my duty is only to *try* to bring about this state of affairs.

This is a simple and attractive picture of the nature of justification and positive epistemic status. I think it is easy to see, however, that it is deeply flawed: for it is utterly clear that aptness for the fulfillment of epistemic duty or obligation is not sufficient for positive epistemic status. Suppose Paul is subject to cognitive dysfunction: then there could be a proposition **A** that has little by way of positive epistemic status for him, but is nonetheless such that believing it is maximally apt for epistemic duty fulfillment for him. Suppose Paul is subject to a cerebral disturbance that causes far-reaching cognitive dysfunction: when he is appeared to by one sense modality, he forms beliefs appropriate to another. When he is aurally appeared to in the way in which one is appeared to upon hearing church bells, for example, he has a nearly ineluctable tendency to believe that there is something that is appearing to him in that fashion, and that that thing is orange—bright orange. This belief, furthermore, seems utterly convincing; it has for him, all the phenomenological *panache* of *modus ponens* itself. He knows nothing about this defect in his epistemic equipment, and his lack of awareness is in no way due to dereliction of epistemic duty. As a matter of fact, Paul is unusually dutiful, unusually concerned about doing his epistemic duty; fulfilling this duty is the main passion of his life. Add that those around him suffer from a similar epistemic deficiency: Paul lives in Alaska and he and all his neighbors have suffered all their lives from similar lesions due to radioactive fallout from a Soviet missile test. Now suppose Paul is aurally appeared to in the way in question and forms the belief that he is being appeared to in that way by something that is orange. Surely this proposition is such that believing it is the right thing to do from the point of view of epistemic duty; nevertheless the proposition has little by way of positive epistemic status for him. Paul is beyond reproach; he has done his duty as he saw it; he is within his epistemic rights; he is permissively justified, and more. Nevertheless there is a kind of positive epistemic status this belief lacks—a kind crucial for knowledge. For that sort of positive epistemic status, it isn't sufficient to satisfy one's duty and do one's epistemic best. Paul can be ever so conscientious about his epistemic duties and still be such that his beliefs do not have that kind of positive epistemic status.

Clearly enough, we can vary the above sorts of examples. Perhaps you think that what goes in *excelsis* with satisfying duty is *effort*; perhaps (in a Kantian vein) you think that genuinely dutiful action must be contrary to inclination. Very well; alter the above cases accordingly. Suppose, for example, that Paul (again, due to cognitive malfunction) nonculpably believes that his nature is deeply misleading. Like the rest of us, he has an inclination, upon being appeared to redly, to believe that there is something red lurking in the neighborhood; unlike the rest of us, he believes that this natural inclination is misleading and that on those occasions there really isn't anything that is thus appearing to him. He undertakes a strenuous regimen to overcome this inclination; after intense and protracted effort he succeeds: upon being appeared to redly he no longer believes that something red is appearing to him. His devotion to duty costs him dearly. The enormous effort he expends takes its toll upon his health; he is subject to ridicule and disapprobation on the part of his fellows; his wife protests his unusual behavior and finally leaves him for someone less epistemically nonstandard. Nonetheless he persists in doing what he nonculpably takes to be his duty. It is obvious, I take it, that even though Paul is unusually dutiful in accepting, on a given occasion, the belief that nothing red is appearing to him, he has little by way of positive epistemic status for that belief.

We may therefore conclude, I think, that positive epistemic status is not or is not merely a matter of aptness for fulfillment of epistemic duty or obligation. Could it be *coherence,* as with Lehrer[18], Bonjour[19], and several Bayesians? Coherentism, of course, comes in many varieties; here I don't have the space to discuss any of them properly. From the present perspective, however, there is at least one crucial difficulty with them all: they all neglect the crucial feature of proper function. According to coherentism, all that is relevant to my beliefs having positive epistemic status for me is a certain internal relationship among them. But surely this is not so. Consider, for example, the case of the Epistemically Inflexible Climber. Paul is climbing Guide's Wall, in the Grand Tetons; having just led the next to last pitch, he is seated on a comfortable ledge, belaying his partner. He believes that Cascade Canyon is down to his left, that the cliffs of Mt. Owen are directly in front of him, that there is a hawk flying in lazy circles 200 feet below him, that he is wearing his new *Fire* rock shoes, and so on. His beliefs, we may stipulate, are coherent. Now imagine that Paul is struck by a burst of high energy cosmic radiation, causing his beliefs to become fixed, no longer responsive to changes in experience. His partner gets him down the wall and, in a last ditch attempt at therapy, takes him to the opera in Jackson, where the Metropolitan Opera on tour is performing "La Traviata" with Pavarotti singing the tenor lead. Paul is appeared to in the same way as everyone else there; he is inundated by waves of golden sound. Sadly enough, the effort at therapy fails; Paul still believes that he is on the belay ledge at the top of the next to last pitch of Guide's Wall, that Cascade Canyon is down to his left, that there is a hawk flying in lazy circles 200 feet below him, and so on. Furthermore, since he believes the very same things he believed when seated on the ledge, his beliefs are coherent. But surely they have very little by way of positive epistemic status for him. Clearly, then, coherence is not sufficient for positive epistemic status.

I turn finally to reliabilism, the last of the three chief contemporary ideas as to the nature of positive epistemic status. The view I have suggested in this paper is closer to reliabilism, especially in the form suggested by William Alston[20], than to either of the other two; indeed, perhaps you think it is a form of reliabilism. I don't propose to argue about labels; still, as I see it, that would be less than wholly accurate. Of course reliability crucially enters into the account I suggest. According to that account, we implicitly think of positive epistemic status as involving our faculties' functioning properly: but clearly we wouldn't think of positive epistemic status in this way if we didn't think that when our faculties function as they ought, then for the most part they are in fact reliable. Still, there is more to a belief's having positive epistemic status than its being reliably produced. There are even more brands of Reliabilism than of Coherentism; and what is true of one may not be true of another. But the leading idea of at least many central brands of reliabilism is that a belief has positive epistemic status if and only if it is produced by a reliable belief producing mechanism or process; and the degree of its positive epistemic status is determined by the degree of reliability of the process that produces it. Thus Alvin Goldman: "The justificational status of a belief," he says, "is a function of the reliability of the process or processes that cause it, where (as a first approximation) reliability consists in the tendency of a process to produce beliefs that are true rather than false."[21]

Here there are problems of several sorts; one of the most important is the dreaded *problem of generality*, developed by Richard Feldman in "Reliability and Justification."[22] But there are other problems as well, problems that arise out of the neglect of the idea of proper function. As we saw above, a crucial part of our notion of positive epistemic status is the idea of a design plan or specifications. But then not just any reliable belief producing process can confer positive epistemic status. Suppose I am struck by a burst of cosmic rays, resulting in the following unfortunate malfunction. Whenever I hear the word 'prime' in any context, I form a belief, with respect to one of the first 1000 natural numbers, that it is not prime. So you say "Pacific Palisades is prime residential area"; or "Prime ribs is my favorite" or "First you must prime the pump" or "(17') entails (14)" or "The prime rate is dropping again" or anything else in which the word occurs; in each case I form a belief, with respect to a randomly selected natural number, that it is not prime. This belief producing process or mechanism is indeed reliable; in the vast majority of cases it produces truth. But it is only accidentally reliable; it just happens, by virtue of a piece of epistemic serendipity, to produce mostly true beliefs. And the force of the suggestion that the process in question is accidentally reliable, I suggest, is just that under the envisaged conditions my faculties are not working in accordance with the design plan or the specifications for human beings; that's what makes the reliability in question *accidental* reliability. Furthermore, it does not confer positive epistemic status. Here the process or mechanism in question is indeed reliable; but my belief— that, say, 41 is not prime—has little or no positive epistemic status. Nor is the problem simply that the belief is false; the same goes for my (true) belief that 631 is not prime, if it is formed in this fashion. So reliable belief formation is not sufficient for positive epistemic status.

By way of conclusion, then: from a theistic perspective, it is natural to see positive epistemic status, the quantity enough of which is sufficient, together with truth, for knowledge in the following way: positive epistemic status accrues to a belief **B** for a person **S** only if **S**'s cognitive environment is appropriate for his cognitive faculties and only if these faculties are functioning properly in producing this belief in him—i.e., only if his cognitive faculties are functioning in the way God designed human cognitive faculties to function, and only if **S** is in the sort of cognitive environment for which human cognitive faculties are designed; and under these conditions the degree of positive epistemic status enjoyed by **B** is proportional to the strength of his inclination to accept **B**. Alternatively: a belief **B** has positive epistemic status for **S** if and only if that belief is produced in **S** by his epistemic faculties working properly (in an appropriate environment); and **B** has more positive epistemic status than **B*** for **S** iff **B** has positive epistemic status for **S** and either **B*** does not or else **S** is more strongly inclined to believe **B** than **B***. Still another way to put the matter: a belief **B** has degree **d** of positive epistemic status for a person **S** if and only if the faculties relevant to producing **B** in **S** are functioning properly (in an appropriate environment), and **S** is inclined to degree **d** to believe **B**.

There remains, of course, an enormous amount to be said and an enormous amount to be thought about. For example: (1) What about *God's* knowledge? God is the premier example of someone who knows; but of course his faculties are not designed either by himself or by someone else. So how shall we think of his knowledge? The answer, I think, lies in the following neighborhood: "Working properly" is used *analogically* when applied to God's cognitive faculties and ours, the analogy being located in the fact that a design plan for a *perfect* knower would specify cognitive powers of the very sort God displays. But of course this notion needs to be developed and worked out in detail. (2) Our spiritual forebears at Princeton used to speak of the *noetic effects of sin.* Clearly (from a Christian perspective) sin has had an important effect upon the function of our cognitive faculties; but just how does this work and how does it bear on specific questions about the degree of positive epistemic status enjoyed by various beliefs? (3) This way of thinking of positive epistemic status, I believe, makes it much easier to understand the degree of positive epistemic status enjoyed by *moral* beliefs and by *a priori* beliefs; but just what sort of account is correct here? (4) How, from this perspective, shall we think of the dreaded Gettier problem? (5) The present account is clearly an *externalist* account of positive epistemic status; but how do internalist factors fit in? (6) From the present perspective, how shall we think about skepticism? (7) How is the present account related to the broadly Aristotelian account of knowledge to be found in Medieval thinkers? (8) How shall we construe *epistemic probability*—more exactly, how shall we construe the relationship between **A** and **B** when **A** is a good non-deductive reason for **B**, or where **B** is epistemically probable with respect to **A**? Here the present account of positive epistemic status is clearly suggestive;[23] but how, precisely, does it work? (9) Over the last few years several philosophers[24] have been arguing that rational belief in God does not require propositional evidence or argument, that it can be properly basic; how shall we think of that claim from the present perspective? These and many others are questions for another occasion.

Endnotes

*Reprinted from *Faith and Philosophy*, Vol. 4, No. 4, October 1987. All rights reserved.

[1] See my "Positive Epistemic Status and Proper Function" in *Topics in Philosophy: vol. II, Epistemology,* ed. James Tomberlin (Northridge: California State University).

[2] See R. Chisholm, *Theory of Knowledge* (New York: Prentice Hall, 2nd Edition) pp. 5ff.

3 See my "Chisholmian Internalism" in *Philosophical Analysis: A Defense by Example*, ed. David Austin (Dordrecht: D. Reidel, 1987).

4 Indeed, it is ludicrous understatement to say that God has a grasp of every proposition and property: from a theistic point of view the natural way to view propositions and properties is as God's thoughts and concepts. (See my "How to be an Anti-realist", *Proceedings of the American Philosophical Association*, Vol. 56, #1, 1983.)

5 In C. S. Lewis' novel *Out of the Silent Planet* the creatures on Mars are of several different types displaying several different kinds of cognitive excellences: some are particularly suited to scientific endeavors, some to poetry and art, and some to interpersonal sensitivity.

6 See my "Positive Epistemic Status and Proper Function" (footnote 1).

7 See his *Theory of Knowledge*, p. 14, and *Foundations of Knowing*, (Minneapolis: University of Minneapolis Press, 1982), p. 7. See also my "Chisholmian Internalism" in *Philosophical Analysis: A Defense by Example (above, footnote 3)*.

8 Must *all* of my cognitive faculties be functioning properly for any belief to have positive epistemic status for me? Surely not. And what about the fact that proper function comes in degrees? How well must the relevant faculties be working for a belief to have positive epistemic status for me? On these questions see "Positive Epistemic Status and Proper Function" (footnote 1).

9 See below, p. 77 [original article had pp. 000].

10 *The Existence of God* (Oxford: at the Clarendon Press, 1979) p. 254. Subsequent references to Swinburne's work will be to this volume.

11 See R. Swinburne, *An Introduction to Confirmation Theory* (London: Methuen & Co. Ltd., 1973).

12 My whole account of positive epistemic status, not just this example, owes much to Thomas Reid with his talk of faculties and their functions and his rejection of the notion (one he attributes to Hume and his predecessors) that self-evident propositions and propositions about one's own immediate experience are the only properly basic propositions.

13 The proposition **there are at least n flying donkeys** is equivalent to the denial of (a) **There are 0 flying donkeys** or . . . **there are just n-1 flying donkeys**. By hypothesis, the probability of each disjunct of (a) is 0; hence by the Additive Axiom the probability of the disjunction is 0, so that the probability of its denial is 1.

14 See my "The Probabilistic Argument from Evil," *Philosophical Studies*, 1979.

15 See my "Chisholmian Internalism" (above, footnote 3) for detailed criticism of Chisholmian internalism; see my "Coherentism and the Evidentialist Objection to Theistic Belief" in *Rationality, Religious Belief, and Moral Commitment*, ed. William Wainwright and Robert Audi (Ithaca: Cornell University Press, 1986) for detailed criticism of coherentism, and see my "Positive Epistemic Status and Proper Function" (above, footnote 1) for criticism of reliabilism.

16 P. 7.

17 P. 14.

18 Keith Lehrer, *Knowledge* (Oxford: Oxford University Press, 1974).

19 Lawrence Bonjour, *The Structure of Empirical Knowledge* (Cambridge: Harvard University Press, 1986).

20 See his "Concepts of Epistemic Justification," *The Monist*, Vol. 68, no. 1 (Jan., 1985) and "An Internalist Externalism" in *Synthese*.

21 "What is Justified Belief?" in *Justification and Knowledge: New Studies in Epistemology*, ed. George Pappas (Dordrecht: D. Reidel, 1979), p. 10.

22 *The Monist*, Vol. 68, #2 (April, 1985) PP. 159ff.

23 See Richard Otte's "Theistic Conception of Probability."

24 See, for example, William Alston's "Christian Experience and Christian Belief," Nicholas Wolterstorff's "Can Belief in God be Rational if it has no Foundations"?,and my "Reason and Belief in God," all in *Faith and Rationality*, ed. N. Wolterstorff and A. Plantinga (Notre Dame: University of Notre Dame Press, 1983).

Study Questions

1.   What does Plantinga mean by "positive epistemic status"? Give account of the various components of Plantinga's answer in your own terms.

2.   What are the eight objections Plantinga lists against his proposal? Which do you take to be the most formidable? Why? Does Plantinga answer the objection in question?

3.   What is an internalist epistemologist?

4.   Is Plantinga's epistemology internalist or externalist? State reasons for your classification.

5.   Plantinga has been characterized as a Reformed epistemologist. What is there about his epistemological theory that justifies this claim?

6

Can Belief in God Be Rational
If It Has No Foundations?

Nicholas Wolterstorff

Nicholas Wolterstorff is professor of philosophy at Yale University, the Divinity School, and is author of *Religion and the Schools, On Universals, Reason Within the Bounds of Religion, Until Justice and Peace Embrace,* and *Faith and Rationality* (coeditor).

One of his main conclusions is that from the fact that it is not rational for some person to believe that God exists it does not follow that he ought to give up that belief. For Wolterstorff, rationality is only prima facie justification, and the lack of it only prima facie impermissability. Moreover, the evidentialist challenge of Locke is untenable.*

Central to Christianity, Judaism, and Islam alike is the conviction that we as human beings are called to believe in God—to trust in him, to rely on him, to place our confidence in him. To believe in God is our fundamental human obligation. Central also is the conviction that only by believing in God can the deepest stirrings of the human heart be satisfied. Duty and fulfillment here coalesce.

But is it rational for us to believe in God? Is it rational for us to place our confidence in him? Can a person believe in God without performing a *sacrificium intellectus?* One cannot belong to the intelligentsia of modern Western society without having that question come to mind.

Presumably it is rational for a person to believe *in* God only if it is rational for him to believe various propositions *about* God—in particular, that there is such a being as God. The rationality of trusting someone presupposes the rationality of believing that that person exists. And among the objections to Christian belief, as well as to Judaic and Muslim, characteristic of the modern intelligentsia is the objection that it is no longer rational, if ever it was, to believe that God exists. We must choose between treasuring our rationality and assenting to God's existence. We cannot have it both ways. The rational person will have to make his way in the world without supposing that there exists any God in whom he *could* trust. Kafka's castle is empty. The noises we hear are only echoes of our own voices.

Tacit in this characteristically modern objection to theistic conviction is the assumption that if it is not rational to believe some (affirmative) proposition about God, then one ought not believe it. There are a good many theologians in this century who—if I read them correctly—would contest this assumption. They would agree with the objectors that believing that God exists requires throwing overboard the demands of rationality, but they would nonetheless refuse to go along with the conclusion of the objectors that we ought then to cease believing that God exists. Divine revelation, they say, has entered our existence, coming as an assault to our rationality. Accordingly, we must now choose by what principle we shall live our lives—reason or revelation. The believer has thrown in his lot with revelation, and rationality no longer has any claim on him. It is a matter of utter indifference to him whether his theistic convictions are rational. Rationality is only a siren tempter.

In my judgment this is a profoundly misguided response to the challenge I have cited, expressing an untenable view as the place of rationality in our human existence—at least when rationality is understood as I shall be understanding it in this discussion. In my judgment the charge that it is irrational to believe that God exists must be taken seriously by the theist. This is one of the theses I shall be defending.

But first let me formulate more amply the objection to theistic conviction which I see as characteristic of the modern Western intellectual. The objection can be seen as presupposing a challenge, call it the *evidentialist challenge* to theism. And this challenge can be thought of as consisting of two claims: first, if it is not rational to accept some proposition about God then one ought not accept it; and second, it is not rational to accept propositions about God unless one does so on the basis of others of one's beliefs which provide adequate evidence for them, and with a firmness not exceeding that warranted by the strength of the evidence. Someone who holds that this challenge is correct and, in addition, holds, concerning a given theistic believer, that the believer does not meet the challenge, may then be said to accept the *evidentialist objection* to the theistic convictions of that believer.

It is the evidentialist objection to theistic belief that I wish to consider in this paper, and especially the evidentialist *challenge* that lies behind the objection. My interest is not so much in whether the challenge is being met by some believers or in whether it can be met; my interest is more in whether the challenge itself is tenable.

An explanation is immediately in order. In what follows I shall often speak of someone *believing* that God exists rather than of someone *accepting the proposition* that God exists. I shall mean the same thing. Often "believe" is used in such a way that from the fact that someone believes something it follows that he does not know it. That is not how I shall be using it. When I speak of someone believing something, it is implied that he does not know it. For—to say it once again—I shall use "believe" as a synonym for "accept."   And surely if someone knows so-and-so, he accepts it.

As I have already tacitly suggested, the evidentialist challenge and objection to theistic conviction are not distributed evenly throughout modern society. They are found mainly among the intelligentsia. And as I have already said, they are peculiarly modern. One finds them not at all—or hardly at all—before the latter half of the seventeenth century. A corollary of this latter fact is that evidentialist apologetics, construed as the attempt to meet the challenge by offering arguments for various (affirmative) theistic propositions, thus to legitimize theistic belief, or by showing that the arguments theistic believers already have are sound ones, thus to show that theistic belief is legitimate, are also unique to modernity. Until the modern age, Christian apologetics consisted mainly, not in giving or defending arguments *for* Christianity, but rather in answering objections to Christianity. It is when the challenge to Christianity is the evidentialist challenge, and when one attempts to cope with the challenge by meeting it or showing that it has already been met, that the offering of "evidence" becomes relevant to the apologist's traditional endeavor. When Tertullian, in his famous and eloquent *Apology*, undertook to answer the objection (among others) that Christians were responsible for the decline in the economy of the Roman Empire, he did not undertake to offer arguments for the truth of Christianity, let alone for the truth of theism.

I

John Locke was among the first to formulate articulately the evidentialist challenge to theistic belief. It will help to set the stage for our discussion if we consider what he says. Reason, says Locke,

> as contradistinguished to faith, I take to be the discovery of the certainty or probability of such propositions or truths, which the mind arrives at by deductions made from such ideas which it has got by the use of its natural faculties, viz., by sensation or reflection.
>
> *Faith,* on the other side, is the assent to any proposition, not thus made out by the deductions of reason, but upon the credit of the proposer, as coming from God in some extraordinary way of communicating. This way of discovering truths to men we call *revelation.* (*An Essay Concerning Human Understanding,* IV, 18, 2)

Reason is *reasoning* for Locke, and clearly he thinks of it as one among others of our belief-forming processes.[1] Faith is another belief-forming process. It, by contrast, consists in accepting something "as coming from God."

Does that mean, then, that reasoning plays no rightful role in faith? Not at all, says Locke. It is worth quoting him at some length on this point.

> But since God, in giving us the light of reason, has not thereby tied up his own hands from affording us, when he thinks fit, the light of revelation in any of those matters wherein our natural faculties are able to give a probable determination, revelation, where God has been pleased to give it, must carry it against the probable conjectures of reason; because the mind, not being certain of the truth of what it does not evidently know, but only yielding to the probability that appears in it, is bound to give up its assent to such a testimony, which, it is satisfied, comes from One who cannot err, and will not deceive. But yet it still belongs to reason to judge of the truth of its being a revelation, and of the signification of the words wherein it is delivered. Indeed, if any thing shall be thought revelation which is contrary to the plain principles of reason and the evident knowledge the mind has of its own clear and distinct ideas, there reason must be hearkened to as a matter within its province: since a man can never have so certain a knowledge that a proposition, which contradicts the clear principles and evidence of his own knowledge, was divinely revealed, or that he understands the words rightly wherein it is delivered, as he has that the contrary is true: and so is bound to consider and judge of it as a matter of reason, and not swallow it, without examination, as a matter of faith. (*Essay*, IV,18,8)
>
> Whatever God hath revealed is certainly true: no doubt can be made of it. This is the proper object of faith; but whether it be a divine revelation or not, reason must judge; which can never permit the mind to reject a greater evidence to embrace what is less evident, nor allow it to entertain probability in opposition to knowledge and certainty. (*Essay*, IV,18,10)[2]

It is self-evident, Locke suggests, that whatever God has revealed is true. This is something on which we can base our reasoning, our inferring. It is not something for which we must *first* have evidence. But that a given deliverance from the mouth or hand of a human being is a revelation of God is something for which, if we are to be entitled to believe it, we must have other beliefs which constitute adequate evidence for it. If the *content* of the purported revelation is self-evidently or demonstrably false, then we must reject it as a revelation of God. If, on the contrary, it only has the status of improbability, then we must weigh up that improbability against the probability that it is a revelation from God. (Presumably it *is* such "weighing-up" that Locke has in mind. On this point he is not wholly explicit.)[3]

Why is this so? If we are entitled to accept without argument that what God reveals is true, then why may we not also accept without argument that the New Testament, say, is a revelation from God? Because, says Locke, we would then have no way of showing that "the enthusiasts" are irresponsible in their believings. If we affirm the evidentialist challenge, we can then go up to the enthusiast and say, "Give us the evidence that your purported revelations are in fact from God." If he cannot comply, then we can justly conclude that he is believing irresponsibly.

> But to examine a little soberly this internal light and this feeling on which they build so much: The question here is, How do I know that God is the revealer of this to me; that this impression is made upon my mind by his Holy Spirit, and that therefore I ought to obey it? If I know not this, how great soever the assurance is, that I am possessed with, it is groundless; whatever light I pretend to, it is but *enthusiasm.* Does it not then stand them upon, to examine upon what grounds they presume it to be a revelation from God? (*Essay,* IV,19,10)[4]

Of course, this challenge to the enthusiasts is also a challenge to Christian believers: if they do not believe on the basis of adequate evidence that the Bible is God's revelation, they too must give up their religion. But Locke was confident that in the case of Christianity the challenge could be met. He himself undertook to meet it in his book *The Reasonableness of Christianity, As Delivered in the Scriptures.*

Thus far we have found Locke saying that a condition of someone's being entitled to accept so-and-so as a revelation from God is that he has inferred from other beliefs of his, which constitute adequate evidence for it, *that it is* a revelation from God. In fact Locke contends that the connection between this entitlement and this condition is even tighter. He holds that the firmness with which one accepts this proposition must be proportioned to the strength of the evidence for it.

> We may as well doubt of our own being, as we can whether any revelation from God be true. So that faith is a settled and sure principle of assent and assurance, and leaves no manner of room for doubt or hesitation. Only we must be sure that it is a divine revelation, and that we understand it right: else we shall expose ourselves to all the extravagancy of enthusiasm, and all the error of wrong principles, if we have faith and assurance in what is not divine revelation. And therefore in those cases, our assent can be rationally no higher than the evidence of its being a revelation, and that this is the meaning of the expressions it is delivered in. If the evidence of its being a revelation, or that this is its true sense, be only on probable

proofs, our assent can reach no higher than as assurance or diffidence, arising from the more or less apparent probability of the proofs. (*Essay*, IV,16,14)

All that has been said thus far presupposes the acceptability of believing that God exists. What, on Locke's view, is the condition for that? Before a person is entitled to believe that such-and-such is a deliverance from God, he must have inferred from adequate evidence that it is that. But what about his prior belief that there is a God? Must it too be supported by adequate reasoning if the person is to be entitled to hold it?

Yes indeed, on Locke's view. God, says Locke, "has given us no innate ideas of himself." He "has stamped no original characters on our mmd, wherein we may read his being." That God exists is not self-evident to us. Yet,

> having furnished us with those faculties our minds are endowed with, he hath not left himself without witness; since we have sense, perception, and reason, and cannot want a clear proof of him as long as we carry ourselves about us. Nor can we justly complain of our ignorance in this great point, since he has so plentifully provided us with the means to discover and know him, so far as is necessary to the end of our being, and the great concernment of our happiness. But though this be the most obvious truth that reason discovers, and though its evidence be (if I mistake not) equal to mathematical certainty; yet it requires thought and attention, and the mind must apply itself to a regular deduction of it from some part of our intuitive knowledge, or else we shall be as uncertain and ignorant of this as of other propositions which are in themselves capable of clear demonstration. (*Essay*, IV,10,1)

Locke then proceeds to argue that each of us knows intuitively that he himself exists, and that "nothing can no more produce any real being, than it can be equal to two right angles." From these two premises he concludes that there must be an eternal being, and he goes on to argue that that eternal being has the characteristics of God. He seems to be of the view that people do in fact believe that God exists on the basis of this argument, and that what he has done is only formulate the argument and show that it is sound.

II

I have said that the evidentialist challenge and objection to theistic conviction, along with the attempt to cope with that challenge by practicing evidentialist apologetics, are peculiar to modernity. Some will question this claim by pointing to the practice of natural theology among the medievals. The reply is that natural theology was a different project from evidentialist apologetics—even though the same arguments may occur in both.

We may take Anselm and Aquinas as typical. Anselm's motto was that of Augustine: *credo ut intelligam.* In the opening pages of his *Proslogion* he makes clear what that means for him. His goal in the book was to come to know, or understand, what already he believed. "I have written the following treatise," he says, "in the person of one who strives to lift his mind to the contemplation of God, and seeks to understand what he believes." (Preface) "For I do not seek to understand that I may believe, but I believe in order to understand." (Chapter 1)

Knowing a proposition was in general, for Anselm, a state of mind preferable to taking that proposition on faith. Hence Anselm's goal in constructing the ontological argument, as the remainder of the *Proslogion*, was to bring it about that what already he believed he now would know. In his view an essential component in this process of transmuting belief (faith) into knowledge (understanding) was constructing proofs.

Aquinas was no different on these matters. He explicated the concept of knowledge somewhat more rigorously than did Anselm: a person knows only what is self-evident to him or evident to his senses, or what has been demonstrated from such. Likewise he conceives faith somewhat more rigorously, as accepting propositions on the authority of God the revealer. But the goal of natural theology for Aquinas was exactly the same as for Anselm: to transmute what already one believed into something known. Demonstration was seen as indispensable to this transmutation project.

Taking Anselm and Aquinas as typical, it becomes clear, then, that the medievals were doing something quite different in their project of natural theology from meeting the evidentialist challenge. They were engaged in the transmutation project of altering belief (faith) into knowledge. No one in their milieu was claiming that it was permissible to believe that God existed only if one did so on the basis of adequate evidence, and with a firmness not exceeding the strength of the evidence. (Nonetheless Aquinas did, in chapter 6 of his *Summa Contra Gentiles,* defend the thesis "that to give assent to the truths of faith is not foolishness even though they are above reason.")

III

A variety of questions can be posed concerning the evidentialist challenge to theistic conviction. (Let us henceforth call this *evidentialism.)* One could ask, for example, what reasons the evidentialist has for holding his position. That is what Alvin Plantinga does in his essay "Reason and Belief in God" in this volume. He there suggests that common to all, or almost all, evidentialists is a certain "model" of rationality, a certain criterion for the application of the concept *rational*—the criterion being that of classical foundationalism. Plantinga then goes on to argue that that criterion is unacceptable. I judge Plantinga to be correct in both these contentions. Almost always when you lift an evidentialist you find a foundationalist. But the careful formulation of classical foundationalism by a number of philosophers in recent years has been accompanied by a growing consensus that it is not a plausible criterion of rational belief.[5]

Another way of considering the tenability of evidentialism would be to formulate and defend a criterion of rational belief alternative to that of classical foundationalism, and then to test the truth of evidentialism by reference to this criterion. That is the approach I shall follow in this essay. If successful, it moves us a stage beyond where Plantinga's discussion leaves us. His discussion puts us in the position of seeing that the most common and powerful argument for evidentialism is classical foundationalism, and of seeing that classical foundationalism is unacceptable. But to deprive the evidentialist of his best defense is not yet to show that his contention is false. It is this next step that I shall undertake to execute.

But before a criterion can be offered for the application of the concept of rational belief, we must be sure that we have clearly in mind the concept itself. And here our situation is surely that our English word "rational" is unusually protean, having a large number of different, albeit connected, senses. We speak of many different sorts of things as rational: rational plans, rational strategies, rational actions, rational persons, rational remarks, rational beliefs. And a large number of different claims are made about these different sorts of entities when we say of them that they are rational. Here it is only rational and nonrational *beliefs* that we will have in view. And the fact that the evidentialist connects the nonrationality of a belief with the obligation not to hold it delimits for us the senses of "rational" relevant to our discussion.

An illuminating way to begin is to consider the following passage from John Locke:

> however faith be opposed to reason, faith is nothing but a firm assent of the mind; which if it be regulated, as is our duty, cannot be afforded to anything but upon good reason, and so cannot be opposite to it. He that believes, without having any reason for believing, may be in love with his own fancies; but neither seeks truth as he ought, nor pays the obedience due to his Maker, who would have him use those discerning faculties he has given him, to keep him out of mistake and error. He that does not this to the best of his power, however he sometimes lights on truth, is in the right but by chance; and I know not whether the luckiness of the accident will excuse the irregularity of his proceeding. This at least is certain, that he must be accountable for

whatever mistakes he runs into: whereas he that makes use of the light and faculties God has given him, and seeks sincerely to discover truth by those helps and abilities he has, may have this satisfaction in doing his duty as a rational creature, that though he should miss truth, he will not miss the reward of it. For he governs his assent right, and places it as he should, who, in any case or matter whatsoever, believes or disbelieves according as reason directs him. He that does otherwise, transgresses against his own light, and misuses those faculties which were given him to no other end, but to search and follow the' clearer evidence and greater probability. (*Essay*, IV,17,24)

What Locke assumes here is that there are duties and responsibilities pertaining to our believings. Just as it is not true that "anything goes" in our actions regarding other human beings, so too it is not true that "anything goes" in our believings.

What must at once be added, however, is that our believings may be subject to duties and responsibilities in a number of different *respects*. (This is a point made by Plantinga in "Reason and Belief in God.") Perhaps there are right and wrong ways of acquiring beliefs. Perhaps there are right and wrong ways of maintaining beliefs. Perhaps some beliefs we ought not to hold because of their injurious effects on our psyches. Perhaps sometimes we hold beliefs with more firmness than we ought (or with less firmness that we are permitted). And if there are obligations pertaining to believings at all, presumably there are some pertaining simply to the having or not having of beliefs.

It is clear that at the center of Locke's attention, and at the core of the evidentialist challenge as he issues it, is this last phenomenon: Some beliefs we ought not to *have*. Some we ought to *have*. Some we are permitted to *have*. Some we are permitted not to *have*. For the sake of convenience we might call these *possession obligations* with respect to our believings (and correlatively, *possession permissions*).

But Locke is also concerned, though less prominently so, with the fact that sometimes we hold beliefs more firmly than we ought—and correspondingly, less firmly than we are permitted. We may call such obligations as these *firmness obligations* with respect to our believings.

Not only does Locke assume that there are duties pertaining to our believings; he also makes a suggestion as to the ground of these obligations—or at least, of the possession obligations. He assumes that we human beings are capable of governing and regulating our assent with the purpose in mind of getting more amply in touch with reality—of increasing our number of true beliefs and of avoiding or eliminating false beliefs. And his thought then is that possession obligations with respect to our believings consist in our obligation to so govern our assent as to get more amply in touch with reality. Fundamentally, then, he thinks of possession obligations along utilitarian lines: they consist in the obligations we have to get more amply in touch with reality, getting more amply in touch with reality being taken, in this context, as a good-in-itself.[6]

It may be remarked, parenthetically, that failure to live up to one's possession and firmness obligations and presumably to all other obligations pertaining to one's believings, when all other things are equal, amounts in Locke's view to disobedience to one's Maker. Living up to them, other things being equal, amounts to obedience. Possession and firmness obligations with respect to our believings are rooted in accountability to our Creator.

Now it would seem that if we have the ability to govern our believings with the goal in mind of getting more amply in touch with reality, then we also have the ability to govern them with other goals in mind. Perhaps we can to some extent govern them with the goal in mind of increasing our peace of mind, or with the goal in mind of staying out of trouble with our government. Correspondingly, perhaps we also have obligations for the governance of our believing with respect to some such goals. Kierkegaard thought, for example, that when it came to religious matters, we ought to hold such beliefs as would most heighten the passion in our lives. To distinguish such obligatiories from those pertaining to governance with the goal in mind of getting more amply in touch with reality, let us call these latter *reality-possession obligations.*

It is clear that Locke connects the concept of rationality he has in mind with the obligations that pertain to our believings—call such obligations our noetic obligations. The rational belief is the belief which does not violate our noetic obligations. The rational belief is the belief which, by reference to our noetic obligations, is permitted, is justified. But if obligations pertain to our beliefs with respect to different dimensions of those beliefs, the question comes to mind whether Locke is perhaps not working with a somewhat more constricted concept of rationality than this catchall concept. I think it clear that he is. For Locke the rational belief is the belief in accord with the reality-possession and firmness obligations that pertain to one's believings. Rationality consists in not violating *those* duties concerning one's believings. To be rational in one's believings amounts to doing as well in the firmness and reality-possession dimensions of one's believings as can rightly be demanded of one. Just as the morally permissible action is the action in accord with the norms for moral action, so the rational belief is the belief in accord with the firmness and reality possession norms for believing.[7]

Rationality, thus conceived, is connected with truth. Locke sees clearly, though, that the connection is indirect. Rationality is not to be identified with truth in beliefs, nor is it to be thought that the two coincide. Someone may light on truth by chance; about that Locke says, ironically, "I know not whether the luckiness of the accident will excuse the irregularity of his proceeding." Conversely, someone may seek "sincerely to discover truth by those helps and abilities he has" and "may have this satisfaction in doing his duty as a rational creature," while yet he misses truth. He will not miss his reward, though, says Locke. For he will, so far forth, have done his duty.

Truth, though a merit in beliefs, is not an unfallible mark of praiseworthiness in the person, nor is falsehood such a mark of blameworthiness. By contrast, rationality in beliefs *is* an infallible mark of praiseworthiness in the person; irrationality, of blameworthiness.[8] Rationality, unlike truth, is a derivative merit in beliefs, deriving its meritoriousness from merit in the believer—that merit being present in the believer, however, only if he pursues as he ought the merit of truth. The merit of rationality in our beliefs is grounded in the proper governance of our assent. Noetic rationality is grounded in practical rationality.

IV

Locke assumes—rightly in my judgment—that we have an obligation to govern our assent with the goal in mind of getting more amply in touch with reality. Likewise he assumes—also rightly, I think—that this goal has the two sides of seeking to increase our stock of true beliefs and of seeking to avoid or eliminate false beliefs. Let us scrutinize these assumptions a bit, beginning with a consideration of that latter assumption. To do so it will be helpful to consider Roderick Chisholm's formulation of our intellectual duties. "Each person," he says, "is subject to two quite different requirements in connection with any proposition he considers: (1) he should try his best to bring it about that if that proposition is true then he believes it; and (2) he should try his best to bring it about that if that proposition is false then he not believe it."[9]

Now suppose one took the second of these two requirements seriously but not the first. That is, suppose one had it as one's sole goal to snare as few falsehoods in one's net of belief as possible. What strategy would then be appropriate? Quite obviously the strategy of undertaking to believe as few as possible of the propositions that cross one's mind. There is nothing better than this that one could do (though even this might well not achieve the result of eliminating all falsehoods, for many of the things we believe, we do so ineluctably). If one wants above all to avoid catching trash fish, one goes fishing as little as possible. But though a serious pursuit of this strategy would be likely to diminish significantly the number of falsehoods believed, that merit would be purchased at the cost of missing out on a great deal of truth. And surely that is an important deficiency in this strategy of incredulity. The extent to which one had gotten in touch with reality would be severely limited.

Suppose, on the other hand, that one took the first of these two requirements seriously but paid no attention to the second. Suppose one had it as one's sole goal to snare as many truths as possible in one's net of belief. What strategy would then be appropriate? Quite obviously the strategy of undertaking to believe as many as possible of the propositions that come to mind—with this proviso: if one cannot believe both a proposition which comes to mind and its contradictory, then one strives to believe that member of the pair, if either, for which one has better evidence. There seems no better strategy than this strategy of gullibility for achieving the goal. If catching as many edible fish as possible is one's only goal, one nets fish indiscriminately—unless one has to make a choice here and there. But though the serious pursuit of this strategy would increase the number of truths one believes, it is also likely to increase substantially one's stock of false beliefs. And that, surely, is a deficiency. False beliefs mark a failure fully to get in touch with reality.

So both goals are necessary: the goal of increasing one's stock of true beliefs and the goal of avoiding or eliminating false beliefs. Accordingly, more subtle strategies will have to be adopted than either that comprehensive strategy of incredulity or that comprehensive strategy of gullibility.

Of course, once we allow that the pursuit of both these goals is necessary for getting in touch with reality, we must also acknowledge the possibility that in specific cases the two goals will yield conflicting results. Upon doing one's best to ascertain whether a proposition is true or false, one may discover that the evidence pro and con is equally balanced. In such a case one has to weigh up which is the worse outcome—that of missing out on truth or that of falling into error.

Yet another matter, pertaining to our obligation to get more amply in touch with reality, must be raised at this point. With respect to which propositions does one have an obligation to bring it about that one believes them if they are true and disbelieves them if they are false? The answer Chisholm gives is *any proposition one considers.* But that seems hardly correct on a couple of counts. Suppose, upon looking at a bean bag, that the thought crosses my mind that it contains exactly 2019 beans. Suppose I then consider that proposition. Is it really the case, in ordinary circumstances, that I then have an obligation to bring it about that I believe this if and only if it is true? Is not the acquisition of true, and the avoidance of false, belief on this matter so unimportant to my life that I have no such obligation—not even *prima facie?* Of course propositions are not in general inherently trivial or important. There may be tasks which you have that make it important for you to seek to bring it about that you believe there are 2019 beans in the bag just in case there are. But I have no such tasks.

Neither is it the case that our obligation to attain truth pertains just to the propositions we *consider.* Some of the propositions we have never considered are nonetheless propositions that we ought to believe. It may be that we *ought* to have considered them—and having considered, to believe. Or alternatively, it may be that though we have no obligation to *consider* them, nonetheless we do have an obligation to *believe* them. After all, there are ways of coming to believe propositions which do not require *considering* those propositions. Many of the things we believe, and ought to believe, have never been *considered* by us. Considering is involved in only some modes of belief acquisition.

But concerning which propositions, then, do we have reality possession obligations? Concerning the ones we each do in fact believe, I would say. But what beyond that? Chisholm is correct in his assumption that the propositions with respect to which we have such obligations are only a limited number and that they vary from person to person. We do not have obligations of rationality concerning reality's entire stock of propositions. And the ones each of us does have are always situated obligations. They are contextual obligations. What determines the variance, however, is not that which each person happens to consider. But if not that, what then?

It is difficult, indeed, to formulate an absolutely general answer to this question. And for our purposes here it is unnecessary to try. But worth observing is that one important factor determining the variance is the person's tasks and obligations in general. Some of my tasks and obligations are such that it becomes essential for their implementation that I seek the truth on certain matters and govern my beliefs accordingly. Of course each person's configuration of tasks and obligations is unique. That, then, is what accounts for a good deal of the variance in the obligations of rationality, and in noetic obligations generally. At the same time, it is true that these configurations do not differ in all respects from person to person, which accounts for a good deal of the commonality in obligations of rationality.

A characteristic error of epistemologists has been to suppose that our noetic obligations are disconnected from our other obligations. The truth is that in good measure the particular shape which the obligation to attain truth and avoid falsehood assumes for each person is determined by his obligations in general. Over and over our general obligations require, for their fulfilment, that we seek to get more amply in touch with some segment of reality. Perhaps there are some matters on which a given person ought to seek to attain true belief and eradicate falsehood whether or not those beliefs will serve some *praxis* of his. But that is not in general true. Our noetic obligations arise from the whole diversity of obligations that we have in our concrete situations. In this way, too, rationality is connected with *praxis*.

One last point. It seems in general not true that each of us has the obligation with respect to certain propositions *to do his best* to bring it about that he believes them if and only if they are true. Doing one's best may be more than can rightly be asked of one—well beyond the call of duty. Indeed, doing one's best with respect to some may interfere with doing one's duty with respect to others. What seems rather to be the case is that each of us has the obligation with respect to certain propositions *to do as well as can rightly be demanded* of us so as to bring it about that we believe them if they are true and disbelieve them if they are false.

Of course, the concept of doing as well as can rightly be demanded of one is, unlike that of doing one's best, a normative concept. This, then, is a second point at which we have found it necessary to introduce normative concepts and considerations where Chisholm had only nonnormative ones—the other being at that point where a determination is made concerning the propositions to which our obligations of rationality pertain.

V

The applicability of the concept of rationality that we are in the process of elucidating presupposes that we human beings are capable of governing our assent, in particular, capable of governing it with the goal in mind of getting more amply in touch with reality. The very image of governing suggests, however, that there are various belief-forming processes or "mechanisms" present in us. A ruler's governance of his subjects does not consist of calling them into existence. It will be important for our subsequent purposes to look more closely at these two phenomena of human nature, that of belief-forming "mechanisms" and that of the capacity for governing these.

It has to be said that the main representatives of the epistemological tradition give us little help here. Though of course they all take for granted the existence of belief-forming "mechanisms" in human beings, they devote scant attention to this phenomenon as such. A characteristic result of this oversight is that the rules they give for "the direction of the mind" prove limited and myopic in application.

To these generalizations Thomas Reid, the eighteenth-century Scottish philosopher, is the great exception. It was Reid's great genius to perceive that if we want to understand knowledge and rationality, we cannot talk only about the abstract relations holding among propositions, along the way making unreflective assumptions about the "mechanisms" which form our beliefs. We must look head-on at the psychological "mechanisms" involved in belief formation. Articulate epistemology requires articulate psychology.

At the very foundation of Reid's approach is his claim that at any point in our lives we each have a variety of dispositions, inclinations, propensities, to believe things—*belief dispositions* we may call them. What accounts for our beliefs, in the vast majority of cases anyway, is the triggering of one and another such disposition. For example, we are all so constituted that upon having memory experiences in certain situations, we are disposed to have certain beliefs about the past. We are all disposed, upon having certain sensations in certain situations, to have certain beliefs about the external physical world. Upon having certain other sensations in certain situations, we are all disposed to have certain beliefs about other persons. Likewise we are all so constituted as to be disposed in certain circumstances to believe what we apprehend people as telling us— the *credulity* disposition, as Reid rather fetchingly called it.

To the belief dispositions of which Reid took note we may add those rather ignoble belief dispositions of which Marx and Freud made so much: our disposition to believe what gives us a sense of security, our disposition to believe what serves to perpetuate our positions of economic privilege, our disposition to adopt clusters of beliefs which function as ideologies and rationalizations to conceal from our conscious awareness the ignobility of those other dispositions, and so on.

The belief dispositions which I have cited thus far are all dispositions which produce their effects *immediately*. We do not normally infer, from other beliefs of ours which we take as good evidence for it, that a person is before us. Rather, upon having certain sensations in certain situations we just immediately believe this. Likewise our memory experiences produce immediately in us certain convictions about the past. Remembering does not consist in going through a process of inferring a belief about the past from other beliefs.

There is, though, another disposition in us of which these remarks are not true. In addition to the features of our constitution thus far mentioned, we are all so constituted that upon judging some proposition which we already believe as being good evidence for another proposition not yet believed, we are disposed to believe that other proposition as well. To this disposition Reid assigned the name of reason. Let me call it the *reasoning disposition*. What the tradition called *mediate* beliefs can now be singled out as those produced by the reasoning disposition, and what it called *immediate* beliefs, those produced by some one of our other belief dispositions.

Not only does Reid call to our attention the various belief dispositions which we actually do, at a given moment in our lives, possess; he also speaks about the origins of these dispositions. It was his conviction, in the first place, that somewhere in the history of each of us are to be found certain belief dispositions with which we were simply "endowed by our Creator." They belong to our human nature. We come with them. They are innate in us. Their existence in us is not the result of conditioning. It must not be supposed, however, that all such nonconditioned dispositions are present in us at birth. Some, possibly most, emerge as we mature. We have the disposition to acquire them upon reaching one and another level of maturation. He says, for example:

> Perhaps a child in the womb, or for some short period of its existence, is merely a sentient being: the faculties by which it perceives an external world, by which it reflects on its own thoughts and existence, and relation to other things, as well as its reasoning and moral

faculties, unfold themselves by degrees; so that it is inspired with the various principles of common sense, as with the passions of love and resentment, when it has occasion for them. (*An Inquiry into the Human Mind,* V,7)

But in addition to our innate, nonconditioned, belief dispositions, we adults all have a number of belief dispositions which we have acquired by way of conditioning. Reid calls attention to a certain range of these as being belief dispositions induced in us by the working of the *inductive principle*. The inductive principle is not itself a belief disposition; it is an innate, nonconditioned disposition for the acquisition of belief dispositions. Reid says, "It is undeniable, and indeed is acknowledged by all, that when we have found two things to have been constantly conjoined in the course of nature, the appearance of one of them is immediately followed by the conception and belief of the other." (*Inquiry,* VI,24) And he adds that it is "a natural, original and unaccountable propensity to believe, that the connections which we have observed in times past, will continue in time to come." (*Inquiry,* II,9) An example that Reid offers, of a belief disposition inculcated in us by this inductive principle of our native constitutions, is this: "When I hear a certain sound, I conclude immediately without reasoning, that a coach passes by. There are no premises from which this conclusion is inferred by any rules of logic. It is the effect of a principle of our nature, common to us with the brutes." (*Inquiry,* IV,1)

Reid's thought concerning the workings of the inductive principle can readily be stated in the language of contemporary psychology. What accounts for some of our beliefs is that a process of classical, or Pavlovian, conditioning has taken place. A regular "schedule" has been established in one's experience between phenomena of type A and phenomena of type B, and now one has the disposition, upon experiencing a phenomenon of type A, to believe that there is also a phenomenon of type B. Hence one has acquired a new belief disposition. It is the disposition to acquire belief dispositions in this manner that Reid calls *the inductive principle*.

Vast numbers of our noninnate belief dispositions are not acquired in this way, however, but rather by way of what we would nowadays call *operant* conditioning, working on our native belief dispositions. In Reid's own thought this comes out most clearly in what he says about the credulity principle. It is a moot point whether the credulity disposition is present in us at birth. But very little maturation is required for it to put in its appearance. "The wise Author of nature," says Reid, "hath planted in the human mind a propensity to rely upon human testimony before we can give a reason for doing so. This, indeed, puts our judgment almost entirely in the power of those who are about us in the first period of life; but this is necessary both to our preservation and to our improvement. If children were so framed as to pay no regard to testimony or authority, they must, in the literal sense, perish for lack of knowledge." (*Essays on the Intellectual Powers of Man*, VI,5)

It was Reid's view that the working of the credulity principle "is unlimited in children" (*Inquiry*, VI,24), in the sense that whatever a child apprehends someone as asserting, he believes. But shortly the principle begins to be "restrained and modified," as Reid puts it. What induces the restraint and modification is the discovery that sometimes the principle produces false beliefs in us. "The principle of credulity is unlimited in children, until they meet with instances of deceit and falsehood." (*Inquiry*, VI,24) Notice: a person's conviction that some of the beliefs produced in him by testimony are false does not *destroy* his disposition to give credence to testimony. Rather, it results in that disposition's becoming restrained and modified. The credulity principle becomes more finely articulated.

We can think of this too in terms of modern conditioning theory. The original, unqualified credulity principle is altered by way of operant conditioning. One's discovery, or conviction, that certain of one's beliefs thus produced are false, functions as an *aversive* consequence, diminishing to the point of extinguishing the workings of the disposition in such cases. That new, slightly altered disposition is then in turn submitted to the same sort of testing, with the person's convictions, concerning some of the beliefs thus produced, that they are false, again functioning as aversive consequences, and his independent discovery that others are true, functioning as reinforcing consequences, until yet another alteration takes place; and so on and on. Eventually the person is no longer disposed to believe what persons of type P speaking under conditions of type C say on topics of type T, whereas other sorts of testimony he is disposed to believe more strongly than ever (and perhaps more strongly disposed to believe than ever).

I find it surprising that Reid does not emphasize that we are constantly acquiring new belief dispositions by the working of operant conditioning on our other innate belief dispositions as well, not only by its working on our credulity disposition. Reid himself notes about memory that we tend to place more confidence in our memories the more vivid, or distinct, they are. But this is almost certainly a matter of learning. And there is much more that can be said than just this. Other things being equal, one learns to place more confidence in one's memories of yesterday's occurrences than of occurrences in the distant past. One learns to place less confidence in the details of one's memory when one was agitated and upset than when one was observing carefully and calmly. And so on. In short, gradually one learns that one's memory is reliable on certain sorts of matters under certain sorts of conditions, and unreliable on other matters or under other conditions; that modifies the belief dispositions attached to one's memory experiences. The revision can be seen as a selective strengthening and weakening of the original disposition, weakening to the point of disappearance for some cases.

The same sort of thing happens in the case of perception. When, as a child, I rode down a paved road on a hot summer day, I often believed that there was water standing on the road ahead, in the distance, because it definitely looked that way. Now I no longer believe that, even when I am in those same circumstances. For I have learned that it *looks* that way as the consequence of heat waves rising from the pavement without really *being* that way. In general what can be said is this: our native belief dispositions all go through stages of increasing articulation as the result of our experience that some beliefs produced by these dispositions are false, others true.

With this picture in mind of our belief-forming dispositions, let us now look at our capacities for governing the workings of these "mechanisms"— in particular, at our capacities for governing their workings with the goal in mind of more amply getting in touch with reality. As we now move to this second level, we leave Reid behind.

To a great extent it is in our power to *govern* the workings of our belief dispositions—not now to alter them, but to govern their workings. And often it is because it is in our power to govern their workings that we are culpable for our believings and our failings to believe. For one thing, it is often in our power to determine whether a triggering event for some disposition will occur. For example, it was in my power to go over and look at the tire; if I had, the sensations received would have triggered in me the belief that the tire was flat. There are also more subtle and interesting examples than ones like this, however. Often it is in our power to bring it about that we will *notice* something when in situations where that is noticeable. For example, one can set oneself, or fail to set oneself, to notice speed-limit signs when entering villages; and setting oneself to do so makes it highly likely that one will. It is for this reason that police officers are often right in holding us accountable for not knowing what the speed limit in a given village is. So too one can try, or fail to try, to *remember* something; and making an effort to remember often makes it much more likely that one will. For this reason one can often rightly be held accountable for not remembering something—for not having correct beliefs on a certain matter. (Strictly speaking, this last case is a case, not of having it in one's power to determine whether a certain belief disposition will be triggered, but of having it in one's power to determine whether a certain belief is *sustained*. Believing is not an event but an enduring state. A full discussion of the matter would systematically distinguish between factors initiating such a state and factors *sustaining* such a state.)

Not only is it often in our power to determine whether a certain triggering event for some belief disposition will occur; likewise it is sometimes in our power, even when an event does occur that characteristically would trigger the disposition, to determine whether or not the disposition will become operative. We can *resolve* or *determine* that a disposition will not become operative, and sometimes at least such a resolution is effective. For example, one can resolve to resist the workings of one's credulity disposition and come to no belief as to what transpired in marital disputes until one has heard out both parties; in the absence of the resolution one would have believed the tale of the first party. Or again: one can resolve to resist the workings of one's memory disposition and no longer to believe that what one seems to remember as having happened when one was in situations of great stress did in fact happen. So, too, one can resolve to resist the workings of one's reasoning disposition and hold no belief about the size of one's checking-account balance until one has gone over the figures at least twice. Obviously, repeatedly resolving to resist the operation of some belief disposition in certain sorts of situations may eventually result in that disposition's being extinguished for those sorts of cases.

The resolve to resist the activation of a belief disposition, even in the presence of an event which, were it not for this resolve, would trigger the disposition, may sometimes take the form of leaving one, not in a state of suspension of belief, but in a state of continuing to believe as one did. Suppose, for example, that a certain belief of Vern's is deeply embedded in the whole structure of his personality, his life-style, his career, and so on. It gives him great comfort. Or he has spent twenty years of work in physics on the premise that this is true. In short, he has deep motivations for hanging on to this belief. Suppose that then someone comes along and presents him with evidence that this belief is false. It would seem that in some such cases it is in Vern's power to accept the evidence and change his mind, but equally in his power to resist changing his mind. That is to say, it is true not merely that in some such cases his mind *is changed* but also that in some such cases it is in his power *to change* his mind, or at least to *let* his mind *be changed*. It is in his power to acknowledge the force of the evidence, give up his resistance to the conclusion, and change his mind; but equally it is in his power to cling stubbornly to what he has always believed and treat the evidence as not conclusive.[10]

And now what about the case so dear to the heart of the classical epistemologist: the case of a person considering some proposition and then deciding to believe it, or to disbelieve it? Perhaps the *considering* is here unimportant. Does it ever happen that we *decide* to believe something? Must a full picture of our belief-forming processes, and of our capacity to govern them, have this sort of case in mind as well?

Perhaps so. Of course it may be that some cases of resolving to resist the working of some belief disposition are also cases of deciding to believe or not to believe so-and-so. Perhaps that is true of the last case considered, the case of Vern. But be that as it may, let us consider a case in which a resolution to resist is not in the picture. Suppose that one is a member of a jury and has agonized long hours over which of two conflicting witnesses to believe on a certain matter. May it be that eventually one *decides to believe* what one of them said and to disbelieve what the other said? One could have made the opposite decision, but as a matter of fact this is what one decides to believe. In some cases of conflicting testimony one just finds oneself persuaded that one witness is speaking truth and the other not. May it be that in other cases one decides? If so, that decision is probably accompanied by a decision to the effect that the *evidence* for the veracity of the one witness is slightly stronger than the evidence for the veracity of the other. This would then be a second point at which a decision to believe occurs in such a case.

So the full picture that emerges is something like this: we each have a variety of belief dispositions, some of which we share with all normal, mature human beings, some of which we do not; some of which we have as part of our native endowment, some of which are the result of one and another form of conditioning, and probably some of which are the result of having resolved to resist the workings of some native or conditioned disposition. In addition, we each have a variety of capacities for governing the workings of these dispositions. To some extent it is in our power to determine whether a certain (sort of) triggering event for a disposition will occur. And to some extent it is in our power to determine whether the disposition will be activated even if an event does occur which characteristically would activate it. Perhaps we also have the capacity in certain (relatively rare) circumstances to *decide* whether to believe something.

It must be clearly noted that rationality, thus conceived, is in good measure person specific and situation specific. When I was young, there were things which it was rational for me to believe which now, when I am older, it is no longer rational for me to believe. And for a person reared in a traditional tribal society who never comes into contact with another society or culture, there will be things rational to believe which for me, a member of the modern Western intelligentsia, would not be rational to believe. Rationality of belief can only be determined in context—historical and social contexts, and, even more narrowly, personal context. It has long been the habit of philosophers to ask in abstract, nonspecific fashion whether it is rational to believe that God exists, whether it is rational to believe that there is an external world, whether it is rational to believe that there are other persons, and so on. Mountains of confusion have resulted. The proper question is always and only whether it is rational for this or that particular person in this or that situation, or for a person of this or that particular type in this or that type of situation, to believe so-and-so. Rationality is always *situated* rationality. (Some thinkers in the modern world seem to have concluded from the fact that a nonsituated theory of rationality is untenable that the concept of rationality itself must be discarded. They have become historicists. We have seen, and will see, no reason whatsoever to draw this conclusion.)

VI

And now it is easy to see why the theist cannot simply dismiss out of hand the charge that his theistic convictions are nonrational. Nonrationality in one's beliefs is the sure sign that some of one's obligations have been violated. Accordingly, a person cannot meet the charge that one of his beliefs is nonrational by announcing that he has chosen not to live by the canons of rationality, anymore than he can meet the charge that he has acted immorally by announcing that he has chosen not to live by moral obligations. He can meet it only by *contesting* the charge.

There is yet a deeper reason why the theist, at least if he is a Christian, Jew, or Muslim, cannot just dismiss out of hand the demands of rationality. Such a person will always perceive our human obligations as related, in one way or another, to the will of God. God wills that we do what we ought to do. When a theist believes nonrationally, he acts in violation of the will of the very God in whom he believes—unless it be the case that there are extenuating circumstances.

However, it is also easy to see now that the charge lodged against the theist, that he holds his theistic convictions nonrationally, is not a *decisive* charge, in the sense that it does not *follow* from the nonrationality of the belief that he ought to give up believing that. We can see, in short, that one of the two principal components in the evidentialist challenge to theistic conviction is untenable.

The most obvious, and perhaps least important, point to make here is that what grounds the nonrationality of some beliefs is not *what* is believed but *how* it is believed: it is believed with the wrong degree of firmness. Hence, from being told that someone holds some one of his beliefs nonrationally one cannot infer that he ought not to believe that.

But second, the nonrationality of a belief—as, following Locke, we have conceived it—results from the fact that one has not done as well as one ought to have done in governing one's belief-forming "mechanisms" toward the goal of getting more amply in touch with reality. But as we have already seen, one can presumably conduct such governance with other goals in mind; and perhaps with respect to such alternative governance there are also obligations. If so, it may well be that though a given belief represents inadequate governance with respect to the goal of getting more amply in touch with reality and is, accordingly, a nonrational belief, it represents *adequate* governance with respect to some other goal. Further, it may well be that governance with respect to that other goal has priority over governance with respect to getting more amply in touch with reality. We in the West for several centuries now have assumed that nothing could take priority in belief governance over our obligation to expand our hold on truth and to avoid or eliminate falsehood in our beliefs. It is difficult to perceive, though, what defense could be given for this. And if the assumption is in fact false, then here is a second way in which it may come about that a person is permitted to believe something that is not rational for him to believe. Maybe in some cases it is even true that he *ought* to believe it in spite of its nonrationality.

Lastly, there is more to life than governing aright the *what* and the *how* of one's assent—and so too there is more to life's obligations than the obligation to govern aright one's belief-forming "mechanisms." Sometimes these other obligations of life take precedence over those governance obligations, again with the result that one is permitted to believe something that is not rational to believe. Perhaps I did not calculate my bank account figures carefully enough for me to believe rationally that the balance is $53.09. But perhaps I had to choose between spending more time calculating and taking my son to see the Phillies play in the World Series. In this conflict of obligations I may have made the right decision, to calculate quickly and go off to the game. Our obligation to govern our assent aright often takes time to carry out, and sometimes the time taken is wrongly taken from the time needed to carry out some other obligation. For this reason, too, from the fact that someone holds a belief nonrationally it does not in general follow that he ought not to hold it.

When we speak of a person as *justified* in holding some belief, often, perhaps always, what we mean is that the person is *permitted to* hold that belief. So another way of putting the point above is that a person may be justified in holding a belief even though he does not hold it rationally. What is true, of course, is that if a person holds a belief rationally, then *other things being equal,* he is justified in holding it—or to put the same point in other words, then he is *prima facie* justified in holding it. But other things may not be equal, with the result that though he holds it rationally, he is nonetheless not justified in holding it. It will sometimes be convenient in what follows to say of the person who believes some proposition rationally that he is *rationally* justified in holding it— from which it does not follow that he is justified *tout court* in holding it.

Now that we have introduced the word "justified" into our discussion, a few cautions should be sounded. For one thing, *being justified* in one's belief that so-and-so is different from *justifying* one's belief that so-and-so. To be justified in believing that so-and-so is to be in a certain *state*. To justify one's belief that so-and-so is to perform a certain *action*. Most of the beliefs we are justified in holding are such that we never justify them—never even attempt to do so. Probably most are such that we could not do so—depending, of course, on the standards adopted for success in performing the action of justifying.

Second, we speak sometimes of one proposition justifying another, but that too is a different matter. One proposition justifies another when it is good evidence for the other. But justification, on the concept I am using, is not a relation between propositions. It is a relation between a *person* and some one of his *believings*.

Last, an unjustified belief of a person is not one that he ought to give up, but one that he ought not to have had. Thinkably, now that he has it, he can give it up. Similarly, the immoral act is not the act that the person ought to undo, nor, always, the act that the person ought to cease doing. It is the act that the person ought not to have done.

VII

Up to this point we have been trying to get before us, as clearly as possible, that concept of rational belief which is characteristically used in the evidentialist objection to theistic conviction. It is not at all an idiosyncratic concept. Though no doubt there are other concepts attached to our English word "rational," there can be little doubt that this is one of them. It is time now that we move to the second stage of our project—that of trying to formulate a *criterion* for the correct application of this concept.

Given our discussion thus far, we can now put somewhat more precisely the contention of the evidentialist. His claim is that theistic conviction, to be rational, must be arrived at, or at least reinforced, by the process of inference. Each of us has a wide variety of belief dispositions, innate and learned. From this whole array the evidentialist picks out the *inference* mechanism as that which must evoke or reinforce theistic conviction if it is to be rational. Only that will do. And of course he adds that the premises from which the inference proceeds must in fact provide adequate evidence for the conclusion.

This provocative contention raises all sorts of questions as to which sorts of beliefs may serve as premises for the inferences. What sorts of propositions are candidates for evidence? With respect to which sorts of propositions must theistic beliefs be evident? Obviously theistic propositions are themselves not eligible. Which ones are? These questions pose many interesting issues, some of which are explored by Plantinga in his essay in this volume. For our purposes we can set them off to the side. For we wish to test evidentialism by matching it up against a criterion for rational belief.

The criterion I propose will actually be a criterion for a somewhat narrower concept than that of rationality as thus far delineated. Here I shall not at all attempt to specify conditions for permissible *firmness* of conviction. I will attempt only to specify conditions for rationally accepting a proposition at all. We are looking simply for the justifying circumstances for the acceptance of propositions.

A criterion which has recently entered the arena of philosophical discussion, after the collapse of classical foundationalism, is that of *reliabilism.* Reliabilism says, roughly, that a given belief of a person is rationally justified if and only if that belief was produced or is sustained in him by a reliable process or mechanism. Just as some thermometers are reliable and some unreliable, so too some belief-producing and belief-reinforcing mechanisms are reliable and some unreliable. Our rationally *justified* beliefs are those produced or reinforced by the reliable mechanisms. Here is how Alvin Goldman, one of the first proponents of the theory, states its basic contention:

> Granted that principles of justified belief must make reference to causes of belief, what kinds of causes confer justifiedness? We can gain insight into this problem by reviewing some faulty processes of belief-formation, i.e., processes whose belief-outputs would be classed as unjustified. Here are some examples: confused reasoning, wishful thinking, reliance on emotional attachment, mere hunch or guesswork, and hasty generalization. What do these faulty processes have in common? They share the feature of *unreliability:* they tend to produce *error* a large proportion of the time. By contrast, which species of belief-forming (or belief-sustaining) processes are intuitively justification-conferring? They include standard perceptual processes, remembering, good reasoning, and introspection. What these processes seem to have in common is *reliability:* the beliefs they produce are generally true. My positive proposal, then, is this. The justificational status of a belief is a function of the reliability of the process or processes that cause it, where (as a first approximation) reliability consists in the tendency of a process to produce beliefs that are true rather than false.[11]

One thing to be kept in mind in reflecting on this theory is that it is not fully accurate to speak simply of reliable and unreliable mechanisms. The situation is rather that a given mechanism is reliable under certain conditions and for certain ranges of inputs and outputs and is unreliable under other conditions and for other input ranges and output ranges. Another thing to be kept in mind is that a mechanism which has produced mainly truth under certain conditions and for certain ranges of inputs and outputs is not yet, thereby, a *reliable* mechanism with respect to such conditions and ranges. For it may be that though it is unreliable for such conditions and ranges, yet, as luck would have it, when it did in fact operate under those conditions and within those ranges, it produced mainly truth. The mechanism which is genuinely reliable for given circumstances and ranges is the one which *would* produce mainly truth under such circumstances and for such ranges. Reliability is an implicitly counterfactual concept.

Perhaps the main challenge facing the reliabilist in the articulation of his theory is that it is not the least bit evident how we are to pick out the mechanism which produced a certain belief—indeed, it is not the least bit evident that in general there is such a thing as *the* mechanism. What, for example, is the mechanism in the case of the child in the primitive tribe who believes something on the say-so of his elders? Is it that of believing something on the say-so of someone else? Of believing something on the say-so of one's elders? Or believing something on the say-so of *those* elders? If the reliabilist theory is to be applicable, we must be told how, for a given belief, we are to pick out the mechanism that we are to scrutinize for reliability, and how we are to select the sort of conditions, and the input/output ranges, with respect to which that mechanism would have to yield mainly truth for the belief to be rationally justified. I understate the point when I say that this is a *daunting* challenge.

But even without that challenge having been met, I think it can be seen, relying on our ordinary intuitive notion of these matters, that reliabilism, no matter how formulated, will not be a correct criterion of rational belief. In the first place, though it is true that a good many more of the beliefs that we intuitively feel to be rationally justified will turn out justified on this criterion than on the criterion of classic foundationalism, nonetheless, the criterion is still too constrictive. For there are unreliable mechanisms which yield rationally justified beliefs. Suppose, for example, that some belief is produced by an unreliable mechanism, but the agent has no good reason to believe it unreliable—and, more strongly yet, has adequate reason to believe that it was produced by a reliable mechanism. Whatever instructions the reliabilists eventually give us, telling us which mechanisms under which circumstances we are here to check out for reliability, it seems possible that such a situation would arise. And if it does, is not the person in whom that unreliable process produces that belief rationally *justified* in thus believing? Is he not doing as well in the use of his belief-governing capacities, toward the goal of getting more amply in touch with reality, as can rightly be demanded of him? If a scientist develops an instrument for acquiring certain information, and if all the evidence available to him points to the reliability of that instrument, even though it is in fact unreliable, is he not rationally justified in believing the deliverances of that instrument? Was he anywhere remiss in the use of his assent-regulating capacities? What more could rightly have been demanded of him?

Just as there can be rationally justified beliefs produced by unreliable mechanisms, so too there can be rationally unjustified beliefs produced by reliable mechanisms. Suppose that some belief of some person is produced by a reliable mechanism, but all the evidence available to the person points to the conclusion that it is unreliable. Suppose, in fact, that the evidence is so strong that the person would be rationally unjustified in believing the mechanism reliable. It would seem that such a situation could in fact arise; if it did, the person would not be rational in continuing to believe the deliverances of that reliable mechanism. Perhaps the case is just the reverse of that considered in the preceding paragraph: A scientist has developed an instrument for obtaining information on certain matters, but on the evidence available to him, the results are largely in error. In fact, however, they are highly accurate—something which is not discovered until, say, fifty years later. If the scientist, against the evidence for his discovery's unreliability, nonetheless continues to believe its deliverances, surely he is rationally unjustified in his belief.

Last, suppose that some belief is produced and sustained in a person by a reliable process, but in this particular case the person has adequate evidence that the belief is false—not evidence that the process producing it is in general unreliable, just evidence that in this particular case the belief produced is false. Surely in this case too the person would not be rational in believing what was in fact reliably produced. And there can be such cases: I may believe something on the say-so of what I know to be a thoroughly reliable authority; nonetheless, I may acquire evidence that in this particular case what I thereby came to believe was mistaken. If so, I ought to give up my belief. (This would be a case in which one reliable process yields the belief Bp, and another the belief *Bnot-p*.) If I fail to do so, I would not be using my belief-governing capacities as well as can rightly be demanded of me.

For these reasons, reliabilism is incapable of filling the void left by the demise of classic foundationalism.[12]

As I now propose to offer my own criterion for rationally justified belief, we must keep clearly in mind the project on which we are engaged. Our project is not to give advice to the person who is wondering whether to believe a certain proposition or whether to keep himself from believing it. Rather we are looking at the person who already has an array of beliefs, so as to give him and others a criterion for picking out those which it is rational for him to hold from those which are not. We are after, not rules for the direction of the mind, but a criterion for separating one's rational beliefs from one's nonrational beliefs.

At the outset a few words should be said about the "ought implies can" principle in its application to beliefs. A rather natural formulation of this principle is that if it is not in a person's power at a given time to cease from believing a certain proposition, then he is rationally justified in believing that proposition. But probably most beliefs are of this sort; I cannot just up and decide to believe that I am not now awake. On the other hand, most of the beliefs a person has at a given time are such that there are some things he *could have done* such that if he had done them, he would not then have the belief. And sometimes these are things he *should have done*. Exactly when they are that is by no means easy to say, however.

The connection between beliefs, volition, and justification is a large dark area, and it would seriously distract me from my main purpose here to enter that area so as to be able to say exactly what the "ought implies can" principle comes to in the area of belief. I think we all feel intuitively that it does come to something. But what exactly that something is, is surely going to prove difficult to say. Let us suppose, though, that some explanation of "could not have" is possible, and let us suppose that some qualifications can be added, so that it turns out true that if a person could not have refrained from believing *p*, then he is rationally justified in believing *p*. Let us then call any belief of a person which, in that sense and with those qualifications, is one he could not have refrained from believing an *ineluctable* belief of his. And let us call the remainder of his beliefs his *eluctable* beliefs. My concern here will be to formulate a criterion for rationally justified *eluctable* beliefs.

One way to get hold of the central contention of the criterion I wish to propose is to note the structure of the objections I have lodged against the reliabilist criterion. The objections were of this sort. If a person has *adequate reason* to cease from some one of his beliefs, then he is rationally unjustified in holding it even if it was produced in him by a reliable process. And if a person *lacks adequate* reason to cease from some one of his beliefs, then he is rationally justified in holding it even if it was produced in him by an unreliable process. The phenomenon of *adequate reason to cease believing* was central in my objections. I suggest that this phenomenon is in fact the central determinant of rationality in beliefs.

Another way to get hold of the theory's central contention is to return to something that Reid said. It will be remembered that Reid thought that there is in all of us a *credulity disposition*—a disposition to believe what we apprehend people as telling us. At first, on Reid's view, this disposition is undifferentiated and unarticulated—as children we believe whatever we apprehend anyone as telling us. But gradually we discover that what certain sorts of people tell us on certain sorts of topics is false. What the rational person then does, says Reid, is resolve to resist the workings of the credulity principle in such cases and no longer accept such testimony. (Eventually this results in the disposition itself being modified.) Says Reid: "when our faculties ripen, we find reason to check that propensity to yield to testimony and to authority, which was so necessary and so natural in the first period of life. We learn to reason about the regard due to them, and see it to be a childish weakness to lay more stress upon them than reason justifies." (*Essays on the Intellectual Powers*, VI,5)

Thus it is Reid's view that we are *prima facie* justified in accepting the deliverances of the credulity disposition until such time as we have adequate reason in specific cases to believe the deliverances false, or until such time as we have adequate reason to believe the deliverances unreliable for certain types of cases. Our situation is not that to be rationally justified in accepting the deliverances of the credulity disposition we need evidence in favor of its reliability. Rather, we are rationally justified in accepting its deliverances until such time as we have evidence of its unreliability for certain types of cases. The deliverances of our credulity disposition are innocent until proved guilty, not guilty until proved innocent.

So, I suggest, it is in general—with one important exception to be mentioned shortly. A person is rationally justified in believing a certain proposition which he does believe unless he has adequate reason to cease from believing it. Our beliefs are rational unless we have reason for refraining; they are not nonrational unless we have reason *for* believing. They are innocent until proved guilty, not guilty until proved innocent. If a person does not have adequate reason to refrain from some belief of his, what could possibly oblige him to give it up? Conversely, if he surrenders some belief of his as soon as he has adequate reason to do so, what more can rightly be demanded of him? Is he not then using the capacities he has for governing his beliefs, with the goal of getting more amply in touch with reality, as well as can rightly he demanded of him?

The exception to which I alluded was this: Suppose that someone has undertaken to alter some native belief disposition, or to cultivate some new belief disposition, for perverse reasons, or for reasons having nothing to do with getting in touch with reality. The extent to which such undertakings, such resolutions, can be successful seems to me severely limited. But no doubt they sometimes have their effect. For example, it may well be that if some person undertakes to disbelieve everything another says, not because of his experience that what the other says is often false, but rather because of his hostility to that person, this will eventually result in his granting the speech of that person less credibility than otherwise he would—*and less than he ought.*

Above I affirmed the innocent-until-proved-guilty principle for beliefs. Here we are dealing with noninnocent belief dispositions. And it seems evident that the outcomes of a noninnocent disposition should not be accorded the honor of innocence until their guilt has been proved.

I suggest that, from the standpoint of rationality and its governing goal of getting in touch with reality, the only acceptable reason for undertaking to revise one of one's belief dispositions is that one justifiably believes it to be unreliable. (It is to be remembered here that many of our belief dispositions get revised by conditioning; we do not *undertake* to revise them.) If one undertakes to revise it for some other reason, and succeeds, then the disposition, with respect to the points of revision, is no longer innocent with respect to rationality. It has been *culpably revised.* Now if a given belief is produced by a culpably revised disposition, and *solely* by such a disposition, then it is not a belief rationally held. Correspondingly, if a person's not believing something in a certain situation is due to the working, or the nonworking, of a culpably revised disposition, then his not-believing is not rational.

The innocent-until-proved-guilty principle which I have affirmed for beliefs must be understood as applying just to those not produced by culpably revised dispositions. A person may well find himself in the situation where he does not have adequate reason to surrender a belief produced by a culpably revised disposition. Nonetheless the belief is not held rationally, for the disposition producing it was not innocent on this matter. What we have so far then is this:

(I) A person S is rational in his eluctable and innocently produced belief Bp if and only if S believes p, and it is not the case that S has adequate reason to cease from believing p.

Rationality in one's beliefs does not await one's believing them on the basis of adequate reasons. Nonetheless, the phenomenon of having reasons does play a central and indispensable role in rationality—a rationality-*removing* role.

But formula (I) is only a first approximation. A number of revisions are necessary before we have a satisfactory criterion. First, though, an explanation is necessary of what I have in mind by "adequate reason." Perhaps it can rightly be said of a person who has the belief that he feels dizzy that he has a *reason* for that belief—namely, *his feeling dizzy*. In that case his reason would be a particular event. Perhaps, too, it can rightly be said of a person who believes that he is seeing a red car, in an ordinary case of perception, that he has a *reason* for this belief—namely, *its seeming to him that he is seeing a red car* (that is, his having a red-car-seeing experience). In this case, too, his reason would be a particular event. In short, sometimes the reason for a belief of ours may be the event which caused the belief (the event which triggered the operative disposition).

But when here I speak of "reason," that is not what I have in mind. I do not mean the disposition-triggering event. What I mean by "reason" is to be explained by reference to the workings of Reid's reasoning disposition. Sometimes what accounts for our believing some proposition p is that we believed some other proposition q which we judged to be good evidence for p. When that occurs, I shall say that the person believes p *for a reason*. And the reason is just the already believed proposition q.[13] Someone believes p for an *adequate* reason, then, if he believes p for a reason, if that reason is evidential support for p, and if the conjunction of that reason with the other things S believes that are relevant to p is also evidential support for p. And last, a person *has* an adequate reason for believing p if there is some proposition q which he believes such that if he believed p for the reason that q, he would believe it for an adequate reason.

It is to be noted that whether a person's belief that q provides him with an adequate reason for his believing p depends, in general, on the other beliefs that person has. Accordingly, it is never strictly speaking true that the reason on the basis of which he believes p *justifies* him in believing p; by itself it does not do that. Suppose, for example, that I believe my brother is on campus, and I do not believe I have ever seen or heard of a close look-alike to him. If I now believe that my brother is standing in the courtyard outside my office, and believe this for the reason that I see someone who looks just like him standing out there, I might very well be rationally justified in my belief. The belief that I see someone who looks just like my brother standing out there might be an adequate reason for believing that my brother is in the courtyard. But suppose now that in addition to all those beliefs I also have the belief that my brother is sitting with me in my office engaged in conversation with me. Then my belief that I see someone who looks just like my brother standing out there in the courtyard would not be adequate reason for believing that he is in the courtyard. If I believed the latter proposition for the reason that the former is true, I would not thereby be rationally justified in believing that latter proposition.

Let us return now to that initial approximation, formula (I). I said that a person is rational in holding some belief of his if and only if it is not the case that among his beliefs there is adequate reason for him to cease from that belief. But this will not quite do. For suppose that though S does not have adequate reason to not believe p, he *ought to have*. The fact that within the totality of his beliefs there is not to be found adequate reason for him to cease from believing p is a fact which itself marks a failure to govern his assent as well as can rightly be demanded of him. For example, perhaps his not having adequate reason to cease from believing p is due to the fact that his calculations were done very hastily, when he *knows* that they were done hastily, knows that hasty calculation is a most unreliable method of arriving at truth, and had it in his power to be less hasty. As a second approximation to a satisfactory criterion we can say this:

(II)   A person S is rational in his eluctable and innocently produced belief Bp if and only if S believes p, and S neither has nor ought to have adequate reason to cease from believing p.

This revision of our initial formulation was made in the light of the conviction that sometimes a person ought to have adequate reason to give up some one of his beliefs when in fact he does not. But may it not sometimes be that the converse is true? May it not sometimes be that a person has adequate reason to cease from some one of his beliefs, when in fact he ought not to have? Suppose that the totality of his beliefs does contain adequate reason to cease from believing p, but suppose that some of those beliefs he ought not to have. He has them only in violation of his rational responsibilities. If that were altered, the totality of his beliefs would no longer constitute adequate reason to cease from believing p. Surely a person in such a situation is in fact justified in believing p.

The point is correct, but no emendation is required. For by definition if S has *adequate* reason for believing p, then within the totality of what he believes there are certain propositions such that if he believed p on the basis of those, his doing so would place him in a *prima facie* justifying circumstance with respect to his belief Bp. But if he is not *prima facie* justified in believing those, then his believing p on their basis cannot make him *prima facie* justified in believing p. Or so at least I shall assume. I shall assume that a person's believing p on the basis of q makes him *prima facie* justified in believing p only if he is *prima facie* justified in believing q. If a person is not justified in holding some one of his beliefs, that defect is passed on to the third and fourth generations of those beliefs that he holds on the basis of that one.[14]

But there are other reasons for revising our formula (II). In making the revisions we shall have to take a fateful step whose full significance will not become evident until later, in section IX.

VIII

Consider the case in which a person has adequate reason to cease from believing p but does not realize that he does. This sort of case comes in two versions. It may be that in failing to realize that he has adequate reason to cease from believing p, he has failed to use his belief-governing capacities as well as can rightly be demanded of him. There it is—right before his eyes. But he does not realize it. And his failure to realize it is due to inexcusable absent-mindedness on his part, or haste, or whatever. On the other hand, his failure to realize the nature of his situation may be wholly excusable. The fact that among his beliefs there is adequate reason to cease from believing p may be so subtle, or the connections so hard to grasp, that he could not rightly be expected to have noticed it.

It is obvious that these two sorts of cases must be treated differently. The latter leaves his justification in believing p unaffected; the former does not. So a third approximation to our desired criterion can be formulated as follows:

(III)   A person S is rational in some eluctable and innocently produced belief Bp of his if and only if S does believe p, and either:
   (i) S neither has nor ought to have adequate reason to cease from believing p, or
   (ii) S does have adequate reason to cease from believing p but does not realize that he does, and is rationally justified in that.

One more qualification is required to reach our final formulation. Suppose a person believes p, and in addition holds the belief, call it C, that his other beliefs provide adequate reason for him to cease from believing p. Suppose also that he is mistaken in that belief C. What does this do to the epistemic status of his belief that p?

Note that this type of case comes in three varieties:

(i)   The person is mistaken and rationally unjustified in the belief C. The belief C is not rationally permissible for him.

(ii) The person is mistaken but rationally justified in the belief C. It is rationally permissible for him to believe C. But it is not rationally obligatory that he believe it. It is rationally permissible for him not to believe it.

(iii) The person is mistaken in the belief C but would not be rationally justified in ceasing from holding C. It is rationally obligatory that he hold it.

It is obvious that case (i) leaves the status of the belief B*p* unmodified. A person's believing that he has adequate reason to cease from believing p, when in so believing he is violating his duties of rationality, does not remove rational justification from his belief that *p*.

It is not so clear what is to be said about case (ii). We are to suppose that a person believes *p* but also happens to hold the belief C that his other beliefs constitute adequate reason to cease from believing *p*. And we are to suppose that he is mistaken, though rational, in that upper-level belief—rationally permitted to hold it, though not obliged to do so. What is permitted of him in this situation?

Ought he to give up his belief that *p*, a belief which he would be fully rational in holding if he did not also have the belief that he has adequate reason to cease from holding it? Does his permissibly, though mistakenly, having that upper-level belief C that his believing *p* is nonrational put him in the situation where he is no longer rational in holding B*p*? Well, why would it do that? Why is it not equally permissible for him to go the other way and surrender that upper-level belief of his? What reason indeed would there be for his being obliged to go one way rather than the other?

Does that mean, then, that he is permitted to go either way? And what about the possibility that he is permitted to continue to believe both?[15] Without decisively resolving the issue, let me assume for our purposes here that it is permissible for him to hang on to his belief that *p*—leaving open the issue of whether this is permissible only if he surrenders the upper-level belief that *p* is not held rationally. There will be no great difficulty in revising our criterion as necessary if this assumption proves incorrect.

Case (iii) clearly does alter the epistemic status of believing *p*, however. If the person is not only justified in believing but also rationally obliged to believe that his other beliefs constitute adequate reason to cease from believing *p*, then he has but one choice: to give up his belief that *p*.

Our criterion then becomes this:

(IV)   A person S is rational in his eluctable and innocently produced belief Bp if and only if S does believe p, and either:

    (i)   S neither has nor ought to have adequate reason to cease from believing p, and is not rationally obliged to believe that he *does* have adequate reason to cease; or

    (ii)   S does have adequate reason to cease from believing p but does not realize that he does, and is rationally justified in that.[16]

My central thesis, now, is this: S will have done as well as can rightly be demanded of him in the use of his belief-governing capacities toward the goal of getting more amply in touch with reality if and only if all of his beliefs are innocently produced and none of those is nonrational on this criterion.[17]

Throughout I have been assuming that we are rational and nonrational not only in our believings but also in our *not* believings. The criterion for rationally not believing is wholly parallel to that for rationally believing:

(V)   A person S is rational in an eluctable and innocently produced case of not believing p if and only if S does not believe p, and either:

    (i)   S neither has nor ought to have adequate reason to believe p, and is not rationally obliged to believe that he *does* have adequate reason to believe p; or

    (ii)   S does have adequate reason to believe p but does not realize that he does, and is rationally justified in that.

IX

The criterion I have offered for rationality in beliefs openly and unabashedly makes use of normative concepts in its formulation. Indeed, it makes use of the very same normative concept for whose application it is a criterion. Accordingly, to understand the criterion one must already grasp the concept, and to apply the criterion one must already know how to apply the concept. These features of our criterion will give some readers pause in accepting it. They will feel that what is wanted out of a criterion has not been achieved.

When one's goal is to *introduce* a concept to someone, then of course one must avoid using the concept in one's introduction. That has not been my aim here. I have presumed that we already have the concept of being rational, of being rationally justified in one's beliefs. Earlier in my discussion I made some clarifying comments about that concept, pointing out its connection to responsibilities, in that way trying to make as clear as possible which concept I had in mind. My hope was that thereby the reader either would acquire the concept or would acquire a clearer view of a concept which already he had. Here in this section my goal has been to formulate a criterion for the application of this concept that the reader already has in mind. It is true, of course, that in trying to formulate a criterion for the application of a normative or evaluative concept one may set as one's goal to make use of no normative or evaluative concepts. That has not been my goal. My goal has simply been to find a criterion which is correct and illuminating. Whether or not the criterion itself makes use of the concept for whose application it is a criterion is, in principle, irrelevant to that goal. A criterion which does not make use of the concept may prove unilluminating; a criterion which does make use of the concept may prove illuminating.

In that it uses the very concept for which it is a criterion, my criterion is similar to the now customary way of thinking of necessity: It is said that a necessarily true (that is, not-possibly-false) proposition is one which is true in all possible worlds. But no one supposes that this formula can be used to introduce the concept of necessity to someone who lacks it; its circularity makes it useless for that purpose. Furthermore, to apply this formula for the not-possibly-false proposition, one must already be able to apply the concept of possibility. Nonetheless, it is evident from the philosophical literature of the last decade and a half that this way of thinking about necessity and possibility has proved extraordinarily illuminating. I intend my criterion to function in a similar way: namely, to provide us with an illuminating way of thinking about rationality and its conditions.

It may be added that reliabilist and foundationalist criteria, if they are to come anywhere near being satisfactory, must also make use of some normative concept. Consider, for example, the reliabilist criterion: S is justified in his belief Bp if and only if S does believe p, and Bp was produced (or is sustained) in S by a reliable mechanism. Suppose that though Bp was not produced in S by a reliable mechanism, nonetheless S believes that it was and is rationally justified in that belief. Surely then S would be rational in believing p. Suppose, conversely, that Bp was produced in S by a reliable mechanism, but S ought to believe it was produced by an unreliable mechanism. Surely S is then *not* rational in believing p.

Or consider the criterion of the classic foundationalist. Suppose that S believes p on the basis of certain incorrigible and self-evident beliefs of his. And suppose that though these beliefs do not provide adequate evidence for p, nonetheless S believes they do and is rationally justified in that. Surely then S is rational in believing p. Suppose, conversely, that those basic beliefs *do* provide adequate evidence for p, but S ought to believe they do not. Surely then S is not rational in believing p.

I conclude that any satisfactory criterion for rational belief will have to be not only a *noetic* criterion, making explicit or tacit reference to the beliefs of the person but also a *normative* noetic criterion, making explicit or tacit use of some such normative concept as that of justification or obligation. In recognition of these facts the criterion I have offered not only takes the phenomenon *of not having adequate reason to surrender one's belief* as the key phenomenon determining rationality; it adds to this an explicitly noetic-normative component.

X

Let me comment briefly on a few other features of the criterion.

(1) The criterion does not assist us in sorting out adequate from inadequate reasons for refraining from beliefs. If at a certain point one is uncertain as to how to make this discrimination, the criterion will not help to resolve that uncertainty; it will not instruct one to resolve it in a certain way. In that respect the criterion is purely formal. But of course the criterion as a whole is not purely formal. It tells us what relation must obtain between a person and some one of his beliefs for him to be rational in holding that belief. In that way it tells us what to look for when trying to determine whether a certain belief of a certain person is rational. Begin, it says, by scrutinizing that person's beliefs to see whether they contain adequate reason for him to give up the belief in question. This is different from what the reliabilist would say, and different from what the classic foundationalist would say.

It would seem that an adequate reason to surrender a certain belief will always be of one or the other of two sorts: It will be evidence that the proposition believed is false or evidence that the disposition which produced the belief is unreliable (for that sort of triggering event, and that sort of outcome, under such circumstances).[18] If that is so, then the next step to take in fleshing out this criterion is to develop a theory of evidence and a theory of reliable belief-producing dispositions. (Incidentally, if it is true that adequate reasons to cease from a belief often consist of evidence that the disposition accounting for the belief is unreliable, then the reliabilist was on the right track in suggesting that rational justification in beliefs has something to do with reliability of belief-producing mechanisms. What it has to do with it, however, is different from what he thought.)

(2) Given its "innocent-until-proved-guilty" posture, the criterion does not say that only those beliefs which a person holds for reasons are ones which he is rational in holding. Beliefs are induced in us by a variety of dispositions; rationality does not attach only to those produced by our reasoning-disposition. Nonetheless, it may well be the case that many of our beliefs are such that we are not rational in holding them unless we do

so for reasons. We must not allow our conviction that this is not true of all beliefs to lead us into supposing that it is true of none.

(3) On the criterion I have offered, a person is rationally justified in all his beliefs until such time as he has acquired certain conceptual equipment and the ability to make use of that equipment. Before that time his system of beliefs may lack a variety of merits, but until, for example, he has grasped (or ought to have grasped) the concept of a reason, he is doing as well in governing his believings as can rightly be demanded of him. Accordingly, there is probably a time in the life of each child when he is rationally justified in all his beliefs. Increase in knowledge makes noetic sin possible.[19]

(4) The criterion offered is clearly not a foundationalist criterion. Fundamental to the foundationalist's vision of the structure of rational belief is the distinction between immediate beliefs and mediate beliefs. As the reader will have surmised, I judge this to be a tenable distinction. And for many purposes it is an important distinction to have in mind. Traditional theories of justified belief and of knowledge, traditional disputes between skeptics and antiskeptics—these often cannot be understood without an understanding of the immediate/mediate distinction. But for a criterion of rational belief the distinction proves otiose. The criterion I have offered is a unified criterion, applying in the same way to mediate and immediate beliefs alike.

Is it then a coherence criterion? Yes, perhaps so. In the central place that it gives to the phenomenon of *no adequate reason to surrender one's belief* it is an example of what John Pollock has called "negative coherence theories." However, in its incorporation of a normative component it goes beyond traditional coherence theories. Perhaps the time has come for us to discard the supposition that the foundationalist/coherentist dichotomy is an illuminating principle of classification.

XI

Frequently an objection of the following sort is lodged against the criterion I have proposed. Suppose a person takes a fancy to a proposition and just up and believes it. Suppose, further, that he neither has nor ought to have any adequate reason to give up that proposition. Then by our criterion he is rational in his belief. But surely he is not.

The truth is that by our criterion he most assuredly is not rational in his belief. The "mechanism" operative in this imaginary case—one may well doubt whether there really is any such "mechanism" and whether anybody really can believe in this fashion, but let that pass—the "mechanism" operative is that of believing what one takes a fancy to. But certainly any normal adult human being not only ought to know but also *does* know that this is a most unreliable "mechanism" of belief formation. Knowing that, he has a very adequate reason indeed for giving up that belief.

XII

Our Reidian approach to epistemology downplays the significance of reasoning. Reasoning is but one among many modes of belief formation. And it is not unique in producing rationally held beliefs. Other "mechanisms" of belief formation produce rational beliefs as well.

Yet in spite of this, *reasons* occupy a central role in the criterion I have offered. Is there not some oddity, some discrepancy, in this? Granted that *having reasons* is not the same as *reasoning*. But they are not unrelated. How does downplaying the role of reasoning fit with emphasizing the role of having reasons?

Well, suppose one wants to dislodge some belief that someone has— perhaps the person just took something on someone else's say-so which one believes to be false. How might one proceed? If it is a matter whose truth can be determined by perception, one might do what one can to put the person in the situation where he himself can determine by perception the truth of the matter. Upon being put in that situation, the person might very well believe the testimony of his senses over the testimony of that other person. He may be so made or conditioned that the perceptual disposition (coupled with the disposition to "see" that the deliverance of the perceptual disposition is in conflict with the deliverance of the credulity disposition) operates more powerfully than the credulity disposition. A hierarchy in the strength of these dispositions would operate in such a case.

Depending on the case, another thing one might try to do is give the person a *reason* for supposing that what was said to him is false. *That* may induce him to give up the belief—the situation again being that whatever are the dispositions behind the reasons, they prove to be more powerful than those which produced and/or sustained the belief in question. Now sometimes when we give someone reasons for believing or not believing so-and-so, we induce new beliefs in that person. Perhaps the person comes to believe things on our say-so. Or what we say prods him into "seeing" connections among his beliefs which he had not seen before. In this latter case, even though what we say induces the belief, the person does not accept it on our say-so. Of course, giving reasons for believing or not believing something does not always induce new beliefs in the person. Sometimes one just brings forcefully to the person's attention what he believed anyway. (Maybe he did not *believe* that he believed it; sometimes that is what one changes.)

I think we can see now why reasons have a special status. It may be that some available perceptual experience would dislodge what a person believes on testimony. I, on the outside, may know of the availability of that experience and may see to it that the person has that experience. But how could the person himself be obliged to obtain this experience without so much as believing, or being obliged to believe, that the experience is available? By contrast, if there is amongst his *beliefs* adequate *reason* to surrender that belief of his which he accepted on testimony, then we can demand of him that he take note of that—unless the connections are too subtle to expect a person of his intelligence to notice them. Reasons have a special status simply because the contents of our minds have a special accessibility to us and ought accordingly to be taken note of. If amongst those contents there are certain beliefs such that if the person becomes fully aware of them and of their connections to that original belief, that original belief (in the absence of culpable resistances) would be inhibited, then he should let that happen. He cannot be expected to range over the whole world in search of what might inhibit his beliefs. He can be expected to range through his own mind, however.

Let us dig deeper yet in these somewhat speculative reflections. Suppose someone believes p, and also has an adequate reason q to believe *not-p*; and suppose further that the person sees all the logical and evidential connections involved in this. Add to this that the dispositions involved have not been culpably revised. Then his situation is that one innocent disposition yields the belief that p, another yields the belief that q, and yet another yields the belief that p conflicts with q. What reason is there in this situation for him to go one way rather than another? Why not give up the belief that q and keep the belief that p, rather than vice versa? Or why not give up the belief that p and q conflict?

Usually we have no choice in the matter. We come with various innate belief dispositions. These gradually become revised, and in good measure they are revised because the deliverance of one disposition conflicts with that of another, and the one yields. Gradually hierarchies of forcefulness develop. We trust vision more than testimony in some circumstances and on some matters; we trust one kind of memory, and one kind of perception, more than another; and so on. And these facts of our nature are the end of the matter. Deeper we cannot go. We cannot *show* that the totality of these dispositions leads us to truth. Of course we can rail against these native dispositions and the hierarchies. of forcefulness that gradually emerge. We can undertake to revise these for some reason other than that they have proved unreliable. The Christian, though, will have a reason for not thus railing, for accepting our native and naturally developed noetic dispositions as trustworthy. He believes that we have been made thus by a good Creator. (Of course, in this very process the Christian is trusting the testimony of inference.) It is true that he may well acknowledge that some of our dispositions are signs of our fallenness, not part of our pristine nature, so that they are unreliable. The dispositions of which Marx and Freud made so much are examples. But the Christian will trust that the unreliability of such as these will show up.

To some this will look alarmingly slippery. Should we not *establish* the reliability of a belief disposition before we trust it—provided, of course, that we *can* restrain our trust in it? Well, how, if we are going to trust no belief disposition whatsoever until proved reliable, are we going to prove it reliable? In the very process we shall have to *assume* that some *are* reliable. Alternatively, suppose we acknowledge this fact and, taking for granted the reliability of some, try to establish the reliability of the others by reference to these? But which shall we pick as the touchstones? Surely any choice here, at this fundamental level, will be completely arbitrary.

Perhaps some of the deep motivation of the classical foundationalist comes to light here. Perhaps he thought that he could get around this unavoidable trust in our noetic dispositions as a whole by starting with propositions that we can "see" to be true, and then by reference to these establish the reliability of those dispositions which produce the acceptance of propositions that we do not just "see" to be true. But a fundamental objection arises immediately. Cannot one have the *experience* of "seeing a proposition to be true" when in fact it is false? And cannot one *think* one has this experience when one has some other?

There is in all of us a complex and natural flow of belief formation. In this natural flow we can and do, and sometimes should, deliberately intervene. The rules of rationality are in effect the rules of such intervention. They instruct us, in effect, to bring our other relevant beliefs into consciousness. Once we have done this, our created nature then once again does its trustworthy work of dispelling the original belief or confirming it (or neither)—provided that we do not culpably interfere.

XIII

And now at last we can return to our beginning. Can belief in God be rational if it has no foundations? Could a person be justified in believing that God exists (or some other affirmative theistic proposition) without the justifying circumstance consisting in the fact that he believes it on the basis of other beliefs of his which he judges to be good evidence for it? Could a person whose belief that God exists is one of his immediate beliefs nonetheless be rationally justified in that belief? Or is it the case that if our theistic convictions are to be rational, they must be formed or reinforced in us exclusively by the "mechanism" of inference?

People come to the conviction that God exists in the most astonishing diversity of ways. Some pick up their theistic convictions from their parents; presumably it is the credulity disposition which is at work in such cases. Some find themselves overcome with a sense of guilt so vast and cosmic that no human being is adequate as its object. Some fall into a mystic trance and find themselves overcome with the conviction that they have met God. Some in suicidal desperation find themselves saying, "Yes, I do believe," whereupon they have a sense of overwhelming peace. The evidentialist proposes slicing through all this diversity. One's belief that God exists is rational only if it is formed or sustained by good inference—by inferring it from others of one's beliefs which in fact provide adequate evidence for it. In the light of the criterion proposed, what is to be said about this claim?

What our criterion instructs us to consider is whether it is possible that there be a person who believes *immediately* that God exists, and at the same time has no adequate reason to surrender that belief. Or more precisely, whether there is a person who at the same time neither has nor ought to believe that he has any adequate reason to surrender that belief. Might a person's being in the situation of believing immediately that God exists represent no failure on his part to govern his beliefs as well as can rightly be demanded of him with respect to the goal of getting more amply in touch with reality?

I see no reason whatsoever to suppose that by the criterion offered the evidentialist challenge is tenable. I see no reason to suppose that people who hold as one of their immediate beliefs that God exists always have adequate reason to surrender that belief—or ought to believe that they do. I see no reason to suppose that holding the belief that God exists as one of one's immediate beliefs always represents some failure on one's part to govern one's assent as well as one ought.

However, those abstract and highly general theses of evidentialism no longer look very interesting, once we regard them in the light of the criterion offered. One of the burdens of this paper has been that issues of rationality are always situation specific. Once the impact of that sinks in, then no longer is it of much interest to spend time pondering whether evidentialism is false. It seems highly likely that it is. But the interesting and important question has become whether some specific person—I, or you, or whoever—who believes immediately that God exists is rational in that belief. Whether a given person is in fact rational in such belief cannot be answered in general and in the abstract, however. It can only be answered by scrutinizing the belief system of the individual believer, and the ways in which that believer has used his noetic capacities.

Perhaps a theistic believer who is not of any great philosophical sophistication has heard a lecture of Anthony Flew attacking religious belief, and perhaps he finds himself unable to uncover any flaws in the argument. Or perhaps he has heard a powerful lecture by some disciple of Freud/Freudianism arguing that religious belief represents nothing more than a surrogate satisfaction of one's need to feel secure, and perhaps, once again, he can find no flaw in the argument. It would appear that if this believer has puzzled over these arguments for a reasonable length of time, has talked to people who seem to him insightful, and so on, and still sees no flaws in the argument, then he is no longer rationally justified in his belief—provided, of course, he does not have evidence in favor of God's existence which counterbalance these. And it makes no difference now by what "mechanism" his theistic convictions were formed in him! By contrast, the person who has never heard of these arguments, and the person who justifiably believes them not sound, is in a relevantly different situation.

It is important to keep in mind here our main earlier conclusion, however. From the fact that it is not rational for some person to believe that God exists it does not follow that he ought to give up that belief. Rationality is only *prima facie* justification; lack of rationality, only *prima facie* impermissibility. Perhaps, in spite of its irrationality for him, the person ought to continue believing that God exists. Perhaps it is our duty to believe more firmly that God exists than any proposition which conflicts with this, and/or more firmly than we believe that a certain proposition *does* conflict with it. Of course, for a believer who is a member of the modern Western intelligentsia to have his theistic convictions prove nonrational is to be put into a deeply troubling situation. There is a biblical category which applies to such a situation. It is a *trial*, which the believer is called to endure. Sometimes suffering is a trial. May it not also be that sometimes the nonrationality of one's conviction that God exists is a trial, to be endured?

XIV

And what, lastly, about the enthusiasts who so vexed Locke? Locke was persuaded that the enthusiasts claiming private revelations were irrational and, accordingly, irresponsible. They were acting in disobedience to their Creator. But if we do not demand of everyone in the field of religion good evidence for their convictions, said Locke, then we will simply have to acknowledge that anything goes. The concept of rational belief will simply have to be discarded. So Locke undertook to provide good evidence for his Christian convictions, and he challenged the enthusiasts to act likewise.

The evidentialist challenge which Locke laid down to the enthusiasts is untenable. But that does not mean that one is speechless in the face of crackpots. It does not mean that anything goes. Rather than demanding evidence from the enthusiast, one offers him adequate reasons for the falsehood of his beliefs. Sometimes he may concede the point and give up his convictions. In other cases, no doubt, he will continue merrily believing. But in this respect the approach implied by our criterion is surely no worse than Locke's. Locke's issuance of the evidentialist challenge was not noticeably effective in snuffing out British "enthusiasm"!

Appendix

A reply to my contention in section IX, that an adequate criterion for rational justification in beliefs will itself have to incorporate, tacitly or explicitly, some normative concept, might go along the following lines. This contention may well be true for the *subjective* concept of rational obligation and justification. Surely it is not true for the *objective* concept. But the standard criteria for rational justification which have been proposed —classic foundationalism, reliabilism, and so on—should be seen as criteria for the *objective* concept. Accordingly, what was said in section IX does not touch these criteria. When these are understood as criteria for objective rational justification, there is no need for them to incorporate some normative concept. The objector might go on to charge that I have served the cause of confusion by failing to distinguish, more sharply than I did, my *no-adequate-reason-for-surrendering* proposal concerning objective rational justification from the normative-noetic qualifications attached so as to make it a criterion for subjective rational justification. I think it will help to unravel the issues here if we turn, for a moment, from the noetic to the moral domain and consider the arguments of those who call for a distinction between objective and subjective obligation within the field of morality. Consider, for example, what Richard B. Brandt says on the matter in his book *Ethical Theory:*

> The definition of "moral obligation" we have outlined makes it possible for a person to make mistakes about his obligation. He may *think* his feeling of obligation is "objectively justified" when in fact it is not. This seems acceptable; we do think that people are sometimes mistaken about their duty or obligation.... Yet there is something wrong, as [an example] will make clear.
> [S]uppose a physician examined a patient suffering from allergies in 1920, when nothing was known of allergies. The physician advised and performed a series of operations (on the patient's nose and sinuses, for example) at considerable cost to the patient in suffering and money. Was the physician's behavior consistent with his moral obligations? We certainly incline to say it was. According to our total theory, as described above, however, it seems he did *not* do his duty, since, if he had been fully informed (including information about allergies), he would have felt obligated to treat for allergies.[20]

Brandt goes on to try to unravel this case by distinguishing between an *objective* and a *subjective* sense of "duty" and "obligation." The physician did his duty, says Brandt, if "duty" is used in the subjective sense. He did not do his duty if "duty" is used in the objective sense.

But is this correct? Is it true that, in some (standard) sense of the word "ought," the physician did not do what he ought to have done? I suggest that it is not. There is no (standard) sense of the word "ought" according to which Brandt's physician did not do what he ought to have done. I am assuming that the issue at stake here is not to be unraveled by the distinction between *prima facie* obligation and all-things-considered obligation.

If there were such an objective concept of obligation as Brandt proposes, one could believe and assert that S ought to do y, while yet with full sincerity advising S not to do y, praising him if he does not do y and blaming him if he does, and treating him as culpable if he does do y. This would be so if one used "ought" in the objective sense. For culpability is thought to attach to the subjective concept of obligation but not to the objective. I suggest, however, that there is no such concept of obligation. Our concept of obligation is inextricably connected with how we treat people: with the advice we give them, with our dispensing of praise and blame, with our treating of them as culpable. If one does believe that S ought to do y, then one cannot with sincerity advise him not to do y, or praise him for not doing y, or treat him as culpable if he does do y. The so-called *subjective* concept of obligation is the only concept of obligation there is.

But can we not simply judge whether the physician's action is or is not enjoined by objective moral law? Certainly we can. But to judge it to be enjoined by objective moral law is to assert, or imply, that he ought to do it. And, once again, one cannot believe that he ought to do it and with sincerity enjoin him not to do it. There is no difference between acting in accord with one's obligation and doing as well as can rightly be expected of one.

There is, indeed, a certain truth which those who make the objective/subjective distinction are trying to get at. In the case of Brandt's example that truth is this: A physician dealing with the same medical case that Brandt's physician was dealing with, but who differed from Brandt's physician *in that he was fully knowledgeable* on all relevant moral and medical facts, would be obliged to act differently from the way Brandt's physician was obliged to act. But quite obviously that does not imply that there is some concept of obligation according to which Brandt's physician is obliged to act as that fully knowledgeable physician would be obliged to act.

Of course, when confronted by Brandt's medical case, we can ask what a fully knowledgeable physician dealing with this medical case would be obliged to do. We can also, if we wish, *stipulate* that sometimes we will use the word "obliged" in such a way that Brandt's physician is "obliged" to do whatever a fully knowledgeable physician dealing with this case would be obliged to do. And we may, if we wish, call this the *objective* sense of "obligation." But that does not tell us what Brandt's physician— who after all is not fully knowledgeable—is obliged to do, using the word "obliged" in its normal English sense. The English word "obliged" is not as a matter of fact used to express that concept.

This analysis of the situation has implications for how we understand standard theories of moral obligation (which are not intentionalistic in character). Such theories should not be viewed as telling us what we— who are far from being fully knowledgeable persons—ought in fact to do. If viewed that way, they are radically deficient. Rather, they are best understood as theories which tell us what a person who is fully knowledgeable on the relevant facts ought to do. To get from that information to what we, in our concrete situations, ought to do, we must in the appropriate way take account of our justified error and ignorance.

Consider, for example, a hedonistic utilitarian who holds that the criterion for right action is the greatest pleasure of the greatest number. Such a theorist does not really have in mind that, of the options that confront a person at a given time, the one which would in fact produce the greatest happiness of the greatest number is the one he ought to perform. Rather, he means something like this: An agent who is fully knowledgeable as to the pleasurable consequences of his various options for action, and as to how the moral law applies to actions having such consequences, ought always to choose that option which yields the greatest happiness of the greatest number. For on the utilitarian's view a fully moral agent will always have it as his goal to bring it about that of those options for action which face him on any occasion, he will perform that one which yields the greatest happiness of the greatest number.

You and I, however, are not fully knowledgeable agents. Furthermore, some of our error and ignorance is justified. Accordingly, even if we have adopted the goal that the utilitarian recommends, it may well turn out that sometimes an alternative which would not yield the most pleasure is nonetheless such that we ought to try to perform it (if we did not try to perform it, given our state of error and ignorance, that would indicate a lack of commitment to the goal); and sometimes an alternative which *would* yield the most pleasure is such that we ought not to try to perform it. Our performing it, given our state of error and ignorance, would indicate that we were not fully committed to the goal of doing what will give the greatest happiness.

In short, it may well be that of some less pleasurable actions it is true that we ought to perform them, and of some more pleasurable actions, that we ought *not* to perform them. But if so, it will not be true that we ought always to do what is (in fact) most pleasure-yielding, and to avoid what is (in fact) less pleasure-yielding. Nonetheless we ought to have it as our goal to make this proposition true: Always we perform (what is in fact) the most pleasure-yielding of the options that confront us.

Similar things are to be said about the obligations of rationality. The person who does in fact have adequate reasons for refraining from his beliefs whenever he ought to have them, and who is fully knowledgeable about the presence and absence of such adequate reasons, ought to surrender a given belief as soon as he has adequate reason to do so. For he, along with everyone else, should have it as his goal to cease believing something as soon as he has adequate reason for doing so—other things being equal. For each proposition p which he believes, he should seek to make it true that he ceases to believe p as soon as he has adequate reason to do so.

But you and I are not such fully knowledgeable epistemic agents. We are often in justifiable error and ignorance on relevant matters. Because of that, there will be propositions we believe for which we have adequate reason to cease believing but which we are nonetheless permitted, even perhaps obliged, to believe; and there will be propositions we believe for which we do *not* have adequate reason to refrain but which we are nonetheless obliged to cease from believing. Almost certainly for each of us there is some proposition p which we believe of which it is not true that we are rational in believing it if and only if we lack adequate reason to refrain. Nonetheless each person should strive to bring it about that there is no proposition which he believes for which he has adequate reason to refrain.

What we learn from the analogy to the moral case is not that the criterion for rational belief which I have proposed is merely a criterion for the subjective sense of obligation. We learn something in the opposite direction: namely, that standard moral theories apply, as formulated, only to a person who is in a certain kind of ideal noetic situation. To apply to us in our factual fallen situations, they would have to take into account what we are and are not rationally justified in believing and in ceasing from believing.

Endnotes

*From *Faith and Rationality: Reason and Belief in God*, edited by A. Plantinga and N. Wolterstorff © 1983 by the University of Notre Dame Press. Reprinted by permission.

1 Sometimes he also includes under reason our faculty for apprehending what is *evident* to us.

2 Cf. *Essay*, IV,19,4: "*Reason* is natural *revelation*, whereby the eternal Father of light, and Fountain of all knowledge communicates to mankind that portion of truth which he has laid within the reach of their natural faculties. *Revelation* is natural *reason* enlarged by a new set of discoveries communicated by God immediately, which reason vouches the truth of, by the testimony and proofs it gives that they come from God. So that he that takes away reason to make way for revelation, puts out the light of both."

[3] Compare this passage: "God, when he makes the prophet, does not unmake the man. He leaves all his faculties in their natural state, to enable him to judge of his inspirations, whether they be of divine origin or no. When he illuminates the mind with supernatural light, he does not extinguish that which is natural. If he would have us assent to the truth of any proposition, he either evidences that truth by the usual methods of natural reason, or else makes it known to be a truth which he would have us assent to by his authority, and convinces us that it is from him, by some marks which reason cannot be mistaken in. Reason must be our last judge and guide in everything. I do not mean that we must consult reason, and examine whether a proposition revealed from God can be made out by natural principles, and if it cannot, that then we may reject it. But consult it we must, and by it examine whether it be a revelation from God or no: and if reason finds it to be revealed from God, reason then declares for it as much as for any other truth, and makes it one of her dictates." (*Essay*, IV,19,14)

[4] Cf. *Essay*, IV,18,11: "If the boundaries be not set between faith and reason, no enthusiasm or extravagancy in religion can be contradicted. — If the provinces of faith and reason are not kept distinct by these boundaries, there will, in matter of religion, be no room for reason at all; and those extravagant opinions and ceremonies that are to be found in the several religions of the world will not deserve to be blamed; for to this crying up of faith in opposition to reason, we may, I think, in good measure, ascribe those absurdities that divide mankind. For men, having been principled with an opinion that they must not consult reason in the things of religion, however apparently contradictory to common sense and the very principles of all their knowledge, have let loose their fancies and natural superstition; and have been by them led into so strange opinions and extravagant practices in religion, that a considerate man cannot but stand amazed at their follies, and judge them so far from being acceptable to the great and wise God, that he cannot avoid thinking them ridiculous and offensive to a sober, good man. So that, in effect, religion, which should most distinguish us from beasts, and ought most peculiarly to elevate us as rational creatures above brutes, is that wherein men most often appear most irrational, and more senseless than beasts themselves."

[5] I have argued for the rejection of classical foundationalism in Nicholas Wolterstorff, *Reason within the Bounds of Religion* (Grand Rapids, MI: Eerdmans, 1976).

[6] Though in principle there may be other obligations that we have with respect to our believings, it is only these governance obligations of which Locke takes note. They are the only ones relevant to his purpose — as indeed to mine.

[7] It is clear from the above that one can attach the word "rational" to other facets of our noetic obligations than these. Perhaps here is also the place to remark that the word "rational" need not be directly hooked up to obligations but can be used simply to pick out a merit in beliefs concerning which one may or may not have obligation. This is connected with the comments about the concept of justification in note 12 below.

[8] Provided the person has, or ought to have, the necessary conceptual equipment. See note 19 below.

[9] Roderick Chisholm, *Theory or Knowledge,* 2nd ed. (Englewood Cliffs, N.J.: Prentice-Hall, 1977), p. 15.

10 There is another analysis of the resistance cases I have cited that ought to be considered. Perhaps the situation is not that the person resists believing, but that he resists acting in appropriate ways on what he does believe. Though I of course acknowledge that there are cases of this sort, it does seem to me that sometimes the resistance is a resistance to the believing. Probably a thorough adjudication between these two analyses would require a perusal of the relevant psychological literature. Such perusal has entered far too little into philosophical epistemology.

11 Alvin Goldman, "What Is Justified Belief?" in George S. Pappas, ed., *Justification and Knowledge* (Dordrecht: D. Reidel, 1979), pp. 9-10.

12 Might it be that the reliabilist, rather than giving a plainly incorrect criterion for rationally justified belief, is formulating a criterion for a different concept of justification than that with which I am dealing? Well, there is evidence that Goldman, for example, *thinks of* the concept of justification differently from how I think of it. He says this: "There may well be propositions which humans have an innate and irrepressible disposition to believe, e.g., 'Some events have causes'. But it seems unlikely that people's inability to refrain from believing such a proposition makes every belief in it justified." ("What Is Justified Belief?" p. 4) Now if a certain belief of a person really is ineluctable, then his holding that belief is no indication that he has failed to use his belief-governing capacities as well as can rightly be demanded of him; for one cannol rightly demand of a person what he cannot do. Accordingly, on the concept of justification with which I have been dealing, such a person is clearly justified in his belief, contrary to what Goldman says. So may it be that the philosophical literature presents us with two different concepts of rationally *justified belief* — not merely various criteria for one concept, but two different concepts for which theorists attempt to offer criteria? The one would be a normative concept. A person is (rationally) justified in believing *p* just in case in doing so he conforms to certain obligations that bear on him. And a reasonable assumption is that if he could not have failed to believe *p*, then he is not obliged not to do so. On this concept a person is, roughly speaking, rationally justified in his beliefs just in case he is doing as well in his believings as can rightly be demanded of him. The other concept of justified belief would be a purely evaluative concept. The word "justified" would pick out a certain merit in beliefs, a desirable feature of beliefs; "unjustified" would pick out a demerit in beliefs, a blemish. And a belief would have these merits and defects whether or not it was in any way within the control of the person to have or not have the belief.

The truth, in my judgment, is that there is no such concept of justification as this purely evaluative concept. The situation is not, I think, that Goldman and others are offering a criterion for a different concept of justified belief from that for which I propose to offer a criterion. The situation is rather that Goldman misapprehends the nature of the concept of justified belief. No doubt this misapprehension plays a role in his adopting the criterion he does.

In a person's system of belief we can pick out certain merits which lie between, as it were, all the beliefs being true and all the beliefs being in accord with what can rightly be demanded of that person. Perhaps some of those merits are picked out with our word "rational." And no doubt one of those in-between merits is that of all the beliefs being well-formed or sustained. But the word "justified" does not pick out that merit. The test cases will be those in which the belief is not reliably formed but in which we agree that the person could not rightly be expected to believe otherwise than he does. So look once more at our example of the young person in a primitive tribe. Can it really correctly be said of him that he is *not justified* in believing as he does? I suggest that there is no sense of the English word "justified" such that that can correctly be said of him.

Incidentally, there is a passage in Goldman's essay in which he himself is on the verge of recognizing that the one and only concept of justification is a normative concept. After considering a case which in his judgment calls for a revision in his unqualified reliabilist theory, he says, "So what we can say about Jones is that *he fails* to use a certain (conditionally) reliable process that he could and should have used. . . So, he failed to do something which, epistemically, he should have done. This diagnosis suggests a fundamental change in our theory. The justificational status of a belief is not only a function of the cognitive processes *actually* employed in producing it; it is also a function of the processes that could and should be employed." (Ibid., p. 29)

^{13} In the sense of "reason" cited in the preceding paragraph the *event* of a person's believing q and believing that it is good evidence for p may be his reason for believing p.

^{14} Suppose that someone who believes p — perhaps because someone told him that p is true — later finds that the evidence for p is exactly balanced with that against p, that is, with that for *not-p*. What then constitute the obligations and permissions of rationality? Well, the "innocent-until-proved-guilty" principle which we are exploring says that he is permitted to continue believing p, for p has not been proved guilty. On the other hand, it would seem that he is also permitted to refrain from believing both p and *not-p*. What he is *not* permitted to do is to proceed to believe *not-p* on the basis of his awareness that the evidence for p and for *not-p* is equally balanced, for he should realize that believing thus is an unreliable "mechanism." (Shortly we shall see more clearly the relevance of this fact.) Of course, if the person had entered this situation believing *not-p* rather than p, then the opposite of all these things is true. Then he is permitted either to continue believing *not-p* or to believe neither p nor *not-p*, but not to believe p on the basis of his awareness that the evidence pro and con *not-p* is equally balanced. This yields what seems initially to be the paradoxical result, that of two people surveying the very same evidence and making the same responsible judgment as to its weight, one may be permitted to believe p but not *not-p*, the other to believe *not-p* but not p.

Consider a different but related case. Suppose that a person who believes neither p nor *not-p* comes responsibly to the conviction that the evidence for these is equal. What ought he to do? Quite clearly, to refrain from believing either p or *not-p*. For to believe either of these on this basis is to believe it on account of what he should realize to be an unreliable "mechanism." Again, suppose that a person who believes *both* p and *not-p* discovers that the evidence for these is equal — and also notices that he believes both, and notices that they cannot both be true. (He may, of course, have been believing both without believing p *and not-p*.) What should, or may, he do? Once again, he is not permitted on the basis of his awareness of his situation to give up one and hang on to the other, for that would be to believe on account of what he should realize to be an unreliable "mechanism." Clearly what he is permitted to do, though, is give up both. But what about the last possibility, that of hanging on to both? Well, the "innocent-until-proved-guilty" principle would in fact seem to say that he is permitted to do this. And though at first this result takes one a bit aback, maybe it is correct. I think, however, that rarely will a person be able to do this — at least for any length of time. And we have already seen that he is not entitled, on the basis of his realization of the situation, to give up either one of them and hang on to the other. He is entitled only to give up both. (Surely such a person would not be rational in believing *p and not-p*. And it is surprising that this would be so, while at the same time it is rational for him to believe both *p* and *not-p*, realizing that they are contradictory.)

15 This last would be most in line with the conclusion drawn in note 14 above.

16 Consider someone who believes that *p* and who earlier held that same belief and held it nonrationally, having adequate reason to cease from holding it. Suppose that in the interim, though he retains the belief B*p*, he forgets those reasons. Suppose also that he is rationally justified in that forgetting; his not believing those reasons later on is rational on his part. And suppose that neither now nor at any time after all those events had transpired was there anything else in his situation relevant to the rationality of this belief than that he once held it in defiance of adequate reasons to give it up and later remembered it but justifiably forgot those reasons. Is he now, at this later point, still nonrational in holding that belief, even though now he neither has nor ought to have adequate reason to cease from that belief? If he is still not rational in holding it, then we have to insert a qualification into the above, assuring that the nonrationality of such a belief remains, even though now the person neither has nor ought to have adequate reason to give it up.

17 With this qualification: As mentioned before, the criterion makes no attempt to specify the rationality of the *firmness* with which beliefs are held.

18 Perhaps the rational person tolerates different degrees of unreliability for different sorts of propositions. This is an important issue which I cannot here explore.

19 Of course, the fact that all of some tiny child's beliefs are rationally *justified* does not imply any praiseworthiness on his part. Though lack of justification implies culpability, justification does not imply praiseworthiness. One could, of course, add some qualification to our criterion for rational belief so that it did imply this. Then, on the criterion, though the tiny child would not be unjustified in his beliefs, he would also not be justified.

20 Richard B. Brandt, *Ethical Theory* (Englewood Cliffs, N.J.: Prentice Hall, 1959), pp. 360-61.

Study Questions

1.   What does Wolterstorff mean when he says that rationality is "only *prima facie* justification"?

2.   What is the evidentialist objection to theistic belief?

3.   What sorts of questions does Wolterstorff raise in response to the evidentialist's stance?

4.   How does Locke fit into the account that is given of "assent"?

5.   Thomas Reid is discussed at length by Wolterstorff. How does Reid fit in with the direction that Wolterstorff wants to take the discussion?

7

In Search of the Foundations
of Theism

Philip L. Quinn

Philip L. Quinn is professor of philosophy at the University of Notre Dame and was the editor of *Faith and Philosophy*, the publication of the Society of Christian Philosophers.

This paper* is a critical and exploratory discussion of Plantinga's claim that certain propositions which self-evidently entail the existence of God could be properly basic. In the critical section, I argue that Plantinga fails to show that the modern foundationalist's criterion for proper basicality, according to which such propositions could not be properly basic, is self-referentially incoherent or otherwise defective. In the exploratory section, I try to build a case for the view that, even if such propositions could be properly basic, they would seldom, if ever, be properly basic for intellectually sophisticated adult theists in our culture.

Foundationalism comes in two varieties. Descriptive foundationalism is a thesis about the structure of a body of beliefs, and normative foundationalism is a thesis about the structure of epistemic justification for a body of beliefs. Both varieties partition a body of beliefs into two subclasses, a foundational class and a founded class. For descriptive foundationalism, the foundational class is the class of basic beliefs. A belief is basic for a person at a time provided it is accepted by that person at that time but is not accepted by that person at that time on the basis of any of his or her other beliefs at that time. For normative foundationalism, the foundational class is the class of properly basic beliefs. A belief is properly basic for a person at a time just in case it is basic for the person at the time and its being basic for the person at the time is contrary to no correct canon of epistemic propriety and results from no epistemic deficiency on his or her part at that time. For descriptive foundationalism, the founded class is the class of beliefs based on basic beliefs, and, for normative foundationalism, the founded class is the class of beliefs properly based on properly basic beliefs.

It surely is possible that, for some human persons at some times, certain propositions which self-evidently entail that God exists are basic. But is it also possible that, for some human persons at some times, certain propositions which self-evidently entail that God exists are *properly* basic? In other words, could such propositions *be*, or at least *be among*, the normative foundations of theism, at least for some people at some times? The answers to these question depend, of course, on what the correct criteria for proper basicality turn out to be.

Recently Alvin Plantinga has been arguing that it is in order for a religious epistemologist to return affirmative answers to these questions.[1] There are two prongs to Plantinga's argument. The first is destructive: it is an attempt to show that certain criteria for proper basicality, according to which propositions which self-evidently entail the existence of God could not be properly basic, are seriously defective and must be rejected. The second is constructive: it is an attempt to elaborate a procedure for justifying criteria for proper basicality which will allow that some propositions self-evidently entailing that God exists could turn out to be properly basic.

This paper has two aims. The first is to criticize Plantinga's argument. In the first section of the paper, I argue for two claims: (1) that Plantinga has failed to show that the criteria for proper basicality he proposes to reject are in any way defective; and (2) that Plantinga's procedure for justifying criteria for proper basicality provides no better reason for adopting criteria according to which some propositions which self-evidently entail the existence of God can be properly basic than for adopting a criterion according to which no such propositions can be properly basic. The paper's second aim is exploratory. Although Plantinga's argument is unsuccessful, it may nevertheless be true that some propositions which self-evidently entail that God exists could be properly basic. And so, in the second section of the paper, I go on to argue, on the hypothesis that this is true, for two additional claims: (1) that actually being properly basic would be a relatively unimportant feature of such propositions because they would be at least as well justified if properly based on other properly basic propositions and could always be so based; and (2) that such propositions would seldom, if ever, be properly basic for intellectually sophisticated adult theists in our culture.

Critique of Plantinga

The criteria for proper basicality Plantinga proposes to reject are those of classical foundationalism. Classical foundationalism is the disjunction of ancient or medieval foundationalism and modern foundationalism. The criterion for proper basicality of ancient or medieval foundationalism is the triply universal claim:

(1) For any proposition p, person S and time t, p is properly basic for S at t if and only if p is self-evident to S at t or is evident to the senses of S at t.

And the criterion for proper basicality of modern foundationalism is this triply universal claim:

(2) For any proposition p, person S and time t, p is properly basic for S at t if and only if p is incorrigible for S at t or is self-evident to S at t.

Although Plantinga thinks the propositions expressed by both (1) and (2) should be rejected on grounds of self-referential incoherence, he actually discusses only the latter proposition at any length. However, it is clear that if his argument for self-referential incoherence succeeds against the proposition expressed by (2), a similar argument will, *mutatis mutandis*, work equally well against the proposition expressed by (1). But what exactly is the argument? And how much does it really prove?

Consider the proposition expressed by (2). What place does it have in the modern foundationalist's own structure of epistemic justification? Is it in the foundational class? Does the modern foundationalist suppose that it is ever properly basic for anyone? If he or she does, then he or she must hold that for someone at some time it is either incorrigible or self-evident. Plantinga believes it to be "neither self-evident nor incorrigible."[2] I agree. I think the proposition expressed by (2) is never incorrigible for or self-evident to me. Are Plantinga and I idiosyncratic in this respect? Could the modern foundationalist claim with any plausibility that we are just plain mistaken on this point? I think the answer to these questions has to be negative. It seems to me perfectly clear that the proposition expressed by (2) is never incorrigible for or self-evident to anyone. Hence, no one, not even a modern foundationalist, is entitled to suppose that the proposition expressed by (2) is ever properly basic for anyone.

Does this suffice to show that modern foundationalism is self-referentially incoherent? Obviously it does not. What would be self-referentially incoherent would be to affirm the proposition expressed by (2), to assert that it is itself never incorrigible for or self-evident to anyone, and also to claim that it is itself properly basic for someone at some time. But this leaves the modern foundationalist with the option of continuing to affirm the proposition expressed by (2) while conceding that it is itself never properly basic for anyone. For all that has been said so far, the proposition expressed by (2), though never properly basic for anyone, is for some people at some times properly based on propositions which, by its own lights, are properly basic for those people at those times. In discussion, Plantinga has claimed that no modern foundationalist has ever given a good argument for the view that the proposition expressed by (2) is, for some people at some times, properly based on propositions which, by its own lights, are properly basic for them then. Maybe this is so. But, even if it is, this does not show that modern foundationalism is self-referentially incoherent. All it shows is that the modern foundationalist has so far not completed the task of justifying the proposition expressed by (2) in the only way that remains open to him or her, namely, by showing how it can, for some people at some times, be properly based on propositions which are, by its own lights, properly basic for them at those times. Can this be done, and, if so, how? More generally, how could any criterion for proper basicality be justified?

Plantinga offers us an explicit answer to the more general question. He says:

> . . . the proper way to arrive at such a criterion is, broadly speaking, *inductive*. We must assemble examples of beliefs and conditions such that the former are obviously properly basic in the latter, and examples of beliefs and conditions such that the former are obviously *not* properly basic in the latter. We must then frame hypotheses as to the necessary and sufficient conditions of proper basicality and test these hypotheses by reference to those examples.[3]

As I understand the proposed procedure, it requires that we do two things. First, we are to assemble the data upon which the induction will be based. A datum may be represented as an ordered pair whose first member is a belief and whose second member is a condition. Positive data are data such that the beliefs that are their first members are obviously properly basic in the conditions that are their second members; negative data are data such that the beliefs that are their first members are obviously not properly basic in the conditions that are their second members. Call the set of data, presumably finite, so assembled 'the initial set.' Second, we are to frame hypotheses stating necessary and sufficient conditions for proper basicality and test them against the data in the initial set. An hypothesis will pass the test posed by the data in the initial set if and only if all of the positive data in the initial set and none of the negative data in that set satisfy its necessary and sufficient conditions for proper basicality. So far, so good.

However, two questions about this procedure quickly arise. First, how do we know that there will be *any* hypothesis at all stating non-trivial necessary and sufficient conditions for proper basicality which will pass the test posed by the data in the initial set? Maybe the initial set will itself be inconsistent or in some other way subtly incoherent. So perhaps we should be allowed to throw data out of the initial set should we discover that it is in some fashion incoherent. But, second, how do we know that there will be *only one* hypothesis stating non-trivial necessary and sufficient conditions for proper basicality which will pass the test posed by the data in the initial set? If the initial set is finite and our hypotheses are universally quantified, as the classical foundationalist's criteria are, then the data in the initial set will underdetermine the truth of hypotheses. In that case, there may very well be several interesting hypotheses which all pass the test posed by the data in the initial set and yet disagree radically about the proper basicality of examples outside the initial set. So perhaps we should also be allowed to add data to the initial set if this will help us to eliminate at least some of those hypotheses that have passed the test posed by the data in the initial set. These considerations make one thing very clear. Plantinga has so far given us only the rough outlines of the first stage of a broadly inductive procedure for arriving at a uniquely justified criterion of proper basicality. Many more details would need to be filled in before we could have any rational assurance that correct application of the procedure would yield exactly one hypothesis about conditions necessary and sufficient for proper basicality that are inductively best supported by, or most firmly based upon, the data in the initial set or in some suitable revision of the initial set.

But, rough though it be, Plantinga's sketch of the first stage of a procedure for justifying criteria of proper basicality is nonetheless well enough developed to permit us to see that it confronts at the outset at least one important difficulty. This is because, as Plantinga himself acknowledges, there is no reason to assume in advance that everyone will agree on what is to go into the initial set. Plantinga says:

> The Christian will of course suppose that belief in God is entirely proper and rational; if he doesn't accept this belief on the basis of other propositions, he will conclude that it is basic for him and quite properly so. Followers of Bertrand Russell and Madelyn Murray O'Hare (*sic!*) may disagree, but how is that relevant? Must my criteria, or those of the Christian community, conform to their examples? Surely not. The Christian community is responsible to its set of examples, not to theirs.[4]

The difficulty is, of course, that this is a game any number can play. Followers of Muhammed, followers of Buddha, and even followers of the Reverend Moon can join in the fun. Even the modern foundationalist can play. When a modern foundationalist, under optimal conditions for visual perception, seems to see a green beachball in front of her, she can claim that one thing which is obviously properly basic for her then is this:

(3) I am being appeared to greenly.

And one thing which is obviously not properly basic for her then, she can say, is this:

(4) I am seeing a green beachball.

After all, as she sees it, the proposition expressed by the latter sentence is for her then properly based, at least in part, on the proposition expressed by the former. And she can then mimic Plantinga's own argument in this fashion: "Followers of G. E. Moore and Alvin Plantinga may disagree, but how is that relevant? Must my criteria, or those of the community of modern foundationalists, conform to their examples? Surely not. The community of modern foundationalists is responsible to its set of examples, not to theirs." It would seem that what is sauce for Russell's goose should also be sauce for Plantinga's gander. Turn about *is*, in this case, fair play.

Ad hominem arguments to one side, the problem is that fidelity to the data in an initial set constructed from intuitions about what is obvious is a very weak constraint on the justification of a criterion for proper basicality. The modern foundationalist can easily choose the data in his or her initial set so that his or her criterion for proper basicality passes the test they pose by making sure (1) that only beliefs that nearly everyone would admit are, in the associated conditions, incorrigible or self-evident are the first members of positive data, and (2) that all beliefs that nearly everyone would, in the associated conditions, not consider incorrigible or self-evident are either the first members of negative data or outside the initial set altogether. How is this to be accomplished?

Suppose a modern foundationalist is contemplating believing that she is being appeared to redly in conditions optimal for visual experience in which she is being appeared to redly. Surely she can plausibly say that it is self-evident to her that that belief would be properly basic for her in those conditions, and clearly she can also reasonably claim that it is self-evident to her that that belief would be self-evident to her in those conditions. Now suppose the same modern foundationalist is contemplating believing that Jove is expressing disapproval in conditions optimal for auditory experience in which she is being appeared to thunderously. Surely she can plausibly say that it is self-evident to her that that belief would not be properly basic for her in those conditions, and clearly she can also reasonably claim that it is self-evident to her that that belief would be neither incorrigible for nor self-evident to her in those conditions. After having assembled a rich initial set of positive and negative data by ringing the changes on these two thought experiments, the modern foundationalist is then in a position to claim, and properly so, that his or her criterion, though not itself properly basic, is properly based, in accord with what Plantinga has told us about proper procedures for justifying criteria for proper basicality, on beliefs that are properly basic by its own lights.

It is important to understand that the data I am supposing the modern foundationalist might use to justify his or her criterion of proper basicality derive from thought experiments about hypothetical situations. My claim is not that when, for instance, a person in fact believes that Jove is expressing disapproval in conditions optimal for auditory experience in which she is being appeared to thunderously, it will then in fact be self-evident to her that that belief is not properly basic for her in those conditions. After all, she may not even wonder whether that belief is properly basic for her in those conditions when she happens to have the belief in the conditions. Rather my claim is that when a modern foundationalist contemplates the hypothetical situation of believing that Jove is expressing disapproval in conditions optimal for auditory experience in which she is being appeared to thunderously, then she can with plausibility maintain that it is self-evident to her that that belief would not in those conditions be properly basic for her. Because I hold that our intuitions about such hypothetical situations often provide the ultimate and decisive test of philosophical generalizations, I think the role of such beliefs about hypothetical situations in confirming or disconfirming philosophical generalizations is best explained on the supposition that they can be, in the right circumstances, self-evident.

In discussion, Plantinga has objected to this line of argument. If I understand his objection, it goes as follows. To say that a belief is properly basic in a set of circumstances is to say, among other things, that in those circumstances a person could accept the belief without displaying some kind of noetic defect. But what constitutes a noetic defect depends upon what constitutes the proper working of one's noetic equipment. So a proposition to the effect that a certain person on a certain occasion is displaying no such defect cannot possibly be self-evident because it cannot be self-evident to one that all one's noetic equipment is in proper working order. Hence, a proposition to the effect that a certain belief is properly basic on a certain occasion cannot possibly be self-evident either.

I concede, of course, that it is not usually self-evident to one that all one's noetic equipment is in proper working order. But if Plantinga's objection is to have any force against my argument, it must apply to the particular hypothetical case I have described above. I believe it does not. Our modern foundationalist is supposed to be contemplating believing that she is being appeared to redly in conditions optimal for visual experience in which she is being appeared to redly. It seems quite clear to me that it could be self-evident to her that she would display no noetic defect in accepting that belief in those conditions. To be sure, her noetic equipment might then have some defects of which she was unaware. She might then, for example, not be able to recognize the taste of ordinary table salt. But that is irrelevant provided she would display none of these defects in accepting the belief that she is being appeared to redly in the specified circumstances. For all that is required is that it could be self-evident to her that she would display no such defect in accepting that belief in those circumstances. Because I believe this requirement can be met, I conclude that Plantinga's objection fails. In short it can be self-evident to one that one is displaying no noetic defect in accepting a certain belief on a certain occasion without it also being self-evident to one then that all one's noetic equipment is in proper working order.

I do not expect that this reply will bring Plantinga's objections to an end. I suspect Plantinga will continue to think the modern foundationalist has made some mistake if he or she proceeds in this fashion to justify his or her criterion for proper basicality. But it is not obvious that this is so; nor is it obvious what precisely the mistake might be. After all, one of the rules of the game specifies that the community of modern foundationalists is permitted to be responsible to its set of examples. Hence, absent a good argument by Plantinga which establishes that a mistake must occur in such a procedure, I think we are entitled to hold that Plantinga's own procedure for justifying criteria for proper basicality provides no better reason for adopting criteria according to which some propositions which self-evidently entail the existence of God can be properly basic than for adopting a criterion, namely, the one proposed by the modern foundationalist, according to which no such propositions can be properly basic.

Of course, nothing I have said rules out the possibility that Plantinga could use the inductive procedure he advocates to justify a criterion of proper basicality according to which some propositions which self-evidently entail that God exists can be properly basic. Indeed, if, as his talk about being responsible to the examples of the Christian community suggests, he would take some such propositions to be the first members of positive data in his initial set and thereafter not delete all such positive data in revising his initial set, it is pretty obvious that Plantinga can succeed in this task, though success at so cheap a price may be thought by some to come uncomfortably close to question-begging. But if Plantinga does succeed in performing this exercise, then I think the conclusion we should draw is that his fight with classical foundationalism has resulted in a stand-off.

What If Belief in God Could Be Properly Basic?

If my critique of Plantinga has been successful, I have shown that he fails to prove that belief in propositions which self-evidently entail God's existence could ever be properly basic for anyone. But it might be true that belief in such propositions could be properly basic, even if Plantinga has not proved it. And if it were, what would be the consequences for religious epistemology? I now turn to an exploration of this issue.

Plantinga's examples of beliefs which could be properly basic in the right conditions include the following items:

(5) God is speaking to me.
(6) God disapproves of what I have done.

and

(7) God forgives me for what I have done.

And according to Plantinga, the right conditions include a component which is, broadly speaking, experiential. He says:

Upon reading the Bible, one may be impressed with a deep sense that God is speaking to him. Upon having done what I know is cheap, or wrong, or wicked I may feel guilty in God's sight and form the belief *God disapproves of what I've done.* Upon confession and repentance, I may feel forgiven, forming the belief *God forgives me for what I've done.*[5]

It strikes me that part of what makes the suggestion that beliefs like those expressed by (5)-(7) could be properly basic in conditions like those partially described in the quoted passage seem attractive is an analogy with an extremely plausible view about how certain Moore an commonsense beliefs are often justified. When I have the experience of seeming to see a hand in front of me in the right conditions, I may be justified in believing

(8) I see a hand in front of me.

This justification may be direct in the sense of being grounded directly in the experience itself without passing through the intermediary of a belief about the way I am being appeared to such as

(9) It seems to me that I see a hand in front of me.

For I may not in the circumstances have entertained, much less accepted, the proposition expressed by (9), but, on the view under consideration, my justification for believing the proposition expressed by (8) is in no way defective on that account. Hence, the proposition expressed by (8) may be basic, and quite properly so, in the right conditions. And if this is, as I believe it to be, an attractive view about how believing the proposition expressed by (8) can be, and sometimes is, justified, then there is an argument from analogy for supposing that propositions like those expressed by (5)-(7) may also be properly basic in conditions which include an experiential component of the right sort for grounding such beliefs. To be sure, there are significant disanalogies. The direct justification of the belief expressed by (8) is grounded in a mode of sensory experience which is now generally believed by non-skeptical epistemologists to be reliable in the right conditions. By contrast, the direct justification of the beliefs expressed by (5)-(7) is grounded in a mode of experience which, though it may be reliable in the right conditions, is not now generally believed by non-skeptical epistemologists to be so. But, although such considerations might be taken to show that the analogical argument is not very strong, it does not deprive the positive analogy of heuristic and explanatory capabilities. I am going to make use of these capabilities in the remainder of the discussion.

When I have the experience of seeming to see a hand in front of me in the right conditions, though the proposition expressed by (8) could then be properly basic for me, it could instead be the case that the proposition expressed by (9) is then properly basic for me and the proposition expressed by (8) is then properly based, at least in part, on the proposition expressed by (9). For when I have that experience in those conditions, I might well be attending mainly to the qualitative aspects of my visual experience with the result that the proposition expressed by (9) is then basic for me. If this happens, the proposition expressed by (9) would clearly be properly basic for me. I might well also then base the proposition expressed by (8) in part on the proposition expressed by (9). And, if this too happens, then the proposition expressed by (8) would be properly based, in part, on the proposition expressed by (9) because the latter proposition does nothing more than serve to articulate that part of the content of my visual experience which is relevant to justifying the former. If the proposition expressed by (8) were indirectly justified by being properly based on the proposition expressed by (9), it would be no less well justified than if it were directly justified by being directly grounded in visual experience. Since, by hypothesis, my visual experience in those conditions suffices to confer a certain degree of justification on the proposition expressed by (8), the amount of justification that reaches the proposition expressed by (8) from that experience will not be less in those conditions if it passes by way of the proposition expressed by (9) than if it is transmitted directly without intermediary. But neither would its justification be any better if indirect in this way. Moreover, it could happen that at a certain time the proposition expressed by (8) is properly basic for me and at a later time it is no longer properly basic, though still justified, for me because in the interval it has come to be properly based on the proposition expressed by (9). For in the interval I might, for example, have come to wonder whether I was justified in believing the proposition expressed by (8) and as a result come to believe the proposition expressed by (9) and to base properly on this belief my belief in the proposition expressed by (8). And if such a process did occur, I think the degree to which the proposition expressed by (8) was justified for me would, other things remaining unaltered, stay constant through it.

By analogy, similar things seem true of the examples that are Plantinga's prime candidates for religious beliefs which could be properly basic. When I am impressed with a deep sense that God is speaking to me, if the proposition expressed by (5) could then be properly basic for me, then it could instead be the case that some other proposition is among those then properly basic for me and the proposition expressed by (5) is then properly based in part on it. Such a proposition is:

(10)   It seems to me that God is speaking to me.

If the proposition expressed by (5) were indirectly justified for me by being properly based on the proposition expressed by (10), its justification would be no better, and no worse, than if it were properly basic and directly justified for me by being directly grounded in my experiential sense that God is speaking to me, other things remaining the same. And it could happen that in the course of time the proposition expressed by (5) changes from being properly basic for me to being properly based in part for me on the proposition expressed by (10) without gain or loss of degree of justification.

So, oddly enough, if certain propositions which self-evidently entail the existence of God can be properly basic for a person at a time, it is epistemically unimportant whether such propositions actually are properly basic for that person at that time. Without loss of degree of justification, such theistic propositions can just as well be properly based, at least in part, on others which are descriptive of the person's experience at the time and are then properly basic for the person. Although such theistic propositions would not need to be based on the evidence of other propositions, they always could be so based. So the cautious philosopher who did so base them would be every bit as justified in believing in the existence of God as the reckless mystic who did not.

There is another salient feature of directly justified Moorean beliefs like the one expressed by (8) which would have an analogue in the case of religious beliefs like those expressed by (5)-(7) if they could be properly basic in the right conditions. This is that the kind of justification conferred on such Moorean beliefs by direct grounding in experience of the right sort is defeasible. So, for example, a potential defeater for the proposition expressed by (8) is this:

(11)   I am now hallucinating a hand.

If propositions such as (8) are taken to be properly basic in the right conditions, then a full specification of those conditions must include reference to the status of potential defeaters such as (11). What would it be reasonable to say about potential defeaters when specifying in fuller detail the right conditions for proper basicality of the proposition expressed by (8)? Several possibilities come to mind.

It might be suggested that conditions are right for the proposition expressed by (8) to be properly basic for me only if none of its potential defeaters is true. This suggestion clearly misses the mark. When I have the experience of seeming to see a hand in front of me, it may be that the proposition expressed by (8) is true and the proposition expressed by (11) is false, and yet I am justified in rejecting the former and accepting the latter because, for instance, I remember taking a large dose of some hallucinogen only an hour ago and hallucinating wildly in the interval. Merely to insist that potential defeaters be false in order for conditions to be right for proper basicality is to require much too little.

Alternatively, it might be suggested that conditions are right for the proposition expressed by (8) to be properly basic for me only if each of its potential defeaters is such that I have some reason to think it is false. Clearly this suggestion errs in the direction of demanding too much. I have never exhaustively enumerated the potential defeaters of the proposition expressed by (8), and I am inclined to doubt that I would ever complete such a task if I began it. I have certainly never mobilized or acquired a reason against each of them. No one I know has ever tried to do such a thing in defense of all of his or her Moorean common sense beliefs. So if such beliefs frequently are properly basic in virtue of being directly grounded in sensory experience, as I think they are, conditions are often right for proper basicality without such an elaborate structure of reasons for the falsity of potential defeaters having been mobilized.

It does, however, seem initially plausible to suppose that conditions are right for the proposition expressed by (8) to be properly basic for me only if I have no sufficiently substantial reasons to think that any of its potential defeaters is true and this is not due to epistemic negligence on my part. Two features of this claim require a bit of explanation. First, if the only reason I have to think that some potential defeater of the proposition expressed by (8) is true is, for instance, that I remember once, long ago, having mistaken a tree's branches for a hand, then that will not usually suffice to undermine the *prima facie* justification the proposition expressed by (8) has in the right experiential conditions to such an extent that that proposition is not properly basic. More generally, since *prima facie* justification comes in degrees, although any good reason one has for thinking one of a proposition's potential defeaters is true will undermine that proposition's *prima facie* justification to some degree, slight reasons will usually not singly undermine it to the extent that it is no longer *prima facie* justified. Instead, it will usually remain *prima facie* justified in the presence of one or a few such reasons but to a lesser degree than it would be in their absence. It takes a sufficiently substantial reason for thinking one of its potential defeaters is true to rob a proposition of proper basicality in conditions in which it would otherwise be properly basic.[6] Second, if I happen to lack sufficiently substantial reasons to think that any potential defeater of the proposition expressed by (8) is true merely because, for example, I have negligently failed to recall that I ingested some hallucinogenic substance only an hour ago and have been hallucinating wildly in the interval, then clearly conditions are not right for the proposition expressed by (8) to be properly basic for me, even though it may in fact be basic for me. More generally, a proposition is not *prima facie* justified if one negligently ignores good reasons for thinking one of its potential defeaters is true which would be sufficiently substantial to undermine the proposition's *prima facie* justification to such an extent that it would not be *prima facie* justified. Such epistemic negligence would constitute an epistemic deficiency.

By analogy, it also seems initially plausible to say that conditions are right for the propositions expressed by (5)-(7) to be properly basic for me only if I have no sufficiently substantial reasons to think that any of their potential defeaters is true and this is not due to epistemic negligence on my part. But there is the rub. A potential defeater of the propositions expressed by (5)-(7) is this:

(12)   God does not exist.

And, unfortunately, I do have very substantial reasons for thinking that the proposition expressed by (12) is true. My reasons derive mainly from one of the traditional problems of evil. What I know, partly from experience and partly from testimony, about the amount and variety of non-moral evil in the universe confirms highly for me the proposition expressed by (12). Of course, this is not indefensible confirmation of the proposition expressed by (12). It could be defeated by other things I do not know. Perhaps it is not even undefeated confirmation. Maybe it even is defeated by other things I do know. Nevertheless, it does furnish me with a very substantial reason for thinking that the proposition expressed by (12) is true. Moreover, I dare say that many, perhaps most, intellectually sophisticated adults in our culture are in an epistemic predicament similar to mine. As I see it, an intellectually sophisticated adult in our culture would have to be epistemically negligent not to have very substantial reasons for thinking that what (12) expresses is true. After all, non-trivial atheological reasons, ranging from various problems of evil to naturalistic theories according to which theistic belief is illusory or merely projective, are a pervasive, if not obtrusive, component of the rational portion of our cultural heritage.

But, even if such reasons are very substantial, are they sufficiently substantial to make it the case that the propositions expressed by (5)-(7) would no longer be properly basic in conditions of the sort described by Plantinga in which, we are supposing, they could have been properly basic but for the presence of such substantial reasons? On reflection, I am convinced that such reasons are, taken collectively, sufficiently substantial, though I confess with regret that I cannot at present back up my intuitive conviction with solid arguments. But I conjecture that many, perhaps most, intellectually sophisticated adults in our culture will share my intuitive conviction on this point. And so I conclude that many, perhaps most, intellectually sophisticated adult theists in our culture are seldom, if ever, in conditions which are right for propositions like those expressed by (5)-(7) to be properly basic for them.

It does not follow from this conclusion that intellectually sophisticated adult theists in our culture cannot be justified in believing propositions like those expressed by (5)-(7). For all that I have said, some such propositions are such that, for every single one of their potential defeaters which is such that there is some very substantial reason to think it is true, there is an even better reason to think it is false. And so, for all I know, some intellectually sophisticated adult theists in our culture could be, or perhaps even are, in the fortunate position, with respect to some such propositions and their potential defeaters, of having, for each potential defeater which some epistemically non-negligent, intellectually sophisticated adult in our culture has a very substantial reason to think is true, an even better reason to think it is false. But if there are such fortunate theists in our culture, they are people who have already accomplished at least one of the main tasks traditionally assigned to natural theology. Although they may know of no proof of the existence of God, they possess reasons good enough to defend some proposition which self-evidently entails the existence of God against all of its potential defeaters which epistemically non-negligent, intellectually sophisticated adults in our culture have very substantial reasons to believe. I tend to doubt that many intellectually sophisticated adult theists in our culture are in this fortunate position for any appreciable portion of their lives.

But suppose someone were in this fortunate position. Such a person would have reasons good enough to defend theistic belief against all of its potential defeaters which epistemically non-negligent, intellectually sophisticated adults in our culture have very substantial reasons to believe, and such reasons would be parts of such a person's total case for the rationality of theistic belief. But would such a person's theistic belief have to be based on such reasons? That depends, of course, on exactly what is involved in basing one belief on others Plantinga is prudently reticent about describing the basing relation; he says only that, "although this relation isn't easy to characterize in a revealing and non-trivial fashion, it is nonetheless familiar."[7] On the basis of the examples Plantinga gives,

I once conjectured in discussion that he thinks the relation is characterized by something like the following principle:

(13) For any person S and distinct propositions p and q, S believes q on the basis of p only if S entertains p, S accepts p, S infers q from p, and S accepts q.[8]

If Plantinga does have in mind some such narrow conception of the basing relation, then our hypothetical fortunate person's theistic belief clearly need not be based on all the reasons, including defenses against potential defeaters which, have very substantial support, in the person's total case for the rationality of theistic belief. After all, some such defenses may consist only of considerations which show that certain atheological arguments are unsound or otherwise defective, and our fortunate person's belief need not be based, in this narrow sense, on such considerations. Indeed, for all I know, it is possible that all our fortunate person's successful defenses against potential defeaters which have substantial support are of this sort. Hence, for all I know, our fortunate person could have a successful total case for the rationality of theistic belief made up entirely of reasons such that belief in some proposition which self-evidently entails the existence of God needs none of them for a basis. Thus, for all I know, on this narrow conception of the basing relation, our fortunate person's theistic belief might be properly basic in the right conditions.

If I were to endorse some such narrow conception of the basing relation, I would have to revise my earlier proposal about when it is plausible to suppose conditions are right for propositions to be properly basic for me. I am inclined to believe that the appropriate thing to say, in light of the line of reasoning developed in the previous paragraph, is that it seems plausible to suppose that conditions are right for propositions like those expressed by (5)-(7) to be, in the narrow sense, properly basic for me only if (i) either I have no sufficiently substantial reason to think that any of their potential defeaters is true, or I do have some such reasons but, for each such reason I have, I have an even better reason for thinking the potential defeater in question is false, and (ii), in either case, my situation involves no epistemic negligence on my part. I could then put the point I am intent on pressing by saying that, depending on which of the two disjuncts in the first clause of this principle one imagines me satisfying, I would have to be non-negligently either rather naive and innocent or quite fortunate and sophisticated in order for conditions to be right for propositions like those expressed by (5)-(7) to be, in the narrow sense, properly basic for me. When I examine my epistemic predicament, I find myself forced to conclude that I am in neither of those extreme situations. Since I have very substantial reasons for thinking the proposition expressed by (12) is true, innocence has been lost. But, because I have not yet done enough to defend theistic belief against potential defeaters which have substantial support, I have not reached the position of our hypothetical fortunate person. Innocence has not, so to speak, been regained. Hence, conditions are not now right for propositions like those expressed by (5)-(7) to be, in the narrow sense, properly basic for me. My conjecture is that many, perhaps most, intellectually sophisticated persons in our culture are in an epistemic predicament similar to mine in this respect for most of their adult lives.

There is, of course, nothing wrong with construing the basing relation in some such narrow fashion provided one is tolerably clear about what one is doing. Surely there is such a relation, and Plantinga is free to use it in his theories if he wishes. But I think it may be more perspicuous, or at least equally illuminating, to look at matters in a slightly different way. Consider again our hypothetical fortunate person who has reasons good enough to defend theistic belief against all of its potential defeaters which epistemically non-negligent, intellectually sophisticated adults in our culture have very substantial reasons to believe. I would say that, for such a person, theistic belief would be based, in a broad sense, on all the reasons which are parts of the person's total case for the rationality of theistic belief. In employing this broad conception of the basing relation, I am aiming to draw attention to the fact that, if the person did not have all those reasons and were like many, perhaps most, intellectually sophisticated adults in our culture, theistic belief would not be rational for the person, or at least its rationality would be diminished to an appreciable extent if some of those reasons were absent. On this broad conception of the basing relation, I would not need to revise the principle concerning the right conditions for certain propositions to be, in the broad sense, properly basic for me, to which I had ascribed initial plausibility, in order to accommodate the hypothetical fortunate person, for the fortunate person's theistic belief would be, in the broad sense, properly based on all the reasons which comprise his or her total case for the rationality of theistic belief. Reasons which are, in the broad sense, part of a basis for theistic belief need not be related to a proposition which self-evidently entails the existence of God in the same way that the premises of an inference are related to its conclusion. They may instead provide part of a basis for theistic belief roughly in the same way a physicist's demonstration that the so-called "clock paradox" does not reveal an inconsistency in Special Relativity provides part of a basis for Special Relativity. Or, to cite what may be a more helpful analogy in the present context, they may provide part of a basis for theistic belief in much the same way Richard Swinburne's argument in *The Coherence of Theism* that the claim that God exists is not demonstrably incoherent provides part of the basis for Swinburne's claim in *The Existence of God* that God's existence is more probable than not.[9] And if I am right about the epistemic predicament of many, perhaps most, intellectually sophisticated adult theists in our culture, for them theistic belief stands in need of at least some basis of this kind if it is to be rational. This may, in the end, be a point on which Plantinga and I have a disagreement which is not merely verbal. I would insist, and Plantinga, for all I know, might not, that many, perhaps most, intellectually sophisticated adult theists in our culture must, if their belief in God is to be rational, have a total case for the rationality of theistic belief which includes defenses against defeaters which have very substantial support.

Conclusion

If theistic belief can be *prima facie* justified by experience at all, then there may be less difference between Plantinga and his opponents than one might at first have thought.[10]   Plantinga locates a proper doxastic foundation for theistic belief at the level of propositions like that expressed by (5); a modern foundationalist would wish to claim that there is a subbasement in the truly proper doxastic structure at the level of propositions like that expressed by (10).

Plantinga's view has the advantage of psychological realism. I doubt that most theists generate their doxastic structures by first entertaining and accepting propositions like that expressed by (10) and then inferring from them, together perhaps with some epistemic principles, propositions like that expressed by (5). Nonetheless, I think there is something to be said on behalf of what I take to be an important insight captured by the modern foundationalist's position, though perhaps not perfectly articulated there. Although it may be a mistake to suppose that a phenomenological belief like the one expressed by (10) must always mediate between experience and a belief like the one expressed by (5) in a properly constructed structure of *prima facie* justification for a belief like the one expressed by (5), experience of the sort that could serve to ground a belief like the one expressed by (5) is itself so thoroughly shaped and penetrated by conceptual elements that, if it grounds a belief like the one expressed by (5) directly, then that belief is based on a cognitive state of the believer, even if that state is not an explicit belief with a phenomenological proposition for its object. Perhaps it is at the level of such cognitive states that we may hope to discover the real evidential foundations in experience for theistic belief.[11]

Brown University

Endnotes

[1] Alvin Plantinga, "Is Belief in God Properly Basic?" *Nous* 15 (1981). Additional discussion related to the charge that modern foundalionalism is self-referentially incoherent may be found in Alvin Plantinga, "Is Belief in God Rational?" *Rationality and Religious Belief*, ed. C. P. Delaney (Notre Dame: University of Notre Dame Press, 1979). Material from both these papers has subsequently been incorporated into Alvin Plantinga, "Rationality and Religious Belief," *Contemporary Philosophy of Religion*, ed. Steven M. Cahn and David Shatz (New York: Oxford University Press, 1982). And some of the same themes are further amplified in Alvin Plantinga, "Reason and Belief in God," *Faith and Rationality*, ed. Alvin Plantinga and Nicholas Wolterstorff (Notre Dame: University of Notre Dame Press, 1983).

[2] Plantinga, "Is Belief in God Properly Basic?" p. 49.

[3] Ibid., p. 50.

[4] *Idem.*

[5] Ibid., p. 40.

[6] I came to appreciate this point as a result of reflecting on comments by Jonathan Malino and William P. Alston.

[7] Plantinga, "Is Belief in God Properly Basic?"; p. 41.

[8] In a more thorough treatment, it would be important to worry about the temporal references in this principle. If I have just looked up the spelling of 'umbrageous' in my dictionary, then my belief about how that word is spelled may now be based on my belief about what my dictionary says. But if I last looked up its spelling many months ago, then my belief about how 'umbrageous' is spelled may now only be based on my belief that I seem to remember seeing it spelled that way in *some dictionary or other*. Presumably bases of the sort specified by this principle can and sometimes do shift with time.

[9] See Richard Swinburne, *The Coherence of Theism* (Oxford: Clarendon Press, 1977) and Richard Swinburne, *The Existence of God* (Oxford: Clarendon Press, 1979).

[10] A recent defense of the view that theistic belief can be *prima facie* justified by experience of certain kinds may be found in William P. Alston, "Religious Experience and Religious Belief," *Nous* 16 (1982).

[11] Some of the material in this paper was included in comments on Plantinga's "Is Belief in God Properly Basic?" I read at the 1981 meeting of the Western Division of the American Philosophical Association. Robert Audi was the other commentator on Plantinga's paper. Earlier versions of the present paper were read in 1984 at the Greensboro Symposium on the Logic of Religious Concepts, where Jonathan Malino was my commentator, and at the University of Notre Dame, where Alvin Plantinga was my commentator. In making various revisions, I have profited by the comments of Audi, Malino and Plantinga and also by written criticism from William P. Alston, Roderick M. Chisholm, George I. Mavrodes and Ernest Sosa.

Study Questions

1.   What does Plantinga mean by the claim that modern foundationalism is "self-referentially incoherent"? Why does Quinn disagree? Which one do you think is right? Why?

2. What are "properly basic propositions" for Plantinga? What does Quinn see wrong with Plantinga's position on the matter?

3. What if belief in God could be properly basic? What does Quinn say about this prospect?

4. On the issues raised regarding the idea of properly basic, which line do you see as stronger, Quinn's or Plantinga's? Why?

5. How would you characterize Classical Foundationalism?

8

Technological Faith
and Christian Doubt

Frederick Ferré

Frederick Ferré is professor of philosophy at the University of Georgia, and is author of *Language, Logic and God*.

Technology, an object of little-considered but intense faith in our modern civilization, has long posed deep problems for Biblical thought. If technology is defined broadly enough, Christian attitudes toward it illuminate conflicting responses to culture itself.* Should technology be regarded as liberating (Cox) or strictly in the domain of sin (Ellul)?

Christian thought needs more clear thinking about technology. What cognitive style, what fundamental values, ought "Christian" technologies to embody? Theologically informed technology assessment will not only help guide society toward a better future and but also give Christians the basis for making ethically sound practical choices today.

Some day historians may look back on the 20th century as an age of unusual faith. I am not now referring to the dramatic revivals of fundamentalism, Jewish, Christian, and Muslim, in the latter decades of the century. Those revivals I take to be primarily reactions against the dominant faith of the century. That dominant faith itself has been an all-pervading and blissful trust in technology. There are many among us who still hardly recognize the degree to which technological faith has characterized our age, but this obliviousness tends to confirm the thesis, since ages tend not to be self-aware of the basic premises on which they stand.

Technological Faith

The gradual awareness of a ubiquitous faith generally emerges together with challenges to it. This was spectacularly true in Christendom at the time of the great Lisbon earthquake, for example, which was used by Voltaire in *Candide* as an occasion for satire against Leibnizian theodicy. Equivalent massive shocks to naïve technological faith have been administered to our culture recently by the epoch-marking events we remember as Three Mile Island and Chernobyl. How could these have happened? How could "they," the experts, have allowed such a breakdown in the order of things? The same sort of pain and searching, amounting to nothing less than a crisis of faith, is observed after major air tragedies, when the computerized efficiency of the air transport system betrays us. Above all, the agony of the *Challenger* explosion before the horrified eyes of millions, with its still-continuing aftermath of recrimination and soul-searching, may stand as a symbol of the spiritual torment of our time, caught unwillingly as many are in recognition that a world-view is in jeopardy. The efforts of the priesthood of the established order, the parade of NASA officials and astronauts and the President himself, reaffirming the creeds of technological faith and urging the continuing validity of technological imperatives, have done little to provide needed balm.

So much has been staked on technological faith that the levels of anxiety produced by discovering that it has, indeed, been faith all along are inevitably high. It would be tedious and unnecessary to enumerate the ways. One obvious example, however, is the faith our society has shown in the ability of the technical experts to cope successfully with nuclear wastes that are now building up and have built up for decades without any really effective solution for the mind-boggling long run over which they need to be safely stored, insulated from the biosphere for tens of thousands of years. Despite warnings, we went ahead with nuclear technology, creating these wastes at an ever-accelerating rate, with the blissful confidence that "they" would come up with a solution—it did not matter that "they" themselves did not ("yet") know just how it would be done. What could be a more touching act of faith? Not only was it a *sacrificium intellectus*, it showed a readiness to sacrifice the future safety of all life on the planet on the blessed assurance that a technological fix would somehow, over more millennia than any civilization has ever been sustained, take care of us and our progeny to the end of time.

Other examples could be given, like the faith that environmental degradation, acid rain, the ozone hole, the greenhouse effect, resource depletion, food production, population control, protection from accidents of biotechnology, the answer to AIDS—all can be entrusted to technological providence. But more examples are not necessary. It is abundantly clear that our civilization is grounded deep on faith and has committed itself, far beyond lip-service, to its creed. When we think about death, our immediate recourse is to medical research, to organ transplants, to the deep freeze of a temporary cryogenic limbo while we await technological resurrection. When we think about sin, we turn to technologies of behavior modification and chemical cures. When we think about providence, we trust in technological progress. We even find evangelists for fusion energy competing with other cults in airports, our contemporary temples. The 20th century may indeed be remembered as an age of unusual faith.

Christian Doubts

Against this faith, however, there has been a long tradition of Christian doubt. Sometimes it appears in amusing ways, as in the earnest debates experienced by my father as a young man in Minnesota over lightning rods. Was it a sin to put lightning rods on one's house and barns? Should God's threat from the skies be deflected by the work of human hands? The theological depth of a position that worries about omnipotence being hindered by a piece of metal and a grounding wire may be questioned, but the general doubt about placing one's faith in technology comes through loud and clear.

This perennial worry is dug deep into the biblical tradition. We find it vividly in the story of the Tower of Babel. There human technological prowess is depicted as a challenge to God. The tower, which was to have its "top in the heavens" (Genesis 11:4, RSV), was just a sample of what human beings could do if they should remain united on a technical project:

> And the Lord said, "Behold, they are one people, and they have all one language, and this is only the beginning of what they will do; and nothing that they propose to do will now be impossible for them" (Genesis 11:6, RSV).

Such prowess was clearly not permissible, so clearly that no reason is thought necessary to be given for its impermissibility.

More generally, the technologies of civilization itself—the word "civil" itself coming from the Latin for "city"—are deeply suspect in the early stories of scripture. Who, after all, is responsible for the first city? It was the major artifact of the murderous Cain.

> Then Cain went away from the presence of the Lord, and dwelt in the land of Nod, east of Eden . . . and he built a city, and called the name of the city after the name of his son, Enoch (Genesis 4:16-17, RSV).

Thus civilization itself bears the mark of Cain. The theme of the wicked city—Sodom, Nineveh, Babylon—runs as a deep pedal point through the biblical saga. We are situated by these stories just outside the urban technological enterprise, positioned with the viewpoint of a suspicious desert nomad looking askance at the corruption brought about by too much ease and by too much fancy know-how.

My honored professor of Old Testament, Philip Hyatt, extended this viewpoint still further, arguing that the "knowledge of good and evil" against which Adam and Eve were warned in the Garden of Eden could not have been knowledge of *moral* good and evil, since to have been able to know that it was "wrong" to eat the fruit of the forbidden tree required prior *moral* comprehension of exactly the same sort. Instead, the forbidden fruit had to be a kind of knowledge that both characterizes God and might be considered wrong to fall into human possession. This double criterion rules out the silly notion that *sexual* knowledge was at issue, since such knowledge could hardly lead to becoming "like God" (Genesis 3:5, RSV). If not sexual and not moral, then perhaps the essence of the forbidden fruit was *technical* knowledge—how to do "good and evil" things, as God only properly should know how to do. The original sin, on the Hyatt hypothesis, would be technical hubris.

This is, of course, highly speculative. It is an interesting speculation, however, despite its variance from the received tradition in which moral, not technological, innocence was lost in Eden. It does cohere well with many other biblical themes, and with myths of other cultures, like the Prometheus story in which fire, the symbol of technological capacity, was stolen from heaven at great cost for human benefit. If it is at all correct, it would place biblical religion on an unalterable collision course not only with technological faith but also with technology itself.

The Great Debate

Christian doubts about technological faith, as a rival religious commitment, have not always led Christians to reject the technological *enterprise* as such. On the contrary, there are among recent articulators of Christian faith strong defenders of the legitimacy of, even the theological mandate for, technology.

One of these voices was that of Harvey Cox. Though Cox himself has become more cautious since *The Secular City* was published in 1965,[2] the book stands as a reminder that Christians may not always feel obliged to stand aloof from the technological world—what Cox calls the "technopolis"—to which they have contributed so much. In fact, if Cox's reading of scripture is correct, biblical spirituality was the key factor in freeing the human spirit from domination by local goblins and allowing the full technological expression of human intelligence to get under way. In the Hebrew-Christian scriptures it is made perfectly clear that God, the only proper object of worship, is not nature but is the transcendent creator of nature. This liberating realization of the transcendence of the sacred had the effect of "desacralizing" the natural resources needed by technological society. God's clarion call to humanity, that we "subdue the earth," made Christianity the primary spiritual vehicle for the coming of the present age.

To Cox's Protestant position can be added the Roman Catholic views of Norris Clarke. Clarke chooses a different theological starting place. He does not begin with the "disenchantment" of nature but with the story of the creation of Adam and Eve in the "image" of God. If humanity is to live up to its status, reflecting in a lesser way the character of God, then the human mission must include God's aspect both as contemplator and as creative worker. As Clarke writes:

> . . . God is at once contemplative and active. He has not only thought up the material universe, with all its intricate network of laws, but he has actively brought it into existence and supports and guides its vast pulsating network of forces. God is both a thinker and a worker, so to speak. So, too, man should imitate God his Father by both thinking and working in the world.[3]

The lesser human role is indicated by the fact that we do not, like God, create *ex nihilo*. Our materials must be found and simply refashioned. But the analogy between our technological work and God's making and doing remains valid. Moreover, Clarke points out, the biblical story of creation includes the human vocation to co-create with God. The first humans— significantly, before the Fall—were given a garden to "till and keep" (Genesis 2:15, RSV). The incarnate God-man, too, was depicted as a tool-user.

> Thus the labor of the young Jesus as a carpenter in Nazareth already lends, in principle, a divine Sanction to the whole technological activity of man through history.[4]

Clarke is conscious of the tendency of humans to abuse technological powers and to exploit them for selfish advantage. Cox, too, mentions this tendency but sets it aside as just immature, "essentially childish and...unquestionably a passing phase."[5] Clarke, in contrast, takes a darker view, acknowledging that theological interpretation of technology must not omit warnings against sin. Christians cannot be naive. Every aspect of human life and practice is subject to distortion and abuse. This is the sad legacy of the Fall. But, Clarke argues, such a warning is properly against the misuse of technology, not against the technological enterprise as a whole or in principle. A proper balance needs to be struck, he argues, so that

> the alert Christian, alive to the full implications of the Christian vision of man, will look on technology with a restrained and carefully qualified optimism, seeing it as at once a great potential good for man by nature and yet in the hands of fallen and selfish human nature an almost equally potent instrument for evil.[6]

A forceful theological counter-attack against any sort of technological optimism, "carefully qualified" or not, comes from Jacques Ellul, who founds his wholly different evaluation of technology on a different rendering of some of the same scriptural passages noted by Cox and Clarke. Ellul, a Calvinist, makes much of the radical break that entered history with the Fall. In paradise, before the estrangement that forced us to survive by the sweat of our brow, there was no laboring, no use of tools. It is impossible for us now, with sin-laden minds, to think back across the bottomless chasm of Original Sin to imagine how Adam and Eve "tilled and kept" the Garden of Eden. But Ellul uses a *reductio ad absurdum* argument to show how wrong it would be to imagine Adam and Eve working with tools in the Garden, as Clarke seems to suppose. "Keeping" or "guarding" Eden (different versions translate this word differently), could not—certainly not in paradise—have involved the use of swords or spears or other weapons. That much is ruled out by the total inappropriateness of armaments in God's pre-Fallen, perfect environment.

But if "guarding" allows of no weapons, then "tilling" allows of no farm machinery. If one is absurd, so is the other. If Paradise is to be even gropingly thought about as a true Paradise, Ellul concludes, we must resolutely omit technology from the picture.

> No cultivation was necessary, no care to add, no grafting, no labor, no anxiety. Creation spontaneously gave man what he needed, according to the order of God who had said, "I give you . . ." (Genesis 1:29).[7]

Technology, then, is *tout court* in the domain of sin. It had no place in Paradise and arose only because of the Fall. To think of human efforts as "co-creating" with God, Ellul holds, is blasphemy. God's creative activity before the Fall was not in need of completing or perfecting. We must not, in our pride over our human technological abilities, forget that "creation as God made it, as it left his hands, was *perfect and finished*."[8] We put on airs when we tell ourselves that we are "working along with" God. If it had not been for human sin, there would have been no need for technology, because "God's work was accomplished, . . . it was complete, . . . there was nothing to add."[9] Ellul's theological condemnation of the technological imperative is complete. In his well-known sociological analyses he makes further important distinctions between the tools of the craft traditions and the all-devouring efficiencies of modern "technique." The former are less objectionable, though by no means theologically mandated; the latter are demonic and out of human control. Both as sociologist and as theologian, Ellul provides no comfort and gives no quarter to the defenders of technology.

Such an uncompromising prophetic voice seems to harmonize well with the Hyatt hypothesis and the chorus of suspicious or negative biblical attitudes we noticed earlier. But there is one serious defect in Ellul's position from a Christian standpoint: there is no final word of good news, no balancing affirmation of redemption to match the stern warnings of judgment and sin. A more balanced position is sought by Egbert Schuurman, another from the Calvinist tradition, when he argues that Ellul leaves us with despair, but that despair is not biblical. As Schuurman puts it:

> It is a constant consolation to know that man on his own and by himself cannot make the meaning of creation, the Kingdom of God, impossible. On the contrary, the fact that the kingdom of God is already on the way means that at any moment people may be converted and led once again to seek the Kingdom—even in a technological society.[10]

Refining the Issues

This swift survey of differing Christian views on the proper Christian stance toward technology and the technological society makes clear how urgently we need to develop our thinking in this area. Theologians can hardly set themselves a more potentially fruitful task than thinking deeply, in a sustained way, about the technological phenomenon from the standpoint of ultimate commitments. Christians seem unable to live comfortably with the technological dimension; but, equally, Christians today are certainly unable to live without it.

A generally acceptable definition of the concept of "technologies" would help this thinking process. To some, the concept seems self-evidently associated with the "high tech" of the 20th century, entailing that all before the industrial revolution be relegated to "crafts" instead of "technologies" proper. To others, the concept seems self-evidently associated with tools of any kind. To the former, technologies are indissolubly linked with science, with all the attitudinal ambivalences this linkage carries. To the latter, technologies are more pervasive, for better or for worse, in the character and typical expressions of the human species.

Without attempting to go into the arguments in any detail here,[11] perhaps a reconciling suggestion may be offered as follows: When we speak of "technologies" in general we must include all the ways in which intelligence implements practical purposes. To include less would be to create a conceptual bifurcation between past and present ways of implementing our purposes that would be insupportable by the evidence on objective reflection. Modern automobiles are different but not absolutely different, after all, from horse-drawn carriages or chariots. On the other hand, it is neither ethnocentric nor myopic to insist on recognizing the vast changes introduced into our practical means by the rise of modern science. A radio bears some but not much similarity, for example, to a jungle drum. Therefore the *genus*, "technology," will stand for all practical implementations of intelligence; the *differentia* will be the kind of intelligence involved, whether habitual-traditional, on the one hand ("craft" technologies), or analytical-scientific ("high" technologies) on the other.

Having a definition that firmly roots the technological phenomenon in human purposes and intelligence helps make it clear to the theologian that technology is nothing alien to the categories of theological discipline. Indeed, looked at in this way, coming to terms with technology is part of the age-old task of Christian faith coming to terms with culture itself. Christianity, and more generally biblical religion, has yet to complete the long process of defining itself unequivocally with respect to the works of human hands. The prophetic tradition, standing outside culture and thundering against its perceived defects, contrasts with the priestly tradition, serving inside culture and seeking to relate the ideals of religion to the realities of social life. Both are part of the fabric of biblical faith. How shall Christ be related to culture? What has Jerusalem to do with Athens? Sharply varying answers have long been given over culture in general, and varying answers should likewise be expected over technological culture, embodying, as it does, the characteristic values and knowledge of human beings at a given time and space.

Asking the question in a new way, however, and with a new sense of urgency, may elicit fresh degrees of clarity. When the question is put today in terms of perennial Christian doubts and modern technological faith, some things newly emerge. Above all, it becomes evident that the extremes will not hold for Christian thinkers. First, Christians cannot, without grave danger to their own faith, embrace the pagan quasi-religion of "technologism." Its anthropology is uncritical; its soteriology is unidimensional; its cosmology is reductionist. Placing unqualified confidence in the works of human hands is technolatry[12] unworthy of Christian conscience. But, second, Christians cannot, without abandoning vital aspects of their faith, participate in wholesale gnostic rejection of intelligent methods for dealing with the material order. Gnostic rejection of materiality is tantamount to the rejection of the reality of incarnation. Gnostic absolute dualisms of good and evil are tantamount to despair over the redeemability of all creation. Somehow the balance for Christians, between remembering human disobedience and trusting in divine redemption, between acknowledging the Fall and accepting the mandate to till a garden and fill a world, must be maintained. Anything less lacks something of the warnings—and the promises—of the full Christian message.

Toward Christian Technologies

A deeper, sustained meditation on the relationship between Christianity and technology, however, will need to press theologians and Christian philosophers to go beyond merely refining their reactions to the actualities of contemporary technological culture. Though no individual or group deliberately makes a culture, yet cultures are not given once and for all but are shaped and reshaped. Though the complex and integrated technologies of our era are not simple voluntary tools, to be picked up and set down at will, yet technologies evolve—sometimes quickly—as knowledge and values change. Is there meaning in the thought that Christian styles of knowledge and Christian fundamental values could inform the technologies of a future culture so pervasively and characteristically that it would be possible to speak of "Christian technologies" as well as "modern technologies" or "high technologies"?

The question rings oddly at first on our ears. We have no logical place for phrases like "Christian Mathematics" or "Christian physics." How, then, could there be a use for an expression like "Christian technologies"? And yet all technologies, as the practical implementations of intelligence, embody characteristic values that always go before and define practical aims. Every artifact is the incarnation of some value, positive or negative. The value may be obvious and widespread, like a preference for protection—from weather and predators and the embodiment of that evaluation in housing technologies. Or the value may be more esoteric, like appreciating a certain level of sonic quality and embodying that value in digital recording technologies. Every technological item is the implementation in this way of some aversion or adversion. The mere fact of it shows that someone, at some time, considered those values permissible and pursuable. By studying classes of technologies in this way we can discover what values are characteristic of a given culture, what sorts of things are at least not taboo. The food-related technologies of a vegetarian society, for example, will be quite different from those of a society of meat-eaters.

Values are one necessary condition for technologies, but values alone are obviously not sufficient to account for them. Simply valuing something will not automatically give us a means to its achievement. Every artifact is the embodiment not only of some value or values but also of some level of *knowledge*, if only the knowledge of an inherited tradition or rule of thumb. The style, what I have come recently to call the "epistemic norms," of such knowledge shows in its technological embodiment. Scientific knowledge, especially, with its emphasis on precision, on quantification, on analysis, may be seen incarnated in the high technologies of our time.[13] These technologies have tended to be powerful and efficient ("efficiency" is itself a concept and a value that reflects the style and norms of scientific knowing), pursuing a clear, often quantitative, objective with singular focus. Our high technologies, invented with Cartesian logic, have thus tended to produce "side effects" unanticipated by the linear methods of knowing that were used in designing them. These effects, in turn, require still more technological solutions, reminding us of the familiar way in which scientific answers lead endlessly to further unanswered questions. They have also tended to be justified by the "bottom line" of quantifiable, material considerations—often measured in money, sometimes in ever-higher speeds or in comparative megadeaths.

If Christianity is truly a distinctive way of thought and life, then what is wrong with Christian thinkers attempting to imagine together what technologies might represent the practical embodiment of characteristic Christian cognitive styles or epistemic norms, and of distinctive Christian values? This, perhaps, is the sense in which it might after all be meaningful to speak of possible "Christian technologies."

Is there a characteristic Christian cognitive style? The question is debatable, since there are so many strands of thought woven into the Christian tapestry. But it might be argued that Christian knowledge, whatever else might characterize it, would at least be *respectful of the integrity of the object known*. This entails that the ways of knowing used by the intensely committed officers of the Inquisition were not Christian. If this is a paradox, so be it. But if it is correct, the normative Christian cognitive style would be compassionate and warm, not remote and cool as has been the approved paradigm for modern knowers since Descartes. It would also, in consequence, be reluctant to cut up wholes in all effort to know the parts out of their relationships. We might call this cognitive style *compassionate holism*.

Is there a distinctive dominant Christian value? Again, debates may be expected, since visions of the essence of Christianity differ. But one long tradition, to which I adhere, has held that agapé, self-forgetful concern for the other, is the one norm by which all the rest are to be measured. If this stress on agapé is accepted, the technologies of a Christian future would be very different from those of Europe and America in the last three hundred years. Private profit as a motivating value would be replaced by community well-being; synthesizing concern for the interlocking multiple effects of technological interventions on society and on the natural environment would replace linear, analytical solutions; qualitative rather than quantitative considerations would rule decisions; the unquestioned dominance of the "bottom line" and of efficiency would be balanced by other concerns.

These thoughts are not predictions of anything likely to come about— surely not without a miracle or a catastrophe or both. They are, rather, designed to suggest the sort of criteria that Christians might well use today and tomorrow in assessing the technological society of which they are, willy-nilly, a part. The technologies that surround us are not all of a piece, cognitively or valuationally. Values embodied in one artifact or system may not at all resemble values incarnated in another. Christians may— should—be selective and discriminating in their evaluations and participations. The powerful technologies of *eros* are today in the ascendant; but if it is not impossible to imagine future technologies of agapé, we may by the same standards be able to identify and strengthen present technologies of compassionate holism. If a "cup of cold water" can be laden with ultimate significance (Matthew 10:42, Mark 9:41), then support for a community's water purification system can be given also in Christ's name. Technology is not remote from religion. It is where we live and breathe and have our worldly being. It is the present practical meeting place for the perennial dialogue between faith and reason.

Christian doubt of technological faith in our time is justified. Such faith represents an overweening and frighteningly shallow approach to life and reality. Christian doubts of technolatry are grounded in a much older alternative faith: trust in a divine Agapé that does not scorn embodiment in matter or in historical praxis. Thus sensible Christian doubt of technolatry does not need to lead to despair of all technology. Much human intelligence has, we know, been implemented for purposes that are ego and pride-driven, offenses to community and abuses of creation. No Christian, aware of the powers of sin in ourselves, will find that distorted outcome surprising. Equally, and on the same grounds, no Christian is likely to suppose that a utopia of Christian agapé-technology awaits us in any realistic historic future. But technology, like human intelligence, is not an all-or-nothing matter. Compassionate holism is a standard Christians can use to measure the technologies of our culture. Then, by combining Christian love with persistent Christian intelligence, it may be possible to look toward a modified technological future with chastened Christian hope.

The University of Georgia

Endnotes

*Reprinted from *Faith and Philosophy*, Vol 8, No. 2, April 1991. All rights reserved.

1 Revised after discussions following presentations at the Eastern Division meeting of The Society of Christian Philosophers, College, Spartanburg, South

Carolina, in April, 1988; at the Western Division of the American Academy of
Religion, Colorado State University, Fort Collins, Colorado, in April, 1988; and at
the annual meeting of the American Theological Society, Princeton, New Jersey,
March, 1989.

2 Harvey Cox, The Secular: *Secularization and Urbanization in Theological
Perspective* (New York: Macmillan, 1965, rev. ed., 1966).

3 W. Norris Clarke, "Technology and Man: A Christian Vision," in *The
Technological Order*, ed. Carl F. Stover (Detroit, Michigan: Wayne State University
Press, 1963). Revised version reprinted in Carl Mitcham and Robert Mackey,
Philosophy and Technology, pp. 247-58.

4 Ibid., p. 252.

5 Cox, op. cit., p. 20.

6 Clarke, op. cit., p. 251.

7 Jacques Ellul, "Technique and the Opening Chapters of Genesis," in *Theology
and Technology: Essays in Christian Analysis and Exegesis*, eds. Carl Mitcham and Jim
Grote (Lanham, MD: University Press of America, Inc., 1984), p. 129.

8 Ibid., p. 125.

9 Ibid., p. 125.

10 Egbert Schuurman, "A Christian Philosophical Perspective on Technology," in
Mitcham and Grote, *Theology and Technology*, op. cit., p. 111.

11 See, however, my *Philosophy of Technology* (Englewood Cliffs, NJ:
Prentice-Hall, Inc., 1988), Chapter 2.

12 See my Shaping the Future (New York: Harper & Row, 1976), especially
Chapter 3, "Limits of Technolatry."

13 See Shaping, the Future, op. cit., especially Chapter 2.

Study Questions

1.   What are the key issues raised by Ferré in contrast to the articles that have
preceded it?

2.   What sorts of Christian doubts does Ferré discuss? How might the theist
respond to these doubts?

3.   What are the issues of the "Great Debate"?

4.   What sorts of refinements does Ferré add regarding a Christian stance on
technology?

5.   What does Ferré mean by "Christian technologies"?

PART II

ARGUMENTS FOR THE EXISTENCE OF GOD

9

Modal Versions of the Ontological Argument

William Rowe

William Rowe is professor of philosophy at Purdue University. In this essay* he critically analyzes Plantinga's version of the ontological argument, appreciating its brilliance but leveling some objections at what it claims to have accomplished.

It has sometimes been thought that two distinct ontological arguments can be found in chapters 2 and 3 of Anselm's *Proslogium*. It is clear that in chapter 2 Anselm intended to set forth an argument for God's existence. He there introduces his concept of God as a being than which none greater is possible, and he advances the principle that existence in reality contributes to the greatness of a being. He then argues that God, as conceived by him, exists in reality—for otherwise a being greater than the greatest possible being would be possible.[1] Having satisfied himself that God's existence has been established, in chapter 3 Anselm turns to consider the mode or way in which God exists. Some things, like cabbages and kings, exist only *contingently*. It is possible that they should not have existed at all. Put in the language of possible worlds, we might say that the possible world that happens to be actual contains cabbages and kings.[2] Other possible worlds, however, do no contain them; and had one of those worlds been the actual world, cabbages and kings would not have existed.

Does God exist only contingently? Anselm thought not, for a being would be greater if it existed in such a way that it logically could not fail to exist. Put in the language of possible worlds, a being would be greater if it is contained in every possible world rather than in just some possible worlds. So if God exists contingently, it would be possible for God to be greater than he is. Since it is not possible for God to be greater than he is, God must exist *necessarily*.

As I have interpreted Anselm, he did not intend in chapter 3 to be offering a further argument for God's existence. Instead, he wanted to determine whether God, whose existence he had already established in chapter 2 exists contingently or necessarily. But whatever his intentions may have been, it is not difficult to see in chapter 3 the makings of a distinct argument for God's existence. For chapter 3 presents us with the principle that *necessary existence*, no less than the *existence in reality* of chapter 2, contributes to the greatness of a being. If it is possible for Anselm's God to possess necessary existence, then that is the sort of existence he does possess—otherwise it would be possible for God to be greater.

Reflection on chapter 3 of Anselm's *Proslogium* has led philosophers to create various modal versions of the ontological argument. Among the most interesting versions is one set forth by Alvin Plantinga. Plantinga's version has the merit of extraordinary simplicity. By defining the concept of maximal greatness in a certain manner, Plantinga is able to boil down his version of the argument to the assertion of a single premise: that there is a possible world in which the property of maximal greatness is instantiated. Another merit of Plantinga's version is that it makes use of the idea of possible worlds, thus reducing the logic of the modal argument to its most intuitive level. Before we consider his version, however, let's prepare ourselves for some of the questions we need to raise by examining two quite simple ontological arguments that are suggested by the reasoning in chapters 2 and 3 of Anselm's *Proslogium*.

Consider two distinct concepts of God that I will call G_1 and G_2. We shall define G_1 as follows:

> G_1 = the concept of an omnipotent, omniscient, wholly good being who is such that he exists with these perfections in the actual world.

G_2 is defined as follows:

> G_2 = the concept of an omnipotent, omniscient, wholly good being who is such that he exists with these perfections in every possible world.

Let us say that a *normal* concept C of a being or kind of being is *satisfied* in a given possible world just in case, were that world actual, that being or a being of that kind would exist. Thus the concept *elephant* is satisfied in our world, but the concept *unicorn* is not. For our world is actual and elephants do exist, but unicorns do not. In some other possible world, however, just the reverse is true—the concept *unicorn* is satisfied, but the concept *elephant* is not. For if that world were actual, at least one unicorn would exist, but no elephants would exist. Armed with this idea of what it is for a normal concept of a being (or kind of being) to be *satisfied* in a possible world, let's consider our two concepts of God introduced above.

With a little reflection, I think we can see that our first concept, G_1, may not be a *normal* concept. To ask whether the normal concept *unicorn* is satisfied in w is simply to ask whether a unicorn would exist if w were actual. Where w is some possible world other than the possible world that is in fact actual, the question of whether the concept *unicorn* is satisfied in w has nothing to do with whether unicorns, elephants, cabbages, or kings exist in the actual world. But this is not so with G_1. Whether G_1 is satisfied in w depends in part on what sorts of beings *actually exist*, what sorts of beings exist in the actual world. It is not enough that w contains an omnipotent, omniscient, wholly good being. For unless *that being* exists in the actual world with just those perfections, G_1 is not satisfied in w. The important point to grasp here is that the satisfaction of G_1 in any possible world depends on the *actual existence* of an omnipotent, omniscient, wholly good being.[3]

The following argument is suggested by the reasoning of *Proslogium 2*:

(1) There is a possible world in which G_1 is satisfied.

Therefore,

(2) There exists an omnipotent, omniscient, wholly good being.

This argument is logically valid. Is its premise true? Well, that depends, as we've seen, on what beings are contained in the actual world. If every existing being has some moral defect, then there is no possible world in which G_1 is *in fact* satisfied.

For an argument to be a *proof* of its conclusion we must know its premise(s) to be true without basing that knowledge on a prior knowledge of its conclusion. Is it logically possible for some human being to know (1) to be true without basing that knowledge on knowing (2) to be true? It would be rash to answer no to this question. For it is difficult to draw *logical* limits to the ways in which human beings might come to know that a certain proposition is true. But perhaps we can say this much. It is exceedingly difficult to see how some human being would in fact come to a knowledge of (1) independently of knowing (2). So it is more than likely true that this argument is not a proof of its conclusion for any human being.

G_2 is a more far-reaching concept than is G_1. For G_1's being satisfied in a possible world w requires that the actual world contain an omnipotent, omniscient, wholly good being but allows that many other possible worlds lack such a being. G_2, however, is satisfied in a possible world w only if every possible world (including the actual world) contains an omnipotent, omniscient, wholly good being. In the spirit of Proslogium 3, if not the letter, we can construct the following argument.

(3) There is a possible world in which G_2 is satisfied.

Therefore,

(4) There necessarily exists an omnipotent, omniscient, wholly good being.

Once we realize that the satisfaction of G_2 in any possible world requires the existence of an omnipotent, omniscient, wholly good being in every possible world, we can appreciate the extraordinary difficulty of viewing this argument as a proof of its conclusion. Perhaps if we know that the actual world contains an omnipotent, omniscient, wholly good being, we might begin to ponder whether this being holds forth in all or just some possible worlds. But it is difficult to see how merely reflecting on the concept G_2 can enable us to know that it is satisfied in some possible world. For, as we've noted, its satisfaction in any possible world depends on what is contained in every possible world. But again, it would be unwise to declare that it is logically impossible for someone to come to know (3) independently of knowing (4), or even (2). But few, I believe, would be inclined to view this argument as a proof of its conclusion.

For reasons we need not consider here, Plantinga prefers to state his modal version of the ontological argument in terms of whether a certain property—the property of being maximally great—is instantiated in any possible world. For a property to be instantiated in a world w is for it to be true that if w were actual some thing would exist having that property. Thus the property of being an elephant is instantiated in our possible world, but the property of being a unicorn is not. Plantinga's property of being maximally great, however, is vastly different from such pedestrian properties as being an elephant or being a unicorn. The question of whether these two properties are instantiated in some possible but nonactual world w doesn't at all depend on whether the actual world contains elephants or unicorns. But Plantinga's property of being maximally great can be instantiated in some possible world w only if the actual world contains a being that is omnipotent, omniscient, and morally perfect. And even this is not enough. Not only must the actual world contain an omnipotent, omniscient, and morally perfect being, but every possible world must contain a being having these marvelous attributes, and it must be the same being who has these attributes in all these different worlds. Once we understand all this, we can see what an extraordinary property it is to which Plantinga has drawn our attention. If any possible world whatever happens to lack an omnipotent, omniscient, and morally perfect being, then Plantinga's extraordinary property is an impossible property and is instantiated in no possible world.

Analogous to our argument concerning concept G_2, the following argument is valid:

(5)   There is a possible world in which maximal greatness is instantiated.

Therefore,

(6) There necessarily exists an omnipotent, omniscient, and morally perfect being.

And, for reasons given in connection with our two earlier arguments, it is extremely unlikely that this argument is a proof of its conclusion.

Consider the property of being in less than perfect company, where it is understood that a person has that property in a world w just in case every person in w (human and nonhuman) has some degree of imperfection, however slight. It may be that we enjoy (or are burdened with) this property in the actual world. But even if we are not, surely, one would think, it is *possible* that this property be instantiated. Surely there is some possible world in which every person has some imperfection, however slight. But if so, then Plantinga's extraordinary property is impossible; there is no possible world in which it is instantiated. If either of these properties is instantiated in some world w, then the other is uninstantiated in w and in every other possible world. Since only one can be instantiated, which, if either, might it be? The instantiation of Plantinga's extraordinary property in a possible world w is *dependent* on what every other possible world contains—every possible world must contain an omnipotent, omniscient, and morally perfect being. The instantiation in w of the property of being in less than perfect company requires only that each person in w have some flaw, however slight. If you know nothing else relevant to your decision and had to bet on which property is possibly instantiated, knowing that both cannot be, which would you bet on?

Although Plantinga accepts the version of the ontological argument that he sets forth, he acknowledges that it is not a proof of its conclusion. It does not, he notes, establish the truth of theism. What then does the argument do? It establishes, Plantinga claims, the rational acceptability of theism. It does this, Plantinga argues, because the premise of the argument, proposition (5), is something that can be believed without violating any rule of reason concerning what we may or may not believe. Since we do no wrong in accepting (5), and since we acknowledge that (5) entails the truth of theism, we do no wrong in accepting the truth of theism. If it is not wrong for me to believe a proposition, then that proposition is rationally acceptable for me.

Perhaps the first point to note about Plantinga's claim is that in his view the premise of an argument may be rationally acceptable and may thus establish the rational acceptability of the argument's conclusion, even though one doesn't know the premise to be true, and even though the truth of the premise is a matter of significant controversy. After all, some who reflect on the amount of tragic evil in our world are committed to the view that the property of being in less than perfect company is instantiated in our world. Others, including a number who believe that there exists an omnipotent, omniscient, and morally perfect being, would insist that there is some possible world in which the property of being in less than perfect company is instantiated. Both groups, therefore, are committed to the denial of Plantinga's premise that there is some possible world in which maximal greatness is instantiated. Still others may hold that there is simply no way of telling whether maximal greatness is possibly instantiated. So the premise of Plantinga's argument is denied by many and held in question by others. Moreover, Plantinga offers no argument for his premise and acknowledges that reflecting on it does not enable us to somehow see that it must be true; he does not claim that after sufficient reflection the inquiring mind somehow comes to find his premise *self-evident*.

What, then, does Plantinga claim for his premise? He claims, as we've seen, that it is not *irrational* to accept it, that in accepting it one does not violate any rules concerning what we may or may not believe. Of course, if it were a rule that one must not accept a premise unless one can prove it or has some good evidence for it, Plantinga would be unjustified in accepting his premise. But the "rule" just mentioned is difficult to defend. Perhaps what Plantinga holds is this: There are circumstances in which it is *permissible* to believe a proposition even though you cannot prove it and don't have good evidence for it. What are these circumstances? Well, one circumstance, surely, is that you have no good reason to think the proposition false. (Some think that the idea of a maximally great being is like the idea of a largest integer—an impossible object. But this may well be wrong. It might be that we have no good reason to think Plantinga's premise false.) The other circumstances that must obtain are difficult to specify. But if we agree with Plantinga about this, then I think we can say that it may be permissible for someone to believe Plantinga's premise. Plantinga says something much stronger. He says it is "evident" that believing his premise is permissible. This claim, I believe, is excessive. We need to be much clearer about the circumstances that must obtain for Plantinga's premise to be acceptable before we declare its acceptability with the unabashed assurance Plantinga here expresses.

Some philosophers declare that the ontological argument in all its versions commits some gross fallacy or contains some obviously false premise. Plantinga's careful work on the argument helps us to see that we can confidently reject such criticisms. But when the argument is set forth with care and rigor, we can see, I believe, how very difficult it is to know or establish the truth of its premise(s). (Indeed, in some versions one has great difficulty in even imagining how one might know the premise(s) without basing such knowledge on a prior knowledge of the conclusion.) I think Plantinga sees this as well. Anselm's high hope of discovering an argument that would conclusively establish God's existence remains unfulfilled, even in Plantinga's skillful hands. As a consolation prize, Plantinga proposes a weak sense of rational acceptability that he claims is satisfied by the premise of his modal version of the argument. Anselm thought that if we really understood the argument it would be obvious that it is a sound demonstration of the existence of God. To reject the argument, therefore, is to be foolish. Plantinga makes no such claim. He holds only that it is clear that one is not foolish to accept it. If I am right, all that has been shown is that it may not be foolish to accept it. To *establish* that it is not foolish requires that we become clear that its premise satisfies all the circumstances (whatever they are) that are required for it to be permissible to believe a proposition even though we cannot prove it and don't have good evidence for it.

Endnotes

*Reprinted from Louis P. Pojman, *Philosophy of Religion: An Anthology,* Belmont, CA: Wadsworth Publishing Company, 1994. © 1994 by Wadsworth, Inc. All rights reserved. Wadsworth Publishing Company, Belmont, California 94002.

[1] This argument has fascinated philosophers and theologians for centuries. For an exposition of the argument and the major objections to it, see my essay, "The Ontological Argument," in my *Philosophy of Religion* (Belmont, CA: Wadsworth, 1978).

[2] The idea of *possible worlds* is explained briefly and clearly in Alvin Plantinga's *God, Freedom and Evil* (New York: Harper & Row, 1974), PP. 34-39.

[3] G_1 is an *abnormal* concept if there is a possible world in which no perfect being exists. For in that case, G_1's being satisfied in w depends in part upon *which* possible world is actual. Suppose possible world w^* contains an omnipotent, omniscient, wholly good being, but possible world w^{**} does not. If w^* is the actual world, then depending on what w contains, G_1 may be satisfied in w. But if w^{**} is the actual world, then no matter what w contains, G_1 is not satisfied in w. G_2, although a more far-reaching concept than G_1, is, however, a *normal* concept. Although its being satisfied in w depends upon what is contained in every other possible world, its being satisfied in w does not depend on *which* possible world is actual.

Study Questions

1.   In terms that you can understand, what is Plantinga's modal version of the ontological argument?

2.   What does Plantinga think that the modal version of the ontological argument accomplishes? Do you think that Rowe agrees? Do you? If so, why? If not, why not?

3. How does Plantinga's version of the modal version of the ontological argument differ from Anselm's in the *Proslogium*?

4. What general positive value does Rowe see in Plantinga's version of the argument?

5. What is it about the ontological argument that makes it ontological? Why is it *a priori* rather than *a posteriori*?

10

Some Emendations of Gödel's Ontological Proof

C. Anthony Anderson

C. Anthony Anderson is professor of philosophy at the University of California, Santa Barbara.

Kurt Gödel's version of the ontological argument was shown by J. Howard Sobel to be defective, but some plausible modifications in the argument result in a version which is immune to Sobel's objection. A definition is suggested which permits the proof of some of Gödel's axioms.*

A new version of the ontological argument for the existence of God was outlined by Kurt Gödel and elaborated by Dana Scott. J. Howard Sobel has given a careful explication of the details and has provided a powerful critique[1]. I believe that Sobel's main objection is conclusive against the argument as sketched by Gödel. But it is possible to correct the argument, making changes which can be independently motivated, and in such a way that the revised argument is immune to the objection. And a definition of one of Gödel's primitive concepts enables the proof of some of his axioms. For the sake of those who do not enjoy symbolism, I give a statement of Gödel's argument and the suggested revisions in the vernacular. Some corollaries and a lemma have been separated off in order to clarify the proof and to isolate the difficulty. A brief statement of the formalities is given in the appendix. To see a full formalization of Gödel's original version, consult Sobel.

I. Gödel's Axioms, Definitions, and Theorems

Axiom 1. A property is positive if and only if its negation is not positive.

The notion of a positive property is taken as a primitive. Gödel suggests two readings—"positive in the moral-aesthetic sense" and positive as involving only "pure attribution." The only further comment in the notes on the first interpretation is to the effect that positiveness in this sense is independent of the "accidental structure of the world." The second notion is said to be "opposed to 'privation' " and to pertain to properties which do not contain privation. (The explanations in Gödel's notes are extremely terse and sometimes cryptic). Even the sympathetic reader still may not find Axiom I intuitively evident. I discuss this below.

Axiom 2. Any property entailed by a positive property is itself positive.

"Entailed" is understood to mean "strictly implied"—in this case, that it is impossible for something to have the one property and not the other. Let us say that a property is consistent if it is possibly exemplified, i.e., if it is possible that there exists an x such that x has that property. And let us say that a property is necessary if it is necessary that everything has the property. Then:

Theorem 1. If a property is positive, then it is consistent.

Proof. Let Φ be a positive property. Then Φ entails the property of self-identity—since every property entails the necessary property of self-identity. Hence, self-identity is positive by Axiom 2. So, by Axiom 1, the negation of self-identity, self-difference, is not positive. But if Φ is inconsistent, it entails self-difference—since an inconsistent property entails everything. This contradicts Axiom 2. So every positive property is consistent.[2]

Q.E.D.

The alleged modal facts used in proving Theorem 1—that a necessary property is entailed by every property and that an inconsistent property entails every property—may strike the modally naive as unintuitive. Indeed, it strikes some of the modally sophisticated thus. But given the explained meaning of "entails," these "paradoxes of strict implication" (as they have been called) are entirely unproblematic. If it is not possible that x lack Φ, then it is not possible that x have Ψ and lack Φ—so any property entails such a property Φ. And if it is not possible that x have Σ, then it is not possible that x has Σ and lacks Ψ. So such a property Σ entails every property.

Definition 1. x is *God-like* if and only if x has every positive property.

Axiom 3. The property of being God-like is positive.

It's worth noticing that there is here an implicit assumption: if we have defined a predicate, then we can straight-away form a name of the property which it expresses. (The technically minded will thus wish to note that it is in effect assumed that anything is counted as a property which can be defined by "abstraction on a formula.")

Corollary 1. The property of being God-like is self-consistent, i.e. possibly exemplified.

Proof: By Axiom 3 and Theorem 1.

Lemma. If something is God-like, then each of its properties is positive.

Proof. Suppose that something x is God-like. Let Ψ be any property of x. If Ψ is not positive, then its negation is (by Axiom 1). By definition, x, being God-like, has every positive property. But then x would exemplify the negation of Ψ—contrary to our assumption that x has Ψ. Hence Ψ is positive.

Q.E.D.

Definition 2. A property Φ is an essence of entity x if and only if x has Φ and Φ entails every property x has.

Gödel was a great admirer of Leibniz[3] and this definition shows that influence. I suggest below that a more conservative characterization of essence better serves the purpose at hand.

Axiom 4. If a property is positive, then it is necessarily positive.[4]

Theorem 2. If something is God-like, then the property of being God-like is an essence of that thing.

Proof: Suppose that something x is God-like and let Ψ be any property of x. Then Ψ is positive by the lemma. Now by definition (of "God-like"), necessarily if Ψ is positive, anything which is God-like has Ψ. Hence, if necessarily Ψ is positive, then necessarily anything which is God-like has Ψ (by modal logic). But by Axiom 4, if Ψ is positive, necessarily Ψ is positive. Therefore, necessarily Ψ is positive. So necessarily anything which is God-like has Ψ—i.e., the property of being God-like entails Ψ. Thus we have shown that any property of x is entailed by the property of being God-like. So, by the definition of "essence," the property of being God-like is an essence of anything which has that property.

Q.E.D.

The modal principle used in the proof of Theorem 2 is that if it is necessary that if P, then Q, then if it is necessary that P, it is necessary that Q.

Corollary 2. If x is God-like and has a property, then that property is entailed by the property of being God-like.

The corollary is immediate by the definition of "essence" and Theorem 2. This consequence of the axioms is at the heart of Sobel's objection, to be explained below.

Definition 3. x *necessarily exists* if and only if every essence of x is necessarily exemplified (i.e., for every Φ, if Φ is an essence of x, then necessarily there exists a y such that y has Φ).

Note that while necessary existence is taken to be a property, it seems perfectly well-defined: it is defined as the property attributed to anything x when it is asserted that every essence Φ of x is such that necessarily $(\exists x)\Phi x$. (Technically, it is definable by abstraction on a second order formula). Actual existence may be taken to be expressed by the natural language counterpart of a quantifier, although one could also define a corresponding property of a thing x: every essence Φ of x is such that something is a Φ.

Axiom 5. The property of necessarily existing is a positive property.

Theorem 3. Necessarily the property of being God-like is exemplified.

Proof: If something x is God-like, then it has every positive property (by definition) and hence (by Axiom 5) it has the property of necessarily existing. That is, if x is God-like, then any essence of x is necessarily exemplified (definition of "necessary existence"). But if x is God-like, then the property of being God-like is an essence of x, by Theorem 2. Therefore, if anything x is God-like, then necessarily the property of being God-like is exemplified. Hence, if something is God-like, then necessarily something is God-like. Since this last has been proved using only necessary truths, it is itself necessary truth. Therefore, if it is possible that something is God-like, then it is possible that necessarily something is God-like (by modal logic). But by Corollary 1, it is possible that something is God-like. Therefore, it is possible that necessarily something is God-like. So, necessarily something is God-like (by the modal logic S5)[5].

Q.E.D.

The principles of modal logic used in this proof are: (1) if it is necessary that if P, then Q, then if it is possible that P, then it is possible that Q, an the principle of S5, (2) if it is possible that it is necessary that P, then it necessary that P.

II. Sobel's Objections

The reasoning is entirely cogent. Unfortunately, too much follows from these axioms. Sobel shows that the axioms engender "modal collapse"— it follows from them that every proposition which is true at all is necessary. Suppose x is God-like and the proposition P is true. Then x has the property of being such that P is true. So by Corollary 2, this property is entailed by the property of being God-like—which latter is necessarily amplified, by Theorem 3. Hence the property of being such that P is true is necessarily amplified. Therefore, it is necessary that P. Again, the reasoning seems correct. (In his formalized version of this argument, Sobel uses the property which anything has when it is self-identical and P is true. Some may find this version slightly more intuitive.) Arguing along similar lines, Sobel concludes that it follows further that everything necessarily exists. Simplifying just a bit, the argument is this. Let x be the necessarily existing God-like being and consider any y distinct from x and having essence Φ. Then the necessarily existing God-like being x has the property of being such that there is something y, distinct from x and having essence Φ. This complex property, being entailed by the necessarily exemplified property of God-likeness, is itself necessarily exemplified and thus it is necessary there is such a y with essence Φ. This last is tantamount to y's necessary existence. I see no reasonable escape from Sobel's conclusions here.

III. Analysis of the Difficulty

Sobel suggests that a natural reaction might be to reject Axiom 5 and to give up on the ontological argument. (Sobel himself believes that ontological arguments have more serious and fundamental difficulties—we do not discuss them here). But Axiom 5 is certainly not the least plausible of the axioms. And on might agree with David Lewis[6] when he says that the ontological arguer is entitled to whatever standards of greatness (or positiveness, in the present case) he wants. Of course one can't then just *stipulate* that Axioms 1 and 2 are true—there might be a clash with the standards or with one another. And positiveness should be theologically significant (as again Lewis notes). But given this, it would be difficult to find fault with Axiom 5. Even without this, Axiom 5 has considerable intrinsic plausibility.

Consider the puzzling Axiom 1. If we separate it into the two conditionals:

(1a) If a property is positive, then its negation is not positive,

(1b) If the negation of a property is not positive, then the property is positive,

we find principles of rather different character. Chisholm and Sosa[7] have developed the logic of intrinsic value as attributed to states of affairs and there are analogies with the idea of a positive property (if we take this latter in the "moral aesthetic" sense). In particular, we can deduce (1a) from the two plausible principles about intrinsic preferability:

(B1) If a property is positive, then it is preferable to (or better than) its negation.

(B2) If a property Φ is preferable to property Ψ, then Ψ is not preferable to Φ.

These are analogous of certain theorems of Chisholm and Sosa[8].

Principle (1b), on the other hand, seems to overlook a possibility: that both a property and its negation should be *indifferent*. For example, *being such that there are stones* does not seem to be intrinsically preferable to its negation nor does its negation seem to be preferable to it—hence neither it nor its negation is positive (according to (B1)). So we should reject Axiom 1, delete the dubious part (1b), and adopt (1a) as our new axiom; call it now "Axiom 1*." Notice that (1b) is used in the proof of the lemma which, by way of Theorem 2, is involved in the proof of the troublesome Corollary 2.[9]

IV. New Definitions and Corresponding Axioms

Another change which seems advisable is this: a property should be defined to be an essence of an entity x when it is a property which entails all and only the *essential* properties of x—those properties which x has necessarily. There's nothing to argue about—here is a different conception of the essence of something, call it "essences*":

Definition 2.* Φ is an *essence** of x if and only if for every property Ψ, x has Ψ necessarily (or essentially) if and only if Φ entails Ψ.[10]

Finally, I advocate that the property of being God-like, call it now "God-likeness*," be defined as follows:

Definition 1.* x is God-like* if and only if x has as essential properties those and only those properties which are positive (i.e., for every Φ, x has Φ necessarily if and only if Φ is positive).

Having only positive properties is, I think, too much to ask. Of an indifferent property and its negation God must have one. But having all and only the positive properties as essential properties is plausibly definitive of divinity.

These changes are theologically very pleasant: the proof of Theorem 1 still goes through (using Axiom 1*, i.e. (1a), in place of the rejected Axiom 1), the proof of the despised Corollary 2 is blocked (depending as it does on the old definition of "essence"), and we can still prove a theorem corresponding to Theorem 2—but now using our new definitions.

Note that the definition of necessary existence now to be used is of the same form as the original definition but has "essence*" in place of "essence." If we call this new notion "necessary existence*," then our new axioms are Axioms 1*, 2, and 4 and, in place of Axioms 3 and 5, respectively:

Axiom 3.* The property of being God-like* is positive, and

Axiom 5.* Necessary existence* is positive. And we prove:

Theorem 2.* If something is God-like*, then the property of being Godlike* is an essence* of that thing.

Proof. Suppose that x is God-like* and necessarily has a property Ψ. Then by definition (of "God-like*"), that property is positive. But necessarily, if is positive, then if anything is God-like*, then it has Ψ— again by the definition of "God-like*," together with the fact that if something has a property necessarily, then it has the property. But if a property is positive, then it is necessarily positive (Axiom 4). Hence, if Ψ is positive, then it is entailed by being God-like* (by modal logic—as in the original Theorem 2). But Ψ is positive and hence is entailed by being

God-like*. Thus we have proved that if an entity is God-like* and has a property essentially, then that property is entailed by the property of being God-like*.

Suppose a property Φ is entailed by the property of being God-like*. Then Φ is positive by Axioms 2 and 3* and therefore, since x is God-like*, x has Φ necessarily (by the definition of "God-like*"). Hence, if something is God-like*, it has a property essentially if and only if that property is entailed by being God-like—i.e., God-likeness* is an essence* of that thing.

Q.E.D.

That the property of being God-like* is necessarily exemplified follows much as before (except that one must use the modal principle "If necessarily P, then P" also in the proof of Theorem 3*). That there is at most one God-like* being also follows: if x and y are both God-like*, then y has the same essential properties as x, including identity with x.

Someone might worry that perhaps the emended axioms still lead to modal collapse. On at least one reasonable way of formalizing the proof, they do not. Symbolic versions of these axioms are satisfiable in a "possible worlds" model of second-order S5 of the sort explained by Nino Cocchiarella[11] and such that "for all P, if P, then necessarily P" is false therein. Take a model containing just two possible worlds w_1 and w_2 and just two (possible) entities a and b. Let a exist at both w_1 and w_2 and let b exist only at w_1. (The contingent entity b is merely possible at w_2). A property is a function which picks out a set of individuals (the extension of the property) at each possible world.[12] Since one cannot represent directly in second-order logic propositions of the form "Φ is positive" (with the property expression in the argument place)[13], let us temporarily define this as "the negation (or complement) of the property Φ entails property Δ" (intuitively, a property is defined as positive if its lack entails a defect). For the purpose of the example, identify property Δ with the property of being a contingent being—the function that picks out the set containing b alone at w_1 and at w_2. It is tedious, but not difficult, to show that being God-like* and necessary existence* are both positive—indeed, they are both identified in the model with that function which picks out a at every possible world (this is also the essence of a), a property whose complement entails (in the model) contingent existence. All the other axioms (using the definition) come out true in this (S5) structure as well. Taking w_1 to be the actual world, there are true but contingent propositions—for example, that there are at least two things.[14]

The idea used in the model suggests a simplification of the axioms. (Actually it was the idea of the simplification that suggested the model). Take as a new primitive the idea of something's being imperfect (or, what is not quite the same, being defective). Then just define a property to be positive if its absence in an entity entails that the entity is imperfect and its presence does not entail that the entity in question is imperfect. A little more formally, we may say that a property Φ is positive if and only if (1) necessarily for every x, if x does not have Φ, then x is imperfect and (2) it is not necessary that for every x, if x has Φ, then x is imperfect[15] A little less formally, we explain that a property is positive if and only if it is necessary for, and compatible with, perfection. Axioms 1*, 2, and 4 are then provable as theorems in modal logic. (The second conjunct in the definition is needed to prove Axiom 1*). But note that, on this definition, to assert that being God-like* is positive is already to assert that being God-like* does not entail any imperfection. And if being God-like* were not self-consistent, then it would entail everything. So asserting that the property is positive is quite close to the outright assertion of self-consistency. Theorem 1 does not then seem to give us much new assurance about the possible exemplification of God-likeness. But there seems to be no epistemic loss and the logical economy gained is of some independent interest.[16]

It is hoped that the suggested changes preserve at least some of the essentials of Gödel's proof. One may doubt that an ontological argument will ultimately succeed and yet still hold that reason demands consideration of the best arguments that can be constructed—on both sides of the question of God's existence. If Kurt Gödel thought that the matter can be settled in the affirmative by proof, perhaps those of us who are interested in the question ought to see what merit we can find in his line of reasoning.[17]

University of Minnesota

Appendix

I. Gödel's Axioms, Definitions, and Theorems

$Pos(\Phi)$: Φ is positive
$\sim S$: It is not the case that S
$\sim\Phi$: The property attributed to anything x when it is asserted that x is not a Φ
$\Box S$: It is necessary that S
$\Diamond S$: It is possible that S
Axiom 1. $Pos(\Phi) \equiv \sim Pos(\sim\Phi)$
      We write $(\Phi \Rightarrow \Psi)$ for $\Box (x)(\Phi(x) \supset \Psi(x))$.
Axiom 2. $Pos(\Phi) \supset [(\Phi \Rightarrow \Psi) \supset Pos(\Psi)]$
Definition 1. $G(x) =$ df $(\Phi)(Pos(\Phi) \supset \Phi(x))$ (God-like)
Axiom 3. $Pos(G)$
Theorem 1. $Pos(\Phi) \supset \Diamond(\exists x)\Phi(x)$
Corollary 1. $\Diamond(\exists x)G(x)$
Lemma. $G(x) \urcorner (\Phi)(\Phi(x) \supset Pos(\Phi))$

Definition 2. Φ Ess x =df Φ(x) . (Ψ)[Ψ(x) ⊃ (Φ⇒Ψ)]   (Essence)
Axiom 4. Pos(Φ) ⊃ □ Pos(Φ)
Theorem 2. G(x) ⊃ (G Ess x)
Corollary 2. G(x) ⊃ [Φ(x) ⊃ (G⇒Φ)]
Definition 3. NE(x) =df (Φ)[Φ Ess x ⊃ □ (∃x)Φ(x)]   (Necessary Existence)
Axiom 5. Pos(NE)

II. Sobel's Objections

It follows that P ⊃ □ P and that (y)NE(y)

III. Analysis of the Difficulty

(la) Pos(Φ) ⊃ ~Pos(~Φ)
(1b) ~Pos(~Φ) ⊃ Pos(Φ)
ΦBΨ : Φ is better than (or preferable to) Ψ
(Bl) Pos(Φ) ⊃ (ΦB~Φ)
(B2) (ΦBΨ) ⊃ ~ (ΨBΦ)

IV. New Definitions and Corresponding Axioms

Definition 1*. G*(x) =df (Φ) [□ Φ(x) ≡ Pos (Φ)]   (God-like*)
Definition 2*. Φ Ess* x =df (Ψ) [□ Ψ(x) ≡ (Φ⇒Ψ)]   (Essence*)
Definition 3*. NE*(x) =df (Φ)[Φ Ess* x ⊃ □ (∃x) Φ (x)]
                                                    (necessary existence*)
(If this symbolism is transcribed into Cocchiarella's logic for the purpose
of constructing a formal proof, the existential quantifier in the definition
of "NE*" should be taken to be an "e-quantifier").
Axiom 3* Pos (G*)
Axiom 5* Pos (NE*)
D(x): x is imperfect (defective)
Definition. Pos (Φ) =df (~Φ⇒Δ). ~(Φ⇒Δ)   (Positive property)

Endnotes

*Reprinted from *Faith and Philosophy*, Vol. 7, No. 3, July 1990. All rights
reserved.
    [1] Jordan Howard Sobel, "Gödel's Ontological Proof," in *On Being and Saying.
Essays for Richard Cartwright*, ed. Judith Jarvis Thomson (Cambridge, Mass. &
London, England: The MIT Press, 1987). Sobel provides detailed renderings of both
Gödel's handwritten note and Scott's elaboration. Apparently the contents of these
have not appeared in print before.
    [2] One of the anonymous referees pointed out that there is a simpler proof of this
which does not require the use of self-identity and self-difference. Suppose Φ were

positive and inconsistent. Then it would entail its own negation, which would have to be positive by Axiom 2. But this contradicts Axiom 1.

3 According to Hao Wang, *Reflections on Kurt Gödel* (Cambridge, Mass. & London: The MIT Press, 1987).

4 Strictly speaking, the proof requires the necessitation of this axiom—that a property is positive entails that it is necessarily positive. In the proof of Theorem 2 below it is asserted that a conditional (namely, "If something is God-like, then necessarily something is God-like.") has been proved using only necessary truths. Other than definitions, the only thing required is that Axiom 4 be necessary. But probably no one who accepts the axioms will shrink from asserting all their necessitations.

5 Because of the arguments of Hugh Chandler ("Plantinga and the Contingently Possible," *Analysis* 36 (1976): 106-109) elaborated by Nathan Salmon (*Reference and Essence* (Princeton University Press and Basil Blackwell, 1981), section 28, pp. 229-52; "Impossible Worlds," *Analysis* 44 (1984); "Modal Paradox: Parts and Counterparts, Points and Counterpoints," in French, Uehling, and Wettstein, eds., *Midwest Studies in Philosophy XI: Studies in Essentialism* (Minneapolis: University of Minnesota Press, 1986): 75-120; and "On the Logic of What Might Have Been," *Philosophical Review*, I have begun to worry that S5 may not be the appropriate modal logic for *de re* modality. For the purpose of proving Theorem 3, it would actually suffice to use the weaker modal logic B, but Salmon (in the last mentioned article) casts doubt on this as well—and in any case it does not appear that the logical weakening corresponds to any epistemic advance. (That the modal principle of B, "If it is possibly necessary that P, then P," will work just as well as S5 for certain modal ontological arguments was to my knowledge first noticed in print by Robert Merrihew Adams, "The Logical Structure of Anselm's Arguments," *The Philosophical Review* 80 (1971): 28-54). These criticisms cause no difficulty in the present case since the only uses of the characteristic principles of S5 are applications to *de dicto* modalities. Perhaps it would be better to isolate the *de re* by introducing a new primitive 'Essentl(F,x)' meaning that F is an essential property of x and then to adopt the axiom: if Essentl(Φ,x), then F(Φ,x). The proofs go through before using 'Essentl(Φ,x)' in place of 'necessarily x has Φ.' Also this would focus (but presumably not alleviate) any worries someone may have about "quantifying in."

6 David Lewis, "Anselm and Actuality," *Noûs* 4 (1970): 175-88. Reprinted in *Readings in the Philosophy of Religion: An Analytic Approach*, ed. Baruch A. Brody (Englewood Cliffs, New Jersey: Prentice Hall, 1974).

7 Roderick M. Chisholm and Ernest Sosa, "On the Logic of 'Intrinsically Better,'" *American Philosophical Quarterly* 3 (1966): 244-249.

8 But notice that the Chisholm-Sosa definition of an "intrinsically good state of affairs as a state of affairs which is preferable to some indifferent state of affairs is not the appropriate analogue of the idea of a positive property. A positive property, in Gödel's sense, is purely positive—it entails only properties which are themselves positive. A good state of affairs, in the Chisholm-Sosa sense, may entail indifferent or even bad states of affairs. A definition which might do is this: a property is positive if and only if ever property Φ it entails is such that Φ is preferable to the negation of Φ. This definition has some of the same advantages and drawbacks as the definition considered below. One additional advantage is that it is then possible to prove Axiom 1 from the principle that preferability is asymmetric. The analogue of this for states of

affairs is an axiom of the Chisholm-Sosa calculus. But which definition is to be used depends largely on theological considerations. Alternatively, one might adopt no definition at all.

[9] There may be something to be said for (Ib) from the point of view of Gödel's other interpretation of positiveness as involving only "pure attribution." I do not fully understand this alternative but one might suppose that (Ib) is a principle of "fullness of being." But, as noted, (Ib) entails the lemma (that if something is God-like, then each of its properties is positive). Below we prove a theorem corresponding to Theorem 2 (which seems crucial to the idea of the main proof), but with new definitions of "God-like" and "essence." There does not follow from this anything corresponding to Corollary 2 (because of the new definition of "essence"), but in the presence of (2b), a correlate of the lemma can still be proved. This and the new version of Theorem 2 again permit an argument like Sobel's to the conclusion that everything which is true is necessary. We assume that most will find this consequence unacceptable.

[10] This definition is equivalent to a definition of essence which is now quite standard: an essence is an essential property of something which only it has in any possible world. Proof sketch: Suppose Φ is a property which entails all and only x's essential properties. Then since Φ entails itself, it is an essential property of x. Further, if something else has Φ (in some possible world), then it would have x's essential property of being identical with x and so would itself be identical with x.

Suppose now that F is an essential property of x which only x has in any possible world. Let Ψ be an essential property of x. Then if, in some possible world, something y has Φ, y is identical with x and thus has Ψ in that world. So Φ entails Ψ. For the converse, assume that Φ entails some property Ψ. Then x will have Ψ in every possible world in which it has Φ. Therefore, since Φ is an essential property of x, Ψ is also an essential property of x. (The reader who wants to formalize this reasoning in the system of Note 11 is advised to take all quantifiers to be "subsistantial" or "possibilist"—see further Note 14).

The use of the idea of an essential property in dealing with the difficulty corresponds to an observation Sobel makes that one might only require of a God-like being that its "intrinsic" properties be positive.

[11] Nino B. Cocchiarella, "A Completeness Theorem in Second Order Modal Logic," Theorea 35 (1969): 81-103.

[12] I do not accept this identification in general. Nothing really turns on it in connection with the use of the model to show that there is no modal collapse. One can think of these functions as the "spectra" of properties without any damage to purpose at hand.

[13] We could of course extend the logic to third order but this would require some elaboration of Cocchiarella's semantics.

[14] One should consult Cocchiarella's article for a detailed and precise account of his semantics for second-order modal logic. But, at least for those having some familiarity with the usual "possible world" approach, the following outline of the semantics may make it possible to see that there is no modal collapse. We are to imagine given a set I of "possible worlds" where each such world has associated with it an "L-model," a triple consisting of a set A (the individuals existing in the world), a set B (the possible individuals; the set of actual individuals must be a subset of this set) and an interpretation function R which assigns appropriate extensions to

the constants of the language—possible individuals to individual constants, sets of possible individuals to one-place predicates and so on. It is worth emphasizing that the denotation of a constant (as given by R) at a world and the extension of a predicate (also given by R) at a world need not consist of individuals which are "actual" at the world. And Cocchiarella's logic has two kinds of quantifiers: what we might call "subsistential quantifiers" which (in the semantics) are construed as ranging over all *possible* individuals (the set B), and "e-quantifiers," "existence quantifiers," which are interpreted at a world as ranging only over the entities which exist in that world (the set A). The logic is interpreted by giving a "world system"—a collection of such L-models, one for each possible world i belonging to I, it being required that the possible individuals of each L-model be the same as those of any other (the possible individuals are the same no matter what world you are in). (Technically the L-models are "indexed"; the set I is the domain of a function which yields an L-model for each i belonging to I). And the existing individuals of all the worlds, taken together, must be a subset of the set of possible individuals. A singular attribute is as usual a function which takes as arguments possible worlds and yields as value in each case a set of possible individuals. And we may take the one-place second-order variables as ranging over all the attributes which correspond to a given world system (Cocchiarella has two kinds of second-order quantifiers, but only one is relevant to our present concern). The n-ary attributes are defined analogously. Ignoring for simplicity some not-immediately-relevant complications of Cocchiarella's actual construction, our desired world system may be taken to contain two possible worlds 1 and 2 and corresponding L-models $A_1 = <\{a,b\}, \{a,b\}, R_1>$ and $A_2 = <\{a\}, \{a,b\}, R_2>$. The first set listed in each case combines the actual individuals of the world, the second contains the possible individuals, and R_1 assigns extensions (from the second set) at the world to the constants and predicates of the language. The singularly attributes of the world system are therefore all the functions whose ranges consists of just the two worlds and whose values are in each case sets of possible individuals. The n-ary attributes (n > 1) of the world system are defined analogously (although we do not actually care about them for the present purpose). Now use the notation 'Φ_{aV} to stand for the attribute that picks out singleton a at the world 1 (corresponding to A_1) and picks out the set of all possible individuals $V = \{a,b\}$ at world 2 (corresponding to A_2), with analogous notation for the other fifteen attributes which exist in this world system. Then take $R_1('\Delta') = R_2('\Delta') = \Phi_{bb}$. It is easy to check that the only positive attributes (those whose negations entail Φ_{bb}) are Φ_{aa}, Φ_{VV}, , Φ_{Va}, and Φ_{aV}, and that the first of these is the attribute corresponding to 'G' and 'NE' and is the unique essence of a. Note well that the appropriate translation of the argument into Cocchiarella's notation will take the existential quantifier in the definition of neccessary existence to be an e-quantifier (an "existence," rather than "subsistence," quantifier) and so too the quantifier in the conclusion of the argument. All other individual quantifiers may be taken to be subsistential and hence to range over all possibles. It is a purely combinatorial task to show that the modified Gödelian axioms all come out true in this model and that there is no modal collapse. And not everything is a necessary existent. Cocchiarella proves that his axioms for second-order S5 are complete in the "Henkin-sense." Given the definition of "positive property," one can completely formalize the present ontological proof in that system. Thus, there is at least one formalization of the present proof using a reasonably adequate logic in which no modal collapse is demonstrable.

[15] The idea of this simplification is based on that of Alan R. Anderson, "A Reduction of Deontic Logic to Alethic Modal Logic," *Mind* 67 (1958): 100-103. The model outlined still shows that there is no modal collapse even if we regard positiveness as thus defined. The positive properties of the model turn out to be the same as before.

[16] I personally do not find Gödel's proof of possibility very reassuring. Consideration of the axioms, especially Axiom 2, may tend to dampen one's confidence in Axioms 3 and 5—that is, if one harbors any real doubt about self-consistency. I don't say that the argument begs the question of possibility; the charge is too difficult to establish. But observe that one cannot just tell by scrutinizing a property what it enables; one might be surprised at a consequence. Thus it may not be so obvious that being God-like is positive, given that positiveness obeys Axiom 2. The best course for ontological arguers may just be to take the possibility as an axiom and rebut attempts to show inconsistency. Of course the model for the modified axioms shows that there is in that case no danger of formal inconsistency.

In some respects Axiom 3 does not seem to do full justice to Gödel's intentions. (Axiom 3 appears in Dana Scott's notes and is presumably his explication of Gödel's sketch). In his notes Gödel assumes instead an axiom that the conjunction of any two positive properties is positive and adds that this is so for any number of conjuncts ("summands")— presumably meaning to include an infinite number as well (See Sobel). If we think of the property of having all positive properties as such a conjunction (instead of what it is—a property involving universal quantification), then the positiveness of being God-like (as defined by Gödel) is included. It may be that a principle along these general lines can be wed to give a plausible argument for the new version of Axiom 3 (with the modified definition of "God-like").

[17] I am grateful to an anonymous referee for substantial improvements in both form and content.

Study Questions

1. What principles of modal logic does C. Anthony Anderson see at work in Kurt Gödel's ontological proof?

2. What problems does J. Howard Sobel see with Gödel's proof?

3. What is the main move of Anderson so as to avoid Sobel's criticism?

4. Does Anderson think that the proof ultimately works?

5. How does Gödel's proof compare with Anselm's modal ontological argument? How does Gödel's proof compare with Plantinga's? On your account, which of the three do you find more attractive?

11

An Examination of the Cosmological Argument

William Rowe

William Rowe is professor of philosophy at Purdue University and the author of several works in philosophy of religion, including *Philosophy of Religion*, from which this selection is taken.* Rowe begins by distinguishing between *a priori* and *a posteriori* arguments and setting the cosmological argument in historical perspective. Next, he divides the argument into two parts: that which seeks to prove the existence of a self-existent being and that which seeks to prove that this self-existent being is the God of theism. He introduces the principle of sufficient reason: "There must be an explanation (a) of the existence of any being, and (b) of any positive fact whatever" and shows its role in the cosmological argument. In the light of this principle, he examines the argument itself and four objections to it.

Stating the Argument

Arguments for the existence of God are commonly divided into *a posteriori* arguments and *a priori* arguments. An *a posteriori* argument depends on a principle or premise that can be known only by means of our experience of the world. An *a priori* argument, on the other hand, purports to rest on principles all of which can be known independently of our experience of the world, by just reflecting on and understanding them. Of the three major arguments for the existence of God—the Cosmological, the Teleological, and the Ontological—only the last of these is entirely *a priori*. In the Cosmological Argument one starts from some simple fact about the world, such as that it contains things which are caused to exist by other things. In the Teleological Argument a somewhat more complicated fact about the world serves as a starting point, the fact that the world exhibits order and design. In the Ontological Argument, however, one begins simply with a concept of God.

Before we state the Cosmological Argument itself, we shall consider some rather general points about the argument. Historically, it can be traced to the writings of the Greek philosophers, Plato and Aristotle, but the major developments in the argument took place in the thirteenth and in the eighteenth centuries. In the thirteenth century Aquinas put forth five distinct arguments for the existence of God, and of these, the first three are versions of the Cosmological Argument.[1] In the first of these he started from the fact that there are things in the world undergoing change and reasoned to the conclusion that there must be some ultimate cause of change that is itself unchanging. In the second he started from the fact that there are things in the world that clearly are caused to exist by other things and reasoned to the conclusion that there must be some ultimate cause of existence whose own existence is itself uncaused. And in the third argument he started from the fact that there are things in the world which need not have existed at all, things which do exist but which we can easily imagine might not, and reasoned to the conclusion that there must be some being that had to be, that exists and could not have failed to exist. Now it might be objected that even if Aquinas' arguments do prove beyond doubt the existence of an unchanging changer, an uncaused cause, and a being that could not have failed to exist, the arguments fail to prove the existence of the theistic God. For the theistic God, as we saw, is supremely good, omnipotent, omniscient, and creator of but separate from and independent of the world. How do we know, for example, that the unchanging changer isn't evil or slightly ignorant? The answer to this objection is that the Cosmological Argument has two parts. In the first part the effort is to prove the existence of a special sort of being, for example, a being that could not have failed to exist, or a being that causes change in other things but is itself unchanging. In the second part of the argument the effort is to prove that the special sort of being whose existence has been established in the first part has, and must have, the features—perfect goodness, omnipotence, omniscience, and so on—which go together to make up the theistic idea of God. What this means, then, is that Aquinas' three arguments are different versions of only the first part of the Cosmological Argument. Indeed, in later sections of his *Summa Theologica* Aquinas undertakes to show that the unchanging changer, the uncaused cause of existence, and the being which had to exist are one and the same being and that this single being has all of the attributes of the theistic God.

We noted above that a second major development in the Cosmological Argument took place in the eighteenth century, a development reflected in the writings of the German philosopher, Gottfried Leibniz (1646-1716), and especially in the writings of the English theologian and philosopher, Samuel Clarke (1675-1729). In 1704 Clarke gave a series of lectures, later published under the title *A Demonstration of the Being and Attributes of God*. These lectures constitute, perhaps, the most complete, forceful, and cogent presentation of the Cosmological Argument we possess. The lectures were read by the major skeptical philosopher of the century, David Hume (1711-1776), and in his brilliant attack on the attempt to justify religion in the court of reason, his *Dialogues Concerning Natural Religion*, Hume advanced several penetrating criticisms of Clarke's arguments, criticisms which have persuaded many philosophers in the modern period to reject the Cosmological Argument. In our study of the argument we shall concentrate our attention largely on its eighteenth century form and try to assess its strengths and weaknesses in the light of the criticisms which Hume and others have advanced against it.

The first part of the eighteenth-century form of the Cosmological Argument seeks to establish the existence of a self-existent being. The second part of the argument attempts to prove that the self-existent being is the theistic God, that is, has the features which we have noted to be basic elements in the theistic idea of God. We shall consider mainly the first part of the argument, for it is against the first part that philosophers from Hume to Russell have advanced very important objections.

In stating the first part of the Cosmological Argument we shall make use of two important concepts, the concept of a *dependent being* and the concept of a *self-existent being*. By *a dependent being* we mean *a being whose existence is accounted for by the causal activity of other things*. Recalling Anselm's division into the three cases: "explained by another," "explained by nothing," and "explained by itself," it's clear that a dependent being is a being whose existence is explained by another. By *a self-existent being* we mean *a being whose existence is accounted for by its own nature*. This idea . . . is an essential element in the theistic concept of God. Again, in terms of Anselm's three cases, a self-existent being is a being whose existence is explained by itself. Armed with these two concepts, the concept of a dependent being and the concept of a self-existent being, we can now state the first part of the Cosmological Argument.

1.   Every being (that exists or ever did exist) is either a dependent being or a self-existent being.
2.   Not every being can be a dependent being.

Therefore,

3.   There exists a self-existent being.

Deductive Validity

Before we look critically at each of the premises of this argument, we should note that this argument is, to use an expression from the logician's vocabulary, *deductively valid*. To find out whether an argument is deductively valid, we need only ask the question: If its premises were true, would its conclusion have to be true? If the answer is yes, the argument is deductively valid. If the answer is no, the argument is deductively invalid. Notice that the question of the validity of an argument is entirely different from the question of whether its premises are in fact true. The following argument is made up entirely of false statements, but it is deductively valid.

1. Babe Ruth is the President of the United States.
2. The President of the United States is from Indiana.

Therefore,

3. Babe Ruth is from Indiana.

The argument is deductively valid because even though its premises are false, if they were true its conclusion would have to be true. Even God, Aquinas would say, cannot bring it about that the premises of this argument are true and yet its conclusion is false, for God's power extends only to what is possible, and it is an absolute impossibility that Babe Ruth be the President, the President be from Indiana, and yet Babe Ruth not be from Indiana.

The Cosmological Argument (that is, its first part) is a deductively valid argument. If its premises are or were true, its conclusion would have to be true. It's clear from our example about Babe Ruth, however, that the fact that an argument is deductively valid is insufficient to establish the truth of its conclusion. What else is required? Clearly that we know or have rational grounds for believing that the premises are true. If we know that the Cosmological Argument is deductively valid, and can establish that its premises are true, we shall thereby have proved that its conclusion is true. Are, then, the premises of the Cosmological Argument true? To this more difficult question we must now turn.

PSR and the First Premise

At first glance the first premise might appear to be an obvious or even trivial truth. But it is neither obvious nor trivial. And if it appears to be obvious or trivial, we must be confusing the idea of a self-existent being with the idea of a being that is not a dependent being. Clearly, it is true that any being is either a dependent being (explained by other things) or it is not a dependent being (not explained by other things). But what our premise says is that any being is either a dependent being (explained by other things) or it is a self-existent being (explained by itself). Consider again Anselm's three cases.

a. explained by another
b. explained by nothing
c. explained by itself

What our first premise asserts is that each being that exists (or ever did exist) is either of sort *a* or of sort *c*. It denies that any being is of sort *b*. And it is this denial that makes the first premise both significant and controversial. The obvious truth we must not confuse it with is the truth that any being is either of sort *a* or not of sort *a*. While this is true it is neither very significant nor controversial.

Earlier we saw that Anselm accepted as a basic principle that whatever exists has an explanation of its existence. Since this basic principle denies that any thing of sort *b* exists or ever did exist, it's clear that Anselm would believe the first premise of our Cosmological Argument. The eighteenth-century proponents of the argument also were convinced of the truth of the basic principle we attributed to Anselm. And because they were convinced of its truth, they readily accepted the first premise of the Cosmological Argument. But by the eighteenth century, Anselm's basic principle had been more fully elaborated and had received a name, the *Principle of Sufficient Reason*. Since this principle (PSR, as we shall call it) plays such an important role in justifying the premises of the Cosmological Argument, it will help us to consider it for a moment before we continue our enquiry into the truth or falsity of the premises of the Cosmological Argument.

The Principle of Sufficient Reason, as it was expressed by both Leibniz and Samuel Clarke, is a very general principle and is best understood as having two parts. In its first part it is simply a restatement of Anselm's principle that there must be an explanation of the *existence* of any being whatever. Thus if we come upon a man in a room, PSR implies that there must be an explanation of the fact that that particular man exists. A moment's reflection, however, reveals that there are many facts about the man other than the mere fact that he exists. There is the fact that the man in question is in the room he's in, rather than somewhere else, the fact that he is in good health, and the fact that he is at the moment thinking of Paris, rather than, say, London. Now, the purpose of the second part of PSR is to require an explanation of these facts, as well. We may state PSR, therefore, as the principle that *there must be an explanation (a) of the existence of any being, and (b) of any positive fact whatever*. We are now in a position to study the role this very important principle plays in the Cosmological Argument.

Since the proponent of the Cosmological Argument accepts PSR in both its parts, it is clear that he will appeal to its first part, PSRa, as justification for the first premise of the Cosmological Argument. Of course, we can and should inquire into the deeper question of whether the proponent of the argument is rationally justified in accepting PSR itself. But we shall put this question aside for the moment. What we need to see first is whether he is correct in thinking that *if* PSR is true then both of the premises of the Cosmological Argument are true. And what we have just seen is that if only the first part of PSR, that is, PSRa, is true, the first premise of the Cosmological Argument will be true. But what of the second premise of the argument? For what reasons does the proponent think that it must be true?

The Second Premise

According to the second premise, not every being that exists can be a dependent being, that is, can have the explanation of its existence in some other being or beings. Presumably, the proponent of the argument thinks there is something fundamentally wrong with the idea that every being that exists is dependent, that each existing being was caused by some other being which in turn was caused by some other being, and so on. But just what does he think is wrong with it? To help us in understanding his thinking, let's simplify things by supposing that there exists only one thing now, A_1, a living thing perhaps, that was brought into existence by something else, A_2, which perished shortly after it brought A_1, into existence. Suppose further that A_2 was brought into existence in similar fashion some time ago by A_3, and A_3 by A_4, and so forth back into the past. Each of these beings is a *dependent* being, it owes its existence to the preceding thing in the series. Now if nothing else ever existed but these beings, then what the second premise says would not be true. For if every being that exists or ever did exist is an A and was produced by a preceding A, then every being that exists or ever did exist would be dependent and, accordingly, premise two of the Cosmological Argument would be false. If the proponent of the Cosmological Argument is correct there must, then, be something wrong with the idea that every being that exists or did exist is an A and that they form a causal series. A_1 caused by A_2, A_2 caused by A_3, A_3 caused by A_4, ... A_n caused by A_{n+1}. How does the proponent of the Cosmological Argument propose to show us that there is something wrong with this view?

A popular but mistaken idea of how the proponent tries to show that something is wrong with the view, that every being might be dependent, is that he uses the following argument to reject it.

1. There must be a *first* being to start any causal series.
2. If every being were dependent there would be no *first* being to start the causal series.

Therefore,

3. Not every being can be a dependent being.

Although this argument is deductively valid, and its second premise is true, its first premise overlooks the distinct possibility that a causal series might be *infinite*, with no first member at all. Thus if we go back to our series of A beings, where each A is dependent, having been produced by the preceding A in the causal series, it's clear that if the series existed it would have no first member, for every A in the series there would be a preceding A which produced it, *ad infinitum*. The first premise of the argument just given assumes that a causal series must stop with a first member somewhere in the distant past. But there seems to be no good reason for making that assumption.

The eighteenth-century proponents of the Cosmological Argument recognized that the causal series of dependent beings could be infinite, without a first member to start the series. They rejected the idea that every being that is or ever was is dependent not because there would then be no first member to the series of dependent beings, but because there would then be no explanation for the fact that there are and have always been dependent beings. To see their reasoning let's return to our simplification of the supposition that the only things that exist or ever did exist are dependent beings. In our simplification of that supposition only one of the dependent beings exists at a time, each one perishing as it produces the next in the series. Perhaps the first thing to note about this supposition is that there is no individual A in the causal series of dependent beings whose existence is unexplained—A_1 is explained by A_2, A_2 by A_3, and A_n by A_{n+1}. So the first part of PSR, PSRa, appears to be satisfied. There is no particular being whose existence lacks an explanation. What, then, is it that lacks an explanation, if every particular A in the causal series of dependent beings has an explanation? If is the series itself that lacks an explanation. Or, as I've chosen to express it, *the fact that there are and have always been dependent beings.* For suppose we ask why it is that there are and have always been As in existence. It won't do to say that As have always been producing other As—we can't explain why there have always been As by saying there always have been As. Nor, on the supposition that only As have ever existed, can we explain the fact that there have always been As by appealing to something other than an A—for no such thing would have existed. Thus the supposition that the only things that exist or ever existed are dependent things leaves us with a fact for which there can be no explanation; namely, the fact that there are and have always been dependent beings.

Questioning the Justification
of the Second Premise

Critics of the Cosmological Argument have raised several important objections against the claim that if every being is dependent the series or collection of those beings would have no explanation. Our understanding of the Cosmological Argument, as well as of its strengths and weaknesses, will be deepened by a careful consideration of these criticisms.

The first criticism is that the proponent of the Cosmological Argument makes the mistake of treating the collection or series of dependent beings as though it were itself a dependent being, and, therefore, requires an explanation of its existence. But, so the objection goes, the collection of dependent beings is not itself a dependent being any more than a collection of stamps is itself a stamp.

A second criticism is that the proponent makes the mistake of inferring that because each member of the collection of dependent beings has a cause, the collection itself must have a cause. But, as Bertrand Russell noted, such reasoning is as fallacious as to infer that the human race (that is, the collection of human beings) must have a mother because each member of the collection (each human being) has a mother.

A third criticism is that the proponent of the argument fails to realize that for there to be an explanation of a collection of things is nothing more than for there to be an explanation of each of the things making up the collection. Since in the infinite collection (or series) of dependent beings, each being in the collection does have an explanation—by virtue of having been caused by some preceding member of the collection—the explanation of the collection, so the criticism goes, has already been given. As David Hume remarked, "Did I show you the particular causes of each individual in a collection of twenty particles of matter, I should think it very unreasonable, should you afterwards ask me, what was the cause of the whole twenty. This is sufficiently explained in explaining the cause of the parts."[2]

Finally, even if the proponent of the Cosmological Argument can satisfactorily answer these objections, he must face one last objection to his ingenious attempt to justify premise two of the Cosmological Argument. For someone may agree that if nothing exists but an infinite collection of dependent beings, the infinite collection will have no explanation of its existence, and still refuse to conclude from this that there is something wrong with the idea that every being is a dependent being. Why, he might ask, should we think that everything has to have an explanation? What's wrong with admitting that the fact that there are and have always been dependent beings is a *brute* fact, a fact having no explanation whatever? Why does everything have to have an explanation anyway? We must now see what can be said in response to these several objections.

Responses to Criticism

It is certainly a mistake to think that a collection of stamps is itself a stamp, and very likely a mistake to think that the collection of dependent beings is itself a dependent being. But the mere fact that the proponent of the argument thinks that there must be an explanation not only for each member of the collection of dependent beings but for the collection itself is not sufficient grounds for concluding that he must view the collection as itself a dependent being. The collection of human beings, for example, is certainly not itself a human being. Admitting this, however, we might still seek an explanation of why there is a collection of human beings, of why there are such things as human beings at all. So the mere fact that an explanation is demanded for the collection of dependent beings is no proof that the person who demands the explanation must be supposing that the collection itself is just another dependent being.

The second criticism attributes to the proponent of the Cosmological Argument the following bit of reasoning.

1. Every member of the collection of dependent beings has a cause or explanation.

Therefore,

2. The collection of dependent beings has a cause or explanation.

As we noted in setting forth this criticism, arguments of this sort are often unreliable. It would be a mistake to conclude that a collection of objects is light in weight simply because each object in the collection is light in weight, for if there were many objects in the collection it might be quite heavy. On the other hand, if we know that each marble weighs more than one ounce, we could infer validly that the collection of marbles weighs more than an ounce. Fortunately, however, we don't need to decide whether the inference from 1 to 2 is valid or invalid. We need not decide this question because the proponent of the Cosmological Argument need not use this inference to establish that there must be an explanation of the collection of dependent beings. He need not use this inference because he has in PSR a principle from which it follows immediately that the collection of dependent beings has a cause or explanation. For according to PSR, every positive fact must have an explanation. If it is a fact that there exists a collection of dependent beings then, according to PSR, that fact too must have an explanation. So it is PSR that the proponent of the Cosmological Argument appeals to in concluding that there must be an explanation of the collection of dependent beings, and not some dubious inference from the premise that each member of the collection has an explanation. It seems, then, that neither of the first two criticisms is strong enough to do any serious damage to the reasoning used to support the second premise of the Cosmological Argument.

The third objection contends that to explain the existence of a collection of things is the same thing as to explain the existence of each of its members. If we consider a collection of dependent beings where each being in the collection is explained by the preceding member which caused it, it's clear that no member of the collection will lack an explanation of its existence. But, so the criticism goes, if we've explained the existence of every member of a collection, we've explained the existence of the collection—there's nothing left over to be explained. This forceful criticism, originally advanced by David Hume, has gained considerable support in the modern period. But the criticism rests on an assumption that the proponent of the Cosmological Argument would not accept. The assumption is that to explain the existence of a collection of things it is *suffcient* to explain the existence of every member in the collection. To see what is wrong with this assumption is to understand the basic issue in the reasoning by which the proponent of the Cosmological Argument seeks to establish that not every being can be a dependent being.

In order for there to be an explanation of the existence of the collection of dependent beings, it's clear that the eighteenth-century proponents would require that the following two conditions be satisfied:

C1.   There is an explanation of the existence of each of the members of the collection of dependent beings.
C2.   There is an explanation of why there are any dependent beings.

According to the proponents of the Cosmological Argument, if every being that exists or ever did exist is a dependent being—that is, if the whole of reality consists of nothing more than a collection of dependent beings—C1 will be satisfied, but C2 will not be satisfied. And since C2 won't be satisfied, there will be no explanation of the collection of dependent beings. The third criticism, therefore, says in effect that if C1 is satisfied, C2 will be satisfied, and, since in a collection of dependent beings each member will have an explanation in whatever it was that produced it, C1 will be satisfied. So, therefore, C2 will be satisfied and the collection of dependent beings will have an explanation.

Although the issue is a complicated one, I think it is possible to see that the third criticism rests on a mistake: the mistake of thinking that if C1 is satisfied C2 must also be satisfied. The mistake is a natural one to make for it is easy to imagine circumstances in which if C1 is satisfied C2 also will be satisfied. Suppose, for example, that the whole of reality includes not just a collection of dependent beings but also a self-existent being. Suppose further that instead of each dependent being having been produced by some other dependent being, every dependent being was produced by the self-existent being. Finally, let us consider both the possibility that the collection of dependent beings is finite in time and has a first member, and the possibility that the collection of dependent beings is infinite in past time, having no first member. Using G for the self-existent being, the first possibility may be diagramed as follows:

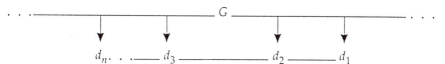

G, we shall say, has always existed and always will. We can think of d_1 as some presently existing dependent being, d_2, d_3, and so forth as dependent beings that existed at some time in the past, and d_n as the first dependent being to exist. The second possibility may be portrayed as follows:

On this diagram there is no first member of the collection of dependent beings. Each member of the infinite collection, however, is explained by reference to the self-existent being G which produced it. Now the interesting point about both these cases is that the explanation that has been provided for the members of the collection of dependent beings carries with it, at least in part, an answer to the question of why there are any dependent beings at all. In both cases we may explain why there are dependent beings by pointing out that there exists a self-existent being that has been engaged in producing them. So once we have learned that the existence of each member of the collection of dependent beings has its existence explained by the fact that G produced it, we have already learned why there are dependent beings.

Someone might object that we haven't really learned why there are dependent beings until we also learn *why* G has been producing them. But, of course, we could also say that we haven't really explained the existence of a particular dependent being, say d_3, until we also learn not just that G produced it but *why* G produced it. The point we need to grasp, however, is that once we admit that every dependent being's existence is explained by G, we must admit that the fact that there are dependent beings has also been explained. So it is not unnatural that someone should think that to explain the existence of the collection of dependent beings is nothing more than to explain the existence of its members. For, as we've seen, to explain the collection's existence is to explain each member's existence and to explain why there are any dependent beings at all. And in the examples we've considered, in doing the one (explaining why each dependent being exists) we've already done the other (explained why there are any dependent beings at all). We must now see, however, that on the supposition that the whole of reality consists *only* of a collection of dependent beings, to give an explanation of each member's existence is not to provide an explanation of why there are dependent beings.

In the examples we've considered, we have gone *outside* of the collection of dependent beings in order to explain the members' existence. But if the only beings that exist or ever existed are dependent beings then each dependent being will be explained by some other dependent being, ad infinitum. This does not mean that there will be some particular dependent being whose existence is unaccounted for. Each dependent being has an explanation of its existence; namely, in the dependent being which preceded it and produced it. So C1 is satisfied: there is an explanation of the existence of each member of the collection of dependent beings. Turning to C2, however, we can see that it will not be satisfied. We cannot explain why there are (or have ever been) dependent beings by appealing to all the members of the infinite collection of dependent beings. For if the question to be answered is why there are (or have ever been) any dependent beings at all, we cannot answer that question by noting that there always have been dependent beings, each one accounting for the existence of some other dependent being. Thus on the supposition that every being is dependent, it seems there will be no explanation of why there are dependent beings. C2 will not be satisfied. Therefore, on the supposition that every being is dependent there will be no explanation of the existence of the collection of dependent beings.

The Truth of PSR

We come now to the final criticism of the reasoning supporting the second premise of the Cosmological Argument. According to this criticism, it is admitted that the supposition that every being is dependent implies that there will be a *brute fact* in the universe, a fact, that is, for which there can be no explanation whatever. For there will be no explanation of the fact that dependent beings exist and have always been in existence. It is this brute fact that the proponents of the argument were describing when they pointed out that if every being is dependent, the series or collection of dependent beings would lack an explanation of *its* existence. The final criticism asks what is wrong with admitting that the universe contains such a brute, unintelligible fact. In asking this question the critic challenges the fundamental principle, PSR, on which the Cosmological Argument rests. For, as we've seen, the first premise of the argument denies that there exists a being whose existence has no explanation. In support of this premise the proponent appeals to the first part of PSR. The second premise of the argument claims that not every being can be dependent. In support of this premise the proponent appeals to the second part of PSR, the part which states that there must be an explanation of any positive fact whatever.

The proponent reasons that if every being were a dependent being, then although the first part of PSR would be satisfied—every being would have an explanation—the second part would be violated; there would be no explanation for the positive fact that there are and have always been dependent beings. For first, since every being is supposed to be dependent, there would be nothing outside of the collection of dependent beings to explain the collection's existence. Second, the fact that each member of the collection has an explanation in some other dependent being is insufficient to explain why there are and have always been dependent beings. And, finally, there is nothing about the collection of dependent beings that would suggest that it is a self-existent collection. Consequently, if every being were dependent, the fact that there are and have always been dependent beings would have no explanation. But this violates the second part of PSR. So the second premise of the Cosmological Argument must be true: Not every being can be a dependent being. This conclusion, however, is no better than the principle, PSR, on which it rests. And it is the point of the final criticism to question the truth of PSR. Why, after all, should we accept the idea that every being and every positive fact must have an explanation? Why, in short, should we believe PSR? These are important questions, and any final judgment of the Cosmological Argument depends on how they are answered.

Most of the theologians and philosophers who accept PSR have tried to defend it in either of two ways. Some have held that PSR is (or can be) known *intuitively* to be true. By this they mean that if we fully understand and reflect on what is said by PSR we can see that it must be true. Now, undoubtedly, there are statements which are known intuitively to be true. "Every triangle has exactly three angles" or "No physical object can be in two different places in space at one and the same time" are examples of statements whose truth we can apprehend just by understanding and reflecting on them. The difficulty with the claim that PSR is intuitively true, however, is that a number of very able philosophers fail to apprehend its truth, and some even claim that the principle is false. It is doubtful, therefore, that many of us, if any, know intuitively that PSR is true.

The second way philosophers and theologians who accept PSR have sought to defend it is by claiming that although it is not known to be true, it is, nevertheless, a presupposition of reason, a basic assumption that rational people make, whether or not they reflect sufficiently to become aware of the assumption. It's probably true that there are some assumptions we all make about our world, assumptions which are so basic that most of us are unaware of them. And, I suppose, it might be true that

PSR is such an assumption. What bearing would this view of PSR have on the Cosmological Argument? Perhaps the main point to note is that even if PSR is a presupposition we all share, the premises of the Cosmological Argument could still be false. For PSR itself could still be false. The fact, if it is a fact, that all of us *presuppose* that every existing being and every positive fact has an explanation does not imply that no being exists, and no positive fact obtains, without an explanation. Nature is not bound to satisfy our presuppositions. As the American philosopher William James once remarked in another connection, "In the great boarding house of nature, the cakes and the butter and the syrup seldom come out so even and leave the plates so clear."

Our study of the first part of the Cosmological Argument has led us to the fundamental principle on which its premises rest, the Principle of Sufficient Reason. Since we do not seem to know that PSR is true, we cannot reasonably claim to know that the premises of the Cosmological Argument are true. They might be true. But unless we do know them to be true they cannot *establish* for us the conclusion that there exists a being that has the explanation of its existence within its own nature. If it were shown, however, that even though we do not *know* that PSR is true we all, nevertheless, presuppose PSR to be true, then, whether PSR is true or not, to be consistent we should accept the Cosmological Argument. For, as we've seen, its premises imply its conclusion and its premises do seem to follow from PSR. But no one has succeeded in *showing* that PSR is an assumption that most or all of us share. So our final conclusion must be that although the Cosmological Argument might be a *sound* argument (valid with true premises), it does not provide us with good rational grounds for believing that among these beings that exist there is one whose existence is accounted for by its own nature. Having come to this conclusion, we may safely put aside the second part of the argument. For even if it succeeded in showing that a self-existent being would have the other attributes of the theistic God, the Cosmological Argument would still not provide us with good rational grounds for belief in God, having failed in its first part to provide us with good rational grounds for believing that there is a self-existent being.

Endnotes

*Reprinted from Louis P. Pojman, *Philosophy of Religion* (Wadsworth Publishing Co., 1978), by permission. © 1994 by Wadsworth, Inc. All rights reserved. Wadsworth Publishing Company, Belmont, California 94002.

1 See St. Thomas Aquinas, *Summa Theologica*, la. 2, 3.

2 David Hume, *Dialogues Concerning Natural Religion*, Part IX, ed. H. D. Aiken (New York: Hafner Publishing Company, 1948), pp. 59-60.

Study Questions

1.   For Rowe, what differences are there between *a priori* and *a posteriori* arguments for God's existence?

2.   What is the Principle of Sufficient Reason (PSR)?

3.   Did the eighteenth-century defenders of the cosmological argument think that the causal series could be infinite?

4.   What is Rowe's verdict regarding PSR?

5.   What is Rowe's opinion regarding the effectiveness of arguments for God's existence?

12

The Argument from Design

Richard G. Swinburne

Richard G. Swinburne is Nolloth Professor of the Philosophy of the Christian Religion at the University of Oxford, and is author of *Revelation; The Concept of Miracle*, co-author of *Personal Identity, Space and Time, An Introduction to Confirmation Theory*; editor of *The Justification of Induction, The Existence of God Faith and Reason, The Coherence of Theism, The Evolution of the Soul*, and *The Christian God*.

In this paper* he tries to show that there are no valid formal objections to the argument from design.

The object of this paper[1] is to show that there are no valid formal objections to the argument from design, so long as the argument is articulated with sufficient care. In particular I wish to analyze Hume's attack on the argument in *Dialogues Concerning Natural Religion* and to show that none of the formal objections made therein by Philo have any validity against a carefully articulated version of the argument.

The argument from design is an argument from the order or regularity of things in the world to a god or, more precisely, a very powerful free non-embodied rational agent, who is responsible for that order. By a body I understand a part of the material Universe subject, at any rate partially, to an agent's direct control, to be contrasted with other parts not thus subject. An agent's body marks the limits to what he can directly control; he can only control other parts of the Universe by moving his body. An agent who could directly control any part of the Universe would not be embodied. Thus ghosts, if they existed, would be non-embodied agents, because there are no particular pieces of matter subject to their direct control, but any piece of matter may be so subject. I use the word 'design' in such a way that it is not analytic that if anything evinces design, an agent designed it, and so it becomes a synthetic question whether the design of the world shows the activity of a designer.

The argument, taken by itself, as was admitted in the *Dialogues* by Cleanthes the proponent of the argument, does not show that the designer of the world is omnipotent, omniscient, totally good, etc. Nor does it show that he is the God of Abraham, Isaac, and Jacob. To make these points further arguments would be needed. The isolation of the argument from design from the web of Christian apologetic is perhaps a somewhat unnatural step, but necessary in order to analyze its structure. My claim is that the argument does not commit any formal fallacy, and by this I mean that it keeps to the canons of argument about matters of fact and does not violate any of them. It is, however, an argument by analogy. It argues from an analogy between the order of the world and the products of human art to a god responsible for the former, in some ways similar to man who is responsible for the latter. And even if there are no formal fallacies in the argument, one unwilling to admit the conclusion might still claim that the analogy was too weak and remote for him to have to admit it, that the argument gave only negligible support to the conclusion which remained improbable. In defending the argument I will leave to the objector this way of escape from its conclusion.

I will begin by setting forward the argument from design in a more careful and precise way than Cleanthes did.

There are in the world two kinds of regularity or order, and all empirical instances of order are such because they evince one or other or both kinds of order. These are the regularities of copresence or spatial order, and regularities of succession, or temporal order. Regularities of copresence are patterns of spatial order at some one instant of time. An example of a regularity of copresence would be a town with all its roads at right angles to each other, or a section of books in a library arranged in alphabetical order of authors. Regularities of succession are simple patterns of behaviour of objects, such as their behaviour in accordance with the laws of nature—for example, Newton's law of gravitation, which holds universally to a very high degree of approximation, that all bodies attract each other with forces proportional to the product of their masses and inversely proportional to the square of their distance apart.

Many of the striking examples of order in the world evince an order which is due both to a regularity of copresence and to a regularity of succession. A working car consists of many parts so adjusted to each other that it follows the instructions of the driver delivered by his pulling and pushing a few levers and buttons and turning a wheel to take passengers whither he wishes. Its order arises because its parts are so arranged at some instant (regularity of copresence) that, the laws of nature being as they are (regularity of succession) it brings about the result neatly and efficiently. The order of living animals and plants likewise results from regularities of both types.

Men who marvel at the order of the world may marvel at either or both the regularities of copresence and of succession. The men of the eighteenth century, that great century of 'reasonable religion', were struck almost exclusively by the regularities of copresence. They marvelled at the design and orderly operations of animals and plants; but since they largely took for granted the regularities of succession, what struck them about the animals and plants, as to a lesser extent about machines made by men, was the subtle and coherent arrangement of their millions of parts. Paley's *Natural Theology* dwells mainly on details of comparative anatomy, on eyes and ears and muscles and bones arranged with minute precision so as to operate with high efficiency, and Hume's Cleanthes produces the same kind of examples: 'Consider, anatomise the eye, survey its structure and contrivance, and tell me from your own feeling, if the idea of a contriver does not immediately flow in upon you with a force like that of sensation'.[2]

Those who argue from the existence of regularities of copresence other than those produced by men, to the existence of a god who produced them are however in many respects on slippery ground when compared with those who rely for their premises on regularities of succession. We shall see several of these weaknesses later in considering Hume's objections to the argument, but it is worth while noting two of them at the outset. First, although the world contains many striking regularities of copresence (some few of which are due to human agency), it also contains many examples of spatial disorder. The uniform distribution of the galactic clusters is a marvellous example of spatial order, but the arrangement of trees in an African jungle is a marvellous example of spatial disorder. Although the proponent of the argument may then proceed to argue that in an important sense or from some point of view (e.g. utility to man) the order vastly exceeds the disorder, he has to argue for this in no way obvious proposition.

Secondly the proponent of the argument runs the risk that the regularities of copresence may be explained in terms of something else by a normal scientific explanation[3] in a way that the regularities of succession could not possibly be. A scientist could show that a regularity of copresence R arose from an apparently disordered state D by means of the normal operation of the laws of nature. This would not entirely 'explain away' the regularity of copresence, because the proponent of this argument from design might then argue that the apparently disordered state D really had a latent order, being the kind of state which, when the laws of nature operate, turns into a manifestly ordered one. So long as only few of the physically possible states of apparent disorder were states of latent order, the existence of many states of latent order would be an important contingent fact which could form a premiss for an argument from design. But there is always the risk that scientists might show that most states of apparent disorder were states of latent order, that is, that if the world lasted long enough considerable order must emerge from whichever of many initial states it began. If a scientist shows that, he would have explained by normal scientific explanation the existence of regularities of copresence in terms of something completely different. The eighteenth-century proponents of the argument from design did not suspect this danger and hence the devastating effect of Darwin's Theory of Evolution by Natural Selection on those who accepted their argument. For Darwin showed that the regularities of copresence of the animal and plant kingdoms had evolved by natural processes from an apparently disordered state and would have evolved equally from any other apparently disordered states. Whether all regularities of copresence can be fully explained in this kind of way no one yet knows, but the danger remains for the proponent of an argument from design of this kind that they can be.

However, those who argue from the operation of regularities of succession other than those produced by men to the existence of a god who produces them do not run into either of these difficulties. Regularities of succession (other than those produced by men) unlike regularities of copresence, are all-pervasive. Simple natural laws rule almost all successions of events. Nor can regularities of succession be given a normal scientific explanation in terms of something else. For the normal scientific explanation of the operation of a regularity of succession is in terms of the operation of a yet more general regularity of succession. Note too that a normal scientific explanation of the existence of regularities of copresence in terms of something different, if it can be provided, is explanation in terms of regularities of succession.

For these reasons the proponent of the argument from design does much better to rely for his premiss more on regularities of succession. St Thomas Aquinas, wiser than the men of the eighteenth century, did just this. He puts forward an argument from design as his fifth and last way to prove the existence of God, and gives his premiss as follows:

"The fifth way is based on the guidedness of nature. An orderedness of actions to an end is observed in all bodies obeying natural laws, even when they lack awareness. For their behaviour hardly ever varies, and will practically always turn out well; which shows that they truly tend to a goal, and do not merely hit it by accident.'[4]   If we ignore any value judgment in 'practically always turn out well', St Thomas' argument is an argument from regularities of succession.

The most satisfactory premiss for the argument from design is then the operation of regularities of succession other than those produced by men, that is, the operation of laws. Almost all things almost always obey simple natural laws and so behave in a strikingly regular way. Given the premiss, what is our justification for proceeding to the conclusion, that a very powerful free non-embodied rational agent is responsible for their behaving in that way? The justification which Aquinas gives is that 'Nothing . . . that lacks awareness tends to a goal, except under the direction of someone with awareness and with understanding; the arrow, for example requires an archer. Everything in nature, therefore is directed to its goal by someone with understanding and this we call "God".'⁵ A similar argument has been given by many religious apologists since Aquinas, but clearly as it stands it is guilty of the grossest *petitio principii*. Certainly *some* things which tend to a goal, tend to a goal because of a direction imposed upon them by someone 'with awareness and with understanding'. Did not the archer place the arrow and pull the string in a certain way the arrow would not tend to its goal. But whether *all* things which tend to a goal tend to a goal for this reason is the very question at issue and that they do cannot be used as a premise to prove the conclusion. We must therefore reconstruct the argument in a more satisfactory way.

The structure of any plausible argument from design can only be the existence of a god responsible for the order in the world is a hypothesis well confirmed on the basis of the evidence, viz. that contained in the premiss which we have now stated, and better confirmed than any other hypothesis. I shall begin by showing that there can be no other possible explanation for the operation of natural laws than the activity of a god and then see to what extent the hypothesis is well confirmed on the basis of the evidence.

Almost all phenomena can, as we have seen, be explained by a normal scientific explanation in terms of the operation of natural laws on preceding states. There is however one other way of explaining natural phenomena, and that is explaining in terms of the rational choice of a free agent. When a man marries Jan rather than Anne, becomes a solicitor rather than a barrister, kills rather than shows mercy after considering arguments in favour of each course, he brings about a state of the world by his free and rational choice. To all appearances this is an entirely different way whereby states of the world may come about than through the operation of laws of nature on preceding states. Someone may object that it is necessary that physiological or other scientific laws operate in order for the agent to bring about effects. My answer is that certainly it is necessary that such laws operate in order for effects brought about directly by the agent to have ulterior consequences. But unless there are some effects which the agent brings about directly without the operation of scientific laws acting on preceding physical states bringing them about, then these laws and states could fully explain the effects and there would be no need to refer to explaining them to the rational choice of an agent. True, the apparent freedom and rationality of the human will *may* prove an illusion. Man may have no more option what to do than a machine and be guided by an argument no more than is a piece of iron. But this has never yet been shown and, in the absence of good philosophical and scientific argument to show it, I assume, what is apparent, that when a man acts by free and rational choice, his agency is the operation of a different kind of causality from that of scientific laws. The free choice of a rational agent is the only way of accounting for natural phenomena other than the way of normal scientific explanation, which is recognised as such by all men and has not been reduced to normal scientific explanation.

Almost all regularities of succession are due to the normal operation of scientific laws. But to say this is simply to say that these regularities are instances of more general regularities. The operation of the most fundamental regularities clearly cannot be given a normal scientific explanation. If their operation is to receive an explanation and not merely to be left as a brute fact, that explanation must therefore be in terms of the rational choice of a free agent. What then are grounds for adopting this hypothesis, given that it is the only possible one?

The grounds are that we can explain some few regularities of succession as produced by rational agents and that the other regularities cannot be explained except in this way. Among the typical products of a rational agent acting freely are regularities both of copresence and of succession. The alphabetical order of books on a library shelf is due to the activity of the librarian who chose to arrange them thus. The order of the cards of a pack by suits and seniority in each suit is due to the activity of the card player who arranged them thus. Among examples of regularities of succession produced by men are the notes of a song sung by a singer or the movements of a dancer's body when he performs a dance in time with the accompanying instrument. Hence knowing that some regularities of succession have such a cause, we postulate that they all have. An agent produces the celestial harmony like a man who sings a song. But at this point an obvious difficulty arises. The regularities of succession, such as songs which are produced by men, are produced by agents of comparatively small power, whose bodies we can locate. If an agent is responsible for the operation of the laws of nature, he must act directly on the whole Universe, as we act directly on our bodies. Also he must be of immense power and intelligence compared with men. Hence he can only be somewhat similar to men having, like them, intelligence and freedom of choice, yet unlike them in the degree of these and in not possessing a body. For a body, as I have distinguished it earlier, is a part of the Universe subject to an agent's direct control, to be contrasted with other parts not thus subject. The fact that we are obliged to postulate on the basis of differences in the effects differences in the causes, men and the god, weakens the argument. How much it weakens it depends on how great these differences are.

Our argument thus proves to be an argument by analogyand to exemplify a pattern common in scientific influence. As are caused by Bs. A*s are similar to As. Therefore—given that there is no more satisfactory explanation of the existence of A*s—they are produced by B*s similarly to Bs. B*s are postulated to be similar in all respects to Bs except in so far as shown otherwise, viz. except in so far as the dissimilarities between As and A*s force us to postulate a difference. A well-known scientific example of this type of inference is as follows. Certain pressures (As) on the walls of containers are produced by billiard balls (Bs) with certain motions. Similar pressures (A*s) are produced on the walls of containers which contain not billiard balls but gases. Therefore, since we have no better explanation of the existence of the pressures, gases consist of particles (B*s) similar to billiard balls except in certain respects—e.g. size. By similar arguments scientists have argued for the existence of many unobservables. Such an argument becomes weaker in so far as the properties which we are forced to attribute to the B*s because of the differences between the As and the A*s become different from those of the Bs. Nineteenth-century physicists postulated the existence of an elastic solid, the aether, to account for the propagation of light. But the way in which light was propagated turned out to have such differences (despite the similarities) from the way in which waves in solids are normally propagated that the physicists had to say that if there was an aether it had very many peculiar properties not possessed by normal liquids or solids. Hence they concluded that the argument for its existence was very weak. The proponent of the argument from design stresses the similarities between the regularities of succession produced by man and those which are laws of nature and so between men and the agent which he postulates as responsible for the laws of nature. The opponent of the argument stresses the dissimilarities. The degree of support which the conclusion obtains from the evidence depends on how great the similarities are.

The degree of support for the conclusion of an argument from analogy does not however depend merely on the similarities between the types of evidence but on the degree to which the resulting theory makes explanation of empirical matters more simple and coherent. In the case of the argument from design the conclusion has an enormous simplifying effect on explanations of empirical matters. For if the conclusion is true, if a very powerful non-embodied rational agent is responsible for the operation of the laws of nature, then normal scientific explanation would prove to be personal explanation. That is, explanation of some phenomenon in terms of the operation of a natural law would ultimately be an explanation in terms of the operation of an agent. Hence (given an initial arrangement of matter) the principles of explanation of phenomena would have been reduced from two to one. It is a basic principle of explanation that we should postulate as few as possible kinds of explanation. To take a more mundane example—if we have as possible alternatives to explain physical phenomena by the operation of two kinds of force, the electromagnetic and the gravitational, and to explain physical phenomena in terms of the operation of only one kind of force, the gravitational, we ought always—*ceteris paribus*—to prefer the later alternative. Since as we have seen, we are obliged, at any rate at present, to use explanation in terms of the free choice of a rational agent in explaining many empirical phenomena, then if the amount of similarity between the order in the Universe not produced by human agents and that produced by human agents makes it at all plausible to do so, we ought to postulate that an agent is responsible for the former as well as for the latter. So then in so far as regularities of succession produced by the operation of natural laws are similar to those produced by human agents, to postulate that a rational agent is responsible for them would indeed provide a simple unifying and coherent explanation of natural phenomena. What is there against taking this step? Simply that celebrated principle of explanation—*entia non sunt multiplicanda praeter necessitatem*—do not add a god to your ontology unless you have to. The issue turns on whether the evidence constitutes enough of a *necessitas* to compel us to multiply entities. Whether it does depends on how strong is the analogy between the regularities of succession produced by human agents and those produced by the operation of natural laws. I do not propose to assess the strength of the analogy but only to claim that everything turns on it. I claim that the inference from natural laws to a god responsible for them is of a perfectly proper type for inference about matters of fact, and that the only issue is whether the evidence is strong enough to allow us to affirm that it is probable that the conclusion is true.

Now that I have reconstructed the argument from design in what is, I hope, a logically impeccable form, I turn to consider Hume's criticisms of it, and I shall argue that all his criticisms alleging formal fallacies in the argument do not apply to it in the form in which I have stated it. This, we shall see, is largely because the criticisms are bad criticisms of the argument in any form but also in small part because Hume directed his fire against that form of the argument which used as its premiss the existence of regularities of copresence other than those produced by men, and did not appeal to the operation of regularities of succession. I shall begin by considering one general point which he makes only in the *Enquiry* and then consider in turn all the objections which appear on the pages of the *Dialogues*.

1.   The point which appears at the beginning of Hume's discussion of the argument in section XI of the *Enquiry* is a point which reveals the fundamental weakness of Hume's sceptical position. In discussing the argument, Hume puts forward as a general principle that 'when we infer any particular cause from an effect, we must proportion the one to the other, and can never be allowed to ascribe to the cause any qualities but what are exactly sufficient to produce the effect.'[6] Now it is true that Hume uses this principle mainly to show that we are not justified in inferring that the god responsible for the design of the Universe is totally good, omnipotent, and omniscient. I accept, as Cleanthes did, that the argument does not by itself lead to that conclusion. But Hume's use of the principle tends to cast doubt on the validity of the argument in the weaker form in which I am discussing it, for it seems to suggest that although we

may conclude that whatever produced the regularity of the world was a regularity-producing object, we cannot go further and conclude that it is an agent who acts by choice, etc., for this would be to suppose more than we need in order to account for the effect. It is, therefore, important to realize that the principle is clearly false on our normal understanding of what are the criteria of inference about empirical matters. For the universal adoption of this celebrated principle would lead to the abandonment of science. Any scientist who told us only that the cause of E had E-producing characteristics would not add an iota to our knowledge. Explanation of matters of fact consists in postulating on reasonable grounds that the cause of an effect has certain characteristics other than those sufficient to produce the effect.

2.   Two objections seem to be telescoped in the following passage of the *Dialogues*. 'When two *species* of objects have always been observed to be conjoined together, I can *infer* by custom the existence of one wherever I *see* the existence of the other; and this I call an argument from experience. But how this argument can have place where the objects, as in the present case, are single, individual, without parallel or specific resemblance, may be difficult to explain.'[7]   One argument here seems to be that we can only infer from an observed A to an unobserved B when we have frequently observed As and Bs together, and that we cannot infer to a B unless we have actually observed other Bs. Hence we cannot infer from regularities of succession to an unobserved god on the analogy of the connection between observed regularities and human agents, unless we have observed at other times other gods. This argument, like the first, reveals Hume's inadequate appreciation of a scientific method. As we saw in the scientific examples which I cited, a more developed science than Hume knew has taught us that when observed As have a relation R to observed Bs, it is often perfectly reasonable to postulate that observed A*s, similar to As have the same relation to unobserved and unobservable B*s similar to Bs.

3.   The other objection which seems to be involved in the above passage is that we cannot reach conclusions about an object which is the only one of its kind, and, as the Universe is such an object, we cannot reach conclusions about the regularities characteristic of it as a whole.[8] But cosmologists are reaching very well-tested scientific conclusions about the Universe as a whole, as are physical anthropologists about the origins of our human race, even though it is the only human race of which we have knowledge and perhaps the only human race there is. The principle quoted in the objections is obviously wrong. There is no space here to analyze its errors in detail but suffice it to point out that it becomes hopelessly confused by ignoring the fact that uniqueness is relative to description. Nothing describable is unique under all descriptions (the Universe is, like the solar system, a number of material bodies distributed in empty space) and everything describable is unique under some description.

4. The next argument which we meet in the *Dialogues* is that the postulated existence of a rational agent who produces the order of the world would itself need explaining. Picturing such an agent as a mind, and a mind as an arrangement of ideas, Hume phrases the objection as follows: 'a mental world or Universe of ideas requires a cause as much as does a material world or Universe of objects."[9]   Hume himself provides the obvious answer to this—that it is no objection to explaining X by Y that we cannot explain Y. But then he suggests that the Y in this case, the mind, is just as mysterious as the ordered Universe. Men never 'thought it satisfactory to explain a particular effect by a particular cause which was no more to be accounted for than the effect itself.'[10]   On the contrary, scientists have always thought it reasonable to postulate entities merely to explain effects, so long as the postulated entities accounted simply and coherently for the characteristics of the effects. The existence of molecules with their characteristic behaviour was 'no more to be accounted for' than observable phenomena, but the postulation of their existence gave a neat and simple explanation of a whole host of chemical and physical phenomena, and that was the justification for postulating their existence.

5.   Next, Hume argues that if we are going to use the analogy of a human agent we ought to go the whole way and postulate that the god who gives order to the Universe is like men in many other respects. 'Why not become a perfect anthropomorphite? Why not assert the deity or deities to be corporeal, and, to have eyes, a nose, mouths, ears, etc.'[11] The argument from design is as we have seen, an argument by analogy. All analogies break down somewhere; otherwise they would not be analogies. In saying that the relation of A to B is analogous to a relation of A* to a postulated B*, we do not claim that B* is in all respects like B, but only in such respects as to account for the existence of the relation and also in other respects except in so far as we have contrary evidence. For the activity of a god to account for the regularities, he must be free, rational, and very powerful. But it is not necessary that he, like men, should only be able to act on a limited part of the Universe, a body, and by acting on that control the rest of the Universe. Hence the postulation of the existence of the god would not explain the operations of those laws: yet to explain the operation of all scientific laws was the point of postulating the existence of the god. The hypothesis that the god is not embodied thus explains more and explains more coherently than the hypothesis that he is embodied. Hume's objection would however have weight against an argument from regularities of copresence which did not appeal to the operation of regularities of succession. For one could suppose an embodied god just as well as a disembodied god to have made the animal kingdom and then left it alone, as a man makes a machine, or, like a landscape gardener, to have laid out the galactic clusters. The explanatory force of such an hypothesis is as great as that of the hypothesis that a disembodied god did these things, and argument from analogy would

suggest the hypothesis of an embodied god to be more probable. Incidentally, a god whose prior existence was shown by the existence of regularities of copresence might now be dead, but a god whose existence was shown by the present operation of regularities of succession could not be, since the existence of an agent is contemporaneous with the temporal regularities which he produces.

6.   Hume urges—why should we not postulate many gods to give order to the Universe, not merely one? 'A great number of men join in building a house or a ship, in rearing a city, in framing a commonwealth, why may not several deities combine in framing a world?'[12] Hume again is aware of the obvious counter-objection to his suggestion—'To multiply causes without necessity is ... contrary to true philosophy'.[13] He claims however that the counter-objection does not apply here, because it is an open question whether there is a god with sufficient power to put the whole Universe in order. The principle, however, still applies whether or not we have prior information that a being of sufficient power exists. When postulating entities, postulate as few as possible. Always suppose only one murderer, unless the evidence forces you to suppose a second. If there were more than one deity responsible for the order of the Universe, we should expect to see characteristic marks of the handiwork of different deities in different parts of the Universe, just as we see different kinds of workmanship in the different houses of a city.

We should expect to find an inverse square law of gravitation obeyed in one part of the universe, and in another part a law which was just short of being in inverse square law—without the difference being explicable in terms of a more general law. But it is enough to draw this absurd conclusion to see how ridiculous the Humean objection is.

7.   Hume argues that there are in the Universe other things than rational agents which bestow order. 'A tree bestows order and organisation on that tree which springs from it, without knowing the order; an animal in the same manner on its offspring.'[14] It would therefore, Hume agrees, be equally reasonable if we are arguing from analogy, to suppose the cause of the regularities in the world 'to be something similar or analogous to generation or vegetation.'[15] This suggestion makes perfectly good sense if it is the regularities of copresence which we are attempting to explain. But as analogous processes to explain regularities of succession, generation or vegetation will not do, because they only produce regularities of copresence—and those through the operation of regularities of succession outside their control. The seed only produces the plant because of the continued operation of the laws of biochemistry.

8.   The last distinct objection which I can discover in the *Dialogues* is the following. Why should we not suppose, Hume urges, that this ordered Universe is a mere accident among chance arrangements of eternal matter? In the course of eternity matter arranges itself in all kinds of ways. We just happen to live in a period when it is characterised by order, and

mistakenly conclude that matter is always ordered. Now, as Hume phrases this objection, it is directed against an argument from design which uses as its premiss the existence of the regularities of copresence. 'The continual motion of matter . . . in less than infinite transpositions must produce this economy or order, and by its very nature, that order, when once established supports itself for many ages if not to eternity'.[16] Hume thus relies here partly on chance and partly on the operation of regularities of succession (the preservation of order) to account for the existence of regularities of copresence. In so far as it relies on regularities of succession to explain regularities of copresence, such an argument has, as we saw earlier, some plausibility. But in so far as it relies on chance, it does not, if the amount of order to be accounted for is very striking. An attempt to attribute the operation of regularities of succession to chance would not thus be very plausible. The claim would be that there are no laws of nature which always apply to matter; matter evinces in the course of eternity all kinds of patterns of behaviour, it is just chance that at the moment the states of the Universe are succeeding each other in a regular way. But if we say that it is chance that in 1960 matter is behaving in a regular way, our claim becomes less and less plausible as we find that in 1961 and 1962 and so on it continues to behave in a regular way. An appeal to chance to account for order becomes less and less plausible, the greater the order. We would be justified attributing a typewritten version of collected works of Shakespeare to the activity of monkeys typing eternally on eternal typewriters if we had some evidence of the existence of an infinite quantity of paper randomly covered with type, as well as the collected works. In the absence of any evidence that matter behaved irregularly at other temporal periods, we are not justified in attributing its present regular behaviour to chance.

In addition to the objections which I have stated, the *Dialogues* contain a lengthy presentation of the argument that the existence of evil in the world shows that the god who made it and gave it order is not both totally good and omnipotent. But this does not affect the argument from design which, as Cleanthes admits, does not purport to show that the designer of the Universe does have these characteristics. The eight objections which I have stated are all the distinct objections to the argument from design which I can find in the *Enquiry* and in the *Dialogues*, which claim that in some formal respect the argument does not work. As well as claiming that the argument from design is deficient in some formal respect, Hume makes the point that the analogy of the order produced by men to the other order of the Universe is too remote for us to postulate similar causes.[17] I have argued earlier that if there is a weakness in the argument it is here that it is to be found. The only way to deal with this point would be to start drawing the parallels or stressing the dissimilarities, and these are perhaps tasks more appropriate for the preacher and the poet than for the philosopher. The philosopher will be content to have shown that though perhaps weak, the argument has some force. How much force depends on the strength of the analogy.

University of Hull

Endnotes

*Reprinted from *Philosophy: The Journal of the Royal Institute of Philosophy,* Vol. XLIII, No. 164, July 1968. Reprinted with the permission of Cambridge University Press.

1 I am most grateful to Christopher Williams and to colleagues at Hull for their helpful criticisms of an earlier version of this paper.

2 David Hume, *Dialogues Concerning Natural Religion,* ed. H. D. Aiken (New York, 1948), p. 28.

3 I understand by a 'normal scientific explanation' one conforming to the pattern of deductive or statistical explanation utilised in paradigm empirical sciences such as physics and chemistry, elucidated in recent years by Hempel, Braithwaite, Popper and others. Although there are many uncertain points about scientific explanation, those to which I appeal in the text are accepted by all philosophers of science.

4 St Thomas Aquinas, *Summa Theologiae,* Ia, 2, 3. Translated by Timothy McDermott, O.P. (London, 1964).

5 Ibid., *loc. cit.*

6 David Hume, *An Enquiry Concerning Human Understanding,* ed. L. A. Selby Bigge, Second Edition, 1902, p. 136.

7 David Hume, *Dialogues Concerning Natural Religion,* ed. H. D. Aiken (New York, 1948), p. 23.

8 For this argument see also *The Enquiry,* pp. 147f.

9 *Dialogues,* p. 33.

10 Ibid., p. 36.

11 Ibid., p. 40.

12 Ibid., p. 39.

13 Ibid., p. 40.

14 Ibid., p. 50.

15 Ibid., p. 47.

16 Ibid., p. 53.

17 See, for example, *Dialogues,* p. 18 and p. 37.

Study Questions

1.   Swinburne observes that there are two sorts of order. What are they?

2.   According to Swinburne, the proponent of the design argument runs a risk regarding "regularities of copresence." What does he mean by this claim?

3.   Where does Swinburne begin his account of the argument from design?

4. Swinburne outlines eight criticisms of Hume. What are they?

5. How do you think Swinburne's responses to Hume's criticisms fare?

13

A Modified Version of the Argument from Religious Experience

Gary Gutting

Gary Gutting is professor of philosophy at the University of Notre Dame and author of *Religious Belief and Religious Skepticism*, from which our selection was taken.* Gutting holds that his argument "establishes the existence of a good and powerful being concerned about us, and justifies a central core of religious belief." The central validity of religion is thereby vindicated. He adds, "hardly anything of any such accounts is justified by knowing that there is a powerful and good being concerned about us." What we discover thereby "falls short of what is asserted by any major religion and of what is held by almost all believers." Gutting develops three criteria that religious experiences must meet: "They must be repeatable; they must be experienced by many in diverse places and cultures."

1. Experiences of God

At least since William James' classic work, it has been a commonplace that there are many varieties of religious experience. Oddly, however, philosophical analysts of religious experiences have often ignored this diversity and treated exceptional instances—mystical experiences and physical visions—as typical or even exhaustive of the type. By contrast, I propose to center my discussion on the particular type of religious experience that, though paid little explicit attention by philosophers, is one of the most common and most important in the lives of believers. This is the sort of experience that psychologists of religion call "direct awareness of the presence of God." James gives the following general characterization of such experiences:

> We may lay it down as certain that in the distinctively religious sphere of experience, many persons (how many we cannot tell) possess the objects of their belief, not in the form of mere conceptions which

their intellect accepts as true, but rather in the form of quasi-sensible realities directly apprehended (*The Varieties of Religious Experience*, p. 65).

James cites a number of instances of this sort of experience:

There was not a mere consciousness of something there, but fused in the central happiness of it, a startling awareness of some ineffable good. Not vague either, not like the emotional effect of some poem, or scene, or blossom, or music, but the sure knowledge of the close presence of a sort of mighty person, and after it went, the memory persisted as the one perception of reality. Everything else might be a dream, but not that. [p. 63].

I remember the night, and almost the very spot on the hilltop, where my soul opened out, as it were, into the Infinite, and there was a rushing together of the two worlds, the inner and the outer. . . . I stood alone with Him who had made me, and all the beauty of the world, and love, and sorrow, and even temptation. I did not seek Him, but felt the perfect unison of my spirit with His. . . . The darkness held a presence that was all the more felt because it was not seen. I could not any more have doubted that He was there than that I was. I felt myself to be, if possible, the less real of the two (p. 70).

Of the following statement, James says, "Probably thousands of unpretending Christians would write an almost identical account":

God is more real to me than any thought or thing or person. I feel his presence positively, and the more as I live in closer harmony with his laws as written in my body and mind. I feel him in the sunshine or rain. . . . I talk to him as to a companion in prayer and praise, and our communion is delightful. He answers me again and again, often in words so clearly spoken that it seems my outer ear must have carried the tone, but generally in strong mental impressions (p. 70).

Finally, a few brief statements taken, James says, at random:

God surrounds me like the physical atmosphere. He is closer to me than my own breath. In him literally I live and move and have my being.

There are times when I seem to stand in his very presence, to talk with him. Answers to prayers have come, sometimes direct and overwhelming in their revelation of his presence and powers. . . .

I have the sense of a presence, strong, and at the same time soothing, which hovers over me. Sometimes it seems to enwrap me with sustaining arms (p. 71).

More systematic studies reveal the same phenomenon. A recent example is a survey of a random sample of a hundred British university students, two-thirds of whom said they have had religious experiences of some sort, with about one-fourth describing their experiences as "awareness of the presence of God."[1] The following are some representative comments by students reporting such experiences:

> It was just about dark and I was looking out of the library window. . . . I was aware of everything going on around me, and I felt that everybody had rejected me—and I felt very alone. But at the same time I was aware of something that was giving me strength and keeping me going. . . protecting me ("Religious Experience Amongst a Group of Post Graduate Students,") (p. 168).
>
> It's something that is there all the time. One's awareness of it is limited by one's willingness to submit to it (p. 168).
>
> When I pray . . . I am not praying in a vacuum; there is a response and I feel that at the time of praying, otherwise I think I'd eventually give it up (p. 170).
>
> At university I began to feel the gay life had nothing to offer, life seemed meaningless and all came to a climax about a month before 1st year exams. I was feeling pretty anxious. One night in my room, as I was going to bed, things were at a bursting point. I said, "I give you my life, whoever you are." I definitely felt somebody was there and something had been done. I felt relief but not much else, emotionally. It was like a re-direction and this was a gradual thing (pp. 172-173).

There is every reason to believe that at least a very large number of such reports are candid, that the experiences reported did in fact take place. The crucial question is whether any of the experiences are veridical, whether there is reason to think that there really is a powerful and benevolent nonhuman being experienced by people reporting religious experiences. But before discussing this issue, we need to become as clear as possible about the nature of the experiences in question. This is especially important because, as noted above, many philosophical critics of religious experience have simply ignored the existence of the sorts of experiences I have cited. Alasdair Macintyre, for example, begins his discussion of religious experience by reducing all such experiences ("visions" in his terminology) to two classes:

> . . . first, those visions which can properly be called such, that is, those where something is seen; and second, those where the experience is of a feeling-state or of a mental image, which are only called visions by an honorific extension of the term.

He then goes on to argue that religious experiences of the second type could never provide evidence for religious claims because "an experience of a distinctively 'mental' kind, a feeling-state or an image cannot of itself yield us any information about anything other than experience" ("Visions," p. 256). With regard to visions properly speaking, Macintyre argues that they of course cannot be themselves literally of God, since he cannot be seen, and that we are never warranted in inferring from an X that we see to a Y that we do not see unless we have on other occasions experienced a correlation between X and Y. Whatever we may think of Macintyre's arguments here (and the second seems particularly weak), it is clear that they do not apply to religious experiences of the sort we are concerned with, since these are neither reports of mere feeling-states or mental images nor claims to have literally seen saints, angels, or the like. Rather, they are experiences that are both *perceptual* (i.e., purporting to be of something other than the experiencer) and *nonsensory* (not of some object of the special senses). As such, they fall into neither of Macintyre's two classes and so escape the objections he raises.

Similarly, Wallace Matson raises difficulties first for the veridicality of experiences of "voices and visions" and second for "mystical" experiences (i.e., extraordinary encounters that cannot be intelligibly described to those who have not had them). We have already noted that the experiences with which we are concerned are not of "visions or voices." But neither are they the mystic's ineffable raptures. Although they sometimes have aspects their subjects feel cannot be fully described, they can all be adequately if not completely expressed by saying that they are of a very powerful and very good nonhuman person who is concerned about us. Accordingly, Matson's objections to the veridicality of mystical experiences—which all derive from their apparently peculiar ineffability—are irrelevant to the experiences we are concerned with. These, to summarize, are not given as mere feelings or images, nor are they literal physical visions or ineffable mystical insights. Rather, they are perceptual but nonsensory experiences, purporting to be of a good and powerful being concerned with us.

But are these experiences actually of such a being? A first crucial point is that no experience that purports to be of an external object, taken simply by itself, makes it reasonable to believe that there is such an object. There are no "phenomenological" features of an experience that will mark it off as of something real. (This is the valid core of Descartes' dream argument: there may be no intrinsic differences between a veridical and a nonveridical perceptual experience.) Given an experience that purports to be of X, we need to know more before we are entitled to believe that X exists. A useful way of putting this point is as follows: given an experience with X as its *intentional object*, we may still ask if it is reasonable to believe that X exists (that X is a real object). However, for this language not to be misleading, we need to note that saying "E has X as its intentional object" does not mean that X exists in some special nonreal way; rather it means that E has the internal character of being an "of-X" experience; i.e., it is the sort of experience that, if veridical, is of a really existing X . . . .

How, then, do of-X experiences support the claim that X exists? Richard Swinburne has recently suggested that such an experience provides *prima facie* evidence for the claim, evidence that will be decisive if there is not some overriding reason in our background knowledge for questioning the experience's veridicality. He formulates this suggestion in a "Principle of Credulity": "I suggest that it is a principle of rationality that (in the absence of special considerations) if it seems (epistemically) to a subject that X is present, then probably X is present; what one seems to perceive is probably so" (*The Existence of God, p.* 245). The "special considerations" that can impugn the veridicality of an of-X experience are of four sorts. There can be considerations that show: (1) "that the apparent perception was made under conditions or by a subject found in the past to be unreliable" (p. 260); (2) "that the perceptual claim was to have perceived an object of a certain kind in circumstances where similar perceptual claims have proved false" (p. 261); (3) "that on background evidence it is probable that X was not present" (p. 261); (4) "that whether or not X was there, X was probably not a cause of the experience of its seeming to me that X was there" (pp. 263-64). Swinburne argues that none of these conditions are conditions under which we have religious experiences (or receive reports of such experiences); so he concludes that the Principle of Credulity warrants the conclusion that God exists.

Swinburne is right in thinking that to understand properly the epistemic relation between of-X experiences and claims that X exists we need to recognize that the experience is *prima facie* evidence for the claim. But I think he misconstrues the sense in which the experience is *prima facie* evidence. He takes *"prima facie"* to mean that the evidence of the experience is by itself decisive unless there is some overriding consideration in our background knowledge. But this claim is too strong.

Suppose, for example, I walk into my study one afternoon and seem to see, clearly and distinctly, my recently deceased aunt sitting in my chair. We may assume that the conditions of this experience (my mental state, the lighting of the room, etc.) are not ones that we have reason to think produce unreliable perceptions. Thus, the first of Swinburne's defeating conditions does not hold. Nor, given normal circumstances, does the second condition hold. Most likely, I have no knowledge at all of circumstances in which experiences of the dead by apparently normal persons have turned out to be nonveridical. (We may even assume that I have never heard of anyone I regard as at all reliable reporting such an experience.) Further, knowing nothing at all about the habits or powers of the dead, I have no reason to think that my aunt could not now be in my study or, if present, could not be seen by me. So Swinburne's third and fourth conditions do not hold for this case. But, although none of the four defeating conditions Swinburne recognizes apply, it is obvious that I am not entitled, without further information, to believe that I have in fact seen my aunt. To be entitled to the belief I would need much more evidence—for example, numerous repetitions of the experience, other people having the same or similar experiences, a long visit in which the appearance behaved in ways characteristic of my aunt, information from the appearance that only my aunt had access to, etc. The mere experience described above provides some slight support for the claim that my aunt is in my room, but, even in the absence of defeating conditions, not nearly enough to warrant believing it.

As this example suggests, an of-X experience in general provides *prima facie* evidence of X's existence only in the sense of supplying some (but not sufficient) support for the claim that X exists. For belief in the claim to be warranted, the solitary of-X experience requires supplementation by additional corroborating experiences. It, along with the additional corroboration, provides an adequate cumulative case for the claim. In cases of kinds of objects of which we have frequently had veridical experiences, we can of course rightly believe that they exist, without further corroboration beyond our seeming to see them. But this is because we have good inductive reason to expect that the further corroborations will be forthcoming. With relatively unfamiliar objects—from elves to deceased aunts to divine beings—this sort of inductive reason is not available; and warranted assent must await further corroboration . . . .

C. B. Martin endorses the sort of view of experiential evidence I am suggesting.[2] He does not require a one-dimensional inference from a subjective experience to its veridicality, but he does insist on the relevance of further "checking procedures" if a subjective experience is claimed to yield an objective truth. For the case of ordinary sense perception (e.g., of a sheet of blue paper), we can, he says, make two sorts of claims. The first is just that the experience as a subjective episode is occurring: "There seems to be a sheet of blue paper." Here the experience is "self-authenticating"; that is, the mere fact of its occurrence is sufficient to establish the truth of the claim based on it. The second sort of claim is that the experience correctly represents an objective state of affairs: "There is a sheet of blue paper." Here, Martin notes, more than just the occurrence of the experience is relevant to the truth of the claim:

> The presence of a piece of blue paper is not to be read off from my experience of a piece of blue paper. Other things are relevant: What would a photograph reveal? Can I touch it? What do others see? It is only when I admit the relevance of such checking procedures that I can lay claim to apprehending the paper, and, indeed, the admission of the relevance of such procedures is what gives meaning to the assertion that I am apprehending the paper. (p. 77).

Presumably, C. B. Martin does not mean that, when I have the experience of seeing a piece of paper, am never entitled to believe that there actually is a piece of paper unless I have in fact carried out further checking procedures. As we have seen, the inductive background of ordinary experience usually obviates the need for such checking. But to claim that the paper is objectively present is to admit the relevance in principle of such checking procedures in the following sense: if such checking procedures should happen not to support the claim, then it becomes questionable; and, if for some reason, the claim is questioned, the procedure can and should be invoked to support it.

It seems to me that Martin, unlike Flew and Swinburne, is employing an essentially correct account of the role of experience in the establishment of objective-truth claims. The main elements of this account are: (1) an "of-X" experience is veridical only if, supposing it to be veridical, we should expect, in suitable circumstances, the occurrence of certain further experiences; (2) if these further experiences do not occur (given the suitable circumstances), we have no basis for accepting the experience as veridical; (3) if, in the relevant circumstances, the experiences occur, we do have a basis for accepting the experience as veridical; (4) if there is some reason for questioning the veridicality of the experience, then appeal to further expected experiences is needed before accepting the experience as veridical.

Since religious beliefs in general and the veridicality of religious experiences in particular are not rationally unquestionable, religious experiences need further corroboration. So here we must, contrary to Swinburne, insist on the need to support the veridicality claim by further checking procedures. Such checking procedures are not further premises in a one-dimensional proof of God's existence; rather, they contribute to a many-dimensional, cumulative experiential case for his reality.

Given this, C. B. Martin goes on to claim that in the case of religious experiences of God no further checking procedures are available: "There are no tests agreed upon to establish genuine experience of God and distinguish it decisively from the ungenuine" ("A Religious Way of Knowing," p. 79). Because this is so, he concludes, religious experiences cannot be rightly taken as establishing the objective reality of God; they show nothing besides the existence of certain human psychological states.

What is puzzling here is Martin's assumption that the need for further checking immediately excludes accepting the veridicality of religious experiences. For surely, at least for the class of experiences we are discussing, there are further experiences that would be expected, given their veridicality. Given the veridicality of the typical experience of a very good and very powerful being concerned about us, we would, for example, expect that: (1) those who have had such experiences once would be likely to have them again; (2) other individuals will be found to have had similar experiences; (3) those having such experiences will find themselves aided in their endeavors to lead morally better lives. All these expectations follow from the nature of the experienced being and its concern for us. If the being has soothed, inspired, or warned me once, it is reasonable to expect that it will do so again in appropriate circumstances. If it is concerned enough to contact me, it is reasonable to think that it will contact others in similar situations. Most important, if it is indeed an extraordinarily good, wise, and powerful being, there is reason to think that intimate contact with it will be of great help in our efforts to lead good lives (just as such contact with a human being of exemplary character and wisdom would be likely to have such a result). Further, for some religious experiences, all these expectations are fulfilled to a very high degree. (1) Many people have numerous "of-God" experiences and some even find themselves having a continual sense of the divine presence. (2) "Of-God" experiences are reported from almost every human culture, and the institutional traditions (e.g., churches) they sustain have been among the most enduring in human history. (3) In very many cases, those having "of-God" experiences undergo major moral transformations and find a purpose and strength of will they previously lacked.

It seems, then, that we can argue that religious experiences of God's presence do establish his existence. The experiences themselves give *prima facie* warrant to the claim that he exists, and the fulfillment of the expectations induced by the assumption that the experiences are veridical provides the further support needed for ultimate warrant. This form of an argument from religious experience could be impressively developed by employing detailed illustrations from the literature of religious experience. But here I want to proceed in a different direction, to examine the underpinnings of the argument by developing and discussing the major philosophical challenges to it . . . .

2. Explaining the Experiences Away

When we are presented with the claim that a given religious experience is truly a revelation of the divine, we are often inclined to point out that the occurrence of the experience can be as well or better explained without the assumption that it was in fact produced by an encounter with God. Thus, we make reference to Freudian projections and wish fulfillments, group-induced expectations, schizophrenic personalities, and even the biochemistry of puberty to account for various religious experiences. Do such explanations truly impugn the veridicality of the experiences they try to account for? An adequate answer requires some reflection on the logic of explanation.

A first crucial point is that no explanation is acceptable unless there is reason to think that the explanandum it yields is true. There are no acceptable explanations of why there are only seven planets. Here there are two importantly different cases. In the first, the above condition is readily satisfied because we have good independent grounds for thinking that the premises of the explanation (the explanans) are true and so can conclude by a sound argument from them to the truth of the explanandum. In the second case, we do not have adequate independent support for the explanans, but rather hope that its successful explanation of the explanandum will help provide such support. In this case, we are justified in regarding the explanation as adequate only if we have good independent reason to think that the explanandum is true.

Let us now apply these comments to attempts to explain away the veridicality of an experience. To claim that an explanation of an experience shows that it is not veridical is to propose an explanans that yields an explanandum asserting the nonveridicality of the experience. The assertion will be justified only if there is reason to think the explanation is adequate, and this will be so only if there is reason to think the explanandum is true. In the first of the cases distinguished in the preceding paragraph, we can rightly regard the explanans itself as establishing the truth of the explanandum, and so the claim that the explanation has shown the nonveridicality of the experience is warranted. Thus, if we know on independent grounds that Jean-Paul has been taking mescaline and that taking mescaline usually causes him to have hallucinations of menacing crustaceans, then we have an explanation of his experience of menacing crustaceans that shows it to be nonveridical. But in the second case this conclusion may not be drawn. If we have no independent support for the claims of the explanans about Jean-Paul's drug use and its probable effects, then, in order to accept the explanation as adequate, we need to have independent support for the claim that Jean-Paul's experiences are nonveridical. In this case, then, the proposed explanation cannot be used to show that the experience it explains is nonveridical.

Our conclusion then must be that we can "explain away" a religious experience only by means of an explanans whose truth we can establish independently of its purported explanatory power. With this in mind, let us examine some standard attempts to explain away religious experiences.

It will be useful to distinguish two sorts of such attempts. The first are based on peculiarities of the individuals who have religious experiences; for example, it may be pointed out that a particular religious mystic shows signs of a psychosis that is typically associated with religious halluci-nations. The second are based on traits common to everyone (or at least everyone belonging to some very broad class); thus, a Freudian might note that we all have unconscious desires to believe in the divine reality allegedly revealed in religious experiences.

The first sort of attempt to explain away religious experiences faces the initial difficulty of severe limitation in scope of application. Even if the "of-God" experiences of some people can be discounted because of their psychological abnormalities, the large number of apparently normal people reporting such experiences makes it extremely unlikely that such an approach could explain away all or even most of these experiences. The approach would be successful only if we had independent reason for thinking that the experiences were nonveridical and could then use this fact to support the hypothesis that there are hidden abnormalities in those who have them. But then, of course, the psychological explanation would presuppose rather than establish the nonveridicality of the experiences it explained.

Furthermore, it is not even clear that the independent establishment of an individual's psychological or physiological abnormalities would ordinarily impugn the veridicality of his religious experiences. The presence of psychotic traits or a history of use of hallucinatory drugs will often impugn the reliability of an individual's sense experiences, because we know that such conditions cause sensory distortions. But it is not so obvious that factors suggesting the unreliability of a person's sense experiences suggest a similar unreliability of his nonsensory experiences. *A priori*, there is just as much reason to think that the abnormalities that inhibit perceptions of material objects might enhance perception of nonmaterial objects. Of course, we might discover correlations between certain psychological traits and the nonveridicality of the religious experiences of those who have them. But this would require some means, other than the appeal to psychological explanations, of determining the nonveridicality of religious experiences; and there is little likelihood that everyone reporting religious experiences would have the traits in question. So there is little reason to think that this first approach to explaining away religious experiences will be successful. What about explanations of religious experiences on the basis of traits common to all human beings? Freud, for example, claims that "religious ideas . . . are fulfillments of the oldest, strongest and most urgent wishes of mankind." For example:

> . . . the benevolent rule of a divine Providence allays our fear of the dangers of life; the establishment of a moral world-order ensures the fulfillment of the demands of justice . . .; and the prolongation of earthly existence in a future life provides the local and temporal framework in which these wish fulfillments shall take place.

Given that we so deeply desire the truth of religious claims, it is not surprising that many people have experiences that seem to support their truth. For, as common sense suggests and depth psychology shows, there are mechanisms whereby the mind is capable, in certain circumstances, of seeing or otherwise experiencing what it wants to. Hence, from a Freudian perspective, there is a relatively straightforward explanation of religious experiences. Moreover, the premises of this explanation (that we desire religious claims to be true, that the mind can produce experiences fulfilling its wishes) have strong support apart from their role in explaining religious experiences. So shouldn't we conclude that this sort of account does undermine the veridicality of religious experiences? No. The difficulty is this: even if we do have independent knowledge of the existence and the nature of the mechanisms of wish fulfillment, the Freudian explanation of any specific religious experience requires not only that these mechanisms exist as *capacities* but that they be actually operative in the occurrences of the experiences being explained. But there is no way of seeing the actual operation of wish-fulfillment mechanisms; we can only postulate them as the best explanation of the occurrence of delusory experiences. Hence, to be entitled to assert the actual operation of wish-fulfillment mechanisms, we must first have good reason to think that the experiences they explain are nonveridical. So the Freudian attempt to explain away religious experience is inevitably question-begging.

The same sort of difficulty faces Marxist explanations, based, for example, on the ideas that religious beliefs support the power of the ruling class and that there are socioeconomic forces capable of causing individuals to have experiences supporting these beliefs. We would need to know that these forces were in fact operative in a given case and to know this independent of information about the nonveridicality of the experiences. Similar strictures apply to any other attempts at general explanations (via social, economic, psychological or other causes) of religious experiences and beliefs. It is not sufficient to show just that such causes could produce the experiences and beliefs. It must also be shown that they are in fact operative in given cases; and it is very hard to see how this can be done without assuming ahead of time that the experiences and beliefs are nonveridical.

It is sometimes suggested—by both Freudians and Marxists—that *all* experiences are psychologically or economically determined. If we knew this to be so, then we would be justified in appealing to economic or psychological causes to explain religious experiences. It is hard to see what evidence could be put forward for these claims of universal determinism. But, given any such claim, we must surely allow that experiences can be veridical (and known to be so) in spite of their being determined, or else fall into an extreme skepticism. But then the mere fact that a religious experience is psychologically or economically determined does not undermine its veridicality.

A final difficulty facing Freudian and Marxist critiques of religious experience—and critiques based on any other general views of human reality and its place in the world—is that their own basic beliefs and the "evidence" they are said to be based on seem at least as susceptible to being explained away as are religious beliefs and experiences. There are after all Freudian explanations of Marxism and Marxist explanations of Freudianism. (Not to mention the possibility of religious explanations of both.) The attempt to discredit general worldviews by proposing explanations themselves based on rival worldviews is a two-edged sword that can easily be turned against those who wield it.

3. Religious Experiences and Religion

So far the objections we have considered have derived from epistemological considerations quite separate from, if not opposed to, the content of religious beliefs. In this section we turn to objections derived from religion itself. I will first examine the suggestion that the true God's transcendence and utter uniqueness make it impossible for him to be the object of a human experience (at least of the relatively straightforward perceptual experiences with which we are concerned).

More precisely, the difficulty can be formulated in this way: any object given in our experience must be properly characterizable in terms of our concepts. (On a Kantian view, the experience is possible only if the object is given under our concepts; on an empiricist view, we could abstract the concepts from the object as experienced.) But it is an essential feature of God that none of our concepts are properly applicable to him. For, if they were, he would be just another thing in our world, even if a preeminent one, and not the creator of this world. So, if a being is given as an object of our experience, one thing we can surely conclude is that it is not the God who created us and whom we worship. We may, on this view, allow for special "mystical experiences" that are not encounters with an external object but rapturous unions with God that, as the mystics insist, cannot be described in human language and concepts. But these are very different from the perceptions of God that are our focus here. Indeed, to the extent that mystical experiences are accepted as true manifestations of God, they show that our more mundane perceptions of a powerful and good person are not.

There are at least three important lines of response to this difficulty. First, it should be noted that the objection does not in fact question the veridicality of experiences of a good and powerful person concerned about us. At best, it shows that there is another religiously relevant being, not encountered in these experiences. If it is true that this unexperienceable being is the primary focus of religious belief, then our "of-God" experiences do not ground the central claim of religion. Nonetheless, the existence of the sort of being revealed in these experiences must be of very great importance for us. Second, even religious views that most emphasize the utter transcendence of God (e.g., some versions of Christianity and Hinduism) allow for the role of mediators (angels, lesser gods) between God and man. So even if our experiences are not strictly of God, they may still be important factors in our relation to him. Finally, there is the possibility—at the heart of Christianity in the doctrine of incarnation—that even a transcendent God might reveal himself to us by taking on a human form. Christians who hold that a man living among us was the transcendent God can hardly reject the possibility that this God could reveal himself to us in nonsensory experiences. This possibility is further supported by the fact that, even if none of our concepts are properly applicable to God, there must be some that are more adequate than others to his reality. Thus, it is surely less of a mistake to say that God is good and powerful than to say that he is neurotic and deciduous. But if this is so, there would seem to be room for an experience—although imperfect—of God in terms of the concepts most appropriate to him.

Another objection drawn from religion is based on the alleged wide diversity in the content of experiences of God and the apparent dependence of this content on the religious traditions of the experiencers. This diversity is undeniable if we take account of the entire range of religious experiences; but it is by far most prominent in the extreme cases of literal visions and the "private revelations" of the most advanced mystics. The Virgin Mary does not appear to Hindus; Moslems do not have mystical encounters with the Trinity. But at best this sort of diversity shows that religious experience does not establish the superiority of one religious tradition over others. The fact remains that in all traditions there are countless experiences of a superhuman loving power concerned about us; and even the otherwise divergent physical and mystical visions share this essential core of content.

There are, it is true, two crucial questions on which there are differences between and even within traditions: Is the divine reality truly other than that of the experiencer? And is the divine reality personal or impersonal? However, the difference between those who answer these questions affirmatively and those who answer them negatively is not so great as it might seem. Even those who emphasize the unity of God and self admit that God is other than the ordinary mundane self of our everyday life. So in spite of their insistence that there is an ultimate unity, they agree that the divine is other than the "finite" or "illusory" self that is transcended in rapturous union with the divine. Given this, they could surely also admit the possibility of an essentially veridical, although incomplete, encounter of the finite self with God. Similarly, those who encounter God as "impersonal" do not claim that he is more like a rock than a human being, but that even the category of 'person' is not adequate to his reality. Even so, there is no reason that an encounter with God as a person could not be partially revelatory of the divine nature or perhaps an experience of a mediator between us and God. So, despite the manifest diversity of religious experiences, there remains a content common to them all; and, apart from very uncommon instances of highly specific revelations via visions or mystical insights, it is possible to accept consistently the essential features of almost all religious experiences.

4. Religious Experiences and the Justification of Religious Belief

People candidly report that they have directly experienced the presence of a good and powerful nonhuman being concerned about us. The experiences are not isolated events in their lives but are followed by other and more intimate encounters with this being, sometimes even to the point of an abiding sense of its presence. These encounters are a source of moral strength and comfort, even more than we would expect from prolonged and intimate contact with the most admirable human. Further, similar experiences with similar effects are reported by great numbers of people from diverse times and places. There is no reason to think that these experiences do not have the perceptual character attributed to them, and there are no explanations of them (as a whole) as delusory that are not question-begging. Further, there are few if any other religious experiences that contradict their central content. Surely, we then have very good reason to believe that at least some of these experiences are veridical and hence that there is a good and powerful being, concerned about us, who has revealed himself to human beings. So much, I think, is established by our discussion so far.

To what extent does this conclusion justify religious belief? If we have in mind the beliefs of the great majority of religious people, the answer is: *very little.* Typically, religious belief includes substantive accounts of the nature of God (e.g., that he is omnipotent, omniscient, all-good, the creator of all things, triune, etc.), of his relations to man (e.g., that he became man to save us, that this salvation is carried out by sacramental acts within specific religious communities), of the moral ideals (self-sacrifice, love for all men) that should animate our lives, and of an afterlife dependent on the moral quality of our lives here on earth. Hardly anything of any such accounts is justified by knowing that there is a powerful and good being concerned about us. We can sum up the situation by saying that "of-God" experiences provide us much more with *access to* than with *accounts of* God. Of course, this access necessarily involves some minimal description of what is encountered, but this description falls far short of what is asserted by any major religion and of what is held by almost all believers.

However, these experiences still have very great significance. First and most importantly, they establish the crucial claim that religion as a pervasive phenomenon of human life is based on a genuine contact with a reality beyond ourselves. As C. D. Broad said after a characteristically judicious assessment of the veridicality of religious experiences:

The claim of any particular religion or sect to have complete or final truth on these subjects seems to me to be too ridiculous to be worth a moment's consideration. But the opposite extreme of holding that the whole religious experience of mankind is a gigantic system of pure delusion seems to me to be almost (though not quite) as farfetched.

Further, the fact that the religious beliefs of mankind derive to at least some extent from an access to the divine warrants our taking seriously the major beliefs of the great world religions. These beliefs have been formed (in part at least) by the sustained and intimate contact of generations of people with a superhuman power; and so, even if they are not to be believed without question, they ought to be carefully and respectfully scrutinized as potential sources of truth. Finally, given the fact that the great world religions seem to be the main loci and sustainers of our access to God, there is good reason for anyone interested in attaining such access or in more deeply understanding what it reveals to take part in the life of some established religious community. (And to these considerations many can add the happiness and moral inspiration they find in the fellowship of a particular religious tradition.)

So it seems that accepting the veridicality of religious experiences can provide good reasons for associating ourselves with the great religious traditions of mankind. There is no *a priori* reason why this association must be with one particular tradition or even a specific church. But for many people there will be specific psychological and social factors that make their participation in just one tradition or church most valuable. Moreover the richness and diversity of the religious life of any one major tradition suggests that most of us will lose little by so restricting our primary commitment. On the contrary, a refusal to participate fully in some specific "form of religious life" may lead to an abstract and superficial religiosity that will fall far short of profiting from what the religious experiences of humankind have to offer. So, for many people at least, there is good reason for a commitment to a particular religious community. . . .

Endnotes

*From *Religious Belief and Religious Skepticism* by Gary Gutting. © 1982 by the University of Notre Dame press. Reprinted by permission. Footnotes edited.

[1] D. Hay, "Religious Experience Amongst a Group of Post-Graduate Students: A Qualitative Study," *Journal for the Scientific Study of Religion* 18 (1979), pp. 164-82.

[2] C. B. Martin, "A Religious Way of Knowing," in A. Flew and A. MacIntyre, eds., *New Essays in Philosophical Theology* (London: Macmillan, 1955). Page references will be given in the text.

Study Questions

1.   Gary Gutting thinks that Swinburne misconstrues the sense in which experience is *prima facie* evidence. Why does he think this?

2.   According to Gutting, how does the logic of explanation figure in giving account of the veridicality of religious experiences?

3.   Gutting draws a comparison between Marxist explanations and religious-experience explanations. What sorts of difficulties do they share?

4.   According to Gutting, what are the objections to the argument from religious experience that arise from epistemological considerations?

5.   What problems, if any, do you see with the three criteria Gutting lists for testing religious experiences?

14

Religious Experience as Self-Transcendence and Self-Deception

Merold Westphal

Merold Westphal is professor of philosophy at Fordham University, and is author of *History and Truth in Hegel's Phenomenology,* and *God, Guilt, and Death.*

Religious experience can be defined as self-transcendence. Models of this decentering of the self are not found in the transcendence of intentionality or in either contemplative or ecstatic self-forgetfulness, since all these leave the self as center. While they play important roles in authentic religion, experience that does not get beyond them is self-deceived and ultimately idolatrous. Only in the ethical claim that places limits on my will to be the center do I encounter the truly other. Even here the form of true religion may assist self-deception about the presence of its substance.*

Perhaps you've heard those lemonade ads that refer to the good old days when we listened to baseball games on the radio. That part reminds me of my own conversion—to lifetime membership in the Diehard Cubs Fan Club. Every summer afternoon, as I sat in front of my grandmother's floor model radio, Bert Wilson would preach the good news, "We don't care who wins, as long as it's the Cubs." And in spite of the fact that in good years they only managed to beat out the Pirates for seventh place, I became a true believer. But when the lemonade ad suggests that it's "sorta cheatin'" to watch baseball on television, I am reminded of something quite different. It was my sophomore year in college and one of the most gifted students I have ever known, whose specialty was the oral interpretation of literature, was giving his senior speech recital. Like an ancient Greek rhapsode, and all in a little under an hour, he gave us *Doctor Zhivago.* For all its visual splendor, like televised baseball, the movie version that I was to see later did not surpass this old-fashioned oral version in dramatic power. The concluding line, taken from one of Pasternak's poems, was utterly shattering and unforgettable. "To live life to the end is no childish task."

Kierkegaard expresses this same conviction that life is the task of a lifetime by satirizing those for whom most of life is supposed to consist in living happily ever after. For such, "when they have arrived at a certain point in their search for truth, life takes on a change. They marry, and they acquire a certain position, in consequence of which they feel that they must in all honor have something finished, that they must have result. . . And so they come to think of themselves as really finished. . . Living in this manner, one is relieved of the necessity of becoming executively aware of the strenuous difficulties which the simplest of propositions about existing *qua* human-being involves" (1941: 78-79; cf. 1980: 55-56).

By arguing that such persons are strangers to religion, no matter how orthodox or pious, Kierkegaard suggests that this enduring adult task has religious import. But what is this task, which is the *sine qua non* of religion, and from which, apparently, only death can release us? The Augustinian tradition, to which Kierkegaard belongs, is united in its answer: self-transcendence. This is why Augustine speaks of the incarnation as the means by which Jesus "might detach from themselves those who were to be subdued and bring them over to Himself, healing the swelling of their pride and fostering their love so that instead of going further in their own self-confidence, they should put on weakness...should cast themselves down upon that divinity which, rising would bear them up aloft" (1963: 155). From this perspective follows the Augustinian beatitude: "Blessed is the man who loves you, who loves his friend in you, and his enemy because of you" (79).

Thomas Merton gives the same answer when he writes, "We do not detach ourselves from things in order to attach ourselves to God, but rather we become detached *from ourselves* in order to see and use all things in and for God" (1972: 21).

Gabriel Marcel puts the point on the horizontal plane in describing the nature and difficulty of admiration, "whose enormous spiritual and even metaphysical significance is still not recognized. The verb *lift* forcefully and accurately denotes the kind of effect admiration evokes in us, or rather realizes in us as a function of the object which evokes it. . . It is clear that the function of admiration is to tear us away from ourselves and from the thoughts we have of ourselves. . . Not so long ago a dramatist affirmed during an interview that admiration was for him a humiliating state which he resisted with all his force. . . An analysis similar to the one Scheler has given of resentment should disclose that there is a burning preoccupation with self at the bottom of this suspicion [of anything superior], a 'but what about me, what becomes of me in that case?'. . . To affirm: admiration is a humiliating state, is the same as to treat the subject as a power existing for itself and taking itself as a center. To proclaim on the other hand, that it is an exalted state is to start from the inverse notion that the proper function of the subject is to emerge from itself and realize itself primarily in the gift of oneself" (1964: 47-49).

Finally, as if to exhibit the agreement between Protestant and Catholic Augustinians on this point, we can return to Kierkegaard himself. His definitions of the self and of faith spell out his understanding of self-transcendence as the lifelong task of life. The self is "a relation that relates itself to itself and in relating itself to itself relates itself to another" (1980: 13-14). This latter relation is faith when "in relating itself to itself and in willing to be itself, the self rests transparently in the power that established it" (49; cf. 14, 30, 82, 131).

Augustine and Merton introduce the basic notion of becoming detached from ourselves. Marcel makes it clear that this involves the transition from a self preoccupied with itself and its position as the center to a self capable of giving itself in admiration and creative fidelity to another. From the point of view of the point of departure, this is a humiliating tearing away from that to which I cling with all my might. From the point of view of the destination, this is a liberating elevation above the narrow horizons defined by the question, But what about me? In short, self-transcendence is the journey from the false self to the true self, with all of its agony and its ecstasy.

In spite of its austere form, Kierkegaard's formula for faith recapitulates these themes and introduces another. First, with Augustine and Merton he is explicit that we are to be detached from ourselves in order to be attached to God. 'Freedom from' is in the service of 'freedom for.' Here we encounter the wonderful ambiguity of the term 'transcendence.' It can mean that which is beyond, the transcendent. Or it can mean going beyond, transcending. For the Augustinian tradition the two are united, and transcending is toward the transcendent. What is beyond my false self is not simply my true self, but the not-myself in proper relation to which it first becomes possible for me to be my true self. Only by losing myself, in the sense of going beyond myself toward the not-myself, do I ever truly find myself.

Second, with Marcel, Kierkegaard is explicit that the relation to the other is a humble, decentering relation. (This is why it is experienced by pride as humiliation.) Self-transcendence means willing to be myself while at the same time willing to let God be God, that is, willing to be myself without insisting on being God. It is the exact opposite of Nietzsche's Zarathustra, who says, "*if* there were gods, how could I endure not to be a god! *Hence* there are no gods" (1966b: 86, "Upon the Blessed Isles"). It means learning to pray

Hallowed be *Thy* name
Thy kingdom come
Thy will be done

without surreptitiously co-opting the name and the kingdom so that *my* will may be done on earth and in heaven.

Finally, for all of its emphasis on the role of the transcendent in self-transcendence, Kierkegaard's account explicitly links relation-to-another to self-relation. Only as self-relating selfhood does the self transcend itself toward its true self in relation to the transcendent. Given the historical linkage of the Augustinian *dubito* to the Cartesian *cogito*, this introduction of inwardness should not take us by surprise. Among its most important implications is that the metaphor of organic development can never be more than a metaphor, and a rather poor one at that, for self-transcendence. The latter presupposes too much in the way of self-awareness and self-involvement (Evans, 1963).

On the other hand, by making self-presence itself a task rather than an achievement, Kierkegaard excludes that total self-presence by virtue of which the self could claim to be the center. This expresses the great gulf fixed between his Augustinianism and its modern, secular counterpart, the Cartesian-Humean (Husserlian-positivist) tradition. In its self-relation the self is not posited as the ground of certainty, the criterion of truth, the self-sufficient and absolute mode of being, in short, the center. If I may be permitted to express the point oxymoronically, to counter Cartesian modernity's arrogant Augustinianism, Kierkegaard develops the inwardness of a decentered Cartesianism. The I of the Augustinian "I think" is always a problem, never a possession nor an Archimedean *pou sto*.

Having given this somewhat extended Augustinian definition of self-transcendence, I now want to suggest that we use it as at least a working definition of religious experience. Religious experience =df self-transcendence, the self-aware, self-involving, self-transforming relation to the ultimately transcendent. While I believe this definition has advantages at the descriptive level for the phenomenological and historical study of religion, the present essay will focus on its prescriptive employment as a norm for distinguishing authentically religious experience from its look alikes. Not all the beliefs, practices, and feelings that are easily recognized as religious are acts of self-transcendence. Prayer, for example, can easily be "a burning preoccupation with self," a solemn repetition of the question, "But what about me, what becomes of me in that case?"

Alterity is a big topic among philosophers these days, and a number of contemporary conversations have reminded us how difficult it is for the human spirit to be "at home [*bei sich*] with itself in its otherness *as such*" (Hegel, 1949: 790, my italics; cf. Taylor, 1987). This formula of Hegel's is strikingly similar to Kierkegaard 's designation of faith as a self-relating that is simultaneously an other-relating. Its "as such" is meant as a reminder that the other is meant to remain other. But for all his emphasis on dialectic as the path of otherness, opposition, negation, contradiction, and so forth, Hegel himself stands accused of taking away with dialectical reconciliation what he first gives in the form of dialectical difference. Dialectic turns out to be a monological self-mediation rather than a dialogical other-mediation (Habermas, 1987 and Desmond, 1987).

In a similar vein, Derridean deconstruction, flying significantly under the banner of *différance*, is a sustained polemic against the metaphysics of presence precisely as the reduction of the different to the same. The debate with Gadamer, for example, can perhaps best be summarized as the reciprocal claims, I am more open to otherness than you are (Michelfelder and Palmer, 1989; cf. Caputo, 1987).

These discussions provide an important context for any contemporary discussion of religious experience as self-transcendence. What is more, reflection on specifically religious experience can make an important contribution to the wider discussion of otherness in general. For, in the first place, the holy, the ultimately transcendent, has appropriately been designated, not merely as other but as "wholly other." It is quintessentially transcendent. Secondly, self-transcendence may be more than casually linked to the transcendent; it may well be the condition and measure of the transcendent. This would mean, not that there is the transcendent only to the degree that we are able to transcend ourselves, but that we experience the transcendent as such, as truly other, only to the degree that we are able to transcend ourselves. Conversely, to the degree that self-transcendence fails, transcendence is only apparent, that is, idolatrous.

In order to explore this hypothesis and to clarify the normative significance of the concept of religious experience as self-transcendence, I want to look at a variety of other modes of experience in order to highlight the tenuousness of transcendence in them. The claim that knowledge is self-transcendence is an good point of departure both because religion is so often identified with religious beliefs and because philosophers so often speak of knowledge as transcendence. For example, Fichte says that "the I forgets itself in the object of its activity. . . *Intuition* is the name of this action, a silent, unconscious contemplation, which loses itself in its object" (Breazeale, 1988: 260). Kojève expands on this idea. "Now, the analysis of 'thought,' 'reason,' 'understanding,' and so on—in general, of the cognitive, contemplative, passive behavior of a being or a 'knowing subject'—never reveals the why or the how of the birth of the word 'I' . . . The man who contemplates is 'absorbed' by what he contemplates; the 'knowing subject' 'loses' himself in the object that is known. Contemplation reveals the object, not the subject. . . The man who is 'absorbed' by the object that he is contemplating can be 'brought back to himself' only by a Desire" (1969: 3). In other words, in desire we are related to the other, for example, something we want to eat, only as the mode in which we are preoccupied with ourselves and satisfying our needs;

but in cognition real transcendence occurs as we lose ourselves and become absorbed in the object.

Since Husserl treats intentionality primarily as cognitive, his claim that intentionality is transcendence can help us make this claim more precise. In the first place there is the transcendence of the physical object to perception. It is transcendent by virtue of exceeding whatever it is able to give of itself "in person," whatever is directly present to perception. It can present its front side, but not its other sides. It can only present itself in adumbrations (*abschattungen*) which it always infinitely exceeds (1983: par. 41-42). In this way the object transcends the perception of it.

Other objects, such as mental processes (*Erlebnisse*) are not given in this way. "*Ein Erlebnis shattet sich niche ab.*" For this reason there is a sharp distinction to be drawn between a mental process and a physical thing (*Ding*), namely that the former "can be perceived in an immanental perception," while the latter is always transcendent (par. 42).

There are also non spatial objects that have their own mode of transcendence. In reflection my intentional object is a cogitatio, one of my own, and we might label this "internal perception." But Husserl prefers the language of immanence and transcendence to that of internal and external. So he says that "by *intentive mental processes related to something immanent,* we understand those to which it is *essential that their intentional objects, if they exist at all, belong to the same stream of mental processes to which they themselves belong...*Intentive mental processes of which that is not the case are directed to something transcendent" (par. 38, his italics). This means that my cognition is transcendent whenever it is directed to an "object" that is not a *cogitatio* or *Erlebnis* of my own. Among such objects are not only spatial objects but essences, other egos, and their *Erlebnisse*.

This seems to be very close to the realism of G. E. Moore, grounded in the distinction between the act and the object of consciousness (1953: ch. XVI and 1959: ch. I-II). Given the way in which both Moore and Husserl distinguish the intentional object (*noema*) from the act that intends it (*noesis*), it is not clear why we shouldn't say that every intentional act involves transcendence. Whether or not that is what they intend us to conclude, we can distinguish three theses about intentionality and transcendence:

1) We encounter transcendence in every intentional object (since the act and the object can always be distinguished).

2) We encounter transcendence in those intentional objects which are not themselves our own *cogitationes* or *Erlebnisse* (since they do not belong to the stream of mental acts that includes the acts that intend them).

3) We encounter transcendence in those intentional objects that are physical, i.e., spatial (since there can only give themselves partially, perspectivally, *abschattungsweise*).

No doubt each of these theses embodies a legitimate and useful concept of transcendence. But none of them gives us the self-transcendence we are looking for, that detachment from self that moves us beyond preoccupation with what Kant calls "the dear self."

The first reason for this is clear if we return briefly to Kojève. The separation of cognition from desire that he attributes to the knowing subject is by no means typical of cognition. Hume, the father of positivism, says, "Reason is, and ought only to be the slave of the passions, and can never pretend to any other office than to serve and obey them" (1888: 415). Nietzsche, the father of post modernism, agrees: "but reason is merely an instrument, and Descartes is superficial" (1966a: 104). If we think of positivism and post modernism as diseases to be eliminated like polio and smallpox, the best we can hope to do is show that Hume and Nietzsche are not right all of the time. We would surely be kidding ourselves to deny that they are right at least most of the time. And whether instrumental reason is to be seen as the glory or the curse of modernity, it is nothing if not preoccupation with the self (personal and collective) and its desires.

But, it may well be objected, did not Fatuity and Kojève speak explicitly about contemplation, making it clear they have disinterested cognition in mind? The Greeks and their modern followers often speak of philosophy as *theoria* in this sense, but at least since the eighteenth century the notion of disinterested contemplation has primarily been developed in relation to aesthetic experience. A tradition that extends from Shaftesbury, Hutcheson, Burke, and Alison through Kant and Schopenhauer to Croce and Edward Bullough has sought to make the transcendence of self-interest the key to aesthetic appreciation (see Westphal, 1984: 131-35). The anti-instrumental, anti-utilitarian theme of this tradition is succinctly expressed by C. S. Lewis , "the many *use* art and the few *receive* it" (1961: 19), and by Oscar Wilde, "All art is quite useless" (1981: xxiv).

The examples Shaftesbury gives of disinterested contemplation make it clear that breaking the link between intentionality and desire is the heart of the matter. It is the absence of the desire to command, the desire to own, the desire to eat, and the desire to touch sexually that makes the perception of beauty disinterested, and Shaftesbury understandably speaks of this as the transcendence of "selfishness," "self-interest," and "self-love" (1964: II, 12628, I, 78, 274-75, 317).

There can be little doubt that in theoretical and aesthetic contemplation we have the self-forgetfulness Fichte and Kojève have in mind, in which the subject sinks from sight, playing at most the role of background or horizon while the object becomes foreground and theme. If we remember that Shaftesbury's primary interest in disinterestedness was not aesthetics but ethics and religion, we may think that we have found what we are looking for (cf. O'Connor, 1972: 151-52). But this model is also too weak.

Contemplative self-forgetfulness takes us beyond instrumental reason, to be sure. Hume and Nietzsche might deny that it ever exists, and we would do well to take their suspicions seriously. But let us retain the hypothesis that it sometimes does occur, at least to a significant degree. The problem begins with Aristotle, whose *Metaphysics* begins with the words, "All men by nature desire to know." It looks as if the link between knowledge and desire has not been cut after all. Of course, the desire to know is not a selfish desire, as if knowledge were a zero sum game. But it is, even when it has no instrumental significance, the desire to satisfy and fulfill the self. To use a Rawlsian distinction (1971: 127-29), it is a desire both of the self (my desire) and in the self (for my satisfaction). For this reason, Aristotle's ethics, including his theory of contemplation as an intellectual virtue, is properly identified as a self-realization theory.

Shaftesbury points us in the same direction. "For though the habit of selfishness and the multiplicity of interested views are of little improvement to real merit or virtue, yet there is a necessity for the preservation of virtue, that it should be thought to have no quarrel with true interest and self-enjoyment" (1964: 274). The point is not that self-realization and self-enjoyment are evil. It is simply that contemplative experience, theoretical or aesthetic, that is properly interpreted in these terms can hardly be a convincing model for religious experience conceived as detachment from self. Disinterestedness may delimit but it does not displace the supremacy of the self, which remains the horizon for contemplative self-forgetfulness. Conversely, if religious experience is to be conceived as self-transcendence, any piety that does not get beyond both instrumental self-seeking and contemplative self-enjoyment is not genuine religious experience.

C. S. Lewis fails to see this point in an otherwise illuminating discussion of heaven in *The Problem of Pain*. People are nervous about "pie in the sky" escapism, he notes. But if there is no "pie in the sky" then Christianity is false, and if there is, then we must deal with it. He writes, "we are afraid that heaven is a bribe, and that if we make it our goal we shall no longer be disinterested. It is not so. Heaven offers nothing that a mercenary soul can desire. It is safe to tell the pure in heart that they shall see God, for only the pure in heart want to." With the right kind of glosses on these claims Lewis could take us beyond disinterestedness to genuine transcendence. But instead of doing so he remains within the dichotomy of disinterested and mercenary. "There are rewards that do not sully motives. A man's love for a woman is not mercenary because he wants to marry her, nor his love for poetry mercenary because he wants to read it, nor his love of exercise less disinterested because he wants to run and leap and walk. Love, by definition, seeks to enjoy its object" (1962: 144-45). By being satisfied as long as enjoyment is not mercenary, Lewis, like Shaftesbury, fails to notice the limitations of enjoyment with reference to transcendence.

The mercenary is one who does what is not enjoyable for the sake of what is. Mercenary behavior is instrumental, means-end behavior. Mercenary love is false love, as when a man loves a woman for her money or a woman loves a man for the security he provides. Disinterested behavior does not have this means-end structure, and disinterested love does not arise from ulterior motives. When the Psalmist prays, "For God alone my soul in silence wait" (62.1), this can be a mercenary prayer meaning, "Only God can get me out of this mess," or it can be a disinterested prayer meaning, "Not even the benefits of divine grace, but only God in person can satisfy me." There is a huge difference between these two prayers, but in both cases the self is concerned with its own satisfaction, and the love that seeks to enjoy its object is caught up in its own enjoyment.

It is Levinas who sees more clearly than anyone that the other enjoyed is not necessarily transcendent, and, consequently, that enjoyment is not necessarily self-transcendence. Echoing the Hegelian formula we noted earlier, Levinas finds us not content merely to be at home with ourselves in familial surroundings (his *chez soi* = Hegel's *bei sich*) but disposed to reach out "toward an alien outside-of-oneself, toward a yonder." He calls this desire for genuine otherness metaphysical desire. But the other thus desired "is not 'other' like the bread I eat, the land in which I dwell, the landscape I contemplate. . .] can 'feed' on these realities and to a very great extent satisfy myself, as though I had simply been lacking them. Their *alterity* is thereby reabsorbed into my own identity as a thinker or a possessor. The metaphysical desire tends toward *something else entirely*, toward the *absolutely other*" (1969: 33).

As this passage indicates, eating is the paradigm of enjoyment and the source of the appearance of transcendence therein. Against all forms of idealism, which interpret knowledge as the primacy of subject over object, the reduction of the latter's otherness to the sameness of the former, alimentation reminds me that I am a body within the world and not just a mind for whom the world is a spectacle. Food overflows its meaning as an object of representation and becomes a condition for the very acts by which such meaning is constituted (127-30). In my dependence on the elements of life I seem to encounter something quite other than myself.

Levinas makes three points about enjoyment so construed that are relevant to our project. First, as Shaftesbury and Lewis have noted, in enjoyment we are beyond self-interest conceived in instrumental or mercenary terms. "Here lies the permanent truth of hedonist moralities: to not seek, behind the satisfaction of need, an order relative to which alone satisfaction would require a value; to take satisfaction, which is the very meaning of pleasure, as a term. The need for food does not have existence as its goal, but food. Biology teaches the prolongation of nourishment into existence; need is naïve" (134).

Second, enjoyment is pure egoism, not self-transcendence. "In enjoyment am absolutely for myself. Egoist without reference to the Other, I am alone without solitude, innocently egoist and alone. Not against the Others, not 'as for me . . .'—but entirely deaf to the Other, outside of all communication and all refusal to communicate—without ears, like a hungry stomach" (134; his ellipsis). I may be dependent on the elements from which I draw my nourishment, but "in the satisfaction of need the alienness of the world that founds me loses its alterity. . . Through labor and possession the alterity of nutriments enters into the same" (129).

Finally, as the phrase 'like a hungry stomach' suggests, eating is but a model of many different modes of enjoyment. As "an ultimate relation with the substantial plenitude of being," enjoyment "embraces all relations with things" (133). I take this to mean not that there is nothing but enjoyment, but that there is no relation that cannot be elevated to/reduced to enjoyment. In spite of the initial distinction between knowledge and enjoyment, Levinas is explicit that cognitive relations can have this structure, especially when they have a contemplative character. Thus, "I but open my eyes and already enjoy the spectacle" (130). And we have already seen him assimilate "the landscape I contemplate" to "the bread I eat." The psalmist who thirsts for the face of God as a deer for streams of water (42:1-2) has surely made spiritual progress over those whose only appetites are for "wine, women, and song." But the journey toward genuine religious experience may not be over.

There is still another mode of self-forgetfulness that turns out to be something less than the self-transcendence we are seeking to clarify. Like contemplation it takes us beyond the mercenary, and it often turns up in religious contexts. We can call it ecstatic self-forgetfulness, as distinct from contemplative. The two are not totally different, for there surely is a contemplative ecstasy, for example, in Yoga.

We can consider play, as interpreted by Gadamer, as something of a transition experience. Since he relates play to the religious festival and claims that "The player experiences the game as a reality that surpasses him" (110, 97-98), there is obvious reference to our own question about religious experience. Even the spectator is able "to forget one's own purposes. . . To be present . . . has a character of being outside oneself." This "ecstasy of being outside oneself [Ecstatic des Aussersichseins]" is "the positive possibility of being wholly with something else. This kind of being present is a self-forgetfulness, and it is the nature of the spectator to give himself in self-forgetfulness to what he is watching" (110-11; cf. 113-14).

More sharply distinct from contemplative self-forgetfulness than Gadamerian play is the Dionysian, as described by Nietzsche. It is not only a self-forgetfulness by contrast with Apollonian self-knowledge; it also dwells among the "wilder emotions" from which Apollonian calm is free (1967: 45, 35). Far from being any kind of spectator sport, it is a realm of *Rausch* (intoxication, delirium, frenzy, transport, ecstasy, rapture) and *Verzückung* (ecstasy, rapture, transport, trance, convulsion). In the "dancers of St. John and St. Vitus," in the Bacchic choruses of the Greeks," and "as far back as Babylon and the orgiastic Sacaea," we find the Dionysian experience in which "everything subjective vanishes into complete self-forgetfulness" (33-37).

There is clearly a dimension of self-transcendence here, even of detachment from self. But ecstatic self-forgetfulness is no more what we are looking for than was contemplative self-forgetfulness. Gadamer tells us as much himself when he writes, "Thus to the ecstatic self-forgetfulness of the spectator there corresponds his continuity with himself. Precisely that in which he loses himself as a spectator requires his own continuity ... the absolute moment in which a spectator stands is at once self-forgetfulness and reconciliation with self. That which detaches him from everything also gives him back the whole of his being" (1975: 113-14).

This sounds so much like the words of Jesus (Mark 8:35) that we might easily think we have found the definition of religious self-transcendence if Gadamer had not also said, in the middle of the passage just quoted, "It is the truth of [the spectator's] own world, the religious and moral world in which he lives, which presents itself to him and in which he recognizes himself." William James is said to have complained that for Josiah Royce "the world is real but not so very damn real." We might say here that the ecstatic self encounters something other than itself, but not so very damn other. In other words, though the elements on which the self feeds here are spiritual rather than physical, we have not gotten beyond the realm of nutrition. Like its contemplative counterpart, ecstatic self-forgetfulness is a species of enjoyment.

That this is also true for Nietzsche's wilder version is perhaps clearest in his linkage of the Dionysian with sexual ecstasy (1967: 36; 1968: sec. 798-801). I do not mean simply that sex is fun. What I have in mind is best expressed in the comment one of my students made to me years ago. After living together for a while, she and her boyfriend had broken up and separated. Though she had no apparent scruples about having lived together, she was obviously not comfortable about the fact that they still secretly got together to have sex. Her explanation/excuse: "the only time I can ever forget myself is when I'm having sex." Her ex-boyfriend was "other but not so very damn other" because he was but an element through which her need was satisfied. That her need was primarily for oblivion rather than for pleasure or intimacy does not take her experience, or Nietzsche's Dionysian of which it is a model, beyond the framework of enjoyment. Self-forgetfulness continues to be a mode of being preoccupied with oneself, in this case with killing for oneself the pain of being oneself.

Although we have not yet found the model that will clarify for us what is essential about the peculiar combination of transcendence and self-transcendence which the Augustinian tradition offers as a normative concept of religious experience, the time has come to introduce our second major theme, self-deception. For it will throw light on our negative results to this point. Our point of departure can be the suspicion Nietzsche directs toward religious experience, even that of religious founders. "One sort of honesty has been alien to all founders of religions and their kind: They have never made their experiences a matter of conscience for knowledge. 'What did I really experience?'. . . None of them has asked such questions, nor do any of our dear religious people ask them even now" (1974: 253).

Paul Ricoeur translates this kind of question into the language of the biblical prophets on the warpath against idolatry as he introduces his own hermeneutics of suspicion. "In our time we have not finished doing away with idols and we have barely begun to listen to symbols. It may be that this situation, in its apparent distress, is instructive: it may be that extreme iconoclasm belongs to the restoration of meaning" (1970: 27). To listen to religious symbols is to open oneself to a claim from what purports to be ultimately transcendent and to entertain the possibility of transcending oneself in that direction. To do away with idols is to take seriously the suspicion that what purports to be listening to religious symbols is actually something quite different, an acoustic illusion in which my own voice is mistaken for the divine voice. When this occurs, religion becomes a disguised form of self-centering or preoccupation with oneself. For corresponding to false-consciousness are false gods, and the deities who are the means or the elements for self-centering are wish-fulfilling projections whose fictitious character does not keep them from being rivals to whatever may be truly sacred (see Westphal, 1987).

Ricoeur's suggestion is that the pursuit of any possibly genuine self-transcendence must include a negative, iconoclastic moment. He calls us to renew the question that Jonathan Edwards put so sharply with reference to the "holy affections" in which "true religion, in great part, consists" (1959: 95)—how can we distinguish the truly holy affections from their counterfeit counterparts? Precisely our failure, to this point, to find an adequate model for the self-transcendence that constitutes genuine religious experience puts us in a good position to see why Nietzsche and Ricoeur and Edwards (like Amos and Jesus) refuse to take everything that offers itself as religious experience at face value. For that failure contains the transcendental deduction, so to speak, of three idols.

To begin with, any religious experience that contents itself with what we have called intentional transcendence can be shown to be idolatrous. Religion that consists of nothing more than doctrinal knowledge of a transcendent creator and savior, for example, no matter how correct and orthodox such doctrine may be, reduces God to one of my clear and distinct ideas. Having already reduced the wholly other to the propositionally possessed, it will complete itself as the instrumental religion in which the truth serves as a security blanket or a weapon against one's opponents and thus as an escape from the call to a decentered selfhood (see Westphal, 1980).

Similarly, insofar as religious experience can be adequately described in terms of either contemplative or ecstatic self-forgetfulness, its gods will be but vehicles of enjoyment, nutritional elements lacking the kind of transcendence in themselves that would make them wholly and genuinely other or enable them to inspire any detachment from self.

To call the gods of such religions idols is to recognize them as convenient fictions masked as transcendent realities. But the iconoclasm that labels them as such should not be misunderstood to be the claim that there is no place in true religion for doctrinal affirmation or for either contemplative or ecstatic self-forgetfulness. On the contrary, I want to insist that there is an important place for each of these in true religion. The point is that by themselves these moments do not make up the true religion we seek. Something is missing, something so essential that without it these important moments of true religion become the embodiment of false. What is it?

There is an important clue in Gadamer's analysis of contemplative and ecstatic self-forgetfulness. Much as Lewis distinguishes the few who receive art from the many who use it, Gadamer emphasizes the "important difference between a spectator who gives himself entirely to the play of art, and someone who merely gapes at something out of curiosity." For the former "the play of art does not simply exhaust itself in the ecstatic emotion of the moment, but has a claim to permanence and the permanence of a claim" (1975: 111-12).

We might take this talk about a claim in purely aesthetic terms, as if the work of art lays claim to be recognized as a classic. But Gadamer seems to have in mind something more nearly like the experience Rilke expresses in his scant, "Archaic Torso of Apollo."

> Never will we know his fabulous head
> where the eyes apples slowly ripened. Yet
> his torso glows: a candelabrum set
> before his gaze which is pushed back and hid,
>> restrained and shining. Else the curving breast
>> could not thus blind you nor through the soft turn
>> of the loins could this smile easily have passed
>> into the bright groins where the genitals burned.
>
> Else stood this stone a fragment and defaced,
> with lucent body from the shoulders falling,
> too short, not gleaming like a lion's fell;
>> nor would this star have shaken the shackles off,

> bursting with light, until there is no place
> that does not see you. You must change your life.
> (MacIntyre, 1957: 92-93)

We are not prepared for these last five words, 'You must change your life.' Like the words, 'To live life to the end is no childish task' at the conclusion of *Doctor Zhivago*, their claim upon us shatters the calm of contemplation and calls us beyond the realm of aesthetic enjoyment to ethical, even religious responsibility. For this reason Gadamer explicates his notion of the claim in terms of Kierkegaard's challenge to contemporaneity with Christ and to hearing the proclamation of the gospel in a sermon, as understood by dialectical theology (1975: 112-13). His earlier notion that "the player experiences the game as a reality that surpasses him" (98), now becomes the notion that in the claim we encounter the "truth" of the "moral and religious world" in which we live (113).

There is an ambiguity here. As a moral and religious claim, this truth seems to have the categorical character that would render it truly other. But, as Kant and Freud insist with the greatest clarity and persuasiveness, the voice of categorical claims may very well be our very own voice. And Gadamer himself qualifies the alterity of the claim by saying, with reference to the spectator, "It is the truth *of his own world*, the religious and moral world *in which he lives*, which presents itself to him and *in which he recognizes himself* (113, my italics). If the truth that claims me is simply the tradition that has already shaped me, the spiritual world in and from which I live, and move, and have my being, its voice is other but not so very damn other. If Gadamer wants us to take seriously his appeal to Kierkegaard and to dialectical theology he must identify a claim that evokes fear and trembling not only from me as an existing individual but from my established order as well (Kierkegaard, 1944: 89; Barth, 1968: 27-54). His lack of enthusiasm for such a task is notorious.

For an unambiguous development of the clue we have found in Gadamer, the idea that it is in the form of a claim upon us that we encounter the otherness of the other, we can return to Levinas' account of metaphysical desire as directed toward "something else entirely, toward the absolutely other" (1969: 33). His analysis of enjoyment as involving self-centering rather than self-transcendence is one of several foils against which he develops the thesis that "the absolutely other is the Other" (39).

Who is this Other? In the first instance it is the one whom I encounter face to face in conversation (39, 71). In other words, the Other is another human being. Because our encounter takes place in language, it can be no animal other, and because it takes place face to face it can be no divine other. Rather, "it is only man who could be absolutely foreign to me" (73; cf. 71-79).

Secondly, the Other is the one whose face and speech I first encounter, beyond all knowing, all using, and all enjoying (38), as a claim, the unconditional constraint upon my freedom that leaves me fully free to accept or reject it and that is expressed in the words, "You shall not commit murder" (199, 216, 262, 303). Only in the realm of ethics, only in "the ethical impossibility of killing [the Other]" (87), do I encounter otherness as truly other.

This claim has a radically decentering intent. "To welcome the Other is to put in question my freedom (85; cf. 51, 43). It reminds me that I am not the center to which all else is peripheral, the end to which all else is the means. In the claims of the Other I am suddenly beyond all objects to be known, all tools to be used, and all elements on which to feed either body or soul.

What is worse, from the perspective of the "dear self," the relation is asymmetrical. It is not a prudent, contractual arrangement among equals in which I offer to spare your life (and liberty) if you agree to spare mine. On the one hand is the asymmetry of loftiness. The unconditional character of the Other's claim can only be expressed in images of height and authority. For this reason, although the Other is human and not divine, Levinas speaks of the Other as "Most-High" (34) and "Master" (72, 75, 86). On the other hand there is the asymmetry of indigence. This is why Levinas also refers to the Other as the stranger, the widow, the orphan, and the poor (77-78). The Other has nothing to offer in exchange for my welcoming, least of all a bribe. With such indigent loftiness it is impossible to negotiate or to strike a deal.

Finally, the face of the Other *"expresses itself,"* it manifests itself *"kath' auto"* (51). We are familiar with this Greek phrase through its Latin equivalent, *per se.* The face of the other expresses itself, and it does so through itself and not through another. This does not consist in its being disclosed, "its being exposed to the gaze that would take it as a theme for interpretation, and would command an absolute position dominating the object. Manifestation *kath' auto* consists in a being telling itself to us independently of every position we would have taken in its regard, *expressing itself"* (65; cf. 67, 74, 77).

The concept of disclosure that Levinas here contrasts with expression *kath' auto* or 'revelation' has Husserlian-Heideggerian connotations. "To recognize truth to be disclosure is to refer it to the horizon of him who discloses...The disclosed being is relative to us and not *kath' auto"* (64). By contrast, the notion of the face as self-revelatory "brings us to a notion of meaning prior to my *Sinngebung* and thus independent of my initiative and my power" (51). Even more important, it is independent of the horizons of meaning we bring with us, the tacit dimensions of our awareness that confer meaning without our noticing it (28).

Levinas knows exactly what he is doing here. He is claiming immediacy for the Other's self-expression. "The immediate is the face to face (52). In spite of all attacks on the "myth of the given," he is claiming that the face is a theory free datum. In willful disregard for the alleged inescapability of the hermeneutical circle, he finds us pointed toward "the possibility of signification without a context" (23). And in spite of all attacks on the metaphysics of presence and the transcendental signifier (Derrida, 1976: 49-50, 69-71; 1981: 19-20, 29, 44), he insists that "the signification of the face is due to an essential coinciding of the existent and the signifier. Signification is not added to the existent. To signify is not equivalent to presenting oneself as a sign, but to expressing oneself, that is, presenting oneself in person" (262).

Such claims are bold heresy in the present philosophical climate. But in spite of the avalanche of criticism they are bound to evoke, Levinas will want to stick by them, for they are the key to his project. Without self-expression *kath' auto*, I could not welcome the Other as such. The Other would be permitted to encounter me only as a meaning relative to my own (present) acts of *Sinngebung* or to the sedimented (past) acts of myself and of others that I bring with me as horizon, context, pre-understanding, *a priori*, tacit dimension, prejudice. Since as thematizing and as operative intentionality would be the condition of the possibility of her appearance, she would clearly be merely phenomenal. No *per se*, no *an sich*. Such an Other is not so very damn other. But as the claim that challenges my centrality in its own term and not in my own, the Other is very other indeed.

This is not the immediacy that ends up as pure indeterminacy (Hegel, 1969 82; cf. 1959: Par. 86). It is concerned with presence, to be sure, but not with sheer presence beyond difference. It is Derrida, pursuing his own agenda of *différance*, who points this out. By virtue of the lofty majesty attributed by Levinas to the Other, the encounter with the Other "does not take the form of an intuitive contact since the Other is present "not as a total presence but as a *trace*" (Derrida, 1978: 95). What we have here is "absolute proximity and absolute distance. . . A community of nonpresence, and therefore of non- phenomenality. . . Only the other, the totally other, can be manifested . . . within a certain non manifestation and *a certain absence*. . . It can be said only of the other that its phenomenon is a certain non phenomenon, *a certain absence*" (90-91, my italics).

This is why Levinas sometimes speaks of the Other simply as "the Stranger who disturbs the being at home with oneself" (1969: 39). Without the additional appellations of widow, orphan, and poor, such a reference evokes Camus rather than the Law and the Prophets and serves to make it clear that the Other, when encountered as truly other, is an intangible intrusion and not an intuitive intelligibility. It is for the same reason that Levinas emphasizes the nudity of the face. This is not to deny that the face may be the bearer of cultural codes, as when an expensive coiffure, a matted beard, or the unmistakable signs of Downs syndrome enable me to assign faces to their place in the social hierarchy. It is simply to deny that the meaning and validity of the Other's claim, "You shall not commit murder," is in any way dependent on these cultural codes. The ethical immediacy of the Other as face has nothing to do with pre-predicative indeterminacy; it is rather a matter of expressing a claim unmediated by the cultural codes that normally censor all claims.

The face as the presence of the Other as absolutely other "is produced concretely as a temptation to total negation, and as the infinite resistance to murder . . . in the hard resistance of these eyes without protection—what is softest and most uncovered (262). If Camus' *The Stranger* renders uncomfortably concrete this "temptation to total negation," the death of the black man, Christmas, in Faulkner's *Light in August* reveals "the infinite resistance to murder . . . in . . . these eyes without protection." A white lynch mob is determined to kill him, in spite of the testimony of the preacher, Hightower, that, "He was here that night. He was with me the night of the murder, I swear to God—"Grimm, their leader, finally corners Christmas, fires five shots into him, and, as he lies dying, castrates him. The others catch up. "But the man on the floor had not moved. He just lay there, with his eyes open and empty of everything save consciousness . . . For a long moment he looked up at them with peaceful and unfathomable and unbearable eyes. Then his face, body, all, seemed to collapse, to fall in upon itself, and from out of the slashed garments about his hips and loins the pent black blood seemed to rush like a released breath . . . upon that black blast the man seemed to rise soaring into their memories forever and ever. They are not to lose it, in whatever peaceful valleys, beside whatever placid and reassuring streams of old age, in the mirroring faces of whatever children they will contemplate old disasters and newer hopes. It will be there, musing, quiet, steadfast, not fading and not particularly threatful, but of itself alone serene, of itself alone triumphant" (1950: 406-407).

From out of the gaze of that black face the whole body of Christmas becomes face, so much so that the black blood that gushes from between his legs is transformed into a breath exuding from that face. According to the cultural codes that are the horizon for white perceptions of that black face, it is possible to interpret this killing, in spite of the victim's humanity, as equivalent to slaughtering a hog, and simultaneously, in spite of the victim's innocence, as a just punishment. If that were the whole story, it would be possible to forget the deed. But those who were there cannot do so, because the face of Christmas, against all the operative cultural codes, expresses unambiguously and unforgettably a claim that they could reject but not refute, "You shall not commit murder."

They can kill him, but they cannot reify him. They cannot reduce his otherness to an object of their knowledge, a tool for their use, or nourishment for their enjoyment. Helpless and humiliated, defeated and dying, he embodies a transcendence unlike any they have ever encountered in church. For the gods they worship are idols, but Christmas is "wholly other."

Here we have the model we have been seeking to help us clarify the Augustinian notion of self-transcendence. This is an Other whose transcendence consists in an unconditional claim that removes me from the center of the universe both ethically by constraining my will and epistemologically by refusing to be constrained by the cultural codes of the world in which I recognize myself.

This is the double decentering that constitutes Augustine's double conversion in Books VII and VIII of the *Confessions*. That independence of cultural codes precludes any account of knowledge as recollection is not only the argument of Augustine's critique of Platonism in Book VII, but also, and in greater detail, of Kierkegaard 's *Fear and Trembling and Philosophical Fragments*, taken jointly. Levinas reprises this argument by sharply distinguishing the ethical, in which I encounter the Other as truly other, from the political, in which I do not, and by repudiating recollection repeatedly as the vehicle of the ethical (1969: 21-24, 43, 51, 61, 171, 180, 204). According to Derrida's apt summary, Levinas sees western philosophy as "dominated since Socrates by a Reason which receives only what it gives itself, a Reason which does nothing but recall itself to itself." In this way "it has always *neutralized* the other, in every sense of the word" (Derrida, 1978: 96; cf. n. 27).

What here separates ethics from politics is what joins it to religion. Thus Kierkegaard's tight linkage in the Postscript of ethics and religion as the life-world of subjectivity, totally different from that of aesthetic-speculative objectivity, finds its echo in Levinas's claim that true religion presupposes ethics (77-78). We cannot truly love God while hating our sister and brother (I John 4:40). If Marcel and Merton are the great Catholic Augustinians of our time, and Kierkegaard the great Protestant Augustinian, Levinas is the great Jewish Augustinian.

The Other whose transcendence Levinas has helped us to specify provides us with the opportunity for a unique self-transcendence. To welcome an Other so unwelcome to the pride that the Augustinian tradition finds to be the heart of our darkness and the darkness of our heart is to become a new person indeed. We are, of course, still in the realm of ethics and not yet talking about religious experience. For this Other is human and not divine. But all we have to do is replace the human with the divine Other to have the normative concept of religious experience we are looking for. Genuine religious experience is the self-transcendence in relation to a divine transcendence that radically decenters us as will, and, correspondingly, as belief and affection. Perhaps this link between the ethical and the religious is the truth behind Kant's claims that "morality does not need religion at all," that "morality leads inevitably to religion," and that "Religion is (subjectively regarded) the recognition of all duties as divine commands" (1960: 3, 7n., 142).

It is now possible to specify just where a couple of earlier formulations that looked so promising came up short. Gadamer's account of ecstatic self forgetfulness in play, art, and religious ritual culminates in these words— "That which detaches him from everything also gives him back the whole of his being" (1975: 113-14). These words evoked for us the claim of Jesus that only those who lose their life will find it. But what Jesus says is this—"whoever loses his life *for my sake and the gospel's* will save it" (Mark 8:35, my italics).

Who is this Jesus, and what is this "gospel of Jesus Christ" (Mark 1:1)? Jesus is the one who has just responded to Peter's "You are the Messiah" with the announcement, to be repeated on two subsequent occasions (9:30-32, 10:32-34, cf. 45), that far from being the Davidic warrior who has come to slay the pharisaical-scribal Goliath of the Galilean synagogue, or the priestly Goliath of the Jerusalem temple, or the imperial Goliath of Rome, he is the Human One who must suffer and die at the hands of these Goliaths. And the good news about him centers in the call to a discipleship of self-denial and joining him on the way of the cross (8:34). By leaving out the crucial words, "for my sake and the gospel's," Gadamer leaves out precisely that decentering of the self as will (to power, cf. 10:35-45) that distinguishes the Markan account of self-transcendence as losing and finding oneself.

Similarly, we can now identify what C. S. Lewis failed to say when he wrote, "Heaven offers nothing that a mercenary soul can desire. It is safe to tell the pure in heart that they shall see God, for only the pure in heart want to" (1962: 144-45). His glosses on this claim, you will recall, were in terms of love as enjoyment of the object of desire. In order to get beyond the self-referential character of enjoyment, we need to specify that the pure in heart are precisely those who have learned to welcome Mark's Jesus as their center. It is safe to tell them of the "pie in the sky" that consists in seeing God not simply because they want to see God. For the God some want to see is an idol, the cosmic legitimizer and guarantor of their own will to power (Peter in Mark 8—"Get behind me, Satan," James and John in Mark 10, the crowd on Palm Sunday). Rather, it is safe to tell them that they shall see God because their purity of heart consists in willing the one thing they cannot will from the center—

Hallowed be *Thy* name
Thy kingdom come
Thy will be done

The enjoyment of God known to such pure hearts is authentic self-transcendence, and the God enjoyed is genuinely transcendent. Transcendence is an ethical category relating to the will, not an ontological category relating to being.

A normative concept of religious experience defined in terms of welcoming Mark's Jesus and learning to pray the prayer of his kingdom may seem too specific, even sectarian, to define religious as distinct from Christian experience. But the generic character of the concept is not compromised by the concreteness of the tradition through which it has been introduced. It is, for example, not difficult to show that the Brahman of the Hindu tradition and the Nirvana of the Buddhist tradition are wholly other in the sense we have now identified, for they confront me as an ethical claim that in both its ascetic and altruistic dimensions defines the false self as the will to be the center.

It would seem, then, that the concept of self-transcendence is useful beyond the biblical framework used here to render it concrete. It focuses attention on the ubiquitous challenge of religion to autonomous selfhood. It is not the task of this essay to spell out in detail the differences and similarities that emerge as the concept is employed across the spectrum of religious phenomena.

Rather the question is whether this generic concept of genuine religious self-transcendence takes us beyond the dangers of religious self-deception? Will it no longer be necessary to ask Nietzsche's question, "What did I really experience?"

Let us make the question even more concrete, returning to the tradition we know best. Suppose I am Thomas à Kempis, and that I offer the following prayer in all sincerity. "O Lord, Thou knowest what is the better way, let this or that be done, as Thou shalt please. Give what Thou wilt, and how much Thou wilt, and when Thou wilt. Deal with me as Thou knowest, and as best pleaseth Thee, and is most for Thy honour. Set me where Thou wilt, and deal, with me in all things just as Thou wilt. I am in Thy hand: turn me round, and turn me back again, even as a wheel. Behold, I am Thy servant, prepared for all things; for I desire not to live unto myself, but unto Thee; and O that I could do it worthily and perfectly" (1900: 127). Can we be confident that this prayer is offered to a truly transcendent God, rather than an idol, and that this prayer belongs to an experience of genuine self-transcendence?

Unfortunately not. We have already stipulated that these words are sincere. We can further stipulate that their sincerity is attested by the appropriate deeds. Our Thomas lives, let us say, an exemplary life of poverty, chastity and obedience. Still, we will be reminded, "However painstaking our work, so long as we omit to surrender ourselves to God while performing it...our efforts build up within us not so much a true spirit of grace but the spirit of a Pharisee" (Charlton, 1966: 137). But how could such words and deeds fail to express a decentering surrender of oneself to God?

The answer is simple. Sincerity is no guarantee against self-deception. Corresponding to the three idols whose transcendental deduction we noted earlier are three modes of religious experience which do not even have the form of true godliness, decentering self-transcendence. This piety, by contrast, has that form so conspicuously that it could be used as its paradigm. But that form may still be but appearance not supported by the reality it professes. Our Thomas may unconsciously be a hypocrite.

To see how this is possible let us recall *The Total Woman*. Perhaps like me you feel you have read this book even though you haven't. It suggests that the way to happiness for a woman is to subordinate herself entirely to the happiness of her lord and master. No, not God, but her husband. The combination of the theological claim that a radically hierarchical relation should exist between husband and wife with an emphasis on the wife's responsibility to keep the husband both sexually stimulated and satisfied, led Martin Marty to summarize his review in four words: fundies in their undies. Some years ago a student of mine wrote a review of this book which revealed the manipulative character of this conspicuous subordination. Again and again the book said, in so many words, Treat your husband as your lord and master and he'll be yours. You'll have no trouble keeping him for yourself or getting him to do what you want. You'll be in control.

The life of the total woman has the form of decentering self-transcendence, but not the substance. She may sincerely hold the beliefs and feel the emotions that her idea calls for, and she may perform a lifetime of sacrificial service for her husband. But this does not keep her from being self-deceived about what she has experienced, nor does it keep her devotion from being manipulative. What appears to her as subordination and service is in fact a complex web of strategic action in the service of her will to power. Secretly, and she keeps this secret even from herself, she is the center of her world.

Exactly the same may be true of our saintly Thomas à Kempis. The form of his piety is that of a decentering self-transcendence. Its inner content may or may not correspond. The form is visible, to others and to him. The content may be hidden from both. If it does not correspond and if he has managed not to notice this, he is self-deceived and the god he serves, so far from being genuinely transcendent, is not only constituted by his intentionality but also constructed by his (hidden) intentions. Such a god, so far from being "wholly other," is not so very damn other at all.

Given the multiple possibilities for self-deception, perhaps we can now see why self-transcendence is the task of a lifetime and why genuine transcendence is so elusive. And perhaps the current preoccupation with alterity among some philosophers is more the expression of hunger than of curiosity.

I want to suggest two conclusions for the philosophy of religion that seem to me to follow from these reflections. If this essay were addressed primarily to pastors or spiritual directors, I would address a very practical issue at this point. While the foregoing has shown, I hope, the need for suspicion and self-examination (since suspicion reduced to a tool for unmasking others becomes thereby a tool for sustaining our own self-deceptions), it has not mentioned the dangers this entails, dangers of morbidity, masochism, and cynicism. Since I do not want to draw too sharp a line between the pastoral and the philosophical, the therapeutic and the theoretical, I pause at least long enough to mention these issues.

But the two conclusions with which I want to conclude concern philosophy as theory. It may seem as if our phenomenological reflections have ignored one of the most intensely debated philosophical questions relating to religious experience, namely whether it can provide good reasons to support religious beliefs. But this is not so. Instead, the account of religious experience we have developed together would seem to place a major obstacle in the way of any positive answer to this question we might seek to develop. Our normative concept suggests that the intentional object of religious experience that lacks either the form or the substance of true godliness will be an idol of one sort or another. Such experience can hardly provide rational support for beliefs that purport to express the genuine transcendence of the truly divine. For religious experience to have any evidential value, it will first have to be shown to be authentic.

There are perhaps two reasons why this task has been conspicuously absent from most discussions. One is its obvious difficulty. The other is the principle of charity, the tendency to consider religious experience innocent until proven guilty. But neither of these is a good reason. An essential task becomes less essential because of its difficulty only in the presence of self-deceptive laziness. And no matter how wonderfully American it may sound, the innocent-until-proven-guilty principle simply ignores 1) the biblical claim that "the heart is deceitful above all things, and desperately corrupt" (Jer. 17:9), 2) the powerful theoretical analyses, only briefly developed in this essay, of self-deception whenever self-transcendence is at issue, and 3) our own "thou art the man" experience in the presence of such analyses.

One way to put this point would be to say that religious experience cannot provide any evidence for truth as objectivity until it has passed the test of truth as subjectivity. This link between the hermeneutics of suspicion and questions of inwardness and authenticity leads to a second conclusion. It puts in question the wisdom of doing business as usual within the religious epistemology industry. No doubt reflection is and ought to be *ancilla vitae*. But when the philosophy of religion, on this issue or any other, so focuses on objectivity as to let issues of subjectivity get forgotten or rendered peripheral, it shows itself to be ancillary to the life of some objectivist culture, Hegelian, positivist, technocratic, or whatever, that is systematically prejudiced against religious experience in general and the life of Christian faith in particular. This fact, if it is indeed a fact, is deserving of more attention than it usually gets among Christians in philosophy.

Fordham University

Endnote

Study Questions

1.   Westphal sees Kierkegaard as adding an element to faith not found in either Augustine or Merton. What is it?

2.   How does Husserl's treatment of intentionality "primarily as cognitive" help Westphal in giving account of "self-transcendence"?

3.   How does the realism of G. E. Moore figure in Westphal's account of "intentional acts"?

4.   Westphal thinks that C. S. Lewis fails to see something important with regard to transcendence. What is it? What do you make of Westphal's point?

5.   How might the theist benefit from Westphal's understanding of the notion of self-transcendence?

For Further Reading

Augustine (1963). *The Confessions of St. Augustine.* Trans. Rex Warner. New York: New American Library.

Barth, Karl (1968). *The Epistle to the Romans.* Trans. Edwyn C. Hoskyns. New York: Oxford University Press.

Breazeale, Daniel, trans. and ed. (1988). *Fichte: Early Philosophical Writings.* Ithaca, NY: Cornell University Press.

Caputo, John D. (1987). *Radical Hermeneutics.* Bloomington, IN: Indiana University Press.

Chariton of Valamo, Igumen, ed. (1966). *The Art of Prayer: An Orthodox Anthology.* Trans. E. Kadloubovsky and E. M. Palmer. London: Faber and Faber.

Derrida, Jacques (1976). *Of Grammatology.* Trans. Gayatri Chakravorty Spivak. Baltimore, MD: Johns Hopkins University Press.

Derrida, Jacques (1978). *Writing and Difference.* Trans. Alan Bass. Chicago: University of Chicago Press.

Derrida, Jacques (1981). *Positions.* Trans. Alan Bass. Chicago: University of Chicago Press.

Desmond, William (1987). *Desire, Dialectic, and Otherness.* New Haven, CT: Yale University Press.

Edwards, Jonathan (1959). *A Treatise Concerning Religious Affections.* New Haven, CT: Yale University Press.

Evans, Donald (1963). *The Logic of Self-Involvement*. London: SCM Press.

Faulkner, William (1950). *Light in August*. New York: Random House.

Gadamer, Hans-Georg (1975). *Truth and Method*. Trans. Garrett Barden and John Cumming. New York: Seabury Press.

Habermas, Jurgen (1987). *The Philosophical Discourse of Modernity*. Trans. Frederick Lawrence. Cambridge, MA: The MIT Press.

Hegel, G. W. F. (1949). *The Phenomenology of Mind*. Trans. J. B. Baillie. London: George Allen & Unwin.

Hegel, G. W. F. (1959). *The Logic of Hegel*. Trans. William Wallace. Oxford: Oxford University Press. Reprinted from the second, revised edition, 1892.

Hegel, G. W. F. (1969). *Hegel's Science of Logic*. Trans. A. V. Miller. London: George Allen & Unwin.

Hume, David (1888). *A Treatise of Human Nature*. Oxford: Clarendon Press.

Husserl, Edmund (1983). *Ideas Pertaining to a Pure Phenomenology and to a Phenomenological Philosophy*, First Book. Trans. F. Kersten. The Hague: Martinus Nijhoff.

Kant, Immanuel (1960). *Religion Within the Limits of Reason Alone*. Trans. Theodore M. Greene and Hoyt H. Hudson. New York: Harper and Brothers.

Kempis, Thomas à (1900). *Of the Imitation of Christ*. London: Oxford University Press.

Kierkegaard, Søren (1941). *Concluding Unscientific Postscript*. Trans. David Swenson and Walter Lowrie. Princeton, NJ: Princeton University Press.

Kierkegaard, Søren (1944). *Training in Christianity*. Trans. Walter Lowrie. Princeton, NJ: Princeton University Press.

Kierkegaard, Søren (1980). *The Sickness Unto Death*. Trans. Howard V. Hong and Edna H. Hong. Princeton, NJ: Princeton University Press.

Kojève, Alexandre (1969). *Introduction to the Reading of Hegel*. Trans. James H. Nichols, Jr. New York: Basic Books.

Levinas, Emmanuel (1969). *Totality and Infinity*. Trans. Alfonso Lingis. Pittsburgh: Duquesne University Press.

Lewis, C. S. (1961). *An Experiment in Criticism*. Cambridge: Cambridge University Press.

Lewis, C. S. (1962). *The Problem of Pain*. New York: Macmillan.

MacIntyre, C. F., trans. (1957). *Rainer Maria Rilke, Selected Poems*. Berkeley, CA: University of California Press.

Marcel, Gabriel (1964). *Creative Fidelity*. Trans. Robert Rosthal. New York Farrar, Strauss and Company.

Merton, Thomas (1972). *New Seeds of Contemplation*. New York: New Directions Books.

Michelfelder, Diane P., and Palmer, Richard E. eds. (1989). *Dialogue and Deconstruction: The Gadamer-Derrida Encounter*. Albany, NY: State University of New York Press.

Moore, G. E. (1953). Some Main Problems of Philosophy. London: George Allen and Unwin.

Moore, G. E. (1959). Philosophical Studies. Patterson, NJ: Littlefield, Adams & Co.

Nietzsche, Friedrich (1966a). *Beyond Good and Evil*. Trans. Waite Kaufmann. New York: Random House.

Nietzsche, Friedrich (1966b). *Thus Spoke Zarathustra*. Trans. Waite Kaufmann. New York: Viking Press.

Nietzsche, Friedrich (1967). *The Birth of Tragedy and The Case of Wagner*. Trans. Walter Kaufmann. New York: Random House.

Nietzsche, Friedrich (1968). *The Will to Power*. Trans. Walter Kaufmann and R. J. Hollingdale. New York: Random House.

15

Religious Experience and Religious Belief

William P. Alston

William P. Alston is professor of philosophy at Syracuse University, and author of, *Perceiving God, Divine Nature and Human Language*, and *Philosophy of Language*. In this essay he argues that religious experience can offer grounds for religious belief.* When compared with the epistemology of sense experience, the epistemology of religious experience has the same epistemic status, notwithstanding justifiable differences. Valid experiences of the former include the criteria of verifiability and predictability, but the fact that God is wholly other stands in the way of these criteria applying to religious experience. He concludes that Christian Epistemic Practice (CP) has basically the same epistemic status as Perceptual Practice (PP) and that "no one who subscribes to the latter is in any position to cavil at the former."

I

Can religious experience provide any ground or basis for religious belief? Can it serve to justify religious belief, or make it rational? This paper will differ from many others in the literature by virtue of looking at this question in the light of basic epistemological issues. Throughout we will be comparing the epistemology of religious experience with the epistemology of sense experience.

We must distinguish between experience directly, and indirectly, justifying a belief. It indirectly justifies belief B_1 when it justifies some other beliefs, which in turn justify B_1. Thus I have learned indirectly from experience that Beaujolais wine is fruity, because I have learned from experience that this, that, and the other bottle of Beaujolais is fruity, and these propositions support the generalization. Experience will directly justify a belief when the justification does not go through other beliefs in this way. Thus, if I am justified, just by virtue of having the visual experiences I am now having, in taking what I am experiencing to be a typewriter situated directly in front of me, then the belief that there is a typewriter directly in front of me is directly justified by that experience.

We find claims to both direct and indirect justification of religious beliefs by religious experience. Where someone believes that her new way of relating herself to the world after her conversion is to be explained by the Holy Spirit imparting supernatural graces to her, she supposes her belief *that the Holy Spirit imparts graces to her* to be indirectly justified by her experience. What she directly learns from experience is that she sees and reacts to things differently; this is then taken as a reason for supposing that the Holy Spirit is imparting graces to her. When, on the other hand, someone takes himself to be experiencing the presence of God, he thinks that his experience justifies him in supposing that God is *what* he is experiencing. Thus, he supposes himself to be directly justified by his experience in believing God to be present to him.

In this paper I will confine myself to the question of whether religious experience can provide direct justification for religious belief. This has implications for the class of experiences we shall be considering. In the widest sense 'religious experience' ranges over any experiences one has in connection with one's religious life, including any joys, fears, or longings one has in a religious context. But here I am concerned with experiences that could be taken to *directly* justify religious beliefs, i.e. experiences that give rise to a religious belief and that the subject takes to involve a direct awareness of what the religious belief is about. To further focus the discussion, let's confine ourselves to beliefs to the effect that God, as conceived in theistic religions, is doing something that is directed to the subject of the experience—that God is speaking to him, strengthening him, enlightening him, giving him courage, guiding him, sustaining him in being, or just being present to him. Call these "M-beliefs" ('M' for 'manifestation').

Note that our question concerns what might be termed a general "epistemic practice", the accepting of M-beliefs on the basis of experience, rather than some particular belief of that sort. I hold that practices, or habits, of belief formation are the primary subject of justification and that particular beliefs are justified only by issuing from a practice (or the activation of a habit) that is justified. The following discussion of concepts of justification will provide grounds for that judgment.

Whether M-beliefs can be directly justified by experience depends, *inter alia*, on what it is to be justified in a belief. So let us take a look at that.

First, the justification about which we are asking is an "epistemic" rather than a "moral" or "prudential" justification. Suppose one should hold that the practice in question is justified because it makes us feel good. Even if this is true in a sense, it has no bearing on epistemic justification. But why not? What makes a justification *epistemic*? Epistemic justification, as the name implies, has something to do with knowledge, or, more broadly, with the aim at attaining truth and avoiding falsity. At a first approximation, I am justified in believing that p when, from the point of view of that aim, there is something O.K., all right, to be approved, about that fact that I believe that p. But when we come to spell this out further, we find that a fundamental distinction must be drawn between two different ways of being in an epistemically commendable position.

On the one hand there is what we may call a "normative" concept of epistemic justification (J_n), "normative" because it has to do with how we stand *vis-à-vis* norms that specify our intellectual obligations, obligations that attach to one *qua* cognitive subject, *qua* truth-seeker. Stated most generally, J_n consists in one's not having violated one's intellectual obligations. We have to say "not having violated" rather than "having fulfilled" because in all normative spheres, being *justified* is a negative status; it amounts to ones behavior not being in violation of the norms. If belief is under direct voluntary control, we may think of intellectual obligations as attaching directly to believing. Thus one might be obliged to refrain from believing in the absence of adequate evidence. But if, as it seems to me, belief is not, in general, under voluntary control, obligations cannot attach directly to believing. However, I do have voluntary control over moves that can influence a particular belief formation, e.g., looking for more evidence, and moves that can affect my general belief forming habits or tendencies e.g., training myself to be more critical of testimony. If we think of intellectual obligations as attaching to activities that are designed to influence belief formation, we may say that a certain epistemic practice is normatively justified provided it is not the case that the practitioner would not have engaged in it had he satisfied intellectual obligations to engage in activities designed to inhibit it. In other words, the practice is justified if and only if the practitioner did not fail to satisfy an obligation to inhibit it.

However epistemologists also frequently use the term 'justified' in such a way that it has to do not with how the subject stands *vis-à-vis* obligations, but rather with the strength of her epistemic position in believing that p, with how likely it is that a belief of that sort acquired or held in that way is true. To say that a practice is justified in this, as I shall say, "evaluative" sense, (J_e) is to say that beliefs acquired in accordance with that practice, in the sorts of circumstances in which human beings typically find themselves, are generally true. Thus we might say that a practice is J_e if and only if it is reliable.

One further complication in the notion of Jt remains to be canvassed. What is our highest reasonable aspiration for being Jn in accepting a belief on the basis of experience? Being Jn no matter what else is the case? A brief consideration of sense perception would suggest a negative answer. I may be justified in believing that there is a tree in front of me by virtue of the fact that I am currently having a certain kind of sense experience, but this will be true only in "favorable circumstances." If I am confronted with a complicated arrangement of mirrors, I may not be justified in believing that there is an oak tree in front of me, even though it looks for all the world as if there is. Again, it may look for all the world as if water is running uphill, but the general improbability of this greatly diminishes the justification the corresponding belief receives from that experience.

What this shows is that the justification provided by one's experience is only defeasibly so. It is inherently liable to be overridden, diminished, or cancelled by stronger considerations to the contrary. Thus the justification of beliefs about the physical environment that is provided by sense experience is a defeasible or, as we might say, *prima facie* justification. By virtue of having the experience, the subject is in a position such that she will be adequately justified in the belief *unless* there are strong enough reasons to the contrary.

It would seem that direct experiential justification for M-beliefs, is also, at most, *prima facie*. Beliefs about the nature and ways of God are often used to override M-beliefs, particularly beliefs concerning communications from God. If I report that God told me to kill all phenomenologists, fellow Christians will, no doubt, dismiss the report on the grounds that God would not give me any such injunction as that. I shall take it that both sensory experience and religious experience provide, at most, *prima facie* justification.

One implication of this stand is that a particular experiential epistemic practice will have to include some way of identifying defeaters. Different theistic religions, even different branches of the same religion, will differ in this regard, e.g., with respect to what sacred books, what traditions, what doctrines are taken to provide defeaters. We also find difference of this kind in perceptual practice. For example, with the progress of science new defeaters are added to the repertoire. Epistemic practices can, of course, be individuated with varying degrees of detail. To fix our thoughts with regard to the central problem of this paper let's think of a "Christian epistemic practice" *(CP)* that takes its defeaters from the Bible, the classic creeds, and certain elements of tradition. There will be differences between sub-segments of the community of practitioners so defined, but there will be enough commonality to make it a useful construct. My foil to *CP*, the practice of forming beliefs about the physical environment on the basis of sense-experience, I shall call "perceptual practice" *(PP)*.

Actually it will prove most convenient to think of each of our practices as involving not only the formation of beliefs on the basis of experience, but also the retention of these beliefs in memory, the formation of rationally self-evident beliefs, and various kinds of reasoning on the basis of all this. *CP* will be the richer complex, since it will include the formation of perceptual beliefs in the usual way, while *PP* will not be thought of as including the distinctive experiential practice of *CP*.

One final preliminary note. J_n is relative to a particular person's situation. If practice P_1 is quite unreliable, I may still be J_n in engaging in it either because I have no way of realizing its unreliability or because I am unable to disengage myself: while you, suffering from neither of these disabilities, are not J_n. When we ask whether a given practice is Jn, we shall be thinking about some normal, reasonably well informed contemporary member of our society.

II

Let's make use of all this in tackling the question as to whether one can be justified in CP and in PP. Beginning with J_n, we will first have to determine more precisely what one's intellectual obligations are *vis-à-vis* epistemic practices. Since our basic cognitive aim is to come into possession of as much truth as possible and to avoid false beliefs, it would seem that one's basic intellectual obligation *vis-à-vis* practices of belief formation would be to do what one can (or, at least, do as much as could reasonably be expected of one) to see to it that these practices are as *reliable* as possible. But this still leaves us with an option between a stronger and a weaker view as to this obligation. According to the stronger demand one is obliged to refrain (or try to refrain) from engaging in a practice unless one has adequate reasons for supposing it to be reliable. In the absence of sufficient reasons for considering the practice reliable, it is not justified. Practices are guilty until proved innocent. While on the more latitudinarian view one is justified in engaging in a practice provided one does not have sufficient reasons for regarding it to be unreliable. Practices are innocent until proved guilty. Let's take J_{ns} as an abbreviation for 'justified in the normative sense on the stronger requirement,' and 'J_{nw}' as an abbreviation for 'justified in the normative sense on the weaker requirement.'

Now consider whether Mr. Everyman is J_{nw} in engaging in PP. It would seem so. Except for those who, like Parmenides and Bradley, have argued that there are ineradicable inconsistencies in the conceptual scheme involved in PP, philosophers have not supposed that we can show that sense perception is not a reliable guide to our immediate surroundings. Sceptics about PP have generally confined themselves to arguing that we can't show that perception is reliable; i.e., they have argued that PP is not J_{ns}. I shall assume without further ado that PP is J_{nw}.

J_{ns} and J_e can be considered together. Although a practice may actually be reliable without my having adequate reasons for supposing so, and *vice versa*, still in considering whether a given practice is reliable, we will be seeking to determine whether there are adequate reasons for supposing it reliable, that is whether Everyman *could* be possessed of such reasons. And if we hold, as we shall, that there are no such reasons, the question of whether they are possessed by one or another subject does not arise.

I believe that there are no adequate noncircular reasons for the reliability of PP but I will not be able to argue that point here. If I had a general argument I would unveil it, but, so far as I can see, this thesis is susceptible only of inductive support, by unmasking each pretender in turn. And since this issue has been in the forefront of the Western philosophical consciousness for several centuries, there have been many pretenders. I do not have time even for criticism of a few representative samples. Instead I will simply assume that PP is not J_{ns}, and then consider what bearing this widely shared view has on the epistemic status of CP.

If J_{nw} is the most we can have for perceptual practice, then if CP is also J_{nw} it will be in at least as strong an epistemic position as the former. (I shall assume without argument that CP can no more be noncircularly shown to be reliable than can PP.) And CP *will* be J_{nw} for S, provided S has no significant reasons for regarding it as unreliable. Are there any such reasons? What might they be? Well, for one thing, the practice might yield a system that is ineradically internally inconsistent. (I am not speaking of isolated and remediable inconsistencies that continually pop up in every area of thought and experience.) For another, it might yield results that come into ineradicable conflict with the results of other practices to which we are more firmly committed. Perhaps some fundamentalist Christians are engaged in an epistemic practice that can be ruled out on such grounds as these. But I shall take it as obvious that one *can* objectify certain stretches of one's experience, or indeed the whole of one's experience, in Christian terms without running into such difficulties.

III

One may grant everything I have said up to this point and still feel reluctant to allow that CP is J_{nw}. CP does differ from PP in important ways, and it may be thought that some of these differences will affect their relative epistemic status. The following features of PP, which it does not share with CP, have been thought to have this kind of bearing.

1. Within PP there are standard ways of checking the accuracy of any particular perceptual belief.

2. By engaging in PP we can discover regularities in the behavior of the objects putatively observed, and on this basis we can, to a certain extent, effectively predict the course of events.

3. Capacity for PP, and practice of it, is found universally among normal adult human beings.

4. All normal adult human beings, whatever their culture, use basically the same conceptual scheme in objectifying their sense experience.

If CP includes PP as a proper part, as I ruled on above, how can it lack these features? What I mean is that there is no analogue of these features for that distinctive part of CP by virtue of which it goes beyond PP. The extra element of CP does not enable us to discover extra regularities, e.g., in the behavior of God, or increase our predictive powers. M-beliefs are not subject to interpersonal check in the same way as perceptual beliefs. The practice of forming M-beliefs on the basis of experience is not engaged in by all normal adults. And so on.

Before coming to grips with the alleged epistemic bearing of these differences, I want to make two preliminary points. (1) We have to engage in PP to determine that this practice has features 1.-4., and that CP lacks them. Apart from observation, we have no way of knowing that, e.g., while all cultures agree in their way of cognizing the physical environment they differ in their ways of cognizing the divine, or that PP puts us in a position to predict while CP doesn't. It might be thought that this is loading the dice in favor of my opponent. If we are to use PP, rather than some neutral source, to determine what features it has, shouldn't the same courtesy of self-assessment be accorded CP? Why should it be judged on the basis of what we learn about it from another practice, while that other practice is allowed to grade itself? To be sure, this is a serious issue only if answers to these questions are forthcoming from CP that differ from those we arrive at by engaging in PP. Fortunately, I can avoid getting involved in these issues by ruling that what I am interested in here is how CP looks from the standpoint of PP. The person I am primarily concerned to address is one who, like all the rest of us, engages in PP, and who, like all of us except for a few outlandish philosophers, regards it as justified. My aim is to show this person that, on his own grounds, CP enjoys basically the same epistemic status as PP. Hence it is consonant with my purposes to allow PP to determine the facts of the matter with respect to both practices. (2) I could quibble over whether the contrast is as sharp as is alleged. Questions can be raised about both sides of the putative divide. On the PP side, is it really true that all cultures have objectified sense experience in the same way? Many anthropologists have thought not. And what about the idea that all *normal* adult human beings engage in the same perceptual practice? Aren't we loading the dice by taking participation in what we regard as standard perceptual practice as our basic criterion for normality? On the CP side, is it really the case that this practice reveals no regularities to us, or only that they are very different from regularities in the physical world? What about the Point that God is faithful to His promises? Or that the pure in heart will see God? However, I believe that when all legitimate quibbles have been duly

registered there will still be very significant differences between the two
practices in these respects. So rather than contesting the factual
allegations, I will concentrate on the *de jure* issue as to what bearing these
differences have on epistemic status.

How could the lack of 1.4. prevent CP from being J_{nw}? Only by
providing an adequate ground in a judgment of unreliability. And why
suppose that? Of course, the lack of these features implies that we lack
certain reasons we might conceivably have had for regarding CP as
reliable. If we could ascertain that PP has those features, without using PP
to do so, that would provide us with strong reasons for judging PP to be
reliable. And the parallel possibility is lacking for CP. This shows that
we cannot have *certain* reasons for taking CP to be reliable, but it doesn't
follow that we have reasons for unreliability. That would follow only if
we could also premise that a practice is reliable *only if* (as well as *if*) it
has 1.-4. And why suppose that?

My position is that it is a kind of parochialism that makes the lack of
1.-4. appear to betoken untrustworthiness. The reality CP claims to put us
in touch with is conceived to be vastly different from the physical
environment. Why should the sorts of procedures required to put us in
effective cognitive touch with this reality not be equally different? Why
suppose that the distinctive features of PP set an appropriate standard for
the cognitive approach to God? I shall sketch out a possible state of
affairs in which CP is quite trustworthy while lacking 1.-4., and then
suggest that we have no reason to suppose that this state of affairs does
not obtain.

Suppose, then, that

   (A)   God is too different from created beings, too "wholly
         other," for us to be able to grasp any regularities in His
         behavior.

Suppose further that

   (B)   for the same reason we can only attain the faintest,
         sketchiest, and most insecure grasp of what God is like.

Finally, suppose that

   (C)   God has decreed that a human being will be aware of His
         presence in any clear and unmistakable fashion only when
         certain special and difficult conditions are satisfied.

If all this is the case, then it is the reverse of surprising that CP should
lack 1.-4. even if it does involve a genuine experience of God. It would lack
1.-2. because of (A). It is quite understandable that it should lack 4.

because of (B). If our cognitive powers are not fitted to frame an adequate conception of God, it is not at all surprising that there should be wide variation in attempts to do so. This is what typically happens in science when investigators are grappling with a phenomenon no one really understands. A variety of models, analogues, metaphors, hypotheses, hunches are propounded, and it is impossible to secure universal agreement. 3. is missing because of (C). If very difficult conditions are set it is not surprising that few are chosen. Now it is compatible with (A)-(C) that

(D) religious experience should, in general, constitute a genuine awareness of the divine

and that

(E) although any particular articulation of such an experience might be mistaken to a greater or lesser extent, indeed even though all such articulations might miss the mark to some extent, still such judgments will, for the most part, contain some measure of truth; they, or many of them, will constitute a useful approximation of the truth;

and that

(F) God's designs contain provision for correction and refinement, for increasing the accuracy of the beliefs derived from religious experience. Perhaps as one grows in the spiritual life ones spiritual sight becomes more accurate and more discriminating; perhaps some special revelation is vouchsafed under certain conditions; and there are many other conceivable possibilities.

If something like all this were the case then *CP* would be trustworthy even though it lacks features 1.-4. This is a conceivable way in which *CP* would constitute a road to the truth, while differing from *PP* in respects 1.-4. Therefore unless we have adequate reason for supposing that no such combination of circumstances obtains, we are not warranted in taking the lack of 1.-4. to be an adequate reason for a judgment of untrustworthiness.

Moreover it is not just that A.-C. constitute a bare possibility. In the practice of *CP* we seem to learn that this is the way things are. As for (A) and (B) it is the common teaching of all the higher religions that God is of a radically different order of being from finite substances and, therefore, that we cannot expect to attain the grasp of His nature and His doings that we have of worldly objects. As for (C), it is a basic theme in Christianity, and in other religions as well, that one finds God within one's experience, to any considerable degree, only as one progresses in the spiritual life. God is not available for *voyeurs*. Awareness of God, and understanding of His nature and His will for us, is not a purely cognitive achievement; it requires the involvement of the whole person; it takes a practical commitment and a practice of the life of the spirit, as well as the exercise of cognitive faculties.

Of course these results that we are using to defend CP are derived from that same practice. But in view of the fact that the favorable features of PP, 1.-4., are themselves ascertained by engaging in PP, our opponent is hardly in a position to fault us on this score. However I have not forgotten that I announced it as my aim to show that even one who engaged only in PP should recognize that CP is J_{nw}. For this purpose, I ignore what we learn in CP and revert to the point that my opponent has no basis for ruling out the conjoint state of affairs A.-F., hence has no basis for taking the lack of 1.-4. to show CP to be untrustworthy, and hence has no reason for denying that CP is J_{nw}.

I conclude that CP has basically the same epistemic status as PP and that no one who subscribes to the latter is in any position to cavil at the former.

Endnote

*Reprinted by permission of the author and of the editor of *Noûs*, Vol. 16 (1982):3-12. Footnotes deleted.

Study Questions

1.   Why does William Alston think that the epistemology of sense experience shares the same epistemic status with the epistemology of religious experience? Do you agree? If so why? If not, why not?

2.   What does Alston mean by the claim that God is wholly other?

3.   What is the "normative" concept of epistemic justification?

4.   How does Alston characterize defeaters?

5.   In what ways do you think Alston's discussion is helpful to the theist's cause?

16

What Good Are Theistic Proofs?

Stephen T. Davis

Stephen T. Davis is professor of philosophy at Claremont McKenna College and is author of *Logic and the Nature of God*. In this essay he first clarifies what a successful proof of the existence of God would be, and then argues that although theists do not need proofs to support their faith, there are aspects of the exercise that are profitable.*

One of the most interesting facts about the enterprise of trying to prove the existence of God is its longevity. In Book X of Plato's *Laws* (written in the fourth century BC) we find a version of what we now call the cosmological argument.[1] Ever since then, philosophers have spent a great deal of time and effort debating various attempts to prove that God exists. The arguments that we call the ontological, cosmological, teleological, and moral proofs have been enormously fascinating to philosophers of every stripe, even to many who have no other particular interest in religion or the philosophy of religion. This interest continues in the twentieth century—scores of books and hundreds of articles have been written on the theistic proofs in the past eighty years or so. One could almost say that debate about the existence of God is a consuming passion of twentieth-century philosophers of religion.

It is odd that this should be the case. For several reasons, theistic proofs are widely criticized and even denigrated—by believers and unbelievers in God alike. First, most (but not quite all) of the participants in the debate concede that none of the theistic proofs succeeds in demonstrating the existence of God. Second, and perhaps for the above reason, it is often pointed out that the theistic proofs are unpersuasive; they just do not succeed in convincing unbelievers. For myself, I do not think I have ever met anyone who was converted to belief in God because of one of the proofs. Third, theologians, religious people, and some philosophers play down or even scoff at the proofs as totally irrelevant to religious faith and practice. Believers don't need the proofs—why try to demonstrate something you already know? And the proofs, it is said, are cold, formal, and philosophical; they do not call for faith or commitment, nor do they meet our spiritual needs. Fourth, the "God" of the theistic proofs, it is said, is a mere philosophical abstraction (a "necessary being," the "Greatest Conceivable Being," the "Prime Mover," etc.) rather than the living God of the Bible. Finally, one recent theologian, Paul Tillich, rejects the proofs because (he says) they end up denying divine transcendence. To say that "God exists," Tillich claims, is to place God on the same level as the creatures. God becomes a "being" like all the other existing "beings" rather than "the ground of being."[2]

What good are the theistic proofs, then? Why bother trying to prove that God exists? Or why bother discussing seriously the attempts of others to do so? Is this not so much wasted effort? In this paper I will attempt to answer these questions. I do not believe that discussing theistic proofs need be a waste of time. That is, I believe the theistic proofs can be religiously and philosophically valuable. That is what I will try to show.

I

It will be helpful to begin by defining some terms. First, let us say that "God" is the God of theism, that is, a unique, eternal, all-powerful, all-knowing, and loving spirit who created the heavens and earth and works for the salvation of human beings. Second, let us say that a "theistic proof" is an argument whose conclusion is identical to or equivalent with the statement "God exists." It tries to prove that God is real or actual, that God exists dependently of our minds. Third, let us say that an argument" is a set of words arranged in a series of sentences in which one sentence consists of the conclusion and the other sentence or sentences consist of the premise or premises, and in which the premise or premises are designed to provide intellectual support for or proof of the conclusion. Fourth, let us say that a "valid" argument is one that makes no error in logic; accordingly, if the premises are true, the conclusion logically must be true. Finally, let us say that a "sound" argument is a valid argument all of whose premises are true.

The next question we need to ask is, What would constitute a good or *successful* theistic proof?[3] Let us see if we can answer this question by considering various theistic proofs. Suppose we begin with the following:

(1)   All the people in Claremont are people;
(2)   Some people believe in God;
(3)   Therefore, God exists.

Now this is obviously a feeble attempt to prove the existence of God. Probably the most noticeable problem with it is that it is invalid—the conclusion does not follow from the premises. Let us then try to remedy this difficulty by coming up with a theistic proof that is formally valid:

(4)   If God exists then God exists;
(5)   God exists;
(6)   Therefore, God exists.

But this argument too is feeble—doubtless few atheists or agnostics will come to believe in the existence of God because of it. It is true that the argument is *formally valid*: if (4) and (5) are true (6) must be true. That is, it is impossible for (4) and (5) to be true and (6) false. But the argument assumes in premise (5) exactly what it is trying to prove; accordingly, no sensible person who doubts the conclusion will grant premise (5). Classically, then, this is an argument that commits the informal fallacy of "begging the question." The argument, then, is *informally invalid*.

Consider also the following two arguments:

(7)   Everything the Bible says is true;
(8)   The Bible says that God exists;
(9)   Therefore, God exists;

and

(10)   Either God exists or $7 + 5 = 13$;
(11) $7 + 5$ does not $= 13$;
(12)   Therefore, God exists.[4]

These arguments too seem to beg the question. As far as the first is concerned, it does so because no one who denies or doubts (9) will grant that both (7) and (8) are true. Premise (8) is perhaps beyond reproach, but (7) will be singularly unappealing to atheists or agnostics. The second argument is a bit more complicated; it is surely formally valid, and those who believe in God, as I do, will hold that it is also sound. Nearly everyone will grant (11), and I for one am happy to grant 10. But the problem again is that no sensible person who denies or doubts the conclusion will grant (10); there is no reason to grant (10) apart from a prior commitment to the existence of God. Thus this argument too begs the question.

Another major informal fallacy is that of "equivocation"—that is, using the same word in two different senses—as for example in the following argument: "The audience gave her a hand: therefore, the audience gave her something; therefore, the audience gave her something with five fingers." A theistic proof that commits the fallacy of equivocation might be stated as follows:

(13) I believe in God;
(14) Therefore, God exists;
(15) Therefore, God exists.

Here the word *exists* is used in two different ways. If premise (13) all by itself is to entail premise (14), then the word *exists* in (14) must mean something like "exists in my mind" (or as Anselm would have said, exists in *intellectu*). But if the above argument is to count as a theistic proof, then the word *exists* in (15) must mean something quite different. It must mean something like "exists independently of my mind" (exists *in re*, as Anselm would have it). Thus this argument too is quite worthless as an attempt to prove the existence of God.

We appear then so far to have arrived at two criteria that a theistic proof must satisfy in order to count as successful: it must be formally valid and it must be informally valid. That is, it must be the case that the truth of the premises logically requires the truth of the conclusion, and it must be the case that the argument avoids question begging, equivocation, and all other informal fallacies. But clearly these criteria are insufficient. Notice the following argument:

(16) Anything everyone believes is true;
(17) Everyone believes in the existence of God;
(18) Therefore, God exists.

This argument seems to me to satisfy both of the above criteria—it is valid both formally and informally—but it is clearly a poor attempt at a theistic proof. It fails, I think, because (16) and (17) are both false—the argument is unsound. (An argument is unsound if any of its premises is false, let alone if both or all of them are.) Thus it seems we must add some third criterion that has something to do with the truth of the premises. But here too we find complications; how exactly shall we specify this third criterion?

Which of the following shall we say that the premises of a successful theistic proof must be?

(a) possibly true;
(b) known to be possibly true;
(c) more reasonable or plausible than their denials;
(d) known to be more reasonable or plausible than their denials;
(e) reasonable or plausible;
(f) known to be reasonable or plausible;

(g)   true;
(h)   known to be true;
(i)   necessarily true; or
(j)   known to be necessarily true?

Some of these candidates can surely be ruled out—(a) and (b) are doubtless too weak; if they were acceptable the (16)-(18) argument might well count as a successful theistic proof, for both (16) and (17) are possibly true and known to be so. Both (c) and (d) are also probably too weak. A premise might be just slightly more plausible than its denial; if so, we will want to deny that any theistic proof in which it appears is successful. And (i) and (j) are doubtless too strong. But where do we go from here? Which of the remaining candidates—(e), (f), (g), or (h)—shall we opt for? What we have concluded so far is that a successful theistic proof is formally and informally valid and satisfies one of the four remaining candidates for the third criterion. Which candidate we pick, it seems to me, will depend on our view as to the purpose of a theistic proof. Let us then ask, What is or ought to be the aim, goal, or purpose of a theistic proof?

II

Here too we find difficulties. There are several ways of envisioning the goal or purpose of a theistic proof. There is perhaps a common assumption behind most discussions of theistic proofs, an assumption made by both defenders and critics of these arguments, namely, that theism is in better epistemic shape, so to speak, if a theistic proof succeeds than it is if none succeeds. But beyond that point of general (but not quite universal) agreement, there are at least three ways in which we might try to define success for a theistic proof.

One possibility is to say that a successful theistic proof is one that *convinces people that God exists*. But which people? (a) Perhaps a successful proof convinces *everyone who hears and follows it* that God exists. But of course it is extremely doubtful that any proof will ever do that. (b) Perhaps then a successful proof is one that convinces every *rational* person who hears and follows it that God exists. This notion is a bit more promising than the first, but the difficulty here is that we will never be able to tell whether a prof is successful because we have no preciser criteria for determining which people are rational. (c) Perhaps we ought to say that a successful proof is one that convinces all rational people *who believe its premises* that God exists. (I am assuming both here and elsewhere that it makes sense to speak of both believers and unbelievers in a proposition p as "being convinced" that p is true; in the second case but not the first a change of mind is involved.) But this is surely too liberal a notion of success. On the basis of this notion, the (7)-(9)

and the (10)-(12) arguments above are probably successful theistic proofs, and that is something we do not want to grant. (d) Perhaps we ought to say that a successful theistic proof is one that convinces at least some of the people who hear and follow it that God exists. But this notion is also too liberal—probably lots of feeble theistic proofs (possibly including some of the ones mentioned above) will convince somebody somewhere that God exists.

Suppose we consider another possibility. A successful theistic proof, we might say, is one that *demonstrates the rationality of belief in God*. That is, it is one that substantiates or provides good grounds for belief in the existence of God. It creates a situation in which rational people who hear and follow the proof may rationally believe in the existence of God. But here too we face the question, To whom is a theistic proof addressed? Does a successful proof demonstrate to everyone the rationality of belief in God? Or just to all rational persons? Or just to all rational persons who believe the premises? Or just to some of the persons who hear and follow the proof?

A third possibility is to define a successful theistic proof as one that *strengthens the faith of theists*, that is, strengthens the conviction of those who already believe in God. But although some theistic proofs probably do achieve this end, and in some cases this might be an end well worth achieving, it is doubtful that we ought to understand success for a theistic proof in this way. For one thing, possibly something like the (7)-(9) argument above would strengthen the faith of some theists, but we will not want to call that argument a successful proof. Furthermore, in the case of the actual theistic proofs discussed by philosophers,—for example, the ontological, cosmological, teleological, and moral arguments—stronger aims than this one are clearly had in mind by the people who propose them.

It seems to me that the second of the above possibilities is by far the most promising. Without claiming that this was precisely what was had in mind by such defenders of theistic proofs as Plato, Anselm, Aquinas, Paley, Kant, and so on, I will hold that the purpose, aim, or goal of a theistic proof is to *demonstrate the rationality of belief in the existence of God*. That is, what a theistic proof aims to do is substantiate the theist's belief in God, give a good reason for it, show that it is credible. And theistic proofs, I suggest, try to demonstrate the rationality of theistic belief to all rational persons (whoever exactly they are).

This causes me to say that the third criterion (besides formal validity and informal validity) of a good or successful theistic proof is either (e) or (f) above. That is, the premises of a good or successful theistic proof must be either *reasonable or plausible or else known to be reasonable or plausible*. Of course a theistic proof would be even more able to demonstrate the rationality of theism if it satisfied the stronger criterion that its premises must be *known to be true*. But I opt for the slightly weaker criterion because there are premises that have not been proved and that may not be known to be true but that, being recognized as at least plausible or rational, can appear as premises in a successful theistic proof.

I think for example of that statement that appears in many versions of the ontological argument, namely, "The Greatest Conceivable Being is a possible being." I would claim to know this statement, but surely many others would dispute such a claim. And I see no way of proving the statement apart from showing that the Greatest Conceivable Being is actual (all actual beings are possible beings). Nevertheless, if this being seems to me to be a possible being, and if I have apparently answered successfully all the known arguments to the contrary, then I know to be plausible the statement, "The Greatest Conceivable Being is a possible being." Accordingly, I can rationally believe the statement, and I can use it as a premise in a successful theistic proof.

Between candidates (e) and (f) for the third criterion of a successful theistic proof, (f) is to be preferred. It is crucial that the premises of a successful theistic proof be not just *plausible* but *known to be plausible*. But known to whom? They must be known by the people to whom the rationality of belief in the existence of God is to be demonstrated (including presumably, the person who offers the proof). If the premises of a theistic proof are plausible but the relevant people do not know them or recognize that they are plausible, the rationality of theism will not be demonstrated to them. Neither believers nor unbelievers in the existence of God will receive the intended benefit, namely, recognition of the rationality of belief in the existence of God.

Of course there may be premises that some people know to be plausible and others don't. (Notoriously, this situation seems frequently to occur in discussions of theistic proofs, e.g., with statements like "Every existing thing has a reason for its existence," or "The universe is like a watch.") If these premises appear in an otherwise successful theistic proof, then the rationality of belief in the existence of God will have been demonstrated to those who know that the premises in question are plausible (if there are any such people) but not to those who do not.

In summary, then, a good or successful theistic proof satisfies the following criteria:

1. It is formally valid;
2. It is informally valid;
3. Its premises are known to be plausible.

A theistic proof that satisfies these criteria (if any such argument ever does) demonstrates the rationality of belief in the existence of God. It shows that rational people can rationally believe in the existence of God.

III

What then would be the result if some logician or philosopher of religion were able to produce a successful, or at least apparently successful, theistic proof? Suppose it were an argument of the form we call *modus ponens* and went something like this:

(19) If p is true, then God exists
(20) p is true;
(21) Therefore, God exists.

Or perhaps the argument might run as follows:

(22) If q is true, it is probable that God exists;
(23) q is true;
(24) Therefore, it is probable that God exists.

Now arguments of this form would surely be formally valid. Suppose that they were also informally valid and that the premises were known to be plausible. What would or should our reaction be?

Our first thought might be to return to the various criticisms mentioned at the outset of this paper that have been raised against theistic proofs. We might wonder what ought to be said about them in the light of the existence of an apparently successful theistic proof. So let us now take a second look at those criticisms. The first point was not so much a criticism as a recognition of the odd fact that debate about theistic proofs thrives despite general but not universal agreement that no actual theistic proof succeeds. But even if all this is true, it constitutes no good argument against the continued thriving of the industry. Perhaps the majority is wrong; perhaps some existing theistic proof succeeds despite the failure of the majority to recognize its success. (I myself hold that there are versions of the ontological argument that have not been refuted.) Or even if the majority is right and no theistic proof succeeds, perhaps engaging in the enterprise of discussing theistic proofs is valuable anyway, that is, for some other reason.

The second point was that theistic proofs don't convince religious skeptics and unbelievers to believe in the existence of God. That is surely true, but perhaps it is merely because no successful theistic proof yet exists; or perhaps it is because defenders of successful theistic proofs have thus far done a poor job of defending them; or perhaps it is because atheists and agnostics are too stubborn. Few arguments possess irresistible force; few coerce people on pain of irrationality, so to speak, into accepting their conclusions. So even if a successful theistic proof existed we should expect (as Norman Malcolm once suggested)[5] few conversions. It is always possible to find some reason to reject an argument whose conclusion one finds repugnant.

The third point was that theistic proofs are irrelevant to religious faith and practice. And it does seem odd to try to prove something that you already know—for example, that San Francisco is north of Los Angeles, or that Napoleon Bonaparte is dead. But perhaps it is not so odd to try to prove something you believe but do not know (which is to how many theists would describe their cognitive on state vis-à-vis the existence of God). And it is surely not at all odd to try to prove something your believe or even know, when the proof is aimed at someone else who neither knows nor believes it. It is also true that the theistic proofs do not do a good job of meeting human spiritual needs—the cosmological argument, for example, calls few people to religious commitment. The teleological argument does not tell us how to worship or pray. The moral argument does not teach us any lessons about forgiving each other. But why is that a problem? Naturally, there are many crucial tasks theistic proofs do not succeed in doing—for example, feeding hungry people. There are even crucial intellectual tasks theistic proofs do not succeed in doing—for example, solving the problem of evil. Is the fact that they fail to do these things a reason for us all to opt out of the debate over theistic proofs? Of course not. Perhaps there are other crucial tasks the theistic proofs can perform. (What they might be I will discuss below.)

The fourth point was that the "God" spoken of in the theistic proofs is a philosophical abstraction rather than the living God of the Bible. And one can appreciate what is being said here. As is well known, Aquinas finishes each of his "five ways" of demonstrating the existence of God with some such statement as, "and this everyone understands to be God." It has been frequently and correctly pointed out that what he claims here is not necessarily true. Despite Aquinas's attempts to argue otherwise, it is logically possible for a first mover, a first cause, and a necessary being that owes its necessity to no other being to exist without possessing such characteristic properties of God as omnipotence, omniscience, compassion, and so on. The beings whose existence Aquinas tries to prove, in short, do not have to be God. Furthermore, the beings spoken of in typical theistic proofs do seem more like metaphysical principles than living beings. But the criticism of theistic proofs we are considering here would be immeasurably stronger, in my view, if it could be shown that such beings as "the Greatest Conceivable Being," "the Designer of the Universe," "the Prime Mover," and so on, cannot be God, that is, if some of their properties are inconsistent with some of the properties of the living God of the Bible. But that has not been shown and (I think) is not true.[6]

The fifth point was Tillich's insistence that God is not a "being" and that to try to prove "the existence of God" is illicitly to place God on the same level as finite beings. But I confess I have never been able to grasp how it lessens or destroys God's transcendence over the creatures to say that God is a being. Why can't we state that God "is a being" and "exists" without denying that God's existence is of a radically different sort than ours? And whether or not we choose to regard God as sharing some of our properties—for example, the property of being a being, the property of knowing the sum of six and five, the property of desiring peace on earth— we will still want to be free to ask whether or not God is real, whether the atheists are right or wrong. And I see no significant danger in using the word *exist* to ask the relevant questions or make the relevant affirmations. As long as we recognize the limitations of all human talk about God, and as long as we recognize that God "exists" in a different sense than we do, the enterprise of proposing, criticizing, and defending theistic proofs can continue.

IV

What good, then, do theistic proofs do? Why spend time arguing about them? I would prefer to approach the question by asking, What good would a successful theistic proof do (if one existed)? Naturally, the question and its answer might be quite different if I were instead to ask, What good is done by the existing theistic proofs discussed by philosophers, that is, the ontological argument, the moral argument, and so on? I choose to proceed in the way I do because the main point behind discussions of these arguments seems to me to be in any case to see whether or not they are successful. Those who defend them think they are or might be (although their notions of "success" sometimes appear to differ from mine); those who criticize them think they are not.

In my view, there are two great benefits that would be derived from a successful theistic proof.[7] The two are closely related; and the first benefit (but not the second) is also derived from discussions of the actual theistic proofs, whether or not any one of them is successful. The first then is this: Theistic proofs show that theists do or at least can make full and thoroughgoing use of their rational faculties in arriving at or continuing in belief in the existence of God. I say this because it is frequently charged (oddly, by some who look sympathetically on religious faith in God as essentially irrational or at least arational, that is, based on an "existential choice" that is not supported by evidence, arguments, or reasons).

The second and most important benefit that would derive from a successful theistic proof is that the belief in the existence of God will have been shown to be rational or intellectually justified. (I do not claim, of course, that this is the *only* way such a belief can be shown to be rational.) The standard criticism of belief in the existence of God, namely, that it is naive or credulous or irrational to believe in the existence of something you can't see or measure or test or prove, will have been answered. I consider that this result will constitute a very great benefit indeed for theism.

If such a proof existed, the temptation for theists would be to use it as an evangelistic device. That is, they might try to use the proof to convince nonbelievers in the existence of God to become believers. And I suppose it is *possible* there might be some converts—a successful theistic proof might at least lead some folk to consider God more seriously than they had been doing, or it might for some folk remove intellectual obstacles to belief in the existence of God. But that, I think, is about all it should be expected to do. As noted above, few arguments are intellectually coercive; I suspect there never will exist a discursive, deductive theistic proof that convinces all the rational people who attend to it.

One reason this is true is that in the face of even a successful theistic proof a stubborn atheist always has the option of denying one of its premises. And in some cases this might be a rational thing for the atheist to do. Similarly, if someone were clever enough to construct from premises I believed a proof of the nonexistence of God, I am quite sure that the first thing I would do would be to consider which of those premises to deny. The strength of my commitment to theism would out-weigh my commitment to at least one of those premises. And, I claim, this might well be the rational thing for me to do.

But just when might it be rational for a person to deny a previously accepted premise in order rationally to reject a conclusion it entails or helps to entail? This is a complicated matter; I will suggest some criteria, but they should be taken as tentative suggestions only. Let us imagine an atheist, Jones, who is faced with the theistic proof with which we began:

(1)   All the people in Claremont are people;
(2)   Some people believe in God;
(3)   Therefore, God exists.

Let us further suppose something that is obviously not in fact true, namely, that this is a *valid* argument. And if it is valid, then it is also *sound*, since surely premises (1) and (2) are true. Now since these premises seem to be not only true but *known to be plausible*, this argument—so we are supposing—meets our requirements of a successful theistic proof. Finally, let us suppose that Jones knows that these premises are plausible. What, then, can or should Jones do in the light of this imagined successful theistic proof?

It seems that Jones has three options. First, Jones might agree that our theistic proof is successful but still deny its conclusion. Second, Jones might agree that our theistic proof is successful and accepts its conclusion, that is, become a theist. Third, Jones might deny that our theistic proof is successful by denying the plausibility of premises (1), (2), or both. (Let us imagine it is the contingently true premise (2) that Jones would decide to dispute.) Now the first option is obviously unacceptable and must be rejected as irrational. The second option, however, is clearly acceptable; in the light of our successful theistic proof, we would want to say, Jones rationally *should* accept the truth of (3).

Whether the third option is acceptable seems to depend on various considerations. First, is Jones willing to pay the price of rationally rejecting (3)? That is, is Jones willing to deny the apparently plausible premise (2)? Second, how important in Jones's world view is the denial of (3)? Is it central or important enough to outweigh the cost of denying premise (2)? Third, how probable is the denial of (3) (i.e., atheism) versus the probability of (2)? I would argue, then, that if Jones is willing to deny (2), and if the denial of (3) is crucial to Jones's world view, and if Jones's best judgment is that the denial of (3) is more probable than the truth of premise (2), then Jones is rational in denying (2), despite its initial plausibility, in order rationally to deny (3).

In short, if you think a statement p is plausible or even true; and if you are utterly convinced that another statement q is false; and if you discover that p entails q; then you can rationally change your mind about p and deny it if you are willing to pay the price of doing so, if the denial of q is crucial to your world view, and if the denial of q seems far more probable to you that the truth or plausibility of p.

V

I have been arguing that rational discussion of theistic proofs is worthwhile. But in the end I do want to say that theistic proofs are very much *optional* for theists. The fact of the matter is this: I enjoy discussing theistic proofs; I consider the enterprise valuable, and I even consider that there do exist successful theistic proofs; nevertheless, the reason I am a theist has almost nothing to do with theistic proofs. It has a great deal to do with experiences I have had that I interpret in terms of the presence of God—experiences I find myself interpreting in terms of divine forgiveness, divine protection, divine guidance. That is why I claim to know that God exists. That is why I would be extremely suspicious of any apparently successful atheistic proof.

Let us return to the move Aquinas makes at the conclusion of each of the five ways—"and this everyone understands to be God." As noted, Aquinas errs in that he has not shown that the Prime Mover, and so on, can be none other than the Judeo-Christian God. Yet we can understand what he is doing here—he is, of course, connecting his philosophy and his theology. His method is first to prove the existence of a first mover, a first cause, and a necessary being who owes its necessity to no other being; he then does an inventory, so to speak, of all the beings he believes on other grounds to exist; finally, he asks, Which of them could be the same being as the being or beings proven in the five ways? The answer he finds, naturally enough, is that only *God* can be a first mover, a first cause, and a necessary being who owes its necessity to no other being. Thus he says, "and this everyone understands to be God."

My own view is that this "connecting" strategy of Aquinas (connecting his philosophical proofs with his theological convictions) is entirely acceptable. And this is surely the (usually implicit) strategy of many of those who offer theistic proofs. If you successfully prove that a given being exists, and if on other grounds there is good reason for you to think this being is God, then you have good reason to hold that you have successfully proved the existence of God. Or at least your proof will have achieved the aim mentioned earlier, namely, the aim of confirming your faith in God.

Endnotes

*Reprinted from *Philosophy of Religion: An Anthology,* 2nd ed, Louis P. Pojman Belmont: Wadsworth Pub. Co., © 1994 by Wadsworth, Inc. All rights reserved. Wadsworth Publishing Company, Belmont, California 94002.The author would like to thank Professors Linda Zagzebski and Bill Alston for helpful comments on an earlier draft of this paper.

1 *The Collected Dialogues of Plato,* ed. Edith Hamilton and Huntington Cairns (New York: Pantheon, 1961), 1455-1479 (894A-899C).

2 See *Systematic Theology,* I (Chicago: Univ. of Chicago Press, 1951), 235-38.

3 Helpful work on this question has been done by George Mavrodes in his *Belief in God* (New York: Random House, 1970), 17-48, and by James F. Ross in his *Philosophical Theology* (Indianapolis: Bobbs-Merrill, 1969), 3-34.

4 This argument is discussed by Alvin Plantinga in *The Nature of Necessity* (Oxford: Clarendon Press, 1974), 217-18.

5 See "Anselm's Ontological Arguments," in *The Existence of God,* ed. John Hick (New York: Macmillan, 1964). 68.

6 See my *Logic and the Nature of God* (London: Macmillan, 1983), 145-53.

7 Another possible benefit of theistic proofs, which I am not able to discuss here, is their use in a cumulative nondeductive argument for the broad truth of the theistic worldview. Some contemporary philosophers have been engaged in making such a case; see, e.g., Basil Mitchell, *The Justification of Religious Belief* (New York: Oxford University Press, 1981) and Richard Swinburne, *The Existence of God* (Oxford: Clarendon Press, 1979).

Study Questions

1.   In Section I of his essay, Stephen Davis lists two criteria that an argument must satisfy for it to be a proof. What are they?

2.   What does Davis add in Section II that he did not have in Section I?

3. How does Davis see Paul Tillich's point that "God is not a 'being?'"

4. According to Davis, what is the value of theistic proofs?

5. What if the theist could provide an argument that is acceptible to an atheist? What follows from this? What if the theist cannot provide such a proof? What follows from this? What if the atheist could provide an argument that counts as a proof that God does not exist for the theist? Would the theist have to abandone belief in God?

17

Does Belief in God Need Proof?

J. Wesley Robbins

J. Wesley Robbins is professor of philosophy at Indiana University, South Bend. The question that he discusses in this paper* is whether William Alston and Alvin Plantinga have succeeded in showing that there is something unreasonable about the exclusion of certain theistic manifestation propositions from the class of propositions that do not need proof. His contention is that they have not succeeded.

In a number of recent and forthcoming papers William Alston and Alvin Plantinga have argued that there are certain theistic propositions (about an immaterial person who exists *a se*; is perfect in goodness, knowledge, and power; and is the creator of the world) such that there is no reasonable epistemological objection to their being accepted without proof.[1] They claim that, in Plantinga's terms, belief in God is properly basic.

The theistic propositions that Alston and Plantinga are talking about are relatively specific and concrete ones, each of which entails the more general proposition that there is a person such as God. These propositions are supposed to need no proof when they are believed in conjunction with some specified nonpropositional, experiential condition. Their acceptance then is not groundless in the sense of being arbitrary or gratuitous. But it is the non-propositional condition that provides the evidential ground in this case, rather than other propositions.

Thus, to cite one of Plantinga's examples, a person beholds the starry heavens and thereupon is strongly inclined to believe that God has created all of this. Or, as in Alston's examples, someone who has certain kinds of non-doxastic religious experience thereupon forms beliefs about God, to the effect that God is speaking to one, guiding one, or just being present to one.

Alston and Plantinga contend that in such cases Christians typically accept such specific propositions about God (which, following Alston, I will refer to as theistic manifestation propositions) as ones that do not

313

need proof. They go on to argue that, epistemologically speaking, there is no reasonable objection to this practice.

Their arguments in this regard are central to a concerted effort on the part of a number of evangelical Christian philosophers to show that Christian theism is in a stronger position intellectually due to the discrediting of a particular theory of knowledge (classical foundationalism) and of an epistemological objection to belief in God that is based on that theory (the evidentialist objection).[2]

Classical foundationalism is a description of what I will refer to as the rational-evidential structure of human thought. According to this description that structure, considered as a group of propositions, is differentiated into those that are evidentially deficient, and thus need the evidential support of other propositions, and those that are evidentially self-sufficient, and thus do not require such support. (In the remainder of this paper I will refer to this as the difference between propositions that need proof and those that do not need proof.)

In addition, the classical foundationalist description of this structure is such that propositions about God (even the manifestation propositions described by Alston and Plantinga) are excluded from the class of those that do not need proof.

Given those two features of rational-evidential structure, the evidentialist objection to belief in God is simply that propositions about God have no place whatsoever in the structure because there is not enough evidence forthcoming from other propositions to compensate for their evidential deficiency.

In their responses to this objection and to its epistemological underpinnings, Alston and Plantinga focus on the exclusion of theistic manifestation propositions from the class of those that do not need proof. They contend, in somewhat different ways, that this exclusion cannot be carried out in a consistent and nonarbitrary way. This being the case, they write off the evidentialist objection itself as an unreasonable one.

The claim that they make in this connection is a rather strong one. It is that any such objection, based on the exclusion of theistic manifestation propositions from the class of those that do not need proof, is liable to be inconsistent or arbitrary and, in either case, unreasonable. This amounts to saying that the rational-evidential structure of human thought is such that belief in God can be guaranteed against any such epistemological objection.

Neither Alston nor Plantinga claim that there is any way to guarantee epistemologically that the theistic manifestation propositions are ones that do not need proof. But they do claim that once they are accepted as propositions that need no proof, there is no consistent and non-arbitrary way to show epistemologically that they are not entitled to such acceptance.

Both parties to this dispute over the epistemological status of theistic manifestation propositions agree that there are certain things that can be said in advance about the rational-evidential structure of human thought. Some of these things have to do, however minimally, with the distinction between propositions that do, and those that do not, need proof. This prior epistemological knowledge can then be used to criticize or to defend other propositions. It can, for instance, be used to defend belief in God against any epistemological objection that is based on the supposition that even theistic manifestation propositions need proof.

The question that I want to discuss in this paper is whether Alston and Plantinga have succeeded in showing that there is something unreasonable about the exclusion of these theistic manifestation propositions from the class of propositions that do not need proof. Have they succeeded in showing that the vocabulary of Christian theism in general, and these theistic propositions in particular, can be guaranteed against any epistemological objection that is based on this exclusion?

My contention is that they have not succeeded. This is because the exclusion can be made without reference to the rational-evidential structure of human thought. Specifically, it can be made without supposing that the difference between propositions that do and those that do not need proof has anything to do with the nature of that structure. If I am correct, then the comfort that Christian theists are finding in the demise of classical foundationalist epistemology is ill-founded.

There are optional ways in which we can describe ourselves as thinkers and inquirers. Here, I want to contrast two such options. One is the epistemological essentialism that underlies both the evidentialist objection as described by Alston and Plantinga and their responses to that objection. The other is what Richard Rorty calls epistemological behaviorism (or pragmatism).

My reason for invoking this contrast is to show, at a minimum, that the description that Alston and Plantinga give of the evidentialist objection to belief in God is an optional one. In particular, the exclusion of theistic manifestation propositions from the class of propositions that do not need proof does not have to be put in essentialist terms. When it is not, but is put in pragmatic terms, then it is neither inconsistent nor arbitrary in the ways described by Plantinga and Alston. Consequently, the objection is not necessarily an epistemologically unreasonable one.

Pragmatism, as Rorty describes it, is ". . . the doctrine that there are no constraints on inquiry save conversational ones—no wholesale constraints derived from the nature of the objects, or of the mind, or language, but only those retail constraints provided by the remarks of our fellow-inquirers."[3] Since these remarks cannot be anticipated and disposed of in advance, "There is no method for knowing *when* one has reached the truth, or when one is closer to it than before."[4]

In other words, pragmatism is simply anti-essentialism so far as truth, knowledge, rationality, evidence, and the like are concerned. It is the denial that there is anything worth saying in advance, in the name of the nature of these things, about which propositions should, and which should not, be believed. In the absence of any such prior knowledge about the rational-evidential structure of human thought, "There is no wholesale epistemological way to direct, or criticize, or underwrite, the course of inquiry."[5]

When the dispute over the epistemological status of theistic manifestation propositions is put in these, pragmatic, terms it boils down to a question about epistemological behavior. The difference, between needing and not needing proof, amounts to the difference between accepting propositions without question, or objection, or demand for proof and not doing that—but questioning, objecting, demanding proof.

But then the determination as to which propositions do not need proof, that is, which are to serve as starting points for rational thought, is contingent upon just this sort of epistemological behavior. There simply will be no way to determine in advance, independently of what people do in this regard, which propositions do, and which do not need proof.

There will, of course, then be no way to determine in advance that the theistic manifestation propositions are ones that need proof as a matter of epistemological principle. But, by the same token, there will be no way to determine in advance that their exclusion from the class of propositions that do not need proof is unreasonable. It is this feature of epistemological pragmatism that leads me to claim, as a minimum, that Alston and Plantinga have not succeeded in showing that the evidentialist objection to belief in God is epistemologically unreasonable.

There is some disagreement between Alston and Plantinga as to just what it is that is unreasonable about the evidentialist objection. According to Plantinga, it is based on a description of rational-evidential structure that is self-referentially incoherent. According to Alston, it is based on a description of that structure which gives arbitrarily different treatment to two sets of propositions that have the same rational-evidential value.

Both men agree with their opponents that this structure must be differentiated into those propositions that do and those that do not need proof. It is this feature of the structure, coupled with the alleged impossibility of identifying its propositional starting points in a way that both excludes theistic manifestation propositions and is consistent and non-arbitrary that, according to both Alston and Plantinga, makes the evidentialist objection an unreasonable one.

According to Plantinga, the rational-evidential structure of human thought will inevitably have propositions in it that do not need proof because the alternative (of a structure in which every proposition is evidentially supported by other propositions) would have a person believing infinitely many propositions. And, in his pithy phrase, ". . . no one has time, these busy days, for that."[6]

As he sees it, the evidentialist objection has typically been made in conjunction with a specific description of the propositional starting points for rational human thought. According to that description, only propositions that are either self-evident or incorrigible are such as to need no proof.

It is this description that, according to Plantinga, makes classical foundationalism self-referentially incoherent as a description of the rational-evidential structure of human thought. In particular, this epistemological principle that supposedly identifies the propositions that do not need proof has no place in the structure described. It is neither self-evident nor incorrigible. Nor is it provable from propositions that are. Consequently, by its own description of rational-evidential structure, classical foundationalism does not have that structure. Thus, an epistemological objection to belief in God posed in its terms is bound to be an unreasonable one.

More generally, Plantinga suggests that the same kind of situation is likely to occur even if some other principle of starting points for rational thought is substituted for the classical foundationalist one. He expresses doubt that ". . . any revealing necessary and sufficient condition for proper basicality follow from clearly self-evident premises by clearly acceptable arguments."[7] But if it is not possible to distinguish those propositions that do not need proof with reference to the nature of rational-evidential structure itself, then any prior epistemological principle which purports to do just that will be in the same predicament as the classical foundationalist one. It will be part of a system of propositions that lacks what it describes as being the rational-evidential structure of human thought.

There is another way in which classical foundationalism might be said to be unreasonable in this connection. If an exception were to be made in the case of its principle of starting points and this were to be accepted as a proposition that needs no proof, even though it is neither self-evident or incorrigible, then that proposition would be no different in that respect than the theistic manifestation propositions which Christians typically accept as ones that need no proof. It would then be quite arbitrary to exclude these theistic propositions from the class of propositions that need no proof while including this epistemological principle.

Given this skepticism as to the prospects of any such prior principle of rational starting points for thought, Plantinga suggests that a principle of starting points will have to be arrived at by an inductive procedure. It will need to be formulated and tested as an hypothesis that is acceptable (unacceptable) as it conforms (fails to conform) to particular examples of propositions that do not need proof. For Christians, such a set of examples will typically include theistic manifestation propositions. So any general principle of starting points that is acceptable to these Christians is going to have to conform to these theistic examples, among others.

Plantinga knows of course that there are people who are not going to be willing to admit that theistic manifestation propositions are examples of propositions that need no proof. Consequently, they will disagree with Christians, to this extent at least, in principle as to which propositions do, and which do not, need proof. What, if anything, is to be done in this case in order to arrive at a generally acceptable description of the propositional starting points of rational thought?

Plantinga's answer is that "The Christian or Jew will of course suppose that belief in God is entirely proper and rational; if he doesn't accept this belief on the basis of other propositions, he will conclude that it is basic for him and quite properly so. Followers of Bertrand Russell and Madelyn Murray O'Hare may disagree, but how is that relevant? Must my criteria [for propositions that need no proof], or those of the believing community, conform to their examples? Surely not. The theistic community is responsible to its set of examples, not to theirs."[8]

Alston is not content to let the matter rest there. He finds Plantinga's dismissal of examples of propositions that do not need proof that conflict with those of the theistic community to be ". . . a bit hard-nosed." He surmises that Plantinga's complacency in this regard stems from his not having ". . . probed deeply enough into the concepts of proper basicality, rationality, and justification to provide the basis for further discussion."[9]

Alston goes on to say that "If we want to critically evaluate a claim to proper basicality, and if, as Plantinga correctly observes, it is not antecedently obvious what the propriety-making characteristics are, we will have to get clear about the kind of propriety involved."[10]

Clearly, these are the remarks of an epistemological essentialist. Alston believes that prior consideration of the rational-evidential structure of human thought will yield more in the way of a principle of starting points than Plantinga has allowed. Such a principle could then, of course, be used to adjudicate exactly the kind of stand-off disagreement over which propositions do not need proof that Plantinga has described.

Alston's account of the rational-evidential structure of human thought is put in terms of epistemic practices. These are specific ways of forming propositional beliefs, where the point of the practices is the attainment of a preponderance of true beliefs over false ones. Such practices are then either generally reliable or unreliable ways of attaining this epistemic goal.

When it comes to determining which is the case (whether particular practices are reliable or unreliable) we have to operate under some rather severe limitations. Any such determination that is carried out on our part is going to involve the use of one or more such practice, whose reliability is taken for granted in the process.

Furthermore, there are some epistemic practices that are especially deeply entrenched for human beings. These are ones in which propositional beliefs are formed directly upon non-doxastic materials and which, in addition, provide unique informational access to some subject-matter. This latter means that the reliability of all other epistemic practices that deal with this subject-matter are dependent upon the reliability of this particular practice and not *vice-versa*. Alston suggests sense perception as one example of such a deeply entrenched epistemic practice, that is, the practice of objectifying sense experience in terms of independently existing physical objects.

Within these limitations, there are two epistemic values that may be assigned to epistemic practices that are to have a place in the rational-evidential structure: strong reasonability (proven reliable) and weak reasonability (not proven unreliable).[11]

Alston suggests that if any of the deeply entrenched (basic) epistemic practices are to have a place in the rational-evidential structure, there is little choice but to admit them as being weakly reasonable. In their case, this is the only one of the two epistemic values that we are likely to be able to apply just because we will not have an independently reliable practice at our disposal in terms of which to prove the reliability of the basic ones.

And thus we have something in the way of a principle of propositional starting points for rational thought that is derived from considerations having to do with the rational-evidential structure of human thought. In general, any epistemic practice (basic or not) that is not proven unreliable is one that is weakly reasonable. And there are certain epistemic practices (basic ones) to which weak reasonability is the only epistemic value that we are likely to be able to apply. The propositional outputs of such basic epistemic practices would then be prime examples of propositions that do not need proof, epistemologically speaking. If the epistemic value of weak reasonability is granted to one basic practice then, by parity of reasoning, that same value should be granted to any similar epistemic practice. It would be arbitrary, and thus unreasonable, to grant this epistemic status in one instance and to withhold it in other instances like it.[12]

Now Christianity itself can be construed as involving epistemic practice(s). It is the practice of objectifying certain ranges of experience in terms of Christian theism. According to both Alston and Plantinga this typically involves the formation of propositional beliefs about God directly upon non-propositional, experiential materials. In other words, Christianity is an epistemic practice at least some of the propositional outputs of which, theistic manifestation propositions, are commonly accepted by its participants as not needing proof.

Alston argues at length that this Christian epistemic practice is a reasonable one in the weak sense of the term. There is, he claims, insufficient reason to conclude that it is unreliable. It thus has exactly the same rational-evidential value as do the epistemic practices that are at the base of the rational-evidential structure of human thought. Consequently, it is as reasonable to accept its basic propositions about God as ones that do not need proof (as a matter of epistemological principle) as it is to accept that propositional outputs of those basic epistemic practices as ones that do not need proof. In other words, it is as reasonable for Christians to accept the manifestation propositions about God (based directly on their religious experience) as ones that do not need proof as it is for anyone to accept perceptual propositions about physical objects (based directly on their sense experience) as ones that do not need proof.[13]

And now there is something more to be said to the Bertrand Russells of the world than Plantinga had allowed. Instead of being left with a stand-off of conflicting examples of propositions that do not need proof, the theistic community has epistemological principle on its side in the first place. Anyone who claims, contrary to the epistemic practice of this community, that even theistic manifestation propositions need proof can quickly be convicted of being unreasonable. They are guilty of treating two sets of propositions (both of which have the same rational-evidential value) in an arbitrarily different manner: claiming that the theistic set needs proof while the other set of propositions, perceptual ones for example, does not need proof.

The evidentialist objection to belief in God is based, as we have seen, on the general exclusion of propositions about God from the class of propositions that do not need proof. In its essentialist versions this exclusion is said to have to do with the character of the rational-evidential structure of human thought. For instance, the classical foundationalist exclusion is based on the notion that only self-evident or incorrigible propositions are suited to be the starting points for rational thought, because they are the only ones for which there is no mistaking the false ones for the true or *vice versa*.

In its pragmatic version, this exclusion would be made for context-specific reasons that involve no reference to the rational-evidential structure of human thought. There is no claim to have a general description, related to that structure, of the sorts of propositions that, essentially, need no proof. Consequently, if and when even theistic manifestation propositions are excluded, on pragmatic grounds, as starting points for rational thought, this exclusion does not involve either the self-referential incoherence or the arbitrariness that Plantinga and Alston, respectively, connect with the evidentialist objection.

An epistemological pragmatist sees human thought and inquiry as operating only with what Rorty calls retail constraints. What is explicitly denied is the availability of any further, deeper constraints provided by the nature of thought or language, for example. To use Rorty's metaphor, human thought and inquiry is a conversation in which the participants say what they have to say to one another without the benefit of translation into, or adjudication by, any neutral vocabulary provided by the over-all rational-evidential structure of their dialogue.

Put in these terms, even the starting points of human thought will be subject only to retail constraints. And people will say what they have to say to one another about those starting points without the benefit of translation into, or adjudication by, any neutral vocabulary provided by the over-all rational-evidential structure of their dialogue.

A conversational objection to one's own starting points for thought takes the form of alternative epistemological behavior concerning which propositions need proof and which do not—questioning those that one typically accepts without question and taking for granted those that one typically puts in question. Such an objection is a retail constraint in the sense of posing a living option to one's own standard ways of starting to think about this, that, or the other subject.

Consider, for example, a theistic community in which, as described by Plantinga, one sort of manifestation proposition consists of propositions to the effect that God approves of this or disapproves of that. These are this community's starting points for thought about moral life. A retail constraint on that practice is posed by the epistemological behavior of other people who unquestioningly accept different non-theistic propositions as starting points for their thinking about moral life (ones, for example, about human approvals and disapprovals). The objection and the constraint need be no more than the contrast, and appeal, of the alternative way of moral life in which the non-theistic vocabulary is embedded.

This contrast and appeal might be put into words addressed to members of the theistic community as follows. "In thinking about and coping with the problems of moral life, you start with a theistic vocabulary and propositions. We don't. We start with a humanistic vocabulary and propositions. Doing it our way has these advantages, and these disadvantages, compared to your way of doing it. So far as we are concerned, your theistic starting point needs proof. It doesn't work as well in this, moral, context, as our humanistic starting point." In this case, a particular sort of theistic manifestation proposition has been put in question as needing proof, in the context of moral life.

A pragmatic version of the general exclusion of theistic propositions from the class of propositions that do not need proof is simply an accumulation of objections, like the one just described, to theistic starting points in a number of different, specific contexts. The claim in each case is that some non-theistic propositions better serve some human purpose, as starting points for thought in this context, than do the theistic propositions that are alleged to need proof. When enough of these context-specific objections are accumulated, then the theistic community is being presented with the claim that in general the theistic manifestation propositions that it currently accepts as not needing proof are in need of proof when they are compared with a variety of non-theistic alternatives in each context.

In this eventuality, these theistic propositions have been placed in exactly the position that is described by Plantinga as underlying the evidentialist objection. They have been put in question by being excluded from the class of propositions that do not need proof. The crucial difference in this case is that this exclusion has been made without reference to any allegedly prior epistemological principle of starting points for rational thought. It has been made solely in terms of alternative, substantive propositions whose status as starting points for thought is a function of epistemological behavior.

I am not suggesting that, in the case of this example, the members of the theistic community have to agree with this pragmatic exclusion of their theistic manifestation propositions from the class of propositions that do not need proof. Neither am I suggesting that in the face of the objection there is any special burden of proof that is placed on them to defend their acceptance of these propositions as ones that do not need proof. I am saying that the constraint is there and that it is an objection to their way of thinking and talking at the level of starting-points. It is an objection to their treating any theistic manifestation propositions as ones that do not need proof. But since it does not even claim that its own starting points for thought need no proof as a matter of epistemological principle (given the character of the rational-evidential structure of human thought), its exclusion of these theistic propositions as starting points for rational thought is neither self-referentially incoherent nor arbitrary in the ways said by Plantinga and Alston to be the case with any evidentialist objection to belief in God.

If members of the theistic community are persuaded in the course of conversation to alter their own epistemological behavior in this regard, they have done nothing that Plantinga or Alston could claim to be unreasonable. In particular, they would not have yielded to an objection to their own belief in God that was unreasonable in the first place.

This pragmatic exclusion of theistic manifestation propositions from the class of propositions that do not need proof clearly is not liable to the sort of self-referential incoherence that Plantinga claims infects any such epistemological exclusion. It is made with the explicit disclaimer of any intention to describe the rational-evidential structure of human thought. Consequently, in no way is it involved in the confusion of providing a description of a structure that it is supposed to exemplify but from which it is excluded by its own description.[14]

On this matter of starting-points for thought, it seems to me that Plantinga is a fellow pragmatist. His disavowal of deductive epistemology in this regard says that the determination as to which propositions do not need proof is going to have to be made without reference to the nature of rational-evidential structure as such. But his proposed inductive epistemology of starting-points is nothing more or less than the canonization of the epistemological behavior of some group of people. That just is epistemological behaviorism. In this case, his claim that it is perfectly reasonable for Christians to accept theistic manifestation propositions as ones that do not need proof amounts to nothing more nor less than the remark that this is exactly what certain Christian people typically do.

In this connection, Plantinga's dictum that members of the theistic community have some kind of overriding commitment to theistic manifestation propositions as examples of propositions that do not need proof is puzzling. Why are Christians responsible to these theistic propositions rather than to, say, some non-theistic religious alternative ones? Unless there is some kind of epistemological magic that attaches to these propositions in particular, it is not at all clear what rationale Plantinga could have for contending that they are to be examples of starting points for Christian thought, come what may in the course of religious inquiry. This is especially so given his own insistence that there is no prior knowledge to be had to the effect that these propositions are such as to need no proof.

Neither is this pragmatically based exclusion of theistic manifestation propositions as starting points for thought liable to Alston's charge of arbitrariness, although the matter is a bit more complicated in this case. Alston's description of the arbitrariness to which such an exclusion is supposed to be liable can be summarized again as follows. The rational-evidential structure of human thought is such that there is an epistemological value (weak reasonability) that is shared by both an epistemic practice that is located at the basis of this structure (sense perception) and Christian epistemic practice, with its theistic manifestation beliefs. It is thus arbitrary, given this epistemological situation, to exclude the theistic manifestation propositions from the class of propositions that need no proof while including propositions about physical objects, when the same epistemic value applies to both.

This charge of arbitrariness is very weak, in the first place, because it is based exclusively on an alleged sameness of epistemic value—both epistemic practices are weakly reasonable. Alston is noncommittal on whether the Christian epistemic practice is also like the perceptual practice in being a basic one. But this in turn means that he must be noncommittal on whether weak reasonability is the only one of the two epistemic values that is likely to be applicable to the Christian practice.

As a result, the question of whether we should settle for weak reasonability in the case of the Christian practice is left open. It all depends on the location of the practice in the structure of human thought. If the practice in question is a basic one—constituting our sole access to the subject matter—then there is little choice but to settle for weak reasonability. If the practice is not a basic one, then the alternative of strong reasonability is available. It is possible for the practice in question to be tested for reliability in terms of another, independent, practice so that the former practice is proven reliable or unreliable.

But then the differential treatment of the theistic manifestation propositions need not be arbitrary. It need only be based on the supposition that there is another independent epistemic practice (in this case, one in which no theistic propositions are accepted without proof) in terms of which the entire Christian epistemic practice (including the acceptance of theistic manifestation propositions without proof) is subject to reliability tests. Unless the Christian practice is, like the perceptual one, a basic epistemic practice, then on Alston's own terms it is fair game for this sort of differential treatment. The moral of this story is that if this arbitrariness charge is going to stick, Alston cannot remain noncommittal on whether the Christian epistemic practice is a basic one.

More importantly, the arbitrariness charge is weak because the idea of an epistemic practice is applied ambiguously to the two cases in question. Alston describes the perceptual practice as involving the formation of beliefs about the immediate physical environment directly upon sensory experience. It provides unique informational access in that "Any other way of finding out about the physical world presupposes the reliability of this [perceptual practice]."[15] But, according to Alston, this practice considered historically has had a variable conceptual-propositional content that allows for change and development. It consists of the objectification of sense experience in terms of some unspecified vocabulary.

The Christian epistemic practice, on the other hand, is described as involving the objectification of religious experience in terms of a specifically Christian theistic vocabulary. This practice is described as having a fixed conceptual-propositional content that does not allow for change and development.

In the perceptual case, Alston says that he favors a developmental view, even at the structural level of basic epistemic practices. He speaks of human cognitive activity as having a history. And he says that he believes that ". . . a careful survey of the whole range of human culture over space and time would reveal that the presently dominant mode of objectifying sense experience is the outcome of a long development in the course of which it had many rivals."[16]

Perceptual epistemic practice is thus a collection of several different ways of thinking about the physical world even at the level of starting points for thought. The presently dominant mode (the common sense physical object vocabulary) involves thinking in terms of macroscopic physical objects and their perceptible properties. But this is one among several, alternative, vocabularies in terms of which to objectify sense experience.

In the religious case, Alston comments that perhaps ". . . the attempt to discern God's presence and activity from religious experience is in the state that the attempt to discern the basic nature of the physical world, by reasoning from what we learn from perception, was in the first 1600 years of our era."[17] But if we think of the religious case in this way as also having a history and as being subject to development, then the most that can be said for the presently dominant mode of objectifying religious experience in our culture (by means of the vocabulary of Christian theism) is that it is ". . . the outcome of a long development in the course of which it had [and continues to have] many rivals."

The Christian epistemic practice thus is strictly comparable to one of the several alternative vocabularies that collectively make up perceptual epistemic practice, understood historically.

What is it, then, that has the epistemological value of weak reasonability in the two cases? Is it some objectifying vocabulary or another, or is it a specific objectifying vocabulary? Alston as much as admits that it is the former in the case of sense perception. But then, even if it is admitted that there are two epistemic practices both of which have the same epistemic value, there is nothing arbitrary about treating the two cases differently so far as their respective specific objectifying vocabularies are concerned. Thus, for example, theistic manifestation propositions can be put in question by excluding them from the class of propositions that do not need proof in favor of some alternative, non-theistic, vocabulary for specifically religious reasons while no such exclusionary claim is made about common sense physical object propositions in the perceptual case, or *vice versa*. Such differential treatment would seem to be entirely within the bounds of reason in the epistemological setting that Alston has described. And it is exactly this sort of context-specific objection made in terms of alternative vocabularies that is characteristic of the pragmatic version of the evidentialist objection to belief in God.

My main objective in this paper has been to show that the evidentialist objection to belief in God is not necessarily based on an unreasonable exclusion of theistic propositions from the class of propositions that do not need proof. I have sought to accomplish that objective by describing a pragmatically based version of that objection, one that is neither self-referentially incoherent nor arbitrary in the ways described by Plantinga and Alston.

I have two concluding remarks about epistemological pragmatism that go beyond the narrow bounds of the topic of this paper. The first has to do with the intellectual difficulties of Christian theism in our culture. It seems to me that pragmatism provides for a better understanding of these difficulties than does epistemological essentialism. If I am right, belief in God is in question in our culture not because of a once and for all objection put in terms of prior philosophical knowledge about knowledge, rationality, and evidence. It is in question because of a piecemeal, gradual accumulation of substantive objections and alternatives that together have shaped our epistemological behavior to the point that propositions about God no longer serve as unquestioned starting points for thought outside of the narrow, privatized boundaries of religious devotional life, if there. The damage, seen in this way, is at once less inevitable and more difficult to repair. It is less inevitable because, contrary to essentialism, there is nothing in the nature of the case that requires or necessitates this exclusion. It is more difficult to repair just because of the piecemeal character of the exclusion. We are looking at a number of different contexts in which, for different reasons, belief in God just is not an unquestioned starting point for thought. If this is a correct assessment, then the demolition of classical foundationalism doesn't even begin to recoup the intellectual strength and position of Christian theism in our culture.

The second comment has to do with the project of Christian revisionism and its intellectual plausibility and integrity. By Christian revisionism I mean the proposed replacement of the theistic vocabulary with a religious alternative, in connection with the Christian life. If Alston and Plantinga are right, then this project is an intellectually needless and pointless exercise, epistemologically speaking, because it is based on an epistemic assessment of theistic propositions that they have shown to be an unreasonable one.

Thus, it is not surprising in this connection to find Plantinga describing Christian thinkers like Tillich and Bultmann as being ". . . professedly Christian theologians, supersophisticates who proclaim the liberation of Christianity from belief in God, seeking to replace it by trust in 'Being itself' or the 'Ground of Being' or some such thing. It remains true, however, that belief in God is the foundation of Christianity."[18]

There is no doubt but that many such Christian revisionist proposals have been couched in epistemologically essentialist terms, including those of classical foundationalism. But the intellectual need for, and plausibility of, these projects does not stand or fall with their essentialist setting. If my pragmatic account of evidentialist objections to belief in God has any merit to it at all, then projects such as those of Tillich and Braithwaite, to name only two, cannot and should not be written off in advance as being epistemologically needless and thus intellectually implausible.[19] Nor should their intellectual, not to mention religious, motivation be attributed to something so unworthy as a desire to be acceptable to the currently fashionable intellectual jet-set.

Indiana University, South Bend

Endnotes

*Reprinted from *Faith and Philosophy*, Vol. 2 No. 3 July 1985. All rights reserved,

[1] William Alston, "Religious Experience and Religious Belief" (RERB), expanded version of paper published in *Noûs,* vol. XVI, no. 1 (March 1982); "Plantinga's Epistemology of Religious Belief" (PERB), in the D. Reidel volume on Plantinga's philosophy edited by James E. Tomberlin and Peter van Inwagen; "Christian Experience and Christian Belief: (CECB), in *Faith and Rationality*, ed. Alvin Plantinga and Nicholas Wolterstorff. Notre Dame: University of Notre Dame Press, 1983.

Alvin Plantinga, "Is Belief in God Rational?" in *Rationality and Religious Belief*, ed. C. Delaney. Notre Dame: University of Notre Dame Press, 1979; "Is Belief in God Properly Basic?" *Nous*, vol. XV, no. 1 (March 1981); "Rationality and Religious Belief" (RRB), in *Contemporary Philosophy of Religion*, ed. Steven Cahn and David Shatz. New York: Oxford University Press, 1982; "Reason and Belief in God" (RBG); in *Faith and Rationality*.

[2] The volume cited above, *Faith and Rationality*, is a collection of papers centered around this theme.

[3] Richard Rorty, "Pragmatism, Relativism, and Irrationalism" in *Consequences of Pragmatism*. Minneapolis: University of Minnesota Press, 1982, p. 165.

[4] Ibid., p. 165f.

[5] Ibid., p. 162.

[6] Plantinga, RBG, p. 39.

[7] Plantinga, RRB, p. 275f.

[8] Ibid., p. 276.

[9] Alston, PERB, p. 24.

[10] Ibid.

[11] I have deliberately collapsed some of Alston's epistemic value distinctions for the sake of brevity.

[12] Alston, CECB, p. 119.

[13] Ibid., p. 120.

[14] Terence Penelhum discusses Plantinga's position in connection with what he calls the parity argument in *God and Skepticism*, chapter 7. Dordrecht: D. Reidel Publishing Co., 1983.

[15] Alston, RERB, p. 13.

[16] Alston, CECB, p. 128.

[17] Alston, PERB, p. 36.

[18] Plantinga, RBG, p. 16.

[19] One of the most straightforward and in-depth Christian revisionist proposals to have come to my attention in recent times, and one which does not depend on epistemologically essentialist doctrines, is that of Don Cupitt in *Taking Leave of God*. New York: The Crossroad Publishing Co., 1981.

Study Questions

1. What is the central question that J. Wesley Robbins addresses?

2. Why does Robbins think that Alston and Plantinga have failed in their apologetic task? What is your opinion of Robbins' claim?

3. Why does Robbins think that Plantinga is a "fellow-Pragmatist"?

4. Robbins makes two points near the end of his paper. What are they?

5. Do you think that belief in God needs proof? If so, why? If not, why not?

PART III

PROBLEMS OF EVIL
AND
STRATEGIES OF DEFENSE

18

Evil and Omnipotence

J. L. Mackie

John L. Mackie was professor of philosophy at Oxford University, and is the author of *The Miracle of Theism*. In this essay* he argues that theists face a logical problem regarding their core of beliefs because the God of Christianity would not allow evil to exist. Since evil exists, God must not.

The traditional arguments for the existence of God have been fairly thoroughly criticised by philosophers. But the theologian can, if he wishes, accept this criticism. He can admit that no rational proof of God's existence is possible. And he can still retain all that is essential to his position, by holding that God's existence is known in some other, non-rational way. I think, however, that a more telling criticism can be made by way of the traditional problem of evil. Here it can be shown, not that religious beliefs lack rational support, but that they are positively irrational, that the several parts of the essential theological doctrine are inconsistent with one another, so that the theologian can maintain his position as a whole only by a much more extreme rejection of reason than in the former case. He must now be prepared to believe, not merely what cannot be proved, but what can be *disproved* from other beliefs that he also holds.

The problem of evil, in the sense in which I shall be using the phrase, is a problem only for someone who believes that there is a God who is both omnipotent and wholly good. And it is a logical problem, the problem of clarifying and reconciling a number of beliefs: it is not a scientific problem that might be solved by further observations, or a practical problem that might be solved by a decision or an action. These points are obvious; I mention them only because they are sometimes ignored by theologians, who sometimes parry a statement of the problem with such remarks as "Well, can you solve the problem yourself?" or "This is a mystery which may be revealed to us later" or "Evil is something to be faced and overcome, not to be merely discussed."

In its simplest form the problem is this: God is omnipotent; God is wholly good; and yet evil exists. There seems to be some contradiction between these three propositions, so that if any two of them were true the third would be false. But at the same time all three are essential parts of most theological positions: the theologian, it seems, at once *must* adhere and *cannot consistently* adhere to all three. (The problem does not arise only for theists, but I shall discuss it in the form in which it presents itself for ordinary theism.)

However, the contradiction does not arise immediately; to show it we need some additional premises, or perhaps some quasi-logical rules connecting the terms "good," "evil," and "omnipotent." These additional principles are that good is opposed to evil, in such a way that a good thing always eliminates evil as far as it can, and that there are no limits to what an omnipotent thing can do. From these it follows that a good omnipotent thing eliminates evil completely, and then the propositions that a good omnipotent thing exists, and that evil exists, are incompatible.

A. Adequate Solutions

Now once the problem is fully stated it is clear that it can be solved, in the sense that the problem will not arise if one gives up at least one of the propositions that constitute it. If you are prepared to say that God is not wholly good, or not quite omnipotent, or that evil does not exist, or that good is not opposed to the kind of evil that exists, or that there are limits to what an omnipotent thing can do, then the problem of evil will not arise for you.

There are, then, quite a number of adequate solutions of the problem of evil, and some of these have been adopted, or almost adopted, by various thinkers. For example, a few have been prepared to deny God's omnipotence, and rather more have been prepared to keep the term "omnipotence" but severely to restrict its meaning, recording quite a number of things that an omnipotent being cannot do. Some have said that evil is an illusion, perhaps because they held that the whole world of temporal, changing things is an illusion, and that what we call evil belongs only to this world, or perhaps because they held that although temporal things *are* much as we see them, those that we call evil are not really evil. Some have said that what we call evil is merely the privation of good, that evil in a positive sense, evil that would really be opposed to good, does not exist. Many have agreed with Pope that disorder is harmony not understood, and that partial evil is universal good. Whether any of these views is *true* is, of course, another question. But each of them gives an adequate solution of the problem of evil in the sense that if you accept it this problem does not arise for you, though you may, of course, have *other* problems to face.

But often enough these adequate solutions are only *almost* adopted. The thinkers who restrict God's power, but keep the term "omnipotence" may reasonably be suspected of thinking, in other contexts, that his power is really unlimited. Those who say that evil is an illusion may also be thinking, inconsistently, that this illusion is itself an evil. Those who say that "evil" is merely privation of good may also be thinking, inconsistently, that privation of good is an evil. (The fallacy here is akin to some forms of the "naturalistic fallacy in ethics, where some think, for example, that "good" is just what contributes to evolutionary progress, and that evolutionary progress is itself good.) If Pope meant what he said in the first line of his couplet, that "disorder" is only harmony not understood, the "partial evil" of the second line must, for consistency, mean "that which, taken in isolation, falsely appears to be evil," but it would more naturally mean "that which, in isolation, really is evil." The second line, in fact, hesitates between two views, that "partial evil" isn't really evil, since only the universal quality is real, and that "partial evil" is really an evil, but only a little one.

In addition, therefore, to adequate solutions, we must recognise unsatisfactory inconsistent solutions, in which there is only a half-hearted or temporary rejection of one of the propositions which together constitute the problem. In these, one of the constituent propositions is explicitly rejected, but it is covertly re-asserted or assumed elsewhere in the system.

B. Fallacious Solutions

Besides these half-hearted solutions, which explicitly reject but implicitly assert one of the constituent propositions, there are definitely fallacious solutions which explicitly maintain all the constituent propositions, but implicitly reject at least one of them in the course of the argument that explains away the problem of evil.

There are, in fact, many so-called solutions which purport to remove the contradiction without abandoning any of its constituent propositions. These must be fallacious as we can see from the very statement of the problem, but it is not so easy to see in each case precisely where the fallacy lies. I suggest that in all cases the fallacy has the general form suggested above: in order to solve the problem one (or perhaps more) of its constituent propositions is given up, but in such a way that it appears to have been retained, and can therefore be asserted without qualification in other contexts. Sometimes there is a further complication: the supposed solution moves to and fro between, say, two of the constituent propositions, at one point asserting the first of these but covertly abandoning the second, at another point asserting the second but covertly abandoning the first. These fallacious solutions often turn upon some equivocation with the words "good" and "evil," or upon some vagueness about the way in which good and evil are opposed to one another, or about how much is meant by "omnipotence." I propose to examine some of these so-called solutions, and to exhibit their fallacies in detail. Incidentally, I shall also be considering whether an adequate solution could be reached by a minor modification of one or more of the constituent propositions, which would, however, still satisfy all the essential requirements of ordinary theism.

(1) "Good cannot exist without evil" or "Evil is necessary as a counterpart to good."

It is sometimes suggested that evil is necessary as a counterpart to good, that if there were no evil there could be no good either, and that this solves the problem of evil. It is true that it points to an answer to the question "Why should there be evil?" But it does so only by qualifying some of the propositions that constitute the problem.

First, it sets a limit to what God can do, saying that God *cannot* create good without simultaneously creating evil, and this means either that God is not omnipotent or that there are *some* limits to what an omnipotent thing can do. It may be replied that these limits are always presupposed, that omnipotence has never meant the power to do what is logically impossible, and on the present view the existence of good without evil would be a logical impossibility. This interpretation of omnipotence may, indeed, be accepted as a modification of our original account which does not reject anything that is essential to theism, and I shall in general assume it in the subsequent discussion. It is, perhaps, the most common theistic view, but I think that some theists at least have maintained that God can do what is logically impossible. Many theists, at any rate, have held that logic itself is created or laid down by God, that logic is the way in which God arbitrarily chooses to think. (This is, of course, parallel to the ethical view that morally right actions are those which God arbitrarily chooses to command, and the two views encounter similar difficulties.) And *this* account of logic is clearly inconsistent with the view that God is bound by logical necessities—unless it is possible for an omnipotent being to bind himself, an issue which we shall consider later, when we come to the Paradox of Omnipotence. This solution of the problem of evil cannot, therefore, be consistently adopted along with the view that logic is itself created by God.

But, secondly, this solution denies that evil is opposed to good in our original sense. If good and evil are counterparts, a good thing will not "eliminate evil as far as it can." Indeed, this view suggests that good and evil are not strictly qualities of things at all. Perhaps the suggestion is that good and evil are related in much the same way as great and small. Certainly, when the term "great" is used relatively as a condensation of "greater than so-and-so," and "small" is used correspondingly, greatness and smallness are counterparts and cannot exist without each other. But in this sense greatness is not a quality, not an intrinsic feature of anything; and it would be absurd to think of a movement in favour of greatness and against smallness in this sense. Such a movement would be self-defeating, since relative greatness can be promoted only by a simultaneous promotion of relative smallness. I feel sure that no theists would be content to regard God's goodness as analogous to this—as if what he supports were not the *good* but the *better*, and if he had the paradoxical aim that all things should be better than other things.

This point is obscured by the fact that "great" and "small" seem to have an absolute as well as a relative sense. I cannot discuss here whether there is absolute magnitude or not, but if there is, there could be an absolute sense for "great," it could mean of at least a certain size, and it would make sense to speak of all things getting bigger, of a universe that was expanding all over, and therefore it would make sense to speak of promoting greatness. But in *this* sense great and small are not logically necessary counterparts: either quality could exist without the other. There would be no logical impossibility in everything's being small or in everything's being great.

Neither in the absolute nor in the relative sense, then, of "great" and "small" do these terms provide an analogy of the sort that would be needed to support this solution of the problem of evil. In neither case are greatness and smallness *both* necessary counterparts *and* mutually opposed forces or possible objects for support and attack.

It may be replied that good and evil are necessary counterparts in the same way as any quality and its logical opposite: redness can occur, it is suggested, only if non-redness also occurs. But unless evil is merely the privation of good, they are not logical opposites, and some further argument would be needed to show that they are counterparts in the same way as genuine logical opposites. Let us assume that this could be given. There is still doubt of the correctness of the metaphysical principle that a quality must have a real opposite: I suggest that it is not really impossible that everything should be, say, red, that the truth is merely that if everything were red we should not notice redness, and so we should have no word "red"; we observe and give names to qualities only if they have real opposites. If so, the principle that a term must have an opposite would belong only to our language or to our thought, and would not be an ontological principle, and, correspondingly, the rule that good cannot exist without evil would not state a logical necessity of a sort that God would just have to put up with. God might have made everything good, though we should not have noticed it if he had.

But, finally, even if we concede that this is an ontological principle, it will provide a solution for the problem of evil only if one is prepared to say, "Evil exists, but only just enough evil to serve as the counterpart of good." I doubt whether any theist will accept this. After all, the *ontological* requirement that non-redness should occur would be satisfied

even if all the universe, except for a minute speck, were red, and, if there
were a corresponding requirement for evil as a counterpart to good, a minute
dose of evil would presumably do. But theists are not usually willing to
say, in all contexts, that all the evil that occurs is a minute and necessary
dose.

(2) "Evil is necessary as a means to good."

It is sometimes suggested that evil is necessary for a good not as a
counterpart but as a means. In its simple form this has little plausibility
as a solution of the problem of evil, since it obviously implies a severe
restriction of God's power. It would be a causal law that you cannot have a
certain end without a certain means, so that if God has to introduce evil as
a means to good, he must be subject to at least some causal laws. This
certainly conflicts with what a theist normally means by omnipotence.
This view of God as limited by *causal* laws also conflicts with the view
that causal laws are themselves made by God, which is more widely held
than the corresponding view about the laws of logic. This conflict would,
indeed, be resolved if it were possible for an omnipotent being to bind
himself, and this possibility has still to be considered. Unless a
favourable answer can be given to this question, the suggestion that evil is
necessary as a means to good solves the problem of evil only by denying one
of its constituent propositions, either that God is omnipotent or that
"omnipotent" means what it says.

(3) "The universe is better with some evil in it than it could be if
there were no evil."

Much more important is a solution which at first seems to be a mere
variant of the previous one, that evil may contribute to the goodness of a
whole in which it is found, so that the universe as a whole is better as it
is, with some evil in it, than it would be if there were no evil. This
solution may be developed in either of two ways. It may be supported by an
aesthetic analogy, by the fact that contrasts heighten beauty, that in a
musical work, for example, there may occur discords which somehow add
to the beauty of the work as a whole. Alternatively, it may be worked out
in connexion with the notion of progress, that the best possible
organisation of the universe will not be static, but progressive, that the
gradual overcoming of evil by good is really a finer thing than would be
the eternal unchallenged supremacy of good. In either case, this solution
usually starts from the assumption that the evil whose existence gives rise
to the problem of evil is primarily what is called physical evil, that is to
say, pain. In Hume's rather half-hearted presentation of the problem of
evil, the evils that he stresses are pain and disease, and those who reply
to him argue that the existence of pain and disease makes possible the

existence of sympathy, benevolence, heroism, and the gradually successful struggle of doctors and reformers to overcome these evils. In fact, theists often seize the opportunity to accuse those who stress the problem of evil of taking a low, materialistic view of good and evil, equating these with pleasure and pain, and of ignoring the more spiritual goods which can arise in the struggle against evils. But let us see exactly what is being done here. Let us call pain and misery "first order evil" or "evil (1)." What contrasts with this, namely, pleasure and happiness, will be called "first order good" or "good (1)." Distinct from this is "second order good" or "good (2)" which somehow emerges in a complex situation in which evil (1) is a necessary component—logically not merely causally, necessary. (Exactly *how* it emerges does not matter: in the crudest version of this solution good [2] is simply the heightening of happiness by the contrast with misery, in other versions it includes sympathy with suffering, heroism in facing danger, and the gradual decrease of first order evil and increase of first order good.) It is also being assumed that second order good is more important than first order good or evil, in particular that it more than outweighs the first order evil it involves. Now this is a particularly subtle attempt to solve the problem of evil. It defends God's goodness and omnipotence on the ground that (on a sufficiently long view) this is the best of all logically possible worlds, because it includes the important second order goods, and yet it admits that real evils, namely first order evils, exist. But does it still hold that good and evil are opposed? Not, clearly, in the sense that we set out originally: good does not tend to eliminate evil in general. Instead, we have a modified, a more complex pattern. First order good (e.g. happiness) *contrasts with* first order evil (e.g. misery): these two are opposed in a fairly mechanical way; some second order goods (e.g. benevolence) try to maximise first order good and minimise first order evil; but God's goodness is not this, it is rather the will to maximise second order good. We might, therefore, call God's goodness an example of a third order goodness, or good (3). While this account is different from our original one, it might well be held to be an improvement on it, to give a more accurate description of the way in which good is opposed to evil, and to be consistent with the essential theist position.

There might, however, be several objections to this solution.

First, some might argue that such qualities as benevolence—and *a fortiori* the third order goodness which promotes benevolence—have a merely derivative value, that they are not higher sorts of good, but merely means to good (1), that is, to happiness, so that it would be absurd for God to keep misery in existence in order to make possible the virtues of benevolence, heroism, etc. The theist who adopts the present solution must, of course, deny this, but he can do so with some plausibility, so I should not press this objection.

Secondly, it follows from this solution that God is not in our sense benevolent or sympathetic: he is not concerned to minimise evil (1), but only to promote good (2); and this might be a disturbing conclusion for some theists.

But, thirdly, the fatal objection is this. Our analysis shows clearly the possibility of the existence of a *second* order evil, an evil (2) contrasting with good (2) as evil (1) contrasts with good (1). This would include malevolence, cruelty, callousness, cowardice, and states in which good (1) is decreasing and evil (1) increasing. And just as good (2) is held to be the important kind of good, the kind that God is concerned to promote, so evil (2) will, by analogy, be the important kind of evil, the kind which God, if he were wholly good and omnipotent, would eliminate. And yet evil (2) plainly exists, and indeed most theists (in other contexts) stress its existence more than that of evil (1). We should, therefore, state the problem of evil in terms of second order evil, and against this form of the problem the present solution is useless.

An attempt might be made to use this solution again, at a higher level, to explain the occurrence of evil (2); indeed the next main solution that we shall examine does just this, with the help of some new notions. Without any fresh notions, such a solution would have little plausibility: for example, we could hardly say that the really important good was a good (3), such as the increase of benevolence in proportion to cruelty, which logically required for its occurrence the occurrence of some second order evil. But even if evil (2) could be explained in this way, it is fairly clear that there would be third order evils contrasting with this third order good: and we should be well on the way to an infinite regress, where the solution of a problem of evil, stated in terms of evil (n), indicated the existence of an evil ($n + 1$), and a further problem to be solved.

(4) "Evil is due to human freewill."

Perhaps the most important proposed solution of the problem of evil is that evil is not to be ascribed to God at all, but to the independent actions of human beings, supposed to have been endowed by God with freedom of the will. This solution may be combined with the preceding one: first order evil (e.g. pain) may be justified as a logically necessary component in second order good (e.g. sympathy) while second order evil (e.g. cruelty) is not *justified*, but is so ascribed to human beings that God cannot be held responsible for it. This combination evades my third criticism of the preceding solution.

The freewill solution also involves the preceding solution at a higher level. To explain why a wholly good God gave men freewill although it would lead to some important evils, it must be argued that it is better on the whole that men should act freely, and sometimes err, than that they should be innocent automata, acting rightly in a wholly determined way.

Freedom that is to say, is now treated as a third order good, and as being more valuable than second order goods (such as sympathy and heroism) would be if they were deterministically produced, and it is being assumed that second order evils, such as cruelty, are logically necessary accompaniments of freedom, just as pain is a logically necessary precondition of sympathy.

I think that this solution is unsatisfactory primarily because of the incoherence of the notion of freedom of the will: but I cannot discuss this topic adequately here, although some of my criticisms will touch upon it.

First I should query the assumption that second order evils are logically necessary accompaniments of freedom. I should ask this: if God has made men such that in their free choices they sometimes prefer what is good and sometimes what is evil, why could he not have made men such that they always freely choose the good? If there is no logical impossibility in a man's freely choosing the good on one, or on several, occasions, there cannot be a logical impossibility in his freely choosing the good on every occasion. God was not, then, faced with a choice between making innocent automata and making beings who, in acting freely, would sometimes go wrong: there was open to him the obviously better possibility of making beings who would act freely but always go right. Clearly, his failure to avail himself of this possibility is inconsistent with his being both omnipotent and wholly good.

If it is replied that this objection is absurd, that the making of some wrong choices is logically necessary for freedom, it would seem that "freedom" must here mean complete randomness or indeterminacy, including randomness with regard to the alternatives good and evil, in other words that men's choices and consequent actions can be "free" only if they are not determined by their characters. Only on this assumption can God escape the responsibility for men's actions; for if he made them as they are, but did not determine their wrong choices, this can only be because the wrong choices are not determined by men as they are. But then if freedom is randomness, how can it be a characteristic of *will*? And, still more, how can it be the most important good? What value or merit would there be in free choices if these were random actions which were not determined by the nature of the agent?

I conclude that to make this solution plausible two different senses of "freedom" must be confused, one sense which will justify the view that freedom is a third order good, more valuable than other goods would be without it, and another sense, sheer randomness, to prevent us from ascribing to God a decision to make men such that they sometimes go wrong when he might have made them such that they would always freely go right.

This criticism is sufficient to dispose of this solution. But besides this there is a fundamental difficulty in the notion of an omnipotent God creating men with free will, for if men's wills are really free this must mean that even God cannot control them, that is, that God is no longer omnipotent. It may be objected that God's gift of freedom to men does not mean that he *cannot* control their wills, but that he always *refrains* from controlling their wills. But why, we may ask, should God refrain from controlling evil wills? Why should he not leave men free to will rightly, but intervene when he sees them beginning to will wrongly? If God could do this, but does not, and if he is wholly good, the only explanation could be that even a wrong free act of will is not really evil, that its freedom is a value which outweighs its wrongness, so that there would be a loss of value if God took away the wrongness and the freedom together. But this is utterly opposed to what theists say about sin in other contexts. The present solution of the problem of evil, then, can be maintained only in the form that God has made men so free that he *cannot* control their wills.

This leads us to what I call the Paradox of Omnipotence: can an omnipotent being make things which he cannot subsequently control? Or, what is practically equivalent to this, can an omnipotent being make rules which then bind himself? (These are practically equivalent because any such rules could be regarded as setting certain things beyond his control, and *vice versa*.) The second of these formulations is relevant to the suggestions that we have already met, that an omnipotent God creates the rules of logic or causal laws, and is then bound by them.

It is clear that this is a paradox: the questions cannot be answered satisfactorily either in the affirmative or in the negative. If we answer "Yes," it follows that if God actually makes things which he cannot control, or makes rules which bind himself, he is not omnipotent once he has made them: there are *then* things which he cannot do. But if we answer "No," we are immediately asserting that there are things which he cannot do, that is to say that he is already not omnipotent.

It cannot be replied that the question which sets this paradox is not a proper question. It would make perfectly good sense to say that a human mechanic has made a machine which he cannot control: if there is any difficulty about the question it lies in the notion of omnipotence itself.

This, incidentally, shows that although we have approached this paradox from the free will theory, it is equally a problem for a theological determinist. No one thinks that machines have free will, yet they may well be beyond the control of their makers. The determinist might reply that anyone who makes anything determines its ways of acting, and so determines its subsequent behaviour: even the human mechanic does this by his *choice* of materials and structure for his machine, though he does not know all about either of these: the mechanic thus determines, though he may not foresee, his machine's actions. And since God is omniscient, and since his creation of things is total, he both determines and foresees the ways in which his creatures will act. We may grant this, but it is beside the point. The question is not whether God *originally* determined the future actions of his creatures, but whether he can *subsequently* control their actions, or whether he was able in his original creation to put things beyond his subsequent control. Even on determinist principles the answers "Yes" and "No" are equally irreconcilable with God's omnipotence.

Before suggesting a solution of this paradox, I would point out that there is a parallel Paradox of Sovereignty. Can a legal sovereign make a law restricting its own future legislative power? For example, could the British parliament make a law forbidding any future parliament to socialise banking, and also forbidding the future repeal of this law itself? Or could the British parliament, which was legally sovereign in Australia in, say, 1899, pass a valid law, or series of laws, which made it no longer sovereign in 1933? Again, neither the affirmative nor the negative answer is really satisfactory. If we were to answer "Yes," we should be admitting the validity of a law which, if it were actually made, would mean that parliament was no longer sovereign. If we were to answer "No," we should be admitting that there is a law, not logically absurd, which parliament cannot validly make, that is, that parliament is not now a legal sovereign. This paradox can be solved in the following way. We should distinguish between first order laws, that is laws governing the actions of individuals and bodies other than the legislature, and second order laws, that is laws about laws, laws governing the actions of the legislature itself. Correspondingly, we should distinguish two orders of sovereignty, first order sovereignty (sovereignty (1)) which is unlimited authority to make first order laws, and second order sovereignty (sovereignty (2)) which is unlimited authority to make second order laws. If we say that parliament is sovereign we might mean that any parliament at any time has sovereignty (1), or we might mean that parliament has both sovereignty (1) and sovereignty (2) at present, but we cannot without contradiction mean both that the present parliament has sovereignty (2) and that every parliament at every time has sovereignty (1), for if the present parliament has sovereignty (2) it may use it to take away the sovereignty (1) of later parliaments. What the paradox shows is that we cannot ascribe to any continuing institution legal sovereignty in an inclusive sense.

The analogy between omnipotence and sovereignty shows that the paradox of omnipotence can be solved in a similar way. We must distinguish between first order omnipotence (omnipotence (1)), that is unlimited power to act, and second order omnipotence (omnipotence (2)), that is unlimited power to determine what powers to act things shall have. Then we could consistently say that God all the time has omnipotence (1), but if so no beings at any time have powers to act independently of God. Or we could say that God at one time had omnipotence (2), and used it to assign independent powers to act to certain things, so that God thereafter did not have omnipotence (1). But what the paradox shows is that we cannot consistently ascribe to any continuing being omnipotence in an inclusive sense.

An alternative solution of this paradox would be simply to deny that God is a continuing being, that any times can be assigned to his actions at all. But on this assumption (which also has difficulties of its own) no meaning can be given to the assertion that God made men with wills so free that he could not control them. The paradox of omnipotence can be avoided by putting God outside time, but the freewill solution of the problem of evil cannot be saved in this way, and equally it remains impossible to hold that an omnipotent God *binds himself* by causal or logical laws.

Conclusion

Of the proposed solutions of the problem of evil which we have examined, none has stood up to criticism. There may be other solutions which require examination, but this study strongly suggests that there is no valid solution of the problem which does not modify at least one of the constituent propositions in a way which would seriously affect the essential core of the theistic position.

Quite apart from the problem of evil, the paradox of omnipotence has shown that God's omnipotence must in any case be restricted in one way or another, that unqualified omnipotence cannot be ascribed to any being that continues through time. And if God and his actions are not in time, can omnipotence, or power of any sort, be meaningfully ascribed to him?

Endnote

*Reprinted from *Mind*, Vol. LXIV, No. 254 (1955). Reprinted by permission of Oxford University Press.

Study Questions

1.   J. L. Mackie thinks that the theist faces a logical problem. What is it?

2.   How does Mackie view giving up one of the beliefs held as a way out of the alleged difficulty for the theist?

3.   What do you think of the revision-of-belief proposal?

4.   What does Mackie think of the free will defense?

5.   What do you think of Mackie's challenge to theism? What follows if the theist cannot answer Mackie's challenge in any helpful way?

19

The Greater Good Defense

Keith E. Yandell

Keith E. Yandell is professor of philosophy at the University of Wisconsin-Madison, and is author of *The Epistemology of Religious Experience*.

Yandell attempts to establish three theses: (1) that the orthodox theist is committed to some version of the greater good defense; (2) that the defense cannot be limited to polemic contexts; (3) that acceptance of the defense is not unreasonable.*

I hope to establish three theses in the argument that follows: first, that the orthodox theist is committed to the truth of some version of a greater good defense; second, that the theist's use of the greater good defense cannot consistently be limited to polemic contexts in which the defense is viewed as merely a logically consistent set of propositions; third, that acceptance of the greater good defense is not unreasonable. The second thesis is an obvious consequence of the first, and my reason for noting it separately will appear shortly.

I

The orthodox theist is committed to the truth of at least these claims:

(1) God exists, and is an all-knowing, all-powerful, all-good Creator and Providence;

(2) There is evil in the world.

As I understand the theistic tradition, (1) is to be understood along the following lines. *God is all-powerful* entails, and is entailed by, *For any proposition P, if P is consistent, and 'God makes P true' is consistent, then God can in fact make P true. God is all-knowing entails,* and is entailed by,

For any proposition P, if it is logically possible that P be known, and that God know that P, then God does in fact know that P. God is all-good entails (among other things) that *God wills that each man attain his greatest good. God is Creator* entails (and *perhaps* is entailed by) *Everything else depends for its existence on God, but not conversely* and *God is providential* entails (among other things) *God controls the course of history so that each man has maximal opportunity to attain his greatest good.*

As I understand the theistic tradition, (2)—that there is evil in the world—is what gives point to talk of repentance and forgiveness, judgement and mercy, damnation and redemption, and hell and heaven. Central, then, if not exhaustive among the evils with which this tradition is concerned are those which seem to frustrate, or actually do frustrate, man's attaining the greatest good available to him, for it is after all the forgiveness, redemption, and attainment of heaven by men which is most in view in theistic thinking and preaching. That man is created in the image of God and that his good is gained through (or compromised by) his imitation of God are basic themes in this context. It seems, then, a relevant (if perhaps partial) theistic characterization of evil to say that anything which frustrates (either prevents or diminishes) a man's attainment of his greatest good is evil. To the degree a man's own free actions and choices frustrate his self-attainment, he is evil. If God brings about, or allows, something to occur which frustrates such development, except insofar as permitting men to frustrate their own development is required for the existence of moral agency, or insofar as such frustration is just punishment, He is not all-good.

I include this very incomplete analysis of a theistic view of the nature of evil for two reasons. For one thing, it serves as a reminder that theism *has* a doctrine of good and evil—one which is relevant to the meaning of *God is all-good* and to the *problem* of evil. For another, this analysis indicates the necessity of, and provides content for, the greater good defense.

Of course it has at times been denied that theism has any ethic, or at any rate any ethic which provides positive meaning to *God is all-good*. Notoriously, negative theology (remarkably tenacious in both Eastern and Western philosophic and religious thought) has made this denial, contending that no proposition of the form *God is* f (where f is any "positive" property at all) is intelligible. For this viewpoint, that God is all-knowing entails that He is not impotent, but not (say) that He can move a mountain. But in a context where *God is not impotent* does not entail *God is potent*, the meaningfulness of *both* propositions is surely open to question. A consequence of this is that (say) *God is just* is not any longer true (or false either). Whatever one thinks of the motivations, philosophical or otherwise, of this view, one thing is clear: if "just" means (at least substantially) the same thing with respect to both Creator and creature, that God is just will involve (what after all Biblical authors affirm) that God is not partial to some, rendering judgment differently in relevantly similar cases, but is fair to all, and so on. That God is just does not involve these things for the negative theologian. What happens to "good" and "just" on this view happens to *all* moral (and non-moral predicates, and so the resultant view is that while God has no vices He has (so far as we can say) no virtues either. Imitation of God is hence impossible. Why worship, or even respect, toward God should remain becomes altogether puzzling, for God the Creator and Providence and Husband of Israel and Father of Jesus Christ becomes the Cosmic Unknown; and it is hard to know how to behave toward cosmic unknowns.

Returning to the main course of the argument, we have seen that the theist accepts (1) and (2). How is this related to the greater good defense? Given (1) and (2), it seems clear that for a theist whatever evil God creates or permits will be justified in the sense that God has a morally sufficient reason for creating or allowing it. Indeed, I take it that *God is good* entails *Insofar as He can God creates or allows no evil which He has no morally sufficient reason for creating or allowing.* But given God's existence and properties, everything that exists—and so everything that is evil—is quite under His control, being created or permitted by an omnicompetent God. So: (3) *Every evil is such that God has a morally sufficient reason for creating or allowing it.* And anyone who holds that (4) *Some evil exists for which there is no morally sufficient reason,* will, if consistent, deny (1), for:

(2) There is evil in the world.

Not—(3) Not every evil is such that God has a morally sufficient reason for creating or allowing it.

So: not—(1) God does not exist or is not an all-knowing, all-powerful, all-good Creator and Providence

is a valid argument. The theist, as indicated, accepts (1) and (2). He thus accepts (3), since (1) and (2) entail (3). So he rejects not—(3). The critic accepts (2), but also thinks that not—(3) is true. So he rejects (1).

The theist, then, accepts:

(3) *Every evil is such that God has a morally sufficient reason for creating or allowing it.*

This not yet the greater good defense. That defense consists of a single though complex proposition. So we must state that proposition and see how it may be derived from (3).

Some evils are related to certain goods, by logical necessity. Thus *Andrew is courageous* entails *Andrew has conquered fear.* If fear is an evil, and courage a virtue (and so a good), then necessarily this virtue exists only if evil exists. It is, of course, only *some fear or other*, not any particular fear, that is entailed. The grounds for regarding fear as an evil are, I take it, that if someone could prevent or eliminate fear on the part of another, and does not, having no morally sufficient reason, then he is morally culpable. The same holds for *producing* fear. A man might escape moral culpability for producing, not preventing, or not eliminating an evil due to ignorance or impotence, or because he knew the evil would produce a justifying good. Only this last escape from culpability is available to an omnicompetent being.

An evil which is related to a good by logical necessity is not therefore justified by that good in the sense that a being who could prevent the evil and did not is not culpable. For the good might be of insufficient value—it might neither counterbalance nor overbalance the evil. So an evil E open to greater-good treatment is such that: (a) there is a good G such that G *exists* entails that E *exists,* and (b) G at least counterbalances E. A good G counterbalances an evil E if and only if G *exists* entails E *exists* and if an agent who creates or permits E for the sake of G performs a morally neutral action (is neither praiseworthy nor blameworthy). A good G overbalances an evil E if and only if G *exists* entails E *exists* and an agent who creates or permits G for the sake of E is thereby morally praiseworthy. That God is all-good presumably entails that He is praiseworthy, and that He is providential presumably entails that He acts in a praiseworthy or morally good manner with respect to men. So the greater good defense can be expressed thusly:

(4)   Every evil is logically necessary to some good which either counterbalances or overbalances it, and some evil is overbalanced by the good to which it is logically necessary.

Alternatively, since E overbalances G if and only if G entails E and an agent who created or permitted E for the sake of G is thereby morally blameworthy, the greater good defense may be expressed via:

(4′)   Every evil is logically necessary to some good, some evil is overbalanced by some good to which it is logically necessary, and *no* evil overbalances the good to which it is logically necessary.

But I will stick to the formulation embodied in (4). How, then, do we get from (3) to (4), and what exactly does (4)—the greater good defense—amount to?

Unless we make explicit appeal to the (admittedly rather general) characterizations of *God is all-good* and *God is providential* offered above, the trip from (3) to (4) is tautologically short. For (3) says that for whatever evil He allows God has a morally sufficient reason. Ringing the changes on "morally sufficient reason", we may rephrase (3) as:

(3a) Every evil God allows is such that He is morally praiseworthy or morally neither praiseworthy nor blameworthy for so doing, and there is some evil such that He is morally praiseworthy for allowing it.

Or: (3b) No evil God allows is such that He is morally blameworthy for allowing it, and there is some evil such that He is morally praiseworthy for allowing it.

But the difference between (3a) and (4), or between (3b) and (4'), is (so far as I can see) the same as that between (3), (3a) and (3b), or between (4) and (4'); that is, the difference is purely verbal. If so, the move from (3) to (4) is trivial.

But if we make explicit appeal to the meaning of *God is all-good and providential,* (4) is not simply (3) recycled. For then (4) says what is more explicitly put as:

(5) Every evil that God allows is logically necessary to some at least counterbalancing good state of affairs, and some evil is overbalanced by the good to which it is logically necessary, where one applicable criterion for a state of affairs being good is that it furthers the growth to moral maturity of some moral agent, and where the evils occurring to each agent are so arranged as to provide him maximal opportunity for moral maturity.

And the inference from (3) to (4), where (4) is taken to be identical to (5), will require this (or some similar) pattern of thought:

1. (3) Every evil is such that God has a morally sufficient reason for creating or allowing it. (from (1) and (2)).
2. God wills that each man attain his greatest good. (entailed by *God is all-good*).
3. Man's greatest good is his realization of his capacities as one made in the *imago dei* and one who is to act always in *imitatio dei.* (Part One of an outline interpretation of theistic ethics.)
4. God controls the course of history so that each man has maximal opportunity to attain his greatest good. (entailed by *God is providential*).

5.   Logically necessary conditions of attaining moral maturity are:
(a) free moral agency, where an agent *A* is free with respect to a
choice *x or not-x* if and only if *A* can in fact choose *x* or choose
not-x; (b) the existence of states of affairs which are evil (in the
sense that it would be blameworthy to allow them without
morally sufficient reason) and which are logically necessary to
states of affairs which are both good (in the sense of being
virtues which comprise, or are logically necessary to, mature
moral character) and at least counterbalancing. (Part Two of an
outline interpretation of theistic ethics.)

6.   Some good overbalances the evil to which it is logically
necessary. (entailed by the theistic claim that God's creation of
men is a good state of affairs).

So: 7.   (5) Every evil that God allows is logically necessary to some at
least counterbalancing state of affairs, and some evil is
overbalanced by the good to which it is logically necessary,
where one applicable criterion for a state of affairs being good is
that it furthers the growth to moral maturity of some moral
agent, and where the evils occurring to each agent are so
arranged as to provide him maximal opportunity for moral
maturity.

Now plainly (1-7) is roughly hewn; there are plenty of loose ends,
uninvestigated consequences, and undefended assumptions. While I cannot
pretend here to tie everything neatly together, I think it worthwhile to
serially note several points relevant to that large and difficult task:

(a)   While of course a theist might object to the outline reading of
theistic ethics offered above, *some* interpretation of "good" is requisite if
(4) (or (3)) is maintained. It is indeed logically possible for someone to
know a proposition of the form *x is f* is true without knowing what f means
(e.g., I might know, on the basis of being told by an expert, that some
particles have negative energy without knowing what "negative energy"
means). So it is possible that one know that God is good without knowing
what "good" means. Or one can know that "good" means, say "of positive
moral value" without knowing what *is* of positive moral value. But the
theist is, I think, not in a position to stay at this aloof level. Theistic
theology and life style, its thinking and preaching, is chock full of moral
content, the source of which it takes to be the nature and will of God. The
theist may confess that the *means* God chooses are mysterious in the sense
that he cannot tell how they will lead to ends God (*ex hypothesi*) takes to
be good. The same may be said for a novice watching a surgeon whom he
trusts. But he cannot consistently pretend total ignorance concerning the
ends the divine surgeon pursues. The commitment and trust required by
worship (in contrast to sheer abasement) require at least a general sense of
the ends God has in view. In sum, a theist who accepts *God is all-good and*

providential accepts thereby a particular concept of goodness and providence—not necessarily the one sketched above, but if not that, then some other. And hence he accepts *some* version of what I have called "the greater good defense" ("defense" because it is in part by appeal to his concept of goodness and providence that the theist endeavours to rebut the charge that evil provides counter-theistic evidence).

(b) It is easy to draw subtly mistaken inferences from *God is all-good* and its theistic kin. Although Aquinas long ago suggested (as a necessary truth I suppose) the claim that *for any world God creates, He can create a better one*, it has often been mistakenly supposed that *necessarily, an all-good God would create the best possible world*. Again, in accord with the principle of treating all men as ends and never only as means, it would seem that if God allows an evil *E* to occur to an agent *A*, *A* must in justice reap an at least counterbalancing good *G* to which *E* is necessary, and this would require further amendment to (5). But it seems to me not clear whether such amendment is justified, for it is (so far as I can see) logically possible that enduring evil for the sake of others is itself of moral worth (or perhaps in that case that very worth is the at least counterbalancing good). In general, it seems clear that exactly what follows from such propositions as (3), (4) or (5) will depend on the particular context of moral theory in which they are embedded.

(c) As has often been noted, a good when added to an evil state of affairs may make the result worse, and the addition of an evil to a good state of affairs may make the result better. This, too, will affect the final statement of (5)-like propositions.[1]

(d) The remarks to this point (and in what follows) assume that some moral propositions are true. But some theists have denied this, though retaining something analogous to theistic ethics. One possibility along these lines concerns non-moral values. Another (not incompatible) line is to try to do more than is usually thought possible with emotivist ethics.[2] But, being an ethical cognitivist, I do not pursue these lines here.

(e) The questions of a theistic view of human nature and a theistic account of morality, and to what degree these are compatible with (and can draw upon) scientific data about human biology and psychology (normal and abnormal, psycho-analytic and social), and the like, are in fact central to what, in the long run, can or cannot be said about the various phases of the problem of evil. Indeed, I think nothing very definitive *can* be said without investigation of these further questions. And plainly any view of man and morality requires attention to the sort of world in which we live, involving answers to the sort of metaphysical questions positivists officially eschewed and covertly answered.

(f) Finally, as I have construed the greater good defense, the free will defense falls under its rubric. For any wrong and free choice God permits an agent *A* to make, it is (*ex hypothesi*) better that God allow moral agency to be misused than that it be temporarily withdrawn, the good of even misused agency (in its cosmic context) being a good that at least counterbalances the evilness of a wrong choice (and perhaps its consequences, or perhaps the consequences of the choice are also related to other justificatory goods).

II

Whereas I have presented (3) as an entailment of orthodox theism, it is often brought into the discussion of God and evil by a less direct route. If one wishes to show that two propositions, A and B, are consistent, one technique is to discover some third proposition C such that the conjunct A *and C* is plainly consistent with B. It then takes no logical genius to see that if A *and C* is consistent with B, A by itself is consistent with B. This is so, whether or not C is true. The truth value of C is quite irrelevant to the appropriateness of its use in this perfectly legitimate technique.[3]

If one wishes to show that *God exists* is not incompatible with *There is evil*, he can note that the conjunct comprised of God *exists* and *Every evil that exists is such that God has a morally sufficient reason for creating or permitting it* is compatible with *There is evil*. In this way, (3) appears as one proposition useful for showing that two other propositions are compatible. For that purpose, as we noted, (3) need not be true. Further, other propositions will be available for the same purpose. One could, for example, appeal to (5), or to (3') *Every evil that exists is such that its non-existence is logically impossible*. The conjunct of this last proposition with *God exists* is itself consistent, and is compatible with *There is evil*. So if one simply wants to argue that *God exists* and *There is evil* are compatible, and in so doing to utilize the technique we have described, use of (3') will be quite as appropriate as use of (3). The fact that (3') is patently false is, in this context, not to the point. If (3) is patently false, that too is irrelevant so far as its use in arguing the point of consistency is concerned.

Nonetheless, as we noted, (1) entails (3) but not (3'). That (3') is false says nothing about (1). But if (3) is false, (1) is also false. Put differently (3) is entailed by orthodox theism, while (3') is certainly not. Thus while use of (3) in showing that (1) and (2) are logically compatible is perfectly legitimate, the theist is committed to (3) in a stronger sense than that in which (3) is one of various propositions he may adopt for legitimate logical manoeuvres, and I think this is worth emphasizing.

III

Having endeavoured to show in what sense and for what reasons the theist is committed to the truth of the greater good defense, and having noted a polemic use of that defense, I turn from exposition to appraisal. Is it reasonable to accept the greater good defense?

Several things seem evident from the outset of reflection on this matter. First, for any specific good G and evil E which are proferred as an example of greater-good-requiring-evil complexes, the example may be questioned. Does the good at least counter-balance the evil? Is the evil logically necessary to the good? Is there no good G' which could replace the state of affairs G *and* E with net moral gain? Is the good in question valuable for its own sake, or simply (so to say) the best alternative available given its corresponding evil? These are matters of moral philosophy. They are also matters on which reasonable men notoriously differ. The theist is, if the above argument is correct, committed to a greater good thesis concerning evils. He is not committed to any particular examples of greater-good-requiring-evils (except, perhaps, at a very general level). But he is committed to there being *some* examples of such complexes, and of course if *no* examples seem forthcoming this casts doubt on whether there are any such cases. But I think there are relevant examples, and have suggested above what I take some of them to be.

Second, there will almost surely be evils for which the theist finds no plausible greater good he can name. But surely this is not surprising. Even if *God exists and has a providential plan* were shown to be a necessary truth, or as well-confirmed a contingent truth as *There is a Pacific Ocean*, it would still be the case that there are evils the theist cannot place with any confidence in any justificatory basket he can name. But this is not evidence that there are evils which fit no such basket whatever.[4]

Third, basic to a theistic treatment of evil is a theistic view of man as *imago dei* and ethics *as imitatio dei*. For at least one central theistic tradition, this places an enormous value on human freedom and moral maturity.[5] One who occupies the perspective of B. F. Skinner's *Beyond Freedom and Dignity* will reject altogether such a view of man, and the theist will view Skinner's view as beneath freedom and dignity. I suspect that the fundamental issue which disturbs believer and non-believer alike with regard to "the problem of evil" is the suspicion that there is no adequate moral theory on which (in conjunction with a correct account of human nature) actual evils could possibly be justified. Unfortunately, systematic and philosophically articulate formulations of theistic ethics are rare, making it hard to confirm or alleviate this suspicion in any definitive way. The following remarks are intended as prolegomena to such alleviation.

Suppose that *if* Andrew's fears result in Andrew becoming courageous, and that *if* Alice's pains result in Alice becoming fortudinous, then these fears and pains are evils related as logically necessary conditions (though not *simpliciter*) to over-balancing goods.[6] One (I think not implausible) way of understanding these remarks will run thusly:

(A)   Andrew's fears and Alice's pains are, considered by themselves, evil—at least in the sense that if an agent who could prevent or remove them did not, and had no morally sufficient reason, he would thereby be morally blameworthy.

(B)   Andrew's free response to his fears, and Alice's to her pains, was morally creative (virtuous) in such a manner that fears-plus-responses and pains-plus-responses were good states of affairs to which evils were necessary (though not *simpliciter*) but which overbalanced their respective evils (which are hence justified).

As we have seen, other fears or pains might have served as well, and other equally lamentable stimuli might have produced other equally valuable virtues, quite compatibly with the truth of (A) or (B).

But suppose Andrew succumbs to his fears and becomes a coward, and Alice curses her pain and becomes a shrew. Then the fears and pains do not exactly shout their moral necessity, and there is something insipid about the reply that Andrew's fears at any rate give him the opportunity to develop courage. The missed chance seems neither worth the price nor proper in a God-made world.

Nonetheless, I think there is considerable force to the reply which is feebly mis-stated along the lines just suggested. From the viewpoint of theistic morality, Andrew's fears and Alice's pains are occasions for free moral growth. As is so for any such occasion, there may be moral failure. But if Andrew becomes a coward, the status of his moral failure should be described (from the indicated perspective) in such terms as:

(C)   It is better that Andrew be given opportunity to respond freely (and so creatively or destructively) to his fears than that he not have this opportunity—there is justificatory value in even the wrong exercise of moral agency.

If Andrew would have done no better given any other occasion of free and morally relevant choice, then not even God could both leave him a free agent and provide him with a better shot at goodness. The alternatives to cowardly Andrew will then be an unfree Andrew or not Andrew at all. Either way, Andrew is no moral agent (at least on the view presently being considered). And the same goes *mutatis mutandis*, for Alice, and for us all.

This view of moral agency, of course, assumes (what seems to me true) that moral agents are necessarily free agents, and that free agents are necessarily not determined. Alternatively, one could hold that (a) in one sense of "free" (say, free$_1$) libertarianism and determinism cannot both be true with respect to any particular choice or action (b) in another sense of "free" (say, free$_2$) libertarianism and determinism can be co-true, (c) correspondingly, there are two possible sorts of moral agents, those who are free$_1$, and those who are free$_2$, with respect to the choices for which they are morally responsible, and (d) it is vastly more valuable that there be free$_1$ agents than that there be free$_2$ agents. I suspect that disagreements concerning the relative worth of different sorts of freedom is as important for the dispute concerning evil as is the hoary controversy as to whether a choice or action may be both free and determined.

Perhaps a theist who argues along the lines of (A) through (C) is committed to such claims as:

(D)   For every moral agent A, A is given those circumstances of moral choice which maximise his opportunity to act in a morally creative way (though he may miserably bungle things anyway).

(E)   There is no set S' of moral agents whose members, had they been created, would have chosen better than the members of the set S of actual persons have chosen.

(F)   For any actual agent A, whatever the actual choices he makes, it is better that A exist (have been created) than otherwise.

Concerning (F), it will perhaps suffice to note that (a) (F) seems plausible with respect to a being *ex hypothesi* created in the *imago dei* and (b) it is compatible with (F) that there be a (possible but not actual) choice C such that an agent who made C would be such that his non-existence was better than his existence.

I think (though I am not sure) that (D), or something like it, is entailed by *God is providential* (and so by (1)). It seems worth noting that in orthodox Christianity, salvation is "by grace, not works"—including the 'work' of a good moral character, so that if theism does entail something like (D), this entailment will have to be understood in terms of a theologically-informed theistic ethic. In spite of some popular versions of heaven, nothing in orthodox theism entails that man-in-heaven is "frozen" at some level of moral development (even the highest). Indeed, being (in *that* sense) "confirmed in righteousness" may be incompatible with being a *person* at all. If these remarks are sound, they too must be considered when unpacking (D).

In sum, then, even cowardly Andrew and shrewish Alice are not so, simply because they were given a test which God (*ex hypothesi*) knew they would fail. Rather, they were granted moral agency (were created as moral agents) even though God (*ex hypothesi*) knew they, in important ways, would misuse it. More carefully, they were created as moral agents even though God (*ex hypothesi*) knew they would not become very good people. (Or perhaps only worse vices than cowardice or shrewhood would justify this harsh a judgment—but then there *are* worse vices.)

Turning briefly to (E)—the claim that no other set S' of moral agents would have produced better choices than the actual set S has—I offer three comments: (a) from the fact that S' is conceivable, it does not follow that S' is creatable;[7] (b) any evidence we have, then, concerning what possible agents might do must be derived from what actual agents have done. The performance of actual persons is our only sample class for the projection of how possible persons, were they created, would use their moral agency. (c) Plainly, it would be fallacious to infer that the members of the reference class (all actual and possible persons) contains some subset of possible persons who would (collectively or distributively) fare morally better (or worse) than have the members of the sample class (all actual persons). This would be analogous to arguing from the fact that all known elephants (the sample class) fear mice to the conclusion that the reference class (all elephants) contains some subset (of unobserved elephants) which delight in the company of their tiny brethren. So either the performance of merely possible persons, were they created, would be of familiar calibre, or we've no idea what they would do. The former alternative substantiates (E) and the latter does it no damage.

Still, it may be felt, even if (A) through (F) are granted, accepting the greater good defense remains unreasonable. For what of the painful death of an infant? And what of the growth to fine moral maturity of a saint who then decays into senility and becomes but the pale shadow of a fully-functioning adult? The road to moral maturity is not only strewn with wrecks; some entrants deceased before they left the driveway and others traverse the road fully only to crash at the end.

I grant the psychological forcefulness of appeal to infant mortality and geriatric disability. Perhaps it is just that forcefulness which not only often prevents us from looking at such matters clearly but makes any such attempt seem crass. It might indeed be crass (and that is charitable) to offer philosophical reflection to a bereaved parent or a grieving child when their need is so clearly for simple kindness. But no good is done by confusing appraisal of putative evidence with counsel to the griefstricken, and each has its proper place. What, then, of the proffered evidence that acceptance of the greater good defense is irrational? While I cannot pretend to deal with all the relevant issues, I offer four comments. First, either the infant is possessed of personal worth or not. If not, only the suffering of the parent is relevant, and (A) through (F) suggest how such suffering may be dealt with along "greater good" lines. If so (and presumably this is the correct alternative), then perhaps the point is that a person has been obliterated before he had a chance to develop—perhaps the idea is that cessation of existence of a potentially mature person is an evil. One question is whether this high value of personal worth can be sustained in a non-theistic perspective, but that issue is too large to broach here. Another question is whether cessation of existence has in fact occurred. At least orthodox Christian theism asserts that it is not, and this is no *ad hoc* assumption made to deal with critical points. Rather, it is intimately intertwined with the themes of mercy and judgment, heaven and hell, and the like which we mentioned above. The thrust of the problem of infant mortality is altogether different for one who accepts either immortality of the soul or resurrection of the body than for one who does not. For the death of an infant (or of anyone) to by itself count as evidence against theism, we must (not merely not have good reason to believe but) have good reason to disbelieve all doctrines of personal survival. I do not myself know of such reasons. Hence I do not take death (infant or other) to constitute evidence against theism.

Second, the case of the senile saint is, it may be suggested, relevantly different. Perhaps the infant is not really a person (a natural extension of some pro-abortion arguments leads to this view). Perhaps the infant does survive to exercise moral agency in (so to say) another context. But the person who attains moral maturity, and then suffers disintegration of his mind as well as his body, raises another matter altogether. A man who really prizes artistic masterpieces does not allow them to go to ruin, even if he can restore them as good as new. If God really prizes moral maturity, why does He then allow even very good men to become senile, or even go mad? Well, I do not know, and I notice that the question does not seem to come up much in the literature. Perhaps no one else knows either, and I should think that it is appeal to such tragic reversals that provides one of the most cogent platforms of criticism of theism. But is this case really any different from that of other evils for which no point or justification can be specified? Perhaps *if* any such case were cogent counter-evidence, then the evil of demised sainthood is that case. But I have argued that such cases are not counter-evidence, and I do not see that identifying the sort of case that would be counter-evidence if any case were provides any counter to that argument.

As a (for the present) final move, we may imagine the critic arguing that the theist, in making the reply just rehearsed, covertly gives up the greater good defense. For the greater good defense is acceptable only if, as a necessary but not sufficient condition, "good" is not equivocal with respect to God and man. But the above defense allows that a good God can do things no good man can do without forfeiting his goodness. So if good at all, God is good in some sense other than that in which man is. Hence farewell to the greater good defense.

Putting the criticism formally, we get this argument:

(A1) If under circumstance c, f applies to all values of x but to no value of y, f means one thing when applied to the values of x and another thing when applied to the values of y.

(A2) Under the circumstance of permitting an infant to die when he can prevent the death (or permitting a saint to become senile or mad when he can prevent it), "good" applies to God but not to man.

So: (A3) "Good" means one thing when applied to God and another thing when applied to man.

In fact, since (A3) entails that "good" is equivocal with respect to God and man, unless some new and relevant sense for "good" as applied to God is provided, "God is good" will be meaningless. But given just (A3), the greater good defense is unacceptable. Does, then, this argument succeed?

It does not. For while (A1) and (A2) *seem* to entail (A3), (A1) is either false (in which case (A1) and (A2) fruitlessly entail (A3)) or true (in which case (A1) and (A2) do not entail (A3)). To see this, consider under what specification of "circumstance" narrowly, allowing for example only those descriptions of states of affairs which include no reference to the motives, intentions, etc. of the agent and no consideration of what effect difference in knowledge and power has on the question of moral appraisal, (A1) will be false. For on (A1), so read, "good" may be applied to a surgeon who operates under emergency conditions rather than running for help, but not to me if under the same circumstances I run for help rather than operate. We may share intent (that the man live) and differ in ways relevant to moral appraisal (medical knowledge and prowess), but this is ruled out of consideration by the present restrictions on "circumstances" in (A1). (A1) will entail that, if the surgeon and I are (in the context of action on the described occasion) good at all, we are good in different senses. Yet this is false. We are both (given all the relevant features of the context) good, though we act differently, for we act for the same good end, each tailoring our actions to both that shared end and our respective talents. Narrowly construed, then, (A1) plus (A2) entails (A3), but this is polemically useless since (A1)—so restricted—is false.

Suppose, then, we do the reasonable thing and allow "circumstances" in (A1) to be widely read so as to include descriptions of the motives, intentions, etc. of agents and (insofar as relevant) differences in their knowledge and power. *Ex hypothesi*, that a man attain moral maturity is an important good. So a good God, and a good man, will allow each man maximal chance to attain this maturity. No man can achieve this end by permitting the death of another, for once dead a man is beyond all influence of his peers. But he is not beyond God's influence. So God sharing the same good end, may act differently, relative to His knowledge and prowess, than any man can act who shares the same end.

Widely read, (A1) is true. But it does not apply in the relevant case, for then "good" applies to God and man in the same circumstances—those in which God and man differ in capacity but coincide in valuation (just as did the surgeon and I in the previous example). Or, if one prefers, when (A1) is widely read, (A2) is false. In any case, (A3) is not, so far as I can see, entailed by any version of this argument (or any other) which is both sound and valid.

The last shred of plausibility is, I think, removed from the criticism under review when we note a further similarity between "God is good" and "Socrates is good." "God" may do duty as a description (then meaning "a being who is omnipotent, omniscient, onmibenevolent, etc.") or a proper name (then functioning as does "Jehovah"). We may designate these uses, respectively, as "$God_{(1)}$" and "$God_{(2)}$". Then x is $God_{(1)}$ entails x is all-good, or (alternatively) *Necessarily, if x is $God_{(1)}$, x is good* is true. But *x is Jehovah* does not entail *x is all-good*, or (alternatively) *Necessarily, if x is $God_{(2)}$, x is good* is false. So *$God_{(2)}$ is all-good* is contingent, as is *Socrates is good*. Further, I take it that *being a saint* entails *being good*. *X is a saint* entails *x is good*, or (alternatively) *Necessarily, if x is a saint then x is good*. Hence *Saint Socrates is good* is a necessary truth. Socrates, *qua* saint, is *necessarily good*, just as Jehovah, *qua* God, is *necessarily all-good*. Socrates, *qua* Socrates, is (at most) *contingently good*, just as Jehovah, *qua* Jehovah, is *contingently good*. And just as Socrates is praised for a goodness he might not have possessed, and so may be credited for possessing, so perhaps Jehovah (or $God_{(2)}$) is praised for a goodness He might not have possessed, and so may be credited for possessing. At least, I see nothing philosophically or theologically objectionable in such a view.[8] But even if I am wrong about this, it is clear that the attempt to show that "good" is equivocal with respect to God and man fails. So far as I can see, so do the other attempts, noted above, to prove that it is unreasonable to accept the greater good defense.

Endnotes

*Reprinted from *Sophia*, October 1974, Essay III.

[1] Cf. John Wisdom, "God and Evil", *Mind* (1935).

[2] See Charles Kielkopf's provocative "Emotivism As A Solution to the Problem of Evil", *Sophia* (July, 1970).

[3] Alvin Plantinga, *God and Other Minds* (Ithaca, 1967), Ch. 5 and 6. George Mavrodes, *Belief in God: A Study in the Epistemology of Religion*, (New York, 1970), Ch. 4, make superb use of this technique.

[4] For reasons detailed in my "A Premature Farewell to Theism", *Religious Studies* (Dec., 1969).

[5] Cf. John Hick, *Evil and the God of Love* (New York, 1966).

[6] On various senses of "justified evil", see my "Ethics, Evils and Theism", *Sophia*, (July, 1969), or *Basic Issues in the Philosophy of Religion* (Boston, 1971), Ch. 2.

[7] As Plantinga, op. cit., notes, while it is logically possible that a world not created by God exists, it is not therefore (or at all) possible that God created a world not created by God.

[8] Cf. Dewey Hoitenga, "Logic and the Problem of Evil", *American Philosophical Quarterly* (April, 1967) for critique of this line of reasoning. For a reply to Hoitenga's critique, see my "Logic and the Problem of Evil: A Reply to Hoitenga" in Keith

Yandell, ed. *God, Man and Religion* (New York, 1972), in which Hoitenga's essay is included.

Study Questions

1.   Keith Yandell outlines the greater good defense. In terms that you can understand, how would you express it?

2   Why does Yandell think that the theist is committed to some version of the greater good defense? Do you agree?

3.   What are the chief divine attributes that figure in the greater good defense?

4.   According to Yandell, what sort of connection must there be between a good and the evil it is viewed as justifying?

5.   What problems do you see with the greater good defense?

20

Evil and Soul-Making

John Hick

John Hick, formerly professor of philosophy at the University of Birmingham, and Professor Emeritus at Claremont Graduate School, is author of *Evil and the God of Love*, from which this essay below was taken.* Hick develops both a free will defense and a soul-making defense in response to the charge that Christian belief is inconsistent because an omniscient, omnipotent, omnibenevolent deity would not allow evil. Evil comes into existence as a result of the misuse of free will, but not through an historic fall. Following Irenaeus, humans have a nature that is in the image of God, but God desires that they grow into his likeness, and this occurs through a process of soul-growth in a world that serves as a "vale of soul-making."

Fortunately there is another and better way. As well as the "majority report" of the Augustinian tradition, which has dominated Western Christendom, both Catholic and Protestant, since the time of Augustine himself, there is the "minority report" of the Irenaean tradition. This latter is both older and newer than the other, for it goes back to St. Irenaeus and others of the early Hellenistic Fathers of the Church in the two centuries prior to St. Augustine, and it has flourished again in more developed forms during the last hundred years.

Instead of regarding man as having been created by God in a finished state, as a finitely perfect being fulfilling the divine intention for our human level of existence, and then falling disastrously away from this, the minority report sees man as still in process of creation. Irenaeus himself expressed the point in terms of the (exegetically dubious) distinction between the "image" and the "likeness" of God referred to in Genesis 1.26: "Then God said, Let us make man in our image, after our likeness." His view was that man as a personal and moral being already exists in the image, but has not yet been formed into the finite likeness of God. By this "likeness" Irenaeus means something more than personal existence as such; he means a certain valuable quality of personal life which reflects finitely the divine life. This represents the perfecting of man, the fulfilment of God's purpose for humanity, the "bringing of many sons to glory," the creating of "children of God" who are "fellow heirs with Christ" of his glory.

And so man, created as a personal being in the image of God, is only the raw material for a further and more difficult stage of God's creative work. This is the leading of men as relatively free and autonomous persons, through their own dealings with life in the world in which He has placed them, towards that quality of personal existence that is the finite likeness of God. The features of this likeness are revealed in the person of Christ, and the process of man's creation into it is the work of the Holy Spirit. In St. Paul's words, "And we all, with unveiled faces, beholding the glory of the Lord, are being changed into his likeness (εικον) from one degree of glory to another; for this comes from the Lord who is the Spirit";[1] or again, "For God knew his own before ever they were, and also ordained that they should be shaped to the likeness (εικον) of his Son."[2] In Johannine terms, the movement from the image to the likeness is a transition from one level of existence, that of animal life (Bios), to another and higher level, that of eternal life (Zoe), which includes but transcends the first. And the fall of man was seen by Irenaeus as a failure within the second phase of this creative process, a failure that has multiplied the perils and complicated the route of the journey in which God is seeking to lead mankind.

In the light of modern anthropological knowledge some form of two-stage conception of the creation of man has become an almost unavoidable Christian tenet. At the very least we must acknowledge as two distinguishable stages the fashioning of homo sapiens as a product of the long evolutionary process, and his sudden or gradual spiritualization as a child of God. But we may well extend the first stage to include the development of man as a rational and responsible person capable of personal relationship with the personal Infinite who has created him. This first stage of the creative process was, to our anthropomorphic imaginations, easy for divine omnipotence. By an exercise of creative power God caused the physical universe to exist, and in the course of countless ages to bring forth within it organic life, and finally to produce out of organic life personal life; and when man had thus emerged out of the evolution of the forms of organic life, a creature had been made who has the possibility of existing in conscious fellowship with God. But the second stage of the creative process is of a different kind altogether. It cannot be performed by omnipotent power as such. For personal life is essentially free and self-directing. It cannot be perfected by divine fiat, but only through the uncompelled responses and willing co-operation of human individuals in their actions and reactions in the world in which God has placed them. Men may eventually become the perfected persons whom the New Testament calls "children of God," but they cannot be created ready-made as this.

The value-judgement that is implicitly being invoked here is that one who has attained to goodness by meeting and eventually mastering temptations, and thus by rightly making responsible choices in concrete situations, is good in a richer and more valuable sense than would be one created *ab initio* in a state either of innocence or of virtue. In the former case, which is that of the actual moral achievements of mankind, the individual's goodness has within it the strength of temptations overcome, a stability based upon an accumulation of right choices, and a positive and responsible character that comes from the investment of costly personal effort. I suggest, then, that it is an ethically reasonable judgement, even though in the nature of the case not one that is capable of demonstrative proof, that human goodness slowly built up through personal histories of moral effort has a value in the eyes of the Creator which justifies even the long travail of the soulmaking process.

The picture with which we are working is thus developmental and teleological. Man is in process of becoming the perfected being whom God is seeking to create. However, this is not taking place—it is important to add—by a natural and inevitable evolution, but through a hazardous adventure in individual freedom. Because this is a pilgrimage within the life of each individual, rather than a racial evolution, the progressive fulfilment of God's purpose does not entail any corresponding progressive improvement in the moral state of the world. There is no doubt a development in man's ethical situation from generation to generation through the building of individual choices into public institutions, but this involves an accumulation of evil as well as of good. It is thus probable that human life was lived on much the same moral plane two thousand years ago or four thousand years ago as it is today. But nevertheless during this period uncounted millions of souls have been through the experience of earthly life, and God's purpose has gradually moved towards its fulfilment within each one of them, rather than within a human aggregate composed of different units in different generations.

If, then, God's aim in making the world is "the bringing of many sons to glory," that aim will naturally determine the kind of world that He has created. Antitheistic writers almost invariably assume a conception of the divine purpose which is contrary to the Christian conception. They assume that the purpose of a loving God must be to create a hedonistic paradise; and therefore to the extent that the world is other than this, it proves to them that God is either not loving enough or not powerful enough to create such a world. They think of God's relation to the earth on the model of a human being building a cage for a pet animal to dwell in. If he is humane he will naturally make his pet's quarters as pleasant and healthful as he can. Any respect in which the cage falls short of the veterinarian's ideal, and contains possibilities of accident or disease, is evidence of either limited benevolence or limited means, or both. Those who use the problem of evil as an argument against belief in God almost invariably think of the world in this kind of way. David Hume, for example, speaks of an architect who is trying to plan a house that is to be as comfortable and convenient as possible. If we find that "the windows, doors, fires, passages, stairs, and the whole economy of the building were the source of noise, confusion, fatigue, darkness, and the extremes of heat and cold" we should have no hesitation in blaming the architect. It would be in vain for him to prove that if this or that defect were corrected greater ills would result: "still you would assert in general, that, if the architect had had skill and good intentions, he might have formed such a plan of the whole, and might have adjusted the parts in such a manner, as would have remedied all or most of these inconveniences.[3]

But if we are right in supposing that God's purpose for man is to lead him from human *Bios*, or the biological life of man, to that quality of *Zoe*, or the personal life of eternal worth, which we seen in Christ, then the question that we have to ask is not, Is this the kind of world that an all-powerful and infinitely loving being would create as an environment for his human pets? or, Is the architecture of the world the most pleasant and convenient possible? The question that we have to ask is rather, Is this the kind of world that God might make as an environment in which moral beings may be fashioned, through their own free insights and responses, into "children of God"?

Such critics as Hume are confusing what heaven ought to be, as an environment for perfected finite beings, with what this world ought to be, as an environment for beings who are in process of becoming perfected. For if our general conception of God's purpose is correct the world is not intended to be a paradise, but rather the scene of a history in which human personality may be formed towards the pattern of Christ. Men are not to be thought of on the analogy of animal pets, whose life is to be made as agreeable as possible, but rather on the analogy of human children, who are to grow to adulthood in an environment whose primary and overriding purpose is not immediate pleasure but the realizing of the most valuable potentialities of human personality.

Needless to say, this characterization of God as the heavenly Father is not a merely random illustration but an analogy that lies at the heart of the Christian faith. Jesus treated the likeness between the attitude of God to man, and the attitude of human parents at their best towards their children, as providing the most adequate way for us to think about God. And so it is altogether relevant to a Christian understanding of this world to ask, How does the best parental love express itself in its influence upon the environment in which children are to grow up? I think it is clear that a parent who loves his children, and wants them to become the best human beings that they are capable of becoming, does not treat pleasure as the sole and supreme value. Certainly we seek pleasure for our children, and take great delight in obtaining it for them; but we do not desire for them unalloyed pleasure at the expense of their growth in such even greater values as moral integrity, unselfishness, compassion, courage, humour, reverence for the truth, and perhaps above all the capacity for love. We do not act on the premise that pleasure is the supreme end of life; and if the development of these other values sometimes clashes with the provision of pleasure, then we are willing to have our children miss a certain amount of this, rather than fail to come to possess and to be possessed by the finer and more precious qualities that are possible to the human personality. A child brought up on the principle that the only or the supreme value is pleasure would not be likely to become an ethically mature adult or an attractive or happy personality. And to most parents it seems more important to try to foster quality and strength of character in their children than to fill their lives at all times with the utmost possible degree of pleasure. If, then, there is any true analogy between God's purpose for his human creatures, and the purpose of loving and wise parents for their children, we have to recognize that the presence of pleasure and the absence of pain cannot be the supreme and overriding end for which the world exists. Rather, this world must be a place of soulmaking. And its value is to be judged, not primarily by the quantity of pleasure and pain occurring in it at any particular moment, but by its fitness for its primary purpose, the purpose of soul-making.

In all this we have been speaking about the nature of the world considered simply as the God-given environment of man's life. For it is mainly in this connection that the world has been regarded in Irenaean and in Protestant thought. But such a way of thinking involves a danger of anthropocentrism from which the Augustinian and Catholic tradition has generally been protected by its sense of the relative insignificance of man within the totality of the created universe. Man was dwarfed within the medieval world-view by the innumerable hosts of angels and archangels above him—unfallen rational natures which rejoice in the immediate presence of God, reflecting His glory in the untarnished mirror of their worship. However, this higher creation has in our modern world lost its hold upon the imagination. Its place has been taken, as the minimizer of men, by the immensities of outer space and by the material universe's unlimited complexity transcending our present knowledge. As the spiritual environment envisaged by Western man has shrunk, his physical horizons have correspondingly expanded. Where the human creature was formerly seen as an insignificant appendage to the angelic world, he is now seen as an equally insignificant organic excrescence, enjoying a fleeting moment of consciousness on the surface of one of the planets of a minor star. Thus the truth that was symbolized for former ages by the existence of the angelic hosts is today impressed upon us by the vastness of the physical universe, countering the egoism of our species by making us feel that this immense prodigality of existence can hardly all exist for the sake of man—though, on the other hand, the very realization that it is not all for the sake of man may itself be salutary and beneficial to man!

However, instead of opposing man and nature as rival objects of God's interest, we should perhaps rather stress man's solidarity as an embodied being with the whole natural order in which he is embedded. For man is organic to the world; all his acts and thoughts and imaginations are conditioned by space and time; and in abstraction from nature he would cease to be human. We may, then, say that the beauties and sublimities and powers, the microscopic intricacies and macroscopic vastnesses, the wonders and the terrors of the natural world and of the life that pulses through it, are willed and valued by their Maker in a creative act that embraces man together with nature. By means of matter and living flesh God both builds a path and weaves a veil between Himself and the creature made in His image. Nature thus has permanent significance; for God has set man in a creaturely environment, and the final fulfilment of our nature in relation to God will accordingly take the form of an embodied life within "a new heaven and a new earth." And as in the present age man moves slowly towards that fulfilment through the pilgrimage of his earthly life, so also "the whole creation" is "groaning in travail," waiting for the time when it will be "set free from its bondage to decay."

And yet however fully we thus acknowledge the permanent significance and value of the natural order, we must still insist upon man's special character as a personal creature made in the image of God; and our theodicy must still centre upon the soul-making process that we believe to be taking place within human life.

This, then, is the starting-point from which we propose to try to relate the realities of sin and suffering to the perfect love of an omnipotent Creator. And as will become increasingly apparent, a theodicy that starts in this way must be eschatological in its ultimate bearings. That is to say, instead of looking to the past for its clue to the mystery of evil, it looks to the future, and indeed to that ultimate future to which only faith can look. Given the conception of a divine intention working in and through human time towards a fulfilment that lies in its completeness beyond human time, our theodicy must find the meaning of evil in the part that it is made to play in the eventual outworking of that purpose; and must find the justification of the whole process in the magnitude of the good to which it leads. The good that outshines all ill is not a paradise long since lost but a kingdom which is yet to come in its full glory and permanence.

Endnotes

    1 II Corinthians 3:18.

[2] Romans 8:29. Other New Testament passages expressing a view of man as undergoing a process of spiritual growth within God's purpose are: Ephesians 2:21; 3:16; Colossians 2:19; I John 3:2; II Corinthians 4:16.

[3] *Dialogues Concerning Natural Religion*, pt. xi. Kemp-Smith's ed. (Oxford: Clarendon Press, 1935), p. 251.

Study Questions

1.   How might one subsume John Hick's soul-making theodicy under the greater good heading?

2.   Hick's theodicy is Irenaean rather than Augustinian. What are the key elements that incline him to the former rather than the latter?

3.   What do you make of the soul-making theodicy?

4.   On Hick's view, what is the difference between "image" and "likeness"?

5.   How might one relate the soul-making theodicy of Hick to the free will defense?

21

The Free Will Defense

Alvin Plantinga

Alvin Plantinga is professor of philosophy at the University of Notre Dame, and author of *God and Other Minds; The Nature of Necessity;* and the two volume work, *Warrant: The Current Debate,* and *Warrant and Proper Function.* He argues that Mackie, and other atheists are wrong to think that the inconsistency strategy works.

He develops a free will defense in two stages that incorporates a possible-worlds ontology and a notion of transworld depravity that he thinks undercuts the charge of inconsistency based on evil.*

1. On the Alleged Contradiction in Theism

In a widely discussed piece entitled "Evil and Omnipotence" John Mackie makes this claim:

> I think, however, that a more telling criticism can be made by way of the traditional problem of evil. Here it can be shown, not that religious beliefs lack rational support, but that they are positively irrational, that the several parts of the essential theological doctrine are *inconsistent* with one another. . . .[1]

Is Mackie right? Does the theist contradict himself? But we must ask a prior question: just what is being claimed here? That theistic belief contains an inconsistency or contradiction, of course. But what, exactly, is an inconsistency or contradiction? There are several kinds. An *explicit* Contradiction is a *proposition* of a certain sort—a conjunctive proposition, one conjunct of which is the denial or negation of the other conjunct. For example:

> Paul is a good tennis player, and it's false that Paul is a good tennis player.

369

(People seldom assert explicit contradictions). Is Mackie charging the theist with accepting such a contradiction? Presumably not; what he says is:

> In its simplest form the problem is this: God is omnipotent; God is wholly good; yet evil exists. There seems to be some contradiction between these three propositions, so that if any two of them were true the third would be false. But at the same time all three are essential parts of most theological positions; the theologian, it seems, at once *must* adhere and *cannot consistently* adhere to all three.

According to Mackie, then, the theist accepts a group or set of three propositions; this set is inconsistent. Its members, of course, are

(1) God is omnipotent
(2) God is wholly good

and

(3) Evil exists.

Call this set A; the claim is that A is an inconsistent set. But what is it for a *set* to be inconsistent or contradictory? Following our definition of an explicit contradiction, we might say that a set of propositions is explicitly contradictory if one of the members is the denial or negation of another member. But then, of course, it is evident that the set we are discussing is not explicitly contradictory; the denials of (1), (2), and (3), respectively, are

(1') God is not omnipotent (or it's false that God is omnipotent)
(2') God is not wholly good

and

(3') There is no evil

none of which is in set A.

Of course many sets are pretty clearly contradictory, in an important way, but not *explicitly* contradictory. For example, set B:

(4) If all men are mortal, then Socrates is mortal
(5) All men are mortal
(6) Socrates is not mortal.

This set is not explicitly contradictory; yet surely *some* significant sense of that term applies to it. What is important here is that by using only the rules of ordinary logic—the laws of propositional logic and quantification theory found in any introductory text on the subject—we can deduce an explicit contradiction from the set. Or to put it differently, we can use the laws of logic to deduce a proposition from the set, which proposition, when added to the set, yields a new set that is explicitly contradictory. For by using the law *modus ponens* (if *p*, then *q*; *p*; therefore *q*) we can deduce

(7)   Socrates is mortal

from (4) and (5). The result of adding (7) to *B* is the set {(4), (5), (6), (7)}. This set, of course, is explicitly contradictory in that (6) is the denial of (7). We might say that any set which shares this characteristic with set *B* is *formally* contradictory. So a formally contradictory set is one from whose members an explicit contradiction can be deduced by the laws of logic. Is Mackie claiming that set *A* is formally contradictory?

If he is, he's wrong. No laws of logic permit us to deduce the denial of one of the propositions in *A* from the other members. Set *A* isn't formally contradictory either.

But there is still another way in which a set of propositions can be contradictory or inconsistent. Consider set *C*, whose members are

(8)   George is older than Paul
(9)   Paul is older than Nick

and

(10)   George is not older than Nick.

This set is neither explicitly nor formally contradictory; we can't, just by using the laws of logic, deduce the denial of any of these propositions from the others. And yet there is a good sense in which it is consistent or contradictory. For clearly it is *not possible* that its three members all be true. It is *necessarily true* that

(11)   If George is older than Paul, and Paul is older than Nick, then George is older than Nick.

And if we add (11) to set *C*, we get a set that is formally contradictory; (8), (9), and (11) yield, by the laws of ordinary logic, the denial of (10).

I said that (11) is *necessarily true*; but what does *that* mean? Of course we might say that a proposition is necessarily true if it is impossible that it be false, or if its negation is not possibly true. This would be to explain necessity in terms of possibility. Chances are, however, that anyone who does not know what necessity is, will be equally at a loss about possibility; the explanation is not likely to be very successful. Perhaps all we can do by way of explanation is to give some examples and hope for the best. In the first place many propositions can be established by the laws of logic alone—for example,

(12)   If all men are mortal and Socrates is a man, then Socrates is mortal.

Such propositions are truths of logic; and all of them are necessary in the sense in question. But truths of arithmetic and mathematics generally are also necessarily true. Still further, there is a host of propositions that are neither truths of logic nor truths of mathematics but are nonetheless necessarily true; (11) would be an example, as well as

(13)   Nobody is taller than himself
(14)   Red is a color
(15)   No numbers are persons
(16)   No prime number is a prime minister

and

(17)   Bachelors are unmarried.

So here we have an important kind of necessity—let's call it "broadly logical necessity." Of course there is a correlative kind of *possibility:* a proposition p is possibly true (in the broadly logical sense) just in case its negation or denial is not necessarily true (in that same broadly logical sense). This sense of necessity and possibility must be distinguished from another that we may call *causal* or *natural* necessity and possibility. Consider

(18)   Henry Kissinger has swum the Atlantic.

Although this proposition has an implausible ring, it is not necessarily false in the broadly logical sense (and its denial is not necessarily true in that sense). But there is a good sense in which it is impossible: it is *causally* or *naturally* impossible. Human beings, unlike dolphins, just don't have the physical equipment demanded for this feat. Unlike Superman, furthermore, the rest of us are incapable of leaping tall buildings at a single bound or (without auxiliary power of some kind) traveling faster than a speeding bullet. These things are *impossible* for us—but not *logically* impossible, even in the broad sense.

So there are several senses of necessity and possibility here. There are a number of propositions, furthermore, of which it's difficult to say whether they are or aren't possible in the broadly logical sense; some of these are subjects of philosophical controversy. Is it possible, for example, for a person never to be conscious during his entire existence? Is it possible for a (human) person to exist *disembodied*? If that's possible, is it possible that there be a person who at *no time at all* during his entire existence has a body? Is it possible to see without eyes? These are propositions about whose possibility in that broadly logical sense there is disagreement and dispute.

Now return to set C. . . . What is characteristic of it is the fact that the conjunction of its members—the proposition expressed by the result of putting "and's" between (8), (9), and (10)—is necessarily false. Or we might put it like this: what characterizes set C is the fact that we can get a formally contradictory set by adding a necessarily true proposition— namely (11). Suppose we say that a set is implicitly contradictory if it resembles C in this respect. That is, a set S of propositions is implicitly contradictory if there is a necessary proposition p such that the result of adding p to S is a formally contradictory set. Another way to put it: S is implicitly contradictory if there is some necessarily true proposition p such that by using just the laws of ordinary logic, we can deduce an explicit contradiction from p together with the members of S. And when Mackie says that set A is contradictory, we may properly take him, I think, as holding that it is implicitly contradictory in the explained sense. As he puts it:

> However, the contradiction does not arise immediately; to show it we need some additional premises, or perhaps some quasi-logical rules connecting the terms "good" and "evil" and "omnipotent." These additional principles are that good is opposed to evil, in such a way that a good thing always eliminates evil as far as it can, and that there are no limits to what an omnipotent thing can do. From these it follows that a good omnipotent thing eliminates evil completely, and then the propositions that a good omnipotent thing exists, and that evil exists, are incompatible.[2]

Here Mackie refers to "additional premises"; he also calls them "additional principles" and "quasi-logical rules"; he says we need them to show the contradiction. What he means, I think, is that to get a formally contradictory set we must add some more propositions to set A; and if we aim to show that set A is implicitly contradictory, these propositions must be necessary truths— "quasi-logical rules" as Mackie calls them. The two additional principles he suggests are

    (19)   A good thing always eliminates evil as far as it can

and

(20)   There are no limits to what an omnipotent being can do.

And, of course, if Mackie means to show that set *A* is implicitly contradictory, then he must hold that (19) and (20) are not merely *true* but *necessarily true*.

But, are they? What about (20) first? What does it mean to say that a being is omnipotent? That he is *all-powerful*, or *almighty*, presumably. But are there no limits at all to the power of such a being? Could he create square circles, for example, or married bachelors? Most theologians and theistic philosophers who hold that God is omnipotent, do not hold that He can create round squares or bring it about that He both exists and does not exist. These theologians and philosophers may hold that there are no *nonlogical* limits to what an omnipotent being can do, but they concede that not even an omnipotent being can bring about logically impossible states of affairs or cause necessarily false propositions to be true. Some theists, on the other hand—Martin Luther and Descartes, perhaps—have apparently thought that God's power is unlimited even by the laws of logic. For these theists the question whether set *A* is contradictory will not be of much interest. As theists they believe (1) and (2), and they also, presumably, believe (3). But they remain undisturbed by the claim that (1), (2), and (3) are jointly inconsistent—because, as they say, God can do what is logically impossible. Hence He can bring it about that the members of set *A* are all true, even if that set is contradictory (concentrating very intensely upon this suggestion is likely to make you dizzy). So the theist who thinks that the power of God isn't limited *at all*, not even by the laws of logic, will be unimpressed by Mackie's argument and won't find any difficulty in the contradiction set *A* is alleged to contain. This view is not very popular, however, and for good reason; it is quite incoherent. What the theist typically means when he says that God is omnipotent is not that there are *no* limits to God's power, but at most that there are no nonlogical limits to what He can do; and given this qualification, it is perhaps initially plausible to suppose that (20) is necessarily true.

But what about (19), the proposition that every good thing eliminates every evil state of affairs that it can eliminate? Is that necessarily true? Is it true at all? Suppose, first of all, that your friend Paul unwisely goes for a drive on a wintry day and runs out of gas on a deserted road. The temperature dips to ⁻10°, and a miserably cold wind comes up. You are sitting comfortably at home (twenty-five miles from Paul) roasting chestnuts in a roaring blaze. Your car is in the garage; in the trunk there is the full five-gallon can of gasoline you always keep for emergencies. Paul's discomfort and danger are certainly an evil, and one which you could eliminate. You don't do so. But presumably you don't thereby forfeit your claim to being a "good thing"—you simply didn't know of Paul's plight. And so (19) does not appear to be necessary. It says that every good thing has a certain property—the property of eliminating every evil that it can. And if the case I described is possible—a good person's failing through ignorance to eliminate a certain evil he can eliminate—then (19) is by no means necessarily true.

But perhaps Mackie could sensibly claim that if you *didn't know* about Paul's plight, then in fact you were *not*, at the time in question, able to eliminate the evil in question; and perhaps he'd be right. In any event he could revise (19) to take into account the kind of case I mentioned:

(19a) Every good thing always eliminates every evil that *it knows about* and can eliminate.

{(1), (2), (3), (20), (19a)}, you'll notice is not a formally contradictory set—to get a formal contradiction we must add a proposition specifying that God *knows about* every evil state of affairs. But most theists do believe that God is omniscient or all-knowing; so if this new set—the set that results when we add to set *A* the proposition that God is omniscient—is implicitly contradictory then Mackie should be satisfied and the theist confounded. (And, henceforth, set *A* will be the old set *A* together with the proposition that God is omniscient.)

But is (19a) necessary? Hardly. Suppose you know that Paul is marooned as in the previous example, and you also know another friend is similarly marooned fifty miles in the opposite direction. Suppose, furthermore, that while you can rescue one or the other, you simply can't rescue both. Then each of the two evils is such that it is within your power to eliminate it; and you know about them both. But you can't eliminate both; and you don't forfeit your claim to being a good person by eliminating only one—it wasn't within your power to do more. So the fact that you don't doesn't mean that you are not a good person. Therefore (19a) is false; it is not a necessary truth or even a truth that every good thing eliminates every evil it knows about and can eliminate.

We can see the same thing another way. You've been rock climbing. Still something of a novice, you've acquired a few cuts and bruises by inelegantly using your knees rather than your feet. One of these bruises is fairly painful. You mention it to a physician friend, who predicts the pain will leave of its own accord in a day or two. Meanwhile, he says, there's nothing he can do, short of amputating your leg above the knee, to remove the pain. Now the pain in your knee is an evil state of affairs. All else being equal, it would be better if you had no such pain. And it is within the power of your friend to eliminate this evil state of affairs. Does his failure to do so mean that he is not a good person? Of course not; for he could eliminate this evil state of affairs only by bringing about another, much worse evil. And so it is once again evident that (19a) is false. It is entirely possible that a good person fail to eliminate an evil state of affairs that he knows about and can eliminate. This would take place, if, as in the present example, he couldn't eliminate the evil without bringing about a *greater* evil.

A slightly different kind of case shows the same thing. A really impressive good state of affairs G will *outweigh* a trivial E—that is, the conjunctive state of affairs G *and* E is itself a good state of affairs. And surely a good person would not be obligated to eliminate a given evil if he could do so only by eliminating a good that outweighed it. Therefore (19a) is not necessarily true; it can't be used to show that set A is implicitly contradictory.

These difficulties might suggest another revision of (19); we might try

> (19b) A good being eliminates every evil E that it knows about and that it can eliminate without either bringing about a greater evil or eliminating a good state of affairs that outweighs E.

Is this necessarily true? It takes care of the second of the two difficulties afflicting (19a) but leaves the first untouched. We can see this as follows. First, suppose we say that a being *properly eliminates* an evil state of affairs if it eliminates that evil without either eliminating an outweighing good or bringing about a greater evil. It is then obviously possible that a person find himself in a situation where he could properly eliminate an evil E and could also properly eliminate another evil E', but couldn't properly eliminate them *both*. You're rock climbing again, this time on the dreaded north face of the Grand Teton. You and your party come upon Curt and Bob, two mountaineers stranded 125 feet apart on the face. They untied to reach their cigarettes and then carelessly dropped the rope while lighting up. A violent, dangerous thunderstorm is approaching. You have time to rescue one of the stranded climbers and retreat before the storm hits; if you rescue both, however, you and your party and the two climbers will be caught on the face during the thunderstorm, which will very likely destroy your entire party. In this case you can eliminate one evil (Curt's being stranded on the face) without causing more evil or eliminating a greater good; and you are also able to properly eliminate the other evil (Bob's being thus stranded). But you can't properly eliminate them *both*. And so the fact that you don't rescue Curt, say, even though you could have, doesn't show that you aren't a good person. Here, then, each of the evils is such that you can properly eliminate it; but you can't properly eliminate them both, and hence can't be blamed for failing to eliminate one of them.

So neither (19a) nor (19b) is necessarily true. You may be tempted to reply that the sort of counterexamples offered—examples where someone is able to eliminate an evil A and also able to eliminate a different evil B, but unable to eliminate them both—are irrelevant to the case of a being who, like God, is both omnipotent and omniscient. That is, you may think that if an omnipotent and omniscient being is able to eliminate each of two evils, it follows that he can eliminate them *both*. Perhaps this is so; but it is not strictly to the point. The fact is the counterexamples show that (19a) and (19b) are not necessarily true and hence can't be used to show that set *A* is implicitly inconsistent. What the reply does suggest is that perhaps the atheologian will have more success if he works the properties of omniscience and omnipotence into (19). Perhaps he could say something like

(19c)   An omnipotent and omniscient good being eliminates every evil that it can properly eliminate.

And suppose, for purposes of argument, we concede the necessary truth of (19c). Will it serve Mackie's purposes? Not obviously. For we don't get a set that is formally contradictory by adding (20) and (19c) to set *A*. This set (call it *A'*) contains the following six members:

(1)   God is omnipotent
(2)   God is wholly good
(2')   God is omniscient
(3)   Evil exists
(19c)   An omnipotent and omniscient good being eliminates every evil that it can properly eliminate

and

(20)   There are no nonlogical limits to what an omnipotent being can do.

Now if *A'* were formally contradictory, then from any five of its members we could deduce the denial of the sixth by the laws of ordinary logic. That is, any five would *formally entail* the denial of the sixth. So if *A'* were formally inconsistent, the denial of (3) would be formally entailed by the remaining five. That is, (1), (2), (2'), (19c), and (20) would formally entail

(3')   There is no evil.

But they don't; what they formally entail is not that there is no evil *at all* but only that

(3'')   There is no evil that God can properly eliminate.

So (19c) doesn't really help either—not because it is not necessarily true but because its addition [with (20)] to set *A* does not yield a formally contradictory set. Obviously, what the atheologian must add to get a formally contradictory set is

(21)   If God is omniscient and omnipotent, then he can properly
        eliminate every evil state of affairs.

Suppose we agree that the set consisting in A plus (19c), (20), and (21) is
formally contradictory. So if (19c), (20), and (21) are all necessarily true,
then set A is implicitly contradictory. We've already conceded that (19c)
and (20) are indeed necessary. So we must take a look at (21). Is this
proposition necessarily true?

No. To see this let us ask the following question. Under what
conditions would an omnipotent being be unable to eliminate a certain evil
E without eliminating an outweighing good? Well, suppose that E is
included in some good state of affairs that outweighs it. That is, suppose
there is some good state of affairs G so related to E that it is impossible
that G obtain or be actual and E fail to obtain. (Another way to put this: a
state of affairs S includes S' if the conjunctive state of affairs S *but not* S' is
impossible, or if it is necessary that S' obtains if S does.) Now suppose
that some good state of affairs G includes an evil state of affairs E that it
outweighs. Then not even an omnipotent being could eliminate E without
eliminating G. But *are* there any cases where a good state of affairs
includes, in this sense, an evil that it outweighs?[3] Indeed there are such
states of affairs. To take an artificial example, let's suppose that E is
Paul's suffering from a minor abrasion and G is your being deliriously
happy. The conjunctive state of affairs, G *and* E—the state of affairs that
obtains if and only if both G and E obtain—is then a good state of affairs:
it is better, all else being equal, that you be intensely happy and Paul
suffer a mildly annoying abrasion than that this state of affairs not
obtain. So G *and* E is a good state of affairs. And clearly G *and* E includes E:
obviously it is necessarily true that if you are deliriously happy and Paul
is suffering from an abrasion, then Paul is suffering from an abrasion.

But perhaps you think this example trivial, tricky, slippery, and
irrelevant. If so, take heart; other examples abound. Certain kinds of
values, certain familiar kinds of good states of affairs, can't exist apart
from evil of some sort. For example, there are people who display a sort of
creative moral heroism in the face of suffering and adversity—a heroism
that inspires others and creates a good situation out of a bad one. In a
situation like this the evil, of course, remains evil; but the total state of
affairs—someone's bearing pain magnificently, for example—may be good.
If it is, then the good present must outweigh the evil; otherwise the total
situation would not be *good*. But, of course, it is not possible that such a
good state of affairs obtain unless some evil also obtain. It is a necessary
truth that if someone bears pain magnificently, then someone is in pain.

The conclusion to be drawn, therefore, is that (21) is not necessarily
true. And our discussion thus far shows at the very least that it is no easy
matter to find necessarily true propositions that yield a formally
contradictory set when added to set A.[4] One wonders, therefore, why the

many atheologians who confidently assert that this set is contradictory make no attempt whatever to *show* that it is. For the most part they are content just to *assert* that there is a contradiction here. Even Mackie, who sees that some "additional premises" or "quasi-logical rules" are needed, makes scarcely a beginning towards finding some additional premises that are necessarily true and that together with the members of set *A* formally entail an explicit contradiction.

2. Can We Show That There Is No Inconsistency Here?

To summarize our conclusions so far: although many atheologians claim that the theist is involved in contradiction when he asserts the members of set *A*, this set, obviously, is neither *explicitly* nor *formally* contradictory; the claim, presumably, must be that it is *implicitly* contradictory. To make good this claim the atheologian must find some necessarily true proposition *p* (it could be a conjunction of several propositions) such that the addition of *p* to set *A* yields a set that is formally contradictory. No atheologian has produced even a plausible candidate for this role, and it certainly is not easy to see what such a proposition might be. Now we might think we should simply declare set *A* implicitly consistent on the principle that a proposition (or set) is to be presumed consistent or possible until proven otherwise. This course, however, leads to trouble. The same principle would impel us to declare the atheologian's claim—that set *A* is *in*consistent—possible or consistent. But the claim that a given set of propositions is implicitly contradictory, is itself either necessarily true or necessarily false; so if such a claim is *possible*, it is not necessarily false and is, therefore, true (in fact, necessarily true). If we followed the suggested principle, therefore, we should be obliged to declare set *A* implicitly consistent (since it hasn't been shown to be otherwise), but we should have to say the same thing about the atheologian's claim, since we haven't shown *that* claim to be inconsistent or impossible. The atheologian's claim, furthermore, is necessarily true if it is possible. Accordingly, if we accept the above principle, we shall have to declare set *A* both implicitly consistent and implicitly inconsistent. So all we can say at this point is that set *A* has not been shown to be implicitly inconsistent.

Can we go any further? One way to go on would be to try to *show* that set *A* is implicitly consistent or possible in the broadly logical sense. But what is involved in showing such a thing? Although there are various ways to approach this matter, they all resemble one another in an important respect. They all amount to this: to show that a set *S* is consistent you think of a *possible state of affairs* (it needn't *actually obtain*) which is such that if it were actual, then all of the members of *S* would be true. This procedure is sometimes called *giving a model of S*. For example, you might construct an axiom set and then show that it is consistent by giving a model of it; this is how it was shown that the denial of Euclid's parallel postulate is formally consistent with the rest of his postulates.

There are various special cases of this procedure to fit special circumstances. Suppose, for example, you have a pair of propositions p and q and wish to show them consistent. And suppose we say that a proposition p_1 *entails* a proposition p_2 if it is impossible that p_1 be true and p_2 false— if the conjunctive proposition p_1 and not p_2 is necessarily false. Then one way to show that p is consistent with q is to find some proposition r whose conjunction with p is both possible, in the broadly logical sense, and entails q. A rude and unlettered behaviorist, for example, might hold that thinking is really nothing but movements of the larynx; he might go on to hold that

P   Jones did not move his larynx after April 30

is inconsistent (in the broadly logical sense) with

Q   Jones did some thinking during May.

By way of rebuttal, we might point out that P appears to be consistent with

R   While convalescing from an April 30 laryngotomy, Jones whiled away the idle hours by writing (in May) a splendid paper on Kant's *Critique of Pure Reason*.

So the conjunction of P and R appears to be consistent; but obviously it also entails Q (you can't write even a passable paper on Kant's *Critique of Pure Reason* without doing some thinking); so P and Q are consistent.

We can see that this is a special case of the procedure I mentioned above as follows. This proposition R is consistent with P; so the proposition P and R is possible, describes a possible state of affairs. But P and R entails Q; hence if P *and* R were true, Q would also be true, and hence both P and Q would be true. So this is really a case of producing a possible state of affairs such that, if it were actual, all the members of the set in question (in this case the pair set of P and Q) would be true.

How does this apply to the case before us? As follows, let us conjoin propositions (1), (2), and (2') and henceforth call the result (1):

(1)   God is omniscient, omnipotent, and wholly good.

The problem, then, is to show that (1) and (3) (evil exists) are consistent. This could be done, as we've seen, by finding a proposition r that is consistent with (1) and such that (1) and (r) together entail (3). One proposition that might do the trick is

> (22) God creates a world containing evil and has a good reason for doing so.

If (22) is consistent with (1), then it follows that (1) and (3) (and hence set A) are consistent. Accordingly, one thing some theists have tried is to show that (22) and (1) are consistent.

One can attempt this in at least two ways. On the one hand, we could try to apply the same method again. Conceive of a possible state of affairs such that, if it obtained, an omnipotent, omniscient, and wholly good God would have a good reason for permitting evil. On the other, someone might try to specify *what God's reason is* for permitting evil and try to show, if it is not obvious, that it is a good reason. St. Augustine, for example, one of the greatest and most influential philosopher-theologians of the Christian Church, writes as follows:

> . . . some people see with perfect truth that a creature is better if, while possessing free will, it remains always fixed upon God and never sins; then, reflecting on men's sins, they are grieved, not because they continue to sin, but because they were created. They say: He should have made us such that we never willed to sin, but always to enjoy the unchangeable truth.
>
> They should not lament or be angry. God has not compelled men to sin just because He created them and gave them the power to choose between sinning and not sinning. There are angels who have never sinned and never will sin.
>
> Such is the generosity of God's goodness that He has not refrained from creating even that creature which He foreknew would not only sin, but remain in the will to sin. As a runaway horse is better than a stone which does not run away because it lacks self-movement and sense perception, so the creature is more excellent which sins by free will than that which does not sin only because it has no free will.[5]

In broadest terms Augustine claims that God could create a better, more perfect universe by permitting evil than He could by refusing to do so:

> Neither the sins nor the misery are necessary to the perfection of the universe, but souls as such are necessary, which have the power to sin if they so will, and become miserable if they sin. If misery persisted after their sins had been abolished, or if there were misery before there were sins, then it might be right to say that the order and government of the universe were at fault. Again, if there were sins but

no consequent misery, that order is equally dishonored by lack of equity.[6]

Augustine tries to tell us *what God's reason is* for permitting evil. At bottom, he says, it's that God can create a more perfect universe by permitting evil. A really top-notch universe requires the existence of free, rational, and moral agents; and some of the free creatures He created went wrong. But the universe with the free creatures it contains and the evil they commit is better than it would have been had it contained neither the free creatures nor this evil. Such an attempt to specify God's reason for permitting evil is what I earlier called a *theodicy*; in the words of John Milton it is an attempt to "justify the ways of God to man," to show that God is just in permitting evil. Augustine's kind of theodicy might be called a Free Will Theodicy, since the idea of rational creatures with free will plays such a prominent role in it.

A theodicist, then, attempts to tell us why God permits evil. Quite distinct from a Free Will Theodicy is what I shall call a Free Will Defense. Here the aim is not to say what God's reason *is*, but at most what God's reason *might possibly be*. We could put the difference like this. The Free Will Theodicist and Free Will Defender are both trying to show that (1) is consistent with (22), and of course if so, then set A is consistent. The Free Will Theodicist tries to do this by finding some proposition r which in conjunction with (1) entails (22); he claims, furthermore, that this proposition is *true*, not just consistent with (1). He tries to tell us what God's reason for permitting evil *really is*. The Free Will Defender, on the other hand, though he also tries to find a proposition r that is consistent with (1) and in conjunction with it entails (22), does *not* claim to know or even believe that r is true. And here, of course, he is perfectly within his rights. His aim is to show that (1) is consistent with (22); all he need do then is find an r that is consistent with (1) and such that (1) and (r) entail (22); whether r is *true* is quite beside the point.

So there is a significant difference between a Free Will Theodicy and a Free Will Defense. The latter is sufficient (if successful) to show that set A is consistent; in a way a Free Will Theodicy goes beyond what is required. On the other hand, a theodicy would be much more satisfying, if possible to achieve. No doubt the theist would rather know what God's reason *is* for permitting evil than simply that it's possible that He has a good one. But in the present context (that of investigating the consistency of set A), the latter is all that's needed. Neither a defense or a theodicy, of course, gives any hint to what God's reason for some *specific* evil—the death or suffering of someone close to you, for example—might be. And there is still another function—a sort of pastoral function[7]—in the neighborhood that neither serves. Confronted with evil in his own life or suddenly coming to realize more clearly than before the *extent* and *magnitude* of evil, a believer in God may undergo a crisis of faith. He may be tempted to follow the advice of Job's "friends"; he may be tempted to "curse God and die." Neither a Free Will Defense nor a Free Will Theodicy is designed to be of much help or comfort to one suffering from such a storm in the soul (although in a specific case, of course, one or the other could prove useful). Neither is to be thought of first of all as a means of pastoral counseling. Probably neither will enable someone to find peace with himself and with God in the face of the evil the world contains. But then, of course, neither is intended for that purpose.

3. The Free Will Defense

In what follows I shall focus attention upon the Free Will Defense. I shall examine it more closely, state it more exactly, and consider objections to it; and I shall argue that in the end it is successful. Earlier we saw that among good states of affairs there are some that not even God can bring about without bringing about evil: those goods, namely, that *entail* or *include* evil states of affairs. The Free Will Defense can be looked upon as an effort to show that there may be a very different kind of good that God can't bring about without permitting evil. These are good states of affairs that don't include evil; they do not entail the existence of any evil whatever; nonetheless God Himself can't bring them about without permitting evil.

So how does the Free Will Defense work? And what does the Free Will Defender mean when he says that people are or may be free? What is relevant to the Free Will Defense is the idea of *being free with respect to an action*. If a person is free with respect to a given action, then he is free to perform that action and free to refrain from performing it; no antecedent conditions and/or causal laws determine that he will perform the action, or that he won't. It is within his power, at the time in question, to take or perform the action and within his power to refrain from it. Freedom so conceived is not to be confused with unpredictability. You might be able to predict what you will do in a given situation even if you are free, in that situation, to do something else. If I know you well, I may be able to predict what action you will take in response to a certain set of conditions; it does not follow that you are not free with respect to that action. Secondly, I shall say that an action is *morally significant*, for a given person, if it would be wrong for him to perform the action but right to refrain or *vice versa*. Keeping a promise, for example, would ordinarily be morally significant for a person, as would refusing induction into the army. On the other hand, having Cheerios for breakfast (instead of Wheaties) would not normally be morally significant. Further, suppose we say that a person is *significantly free*, on a given occasion, if he is then free with respect to a morally significant action. And finally we must distinguish between *moral evil* and *natural evil*. The former is evil that results from free human activity; natural evil is any other kind of evil.[8]

Given these definitions and distinctions, we can make a preliminary statement of the Free Will Defense as follows. A world containing creatures who are significantly free (and freely perform more good than evil actions) is more valuable, all else being equal, than a world containing no free creatures at all. Now God can create free creatures, but He can't *cause* or *determine* them to do only what is right. For if He does so, then they aren't significantly free after all; they do not do what is right *freely*. To create creatures capable of *moral good*, therefore, He must create creatures capable of moral evil; and He can't give these creatures the freedom to perform evil and at the same time prevent them from doing so. As it turned out, sadly enough, some of the free creatures God created went wrong in the exercise of their freedom; this is the source of moral evil. The fact that free creatures sometimes go wrong, however, counts neither against God's omnipotence nor against His goodness; for He could have forestalled the occurrence of moral evil only by removing the possibility of moral good.

I said earlier that the Free Will Defender tries to find a proposition that is consistent with

(1)   God is omniscient, omnipotent, and wholly good

and together with (1) entails that there is evil. According to the Free Will Defense, we must find this proposition somewhere in the above story. The heart of the Free Will Defense is the claim that it is *possible* that God could not have created a universe containing moral good (or as much moral good as this world contains) without creating one that also contained moral evil. And if so, then it is possible that God has a good reason for creating a world containing evil.

Now this defense has met with several kinds of objections. For example, some philosophers say that *causal determinism* and *freedom*, contrary to what we might have thought, are not really incompatible.[9] But if so, then God could have created free creatures who were free, and free to do what is wrong, but nevertheless were causally determined to do only what is right. Thus He could have created creatures who were free to do what was wrong, while nevertheless preventing them from ever performing any wrong actions—simply seeing to it that they were causally determined to do only what is right. Of course this contradicts the Free Will Defense, according to which there is inconsistency in supposing that God determines free creatures to do only what is right. But is it really possible that all of a person's actions are causally determined while some of them are free? How could that be so? According to one version of the doctrine in question, to say that George acts freely on a given occasion is to say only this: *if George had chosen to do otherwise, he would have done otherwise.* Now George's action *A* is causally determined if some event *E*—some event beyond his control—has already occurred, where the state of affairs consisting in *E*'s occurrence conjoined with George's *refraining* from performing *A*, is a causally impossible state of affairs. Then one can consistently hold both that all of a man's actions are causally determined and that some of them are free in the above sense. For suppose that all of a man's actions are causally determined and that he *couldn't*, on any occasion, have made any choice or performed any action different from the ones he did make and perform. It could still be true that if he *had* chosen to do otherwise, he would have done otherwise. Granted, he couldn't have chosen to do otherwise; but this is consistent with saying that *if* he had, things would have gone differently.

This objection to the Free Will Defense seems utterly implausible. One might as well claim that being in jail doesn't really limit one's freedom on the grounds that if one were *not* in jail, he'd be free to come and go as he pleased. So I shall say no more about this objection here.[10]

A second objection is more formidable. In essence it goes like this. Surely it is possible to do only what is right, even if one is free to do wrong. It is *possible*, in that broadly logical sense, that there would be a world containing free creatures who always do what is right. There is certainly no *contradiction* or *inconsistency* in this idea. But God is omnipotent; his power has no nonlogical limitations. So if it's possible that there be a world containing creatures who are free to do what is wrong but never in fact do so, then it follows that an omnipotent God could create such a world. If so, however, the Free Will Defense must be mistaken in its insistence upon the possibility that God is omnipotent but unable to create a world containing moral good without permitting moral evil. J. L. Mackie . . . states this objection:

> If God has made men such that in their free choices they sometimes prefer what is good and sometimes what is evil, why could he not have made men such that they always freely choose the good? If there is no logical impossibility in a man's freely choosing the good on one, or on several occasions, there cannot be a logical impossibility in his freely choosing the good on every occasion. God was not, then, faced with a choice between making innocent automata and making beings who, in acting freely, would sometimes go wrong; there was open to him the obviously better possibility of making beings who would act freely but always go right. Clearly, his failure to avail himself of this possibility is inconsistent with his being both omnipotent and wholly good.[11]

Now what, exactly, is Mackie's point here? This. According to the Free Will Defense, it is possible both that God is omnipotent and that He was unable to create a world containing moral good without creating one containing moral evil. But, replies Mackie, this limitation on His power to create is inconsistent with God's omnipotence. For surely it's *possible* that there be a world containing perfectly virtuous persons—persons who are significantly free but always do what is right. Surely there are *possible worlds* that contain moral good but no moral evil. But God, if He is omnipotent, can create any possible world He chooses. So it is *not* possible, contrary to the Free Will Defense, both that God is omnipotent and that He could create a world containing moral good only by creating one containing moral evil. If He is omnipotent, the only limitations of His power are *logical* limitations; in which case there are no possible worlds He could not have created.

This is a subtle and important point. According to the great German philosopher G. W. Leibniz, *this* world, the actual world, must be the best of all possible worlds. His reasoning goes as follows. Before God created anything at all, He was confronted with an enormous range of choices; He could create or bring into actuality any of the myriads of different possible worlds. Being perfectly good, He must have chosen to create the best world He could; being omnipotent, He was able to create any possible world He pleased. He must, therefore, have chosen the best of all possible worlds; and hence *this* world, the one He did create, must be the best possible. Now Mackie, of course, agrees with Leibniz that God, if omnipotent, could have created any world He pleased and would have created the best world he could. But while Leibniz draws the conclusion that this world, despite appearances, must be the best possible, Mackie concludes instead that there is no omnipotent, wholly good God. For, he says, it is obvious enough that this present world is not the best of all possible worlds.

The Free Will Defender disagrees with both Leibniz and Mackie. In the first place, he might say, what is the reason for supposing that there *is* such a thing as the best of all possible worlds? No matter how marvelous a world is—containing no matter how many persons enjoying unalloyed bliss—isn't it possible that there be an even better world containing even more persons enjoying even more unalloyed bliss? But what is really characteristic and central to the Free Will Defense is the claim that God, though omnipotent, could not have actualized just any possible world He pleased.

4. Was It Within God's Power to Create Any Possible World He Pleased?

This is indeed the crucial question for the Free Will Defense. If we wish to discuss it with insight and authority, we shall have to look into the idea of *possible worlds*. And a sensible first question is this: what sort of thing is a possible world? The basic idea is that a possible world is a *way things could have been*; it is a *state of affairs* of some kind. Earlier we spoke of states of affairs, in particular of good and evil states of affairs. Suppose we look at this idea in more detail. What sort of thing is a state of affairs? The following would be examples:

Nixon's having won the 1972 election
7 + 5's being equal to 12
All men's being mortal

and

Gary, Indiana's, having a really nasty pollution problem.

These are *actual* states of affairs: states of affairs that do in fact *obtain*. And corresponding to each such actual state of affairs there is a true proposition—in the above cases, the corresponding propositions would be *Nixon won the 1972 presidential election, 7 + 5 is equal to 12, all men are mortal,* and *Gary, Indiana, has a really nasty pollution problem.* A proposition *p corresponds* to a state of affairs *s,* in this sense, if it is impossible that *p* be true and *s* fail to obtain and impossible that *s* obtain and *p* fail to be true.

But just as there are false propositions, so there are states of affairs that do *not* obtain or are *not* actual. *Kissinger's having swum the Atlantic* and *Hubert Horatio Humphrey's having run a mile in four minutes* would be examples. Some states of affairs that do not obtain are *impossible*: e.g. *Hubert's having drawn a square circle, 7 + 5's being equal to 75,* and *Agnew's having a brother who was an only child.* The propositions corresponding to these states of affairs, of course, are necessarily false. So there are states of affairs that *obtain* or *are actual* and also states of affairs that don't obtain. Among the latter some are *impossible* and others are *possible*. And a possible world is a possible state of affairs. Of course not every possible state of affairs is a possible world; *Hubert's having run a mile in four minutes* is a possible state of affairs but not a possible world. No doubt it is an *element* of many possible worlds, but it isn't itself inclusive enough to be one. To be a possible world, a state of affairs must be very large—so large as to be *complete* or *maximal.*

To get at this idea of completeness we need a couple of definitions. As we have already seen . . . a state of affairs *A includes* a state of affairs *B* if it is not possible that *A* obtain and *B* not obtain or if the conjunctive state of affairs *A but not B*—the state of affairs that obtains if and only if *A* obtains and *B* does not—is not possible. For example, *Jim Whittaker's being the first American to climb Mt. Everest* includes *Jim Whittaker's being an American.* It also includes *Mt. Everest's being climbed, something's being climbed, no American's having climbed Everest before Whittaker did,* and the like. *Inclusion* among states of affairs is like *entailment* among propositions; and where a state of affairs *A* includes a state of affairs *B*, the proposition corresponding to *A* entails the one corresponding to *B*. Accordingly, *Jim Whittaker is the first American to climb Everest* entails *Mt. Everest has been climbed, something has been climbed,* and *no American climbed Everest before Whittaker did.* Now suppose we say further that a state of affairs *A* precludes a state of affairs *B* if it is not possible that both obtain, or if the conjunctive state of affairs *A and B* is impossible. Thus *Whittaker's being the first American to climb Mt. Everest* precludes *Luther Jerstad's being the first American to climb Everest,* as well as *Whittaker's never having climbed any mountains.* If *A* precludes *B*, then *A*'s corresponding proposition entails the denial of the one corresponding to *B*. Still further, let's say that the *complement* of a state of affairs is the state of affairs that obtains just in case *A* does not obtain. [Or we might say that the complement (call it -*A*) of *A* is the state of affairs corresponding to the *denial* or *negation* of the proposition corresponding to *A*.] Given these definitions, we can say what it is for a state of affairs to be *complete*: *A* is a complete state of affairs if and only if for every state of affairs *B*, either *A includes B or A precludes B*. (We could express the same thing by saying that if *A* is a complete state of affairs, then for every state of affairs *B*, either *A* includes *B* or *A* includes -*B*, the complement of *B*.) And now we are able to say what a possible world is: a possible world is any possible state of affairs that is complete. If *A* is a possible world, then it says something about everything; every state of affairs *S* is either included in or precluded by it.

Corresponding to each possible world *W*, furthermore, there is a set of propositions that I'll call *the book on W*. A proposition is in the book on *W* just in case the state of affairs to which it corresponds is included in *W*. Or we might express it like this. Suppose we say that a proposition *P is true in a world W* if and only if *P would have been true if W had been actual*—if and only if, that is, it is not possible that *W* be actual and *P* be false. Then the book on *W* is the set of propositions true in *W*. Like possible worlds, books are complete; if *B* is a book, then for any proposition *P*, either *P* or the denial of *P* will be a member of *B*. A book is a *maximal consistent set* of propositions; it is so large that the addition of another proposition to it always yields an explicitly inconsistent set.

Of course, for each possible world there is exactly one book corresponding to it (that is, for a given world *W* there is just one book *B* such that each member of *B* is true in *W*); and for each book there is just one world to which it corresponds. So every world has its book.

It should be obvious that exactly one possible world is actual. At *least* one must be, since the set of true propositions is a maximal consistent set and hence a book. But then it corresponds to a possible world, and the possible world corresponding to this set of propositions (since it's the set of *true* propositions) will be actual. On the other hand there is at *most* one actual world. For suppose there were two: *W* and *W'*. These worlds cannot include all the very same states of affairs; if they did, they would be the very same world. So there must be at least one state of affairs S such that W includes S and W' does not. But a possible world is maximal; W', therefore, includes the complement S of S. So if both W and W' were actual, as we have supposed, then both S and $-S$ would be actual—which is impossible. So there can't be more than one possible world that is actual.

Leibniz pointed out that a proposition p is necessary if it is true in every possible world. We may add that p is possible if it is true in one world and impossible if true in none. Furthermore, p *entails* q if there is no possible world in which p is true and q is false, and p *is consistent with* q if there is at least one world in which both p and q are true.

A further feature of possible worlds is that people (and other things) *exist* in them. Each of us exists in the actual world, obviously; but a person also exists in many worlds distinct from the actual world. It would be a mistake, of course, to think of all of these worlds as somehow "going on" at the same time, with the same person reduplicated through these worlds and actually existing in a lot of different ways. This is not what is meant by saying that the same person exists in different possible worlds. What is meant, instead, is this: a person Paul exists in each of those possible worlds W which is such that, if W *had been actual*, Paul would have existed—actually existed. Suppose Paul had been an inch taller than he is, or a better tennis player. Then the world that does in fact obtain would not have been actual; some other world—W', let's say—would have obtained instead. If W' had been actual, Paul would have existed; so Paul exists in W'. (Of course there are still other possible worlds in which Paul does not exist—worlds, for example, in which there are no people at all.) Accordingly, when we say that Paul exists in a world W, what we mean is that Paul *would have* existed had W been actual. Or we could put it like this: Paul exists in each world W that includes the state of affairs consisting in Paul's existence. We can put this still more simply by saying that Paul exists in those worlds whose books contain the proposition Paul exists.

But isn't there a problem here? *Many* people are named "Paul": Paul the apostle, Paul J. Zwier, John Paul Jones, and many other famous Pauls. So who goes with "Paul exists"? Which Paul? The answer has to do with the fact that books contain *propositions*—not sentences. They contain the sort of thing sentences are used to express and assert. And the same sentence—"Aristotle is wise," for example—can be used to express many different propositions. When Plato used it, he asserted a proposition predicating wisdom of his famous pupil; when Jackie Onassis uses it, she asserts a proposition predicating wisdom of her wealthy husband. These are distinct propositions (we might even think they differ in truth value); but they are expressed by the same sentence. Normally (but not always) we don't have much trouble determining which of the several propositions expressed by a given sentence is relevant in the context at hand. So in this case a given person, Paul, exists in a world W if and only if W's book contains the proposition that says that *he*—that particular person—exists. The fact that the sentence we use to express this proposition can also be used to express *other* propositions is not relevant.

After this excursion into the nature of books and worlds we can return to our question. Could God have created just any world He chose? Before addressing the question, however, we must note that God does not, strictly speaking, *create* any possible worlds or states of affairs at all. What He creates are the heavens and the earth and all that they contain. But He has not created states of affairs. There are, for example, the state of affairs consisting in God's existence and the state of affairs consisting in His nonexistence. That is, there is such a thing as the state of affairs consisting in the existence of God, and there is also such a thing as the state of affairs consisting in the nonexistence of God, just as there are the two propositions *God exists* and *God does not exist*. The theist believes that the first state of affairs is actual and the first proposition true, the atheist believes that the second state of affairs is actual and the second proposition true. But, of course, both propositions *exist*, even though just one is true. Similarly, there are two states of affairs here, just one of which is actual. So both states of affairs *exist*, but only one *obtains*. And God has not created either one of them since there never was a time at which either did not exist. Nor has He created the state of affairs consisting in the earth's existence; there was a time when *the earth* did not exist, but none when the state of affairs consisting in the earth's existence didn't exist. Indeed, God did not bring into existence any states of *affairs* at all. What He did was to perform actions of a certain sort—creating the heavens and the earth, for example—which resulted in the *actuality* of certain states of affairs. God *actualizes* states of affairs. He actualizes the possible world that does in fact obtain; He does not create it. And while He has created Socrates , He did not create the state of affairs consisting in Socrates' existence.[12]

Bearing this in mind, let's finally return to our question. Is the atheologian right in holding that if God is omnipotent, then he could have actualized or created any possible world He pleased? Not obviously. First, we must ask ourselves whether God is a *necessary* or a *contingent* being. A *necessary* being is one that exists in every possible world—one that would have existed no matter which possible world had been actual; a contingent being exists only in some possible worlds. Now if God is not a necessary being (and many, perhaps most, theists think that He is not), then clearly enough there will be many possible worlds He could not have actualized—all those, for example, in which He does not exist. Clearly, God could not have created a world in which He doesn't even exist.

So, if God is a contingent being then there are many possible worlds beyond His power to create. But this is really irrelevant to our present concerns. For perhaps the atheologian can maintain his case if he revises his claim to avoid this difficulty; perhaps he will say something like this: if God is omnipotent, then He could have actualized any of those possible worlds *in which He exists*. So if He exists and is omnipotent, He could have actualized (contrary to the Free Will Defense) any of those possible worlds in which He exists and in which there exist free creatures who do no wrong. He could have actualized worlds containing moral good but no moral evil. Is this correct?

Let's begin with a trivial example. You and Paul have just returned from an Australian hunting expedition: your quarry was the elusive double-wattled cassowary. Paul captured an aardvark, mistaking it for a cassowary. The creature's disarming ways have won it a place in Paul's heart; he is deeply attached to it. Upon your return to the States you offer Paul $500 for his aardvark, only to be rudely turned down. Later you ask yourself, "What would he have done if I'd offered him $700?" Now what is it, exactly, that you are asking? What you're really asking in a way is whether, under a *specific set of conditions*, Paul would have sold it. These conditions include your having offered him $700 rather than $500 for the aardvark, everything else being as much as possible like the conditions that did in fact obtain. Let S' be this set of conditions or state of affairs. S' includes the state of affairs consisting in your offering Paul $700 (instead of the $500 you did offer him); of course it does not include his *accepting* your offer, and it does not include his *rejecting* it; for the rest, the conditions it includes are just like the ones that did obtain in the actual world. So, for example, S' includes Paul's being free to accept the offer and free to refrain; and if in fact the going rate for an aardvark was $650, then S' includes the state of affairs consisting in the going rate's being $650. So we might put your question by asking which of the following conditionals is true:

(23) If the state of affairs S' had obtained, Paul would have accepted the offer

(24) If the state of affairs S' had obtained, Paul would not have accepted the offer.

It seems clear that at least one of these conditionals is true, but naturally they can't both be; so exactly one is.

Now since S' includes neither Paul's accepting the offer not his rejecting it, the antecedent of (23) and (24) does not entail the consequent of either. That is,

(25) S' obtains

does not entail either

(26) Paul accepts the offer

or

(27)   Paul does not accept the offer.

So there are possible worlds in which both (25) and (26) are true, and other possible worlds in which both (25) and (27) are true.

We are now in a position to grasp an important fact. Either (23) or (24) is in fact true; and either way there are possible worlds God could not have actualized. Suppose, first of all, that (23) is true. Then it was beyond the power of God to create a world in which (1) Paul is free to sell his aardvark and free to refrain, and in which the other states of affairs included in S' obtain, and (2) Paul does not sell. That is, it was beyond His power to create a world in which (25) and (27) are both true. There is at least one possible world like this, but God, despite His omnipotence, could not have brought about its actuality. For let W be such a world. To actualize W, God must bring it about that Paul is free with respect to this action, and that the other states of affairs included in S' obtain. But (23), as we are supposing, is true; so if God had actualized S' and left Paul *free* with respect to this action, he would have sold: in which case W would not have been actual. If, on the other hand, God had *brought it about* that Paul didn't sell or had *caused him* to refrain from selling, then Paul would not have been free with respect to this action; then S' would not have been actual (since S' includes Paul's being free with respect to it), and W would not have been actual since W includes S'.

Of course if it is (24) rather than (23) that is true, then another class of worlds was beyond God's power to actualize—those, namely, in which S' obtains and Paul *sells* his aardvark. These are the worlds in which both (25) and (26) are true. But either (23) or (24) is true. Therefore, there are possible worlds God could not have actualized. If we consider whether or not God could have created a world in which, let's say, both (25) and (26) are true, we see that the answer depends upon a peculiar kind of fact; it depends upon what Paul would have freely chosen to do in a certain situation. So there are any number of possible worlds such that it is partly up to Paul whether God can create them.[13]

That was a past tense example. Perhaps it would be useful to consider a future tense case, since this might seem to correspond more closely to God's situation in choosing a possible world to actualize. At some time t in the near future Maurice will be free with respect to some insignificant action—having freeze-dried oatmeal for breakfast, let's say. That is, at time t Maurice will be free to have oatmeal but also free to take something else—shredded wheat, perhaps. Next, suppose we consider S', a state of affairs that is included in the actual world and includes Maurice's being free with respect to taking oatmeal at time t. That is, S' includes Maurice's being free at time t to take oatmeal and free to reject it. S' does not include Maurice's taking oatmeal, however; nor does it include his rejecting it. For the rest S' is as much as possible like the actual world. In particular there are many conditions that do in fact hold at time t and are *relevant* to his choice—such conditions, for example, as the fact that he hasn't had oatmeal lately, that his wife will be annoyed if he rejects it, and the like; and S' includes each of these conditions. Now God no doubt knows what Maurice will do at time t, if S obtains; He knows which action Maurice would freely perform if S were to be actual. That is, God knows that one of the following conditionals is true:

(28)   If S' were to obtain, Maurice will freely take the oatmeal

or

(29)   If S' were to obtain, Maurice will freely reject it.

We may not know which of these is true, and Maurice himself may not know; but presumably God does.

So either God knows that (28) is true, or else He knows that (29) is. Let's suppose it is (28). Then there is a possible world that God, though omnipotent, cannot create. For consider a possible world W' that shares S' with the actual world (which for ease of reference I'll name "Kronos") and in which Maurice does *not* take oatmeal. (We know there is such a world, since S' does not include Maurice's taking the oatmeal.) S' obtains in W' just as it does in Kronos. Indeed, everything in W' is just as it is in Kronos up to time t. But whereas in Kronos Maurice takes oatmeal at time t, in W' he does not. Now W' is a perfectly possible world; but it is not within God's power to create it or bring about its actuality. For to do so He must actualize S'. But (28) is in fact true. So if God actualizes S' (as He must to create W') and leaves Maurice free with respect to the action in question, then he will take the oatmeal; and then, of course, W' will not be actual. If, on the other hand, God causes Maurice to *refrain* from taking the oatmeal, then he is not *free* to take it. That means, once again, that W' is not actual; for in W' Maurice is free to take the oatmeal (even if he doesn't do so). So if (28) is true, then this world W' is one that God can't actualize, it is not within His power to actualize it even though He is omnipotent and it is a possible world.

Of course, if it is (29) that is true, we get a similar result; then too there are possible worlds that God can't actualize. These would be worlds which share S' with Kronos and in which Maurice does take oatmeal. But either (28) or (29) is true; so either way there is a possible world that God can't create. If we consider a world in which S' obtains and in which Maurice freely chooses oatmeal at time t, we see that whether or not it is within God's power to actualize it depends upon what Maurice would do if he were free in a certain situation. Accordingly, there are any number of possible worlds such that it is partly up to Maurice whether or not God can actualize them. It is, of course, up to God whether or not to create Maurice and also up to God whether or not to make him free with respect to the action of taking oatmeal at time t. (God could, if He chose, cause him to succumb to the dreaded *equine obsession*, a condition shared by some people and most horses, whose victims find it *psychologically impossible* to refuse oats or oat products.) But if He creates Maurice and creates him free with respect to this action, then whether or not he actually performs the action is up to Maurice—not God.[14]

Now we can return to the Free Will Defense and the problem of evil. The Free Will Defender, you recall, insists on the possibility that it is not within God's power to create a world containing moral good without creating one containing moral evil. His atheological opponent—Mackie, for example—agrees with Leibniz in insisting that *if* (as the theist holds) God is omnipotent, then it *follows* that He could have created any possible world He pleased. We now see that this contention—call it "Leibniz' Lapse"—is a mistake. The atheologian is right in holding that there are many possible worlds containing moral good but no moral evil; his mistake lies in endorsing Leibniz' Lapse. So one of his premises—that God, if omnipotent, could have actualized just any world He pleased—is false.

5. Could God Have Created a World Containing Moral Good but No Moral Evil?

Now suppose we recapitulate the logic of the situation. The Free Will Defender claims that the following is possible:

(30)   God is omnipotent, and it was not within His power to create a world containing moral good but no moral evil.

By way of retort the atheologian insists that there are possible worlds containing moral good but no moral evil. He adds that an omnipotent being could have actualized any possible world he chose. So if God is omnipotent, it follows that He could have actualized a world containing moral good but no moral evil, hence (30), contrary to the Free Will Defender's claim, is not possible. What we have seen so far is that his second premise—Leibniz' Lapse—is false.

Of course, this does not settle the issue in the Free Will Defender's favor. Leibniz' Lapse (appropriately enough for a lapse) is false; but this doesn't show that (30) is possible. To show this latter we must demonstrate the possibility that among the worlds God could not have actualized are all the worlds containing moral good but no moral evil. How can we approach this question?

Instead of choosing oatmeal for breakfast or selling an aardvark, suppose we think about a morally significant action such as taking a bribe.

Curley Smith, the mayor of Boston, is opposed to the proposed freeway route; it would require destruction of the Old North Church along with some other antiquated and structurally unsound buildings. L. B. Smedes, the director of highways, asks him whether he'd drop his opposition for $1 million. "Of course," he replies. "Would you do it for $2?" asks Smedes. "What do you take me for?" comes the indignant reply. "That's already established," smirks Smedes; "all that remains is to nail down your price." Smedes then offers him a bribe of $35,000; unwilling to break with the fine old traditions of Bay State politics, Curley accepts. Smedes then spends a sleepless night wondering whether he could have bought Curley for $20,000.

Now suppose we assume that Curley was free with respect to the action of taking the bribe—free to take it and free to refuse. And suppose, furthermore, that he would have taken it. That is, let us suppose that

(31)   If Smedes had offered Curley a bribe of $20,000, he would have accepted it.

If (31) is true, then there is a state of affairs S' that (1) includes Curley's being offered a bribe of $20,000; (2) does not include either his accepting the bribe or his rejecting it; and (3) is otherwise as much as possible like the actual world. Just to make sure S' includes every relevant circumstance, let us suppose that it is a *maximal world segment*. That is, add to S' any state of affairs compatible with but not included in it, and the result will be an entire possible world. We could think of it roughly like this: S' is included in at least one world W in which Curley takes the bribe and in at least one world W' in which he rejects it. If S' is a maximal world segment, then S' is what remains of W when *Curley's taking the bribe* is deleted; it is also what remains of W' when *Curley's rejecting the bribe* is detected. More exactly, if S' is a maximal world segment, then every possible state of affairs that includes S', but isn't included by S', is a possible world. So if (31) is true, then there is a maximal world segment S' that (1) includes Curley's being offered a bribe of 520,000; (2) does not include either his accepting the bribe or his rejecting it; (3) is otherwise as much as possible like the actual world—in particular, it includes Curley's being free with respect to the bribe, and (4) is such that if it were actual then Curley would have taken the bribe. That is,

(32)   if S' were actual, Curley would have accepted the bribe is true.

Now, of course, there is at least one possible world W' in which S' is actual and Curley does not take the bribe. But God could not have created W'; to do so, He would have been obliged to actualize S', leaving Curley free with respect to the action of taking the bribe. But under these conditions Curley, as (32) assures us, would have accepted the bribe, so that the world thus created would not have been S'.

Curley, as we see, is not above a bit of Watergating. But there may be worse to come. Of course, there are possible worlds in which he is significantly free (i.e., free with respect to a morally significant action) and never does what is wrong. But the sad truth about Curley may be this. Consider W', any of these worlds: in W' Curley is significantly free, so in W' there are some actions that are morally significant for him and with respect to which he is free. But at least one of these actions—call it A—has the following peculiar property. There is a maximal world segment S' that obtains in W' and is such that (1) S' includes Curley's being free re A but neither his performing A nor his refraining from A; (2) S' is otherwise as much as possible like W'; and (3) if S' had been actual, Curley would have gone wrong with respect to A.[15] (Notice that this third condition holds in fact, in the actual world; it does not hold in that world W'.)

This means, of course, that God could not have actualized W'. For to do so He'd have been obliged to bring it about that S' is actual; but then Curley would go wrong with respect to A. Since in W' he always does what is right, the world thus actualized would not be W'. On the other hand, if God causes Curley to go right with respect to A or *brings it about that* he does so, then Curley isn't free with respect to A; and so once more it isn't W' that is actual. Accordingly God cannot create W'. But W' was just any of the worlds in which Curley is significantly free but always does only what is right. It therefore follows that it was not within God's power to create a world in which Curley produces moral good but no moral evil. Every world God can actualize is such that if Curley is significantly free in it, he takes at least one wrong action.

Obviously Curley is in serious trouble. I shall call the malady from which he suffers transworld depravity. (I leave as homework the problem of comparing transworld depravity with what Calvinists call "total depravity.") By way of explicit definition:

(33) A person P *suffers from transworld depravity* if and only if the following holds: for every world W such that P is significantly free in W and P does only what is right in W, there is an action A and a maximal world segment S' such that

(1) S' includes A's being morally significant for P
(2) S' includes P's being free with respect to A
(3) S' is included in W and includes neither P's performing A nor P's refraining from performing A

and

(4) If S' were actual, P would go wrong with respect to A.

(In thinking about this definition, remember that (4) is to be true in fact, in the actual world—not in that world *W*.)

What is important about the idea of transworld depravity is that if a person suffers from it, then it wasn't within God's power to actualize any world in which that person is significantly free but does no wrong—that is, a world in which he produces moral good but no moral evil.

We have been here considering a crucial contention of the Free Will Defender: the contention, namely, that

(30)   God is omnipotent, and it was not within His power to create a world containing moral good but no moral evil.

How is transworld depravity relevant to this? As follows. Obviously it is possible that there be persons who suffer from transworld depravity. More generally, it is possible that everybody suffers from it. And if this possibility were actual, then God, though omnipotent, could not have created any of the possible worlds containing just the persons who do in fact exist, and containing moral good but no moral evil. For to do so He'd have to create persons who were significantly free (otherwise there would be no moral good) but suffered from transworld depravity. Such persons go wrong with respect to at least one action in any world God could have actualized and in which they are free with respect to morally significant actions; so the price for creating a world in which they produce moral good is creating one in which they also produce moral evil.

Endnotes

*Reprinted from *God, Freedom, and Evil* by Alvin Plantinga (New York: Harper & Row, 1974). Reprinted by permission of the author. Footnotes edited. The numbering of the sections has been changed because the first section in the book was omitted which deals with Hume's account of the theist's problem of evil.

1 John Mackie, "Evil and Omnipotence," in *The Philosophy of Religion*, ed. Basil Mitchell (London: Oxford University Press, 1971), p. 92. [See previous reading.]

2 Ibid., p. 93. [*Philosophy of Religion: Selected Readings*, Second Edition, p. 224.]

3 More simply, the question is really just whether any good state of affairs includes an evil; a little reflection reveals that no good state of affairs can include an evil that it does *not* outweigh.

4 In Plantinga, *God and Other Minds* (Ithaca, N.Y.: Cornell University Press, 1967), chap.5, I explore further the project of finding such propositions.

5 *The Problem of Free Choice*, Vol. 22 of *Ancient Christian Writers* (Westminster, Md.: The Newman Press, 1955), bk. 2, pp. 14-15.

6 Ibid., bk. 3, p. 9.

7 I am indebted to Henry Schuurman (in conversation) for helpful discussion of the difference between this pastoral function and those served by a theodicy or a defense.

8 This distinction is not very precise (how, exactly, are we to construe "results from"?), but perhaps it will serve our present purposes.

9 See, for example, A. Flew, "Divine Omnipotence and Human Freedom," in *New Essays in Philosophical Theology*, eds. A. Flew and A. MacIntyre (London: SCM, 1955), pp. 150-53.

10 For further discussion of it see Plantinga, *God and Other Minds*, pp. 132-35.

11 Mackie, in *The Philosophy of Religion*, pp. 100-101.

12 Strict accuracy demands, therefore, that we speak of God as *actualizing* rather than creating possible worlds. I shall continue to use both locutions, thus sacrificing accuracy to familiarity. For more about possible worlds see my book *The Nature of Necessity* (Oxford: The Clarendon Press, 1974), chaps. 4-8.

13 For a fuller statement of this argument see Plantinga, *The Nature of Necessity*, chap. 9, secs. 4-6.

14 For a more complete and more exact statement of this argument see Plantinga, *The Nature of Necessity*, chap. 9, secs. 4-6.

15 A person goes wrong with respect to an action if he either wrongfully performs it or wrongfully fails to perform it.

Study Questions

1.   What is the alleged contradiction challenge that Alvin Plantinga addresses?

2.   What are the two stages to Plantinga's free will defense?

3.   According to Plantinga, why is it not within God's power to create "any possible world he pleases"?

4.   What do you make of Plantinga's notion of "transworld identity"?

5.   In what ways is Plantinga's notion of "transworld depravity" different from John Calvin's notion of "total depravity?" What problems, if any, do you see for the theist who wants to work with the notion of "transworld depravity"?

22

Evil—A Religious Mystery:
A Plea for a More Inclusive
Model of Theodicy

Louis Dupré

Louis Dupré is professor of philosophy at Yale University and is author of *The Other Dimension*.

Major problems in modern theodicy derive from a rationalist conception of God—alien to living faith—and from an abstract, theologically neutral definition of good and evil. The alternative model here proposed rests on a more intimate union of finite with infinite Being which, on the one hand, allows the creature a greater autonomy and responsibility, and, on the other hand, enables the Creator to share in the suffering of his creatures and thereby to redeem them.*

1. The Concrete-Religious Versus the Rationalist-Abstract Approach

Theodicy today enjoys the dubious reputation of a failed experiment. Few outside the small circle of persistent believers in it would grant that it has succeeded in accomplishing what it set out to do. That failure has become more painfully apparent as our sensitivity to, as well as the increased visibility of, evil, both moral and physical, have intensified our questioning. The sheer magnitude of evil which our age has witnessed in death camps, nuclear warfare, internecine tribal or racial conflicts, have lowered our tolerance level for what once was accepted as a necessary part of life. Indeed, the presence of evil has impressed itself more powerfully than the presence of God upon the minds of many of our contemporaries for whom the primary question is no longer how God can tolerate so much evil, but rather how the more tangible reality of evil still allows the possibility of God's existence. Beyond religious and ideological differences our contemporaries have attained a remarkable agreement that evil "was not meant to be," that it constitutes an alien invasion into our lives. To an unprecedented degree we feel the need to "justify" the presence of evil in our world. Yet we have lowered or abandoned our expectations to receive an adequate answer to the question *Unde malum?* from philosophy. Indeed, speculative attempts to reduce the question to a theoretical issue tend to render the reality of evil less rather than more acceptable.

Evil invites philosophical speculation, yet it is the cliff on which philosophy suffers shipwreck. By a paradox unique to our time we remain simultaneously aware of both terms of the opposition. Schopenhauer anticipated the paradox when he wrote: "Without doubt it is the knowledge of death, and along with this the consideration of the suffering and misery of life, which gives the strongest impulse to philosophical reflection and metaphysical explanation of the world. If our life were endless and painless, it would perhaps occur to no one to ask why the world exists, and is just this kind of world it is."[1] Two distinct philosophical reactions have emerged. Some contemporary thinkers attempt to repair by one philosophy the damage wrought by another, believing that what has been philosophically misstated can be philosophically corrected. Logicians have endeavored to point out the many non sequiturs that lead to the conclusion "Hence an omnipotent, omniscient, good God cannot exist." Rightly. A remedial strategy alone does not suffice, however, particularly not when its authors fail to question the more fundamental anthropomorphic premises which inspired the objections. But even those who succeed in replacing a simplistic conception of God by a philosophically more coherent one, do not dispel our basic doubt whether any kind of autonomous philosophical speculation would be capable of meeting a difficulty born in metaphysical despair. The philosopher may, of course, dismiss such doubts as unreasonable and insist that on his terrain the discussion must be restricted by the clearly defined limits of logical argument.

To be sure, such basic work is needed. But a more fundamental problem remains: theodicy is based upon a concept of religion in which the believer will hardly recognize his or her own. As Kant defined it, theodicy consists in "the defense of the supreme wisdom of the Creator (*Urheber*) of the world against the charges raised by reason on the basis of what conflicts with a meaningful order (*Zweckwidrig*) in the world."[2] The God hereby presented is not merely "less" than the "Father" whom Jesus revealed or than the God of Israel: He essentially differs from either. To be sure, there is nothing wrong with an attempt to articulate philosophically the dependence of creation on God, while leaving all other aspects out of consideration. If finite being depends on an omnipotent, wise Creator, that dependence is worth investigating. The problem begins, however, when that dependence is conceived *exclusively* in terms of *efficient* causality. The link between God and the creature is obviously more intimate than that between an efficient cause (as modern thought conceived of it) and its effect.[3] To represent it *exclusively* in causal terms makes it extremely difficult, if not impossible, to justify any suffering avoidable in the creation of an all-wise, omnipotent God. The so-called physico-theological argument whereby the mind proves the existence of God on the basis of the cosmos, becomes then inverted into a normative rule that determines the limits of divine action in the world. One of the modes in which God relates to creation comes thereby to function as the very standard of his activity with respect to the cosmos and all that is in it.

A theodicy based upon such a narrowly conceived, purely causal relation differs, of course, from the older one that rested upon a more inclusive relationship between God and creation. In the following pages I intend to return to that older tradition (medieval and, in part already Platonic) by taking account of other, specifically religious modes of conceiving that relation. Such an approach, though more modest in its claims than the rationalist one tends to be, may in the end prove more religiously appropriate and therefore also more fruitful. As Brian Hebbelthwaite observed: "One has actually to meet religious people, Buddhists, Hindus, Christians, Jews, Muslims, and see how they in fact confront the world's evil, if one is going to grasp something of the resources of religion for coping with suffering and wrong."[4] It should be clear from the outset: to adopt this approach is not to renege on philosophical theology, but to expand it beyond the rationalist limits within which a purely causal, basically deist philosophy has constrained it. The method of philosophy imposes certain restrictions upon such a use of "dogmatic" material, for unless the philosopher detaches his religious sources from the absolute authority they enjoy within the religious community, philosophy loses its autonomy and becomes transformed into theology. Scripture, theology, and mystical speculation provide *models* for conveying a concrete content to our relation with a transcendent absolute.[5] They do not replace critical reflection.

A further challenge confronting a religiously "inclusive" approach is that the religious sources which direct its search date from a remote past and often present an anthropomorphic image of God which today's educated believer may find hard to take as literal truth. This applies, of course, most obviously to the older books of the Bible, but even the more recent ones of the New Testament create problems of interpretation. A literal reading of some of the historical narratives may considerably add to the difficulties of a philosophical theodicy, rather than reducing them. I must confess that in this respect I find the methods of those Christian philosophers who commendably react against a deist rationalism often seriously wanting in the interpretation of ancient texts. Too many appear unwilling to accept that the meaning of a text lies in the total context. Applied to canonical texts dating from a remote past this principle would appear to require some acquaintance not only with the literary context, but also with the historical one. The meaning of a passage in archaic writings such as the books of the Pentateuch cannot be gathered by the same methods we use for analyzing a modern study of history. To treat an ancient narrative as a critically historical discourse can only set philosophical reflection on the wrong track from the start. One may attempt to extricate oneself from those self-inflicted problems by arguing that none of the improbable assumptions inherent in a literal reading is "demonstrably false."[6] But no discipline known to me has ever profited from accepting highly unlikely claims as true as long as they cannot be positively demonstrated to be false.

On the opposite side, however, the question arises whether a rationally "edited" reading of ancient sacred texts would not lead us right back to the kind of rationalist theodicy we are trying to avoid. Can we still claim to be more intrinsically religious than rationalists when we leave out what cultural or personal taste finds hard to accept? Which principles enable us to discern the essential, religious message from the anthropomorphic metaphor? This much appears certain: a liberal exegesis has taken critical liberties which would fundamentally obstruct any attempt to base theodicy upon a scriptural idea of God. What then must be the criterion for responsibly reading the Bible as an account of divine action? To eliminate all "anthropomorphism," as the Enlightenment attempted, leaves us with no more than the lifeless skeleton on which deism built its idea of God. Moreover, in the case of the religiously more inclusive model of theodicy here presented, it would in principle deny the most fundamental datum of Jewish, Christian, and Moslem religious anthropology, namely that God has created man in his own image and likeness. Despite these difficulties I do not believe that preserving the biblical principle forces us literally to accept the more primitive metaphors in which this principle has been concretely presented. Among them we count biblical images of God's all too human emotions (jealousy, anger, etc.), his abrupt and by human standards arbitrary decisions and subsequent repentance, his creation of cosmos and persons in the manner of physical fashioning (in *Genesis* 2, as a potter working with clay). It is not possible to define once and for all at which point representations become unacceptably anthropomorphic. The rational demands of interpretation develop under the impact of new scientific theories about cosmos and person, but also of theological and metaphysical refinement. What to the J writer of *Genesis* appeared perfectly acceptable may no longer appear so to us. But it seems not unreasonable to generalize that a representation becomes unsatisfactory when even serious believers perceive it as conflicting with the ideas of God, person, and cosmos which centuries of philosophical, theological, and scientific reflection have left us. It would be difficult conclusively to demonstrate the falsehood of such representations, as fundamentalist interpreters challenge us to do. Yet much of what is not demonstrably false may strike an educated believer in our time as improbable beyond falsehood. At least in the area of theodicy little may be gained from the use of canonical texts for the support of representations which believing philosophers would find it hard to accept as literal truth. Even if such representations are no more than highly improbable to the educated, they cease to be useful for the particular task of theodicy which consists in making the idea of God more (rather than less) acceptable in the face of evil.

Finally, and most importantly, we must remind ourselves that not all religious traditions share the same assumptions about the origin and significance of evil, and hence that there is no single "religious answer" to evil. Positions vary from a strong affirmation of evil as an ultimate principle coequal with the good in Manicheism, to a denial of its reality as an illusion in the more radical Buddhist and Vedantic monist schools. Between these two extremes theist responses range from an evil inherent in the finite condition as such, to evil as the sole responsibility of the human race (through the fall and subsequent sins). Evil provokes, of course, the strongest reaction among such monotheists as Jews, Christians, and Moslems who consider all finite being the creation of a free God. Here again the nature and urgency of the crisis have resulted in a variety of responses. Judaism alone presents several models. According to the archaic retaliation model, God inflicts suffering as a punishment for human sin. But, one might wonder, why should humans, created by God, commit sin? Israel never ceased to struggle with this question, and many felt compelled to look in a different direction. One alternative model delays the overcoming of evil till a future time of history. But why should creation have to pass through evil in order to achieve final good? In the face of such major difficulties two different models emerged. The Book of Job concludes that humans are not in a position to question God's inscrutable decrees, while Deutero-Isaiah, in his description of the suffering servant, equally desisting from seeking the origin of suffering or its future goal, considers suffering itself intrinsically redemptive.

Christianity adopted all four of these models but connected the idea of punishment primarily to Adam's fall, while grounding the idea of redemptive suffering in the passion and death of Christ. In addition, early theologians combined those scriptural positions with the prevailing philosophical ones (mainly Neoplatonic and Stoic). Thus they adopted the Neoplatonic interpretation according to which evil consists in a lack of being—*a privatio boni*. As John Hick has shown, this solution, suitable for an order of being in which necessary emanations move down from the One, causes serious difficulties in a universe *freely* created by God.[7] While the Neoplatonic *One* is not responsible for all the ills inherent in the lower hypostases that with absolute necessity emanate from it, a free, omnipotent Creator *chooses* what is to exist. Augustine who was chiefly responsible for establishing this privative conception of evil in the West, attempted to counter the objection by means of a Greek aesthetics of form. Contrast, for him, including the contrast between good and evil, adds to the perfection of the created form. Needless to say, an aesthetic principle of perfection that requires the presence of physical pain and moral evil and that results in the final damnation of most moral agents, hardly corresponds to the Christian idea of God's goodness or to that of the individual's responsibility. The God of love preached in the Gospel of salvation here has made room for an Olympian Artist of dreamlike form. Nor does one soften that grim picture much by declaring that the Creator merely allows moral evil, as long as one holds God to be capable of freely creating a world that contains less suffering and less moral evil. "One cannot say that God both is blameless in respect of the natural evil in our world, because He alone allows it as something inseparable from the world's good, and that He could, had He wished, have created a better world in which there would have been less natural evil."[8] Augustine obviates any divine obligation to create a better world by the idea of contrast, while he uses the *privatio boni* (hardly suitable for aesthetic contrast) to acquit God from any complicity with the evil needed for that contrast.

2. Created Autonomy Versus Causal Determinism

The positions that in the wake of theological and philosophical controversies came to prevail in much of Western thought under the direct or indirect impact of St. Augustine resulted in the following questionable theses.

1. God creates the intelligent agent free, yet predestines him or her to damnation or salvation.
2. The good exists as an independent value prior to the Creator's choice.
3. God remains unaffected by the finite reality.

All of these theses would at a later time and in modified form find their way into the rationalist assumptions of the theodicy formulated in seventeenth and eighteenth century philosophy which, to a great extent, is still surviving today. The modern assumptions may be summarized as follows:

1. While the Creator is the efficient cause of creation, the autonomy of the creature is severely restricted. Even the exercise of free will must somehow be determined by the causal impact of an omnipotent, omniscient Creator.
2. Ideals of goodness and value preexist our pursuit of them. The free agent may ratify or reject them, but does not constitute them.

3. The Creator stands entirely outside His creation and remains untouched by suffering and the effects of moral evil.

The alternative model presented in this essay rejects all three of these assumptions in favor of more authentically Christian and, I hope, more coherently philosophical principles. Yet before confronting the two models to one another we need to consider the original theological theses as well as the philosophical assumptions more closely.

The controversy over divine predestination did not reach a critical stage until the sixteenth century, when Calvin denied the exercise of free choice in the order of grace and when Thomists and Molinists initiated their acrimonious dispute *de auxiliis*. For Banez and his Thomist followers, God's position as the absolutely universal cause of creation entailed that He had to be responsible for at least a "negative reprobation" of some, previous to any personal merits and demerits. God causes no evil, but decides not to cause the good that would prevent evil from occurring. Left to its own fallen and fallible liberty, the finite will without God's efficacious grace *inevitably* sins. To this determinism Molina and his school, anxious to preserve human responsibility, opposed a free human causality next to, and partly in competition with, divine causality. These conflicting positions share the burden of an impossible task: in one case reconciling total divine causality with human responsibility for evil, in the other, squaring total human responsibility with divine causality.

The second thesis posits the *good* as an ideal *apriori*, preceding God's creative act, and thus imposing upon a moral God the obligation to create the universe which approaches this ideal as closely as a finite composition is able to. The same necessity which determines the divine being thereby extends to creation, leaving no room for either divine freedom or finite contingency. Leibniz who formulated the position into a clearly articulated principle, attempted to escape its pantheistic implications by distinguishing between the "absolute" necessity to create the best possible world (which he denied) and the "moral" necessity by which God owed it to his goodness to create the best possible (which he affirmed). In this rationalist scenario, God contemplates the non-existent essences of several possible worlds, after which He decides to create the actual world in accordance with His goodness—though He was not intrinsically forced to do so.[9] Even if we leave out of consideration the untenable real distinction between God's goodness and His omnipotence, we must still question Leibniz's interpretation of divine omnipotence. Does it refer to God's power to do "anything at all"? That is hardly meaningful, and Leibniz himself hastens to restrict it to what is logically possible and compossible with God's other attributes. If God is supremely good, He is not able to do evil. We should then restrict our definition of omnipotence so as to define God's ability to do anything He wills *in accordance with His divine nature*.

But even then the term "anything He wills" raises further questions. God's "acting" expresses His nature; it serves not, as it does for me, as a means to satisfy particular wants or desires by the attainment of goals that lie outside me. A wide gap separates what I *am* from what I attempt to attain by means of acts devised to complement my experienced deficiency. None of this applies to God. Nor am I from my own position able to conceive what God's acting implies or does not imply. All I can do is look at the concrete, visible result of that divine action which we call *creation*. But here precisely theodicy ought to follow a procedure opposite to the one it usually follows when it decrees that the world must conform to those standards of human rationality which it has *a priori* set up for God. A genuine, religious theodicy *begins* by accepting creation *as it is* (including its evil) as a visible expression of God's nature, rather than by dictating *a priori* what a divine expression must be like. As we shall see, such an attitude does not condemn theodicy to blind faith, for it must critically examine what it may learn of the divine nature on the basis of this created expression, and it may conceivably conclude that this created expression fails to meet even minimal human standards of goodness. But it should do so on the basis of the total evidence (including the one provided in the specifically religious experience of faith) rather than of an *a priori*, narrowly rationalist definition of what God ought to be and therefore ought to do.

Returning then to Leibniz's argument, it should be clear that the idea of a divine choice with an antecedent moment of deliberation and a consequent moment of decision, patterned after the model of human persons deliberating about several alternatives, is itself heavily anthropomorphic. Kolakowski puts it well:

> In God Himself essence and existence converge and this implies that His will is identical with His essence. God neither obeys rules which are valid regardless of His will nor produces these rules according to His whims or as the result of deliberating various options; He is those rules. Unlike humans God never faces alternative possibilities and then freely decides which of them He ought to choose; His decisions are necessary aspects of His Being—and therefore they could not have been different from what they are; yet they are free in the sense that no superior powers, no norms of validity independent of God, bind Him. He *is* what He does, decides, orders. Consequently we may say neither that the definitions of what is good and true precede God, . . . nor that He precedes them.[10]

In addition to these intra-divine difficulties of God "choosing" the best possible world, there are others inherent in the very concept of "best possible world." Bergson pointed them out and dismissed the entire idea in a few lapidary sentences.

> I can, at a stretch, represent something in my mind when I hear of the sum-total of existing things, but in the sum-total of the non-existent I can see nothing but a string of words. So that here again the objection is based on a pseudo-idea, a verbal entity. But we can go further still: the objection arises from a whole series of arguments implying a radical defect of method. A certain representation is built up *a priori*, and it is taken for granted that this is the idea of God; from thence are deduced the characteristics that the world ought to show; and if the world does not actually show them, we are told that God does not exist.[11]

One imposes no undue restrictions upon divine perfection by declaring God unable to achieve what conflicts with the nature of the finite. But finite being is intrinsically imperfect and any attempt to measure its perfection depends itself on finite, hence intrinsically, imperfect norms. Thus the idea of the best possible world imposes upon the Creator a subjective, human standard.

The most serious problems begin when modern theodicy attempts to square the idea of a perfect Creator with the creation of free agents capable of perpetrating moral evil and inflicting suffering upon other creatures. On this issue the modern assumption leads to the most questionable conclusions. Both theodicy's adversaries and advocates hold a concept of freedom that from the start sets the discussion on the wrong track. Thus Antony Flew argues that for an action to be free it suffices that it not be compelled—which, for him, entails not that it is unpredictable, but that the person nevertheless could have acted differently had he chosen to do so. From these premises he concludes that an omnipotent Creator could have created persons who would always (or more often) have acted rightly.[12] J. L. Mackie concurs: human beings could have been so constituted as freely to choose the good. The idea of a God who could not control men's actions leads to what he calls the "paradox of omnipotence."[13] How the idea of a will determined always to choose the good remains compatible with freedom escapes me. Nor do I see how in a theory of predetermined freedom evil could avoid being ultimately attributable to God."[14] Yet the most questionable concept appears to be that of a finite freedom created with a built-in resistance to evil. Freedom is far more than the power to say yes or no to divinely pre-established values with or without a divine impulse toward one or the other. Its signal characteristic consists not in the power to ratify pre-established values but in the ability to create them. Freedom can tolerate contingency and an extremely restricted field of operation. But to interfere with its creative power is to replace freedom by causality. Creativity constitutes its very essence. Both theists and atheists admit freedom to be "given," but it is not given in the way of causal determination. Even a wholly pre-established order of values reduces its scope. Most of us agree on that point when it comes to humanly induced unconscious conditioning (including hypnosis), such as B. F. Skinner proposes for the improvement of society as a whole. But the same objection holds true for any divine "conditioning." Even a divinely pre-established order leaves man none but a negative creativity (as Sorter perceived). Yet, strangely enough, this inauthentic, reduced freedom of choice, the very same one the secular critics of theodicy reject in predestinationist theologies, is the one they propose as the only one compatible with the existence of a good God.

God creates neither values nor strong or weak inclinations to choose them; He creates creators who depend on a divine source for the exercise of their creative spontaneity, but not for its determination. Nor need such a theory result in the kind of atheism it has entailed in some existentialist philosophies. For an essential part of the free agent's creative project consists in practically recognizing his overall *dependence.* Failure to do so deprives us of an absolute in determining the hierarchy of values, while forcing us to elevate relative values into absolutes. Now, a freedom responsible for creating its own values remains intrinsically and irrevocably able to erect false absolutes and even to invert the creative impulse into an annihilating power. Genuine freedom is endowed with a capacity unlimited for evil as well as for good. In creating free agents God has released a power which may turn against Himself. In Berdyaev's words: "Evil presupposes freedom and there is no freedom without the freedom of evil, that is to say, there is no freedom in the state of compulsory good."[15] Leibniz understood this better than some of his followers.

The real issue concerning freedom is not whether it deserved to be created, but whether God's necessary being is compossible with such an unrestricted creaturely autonomy as freedom requires. Since that issue obviously falls outside the limits of theodicy, we need not enter into it. Nor is it a problem for theodicy to solve whether there may exist spiritual beings endowed with a clearer sense of freedom's potential and therefore less inclined to pervert its creative autonomy (e.g., angels). Its own question concerns the compatibility of free agents *as we know them* with the easiness of a good and wise Creator. Moreover, theodicy should be concerned only with the *compatibility* of the world *as it is*, not with the possibility of proving the existence of God on the basis of this world's perfection. Symptomatic for the confusion that often occurs between the two is that many modern treatises of theodicy begin with a discussion of Hume's *Dialogues Concerning Natural Religion.* Whatever Hume's intention may have been, he did not write an anti-theodicy, that is, a refutation of any possibility to defend the idea of God in the face of evil in creation. The *Dialogues* deflate the exaggerated claims of a natural theology which on the basis of a purely philosophical speculation concerning order and purpose in the world concludes to the existence of God. Even on those terms we should beware of overstating the case. Does Philo, the most skeptical of the three participants in the dialogue, after having invalidated all arguments presented in favor of a benevolent Providence, not concede in the end: "In many views of the universe and of its parts, particularly the latter, the beauty and fitness of final causes strike us with such irresistible force, that all objections appear (what I believe they really are) mere cavils and sophisms; nor can we then imagine how it was ever possible for us to repose any weight on them."[16] One may, of course, dismiss this statement as the expression of a thorough skepticism whereby Philo, after having first invalidated the arguments of the other interlocutants, in the end scuttles his own. But we may also read this as a sincere attempt to attain "synoptically," that is, by an immediate, total impression, what analytic inference withholds. If this reading is correct, an "illative sense" would provide what analysis alone fails to supply, namely, certitude concerning the existence of an intelligent Designer who may be infinitely perfect and good (though these attributes cannot be established by natural reason alone).[17]

The implications of Hume's argument so understood would be less constrictive for philosophical theodicy than much contemporary fideism which, rightly dissatisfied with the rationalist theodicy, prefers to leave the justification of God in the face of evil *entirely* to faith. The philosopher cannot remain satisfied with such a total abdication of reason: the presence of evil must be shown not to exclude the idea of a good Creator. Nor will the philosopher be satisfied with defining "divine goodness" by standards that have nothing in common with our human conception of goodness, an equivocity that, as John Stuart Mill pointed out, would merely result in "an incomprehensible attribute of an incomprehensible substance."[18] The philosopher rightly insists that the idea of an omnipotent, good God be shown to be compatible with the actual existence of evil. Reason modestly yet legitimately demands only to perceive how an open conflict between a good God and an evil world is *not inevitable*.

Even that modest goal philosophy cannot meet unless it adequately answers the objection of God's supreme indifference to the suffering of his creatures. To do so becomes nearly impossible for one who accepts the third of the Augustinian theses, especially after it became combined with the idea of the Creator as efficient cause in the modern sense. But even medieval scholasticism in denying any real relation between God and the world had placed itself in an unfavorable position for defending the Creator against the charge of supreme indifference. For such a defense to be effective philosophy would have to accept that the sufferings of creation, including the suffering caused by human evil, affect the Creator himself. A number of philosophical systems broadly comprehended under the general name of "process philosophy" have attempted to justify such a divine participation in finite processes. Despite essential disagreements concerning the relation between the finite and the infinite, divine personhood, the role and ultimate destiny of human individuals, all these systems share Whitehead's overall vision of the real as a creative process, whereby God comes to be with his creation rather than above it. In Whitehead's terms: "He shares with every new creation its actual world."[19] Indeed, only through the creative process does God attain that full actuality to which Whitehead refers as God's "consequent" nature. Rather than being an unchanging, transcendent Prime Mover, God is the actual entity from which each creative development in time "receives that initial aim from which its self-causation starts."[20] Various philosophers have interpreted this divine participation in various ways, ranging from an impersonal "creative event," the source of all human good (Wieman), to a creative personalism (Brightman). But only when the idea of a personal God is preserved can process philosophy contribute toward making the monotheist position with respect to evil more acceptable.

Peter Bertocci in *The Goodness of God* shows a clear appreciation of the importance of safeguarding this personal character and bases his argument on the premise that a creative force resulting in human persons must itself be personal. But such a Creator-Person need not be conceived as self-sufficient, uninhibited by restraints other than those He imposes upon Himself. If personhood reaches its highest realization in interpersonal communication, then the perfection of the divine Creator would likewise be enhanced, rather than weakened, in responding to persons. Furthermore, such a divine Person exposes himself to risks analogous to those run by humans in their attempts to create good—what Bertocci calls "creative insecurity."

> Insecurity inheres in the very nature of being a person whose actual freedom of personal choice is involved in the pursuit of truth and goodness. Intrinsic to the good for persons is the insecurity that can become creative, because values are compenetrating, and because persons themselves can choose orchestration-within-pattern as they change and grow.[21]

Bertocci supports this bold application of the personalist principle to the Absolute by an even more daring thesis. As he reads it, the insecurity of the creative act expresses a fundamental uncertainty in the very nature of the Creator-Person. A refractory element, not a "flaw" in the divine or an impediment imposed upon the divine, but the essential passivity inherent in the very act whereby the Absolute gives birth to the relative, prevents the Creator from achieving His goals without at the same time having to allow the possible intrusion of suffering and evil.

3. A Passive, Suffering God

In this section I intend to show that such an idea of a God who renders Himself passive in the act of creation presents a more solid, as well as a more concretely religious basis for theodicy than a first cause untouched by the suffering of creation and unmoved by the effects of moral evil. The doctrine of the passion and death of Christ lends indirect, though strong, support to this position, as it rests upon the very notion of God who suffers and dies. But in all three monotheist faiths mystical and theosophical traditions have held that with creation some passivity enters God's very essence. For infinite, perfect Being to give rise to being other than itself means not adding to itself (as St. Thomas already clearly stated: *non datur plus esse*), but causing an emptiness within its own fullness wherein "otherness" can subsist. Only through an "annihilation" (Blondel) of infinite Being can the finite be *another* being. Though finite being must remain *within* the infinite, perfect Being from which it draws its entire sustenance, as *other* it assumes a certain independence. By allowing it to be in its own right infinite Being ceases to wield unlimited power over it, and comes to stand in a relation that is no longer exclusively active.

Now philosophers who adopt Aristotle's definition of God as pure act tend to exclude passivity from God as incommensurable with divine perfection. Yet if we understand pure act as the opposite of passivity, it becomes itself imperfect. For to "act," as opposed to being acted upon, means to "re-act" to events and circumstances in a manner that forces the acting subject to go out toward the other than itself in order to return to itself in a different manner. Obviously, this kind of acting wherein the agent thus loses himself in order to find himself anew does not apply to God as *He is in Himself*. Resting within itself a perfect, infinite Being as such cannot be called active any more than passive, as Nicholas of Cusa showed in his theory of the divine coincidence of opposites. In creation, however, the two moments of activity and passivity simultaneously emerge. Though the act of creation requires itself no external support and in this respect may be called entirely "active, in the very "otherness" of the created being, God places Himself in a position where He is forced to react and thereby to relate passively as well as actively. Aristotelians avoid this conclusion by asserting that God has no *real* relation to the world. But such a claim, intelligible enough within Aristotle's theory of an uncreated cosmos, makes little sense within a creationist theology.

On the other side, to introduce passivity in God and autonomy in the creature is not sufficient for solving the problem of theodicy. Indeed, even the deist with his remote, *laissez-faire* God implicitly or explicitly holds that, once having created the world, God leaves all initiative to the creatures, restricting his own activity to preservation and support. If there were no further divine intervention, the issue would, once again, be reduced to the simple dilemma we have rejected in the first part: *Either* the world is as good as it can possibly be, and to be so, however imperfect, is better than not to be. In that case God is justified. *Or* the world could have been better than it is, and then we must conclude that an omnipotent, wise, and good God did not create it. For the believer, the "passivity" of the Creator is of a very different nature. Rather than creating and then leaving creation to its own devices, God never stops *reacting* to the creature's initiative. Monotheist theologies have expressed the interaction between God and creation in several ways. Christians affirm this ever renewed divine action by saying that God *redeems* what He has created. Unfortunately, in theodicy believers often use the concept of redemption for stopping the gaps of ignorance that remain after they have depleted their supply of rational justifications for suffering and evil. Thus they end up yielding to the duplicity which Mill denounced, by calling "good" in an invisible order (that, in a future world, may become manifest) what by ordinary standards cannot but count as "bad." Rather than whitewashing evil by such an *argumentum ex ignorantia*—as irrefutable as it is unprovable—the believer should, from the start, admit that this world contains a great deal of unexplainable suffering, that creatures endowed with a free will remain perfectly capable of causing unqualified evil and often avail themselves of this possibility. Rather than using the term "redemption" to make suffering and evil vanish into an invisible realm of goodness, the Christian philosopher ought to show, what the ordinary faithful have always maintained, namely that in his redemptive action God *reacts* to *real* suffering and *real* evil. To be effective in theodicy the idea of redemption must be integrated with that of creation as one continuous, active relation of God to His creatures. Such a view, contrary to the deist's, envisions divine activity as an open-ended, ever renewed dialogue with creation. At each moment of time God creatively responds to the conditions shaped by His creatures in the preceding moment. A divine response then counteracts existing evil by constantly presenting us with new occasions for the accomplishment of good or the redemption of evil. Without having to interfere with the creature's autonomy. God's response provides ever novel opponents for converting evil into goodness. Christian writers have consistently upheld this divine ability to restore creation to new innocence. Thus Jacques Maritain suggestively argues:

> Each time that a free creature undoes for its part the work that God makes, God remakes to that extent—for the better—this work and leads it to higher ends. Because of the presence of evil on earth, everything on earth, from the beginning to the end of time, is in perpetual recasting.[22]

To be sure, the ways in which God actively counteracts evil in a creation increasingly threatened by it, cannot be "justified" on the basis of an abstract concept of human nature. Theology may inform us that God offers ever new opportunities for converting past evil into future goodness. It may show how, in a condition antagonistic to good, such a reversal must necessarily take the form of a struggle, an *agon*. According to Christian doctrine, God himself had to provide both the means and the model of this conversion by suffering and dying under the power of evil. But in thus linking the mystery of evil to the even greater mystery of redemption we have decidedly left the domain of philosophy and introduced considerations not available to a purely philosophical reflection on reality as it is universally manifest.

The admission of dogmatic doctrines into a universal, philosophical reflection ought to be justified more thoroughly than this essay allows.[23] Here I mention only one critically significant reason that forces us to admit them at least to some extent. The very standards by which we measure what does and what does not count as "good" depend upon the acceptance or rejection of an intrinsically religious hierarchization of values. Any attempt to erect a system of values upon a religiously neutral basis, common to believers and unbelievers, fails precisely in the area where theodicy matters most, namely, in deciding what must count as *definitive* evil. In a recent essay Marilyn McCord Adams has shown how ontological commitments affect descriptions of values. Moral theories that omit any reference to a transcendent norm differ from value systems ruled by a relation to transcendent Being. More specifically, varying ontological commitments "widen or narrow the range of options for defeating evil with good.[24] The believer, not satisfied with exclusively immanent goods may value an intimate sense of God's presence, acquired through much pain and suffering, more highly than a satisfaction of immediate needs. But different value systems result in different judgments concerning standards of good and evil.[25] In his evaluation of what constitutes unnecessary evil and what constitutes ultimate goodness, the believer often fundamentally disagrees with the nonbeliever. Diametrically opposed attitudes concerning the desirability of terminating an unwanted pregnancy become intelligible only if we take this fundamental disagreement on values into account. To recognize major differences in the perception of what in the final analysis constitutes evil need not result in the kind of verbal equivocity on good and evil denounced by J. S. Mill. Yet it should caution us against deciding prematurely what must count as *unredeemably* evil and what as *unconditionally* good. Once we introduce value judgments based on factors that fall beyond the range of a "common" appraisal of what benefits or harms human nature, we admit intrinsically private factors that make a *universal* philosophical theodicy, identical for believers and unbelievers, impossible.

Instead of continuing to attempt such an impossible enterprise, the believing philosopher should not hesitate to include the redemptive vision of his faith in his speculation. From that broadened perspective the experience of evil and suffering, however burdensome, can never lead to a final conclusion concerning life's balance of good and evil. Nor is such a position based upon a purely fideist anticipation of future well-being. For the believer may actually *experience* suffering itself as redemptive, that is, as endowed with more than a merely negative meaning. "Grace and nature not being two closed worlds, but two worlds open to one another and in mutual communication, it might happen that the greater progress (of the wheat over that of the cockle) would occur more in the order of grace than in that of nature."[26] To refer to different modes of experiencing is not to advance an unsupported claim, but merely to assert what eminent psychologists, beginning with William James, have persistently asserted.

The distinction here proposed finds unambiguous theological support in the doctrine of redemptive suffering which, for Jews, Christians, and Moslems transforms the meaninglessness of suffering and evil into different patterns of meaning and goodness. In its most radical form, expressed in the New Testament theology of Christ's passion and death, the mystery of redemptive suffering allows God himself to participate in human distress. No writer has pursued the theme of suffering redemptive through God's participation in it further than Dostoevsky. Essays on theodicy routinely refer to Ivan Karamazov's charge against a God who tolerates unredeemable suffering—the pain of innocent children and animals who lack the capacity to learn from pain. Usually they fail to mention Alyosha's later reply. Alyosha admits the full scandal of innocent pain and, even as his brother, refuses to accept it. But he assumes this scandal into the even greater one of God's own suffering. When, dying on the cross, Christ feels abandoned by his Father, the tragic conflict enters God's own Being. In this intra-divine theology crucis God is set against God, as in Goethe's dark saying: *Nemo contra Deum nisi Deus ipse.* ("No one against God but God himself."[27] In Christ God assumes all human suffering and takes upon Himself the burden of compensating for all moral evil. In addition, as the legend of the Grand Inquisitor suggests, He faces the failure of a salvation that surpasses the capacity for acceptance of most of those to whom it is offered. This greater scandal does not "justify" evil, but it makes God a participant in our pain, as Christian theologies have consistently implied, and mystical and theosophical ones have explicitly stated.

Gnostic and theosophical doctrines in the three monotheist religions have, in an even more daring way than Christian orthodoxy, introduced the mystery of evil into God's inner life. In contrast to orthodox beliefs, they attribute the possibility of evil (though not its actuality) to an intradivine multiplicity the harmony of which became disturbed by an unknown cause. The resulting conflict gave birth to that realm of unrest and disharmony which is the physical universe.[28] Variously formulated in Jewish, Christian, and pagan myths during the first centuries of our era, this gnostic doctrine found its most radical expression in kaballah mysticism, as it developed between the thirteenth century (the Zohar) and the sixteenth century (Isaac Luria). The German theosophist Jacob Boehme attempted to incorporate it in Lutheran theology by presenting the intradivine conflict as an opposition between God's wrath and God's mercy.[29] We hear a final major echo of it in Blake's *Prophetic Books* according to which a fragmentation of the divine harmony has caused an intra-divine conflict resulting in the creation of the physical universe.[30]

We may of course dismiss such daring speculations as unworthy of philosophical attention. But before doing so we ought to consider that major philosophers, beginning with Plato, have persistently turned to ancient mythical and religious interpretations that trace the origin of good and evil to a single transcendent source. Even some modern philosophers have attempted to trace the opposition between good and evil to a separation of complementaries harmoniously united in the Absolute. Thus in Karl Jaspers's memorable treatment of "The Law of the Day and the Passion for the Night," night and day appear as two complementary elements within the Absolute: intelligible but limited clarity and dark desire of the infinite. The diurnal law "regulates our existence, demands clarity, consistency, and loyalty, binds us to reason and to the idea, to the One and to ourselves."[31] The night functions as the negative desire to transcend finitude, limit, temporality. Though irreducible to the law of the day, the passion for the night is an equally essential constituent of human existence. In mythical (and highly controversial) language such reflections on complementarity within the Absolute articulate what I have described as the "passivity" that enters infinite Being when it gives birth to the finite. Orthodox monotheist theologies have never accepted the gnostic equation of creation with the fall. Nor do they accept conflicts "within" the Godhead to account for the existence of evil in creation. Rightly, because the gnostic myths and their theosophical interpretations result in theological inconsistencies as well as in morally problematic positions. But the underlying assumption that the *possibility* of evil cannot be explained unless we trace it back to the divine act of creation itself rests on a profound insight, no more irrational than God's own participation in human suffering.

Still, the philosopher cannot but wonder, what such theosophical speculations contribute to the kind of strictly rational reflection he or she is committed to. Passivity in God and otherness in the creature neither explain the actual origin of physical evil nor do they justify its existence. Neither do gnostic or theosophical doctrines provide the philosopher with such an explanation or justification. It would be unreasonable to expect from them rational explanations which reason itself has been powerless to provide. Theosophical doctrines do not reduce the "mysteriousness" of evil. If anything, they deepen it. What they may accomplish, however, is to extend the boundaries within which theology and the philosophy that has followed its lead conceive of that mystery. While the traditional theistic position has attributed the source of evil entirely to the creature—either as a result of sin or as an inevitable effect of finitude, theosophical doctrines force us to consider also the divine act of creation itself and the momentous transition it constitutes in Being from the one to the many. This very transition entails the possibility of opposition (and sufferings) not only among differently disposed and variously oriented creatures, but even within each single living organism with its own multiplicity of tendencies, drives, and instincts.

Theosophical doctrines, however, tend to go beyond tracing the mere *possibility* of physical evil to the creative act. Most of them attribute the *actuality* of evil to a mysterious darkness within God's nature. Here philosophy can and should not follow them. Claims of a revelation, altogether inaccessible to reason, have no legitimate place in philosophy. Any appeal to a "secret" knowledge restricted to a special enlightenment of few, remains in principle incompatible with the public goals and universal methods of philosophical reflection. Nor could such privileged enlightenment constitute an additional source of *positive knowledge* for the theistic philosopher. Gnostic speculation can do no more than open up perspectives different from the ones traditionally considered and invite the philosopher to explore them within his/her own discipline. In the case of physical evil it draws attention to the divine creative act itself. Such a reorientation of the philosophical attention may be highly useful for the conception of new, more fruitful models in defining the issue. Specifically, in theodicy, it may force us to think of the creative act as being more complex than a simple divine *fiat*. Since the purview of this article limits it to a critique of traditional approaches and a suggestion of an alternative model for theodicy, this is not the proper place to develop its philosophical consequences. But it appears that a philosophical theology of the process type would be better equipped to accommodate the inherent ambiguity of the creative act with respect to physical evil than one of the traditional type which too absolutely separates the Creator from His creation.

Conclusion

The theologically inclusive model of theodicy here defended requires the concrete religious context of faith for any rational reflection on a mystery that attains its full poignancy only within religion itself. As Hegel once remarked, only in actual worship are believers capable of overcoming evil. It differs from those philosophical theodicees which allege to be based upon a rational, but in fact rationalist, idea of God, far removed from living faith, if not in actual conflict with it. Theological inclusiveness does not force us to abandon the rational methods and goals of philosophy. True enough, on the cross philosophy suffers shipwreck, believers and unbelievers unanimously declare. But that does not dispense the believing philosopher from the task of showing that, within a concrete, theological context, belief in a good God is compatible with the existence of evil. In addition, the philosopher must examine whether the theological theses which form the context for the believer's concrete evaluation of what must count as a good or an evil remain in conformity with reason. Interpretations of Jesus's redemptive suffering as a satisfaction exacted by an angry God or a ransom paid to the devil do not satisfy that demand. But no such objections can be raised against the central Christian idea of God uniting Himself to finite nature and descending in person into the abyss of human suffering and moral evil. In taking account of the mystery of evil and redemption, as faith presents it and as the believer, to a greater or lesser extent, actually experiences it, the Christian philosopher admits a complexity of the issue which the rationalist ignores. In giving birth to the finite, God himself inevitably assumes a certain passivity in regard to the autonomy of finite being, a passivity that may render Him vulnerable and that indeed, according to the Christian mystery of the Incarnation, has induced Him personally to share the very suffering of finite being.[32]

Yale University

Endnotes

*Reprinted from *Faith and Philosophy*, Vol. 7, No. 3, July 1990. All rights reserved.

[1] Arthur Schopenhauer: *The World as Will and Representation*. Supplemental Ch. XVII (added to Section 15).

[2] Kant: *Werke* (Berlin Akademie edition) VIII, p. 255.

[3] I have developed this point in "Transcendance et objectivisme" in *Archivio di Filosofia* (Rome) 1977, pp. 265-72.

[4] Brian Hebblethwaite: Evil, Suffering and Religion (London: Sheldon Press, 1976), p. 10.

[5] For a justification of such a "hypothetical" use of intrinsically religious sources in philosophy the reader may consult my "Blondel's Reflection on Experience," in *A Dubious Heritage. Philosophy of Religion After Kant* (New York: The Paulist Press, 1977).

[6] As Eleanore Stump does in "The Problem of Evil," *Faith and Philosophy* 2 (1985), pp. 392-423, where she makes the highly dubious claim concerning the Cain and Abel story in Genesis: "To the extent to which Christians are committed to accepting the Bible as the revealed word of God, to that extent they are committed to accepting this story as veridical also" (413). "Veridical" here stands for historically true.

[7] John Hick: *Evil and the God of Love* (San Francisco: Harper & Row, 1978), pp. 70-78.

[8] John Hick: Ibid., p. 105.

[9] *Cf.*, William Rowe's critical analysis, "Rationalistic Theology and Some Principles of Explanation," in *Faith and Philosophy* 1 (1984: 4), p. 361.

[10] Leszek Kolakowski: *Religion* (Oxford University Press, 1982), p. 25.

[11] Henry Bergson: *The Two Sources of Morality and Religion*, trans. Ashley Andra and Cloudesly Brereton (Garden City: Doubleday, 1951), p. 261. *See also* James Felt's pertinent remarks in "God's Choice: Reflections on Evil in a Created World," *Faith and Philosophy* 1 (1984: 4), pp. 370-77.

[12] Antony Flew: "Divine Omnipotence and Human Freedom," in *New Essays in Philosophical Theology*, ed. Flew and MacIntyre (London: SCM Press, 1965), p. 152.

[13] J. L. Mackie: "Evil and Omnipotence," *Mind* LXIV, No. 254 (1955), pp. 200-12. Reprinted in *God and Evil*, ed. Nelson Pike (Englewood Cliffs, NJ: Prentice Hall, 1964), pp. 46-60. Reference to p. 57.

[14] *See* Alfred North Whitehead: *Religion in the Making* (New York: Meridian Books, 1961), p. 92.

[15] Nicholas Berdyaev: *The Divine and the Human*, trans. R. M. French (London: Geoffrey Bles, 1948), p. 92.

[16] Ed. N. Kemp Smith (Indianapolis: Library of the Liberal Arts, 1947), p. 202.

[17] I owe the comparison with Newman's "illative sense" (which was undoubtedly influenced by Hume) to my student, Steven Fields.

[18] John Stuart Mill: *An Examination of Sir William Hamilton's Philosophy* (London: Longmans, Green, 1872), p. 128.

[19] Alfred North Whitehead: *Process and Reality* (New York: Macmillan, 1929), p. 521.

[20] Ibid., p. 374.

[21] Peter Bertocci: *The Goodness of God* (Washington, DC: University Press of America, 1981), p. 267. John Dewey made the point in a general way when writing: "No mode of action can...give anything approaching absolute servitude; it provides insurance but no assurance. *The Quest for Certainty* (1929) (New York: G. P. Putnam's Sons—Capricorn Books, 1960), p. 33.

[22] Jacques Maritain: *God and the Permission of Evil*, tran. Joseph Evans (Milwaukee: Bruce, 1966), p. 86.

[23] For a more substantial discussion: Louis Dupré: *The Other Dimension* (New York: Doubleday, 1972), Ch. 3, "Religious Faith and Philosophical Reflection."

[24] Marilyn McCord Adams: "Problems of Evil: More Advice to Christian Philosophers," in *Faith and Philosophy* 5 (April, 1988), p. 129.

[25] Alvin Plantinga argued for this position already in "The Probabilistic Argument from Evil," in *Philosophical Studies* 35 (1979), pp. 46-47.

[26] Maritain: *ibid.*, p. 89.

[27] *Cf.*, Luigi Pareyson: "La sofferenza inutile in Dostoevskij," in *Giornale di metafisica* 4 (1982), pp. 123-70.

[28] *Cf.*, Hans Jonas: *The Gnostic Religion* (Boston: Beacon Press, 1963). Also, Claude Tresmontant: *A Study of Hebrew Thought* (New York: Desclee de Brouwer, 1960), especially pp. 13-14 for a comparison with more orthodox Christian and Jewish theologies of creation.

[29] Jacob Boehme: *Six Theosophic Points*, trans. John Earle (Ann Arbor: University of Michigan, 1958); Heinrich Bornkamm: *Luther und Boehme* (Bonn, 1925); and Cyril O'Regan: *The Trinity in Hegel's Philosophy* (Yale University, 1989, unpublished dissertation), Ch. 7.

[30] "Without contraries is no progression. Attraction and repulsion, reason and energy love and hate are necessary to human existence. From the contraries spring what the religious call good and evil. Good is the passive that obeys reason; evil is the active springing from energy." William Blake: *The Marriage of Heaven and Hell* (beginning).

[31] Karl Jaspers: *Philosophy* III, trans. E. B. Ashton (Chicago: University of Chicago Press, 1971), p. 90.

[32] My special thanks to William Alston and Alvin Plantinga for their kind, constructive, and incisive criticism.

Study Questions

1. How would you summarize Louis Dupré's account of the "concrete-religious" and the "rationalist-abstract"?

2. Dupré offers an alternate model to the revised Augustinian one. What is it?

3. What does Dupré mean by the "passivity" of God?

4. What problems do you see facing the theist who attributes good and evil to a single source?

5. In what ways does Dupré think that his discussion aids the theist's cause?

23

The Inductive Argument from Evil and the Human Cognitive Condition

William P. Alston

William P. Alston is professor of philosophy at Syracuse University, and is author of *Philosophy of Language, Epistemic Justification: Essays in the Theory of Knowledge, Perceiving God, Divine Nature and Human Language*; is editor of *Religious and Philosophical Thought*; and is co-editor of *The Problems of Philosophy*, and *Readings in Twentieth-Century Philosophy*.

In this paper* William Alston contributes to a criticism of the inductive argument from evil, based on a low estimate of human cognitive capacities in a certain application.

I

The recent outpouring of literature on the problem of evil has materially advanced the subject in several ways. In particular, a clear distinction has been made between the "logical" *argument against the existence of God"* ("atheological argument") from evil, which attempts to show that evil is logically incompatible with the existence of God, and the "inductive" ("empirical", "probabilistic") argument, which contents itself with the claim that evil constitutes (sufficient) empirical evidence against the existence of God. It is now acknowledged on (almost) all sides that the logical argument is bankrupt, but the inductive argument is still very much alive and kicking.

In this paper I will be concerned with the inductive argument. More specifically, I shall be contributing to a certain criticism of that argument, one based on a low estimate of human cognitive capacities in a certain application. To indicate the point at which this criticism engages the argument, I shall use one of the most careful and perspicuous formulations of the argument in a recent essay by William Rowe (1979).

1. There exist instances of intense suffering which an omnipotent, omniscient being could have prevented without thereby losing some greater good or permitting some evil actually bad or worse.
2. An omniscient, wholly good being would prevent the occurrence of any intense suffering it could, unless it could not do so without thereby losing some greater good or permitting some evil equally bad or worse
3. There does not exist an omnipotent, omniscient, wholly good being (p. 336).

Let's use the term 'gratuitous suffering' for any case of intense suffering, E, that satisfies premise 1, that is, which is such that an omnipotent, omniscient being could have prevented it without thereby losing some greater good or permitting some evil equally bad or worse.[1] 2 takes what we might call the "content" of 1 (losing a greater good or permitting some worse or equally bad evil) as a necessary condition for God to have a sufficient reason for permitting E. E's being gratuitous, then, is the contradictory of the possibility of God's having a sufficient reason to permit it, and equivalent to the impossibility of God's having a sufficient reason for permitting it. I will oscillate freely between speaking of a particular case of suffering, E, being gratuitous, and speaking of the impossibility of God's having a sufficient reason for permitting E. I shall call a proponent of an inductive argument from evil the "critic".

The criticism I shall be supporting attacks the claim that we are rationally justified in accepting 1, and it does so on the grounds that our epistemic situation is such that we are unable to make a sufficiently well grounded determination that 1 is the case. I will call this, faute de mieux, the *agnostic* thesis, or simply *agnosticism*. The criticism claims that the magnitude or complexity of the question is such that our powers, access to data, and so on are radically insufficient to provide sufficient warrant for accepting 1. And if that is so, the inductive argument collapses.[2]

How might one be justified in accepting 1? The obvious way to support an existential statement is to establish one or more instantiations and then use existential generalization. This is Rowe's tack, and I don't see any real alternative. Thus Rowe considers one or another case of suffering and argues, in the case of each, that it instantiates 1. I will follow him in this approach. Thus to argue that we cannot be justified in asserting 1, I shall argue that we cannot be justified in asserting any of its instantiations, each of which is of the form

1A. E is such that an omnipotent, omniscient being could have prevented it without thereby losing some greater good or permitting some evil equally bad or worse.

In the sequel when I speak of being or not being justified in accepting 1, it must be remembered that this is taken to hang on whether one is, or can be justified, in accepting propositions of the form 1A.

Does the agnostic thesis, in my version, also claim that we are unable to justifiably assert the denial of 1, as we would have to do to develop a successful theodicy? It is no part of my task in this paper to address this question, but I will make a couple of remarks. First, my position is that we could justifiably believe, or even know, the denial of 1, and that in one of two ways. We might have sufficient grounds for believing in the existence of God—whether from arguments of natural theology, religious experience or whatever—including sufficient grounds for taking God to be omnipotent, omniscient, and perfectly good, and that could put us in a position to warrantedly deny 1. Or God might reveal to us that 1 is false, and we might be justified in accepting the message as coming from God. Indeed, revelation might not only provide justification for denying 1, but also justification for beliefs about what God's reasons are for permitting this or that case of suffering or type of suffering, thereby putting us in a position to construct a theodicy of a rather ambitious sort.[3] If, however, we leave aside the putative sources just mentioned and restrict ourselves to what we can do by way of tracing out the interconnections of goods and evils in the world by the use of our natural powers, what are we to say? Well, the matter is a bit complicated. Note that 1 is an existential statement, which says that there are instances of intense suffering of which a certain negative claim is true. To deny 1 would be to say that this negative claim is false for *every* case of intense suffering. And even if we could establish the non-gratuitousness of certain cases by tracing out interconnections—and I don't see that this is necessarily beyond our powers—that would not be sufficient to yield the denial of 1. To sum up: I think that examining the interconnections of good and evil in the world by our natural powers cannot suffice to establish either 1 or its negation.[4] For particular cases of suffering we might conceivably be able to establish non-gratuitousness in this way, but what I shall argue in this paper is that no one can justifiably assert gratuitousness for any case.

II

Before setting out the agnostic thesis in more detail and adding my bit to the case for it, let me make some further comments about the argument against which the criticism is directed and variants thereof.

A. The argument is stated in terms of intense suffering, but it could just as well have appealed to anything else that can plausibly be claimed to be undesirable in itself. Rowe focuses on intense suffering because he thinks that it presents the greatest difficulty for anyone who tries to deny a premise like 1. I shall follow him in this, though for concision I shall often simply say 'suffering' with the 'intense' tacitly understood.

B. Rowe doesn't claim that all suffering is gratuitous, but only that some is. He takes it that even one case of gratuitous suffering is incompatible with theism. I go along with this assumption (though in E, I question whether Rowe has succeeded in specifying necessary and sufficient conditions for gratuitousness, and for God's having a sufficient reason for permitting suffering). As already noted, Rowe does not argue for 1 by staying on its level of unspecificity; rather he takes particular examples of suffering and argues in the case of each that it is gratuitous; from there it is a short step of existential generalization to 1. In (1979) and subsequent papers Rowe focuses on the case of a fawn trapped in a forest fire and undergoing several days of terrible agony before dying (hereinafter 'Bambi'). In (1988) he adds to this a (real life) case introduced by Bruce Russell (1989), a case of the rape, beating, and murder by strangulation of a 5-year old girl ('Sue') by her mother's boyfriend. Since I am specifically interested in criticizing Rowe's argument I will argue that we are not justified, and cannot be justified, in judging these evils to be gratuitous. It will turn out that some of my discussion pertains not to Rowe's cases but to others. I will signal the reader as to how to understand the dummy designator, 'E', in each part of the paper.

C. The argument deals with a classical conception of God as omnipotent, omniscient and perfectly good; it is designed to yield the conclusion that no being with those characteristics exists. I shall also be thinking of the matter in this way. When I use 'God' it will be to refer to a being with these characteristics.

D. There are obvious advantages to thinking of the inductive argument from evil as directed against the belief in the existence of God as God is thought of in some full blown theistic religion, rather than as directed against what we may call "generic theism". The main advantage is that the total system of beliefs in a religion gives us much more to go on in considering what reasons God might possibly have for permitting E. In other terms, it provides much more of a basis for distinguishing between plausible and implausible theodicies. I shall construe the argument as directed against the traditional Christian belief in God.[5] I choose Christianity for this purpose because (a) I am more familiar with it than other alternatives, as most of my readers will be, and (b) most of the philosophical discussions of the problem of evil, both historically and currently, have grown out of Christian thought.

E. Rowe does not claim to know or to be able to prove that 1 is true. With respect to his fawn example he acknowledges that "Perhaps, for all we know, there is some familiar good outweighing the fawn's suffering to which that suffering is connected in a way we do not see" (1979, p. 337). He only claims that we have sufficient rational grounds for believing that the fawn's suffering is gratuitous, and still stronger rational grounds for holding that at least some of the many cases of suffering that, so far as we can see, instantiate 1 actually do so.[6] Not all of Rowe's fellow atheologians are so modest, but I will concentrate my fire on his weaker and less vulnerable version.

F. A final comment will occupy us longer. Rowe obviously supposes, as premise 2 makes explicit, that cases of "gratuitous" evil count decisively against the existence of God. That is, he takes it that an omnipotent, omniscient, and perfectly good God would not permit any gratuitous evil; perhaps he regards this as conceptually or metaphysically necessary. Thus he holds that God could have no other reason for permitting suffering except that preventing it would involve losing some greater good or permitting some equally bad or worse evil.[7] But this is highly controversial. It looks as if there are possible divine reasons for permitting evil that would be ruled out by (2). (i) Suppose that God could bring about a greater good only by permitting any one of several equally bad cases of suffering. Then no one is such that by preventing it He would lose that greater good. And if we stipulate that God has a free choice as to whether to permit any of these disjuncts, it is not the case that to prevent it would be to permit something equally bad or worse; that might or might not ensue, depending on God's choice. But if we are to allow that being necessary for a greater good can justify permission of evil, it looks as if we will have to allow this case as well. (ii) More importantly, human free will complicates God's strategies for carrying out His purposes. As we will be noting later in the paper, if God has a policy of respecting human free will, He cannot guarantee human responses to His initiatives where those responses would be freely made if at all.[8] Hence if God visits suffering on us in an attempt to turn us from our sinful ways, and a particular recipient doesn't make the desired response, God could have prevented that suffering without losing any greater good (no such good was forthcoming), even though we might reasonably take God to be justified in permitting the suffering, provided that was His best strategy in the situation, the one most likely to get the desired result. (iii) Look at "general policy" theodicies.[9] Consider the idea that God's general policy of, e.g., usually letting nature take its course and not interfering, even when much suffering will ensue, is justified by the overall benefits of the policy. Now consider a particular case of divine non-intervention to prevent intense suffering. Clearly, God could have intervened in this case without subverting the general policy and losing its benefits. To prevent this particular suffering would not be to lose some greater good or permit something worse or equally bad. And yet it seems that general policy considerations of the sort mentioned could justify God in refraining from intervening in this case. For if it couldn't, it could not justify His non-intervention in any case, and so He would be inhibited from carrying out the general policy.[10]

Since my central aim in this paper is not to refine principles like 2 in microscopic detail, I will take a shortcut in dealing with these difficulties. (i) can be handled by complicating the formula to allow the permission of any member of a disjunction, some member of which is necessary for a greater good. Consider it done. (ii) and (iii) can be accommodated by widening the sphere of goods for which the evil is necessary. For cases of the (ii) sort, take the greater good to be having as great a chance as possible to attain salvation, and let's say that this good is attained whatever the response. As for (iii), we can say that E is permitted in order to realize the good of maintaining a beneficial general policy except where there are overriding reasons to make an exception, and the reasons in this case are not overriding. With these modifications we can take Rowe to have provided a plausible formulation of necessary conditions for divine sufficient reasons for permitting E. But if you don't think I have successfully defended my revision of *Rowe*, then you may think in terms of an unspecific substitute for I like "There are instances of suffering such that there is no sufficient reason for God to allow them". That will still enable me to argue that no one is in a position to justifiably assert that God could have no sufficient reason for allowing E.

III

Clearly the case for 1 depends on an inference from "So far as I can tell, p" to "p" or "Probably, p". And, equally clearly, such inferences are sometimes warranted and sometimes not. Having carefully examined my desk I can infer 'Jones' letter is not on my desk 'from' So far as I can tell, Jones 'letter is not on my desk'. But being ignorant of quantum mechanics I cannot infer 'This treatise on quantum mechanics is well done' from 'So far as I can tell, this treatise on quantum mechanics is well done'. I shall be contending that our position vis-à-vis 1 is like the latter rather than like the former.

I am by no means the first to suggest that the atheological argument from evil is vitiated by an unwarranted confidence in our ability to determine that God could have no sufficient reason for permitting some of the evils we find in the world. A number of recent writers have developed the theme.[11] I endorse many of the reasons they give for their pessimism. Wykstra points out that our cognitive capacities are much more inferior to God's than is a small child's to his parents; and in the latter case the small child is often unable to understand the parents' reasons for inflicting punishment or for requiring him to perform tasks that are distasteful to him (88). Ahern points out that our knowledge of the goods and evils in the world (51-5) and of the interconnections between things (57, 72-3) are very limited. Fitzpatrick adduces the deficiencies in our grasp of the divine nature (25-28). This is all well taken and, I believe, does provide support for the agnostic thesis. But then why am I taking pen in hand to add to this ever swelling stream of literature? For several reasons. First, I will not be proceeding on the basis of any general skepticism about our cognitive powers either across the board or generally with respect to God. I will, rather, be focusing on the peculiar difficulties we encounter in attempting to provide adequate support for a certain very ambitious negative existential claim, viz., that there is (can be) no sufficient divine reason for permitting a certain case of suffering, E.[12] I will be appealing to the difficulties of defending a claim of this particular kind, rather than to more generalized human cognitive weaknesses. Second, much of the literature just alluded to has centered around Wykstra's claim that to be justified in asserting 1 it would have to be the case that if 1 were false that would be indicated to one in some way.[13] By contrast I will not be proceeding on the basis of any such unrestrictedly general epistemological principle. Third, I will lay out in much more detail than my predecessors the range of conceivable divine reasons we would have to be able to exclude in order to be justified in asserting 1. Fourth, I can respond to some of the defenses the likes of Rowe have deployed against the agnostic criticism.

VI

Now, at last, I am ready to turn to my central project of arguing that we cannot be justified in accepting 1A. As already noted, I will be emphasizing the fact that this is a negative existential claim. It will be my contention that to be justified in such a claim one must be justified in excluding all the live possibilities for what the claim denies to exist. What 1A denies is that there is any reason God could have for permitting it. I will argue that we are not, and cannot, be justified in asserting that none of these possibilities are realized. I will draw on various theodicies to compile a (partial) list of the reasons God might conceivably have for permitting E. That will provide me with a partial list of the suggestions we must have sufficient reason to reject in order to rationally accept 1. Note that it is no part of my purpose here to develop or defend a theodicy. I am using theodicies only as a source of *possibilities* for divine reasons for evil, possibilities the realization of which the atheologian will have to show to be highly implausible if his project is to succeed.

Since I am criticizing Rowe's argument I am concerned to argue that we are not justified in asserting 1A for the particular kinds of suffering on which Rowe focuses. And we should not suppose that God would have the same reason for permitting every case of suffering.[14] Hence it is to be expected that the reasons suggested by a given theodicy will be live possibilities for some cases of evil and not others. I am, naturally, most interested in suggestions that constitute live possibilities for divine reasons for permitting Bambi's and Sue's suffering. And many familiar theodicies do not pass this test. (This is, no doubt, why these cases were chosen by Rowe and Russell.) Bambi's suffering, and presumably Sue's as well, could hardly be put down to punishment for sin, and neither case could seriously be supposed to be allowed by God for the sake of character building. Nevertheless, I shall not confine the discussion to live possibilities for these two cases. There are two reasons for this. First, a discussion of other theodicies will help to nail down the general point that we are typically unable to exclude live possibilities for divine reasons in a particular case. Second, these discussions will provide ammunition against atheological arguments based on other kinds of suffering.

Thus I shall first consider theodical suggestions that seem clearly not to apply to Bambi or Sue. Here I shall be thinking instead of an adult sufferer from a painful and lengthy disease (fill in the details as you like) whom I shall call 'Sam'. Having argued that we are not in a position to exclude the possibility that God has reasons of these sorts for permitting Sam's suffering, I shall pass on to other suggestions that do constitute genuine possibilities for Bambi and/or Sue.

V

I begin with a traditional theme, that human suffering is God's punishment for sin. Though it hardly applies to Bambi or Sue, it may be a live possibility in other cases, and so I will consider it. The punishment motif has tended to drop out of theodicies in our "soft-on-criminals" and "depravity-is-a-disease" climate, but it has bulked large in the Christian tradition.[15] It often draws the criticism that, so far as we can see, degree or extent of suffering is not nicely proportioned to degree of guilt. Are the people of Vietnam, whose country was ravaged by war in this century, markedly more sinful than the people of Switzerland, whose country was not? But, remembering the warnings of the last section, that does not show that this is never God's reason for permitting suffering, and here we're concerned with a particular case, Sam. Let's say that it seems clear, so far as we can tell, that Sam's suffering is not in proportion to his sinfulness. Sam doesn't seem to have been a bad sort at all, and he has suffered horribly. Can we go from that to "Sam's suffering was not a punishment for sin", or even to "It is reasonable to suppose that Sam's suffering was not a punishment for sin". I suggest that we cannot.

First, we are often in a poor position to assess the degree and kind of a certain person's sinfulness, or to compare people in this regard. Since I am thinking of the inductive argument from evil as directed against Christian belief in God, it will be appropriate to understand the punishment-for-sin suggestion in those terms. Two points about sin are particularly relevant here. (I) Inward sins—one's intentions, motives, attitudes—are more serious than failings in outward behavior.[16] (2) The greatest sin is a self-centered refusal or failure to make God the center of one's life. (2) is sharply at variance with standard secular bases for moral judgment and evaluation. Hence the fact that X does not seem, from that standpoint, more wicked than Y, or doesn't seem wicked at all, does nothing to show that God, or a Christian understanding of God, would make the same judgment. Because of (1) overt behavior is not always a good indication of a person's condition, sin-wise. This is not to say that we could not make a sound judgment of a person's inner state if we had a complete record of what is publicly observable concerning the person. Perhaps in some instances we could, and perhaps in others we could not. But in any event, we rarely or never have such a record. Hence, for both these reasons our judgments as to the relation between S's suffering and S's sinfulness are usually of questionable value.

Second, according to Christianity, one's life on earth is only a tiny proportion of one's total life span. This means that, knowing nothing about the immeasurably greater proportion of Sam's life, we are in no position that deny that the suffering qua punishment has not had a reformative effect, even if we can see no such effect in his earthly life.[17]

I might be accused of begging the question by dragging in Christian convictions to support my case. But that would be a misunderstanding. I am not seeking to prove, or give grounds for, theism or Christianity. I am countering a certain argument against Christian theism. I introduce these Christian doctrines only to spell out crucial features of what is being argued against. The Christian understanding of sin, human life, God's purposes, and so on, go into the determination of what the critic must be justified in denying if she is to be justified in the conclusion that Sam's suffering would not have been permitted by God.

VI

I have led off my survey of theodical suggestions with the punishment motif, despite the fact that it is highly controversial and the reverse of popular. Nor would I want to put heavy emphasis on it were I constructing a theodicy. I have put my worst foot forward in order to show that even here the critic is in no position to show that Sam's suffering is not permitted by God for this reason. If the critic can't manage even this, he will presumably be much worse off with more plausible suggestions for divine reasons, to some of which I now turn.

One of the most prominent theodical suggestions is that God allows suffering because He is interested in a "vale of soulmaking". He takes it that by confronting difficulties, hardships, frustrations, perils, and even suffering and only by doing this, we have a chance to develop such qualities of character as patience, courage, and compassion, qualities we would otherwise have no opportunity to develop. This line has been set forth most forcefully in our time by John Hick in *Evil and the God of Love* revised edition, (1978), a book that has evoked much discussion. To put the point most generally, God's purpose is to make it possible for us to grow into the kind of person that is capable of an eternal life of loving communion with Himself. To be that kind of person one will have to possess traits of character like those just mentioned, traits that one cannot develop without meeting and reacting to difficulties and hardships, including suffering. To show that E would not be permitted by God, the critic has to show that it does not serve the "soul-making" function.

To get to the points I am concerned to make I must first respond to some standard objections to this theodicy. (1) God could surely just create us with the kind of character needed for fellowship with Himself, thereby rendering the hardships and suffering unnecessary. Hick's answer is that what God aims at is not fellowship with a suitably programmed robot, but fellowship with creatures who freely choose to work for what is needed and to take advantage of the opportunity thus engendered. God sees the realization of this aim for some free creatures,[18] even at the cost of suffering and hardship for all, as being of much greater value than any alternative, including a world with no free creatures and a world in which the likes of human beings come off the assembly line pre-sanctified. As usual, I am not concerned to defend the claim that this is the way things are, but only to claim that we are in no position to deny that God is correct in this judgment. (For a discussion of difficulties in carrying out comparative evaluation of total universes, see the end of section IX.)

(2) "If God is using suffering to achieve this goal, He is not doing very well. In spite of all the suffering we undergo, most of us don't get very far in developing courage, compassion, etc." There are two answers to this. First, we are in no position to make that last judgment. We don't know nearly enough about the inner springs of peoples' motivation, attitudes, and character, even in this life. And we know nothing about any further development in an after-life. Second, the theism under discussion takes God to respect the free will of human beings. No strategy consistent with that can guarantee that all, or perhaps any, creatures will respond in the way intended. Whether they do is ultimately up to them. Hence we cannot argue from the fact that such tactics often don't succeed to the conclusion that God wouldn't employ them. When dealing with free creatures God must, because of self-imposed limitations, use means that have some considerable likelihood of success, not means that cannot fail. It is amazing that so many critics reject theodicies like Hick's on the grounds of a poor success rate. I don't say that a poor success rate could not, under any circumstances, justify us in denying that God would permit E for the sake of soulmaking. If we really did know enough to be reasonably sure that the success rate is very poor *and* that other devices open to God would be seen by omniscience to have a significantly greater chance of success, *then* we

could conclude that Hick's line does not get at what God is up to. But we are a very long way indeed from being able to justifiably assert this.

We cannot take the kind of reason stressed by Hick to be a live possibility for the Bambi and Sue cases. The former is much more obvious than the latter, but even in the latter case Sue has no chance to respond to the suffering in the desired way, except in an after life, and it strains credulity to suppose that God would subject a 5-year old to *that* for the sake of character building in the life to come. Hence once more, and until further notice, we will stick with Sam.

Let's stipulate that Sam's suffering does not appear, on close examination, to be theistically explainable as aimed by God at "soulmaking". He seems already to have more of the qualities of character in question than most of us, or the amount of suffering seems to be too much for the purpose, or to be so great as to overwhelm him and make character development highly unlikely. And so our best judgment is that God wouldn't be permitting his suffering for that reason. But that judgment is made in ignorance of much relevant information. Perhaps a more penetrating picture of Sam's spiritual condition would reveal that he is much more in need of further development than is apparent to us from our usual superficial perspective on such matters. Since we don't see his career after death, we are in a poor position to determine how, over the long run, he reacts to the suffering; perhaps if we had that information we would see that this suffering is very important for his full development. Moreover, we are in a poor position, or no position, to determine what is the most effective strategy for God to use in His pursuit of Sam. We don't know what alternatives are open to God, while respecting Sam's freedom, or what the chances are, on one or another alternative, of inducing the desired responses. We are in a poor position to say that this was too much suffering for the purpose, or to say how much would be just right. And we will continue to be in that position until our access to relevant information is radically improved.

Thus we cannot be justified in holding that Sam's suffering is not permitted by God in order to further His project of soul-making. There is an allied, but significantly different theodical suggestion by Eleonore Stump concerning which I would make the same points. Briefly, and oversimply, Stump's central suggestion is that the function of natural evil in God's scheme is to bring us to salvation, or, as she likes to put it, to contribute to the project of "fixing our wills", which have been damaged by original sin. Natural evil tends to prod us to turn to God, thereby giving Him a chance to fix our wills.

> Natural evil—the pain of disease, the intermittent and unpredictable destruction of natural disasters, the decay of old age, the imminence of death—takes away a person's satisfaction with himself.It tends to humble him, show him his frailty, make him reflect on the transience

of temporal goods, and turn his affections towards other-worldly things, away from the things of this world. No amount of moral or natural evil, of course, can *guarantee* that a man will seek God's help. If it could, the willing it produced would not be free. But evil of this sort is the best hope, I think, and maybe the only effective means, for bringing men to such a state (Stump, 1985, p. 409).

Objections will be raised somewhat similar to those that have been made to Hick. A perfectly good God wouldn't have let us get in this situation in the first place. God would employ a more effective technique.[19]   There's too much suffering for the purpose. It is not distributed properly. And so on. These will answered in the same way as the analogous objections to Hick. As for Sam, if we cannot see how his suffering was permitted by God for the reason Stump suggests, I will do a rerun of the parallel points concerning Hick's soul making suggestion.

Closely related suggestions have been made by Marilyn McCord Adams in her essay, "Redemptive Suffering: A Christian Solution to the Problem of Evil" (1986). She takes martyrdom as her model for redemptive suffering, though she by no means wishes to limit her discussion to martyrdom strictly so called. ". . . the redemptive potential of many other cases that, strictly speaking, are not martyrdoms can be seen by extrapolation" (p. 261). In other words her suggestion is that the benefits for the martyr and others that can flow from martyrdom in the strict sense, can also flow from suffering that does not involve undergoing persecution for the faith. Her bold suggestion is that "martyrdom is an expression of God's righteous love toward the onlooker, the persecutor, and even the martyr himself" (257). Here I want to focus on her account of the benefits to the martyr. ". . . the threat of martyrdom is a time of testing and judgment. It makes urgent the previously abstract dilemma of whether he loves God more than the temporal goods that are being extracted as a price . . . the martyr will have had to face a deeper truth about himself and his relations to God and temporal goods than ever he could in fair weather . . . the time of trial is also an opportunity for building a relationship of trust between the martyr and that to which he testifies. Whether because we are fallen or by the nature of the case, trusting relationships have to be built up by a history of interactions. If the martyr's loyalty to God is tested, but after a struggle he holds onto his allegiance to God and God delivers him (in his own time and way), the relationship is strengthened and deepened" (259). Adams is modest in her claims. She does not assert that all cases of suffering are analogous to martyrdom in these respects. "Some are too witless to have relationships that can profit and mature through such tests of loyalty. Some people are killed or severely harmed too quickly for such moral struggles to take place. At other times the victim is an unbeliever who has no explicit relationship with God to wrestle with."[20]   However none of these disqualifications apply to her boldest suggestion, that given the Christian doctrine of the suffering of God incarnate on the cross, "temporal suffering itself is a vision into the inner life of God" (264), a theme that she takes from Christian mysticism. That value of suffering, if such it be, can be enjoyed by any sufferer, whatever the circumstances. To be sure, one might not realize at the time that the suffering has that significance. But if one reaches the final term of Christian development, "he might be led to reason that the good aspect of an experience of deep suffering [the aspect just pointed to] is great enough that, from the standpoint of the beatific vision, the victim would not wish the experience away from his life history, but would, on the contrary, count it as an extremely valuable part of his life" (265). It should also be noted that Adams does not suggest that God's reasons for permitting suffering in any particular case are restricted to one of the considerations she has been presenting, or indeed to all of the points she makes.

If we were to try to decide whether Sam's suffering is permitted by God for any of these reasons, we would be in a poor position to make a negative judgment for reasons parallel to those brought out in the discussion of Hick. Given the limits of our access to the secrets of the human heart and the course of the after life, if any, we are, in many instances, in no position to assert with any confidence that this suffering does not have such consequences, and hence that God does not permit it (at least in part) for the sake of just those consequences.

VII

Thus far I have been restricting myself to conceivable divine reasons for suffering that involve the use of that suffering to bring about good for the *sufferer*. This is obvious except for the punishment reason. As for that one, this claim is equally obvious if we are thinking of punishment in terms of reformation of the punishee,[21] but what about a "retributive" theory, according to which the rationale of punishment is simply that the sinner *deserves* to suffer for his sin, that justice demands this, or that a proportionate suffering for wickedness is intrinsically good? Well, though one might balk at describing this as a *good* for the sufferer, it remains that such good as is aimed at and effected by the punishment, on this conception, terminates with the sufferer and does not extend to the welfare of others.

Where divine reasons are restricted this narrowly, the critic is operating on the most favorable possible terrain. If he has any hope of making his case it will be here, where the field of possibilities that must be excluded is relatively narrow. What we have seen is that wherever the reasons we have canvassed are live possibilities, even this is too much for his (our) powers. Our ignorance of relevant facts is so extensive, and the deficiencies in our powers of discernment are so fundamental, as to leave us without any sufficient basis for saying, with respect to a particular case of suffering, that God does not permit it for reasons such as these.

To be sure, this is cold comfort for the critic of Rowe's argument since, as noted earlier, the possibilities we have been canvassing do not seem to be live possibilities for Bambi or Sue. The only real chance for an exception is Adams' suggestion that the experience of suffering constitutes a vision of the inner life of God. Since this is not confined to those who identify it as such, it could apply to Sue, and perhaps to Bambi as well, though presumably only Sue would have a chance to recognize it and rejoice in it, retrospectively, in the light of the beatific vision. However, I don't want to insist on this exception. Let us say that a consideration of the theodicies thus far canvassed does nothing to show that we can't be justified in affirming an instantiation of 1 for Bambi or Sue.

Nevertheless, that does *not* show that we can be justified in excluding the possibility that God has no patient-centered reason for permitting Bambi's or Sue's suffering. It doesn't show this because we are not warranted in supposing that the possible reasons we have been extracting from theodicies exhaust the possibilities for patient-centered reasons God might have for permitting Bambi's or Sue's suffering. Perhaps, unbeknownst to us, one or the other of these bits of suffering is necessary, in ways we cannot grasp, for some outweighing good of a sort with which we are familiar, e.g., supreme fulfillment of one's deepest nature. Or perhaps it is necessary for the realization of a good of which we as yet have no conception. And these possibility are by no means remote ones. "There are more things in heaven and earth, Horatio, than are dreamt of in your philosophy." Truer words were never spoken. They point to the fact that our cognitions of the world, obtained by filtering raw data through such conceptual screens as we have available for the nonce, acquaint us with only some indeterminable fraction of what is there to be known. The progress of human knowledge makes this evident. No one explicitly realized the distinction between concrete and abstract entities, the distinction between efficient and final causes, the distinction between knowledge and opinion, until great creative thinkers adumbrated these distinctions and disseminated them to their fellows. The development of physical science has made us aware of a myriad of things hitherto undreamed of, and developed the concepts with which to grasp them— gravitation, electricity, electromagnetic fields, space-time curvature, irrational numbers, and so on. It is an irresistible induction from this that we have not reached the final term of this process, and that more realities, aspects, properties, structures remain to be discerned and conceptualized. And why should values, and the conditions of their realization, be any exception to this generalization? A history of the apprehension of values could undoubtedly be written, parallel to the history just adumbrated, though the archeology would be a more difficult and delicate task.

Moreover, remember that our topic is not the possibilities for future human apprehensions, but rather what an omniscient being can grasp of modes of value and the conditions of their realization. Surely it is eminently possible that there are real possibilities for the latter that exceed anything we can anticipate, or even conceptualize. It would be exceedingly strange if an omniscient being did not immeasurably exceed our grasp of such matters. Thus there is an unquestionably live possibility that God's reasons for allowing human suffering may have to do, in part, with the appropriate connection of those sufferings with goods in ways that have never been dreamed of in our theodicies. Once we bring this into the picture, the critic is seen to be on shaky ground in denying, of Bambi's or Sue's suffering, that God could have any patient-centered reason for permitting it, even if we are unable to suggest what such a reason might be.[22]

This would be an appropriate place to consider Rowe's argument that we can be justified in excluding the possibility that God permits one or another case of suffering in order to obtain goods of which we have no conception. In his latest article on the subject (1988) Rowe claims that the variant of 1 there put forward:

Q. No good state of affairs is such that an omnipotent, omniscient being's obtaining it would morally justify that being in permitting E1 or E2 (p. 120).[23]

can be derived probabilistically from:

P. No good state of affairs we know of is such that an omnipotent, omniscient being's obtaining it would morally justify that being's permitting E1 or E2 (p. 121).

I have been arguing, and will continue to argue, that Rowe is not justified in asserting P, since he is not justified in supposing that none of the particular goods we have been discussing provide God with sufficient reason for permitting the suffering of Bambi and Sue. But even if Rowe were justified in asserting P, what I have just been contending is that the argument from P to Q does not go through. In defending the argument Rowe says the following.

My answer is that we are justified in making this inference in the same way we are justified in making the many inferences we constantly make from the known to the unknown. All of us are constantly inferring from the A's we know of to the A's we don't know of. If we observe many A's and all of them are B's we are justified in believing that the A's we haven't observed are also B's. If I encounter a fair number of pit bulls and all of them are vicious, I have reason to believe that all pit bulls are vicious (1988, pp. 123-24).

But it is just not true that Rowe's inference from known goods to all goods is parallel to inductive inferences we "constantly make". Typically when we generalize from observed instances, at least when we are warranted in doing so, we know quite a lot about what makes a sample of things like that a good base for general attributions of the properties in question. We know that temperamental traits like viciousness or affectionateness are often breed-specific in dogs, and so when a number of individuals of a breed are observed to exhibit such a trait it is a good guess that it is characteristic of that breed. If, on the other hand, the characteristic found throughout the sample were a certain precise height or a certain sex, our knowledge indicates that an inference that all members of that breed are of that height or of that sex would be foolhardy indeed. But, as I have been arguing, an inference from known goods lacking J to all goods (including those we have never experienced and even those of which we have no conception) is unlike both the sorts just mentioned in the way they resemble one another, viz., our possession of knowledge indicating which characteristics can be expected to be (fairly) constant in the larger population. We have no background knowledge that tells us the chances of J's being a "goods-specific" characteristic, one that can reasonably be expected to be present in all or most goods if it is found in a considerable sample. Hence we cannot appeal to clearly warranted generalizations in support of this one. Rowe's generalization is more like inferring from the fact that no one has yet produced a physical theory that will unify relativity and quantum mechanics, to the prediction that no one will ever do so, or inferring, in 1850, from the fact no one has yet voyaged to the moon that no one will ever do so. We have no way of drawing boundaries around the total class of goods; we are unable to anticipate what may lie in its so-far-unknown sub-class, just as we are unable to anticipate future scientific developments and future artistic innovations. This is not an area in which induction by simple enumeration yields justified belief.[24]

VIII

It is now time to move beyond the restriction on divine reasons to benefits to the sufferer. The theodical suggestions we will be discussing from here on do not observe this restriction. Since I am moving onto territory less favorable to my opponent, I must give some indication of what might justify dropping the restriction. For my central purposes in this paper I do not need to show that the restriction is unjustified. I take myself to have already shown that the critic is not entitled to his "no sufficient divine reasons" thesis even with the restriction. But I do believe that the restriction is unwarranted, and I want to consider how the land lies with respect to conceivable divine reasons of other sorts. As a prelude to that I will point out the main reasons for and against the restriction to benefits to the sufferer.

On the pro side by far the main consideration is one of justice and fairness. Why should suffering be laid on me for the sake of some good in which I will not participate, or in which my participation is not sufficient to justify my suffering? Wouldn't God be sacrificing me to His own ends and/or to the ends of others if that were His modus operandi, and in that case how could He be considered perfectly good?

> Undeserved suffering which is uncompensated seems clearly unjust; but so does suffering compensated only by benefits to someone other than the sufferer...other things being equal, it seems morally permissible to allow someone to suffer involuntarily only in case doing so is a necessary means or the best possible means in the circumstances to keep the sufferer from incurring even greater harm.[25]

I agree with this to the extent of conceding that a perfectly good God would not wholly sacrifice the welfare of one of His intelligent creatures simply in order to achieve a good for others, or for Himself. This would be incompatible with His concern for the welfare of each of His creatures. Any plan that God would implement will include provision for each of us having a life that is, on balance, a good thing, and one in which the person reaches the point of being able to see that his life as a whole is a good for him. Or at least, where free creaturely responses have a significant bearing on the overall quality of the person's life, any possible divine plan will have to provide for each of us to have the chance (or perhaps many chances) for such an outcome, if our free responses are of the right sort. Nevertheless, this is compatible with God having as part of his reason for permitting a given case of suffering that it contributes to results that extend beyond the sufferer.[26] So long as the sufferer is amply taken care of, I can't see that this violates any demands of divine justice, compassion, or love. After all, parents regularly impose sacrifices on some of their children for the overall welfare of the family. Of course, in doing so they are acting out of a scarcity of resources, and God's situation is enormously different in this respect. Nevertheless, assuming that Sue's suffering is necessary even for God to be able to achieve a certain good state of affairs, then, provided that Sue is taken care of in such a way that she will eventually come to recognize the value and justifiability of the proceeding and to joyfully endorse it (or at least has ample opportunities to get herself into this position), I cannot see that God could be faulted for setting things up this way.[27]

From now on I will be considering possible divine reasons that extend beyond benefit to the sufferer. Though in line with the previous paragraph I will not suppose that any of these (so far as they exclusively concern persons other than the sufferer) could be God's whole reason for permitting a bit of suffering, I will take it as a live possibility that they could contribute to a sufficient divine reason. The theodicies to be considered now will give us more specific suggestions for Bambi and Sue.

I will begin with the familiar free will theodicy, according to which God is justified in permitting creaturely wickedness and its consequences because he has to do so if he is bestow on some of his creatures the incommensurable privilege of being responsible agents who have, in many areas, the capacity to choose between alternatives as they will, without God, or anyone or anything else (other than themselves), determining which alternative they choose. The suggestion of this theodicy is that it is conceptually impossible for God to create free agents and also determine how they are to choose, within those areas in which they are free. If He were so to determine their choices they would, ipso facto, not be free. But this being the case, when God decided to endow some of His creatures, including us, with free choice, He thereby took the chance, ran the risk, of our sometimes or often making the wrong choice, a possibility that has been richly realized. It is conceptually impossible for God to create free agents and not subject Himself to such a risk. Not to do the latter would be not to do the former. But that being the case, He, and we, are stuck with whatever consequences ensue. And this is why God permits such horrors as the rape, beating, and murder of Sue. He does it not because that particular wicked choice is itself necessary for the realization of some great good, but because the permission of such horrors is bound up with the decision to give human beings free choice in many areas, and that (the capacity to freely choose) is a great good, such a great good as to be worth all the suffering and others evils that it makes possible.[28]

This theodicy has been repeatedly subjected to radical criticisms that, if sound, would imply that the value of creaturely free will is not even a possible reason for God's allowing Sue's attacker to do his thing. For one thing, it has been urged that it is within God's power to create free agents so that they always choose what is right. For another, it has been denied or doubted that free will is of such value as to be worth all the sin and suffering it has brought into the world. In accord with my general policy in this paper, I will not attempt to argue that this theodicy does succeed in identifying God's reasons for permitting wrongdoing and its results, but only that the possibility of this cannot be excluded. Hence I can confine myself to arguing that these criticisms do not dispose of that possibility. Though lack of space prevents a proper discussion, I will just indicate what I would say in such a discussion. On the first point, if we set aside middle knowledge as I am doing in this paper, it is logically impossible for God to create beings with genuine freedom of choice and also guarantee that they will always choose the right. And even granting middle knowledge Plantinga (1974) has established the *possibility* that God could not actualize a world containing free creatures that always do the right thing. As for the second point, though it may be beyond our powers to show that free will has sufficient value to carry the theodical load, it is surely equally beyond our powers to show that it does not.[29]

Thus we may take it to be a live possibility that the maintenance of creaturely free will is at least part of God's reason for permitting wrongdoing and its consequences. But then the main reason one could have for denying that this is at least part of why God would allow the attack on Sue is that God could, miraculously or otherwise, prevent any one incipient free human action without losing the value of human free will. Clearly a divine interference in normal human operations in this one instance is not going to prevent even Sue's attacker from being a free moral agent in general, with all that that involves. This point is supported by the consideration that, for all we know, God does sometimes intervene to prevent human agents from doing wicked things they would otherwise have done, and, so the free will theodicist will claim, even if that is the case we do enjoy the incommensurable value of free choice. We can also think of it this way. It is perfectly obvious that the scope of our free choice is not unlimited. We have no effective voluntary control over, e.g., our genetic constitution, our digestive and other biological processes, and much of our cognitive operations. Thus whatever value the human capacity for free choice possesses, that value is compatible with free choice being confined within fairly narrow limits. But then presumably a tiny additional constriction such as would be involved in God's preventing Sue's attacker from committing that atrocity would not render things radically different, free-will-wise, from what they would have been without that. So God could have prevented this without losing the good emphasized by this theodicy. Hence we can be sure that this does not constitute a sufficient reason for His not preventing it.

To be sure, if God were to act on this principle in every case of incipient wrongdoing, the situation would be materially changed. Human agents would no longer have a real choice between good and evil, and the surpassing worth that attaches to having such a choice would be lost. Hence, if God is to promote the values emphasized by the free will theodicy, He can intervene in this way in only a small proportion of cases. And how are these to be selected? I doubt that we are in a position to give a confident answer to this question, but let's assume that the critic proposes that the exceptions are to be picked in such a way as to maximize welfare, and let's go along with that. Rowe's claim would then have to be that Sue's murder was so horrible that it would qualify for the class of exceptions. But that is precisely where the critic's claims far outrun his justification. How can we tell that Sue falls within the most damaging n% of what would be cases of human wrongdoing apart from divine intervention. To be in a position to make such a judgment we would have to survey the full range of such cases and make reliable assessments of the deleterious consequences of each. Both tasks are far beyond our powers. We don't even know what free creaturely agents there are beyond human beings, and with respect to humans the range of wickedness, past, present, and future, is largely beyond our ken. And even with respect to the cases of which we are aware we have only a limited ability to assess the total consequences. Hence, by the nature of the case, we are simply not in a position to make a warranted judgment that Sue's case is among the n% worst cases of wrongdoing in the history of the universe. No doubt, it strikes us as incomparably horrible on hearing about it, but so would innumerable others. Therefore, the critic is not in a position to set aside the value of free will as at least part of God's reason for permitting Sue's murder.

IX

Next I turn to theodicies that stress benefit to human beings other than the sufferer or to humanity generally.[30] And first let's return to Marilyn Adams 'discussion of martyrdom in (1986). In addition to her account, already noted, of martyrdom as a vehicle of God's goodness to the martyr, she discusses "Martyrdom as a vehicle of God's goodness to the onlooker". "For onlookers, the event of martyrdom may function as a prophetic story, the more powerful for being brought to life. The martyr who perseveres to the end presents an inspiring example. Onlookers are invited to see in the martyr the person they ought to be and to be brought to a deeper level of commitment. Alternatively, onlookers may see themselves in the persecutor and be moved to repentance. If the onlooker has ears to hear the martyr's testimony, he may receive God's redemption through it" (p. 257). She also suggests that martyrdom may be redemptive for the persecutor. "First of all, the martyr's sacrifice can be used as an instrument of divine judgment, because it draws the persecutor an external picture of what he is really like—the more innocent the victim, the clearer the focus...In attempting to bring reconciliation out of judgment, God may find no more promising vehicle than martyrdom for dealing with the hard-hearted" (p. 258). (Again, in making these suggestions for a theodicy of suffering, Adams is not restricting their scope to martyrdom strictly so called.) To be sure, sometimes there is no persecutor, but often there is, as in child and wife abuse. And there is always the possibility, and usually the actuality, of onlookers.[31]

Can the critic be justified in holding that Sue's suffering, e.g., would not be permitted by God at least in part for reasons of these sorts? Once more, even if we cannot see that Sue's suffering brings these kinds of benefits to her attacker or to onlookers, our massive ignorance of the recesses of the human heart and of the total outcomes, perhaps through eternity, for all such people, renders us poor judges of whether such benefits are indeed forthcoming. And, finally, even if no goods of these sorts eventuate, there is once more the insoluble problem of whether God could be expected to use a different strategy, given His respect for human free will. Perhaps that was (a part of) the strategy that held out the best chance of evoking the optimal response from these particularly hard-hearted subjects.

Next I want to consider a quite different theodicy that also sees God's reasons for permitting suffering in terms of benefits that are generally distributed, viz., the appeal to the benefits of a lawlike natural order, and the claim that suffering will be an inevitable byproduct of any such order. I choose the exposition of this theodicy in Bruce Reichenbach in *Evil and a Good God* (1982).

> . . . creation, in order to make possible the existence of moral agents . . . had to be ordered according to some set of natural laws (p. 101).

The argument for this is that if things do not happen in a lawlike fashion, at least usually, agents will be unable to anticipate the consequences of their volitions, and hence will not be able to effectively make significant choices between good and evil actions. Reichenbach continues:

> Consequently, the possibility arises that sentient creatures like ourselves can be negatively affected by the outworkings of these laws in nature, such that we experience pain, suffering, disability, disutility, and at times the frustration of our good desires. Since a world with free persons making choices between moral good and evil and choosing a significant amount of moral good is better than a world without free persons and moral good and evil, God in creating had to create a world which operated according to natural laws to achieve this higher good. Thus, his action of creation of a natural world and a natural order, along with the resulting pain and pleasure which we experience, is justified. The natural evils which afflict us—diseases, sickness, disasters, birth defects—are all the outworking of the natural system of which we are a part. They are the byproducts made possible by that which is necessary for the greater good (100-01).

This is a theodicy for natural evil, not for the suffering that results from human wickedness. Hence it has possible application to Bambi, but not to Sue, and possible application to any other suffering that results from natural processes that are independent of human intentional action.

Let's agree that significant moral agency requires a natural lawful order. But that doesn't show that it is even possible that God had a sufficient reason to allow Bambi's suffering. There are two difficulties that must be surmounted to arrive at that point.

First, a natural order can be regular enough to provide the degree of predictability required for morally significant choice even if there are exceptions to the regularities. Therefore, God could set aside the usual consequences of natural forces in this instance, so as to prevent Bambi's suffering, without thereby interfering with human agents' reasonable anticipations of the consequences of their actions. So long as God doesn't do this too often, we will still have ample basis for suppositions as to what we can reasonably expect to follow what. But note that by the same line of reasoning God cannot do this too often, or the desired predictability will not be forthcoming. Hence, though any one naturally caused suffering could have been miraculously prevented, God certainly has a strong prima facie reason in each case to refrain from doing this; for if He didn't He would have no reason for letting nature usually take its course. And so He has a possible reason for allowing nature to take its course in the Bambi case, a reason that would have to be overridden by stronger contrary considerations.

This means that in order to be justified in supposing that God would not have a sufficient reason to refrain from intervening in this case, we would have to be justified in supposing that God would have a sufficient reason to make, in this case, an exception to the general policy. And how could we be justified in supposing that? We would need an adequate grasp of the full range of cases from which God would have to choose whatever exceptions He is going to make, if any, to the general policy of letting nature take its course. Without that we would not be in a position to judge that Bambi is among the n% of the cases most worthy of being miraculously prevented.[32] And it is abundantly clear that we have and can have no such grasp of this territory as a whole. We are quite unable, by our natural powers, of determining just what cases, or even what kinds of cases, of suffering there would be throughout the history of the universe if nature took its course. We just don't know enough about the constituents of the universe even at present, much less throughout the past and future, to make any such catalogue. And we could not make good that deficiency without an enormous enlargement of our cognitive capacities. Hence we are in no position to judge that God does not have sufficient reason (of the Reichenbach sort) for refraining from interfering in the Bambi case.[33]

But all this has to do with whether God would have interfered with the natural order, as it actually exists, to prevent Bambi's suffering. And it will be suggested, secondly, that God could have instituted a quite different natural order, one that would not involve human and animal suffering, or at least much less of it. Why couldn't there be a natural order in which there are no viruses and bacteria the natural operation of which results in human and animal disease, a natural order in which rainfall is evenly distributed, in which earthquakes do not occur, in which forests are not subject to massive fires? To be sure, even God could not bring into being just the creatures we presently have while subjecting their behavior to different laws. For the fact that a tiger's natural operations and tendencies are what they are is an essential part of what makes it the kind of thing it is.[34] But why couldn't God have created a world with different constituents so as to avoid subjecting any sentient creatures to disease and natural disasters? Let's agree that this is possible for God. But then the critic must also show that at least one of the ways in which God could have done this would have produced a world that is better on the whole than the actual world. For even if God could have instituted a natural order without disease and natural disasters, that by itself doesn't show that He would have done so if He existed. For if that world had other undesirable features and/or lacked desirable features in such a way as to be worse, or at least no better than, the actual world, it still doesn't follow that God would have chosen the former over the latter. It all depends on the overall comparative worth of the two systems. Once again I am not concerned to argue for Reichenbach's theodicy, which would, on the rules by which we are playing, require arguing that no possible natural order is overall better than the one we have. Instead I merely want to show that the critic is not justified in supposing that some alternative natural order open to God that does not involve suffering (to the extent that we have it) is better on the whole.

There are two points I want to make about this, points that have not cropped up earlier in the paper. First, it is by no means clear what possibilities are open to God. Here it is important to remember that we are concerned with metaphysical possibilities (necessities . . .), not merely with conceptual or logical possibilities in a narrow sense of 'logical'. The critic typically points out that we can consistently and intelligibly conceive a world in which there are no diseases, no earthquakes, floods, or tornadoes, no predators in the animal kingdom, while all or most of the goods we actually enjoy are still present. He takes this to show that it is possible for God to bring about such a world. But, as many thinkers have recently argued,[35] consistent conceivability (conceptual possibility) is by no means sufficient for metaphysical possibility, for what is possible given the metaphysical structure of reality. To use a well worn example, it may be metaphysically necessary that the chemical composition of water is H_2O since that is what water essentially is, even though, given the ordinary concept of water, we can without contradiction or unintelligibility, think of water as made of up of carbon and chlorine. Roughly speaking, what is conceptually or logically (in a narrow sense of 'logical') possible depends on the composition of the concepts, or the meanings of the terms, we use to cognize reality, while metaphysical possibility depends on what things are like in themselves, their essential natures, regardless of how they are represented in our thought and language.

It is much more difficult to determine what is metaphysically possible or necessary than to determine what is conceptually possible or necessary. The latter requires only careful reflection on our concepts. The former requires—well, it's not clear what will do the trick, but it's not something we can bring off just by reflecting on what we mean by what we say, or on what we are committing ourselves to by applying a certain concept. To know what is metaphysically possible in the way of alternative systems of natural order, we would have to have as firm a grasp of this subject matter as we have of the chemical constitution of familiar substances like water and salt. It is clear that we have no such grasp. We don't have a clue as to what essential natures are within God's creative repertoire, and still less do we have a clue as to which combinations of these into total lawful systems are doable. We know that you can't have water without hydrogen and oxygen and that you can't have salt without sodium and chlorine. But can there be life without hydrocarbons? Who knows? Can there be conscious, intelligent organisms with free will that are not susceptible to pain? That is, just what is metaphysically required for a creature to have the essential nature of a conscious, intelligent, free agent? Who can say? Since we don't have even the beginnings of a canvass of the possibilities here, we are in no position to make a sufficiently informed judgment as to what God could or could not create by way of a natural order that contains the goods of this one (or equal goods of other sorts) without its disadvantages.

One particular aspect of this disability is our inability to determine what consequences would ensue, with metaphysical necessity, on a certain alteration in the natural order. Suppose that predators were turned into vegetarians. Or rather, if predatory tendencies are part of the essential natures of lions, tigers, and the like, suppose that they were replaced with vegetarians as much like them as possible. How much like them is that? What other features are linked to predatory tendencies by metaphysical necessity? We may know something of what is linked to predation by natural necessity, e.g., by the structure and dispositional properties of genes. But to what extent does metaphysical possibility go beyond natural possibility here? To what extent could God institute a different system of heredity such that what is inseparable from predation in the actual genetic code is separable from it instead? Who can say? To take another example, suppose we think of the constitution of the earth altered so that the subterranean tensions and collisions involved in earthquakes are ruled out. What would also have to be ruled out, by metaphysical necessity? (Again, we know something of what goes along with this by natural necessity, but that's not the question.) Could the earth still contain soil suitable for edible crops? Would there still be mountains? A system of flowing streams? We are, if anything, still more at a loss when we think of eradicating all the major sources of suffering from the natural order. What metaphysical possibilities are there for what we could be left with? It boggles the (human) mind to contemplate the question.[36]

The second main point is this. Even if we could, at least in outline, determine what alternative systems of natural order are open to God, we would still be faced with the staggering job of comparative evaluation. How can we hold together in our minds the salient features of two such total systems sufficiently to make a considered judgment of their relative merits? *Perhaps* we are capable of making a considered evaluation of each feature of the systems (or many of them), and even capable of judicious comparisons of features two-by-two. For example, we might be justified in holding that the reduction in the possibilities of disease is worth more than the greater variety of forms of life that goes along with susceptibility to disease. But it is another matter altogether to get the kind of overall grasp of each system to the extent required to provide a comprehensive ranking of those systems. We find it difficult enough, if not impossible, to arrive at a definitive comparative evaluation of cultures, social systems, or educational policies. It is far from clear that even if I devoted my life to the study of two primitive cultures, I would thereby be in a position to make an authoritative pronouncement as to which is better on the whole. How much less are we capable of making a comparative evaluation of two alternative natural orders, with all the indefinitely complex ramification of the differences between the two.[37]

Before leaving this topic I want to emphasize the point that, unlike the theodicies discussed earlier the natural law theodicy bears on the question of animal as well as human suffering. If the value of a lawful universe justifies the suffering that results from the operation of those laws, that would apply to suffering at all levels of the great chain of being.

X

I have been gleaning suggestions from a variety of theodicies as to what reasons God might have for permitting suffering. I believe that each of these suggestions embody one or more sorts of reasons that God might conceivably have for some of the suffering in the world. And I believe that I have shown that none of us are in a position to warrantedly assert, with respect to any of those reasons, that God would not permit some cases of suffering for that reason. Even if I am mistaken in supposing that we cannot rule out some particular reason, e.g. that the suffering is a punishment for sin, I make bold to claim that it is extremely unlikely that I am mistaken about all those suggestions. Moreover, I have argued, successfully I believe, that some of these reasons are at least part of possible divine reasons for Rowe's cases, Bambi and Sue, and that hence we are unable to justifiably assert that God does not have reasons of these sorts for permitting Rowe-like cases.

However that does not suffice to dispose of Rowe's specific argument, concerned as it is with the Bambi and Sue cases in particular. For I earlier conceded, for the sake of argument, that (1) none of the sufferer-centered reasons I considered could be any part of God's reasons for permitting the Bambi and Sue cases, and (2) that nonsufferer-centered reasons could not be the whole of God's reasons for allowing any case of suffering. This left me without any specific suggestions as to what might be a fully sufficient reason for God to permit those cases. And hence showing that no one can be justified in supposing that reasons of the sort considered are not at least part of God's reasons for one or another case of suffering does not suffice to show that no one can be justified in supposing that God could have no sufficient reason for permitting the Bambi and Sue cases. And hence it does not suffice to show that Rowe cannot be justified in asserting 1.

This lacuna in the argument is remedied by the point that we cannot be justified in supposing that there are no other reasons, thus far unenvisaged, that would fully justify God in permitting Rowe's cases. That point was made at the end of section vii for sufferer-centered reasons, and it can now be made more generally. Even if we were fully entitled to dismiss all the alleged reasons for permitting suffering that have been suggested, we would still have to consider whether there are further possibilities that are undreamt of in our theodicies. Why should we suppose that the theodicies thus far excogitated, however brilliant and learned their authors, exhaust the field. The points made in the earlier discussion about the impossibility of anticipating future developments in human thought can be applied here. Just as we can never repose confidence in any alleged limits of future human theoretical and conceptual developments in science, so it is here, even more so if possible. It is surely reasonable to suppose that God, if such there be, has more tricks up His sleeve than we can envisage. Since it is in principle impossible for us to be justified in supposing that God does not have sufficient reasons for permitting E that are unknown to us, and perhaps unknowable by us, no one call be justified in holding that God could have no reasons for permitting the Bambi and Sue cases, or any other particular cases of suffering.[38]

This last point, that we are not warranted in supposing that God does not have sufficient reasons unknown to us for permitting E, is not only an essential part of the total argument against the justifiability of 1. It would be sufficient by itself. Even if all my argumentation prior to that point were in vain and my opponent could definitively rule out all the specific suggestions I have put forward, she would still face the insurmountable task of showing herself to be justified in supposing that there are no further possibilities for sufficient divine reasons. That point by itself would be decisive.

XI

In the case of each of the theodical suggestions considered I have drawn on various limits to our cognitive powers, opportunities, and achievements in arguing that we are not in a position to deny that God could have that kind of reason for various cases of suffering. In conclusion it may be useful to list the cognitive limits that have formed the backbone of my argument.

1. *Lack of data.* This includes, inter alia, the secrets of the human heart, the detailed constitution and structure of the universe, and the remote past and future, including the afterlife if any.

2. *Complexity greater than we can handle.* Most notably there is the difficulty of holding enormous complexes of fact—different possible worlds or different systems of natural law—together in the mind sufficiently for comparative evaluation.

3. *Difficulty of determining what is metaphysically possible or necessary.* Once we move beyond conceptual or semantic modalities (and even that is no piece of cake) it is notoriously difficult to find any sufficient basis for claims as to what is metaphysically possible, given the essential natures of things, the exact character of which is often obscure to us and virtually always controversial. This difficulty is many times multiplied when we are dealing with tota possible worlds or total systems of natural order.

4. *Ignorance of the full range of possibilities.* This is always crippling when we are trying to establish negative conclusions. If we don't know whether or not there are possibilities beyond the ones we have thought of, we are in a very bad position to show that there can be no divine reasons for permitting evil.

5. *Ignorance of the full range of values.* When it's a question of whether some good is related to E in such a way as to justify God in permitting E, we are, for the reason mentioned in 4., in a very poor position to answer the question if we don't know the extent to which there are modes of value beyond those of which we are aware. For in that case, so far as we can know, E may be justified by virtue of its relation to one of those unknown goods.

6. *Limits to our capacity to make well considered value judgments.* The chief example of this we have noted is the difficulty in making comparative evaluations of large complex wholes.

It may seem to the reader that I have been making things too difficult for the critic, holding him to unwarrantedly exaggerated standards for epistemic justification. "If we were to apply your standards across the board", he may complain, "it would turn out that we are justified in believing little or nothing. That would land us in a total skepticism. And doesn't that indicate that your standards are absurdly inflated?" I agree that it would indicate that if the application of my standards did have that result, but I don't agree that this is the case. The point is that the critic is engaged in attempting to support a particularly difficult claim, a claim that there isn't something in a certain territory, while having a very sketchy idea of what is in that territory, and having no sufficient basis for an estimate of how much of the territory falls outside his knowledge. This is very different from our more usual situation in which we are forming judgments and drawing conclusions about matters concerning which we antecedently know quite a lot, and the boundaries and parameters of which we have pretty well settled. Thus the attempt to show that God could have no sufficient reason for permitting Bambi's or Sue's suffering is quite atypical of our usual cognitive situation; no conclusion can be drawn from our poor performance in the former to an equally poor performance in the latter.[39]

I want to underline the point that my argument in this paper does not rely on a general skepticism about our cognitive powers, about our capacity to achieve knowledge and justified belief. On the contrary, I have been working with what I take to be our usual nonskeptical standards for these matters, standards that I take to be satisfied by the great mass of our beliefs in many areas. My claim has been that when these standards are applied to the kind of claim exemplified by Rowe's 1, it turns out this claim is not justified and that the prospects for any of us being justified in making it are poor at best. This is because of the specific character of that claim, its being a negative existential claim concerning a territory about the extent, contents, and parameters of which we know little. My position no more implies, presupposes, or reflects a general skepticism than does the claim that we don't know that there is no life elsewhere in the universe.

This completes my case for the "agnostic thesis", the claim that we are simply not in a position to justifiably assert, with respect to Bambi or Sue or other cases of suffering, that God, if He exists, would have no sufficient reason for permitting it. And if that is right, the inductive argument from evil is in no better shape that its late lamented deductive cousin.

Endnotes

*"The Inductive Argument from Evil and the Human Cognitive Condition," by William P. Alston, appeared in *Philosophical Perspectives, 5, Philosophy of Religion, 1991,* edited by James E. Tomberlin (copyright by Ridgeview Publishing Co., Atascardero, CA). Reprinted by permission of Ridgeview Publishing Company.

1 The term 'gratuitous' is used in different ways in the literature. Lately it has sprouted variations My use of the term is strictly tied to Rowe's 1.

2 In (1979) Rowe considers this criticism. He says of it: "I suppose some theists would be content with this rather modest response...But given the validity of the basic

argument and the theist's likely acceptance of (2), he is thereby committed to the view that (1) is false, not just that we have no good reasons for accepting (1) as true" (338). No doubt, the theist is committed to regarding (1) as false, at least on the assumption that it embodies necessary conditions for God's having sufficient reason for permitting suffering (on which see F in the next section). But Rowe does not explain why he thinks that showing that we are not justified in asserting 1 does not constitute a decisive reason for rejecting his argument.

3 There is considerable confusion in the literature over what it takes to have a theodicy, or, otherwise put, what a reasonable level of aspiration is for theodicy. Even if we were vouchsafed an abundance of divine revelations I cannot conceive of our being able to specify God's reason for permitting each individual evil. The most that could sensibly be aimed at would be an account of the sorts of reasons God has for various sorts of evil. And a more modest, but still significant, ambition would be to make suggestions as to what God's reasons might be, reasons that are plausible in the light of what we know and believe about God, His nature, purposes, and activities. See Stump, 1990.

4 In arguing for 1 in (1979) Rowe proceeds as if he supposed that the only alternatives are (a) its being reasonable to believe 1 and (b) its being reasonable to believe not-1. "Consider again the case of the fawn's suffering. Is it reasonable to believe that there is some greater good so intimately connected to that suffering that even an omnipotent, omniscient being could not have obtained that good without permitting that suffering or some evil at least as bad? It certainly does not appear reasonable to believe this. Nor does it seem reasonable to believe that there is some evil at least as bad as the fawn's suffering such that an omnipotent being simply could not have prevented it without permitting the fawn's suffering. But even if it should somehow be reasonable to believe either of these things of the fawn's suffering, we must then ask whether it is reasonable to believe either of these things of *all* the instances of seemingly pointless human and animal suffering that occur daily in our world. And surely the answer to this more general question must be no. . . It seems then that although we cannot *prove* that (1) is true, it is nevertheless, altogether *reasonable* to believe that (1) is true, that (1) is a *rational* belief" (337-38). The form of this argument is: "It is not rational to believe that p. Therefore it is rational to believe that not-p." But this is patently lacking in force. There are many issues on which it is rational to believe neither p nor not-p. Take p to be, e.g, the proposition that it was raining on this spot exactly 45,000 years ago.

5 The qualifier 'traditional' adheres to the restrictions laid down in D and excludes variants like process theology. Admittedly, "traditional Christianity" contains a number of in-house variants, but in this paper I will appeal only to what is common to all forms of what could reasonably be called "traditional Christianity".

6 Rowe does not often use the term 'justified belief', but instead usually speaks of its being *rational* to hold a belief. I shall ignore any minor differences there may be between these epistemic concepts.

7 The point at issue here is whether being non-gratuitous in this sense is necessary for divine permission. But there is also a question as to whether it is sufficient. Would any outweighing good for which a particular bit of suffering is necessary, however trivial and insignificant that good, justify that suffering? Suppose that some minor suffering on my part is necessary for my enjoying my dinner to the extent I did, and that the enjoyment outweighs the suffering? Would that give God a

reason for permitting the suffering? I doubt it. Again, suppose that it is necessary for some greater good, but that the universe as whole would be better without E and the greater good than with them? Would God be justified in permitting E? (Note that in (1986) Rowe's substitute for 1 is in terms of the world as a whole: "There exists evils that O [God] could have prevented, and had O prevented them the world as a whole would have been better") (228). However I am not concerned here with what is sufficient for God to have a reason for permitting evil, only with what is necessary for this.

8 This presupposes that God does not enjoy "middle knowledge". For if He did, He could see to it that suffering would be imposed on people only where they will in fact make the desired response. I owe this point to William Hasker.

9 Such a theodicy will be discussed in section ix.

10 There are also more radical objections to Rowe's 2. I think particularly of those who question or deny the principle that God would, by virtue of His nature, create the best possible universe or, in case there can be no uniquely best possible universe, would create a universe that comes up to some minimal evaluative level. See, e.g., R. Adams (1987). On these views an argument like Rowe's never gets out of the starting gate. Though I have some sympathy with such views I will not take that line in this paper.

11 See, e.g., Ahern (1971), Fitzpatrick (1981), Reichenbach (1982), Wykstra (1984).

12 To be sure, 1 is in the form of a positive existential statement. However when we consider an instantiation of it with respect to a particular case of suffering, E, as Rowe does in arguing for it, it turns out to be a negative existential statement about E, that *there is no sufficient divine reason for permitting E.* It is statements of this form that, so I claim, no one can be justified in making.

13 Wykstra labors under the additional burden of having to defend a thesis as to the conditions under which one is justified in making an assertion of the form "It appears that p", and much of the considerable literature spawned by his article is taken up with this side-issue.

14 Hence the very common procedure of knocking down theodical suggestions, one by one, by pointing out, in the case of each, that there are evils it does not cover, will not suffice to make the critic's case. For it may be that even though no one divine reason covers all cases each case is covered by some divine reason.

15 It is often dismissed nowadays on the grounds that it presupposes a morally unacceptable theory of punishment, viz., a retributive conception. But it need not make any such presupposition; whatever the rationale of punishment, the suggestion is that (in some cases) God has that rationale for permitting suffering. Though it must be admitted that the "retributive" principle that *it is intrinsically good that persons should suffer for wrongdoing* makes it easier to claim that suffering constitutes justifiable punishment than a reformatory theory does, where a necessary condition for the justification of punishment is the significant chance of an improvement of the punishee. For purposes of this discussion I will not choose between different theories of punishment.

16 I don't mean to suggest that a person's inner sinfulness or saintliness cannot be expected to manifest itself in behavior. Still less do I mean to suggest that one could be fully or ideally living the life of the spirit, whatever her outward behavior.

[17] Rowe writes: "Perhaps the good for which *some* intense suffering is permitted cannot be realized until the end of the world, but it certainly seems likely that much of this good could be realized in the lifetime of the sufferer...In the absence of any reason to think that O [God] would need to postpone these good experiences, we have reason to expect that many of these goods would occur in the world we know" (1986, 244-45). But why suppose that we are entitled to judge that justifying goods, if any, would be realized during the sufferer's earthly life, unless we have specific reasons to the contrary? Why this initial presumption? Why is the burden of proof on the suggestion of the realization of the goods in an after-life? Rowe doesn't say, nor do I see what he could say.

[18] Actually, Hick is a universalist and believes that all free creatures will attain this consummation; but I do not take this thesis as necessary for the soul making theodicy.

[19] Stump gives her answer to this one in the passage quoted.

[20] All these disclaimers may well apply to Sue.

[21] Here, of course, as in the other cases in which God's action is designed to evoke a free response from the patient, there is no guarantee that the reformation will be effected. But it still remains true that the good aimed at is a good for the sufferer.

[22] There is, to be sure, a question as to why, if things are as I have just suggested they may be, God doesn't fill us in on His reasons for permitting suffering. Wouldn't a perfectly benevolent creator see to it that we realize why we are called upon to suffer? I acknowledge this difficulty, in fact it is just another form taken by the problem of evil. And I will respond to it in the same way. Even if we can't see why God would keep us in the dark in this matter, we cannot be justified in supposing that God does not have sufficient reason for doing so.

[23] El is Bambi's suffering and E2 is Sue's suffering. There are, of course, various differences between Q and 1. For one thing, Q, unlike I makes reference to God's being morally justified. For another, Q has to do with God's *obtaining* particular goods, apparently leaving out of account the cases in which cooperation from human free choice is required. However these differences are not germane to the present point.

[24] Cf. the criticism of Rowe's move from P to Q in Christlieb (forthcoming). Note too that Rowe restricts his consideration of the unknown to "good states of affairs" we do not know of. But, as is recognized in my discussion, it is an equally relevant and equally live possibility that we do not grasp ways in which good states of affairs we know of are connected with cases of suffering so to as to provide God with a reason for permitting the latter. Both types of unknown factors, if realized, would yield divine reasons for permitting suffering of which we are not cognizant.

[25] Stump (1990), p. 66. Many other thinkers, both theistic and atheistic, concur in this judgment.

[26] Note that we are assuming (what seems to be obvious) that God might have a number of reasons for permitting a particular case of suffering, no one of which reasons is sufficient by itself though the whole complex is. This obvious possibility is often ignored when critics seek to knock down theodical suggestions one by one.

[27] In "Victimization and the Problem of Evil" [forthcoming], Thomas F. Tracy persuasively argues that although "God must not actualize a world that contains persons whose lives, through no fault of their own, are on balance an evil (i.e., an intrinsic disvalue) for them rather than a good" (20), nevertheless, we cannot also claim that "God must not actualize a world in which a person suffers some evil E if

the elimination of E by God would result in a better balance *for this individual* of the goods God intends for persons and the evils God permits" (23).

28 The reader may well wonder why it is only now that I have introduced the free will theodicy, since it has such an obvious application to Sue's case. The reason is that I wanted at first to focus on those suggestions that confined the rationale of suffering to benefit to the sufferer.

29 On this point, see the discussion in the next section of our inability to make evaluative comparisons on the scale required here.

30 Or to other creatures. Most discussions of the problem of evil are markedly anthropocentric, in a way that would not survive serious theological scrutiny.

31 These suggestions will draw many of the objections we have already seen to be levelled against Hick's, Stump's, and Adams' sufferer-centered points. See section vi for a discussion of these objections.

32 There are also questions as to whether we are capable of making a reasonable judgment as to which cases from a given field have the strongest claim to being prevented. Our capacity to do this is especially questionable where incommensurable factors are involved, e.g., the worth of the subject and the magnitude of the suffering. But let this pass.

33 The reader will, no doubt, be struck by the similarity between this problem and the one that came up with respect to the free will theodicy. There too it was agreed that God can occasionally, but only occasionally, interfere with human free choice and its implementation without sacrificing the value of human free will. And so there too we were faced with the question of whether we could be assured that a particular case would be a sufficiently strong candidate for such interference that God would have sufficient reason to intervene.

34 Reichenbach, 110-11.

35 See, e.g., Kripke (1972), Plantinga (1974).

36 I hope it is unnecessary to point out that I am not suggesting that we are incapable of making any reasonable judgments of metaphysical modality. Here, as elsewhere, my point is that the judgments required by the inductive argument from evil are of a very special and enormously ambitious type and that our cognitive capacities that serve us well in more limited tasks are not equal to this one. (For more on this general feature of the argument see the final section.) Indeed, just now I contrasted the problem of determining what total systems of nature are metaphysically possible with the problem of the chemical composition of various substances, where we are in a much better position to make judgments of metaphysical modality.

37 This point cuts more than one way. For example, theodicists often confidently assert, as something obvious on the face of it, that a world with free creatures, even free creatures who often misuse their freedom, is better than a world with no free creatures. But it seems to me that it is fearsomely difficult to make this comparison and that we should not be so airily confident that we can do so. Again, to establish a natural law theodicy along Reichenbach's lines one would have to show that the actual natural order is at least as beneficial as any possible alternative; and the considerations I have been adducing cast doubt on our inability to do this. Again, please note that in this paper I am not concerned to defend any particular theodicy.

38 For Rowe's objection to this invocation of the possibility of humanly unenvisaged divine reasons for permitting suffering, and my answer thereto, see the end of section vii.

[39] See the end of section vii for a similar point.

Study Questions

1.   What does William Alston mean by "gratuitous suffering"?

2.   What are the six points Alston makes by way of setting the stage for further discussion of William Rowe's inductive argument from evil?

3.   Alston takes a stand on the matter of the "punishment motif." What is it?

4.   What objections does Alston respond to in connection with Hick's "vale of soul making" theme?

5.   What do you think of Alston's contention that a perfectly good God would not "wholly sacrifice the welfare of one of His intelligent creatures simply in order to achieve a good for others or for Himself?"

For Further Reading

1.   Adams, Marilyn McCord, "Redemptive Suffering: A Christian Approach to the Problem of Evil", in *Rationality, Religious Belief, and Moral Commitment*, ed. R. Audi & W.J. Wainwright (Ithaca, NY: Cornell U. Press, 1986).

2.   Adams, Robert M., "Must God Create the Best?", in *The Virtue of Faith and Other Essays in Philosophical Theology* (New York: Oxford University Press, 1987).

3.   Ahern, M.B., *The Problem of Evil* (London: Routledge & Kegan Paul, 1971).

4.   Christlieb, Terry, "Which Theism's Face an Evidential Problem of Evil?", *Faith and Philosophy*, forthcoming.

5.   Fitzpatrick, F.J., "The Onus of Proof in Arguments about the Problem of Evil", *Religious Studies*, 17 (1981).

6.   Hasker, William, "The Necessity of Gratuitous Evil", *Faith and Philosophy*.

7.   Hick, John, *Evil and the God of Love*, rev. ed. (New York: Harper & Row, 1978).

8.   Keller, James, "The Problem of Evil and the Attributes of God", *Int. Journ. Philos. Relig.*, 26 (1989).

9.   Kripke, Saul A., "Naming and Necessity", in *Semantics of Natural Language*, ed. Donald Davidson & Gilbert Harman (Dordrecht: D. Reidel Pub. Co., 1972).

10.   Plantinga, Alvin, *The Nature of Necessity* (Oxford: Clarendon Press, 1974).

11.   Reichenbach, Bruce, *Evil and a Good God* (New York: Fordham University Press, 1982).

12.   Rowe, William L., "The Problem of Evil and Some Varieties of Atheism", *Amer. Phlios. Quart.*, 16, no. 4 (October, 1979).

13. Rowe, William L., "The Empirical Argument from Evil", in *Rationality, Religious Belief, and Moral Commitment,* ed. R. Audi & W. J. Wainwright (Ithaca, NY: Cornell U. Press, 1986).

14. Rowe, William L., "Evil and Theodicy", *Philosophical Topics,* 16, no. 2 (Fall, 1988).

15. Russell, Bruce, "The Persistant Problem of Evil", *Faith and Philosophy,* 6, no. 2 (April, 1989).

16. Stump, Eleonore, "The Problem of Evil", *Faith and Philosophy,* 2, no. 4, Oct., 1985).

17. Stump, Eleonore, "Providence and Evil", in *Christian Philosophy,* ed. Thomas P. Flint (Notre Dame, IN: University of Notre Dame Press, 1990).

18. Tracy, Thomas F. "Victimization and the Problem of Evil", *Faith and Philosophy.*

19. Wykstra, Stephen, "The Human Obstacle to Evidential Arguments from Suffering: On Avoiding the Evils of 'Appearance'", *Int. Journ. Philos. Relig.,* 16 (1984).

24

The Inscrutable Evil Defense Against the Inductive Argument from Evil

James F. Sennett

James F. Sennett is professor of philosophy at Palm Beach Atlantic College and is author of *Modality, Probability, and Rationality*.

In this paper* I offer a defense against the inductive argument from evil as developed by William Rowe. I argue that a key assumption in Rowe's argument—that the goods we know of offer us good inductive grounds to make certain inferences about the goods there are—is not justified. Particularly, I argue that inscrutable evil—evil such that any good it might serve is not open to human scrutiny—is not, in and of itself, good reason to believe that there is any unjustified evil. I then develop the defense by introducing the notion of a relevant inductive sample and arguing that there is good reason to assume that the goods we know of are not a relevant inductive sample of the goods there are—a fact that compromises any strength Rowe's argument might seem to have.

It is the purpose of this paper to present a defense against the inductive argument from evil—the argument that the presence of evil in the world inductively supports or makes likely the claim that an omnicompetent God does not exist.[1] I will concentrate on the argument offered by William Rowe, though I believe that my defense can be revised so as to meet the objections of any other plausible inductive argument.[2] I focus on Rowe because he is undoubtedly the dean of contemporary analytic philosophers working in this field, and because I see his argument to be the clearest, most easily understood, and most intuitively appealing of those available.

In calling my position a "defense," I take advantage of the very useful distinction between defense and theodicy, made famous by Alvin Plantinga.[3] A theodicy purports to offer reasons for God's allowance of evil, while a defense has a much more modest task. It seeks simply "to establish that a given formulation of the problem of evil fails to show theism to be inconsistent or improbable."[4] A defense against the deductive argument from evil, such as the free will defense, only needs to describe possible states of affairs that entail that God coexists with evil. These states do not need to be actual (indeed, they do not even need to be probable), nor do they need to describe what the justification for evil in those states might be. A defense against the inductive argument from evil would likewise describe a state of affairs entailing that God and evil coexist. However, such a defense must be more than simply possible. It must be likely or probable enough to outweigh the likelihood involved in the argument.[5] Still, a defense need not offer an explanation for evil. It need only provide a scenario under which God's allowing evil is plausible, whatever his justification might be.

I

In its most recent form, Rowe's inductive argument from evil considers specific cases of natural evil (a fawn dying a slow, agonizing death in a naturally caused forest fire) and moral evil (the brutal rape and fatal beating of an innocent five-year-old girl).[6] Calling the first "E1" and the second "E2," Rowe argues that

> P: No good state of affairs we know of is such that an omnipotent, omniscient being's obtaining it would morally justify that being's permitting E1 or E2

is true and constitutes good reason for inferring

> Q: No good state of affairs is such that an omnipotent, omniscient being's obtaining it would morally justify that being in permitting E1 or E2.[7]

Q, together with the assumption that an omnicompetent God would allow only morally justified evil (an assumption I will grant in this paper),[8] entails that such a God does not exist.

Notice that the only real difference between P and Q is that the words "we know of" appear in the former and not in the latter. Inherent in the inference from P to Q is the assumption that what we know about good and evil is good reason to draw certain conclusions about the nature of all good and evil, including that about which we have no knowledge. Rowe presents a perfectly natural justification for this assumption:

> [W]e are justified in making this inference in the same way we are justified in making the many inferences we constantly make from the known to the unknown. All of us are constantly inferring from the A's

we know of to the A's we don't know of. If we observe many A's and all of them are B's we are justified in believing that the A's we haven't observed are also B's.[9]

According to Rowe, the inference from P to Q is as natural, permissible, and rational as many others made on a daily basis—for example, the conclusion that all pit bulls are vicious, given that many have been found to be vicious.[10] Rowe admits that this inference is susceptible to defeating information, but so are all such inferences. This fact alone certainly does not block the rationality of other inductive generalizations. Hence, in the absence of defeating information, P renders Q more likely, more rationally acceptable, than its negation. Since Q entails the denial of God's existence, P apparently makes the denial of God's existence more rational than its acceptance.

Consider the notion of inscrutable evil: evil such that human beings are unable to discern any divine justification for it—that is, any reason an omnicompetent God might have for allowing it.[11] The genius of Rowe's argument can be represented as the charge that

P*: There is inscrutable evil

inductively supports

Q*: There is unjustified evil.

For sake of simplicity and clarity, I will work with this formulation of the argument throughout this paper.[12]

II

Stephen Wykstra points out that Rowe's argument works only if he is justified in believing that, were God to exist, the phenomena of inscrutable evil would appear to us differently from the way they in fact do.[13] But, Wykstra argues, there is no justification for such a claim. Wykstra speaks of goods that are "beyond our ken"—that is, goods that we cannot recognize or understand as goods. Since God can recognize and understand such goods, Wykstra maintains that, if theism is true, then it is likely that the goods served by many instances of suffering will be just such goods—those beyond our ken. Thus, we should expect that many of the instances of suffering we see will not appear to us to be justified. Therefore, Rowe's assumption that the existence of God would make it likely that many evils would appear to us differently than they do (i.e., many evils that do not now appear to us as justified either would not occur or would appear to us as justified) is unfounded.

In response, Rowe finds fault with Wykstra's move from "[God] can grasp goods beyond our ken," to "It is likely that the goods in relation to which [God] permits many sufferings are beyond our ken." Rowe asserts that this move makes sense only if "the goods in question *have not occurred*, or . . . remain quite unknown to us [once they have occurred]." But, Rowe asserts, there is little in the assumption of theism that warrants either of these claims.

> The mere assumption that [God] exists gives us no reason whatever to suppose *either* that the greater goods in virtue of which he permits most sufferings are goods that come into existence far in the future of the sufferings we are now aware of or that, once they do obtain, we continue to be ignorant of them and their relation to the sufferings.[14]

That is, Rowe charges that Wykstra's defense requires that he have reasons for

(1) All inscrutable evil serves goods that are beyond our ken,

and there is no such reason, even given the existence of God. But Rowe is mistaken in thinking that Wykstra must have reasons for (1) in order to make a case against the inference of Q* from P*. All that is required is that (1) be no less likely than not—that is, that there is not reason sufficient to justify denial of it. Since the existence of God entails that there is no unjustified evil, the existence of God plus the existence of inscrutable evil entails (1). That is, if God *does* exist, any inscrutable evil must be due to the fact that the goods that justify such evil are goods that we cannot discern as goods. There is no reason to assume that such a scenario is either impossible or *a priori* improbable. Therefore, at worst the existence of God *simpliciter* offers no reason to assume (1) to be more or less likely to be true. Hence, evidence that God does not exist must consist not only of the presence of inscrutable evil, but also of reason to assume that (1) is less likely than not. As long as (1) is considered no more likely to be false than true, one does not have a case for the denial of theism.

This line of thought is what I call "The Inscrutable Evil Defense." The key premise of my argument is

(2) If God exists and is omnicompetent, then it is at least no less likely than not that all inscrutable evils serve goods beyond our ken.

(2) is the claim just argued fore—that theism is at worst neutral with regards to (1). But more can be said on behalf of (2). Specifically, given that there is no reason to think that all evil will serve discernible goods, there is no reason to deny, and perhaps some reason to assert, that the line of demarcation between inscrutable evils and other evils just is the line of

demarcation between evils serving goods beyond our ken and those serving goods we can discern. That is, the reason why these evils are inscrutable is precisely that they are the ones serving indiscernible goods. There is no *prima facie* reason to reject this assumption in favor of an atheistic deduction. At the very least, such an assumption is no less likely than not. This alone entails (2).

Now, (2) maintains that God's existence renders (1) at *least* no less likely than not, given God's existence. If it is *simply* no less likely than not, or only more likely to an inductively insignificant degree, then the existence of God and (1) together do not inductively support ¬P*. On the other hand, if it renders (1) more likely than not to an inductively significant degree, then the existence of God and (1) together inductively support P*. Hence, (2) entails

> (3) Either the existence of an omnicompetent God and (1) together inductively support P*, or they do not inductively support its denial.

(3) entails that P* must be accompanied by some reason to assume that (1) is less likely than not in order to make a case against theism. Absent such reason, P* alone cannot make a case against theism. So, it follows from (3) that

> (4) P* alone does not make the existence of God less likely than not.

Now, Q* entails that God does not exist. Therefore, P* would make Q* more likely than not only if P* would make it more likely than not that God does not exist.[15] But we see by (4) that P* does no such thing. Therefore, we can conclude

> (5) Inscrutable evil is not good evidence for unjustified evil (i.e., ~P does not inductively support ~Q).

Without the assumption that (1) is less likely than not, Rowe's argument does not go through.

III

In this section I will explore the exact nature of the defect in Rowe's reasoning from P* to Q*, which is exploited by the Inscrutable Evil Defense. Concerning the analogous inference of *All pit bulls are vicious* from the evidence *I have encountered a fair number of pit bulls and they were all vicious* (alluded to in section I above), Rowe points out that the evidence justifying the inference could be defeated by discovering that "all the pit bulls I've encountered have been trained for fighting...[and] there are many pit bulls that are not so trained."[16] The defeat Rowe alludes to is evidence that the sample of pit bulls to which he has been exposed is not a relevant sample for the inductive inference he makes. Prior to acquaintance with such evidence, Rowe is *prima facie* justified in believing that his sample is relevant for the inference. But if he encounters the evidence, he loses his justification. So, in the absence of defeating evidence, Rowe has no reason to believe

(6) The pit bulls I have encountered do not constitute a relevant inductive sample for the inference in question.

This lack of reason for (6) (among other things) gives him *prima facie* justification for making the inference.

Likewise, Rowe is *prima facie* justified in making the inference from P* to Q*, in part, because he has no reason to believe

(7) The goods we know of do not constitute a relevant inductive sample of the goods there are,

which is the analogue to (6) for this inference. The truth of (7) would defeat the support of Q* by P*. That is, the conjunction of P* and (7) would not inductively support Q*. So, if one is justified in believing (7), then one is not justified in inferring Q* from P*.

I will now present three arguments that, coupled with the assumption that an omnicompetent God exists, each constitute good reason for believing (7). As such, these arguments constitute, separately and conjointly, evidence sufficient to defeat the inference from P* to Q* for anyone properly appreciative of them.

First, the existence of an omnicompetent God entails that there is at least one super-human intelligence and moral sensitivity in the universe. Therefore, there is some being capable of grasping concepts, ideas, or situations infinitely above what we are able to grasp. Yet one assuming that (7) is false assumes that human moral sensitivities are capable of grasping enough truth from the goods they can discern to make very large generalizations about all the goods there are. Such an attitude displays a human chauvinism that is certainly out of place in a world of super-human moral sensitivities. Given omnicompetence, there is reason to believe that (7) is true and to reject the inference from P* to Q* as unjustified.

Second, Judaeo-Christian tradition teaches that humanity is "fallen," and that among the consequences of this fallenness is a perverted moral outlook—one that often mistakes good for evil and evil for good—and one that cannot begin to fathom the purposes of God. From such a viewpoint, belief of (7) is virtually mandatory. Far from being part of a relevant inductive sample, many of the "goods" we know of may not even be goods at all. Our moral sensitivities are not only too limited to justify denial of (7), as in the first argument above. They are also "out of tune," and at times deliver unreliable pronouncements. Hence, at least one representative theistic tradition offers good evidence to believe (7).

One important objection to this argument must be addressed before I go on. Rowe argues that no expansion of theism (such as the Judaeo-Christian tradition) is any more likely than basic theism (i.e., the belief that an omnicompetent God exists), given the existence of inscrutable evil.[17] Since any expanded theism entails basic theism, the former will be at least as improbable as the latter, given the existence of inscrutable evil.[18] However, Rowe also discusses a response to this claim from Robert Adams, who argues that one must simply make a judgment between two hypotheses: (i) that basic theism is significantly less probable given inscrutable evil than it is prior to such consideration; and (ii) that a given expanded theism is not significantly less probable than basic theism. Rowe assumes that the first hypothesis is true, and therefore concludes that the second, even if true, does not help the theist's case. But, Adams points out, it is not clear that this is the only, or even the most rational, course to take. If instead we first assume that (ii) is true, then if the expanded theism under consideration succeeds in explaining the presence of inscrutable evil, there is little reason to believe that (i) is true, or to be worried about it if it is.

Rowe responds that one pursuing Adams' strategy must

> *argue* that E [the evidence of inscrutable evil] does not significantly disconfirm RST [Restricted Standard Theism—i.e., basic theism] by showing that there are not implausible hypotheses that, when added to RST, produce a result that both accounts for E and is not significantly less probable than is RST itself. To pursue this...way would be to endeavor to give some not implausible suggestions concerning [God's] reasons for permitting E. Whether the theist can succeed in this task remains to be seen.[19]

But again Rowehas described the task before the theist too strongly. The theist need not provide an expanded theism that gives "suggestions concerning [God's] reasons for permitting E." All she needs to do is provide "not implausible" suggestions concerning the relationship between God and the world that make it likely that there would be inscrutable evil— regardless of the actual purposes God has in permitting it. (Rowe seems to have conflated the distinct tasks of theodicy and defense, identified in the introduction to this paper.) The version of expanded theism I have employed here—basic theism plus the doctrine of the fall—offers a "not implausible" reason to assume that there would be inscrutable evil, and therefore accomplishes the task at hand.[20]

But perhaps the best argument for (7) is one from analogy. The goods my ten-year-old daughter knows of are in no way a relevant inductive sample of the goods I know of. This fact causes conflict and consternation between us at times, and may even drive her to the conclusion that some of my decisions and actions, which bring what she discerns as evil into her life, cannot possibly serve any good purpose—a conviction as inescapable to her mind as is Q* to Rowe's mind. This fact is due to my daughter's developmental status, which prevents her from perceiving or conceiving the evidence that would defeat the support her observations give to her conclusion that I am causing her evil for no good purpose.

Certainly there is at least as much difference between human moral posture and that of an omnicompetent God as there is between those of my daughter and me. Hence, the evidence of disparity between my daughter's moral perspective and mine is good evidence for a similar disparity between mine and God's. Since such a disparity defeats the assumption that the goods she knows of are a relevant inductive sample of the goods I know of, it also defeats the assumption that the goods I know of are a relevant inductive sample of the goods God knows of (i.e., of the goods there are). That is, it is good evidence for (7). But, of course, if (7) is true, then the argument from P* to Q* is no stronger than the argument about pit bulls, given the defeating evidence (that is, not strong at all). The sample is not sufficient to support the induction.[21]

IV

I have not argued that no one can justifiably infer Q* from P*. However, my argument does have the consequence that anyone justified in making the inference is in such a situation purely because of an unappealing sort of epistemic ignorance. The defeaters I have introduced are not so obscure or esoteric as to be available only to the scholar or the deep thinker. In fact, they are quite obvious and natural within the theistic tradition. A minor excursion into possible rebuttals that the theistic community could offer to Rowe's argument would reveal these and similar retorts. In fact, I maintain that such defeaters are so readily available that most people who would feel tempted to make the inference from P* to Q* could uncover them with only a minimum of effort. If this is so, such people may be guilty of epistemic neglect in not making the minimal effort to uncover them, and therefore unjustified in making the inference anyway. After all, the issue at stake here—the existence of God—is important enough to call forth at least a minimum of inquiry from one who would dare to make an inference to a conclusion on the matter.

So a trilemma faces the one who would ground her atheism in the inference from P* to Q*. Either she has reason to believe (7) or she does not. If she does, then she is not justified in making the inference. If she does not, then there are two possibilities. At best she lacks such reason due to ignorance, and therefore is not in the most desirable epistemic situation. She is justified in making the inference from P* to Q* only by default, and not because of any competence in reasoning. At worst she lacks reason for (7) because of epistemic negligence in failing to uncover the relevant defeaters. In this case she is unjustified in her failure to believe (7) and unjustified in inferring Q* from P*. Either way, the power of Rowe's inductive argument for undergirding atheism has been severely compromised.[22]

Palm Beach Atlantic College

Endnotes

*Reprinted by permission from the author, *Faith and Philosophy*, Vol. 10, No. 2, April 1993. All rights reserved.

[1] The term "omnicompetence" names that property borne by an object just in case it is omniscient, omnipotent, and morally perfect.

[2] A powerful, though extremely technical, argument is offered by Paul Draper in "Pain and Pleasure: An Evidential Problem for Theists," *Nous* 23 (1989), pp. 331-50. I am confident that my defense can be translated into the probability calculus and shown to be an effective defense against Draper. This is a project I hope to undertake some time—though I know it will be, as they say, no mean task.

[3] *The Nature of Necessity* (Oxford: Clarendon Press, 1974), p. 192. Plantinga attributes this distinction to Henry Schuurman.

[4] Michael Peterson, et al., *Reason and Religious Belief: An Introduction to the Philosophy of Religion* (New York: (Oxford University Press, 1991), p. 100.

[5] Robert Adams makes this point nicely in "Plantinga on the Problem of Evil," in James Tomberlin and Peter van Inwagen, eds., *Alvin Plantinga* (Dordrecht: D. Reidell, 1985), pp. 242f.

[6] Rowe's argument was originally presented in *Philosophy of Religion: An Introduction* (Belmont, CA: Wadsworth, 1978), pp. 86-92. This argument was later developed and expanded in "The Problem of Evil and Some Varieties of Atheism." *American Philosophical Quarterly* 16 (1979), pp. 335-41. Rowe responded to some important criticisms and presented a new formulation of the argument in "The Empirical Argument from Evil," in Robert Audi and William Wainwright, eds., *Rationality, Religious Belief, and Moral Commitment* (Ithaca, NY: Cornell University Press, 1986), pp. 227-47. His latest formulation at the time of this writing is in "Evil and Theodicy," *Philosophical Topics* 162 (1988), pp. 119-32. While these latter two formulations differ in emphasis, the argument remains pretty much the same as it was in "The Problem of Evil and Some Varieties of Atheism." Rowe has responded to more criticisms and clarified some relevant issues in "Ruminations About Evil," *Philosophical Perspectives* 5 (1991): 69-88.

[7] "Evil and Theodicy," pp. 120ff. In "The Problem of Evil and Some Varieties of Atheism," Rowe offers the following argument:

(i) There exist instances of intense suffering which an omnipotent, omniscient being could have prevented without thereby losing some greater good or permitting some evil equally bad or worse.

(ii) An omniscient, wholly good being would prevent the occurrence of any intense suffering it could, unless it could not do so without thereby losing some greater good or permitting some evil equally bad or worse.

Therefore

(iii) There does not exist an omnipotent, omniscient, wholly good being.

This argument is deductive. The induction lies in the defense of the first premise. The argument from P to Q in the text is an argument for this premise.

[8] For an important attack on this assumption, see William Hasker, "The Necessity of Gratuitous Evil," *Faith and Philosophy* 9 (1992): 23-44. Rowe has responded to Hasker in section III of "Ruminations on Evil."

[9] "Evil and Theodicy," pp. 123f.

[10] Ibid., p. 124.

[11] Throughout this paper I will speak of "justified" and "unjustified" evil with this sense in mind.

[12] This revision actually strengthens Rowe's case. In the original argument, lack of known justification for a given evil is taken as evidence that that evil is unjustified. In my reformulation, the fact of inscrutable evil in general is taken as evidence that at least some of it is unjustified. My revision allows, as Rowe's original formulation does not, that some of the inscrutable evil considered is in fact justified. It only suggests that it is more reasonable to assume that some inscrutable evil is unjustified than to assume that all of it is justified.

[13] "The Humean Obstacle to Evidential Arguments from Suffering: On Avoiding the Evils of 'Appearance,' " *International Journal for Philosophy of Religion* 16 (1984), pp. 73-93.

[14] "The Empirical Argument from Evil," p. 238.

[15] It is a theorem of the probability calculus that, if $P(A/B)=n$ and A entails C, then $P(C/B) \geq n$. Therefore, since Q^* entails *God does not exist* ($\neg G$), $P(Q^*/P^*) > 1/2$ only if $P(\neg G/P^*) > 1/2$. The latter is false, and so, therefore, is the former.

[16] "Evil and Theodicy," p. 124.

[17] "The Empirical Argument from Evil," pp. 239f.

[18] It is a theorem of the probability calculus that, if A entails B, then $P(A/C) \leq P(B/C)$.

[19] "The Empirical Argument from Evil," p. 240, n. 16.

[20] It is arguable, I suppose, that this version of expanded theism is in fact significantly less probable than basic theism. I believe that there are good reasons for denying this claim, though I will not broach them here. Since it to say that, even if this version of expanded theism is significantly less probable than basic theism, the first and third arguments I give for (7) are grounded only in basic theism—deriving only from logical consequences of omniscience and moral perfection—and therefore do not rely on any such expansion.

[21] Rowe has responded in conversation that my daughter may well understand that I am unable to bring about the good I seek without allowing the evil in question. But omnicompetence precludes us believing this of God, at least in many cases. The point here, however, is that the great disparity in the moral perspectives my daughter and I possess precludes her from understanding that there is *any* good being served *at*

all by the evil. *A fortiori*, such a lack of perspective will also preclude her understanding how that good could be served without the evil. So also with our moral perspective *vis à vis* God's. If we can discern no good *at all* that would be served by inscrutable evil, why is it surprising that we cannot perceive a good for which such evil is a necessary condition? If the gap in moral perspective allows that inscrutable evil may indeed serve some indiscernible good, why should it not also allow that it is a necessary condition for this good, and hence justified by it?

22 I thank Robert Audi, Al Casullo, Phil Hugly, Al Plantinga, and William Rowe for helpful conversations on these issues and comments on previous drafts of this paper. I also thank Rowe for pre-publication access to "Ruminations on Evil." Finally, I thank Philip Quinn and two anonymous referees for *Faith and Philosophy* for great help in bringing the manuscript to publishable form.

Study Questions

1.   How would you distinguish the deductive argument from evil from the inductive one?

2.   What for James Sennett, is "inscrutable evil"? Do you think this expression is more advantageous for the theist's cause than "unjustified evil?" Why?

3.   What does Sennett mean by the expression, "omnicompetent"?

4.   How does Sennett judge the theist fares when confronted with William Rowe's argument? How do you think the theist fares?

5.   Which strategy do you think counts more incisively against the theist, the deductive or inductive? Why?

PART IV

THE ATTRIBUTES OF GOD

25

Some Puzzles Concerning Omnipotence

George Mavrodes

George Mavrodes is professor of philosophy at the University of Michigan and author of *Belief in God*. In this essay* he applies the Thomistic conception of divine omnipotence to the paradox of the stone, and argues that there is no problem because the task contemplated in the paradox involves self-contradictory descriptions.

The doctrine of God's omnipotence appears to claim that God can do anything. Consequently, there have been attempts to refute the doctrine by giving examples of things which God cannot do; for example, He cannot draw a square circle.

Responding to objections of this type, St. Thomas pointed out that "anything" should be here construed to refer only to objects, actions, or states of affairs whose descriptions are not self-contradictory.[1] For it is only such things whose nonexistence might plausibly be attributed to a lack of power in some agent. My failure to draw a circle on the exam may indicate my lack of geometrical skill, but my failure to draw a square circle does not indicate any such lack. Therefore, the fact that it false (or perhaps meaningless) to say that God could draw one does no damage to the doctrine of His omnipotence.

A more involved problem, however, is posed by this type of question: can God create a stone too heavy for Him to lift? This appears to be stronger than the first problem, for it poses a dilemma. If we say that God can create a stone, then it seems that there might be such a stone. And if there might be a stone too heavy for Him to lift, then He is evidently not omnipotent. But if we deny that God can create such a stone, we seem to have given up His omnipotence already. Both answers lead us to the same conclusion.

Further, this problem does not seem obviously open to St. Thomas' solution. The form "x is able to draw a square circle" seems plainly to involve a contradiction, while "x is able to make a thing too heavy for x to lift" does not. For it may easily be true that I am able to make a boat too heavy for me to lift. So why should it not be possible for God to make a stone too heavy for Him to lift?

Despite this apparent difference, this second puzzle *is* open to essentially the same answer as the first. The dilemma fails because it consists of asking whether God can do a self-contradictory thing. And the reply that He cannot does no damage to the doctrine of omnipotence.

The specious nature of the problem may be seen in this away. God is either omnipotent or not.[2] Let us assume first that He is not. In that case the phrase "a stone too heavy for God to lift" may not be self-contradictory. And then, of course, if we assert either that God is able or that He is not able to create such a stone, we may conclude that He is not omnipotent. But this is no more than the assumption with which we began, meeting us again after our roundabout journey. If this were all that the dilemma could establish it would be trivial. To be significant it must derive this same conclusion *from the assumption that God is omnipotent;* that is, it must show that the assumption of the omnipotence of God leads to a *reductio.* But does it?

On the assumption that God is omnipotent, the phrase "a stone too heavy for God to lift" becomes self-contradictory. For it becomes "a stone which cannot be lifted by Him whose power is sufficient for lifting anything." But the "thing" described by a self-contradictory phrase is absolutely impossible and hence has nothing to do with the doctrine of omnipotence. Not being an object of power at all, its failure to exist cannot be the result of some lack in the power of God. And, interestingly, it is the very omnipotence of God which makes the existence of such a stone absolutely impossible, while it is the fact that I am finite in power which makes it possible for me to make a boat too heavy for me to lift.

But suppose that some die-hard objector takes the bit in his teeth and denies that the phrase "a stone too heavy for God to lift" is self-contradictory, even on the assumption that God is omnipotent. In other words, he contends that the description "a stone too heavy for an omnipotent God to lift" is self-coherent and therefore describes an absolutely possible object. Must I then attempt to prove the contradictory which I assume above as intuitively obvious? Not necessarily. Let me reply simply that if the objector is right in this contention, then the answer to the original question is "Yes, God can create such a stone." It nay seem that this reply will force us into the original dilemma. But it does not. For now the objector can draw no damaging conclusion from this answer. And the reason is that he has just now contended that such a stone is compatible with the omnipotence of God. Therefore, from the possibility of God's creating such a stone it cannot be concluded that God is not omnipotent. The objector cannot have it both ways. The conclusion which he himself wishes to draw from an affirmative answer to the original question is itself the required proof that the descriptive phrase which appears there is self-contradictory. And "it is more appropriate to say that such things cannot be done, than that God cannot do them."[3]

The specious nature of this problem may also be seen in a somewhat different way.[4] Suppose that some theologian is convinced by this dilemma that he must give up the doctrine of omnipotence. But he resolves to give up as little as possible, just enough to meet the argument. One way he can do so is by retaining the infinite power of God with regard to lifting, while placing a restriction on the sort of stone He is able to create. The only restriction required here, however, is that God must not be able to create a stone too heavy for Him to lift. Beyond that the dilemma has not even suggested any necessary restriction. Our theologian has, in effect, answered the original question in the negative, and he now regretfully supposes that this has required him to give up the full doctrine of omnipotence. He is now retaining what he supposes to be the more modest remnants which he has salvaged from that doctrine.

We must ask, however, what it is which he has in fact given up. Is it the unlimited power of God to create stones? No doubt. But what stone is it which God is now precluded from creating? The stone too heavy for Him to lift, of course. But we must remember that nothing in the argument required the theologian to admit any limit on God's power with regard to the lifting of stones. He still holds that to be unlimited. And if God's power to lift is infinite, then His power to create may run to infinity also without outstripping that first power. The supposed limitation turns out to be no limitation at all, since it is specified only by reference to another power which is itself infinite. Our theologian need have no regrets, for he has given up nothing. The doctrine of the power of god remains just what it was before.

Nothing I have said above, of course, goes to prove that God is, in fact, omnipotent. All I have intended to show is that certain arguments intended to prove that He is not omnipotent fail. They fail because they propose, as tests of Gods' power, putative tasks whose descriptions are self-contradictory. Such pseudo-tasks, not falling within the realm of possibility , are not objects of power at all. Hence the fact that they cannot be performed implies no limit on the power of God, and hence no defect in the doctrine of omnipotence.

Endnotes

*Reprinted from *The Philisophical Review*, 73 (1964).

[1] St. Thomas Aquinas, *Summa Theologiae*, Ia, q. 25, a. 3.

[2] I assume, of course, the existence of God, since that is not being brought in question here.

[3] St. Thomas, *loc. cit.*

[4] But this method rests finally on the same logical relations as the preceding one.

Study Questions

1. How does Thomas Aquinas unpack the notion of "anything" in connection with defining "omnipotence?"

2. Mavrodes judges that the second puzzle is open to the same answer as the first. What is it?

3. Why does Mavrodes think that the problem regarding God's omnipotence and the paradox of the stone is not open to Thomas Aquinas' solution?

4. What does Mavrodes think he has achieved in the discussion?

5. Do you think Mavrodes has succeeded in his task?

26

Omnipotence and Almightiness

Peter Geach

Peter Geach is professor of philosophy at Leeds University and is author of *Providence and Evil*. In this essay* he draws a distinction between the notion of omnipotence and almightiness, and argues that the latter is a Biblical concept but the former isn't. He considers four accounts of omnipotence and finds each involving significant problems.

It is fortunate for my purposes that English has the two words "almighty" and "omnipotent," and that apart from any stipulation by me the words have rather different associations and suggestions. "Almighty" is the familiar word that comes in the creeds of the Church; "omnipotent" is at home rather in formal theological discussions and controversies, e.g. about miracles and about the problem of evil. "Almighty" derives by way of Latin "omnipotens" from the Greek word *"pantokrator"*; and both this Greek word, like the more classical *"pankrates,"* and "almighty" itself suggest God's having power over all things. On the other hand the English word "omnipotent" would ordinarily be taken to imply ability to do everything; the Latin word "omnipotens" also predominantly has this meaning in Scholastic writers, even though in origin it is a Latinization of *"pantocrator."* So there already is a tendency to distinguish the two words; and in this paper I shall make the distinction a strict one. I shall use the world "almighty" to express God's power over all things, and I shall take "omnipotence" to mean ability to do everything.

I think we can in a measure understand what God's almightiness implies, and I shall argue that almightiness so understood must be ascribed to God if we are to retain anything like traditional Christian belief in God. The position as regards omnipotence, or as regards the statement "God can do everything," seems to me to be very different. Of course even "God can do everything" may be understood simply as a way of magnifying God by contrast with the impotence of man. McTaggart

473

described it as "a piece of theological etiquette" to call God omnipotent: Thomas Hobbes, out of reverence for his Maker, would rather say that "omnipotent" is an attribute of honour. But McTaggart and Hobbes would agree that "God is omnipotent" or "God can do everything" is not to be treated as a proposition that can figure as premise or conclusion in a serious theological argument. And I too wish to say this. I have no objection to such ways of speaking if they merely express a desire to give the best honour we can to God our Maker, whose Name only is excellent and whose praise is above heaven and earth. But theologians have tried to prove that God can do everything, or to derive conclusions from this thesis as a premise. I think such attempts have been wholly unsuccessful. When people have tried to read into "God can do everything" a signification not of Pious Intention but of Philosophical Truth, they have only landed themselves in intractable problems and hopeless confusions; no graspable sense has ever been given to this sentence that did not lead to self-contradiction or at least to conclusions manifestly untenable from a Christian point of view.

I shall return to this; but I must first develop what I have to say about God's almightiness, or power over all things. God is not just more powerful than any creature; no creature can compete with God in power, even unsuccessfully. For God is also the source of all power; any power a creature has comes from God and is maintained only for such time as God wills. Nebuchadnezzar submitted to praise and adore the God of heaven because he was forced by experience to realize that only by God's favour did his wits hold together from one end of a blasphemous sentence to the other end. Nobody can deceive God or circumvent him or frustrate him; and there is no question of God's trying to do anything and failing. In Heaven and on Earth, God does whatever he will. We shall see that some propositions of the form "God cannot do so-and-so" have to be accepted as true; but what God cannot be said to be able to do he likewise cannot will to do; we cannot drive a logical wedge between his power and his will, which are, as the Scholastics said, really identical, and there is no application to God of the concept of trying but failing.

I shall not spend time on citations of Scripture and tradition to show that this doctrine of God's almightiness is authentically Christian; nor shall I here develop rational grounds for believing it is a true doctrine. But it is quite easy to show that this doctrine is indispensable for Christianity, not a bit of old metaphysical luggage that can be abandoned with relief. For Christianity requires an absolute faith in the promises of God: specifically, faith in the promise that some day the whole human race will be delivered and blessed by the establishment of the Kingdom of God. If God were not almighty, he might will and not do; sincerely promise, but find fulfilment beyond his power. Men might prove untamable and incorrigible, and might kill themselves through war or pollution before God's salvific plan for them could come into force. It is useless to say that after the end of this earthly life men would live again; for as I have argued elsewhere, only the promise of God can give us any confidence that there will be an afterlife for men; and if God were not almighty, this promise too might fail. If God is true and just and unchangeable and almighty, we can have absolute confidence in his promises: otherwise we cannot—and there would be an end of Christianity.

A Christian must therefore believe that God is almighty; but he need not believe that God can do everything. Indeed, the very argument I have just used shows that a Christian must not believe that God can do everything: for he may not believe that God could possibly break his own word. Nor can a Christian even believe that God can do everything that is logically possible; for breaking one's word is certainly a logically possible feat.

It seems to me, therefore, that the tangles in which people have enmeshed themselves when trying to give the expression "God can do everything" an intelligible and acceptable content are tangles that a Christian believer has no need to enmesh himself in; the spectacle of others enmeshed may sadden him, but need not cause him to stumble in the way of faith. The denial that God is omnipotent, or able to do everything, may seem dishonouring to God; but when we see where the contrary affirmation, in its various forms, has led, we may well cry out with Hobbes: "Can any man think God is served with such absurdities? As if it were an acknowledgment of the Divine Power, to say, that which is, is not; or that which has been, has not been."

I shall consider four main theories of omnipotence. The first holds that God can do everything absolutely; everything that can be expressed in a string of words that makes sense; even if that sense can be shown to be self-contradictory, God is not bound in action, as we are in thought, by the laws of logic. I shall speak of this as the doctrine that God is absolutely omnipotent.

The second doctrine is that a proposition . . . "God can do so-and-so" is true when and only when "so-and-so" represents a logically consistent description.

The third doctrine is that "God can do so-and-so" is true just if "God does so-and-so" is logically consistent. This is a weaker doctrine than the second; for "God is doing so-and-so" is logically consistent only when "so-and-so" represents a logically consistent description, but on the other hand there may be consistently describable feats which it would involve contradiction to suppose done *by God*.

The last and weakest view is that the realm of what can be done or brought about includes all future possibilities, and that whenever "God will bring so-and-so about is logically possible, "*God can* bring so-and-so about" is true.

The first sense of "omnipotent" in which people have believed God to be omnipotent implies precisely: ability to do absolutely everything describable. You mention it, and God can do it. McTaggart insisted on using "omnipotent" in this sense only; from an historical point of view we may of course say that he imposed on the word a sense which it, and the corresponding Latin word, have not always borne. But Broad seems to me clearly unjust to McTaggart when he implies that in demolishing this doctrine of omnipotence McTaggart was just knocking down a man of straw. As Broad must surely have known, at least one great philosopher, Descartes, deliberately adopted and defended this doctrine of omnipotence: what I shall call the doctrine of absolute omnipotence.

As Descartes himself remarked, nothing is too absurd for some philosopher to have said it some time; I once read an article about an Indian school of philosophers who were alleged to maintain that it is only a delusion, which the wise can overcome, that anything exists at all—so perhaps it would not matter all that much that a philosopher is found to defend absolute omnipotence. Perhaps it would not matter all that much that the philosopher in question was a very great one; for very great philosophers have maintained the most preposterous theses. What does make the denial of absolute omnipotence important is not that we are thereby denying what a philosopher, a very great philosopher, thought he must assert, but that this doctrine has a live influence on people's religious thought–I should of course say, a pernicious influence. Some naive Christians would explicitly assert the doctrine; and moreover, I think McTaggart was right in believing that in popular religious thought a covert appeal to the doctrine is sometimes made even by people who would deny it if it were explicitly stated to them and its manifest consequences pointed out.

McTaggart may well have come into contact with naive Protestant defenders of absolute omnipotence when he was defending his atheist faith at his public school. The opinion is certainly not dead, as I can testify from personal experience. For many years I used to teach the philosophy of Descartes in a special course for undergraduates reading French; year by year, there were always two or three of them who embraced Descartes' defence of absolute omnipotence *con amore* and protested indignantly when I described the doctrine as incoherent. It would of course have been no good to say I was following Doctors of the Church in rejecting the doctrine; I did in the end find a way of producing silence, though not, I fear, conviction, and going on to other topics of discussion; I cited the passages of the Epistle to the Hebrews which say explicitly that God cannot swear by anything greater than himself (vi.13) or break his word (vi.18). Fortunately none of them ever thought of resorting to the ultimate weapon which, as I believe George Mavrodes remarked, is available to the defender of absolute omnipotence; namely, he can always say: "Well, you've stated a difficulty, but of course being omnipotent God can overcome that difficulty, though I don't see how." But what I may call, borrowing from C. S. Lewis's story, victory by the

Deplorable Word is a barren one; as barren as a victory by an incessant demand that your adversary should prove his premises or define his terms.

Let us leave these naive defenders in their entrenched position and return for a moment to Descartes. Descartes held that the truths of logic and arithmetic are freely made to be true by God's will. To be sure we clearly and distinctly see that these truths are necessary; they are necessary in our world, and in giving us our mental endowments God gave us the right sort of clear and distinct ideas to see the necessity. But though they are necessary, they are not necessarily necessary; God could have freely chosen to make a different sort of world, in which other things would have been necessary truths. The possibility of such another world is something we cannot comprehend, but only dimly apprehend; Descartes uses the simile that we may girdle a tree-trunk with our arms but not a mountain—but we can touch the mountain. Proper understanding of the possibility would be possessed by God, or, no doubt, by creatures in the alternative world, who would be endowed by God with clear and distinct ideas corresponding to the necessities of their world.

In recent years, unsound philosophies have been defended by what I may call shyster logicians: some of the more dubious recent developments of modal logic could certainly be used to defend Descartes. A system in which "possibly p" were a theorem—in which everything is possible—has indeed never been taken seriously; but modal logicians have taken seriously systems in which "possibly possibly p," or again "it is not necessary that necessarily p," would be a theorem for arbitrary interpretation of "p." What is more, some modern modal logicians notoriously take possible worlds very seriously indeed; some of them even go to the length of saying that what you and I vulgarly call the actual world is simply the world we happen to live in. People who take both things seriously—the axiom "possibly possibly p" and the ontology of possible worlds—would say: You mention any impossibility, and there's a possible world in which that isn't impossible but possible. And this is even further away out than Descartes would wish to go; for he would certainly not wish to say that "It is possible that God should not exist" is even *possibly* true. So *a fortiori* a shyster logician could fadge up a case for Descartes. But to my mind all that this shows is that modal logic is currently a rather disreputable discipline: not that I think modal notions are inadmissible—on the contrary, I think they are indispensable—but that current professional standards in the discipline are low, and technical ingenuity is mistaken for rigour. On that showing, astrology would be rigorous.

Descartes' motive for believing in absolute omnipotence was not contemptible: it seemed to him that otherwise God would be *subject to* the inexorable laws of logic as Jove was to the decrees of the Fates. The nature of logical truth is a very difficult problem, which I cannot discuss here.

The easy conventionalist line, that it is our arbitrary way of using words that makes logical truth, seems to me untenable, for reasons that Quine among others has clearly spelled out. If I could follow Quine further in regarding logical laws as natural laws of very great generality—revisable in principle, though most unlikely to be revised, in a major theoretical reconstruction—then perhaps after all some rehabilitation of Descartes on this topic might be possible. But in the end I have to say that as we cannot say how a non-logical world would look, we cannot say how a supra-logical God would act or how he could communicate anything to us by way of revelation. So I end as I began: a Christian need not and cannot believe in absolute omnipotence.

It is important that Christians should clearly realize this, because otherwise a half-belief in absolute omnipotence may work in their minds subterraneously. As I said, I think McTaggart was absolutely right in drawing attention to this danger. One and the same man may deny the doctrine of absolute omnipotence when the doctrine is clearly put to him, and yet reassure himself that God can certainly do so-and-so by using merely the premise of God's omnipotence. And McTaggart is saying this is indefensible. At the very least this "so-and-so" must represent a logically consistent description of a feat; and proofs of logical consistency are notoriously not always easy. Nor, as we shall see, are our troubles at an end if we assume that God can do anything whose description is logically consistent.

Logical consistency in the description of the feat is certainly a necessary condition for the truth of "God can do so-and-so": if "so-and-so" represents an inconsistent description of a feat, then "God can do so-and-so" is certainly a false and impossible proposition, since it entails "It could be the case that so-and-so came about"; so, by contraposition, if "God can do so-and-so" is to be true, or even logically possible, then "so-and-so" must represent a logically consistent description of a feat. And whereas only a minority of Christians have explicitly believed in absolute omnipotence, many have believed that a proposition of the form "God can do so-and-so" is true whenever "so-and-so" represents a description of a logically possible feat. This is our second doctrine of omnipotence. One classic statement of this comes in the *Summa Theologica* 1a q. xxv art. 3. Aquinas rightly says that we cannot explain "God can do everything" in terms of what is within the power of some agent; for "God can do everything any created agent can do," though true, is not a comprehensive enough account of God's power, which exceeds that of any created agent; and "God can do everything God can do" runs uselessly in a circle. So he puts forward the view that if the description "so-and-so" is in itself possible through the relation of the terms involved—if it does not involve contradictories' being true together—then "God can do so-and-so" is true. Many Christian writers have followed Aquinas in saying this; but it is not a position consistently maintainable. As we shall see, Aquinas did not manage to stick to the position himself.

Before I raise the difficulties against this thesis, I wish to expose a common confusion that often leads people to accept it: the confusion between self-contradiction and gibberish. C. S. Lewis in *The Problem of Pain* says that meaningless combinations of words do not suddenly acquire meaning simply because we prefix to them the two other words "God can," and Antony Flew has quoted this with just approval. But if we take Lewis's words strictly, his point is utterly trivial, and nothing to our purpose. For gibberish, syntactically incoherent combination of words, is quite different from self-contradictory sentences or descriptions; the latter certainly have an intelligible place in our language.

It is a common move in logic to argue that a set of premises A, B, C together yield a contradiction, and that therefore A and B as premises yield as conclusion the contradictory of C; some logicians have puritanical objections to this manoeuvre, but I cannot stop to consider them; I am confident, too, that neither Aquinas nor Lewis would share these objections to *reductio ad absurdum*. If, however, a contradictory formula were gibberish, *reductio ad absurdum* certainly would be an illegitimate procedure—indeed it would be a nonsensical one. So we have to say that when "so-and-so" represents a self-contradictory description of a feat, "God can do so-and-so" is likewise self-contradictory, but that being self-contradictory it is not gibberish, but merely false.

I am afraid the view of omnipotence presently under consideration owes part of its attractiveness to the idea that then "God can do so-and-so" would never turn out false, so that there would be no genuine counterexamples to "God can do everything." Aquinas says, in the passage I just now cited: "What implies contradiction cannot be a word, for no understanding can conceive it." Aquinas, writing seven centuries ago, is excusable for not being clear about the difference between self-contradiction and gibberish; we are not excusable if we are not. It is not gibberish to say "a God can bring it about that in Alcala there lives a barber who shaves all those and only those living in Alcala who do not shave themselves"; this is a perfectly well-formed sentence, and not on the face of it self-contradictory; all the same, the supposed feat notoriously is self-contradictory, so this statement of what God can do is not nonsense but false.

One instance of a description of a feat that is really but not overtly self-contradictory has some slight importance in the history of conceptions of omnipotence. It appeared obvious to Spinoza that *God can bring about everything that God can bring about*, and that to deny this would be flatly incompatible with God's omnipotence (Ethics 1.17, scholium). Well, the italicized sentence is syntactically ambiguous. "Everything that God can bring about God can bring about" is one possible reading of the sentence, and this is an obvious, indeed trivial predication about God, which must be true if there is a God at all. But the other way of taking the sentence relates to a supposed feat of *bringing about everything that God can bring about—all* of these bringable-about things together—and it says that God is capable of this feat. This is clearly the way Spinoza wishes us to take the sentence. But taken this way, it is not obvious at all; quite the contrary, it's obviously false. For among the things that are severally possible for God to bring about, there are going to be some pairs that are not *com*possible, pairs which it is logically impossible should both come about; and then it is beyond God's power to bring about such a pair together—let alone, to bring about all the things together which he can bring about severally.

This does not give us a description of a *logically possible* feat which God cannot accomplish. However, there is nothing easier than to mention feats which are logically possible but which God cannot do, if Christianity is true. Lying and promise-breaking are logically possible feats: but Christian faith, as I have said, collapses unless we are assured that God cannot lie and cannot break his promises.

This argument is an *ad hominem* argument addressed to Christians; but there are well-known logical arguments to show that on any view there must be some logically possible feats that are beyond God's power. One good example suffices: making a thing which its maker cannot afterwards destroy. This is certainly a possible feat, a feat that some human beings have performed. Can God perform the feat or not? If he cannot there is already some logically possible feat which God cannot perform. If God can perform the feat, then let us suppose that he does: *ponatur in esse*, as medieval logicians say. Then we are supposing God to have brought about a situation in which he *has* made something he cannot destroy; and in that situation destroying this thing is a *logically* possible feat that God cannot accomplish, for we surely cannot admit the idea of a creature whose destruction is logically *impossible*.

There have been various attempts to meet this argument. The most interesting one is that the proposition "God cannot make a thing that he cannot destroy" can be turned round to "Any thing that God can make he can destroy"—which does not even look like an objection to God's being able to do everything logically possible. But this reply involves the very same bracketing fallacy that I exposed a moment ago in Spinoza. There, you will remember, we had to distinguish two ways of taking "God can bring about everything that God can bring about":

A.   Everything that God can bring about, God can bring about.
B.   God can bring about the following feat: to bring about everything that God can bring about.

And we saw that A is trivially true, given that there *is* a God, and B certainly false. Here, similarly, we have to distinguish two senses of "God cannot make a thing that its maker cannot destroy":

A. Anything that its maker cannot destroy, God cannot make.
B. God cannot bring about the following feat: to make something that its maker cannot destroy.

And here A does contrapose, as the objectors would have it, to "Anything that God can make, its maker can destroy," which on the face of it says nothing against God's power to do anything logically possible. But just as in the Spinoza example, the B reading purports to describe a single feat, *bringing about everything that God can bring about* (this feat, I argued, is impossible for God, because logically impossible): so in our present case, the B reading purports to describe a single feat, making something that its maker cannot destroy. This, as I said, is a logically possible feat, a feat that men sometimes do perform; so we may press the question whether this is a feat God can accomplish or not; and either way there will be some logically possible feat God cannot accomplish. So this notion of omnipotence, like the Cartesian idea of absolute omnipotence, turns out to be obviously incompatible with Christian faith, and moreover logically untenable.

Let us see, then, if we fare any better with the third theory: the theory that the only condition for the truth of "God can do so-and-so" is that "God does so-and-so" or "God is doing so-and-so" must be logically possible. As I said, this imposes a more restrictive condition than the second theory: for there are many feats that we can consistently suppose to be performed but cannot consistently suppose to be performed by God. This theory might thus get us out of the logical trouble that arose with the second theory about the feat: *making a thing that its maker cannot destroy*. For though this is a logically possible feat, a feat some creatures do perform, it might well be argued that "God has made a thing that its maker cannot destroy" is a proposition with a buried inconsistency in it; and if so, then on the present account of omnipotence we need not say "God can make a thing that its maker cannot destroy."

This suggestion also, however, can easily be refuted by an example of great philosophical importance that I borrow from Aquinas. "It comes about that Miss X never loses her virginity" is plainly a logically possible proposition: and so also is "God brings it about that Miss X never loses her virginity." All the same, if it so happens that Miss X already has lost her virginity, "God can bring it about that Miss X never loses her virginity" is false (1a q. xxv art. 4 ad 3 um). Before Miss X had lost her virginity, it would have been true to say this very thing; so what we can truly say about what God can do will be different at different times. This appears to imply a change in God, but Aquinas would certainly say, and I think rightly, that it doesn't really do so. It is just like the case of Socrates coming to be shorter than Theaetetus because Theaetetus grows up; here, the change is on the side of Theaetetus not of Socrates. So in our case, the change is really in Miss X not in God; something about her passes from the realm of possibility to the realm of *fait accompli*, and thus no longer comes under the concept of the accomplishable—*deficit a ratione possibilium* (Aquinas, loc. cit., ad 2 um). I think Aquinas's position here is strongly defensible; but if he does defend it, he has abandoned the position that God can do everything that it is not a priori impossible *for God to do*, let alone the position that God can bring about everything describable in a logically consistent way.

Is it a priori impossible for God to do something wicked? And if not, *could* God do something wicked? There have been expressed serious doubts about this: I came across them in that favourite of modern moral philosophers, Richard Price. We must distinguish, he argues, between God's natural and his moral attributes: if God is a free moral being, even as we are, it must not be absolutely impossible for God to do something wicked. There must be just a chance that God should do something wicked: no doubt it will be a really infinitesimal chance—after all, God has persevered in ways of virtue on a vast scale for inconceivably long—but the chance must be there, or God isn't free and isn't therefore laudable for his goodness. The way this reverend gentleman commends his Maker's morals is so startling that you may suspect me of misrepresentation; I can only ask any sceptic to check in Daiches Raphael's edition of Price's work! Further comment on my part is I hope needless.

A much more restrained version of the same sort of thing is to be found in the Scholastic distinction between God's *potentia absoluta* and *potentia ordinata*. The former is God's power considered in abstraction from his wisdom and goodness, the latter is God's power considered as controlled in its exercise by his wisdom and goodness. Well, as regards a man it makes good sense to say: "He has the bodily and mental power to do so-and-so, but he certainly will not, it would be pointlessly silly and wicked." But does anything remotely like this make sense to say about Almighty God? If not, the Scholastic distinction I have cited is wholly frivolous.

Let us then consider our fourth try. Could it be said that the "everything" in "God can do everything" refers precisely to things that are not in the realm of *fait accompli* but of futurity? This will not do either. If God can promulgate promises to men, then as regards any promises that are not yet fulfilled we know that they certainly will be fulfilled: and in that case God clearly has not a *potentia ad utrumque*—a two-way power of either actualizing the event that will fulfill the promise or not actualizing it. God can then only do what will fulfill his promise. And if we try to evade this by denying that God can make promises known to men, then we have once more denied something essential to Christian faith, and we are still left with something that God cannot do.

I must here remove the appearance of a fallacy. God cannot but fulfil his promises, I argued; so he has not a two-way power, *potentia ad utrumque,* as regards these particular future events. This argument may have seemed to involve the fallacy made notorious in medieval logical treatises, of confusing the necessity by which something follows—*necessitas consequentiae*—with the necessity of that very thing which follows—*necessitas conseguentis.* If it is impossible for God to promise and not perform, then if we know God has promised something we may infer with certainty that he will perform it. Surely, it may be urged, this is enough for Christian faith and hope; we need not go on to say that God *cannot not* bring about the future event in question. If we do that, are we not precisely committing the hoary modal fallacy I have just described?

I answer that there are various senses of "necessary." The future occurrence of such-and-such, when God has promised that such-and-such shall be, is of course not logically necessary; but it may be necessary in the sense of being, as Arthur Prior puts it, now unpreventable. If God has promised that Israel shall be saved, then there is nothing that anybody, even God, can do about that; this past state of affairs is now unpreventable. But it is also necessary in the same way that if God has promised then he will perform; God cannot do anything about that either—cannot make himself liable to break his word. So we have as premises "Necessarily p" and "Necessarily if p then q," in the same sense of "necessarily"; and from these premises it not merely necessarily follows that q—the conclusion in the necessitated form, "Necessarily q" with the same sense of "necessarily," follows from the premises. So if God has promised that Israel shall be saved, the future salvation of Israel is not only certain but inevitable; God must save Israel, because he cannot not save Israel without breaking his word given in the past and he can neither alter the past nor break his word.

Again, in regard to this and other arguments, some people may have felt discomfort at my not drawing in relation to God the sort of distinction between various applications of "can" that are made in human affairs: the "can" of knowing how to, the "can" of physical power to, the "can" of opportunity, the "can" of what fits in with one's plans. But of course the way we make these distinct applications of "he can" to a human agent will not be open if we are talking about God. There is no question of God's knowing how but lacking the strength, or being physically able to but not knowing how; moreover (to make a distinction that comes in a logical example of Aristotle's) though there is a right time when God may bring something about, it is inept to speak of his then having the opportunity to do it. (To develop this distinction: if "x" stands for a finite agent and "so-and-so" for an act directly in x's power, there is little difference between "At time t it is suitable for x to bring so-and-so about" and "It is suitable for x to bring so-and-so about at time t"; but if "x" means God, the temporal qualification "at time r can attach only to what is brought about;

God does not live through successive times and find one more suitable than another.)

These distinct applications of "can" are distinct only for finite and changeable agents, not for a God whose action is universal and whose mind and character and design are unchangeable. There is thus no ground for fear that in talking about God we may illicitly slip from one sort of "can" to another. What we say God can do is always in respect of his changeless supreme power.

All the same, we have to assert different propositions at different times in order to say truly what God can do. What is past, as I said, ceases to be alterable even by God; and thus the truth-value of a proposition like "God can bring it about that Miss X never loses her virginity" alters once she has lost it. Similarly, God's promise makes a difference to what we can thereafter truly say God can do; it is less obvious in this case that the real change involved is a change in creatures, not in God, than it was as regards Miss X's virginity, but a little thought should show that the promulgation or making known of God's intention, which is involved in a promise, is precisely a change in the creatures to whom the promise is made.

Thus all the four theories of omnipotence that I have considered break down. Only the first overtly flouts logic; but the other three all involve logical contradictions, or so it seems; and moreover, all these theories have consequences fatal to the truth of Christian faith. The last point really ought not to surprise us; for the absolute confidence a Christian must have in God's revelation and promises involves, as I said at the outset, both a belief that God is almighty, in the sense I explained, and a belief that there are certain describable things that God cannot do and therefore will not do.

If I were to end the discussion at this point, I should leave an impression of Aquinas's thought that would be seriously unfair to him; for although in the passage I cited Aquinas appears verbally committed to our second theory of omnipotence, it seems clear that this does not adequately represent his mind. Indeed, it was from Aquinas himself and from the *Summa Theologica* that I borrowed an example which refutes even the weaker third theory, let alone the second one. Moreover, in the other Summa (Book II, c. xxv) there is an instructive list of things that *Deus omnipotens* is rightly said not to be able to do. But the mere occurrence of this list makes me doubt whether Aquinas can be said to believe, in any reasonable interpretation, the thesis that God can do everything. That God is almighty in my sense Aquinas obviously did believe; I am suggesting that here his "omnipotens" means "almighty" rather than "omnipotent." Aquinas does not say or even imply that he has given an *exhaustive* list of kinds of case in which "God can do so-and-so" or "God can make so-and-so" turns out false; so what he says here does not commit him to "God can do everything" even in the highly unnatural sense "God can do everything that is not excluded under one or other of the following heads."

I shall not explore Aquinas's list item by item, because I have made open or tacit use of his considerations at several points in the foregoing and do not wish to repeat myself. But one batch of items raises a specially serious problem. My attention was drawn to the problem by a contribution that the late Mr. Michael Foster made orally during a discussion at the Socratic Club in Oxford. Aquinas tells us that if "doing so-and-so" implies what he calls passive potentiality, then "God can do so-and-so" is false. On this ground he excluded all of the following:

- God can be a body or something of the sort.
- God can be tired or oblivious.
- God can be angry or sorrowful.
- God can suffer violence or be overcome.
- God can undergo corruption.

Foster pointed out that as a Christian Aquinas was committed to asserting the contradictory of all these theses. *Contra factum non valet ratio*; it's no good arguing that God cannot do what God has done, and in the Incarnation God did do all these things Aquinas said God cannot do. The Word that was God was made flesh (and the literal meaning of the Polish for this is: The Word became a body!); God the Son was tired and did sink into the oblivion of sleep; he was angry and sorrowful; he was bound like a thief, beaten, and crucified; and though we believe his Body did not decay, it suffered corruption in the sense of becoming a corpse instead of a living body—Christ in the Apocalypse uses of himself the startling words "I became a corpse," "*egenomen nekros*," and the Church has always held that the dead Body of Christ during the *triduum mortis* was adorable with Divine worship for its union to the Divine Nature.

Foster's objection to Aquinas is the opposite kind of objection to the ones I have been raising against the various theories of omnipotence I have discussed. I have been saying that these theories say by implication that God can do certain things which Christian belief requires one to say God *cannot* do; Foster is objecting that Aquinas's account says God *cannot* do some things which according to Christian faith God *can* do and has in fact done.

It would take me too far to consider how Aquinas might have answered this objection. It would not of course be outside his intellectual milieu; it is the very sort of objection that a Jew or Moor might have used, accepting Aquinas's account of what God cannot do, in order to argue against the Incarnation. I shall simply mention one feature that Aquinas's reply would have had: it would have to make essential use of the particle "as," or in Latin "*secundum quod*." God did become man, so God can become man and have a human body; but God as God cannot be man or have a body.

The logic of these propositions with "as" in them, reduplicative propositions as they are traditionally called, is a still unsolved problem, although as a matter of history it was a problem raised by Aristotle in the *Prior Analytics*. We must not forget that such propositions occur frequently in ordinary discourse; we use them there with an ill-founded confidence that we know our way around. Jones, we say, is Director of the Gnome Works and Mayor of Middletown; he gets a salary as Director and an expense allowance as Mayor; he signs one letter as Director, another as Mayor. We say all this, but how far do we understand the logical relations of what we say? Very little, I fear. One might have expected some light and leading from medieval logicians; the theological importance of reduplicative propositions did in fact lead to their figuring as a topic in medieval logical treatises. But I have not found much that is helpful in such treatments as I have read.

I hope to return to this topic later. Meanwhile, even though it has nothing directly to do with almightiness or omnipotence, I shall mention one important logical point that is already to be found in Aristotle. A superficial grammatical illusion may make us think that "A as P is Q" attaches the predicate "Q" to a complex subject "A as P." But Aristotle insists, to my mind rightly, on the analysis: "A" subject, "is as P, Q" predicate—so that we have not a complex subject-term, but a complex predicate-term; clearly, this predicate entails the simple conjunctive predicate "is both P and Q" but not conversely. This niggling point of logic has in fact some theological importance. When theologians are talking about Christ as God and Christ as Man, they may take the two phrases to be two logical subjects of predication, if they have failed to see the Aristotelian point; and then they are likely to think or half think that Christ as God is one entity or *Gegenstand* and Christ as Man is another. I am sure some theologians have yielded to this temptation, which puts them on a straight road to the Nestorian heresy.

What Aquinas would have done, I repeat, to meet Foster's objection in the mouth of a Jew or Moor is to distinguish between what we say God can do, *simpliciter*, and what we say God as God can do, using the reduplicative form of proposition. Now if we do make such a distinction, we are faced with considerable logical complications, particularly if we accept the Aristotelian point about the reduplicative construction. Let us go back to our friend Jones: there is a logical difference between:

1. Jones as Mayor can attend this committee meeting.
2. Jones can as Mayor attend this committee meeting.

as we may see if we spell the two out a little:

1. Jones as Mayor has the opportunity of attending the committee meeting.

2. Jones has the opportunity of (attending this committee meeting as Mayor).

We can easily see now that 1 and 2 are logically distinct: for one thing, if Jones is not yet Mayor but has an opportunity of becoming Mayor and *then* attending the committee meeting, 2 would be true and 1 false. And if we want to talk about what Jones as Mayor *cannot* do, the complexities pile up; for then we have to consider how the negation can be inserted at one or other position in a proposition of one of these forms, and how all the results are logically related.

All this is logical work to be done if we are to be clear about the implications of saying that God can or cannot do so-and-so, or again that God *as God* can or cannot do so-and-so. It is obvious, without my developing the matter further, that the logic of all this will not be simple. It's a far cry from the simple method of bringing our question "Can God do so-and-so?" under a reassuring principle "God can do *everything*." But I hope I have made it clear that any reassurance we get that way is entirely spurious.

Endnote

*Reprinted from *Philosophy The Journal of the Royal Institute of Philosophy*, 48 (1973) by permission of Cambridge University Press.

Study Questions

1. What is the difference, for Peter Geach, between "omnipotence" a "almightiness"?

2. Geach discusses four views of omnipotence. What are they?

3. How does Rene Descartes' view of the truths of logic and arithmetic figure in the discussion?

4. According to Richard Price, why is God praiseworthy for his acts of goodness?

5. What are the senses of "necessary" Geach discusses?

27

Middle Knowledge

William Hasker

William Hasker is professor of philosophy at Huntington College, and is author of *God, Time, and Knowledge* and *Metaphysics: Constructing a Worldview*; co-author of *Reason and Religious Belief,* and *The Openness of God: A Biblical Alternative to the Traditional Conception of God.*

This selection is an adaptation, with minor changes, of chapter 2* of *God, Time, and Knowledge,* where he considers the doctrine of middle knowledge as it emerged in the sixteenth-century controversy and mentions some of the arguments pro and con that were put forward. Then he considers the doctrine as it has been reinvented by Plantinga. Finally, he considers objections to the theory, one of which he thinks is decisive.

Introduction

The theory of divine middle knowledge offers a particular way of understanding the traditional view that God has complete foreknowledge of everything that will ever happen. Middle knowledge assumes, first of all, that human beings possess free will in the libertarian sense—that they are capable, on occasion, of performing actions that are not predetermined by anything whatever, either by natural causes or by the will and decrees of God. But it goes on to ascribe to God a very special kind of knowledge concerning these free actions. It holds that God knows in advance all of the free choices and free actions that will ever be performed by his creatures. But beyond that, it holds that God knows what choices *would* have been made by any of these creatures, in any situation of libertarian free choice that they *might* have found themselves in, even if the situations in question never arose and the choices were never made. Indeed, it holds that God has this knowledge, not only concerning his *actual* free creatures, but concerning all the *possible* free creatures which he might have created but in fact has not created.

The theory of middle knowledge seems to offer some important advantages for theology, but it also raises major difficulties which have made it a center of controversy. It is the purpose of this selection to explore these issues. In the first section, we take an overview of the "classical theory" of middle knowledge, as it was first introduced by the Jesuit theologian Luis de Molina in the sixteenth century. Then, we turn to the version of the theory that has become prominent—originally through the influence of Alvin Plantinga—in recent analytical philosophy of religion. The third section explores certain objections which cast doubt on the viability of the theory, and the final section develops a particular argument which, if successful, shows conclusively that the theory of middle knowledge cannot be true.

The selection is an adaptation, with very minor changes, of chapter 2 of my book, *God, Time, and Knowledge* (Ithaca: Cornell University Press, 1989). There are references in the notes to some of the other chapters of the book, but the material presented here is self-contained on all of the main points. The text contains numerous references to previous discussions, but the reader might also wish to consult some more recent writings on the topic. Thomas Flint, "Hasker's *God, Time, and Knowledge*" (*Philosophical Studies* 60 (1990): 103-15), provides a general critique of the approach taken in this selection, especially the argument in section 4. My "Response to Thomas Flint" (*Philosophical Studies* 60 (1990): 117-26), replies to Flint's concerns. Robert M. Adams' "An Anti-Molinist Argument" (*Philosophical Perspectives* 5 (1991): 343-53) develops an argument parallel to the one given in section 4, arriving at the same conclusion by a somewhat different route. Rod Bertolet's "Hasker on Middle Knowledge" (*Faith and Philosophy* 10 (1993): 3-17) discusses the objections to middle knowledge given in section 3. My own most recent contribution is "Middle Knowledge: A Refutation Revisited," which as I write this is forthcoming in *Faith and Philosophy*.

Middle Knowledge

The theory of divine middle knowledge depends on the truth of theological compatibilism, the view that comprehensive divine fore-knowledge and human free will are logically consistent with each other. But it also serves to strengthen theological compatibilism in at least two ways. For one thing, it offers an account of *how* God is able to know future free actions, and the account of this given by middle knowledge is free of some of the difficulties—for instance, retroactive causation—that plague other accounts of the matter. More important, middle knowledge provides the key to a uniquely powerful conception of the operation of divine providence, almost certainly the strongest view of providence that is possible short of complete theological determinism. In contrast with this, it can be argued that foreknowledge *without* middle knowledge—"simple foreknowledge"—does *not* offer the benefits for the doctrine of providence that its adherents have sought to derive from it. In view of this, it could be argued that a good many theists who are not explicit adherents of middle knowledge nevertheless hold to a conception of divine providence that implicitly commits them to this theory.[1] And if this is so, a refutation of middle knowledge substantially weakens the doctrine of foreknowledge by removing one of its principal motivations.

Our procedure in this chapter will be as follows: First, we shall consider the doctrine as it emerged in the sixteenth-century controversy and mention briefly some of the arguments pro and con that were put forward at that time. Then, we shall turn to the modern form of the doctrine as it has been revived—or rather, reinvented[2]—by Alvin Plantinga. Finally, a series of objections to this theory will be considered, leading up to one that I consider decisive.

The Classical Theory

The theory of middle knowledge holds that, for each possible free creature that might exist, and for each possible situation in which such a creature might make a free choice, there is a truth, known to God prior to and independent of any decision on God's part, concerning what definite choice that creature would freely make if placed in that situation. In effect, middle knowledge extends the doctrine of divine foreknowledge to include knowledge of the outcome of choices that *might have been* made but in fact were not.

On casual consideration, middle knowledge may appear to be simply an obvious implication of divine omniscience: If God knows everything, how could he fail to know *this*? And by the same token, it may seem relatively innocuous. Both impressions, however, are mistaken. Middle knowledge is not a straightforward implication of omniscience, because it is not evident that the truths postulated by this theory exist to be known. In ordinary foreknowledge, it may be argued, what God knows is the agent's *actual decision* to do one thing or another. But with regard to a situation that never in fact arises, no decision is ever made, and none exists for God to know. And if the decision in question is supposed to be a *free* decision, then all of the circumstances of the case (including the agent's character and prior inclinations) are consistent with any of the possible choices that might be made. Lacking the agent's *actual* making of the choice, then, there is nothing that disambiguates the situation and makes it true that some one of the options is the one that *would be* selected. This line of argument indicates the single most important objection that the proponent of middle knowledge must seek to answer.

But the very same feature that makes middle knowledge problematic (viz., that God can know the outcome of choices that are never actually made) also makes it extraordinarily useful for theological purposes. Consider the following counterfactual: "If A were in circumstances C, she would do X." According to middle knowledge, God knows the truth of this *whether or not* A ever actually *is* placed in circumstances C; indeed, God knows this whether or not A even exists, so that his knowledge about this is entirely independent of any of *God's own decisions* about creation and providence. But this, of course, makes such knowledge ideal for God to use in *deciding* whether or not to create A, and, if he does create her, whether or not to place her in circumstances C. As Molina says:

> God in his eternity knew by natural knowledge all the things that he could do: that he could create this world and infinitely many other worlds . . . [and] given his complete comprehension and penetrating insight concerning all things and causes, he saw what would be the case if he chose to produce this order or a different order; how each person, left to his own free will, would make use of his liberty with such and such an amount of divine assistance, given such and such opportunities, temptations and other circumstances, and what he would freely do, retaining all the time the ability to do the opposite in the same opportunities temptations and other circumstances.[3]

Another way to look at the matter is this: It is evident that, if God had created a thoroughly deterministic world, his creative plan would have involved no risks whatsoever; all of the causal antecedents of such a world would be set up to produce exactly the results God intended. But it seems extremely plausible that in a world involving libertarian free choice, some risks are inevitable: God in creating such a world makes it possible for us to freely bring about great good, but also great evil—and which we in fact choose is up to us, not to God. Thus, the frequently heard statement that God "limits his power" by choosing to create free creatures. But according to the theory of middle knowledge, this is not quite correct. To be sure, it is still the creatures, not God, who determine their own free responses to various situations. But God, in choosing to create them and place them in those situations, knew exactly what their responses would be; he views the future, not as a risk taker seeking to optimize probable outcomes, but as a planner who knowingly accepts and incorporates into his plan exactly those outcomes that in fact *occur*—though, to be sure, some of them may not be the outcomes he would most prefer. The element of risk is entirely eliminated.

As we have already seen, the chief difficulty that the proponent of middle knowledge must confront is the contention that the truths God is alleged to know, commonly called "counterfactuals of freedom," do not exist to be known. Most of the arguments for counterfactuals of freedom seem to depend on general considerations of philosophical plausibility, but in the medieval controversy there were also arguments based on Scripture. A favorite text for this purpose is found in I Samuel 23, which recounts an incident in the troubled relationship of David with King Saul.[4] David, currently in occupation of the city of Keilah, consults Yahweh by means of the ephod about the rumors that Saul intends to attack the city:

> "Will Saul come down, as thy servant has heard? O LORD, the God of Israel, I beseech thee, tell thy servant. "And the LORD said, "He will come down." Then said David, "Will the men of Keilah surrender me and my men into the hand of Saul?" And the LORD said, "They will surrender you." (I Samuel 23:11-12, RSV)

The advocates of middle knowledge took this passage as evidence that God knew the following two propositions to be true:

(1)   If David stayed in Keilah, Saul would besiege the city.
(2)   If David stayed in Keilah and Saul besieged the city, the men of Keilah would surrender David to Saul.

But (given the assumption that Saul and the men of Keilah would act freely in performing the specified actions), these two propositions are counterfactuals of freedom, and the incident as a whole is a dramatic demonstration of the existence and practical efficacy of middle knowledge.

But this argument is hardly compelling. As Anthony Kenny points out, the ephod seems to have been a yes-no device hardly possessing the subtlety required to distinguish between various possible conditionals that might have been asserted in answer to David's questions. Kenny, indeed, suggests that we may understand material conditionals here,[5] but that seems hardly likely, since on that construal both conditionals would be true simply in virtue of the fact that their antecedents are false. Much more plausible candidates are given by Robert Adams:

(3)   If David stayed in Keilah, Saul would *probably* besiege the city.
(4)   If David stayed in Keilah and Saul besieged the city, the men of Keilah would *probably* surrender David to Saul.

As Adams points out, "(3) and (4) are enough for David to act on, if he is prudent, but they will not satisfy the partisans of middle knowledge."[6] The prospects for a scriptural proof of middle knowledge, therefore, do not seem promising.

But of course, the argument just given shows only that the responses to David's questions *need not* be taken as asserting counterfactuals of freedom, not that they *cannot* be so understood. And there are not lacking situations in everyday life in which it seems plausible that we are taking counterfactuals of freedom to be true. Plantinga, for example, says he believes that "If Bob Adams were to offer to take me climbing at Tahquitz Rock the next time I come to California, I would gladly (and freely) accept."[7] And Adams notes that "there does not normally seem to be any uncertainty at all about what a butcher, for example, would have done if I had asked him to sell me a pound of ground beef, although we suppose he would have had free will in the matter."[8]

So the discussion of examples seems to end in a stand-off. Still, the proponent of middle knowledge needs to address the question mentioned earlier: How is it possible for counterfactuals of freedom to be *true?* What is the truth maker for these propositions? At this point the advocate of middle knowledge is presented with an attractive opportunity, but one that it is imperative for her to resist. The opportunity is simply to claim that counterfactuals of freedom are true in virtue of the *character and psychological tendencies* of the agents named in them. The attractiveness of this is evident in that in nearly all of the cases where we are disposed to accept such counterfactuals as true, the epistemic grounds for our acceptance would be found precisely in our knowledge of such psychological facts—Saul besieging Keilah, Adams's compliant butcher, and Plantinga climbing Tahquitz Rock are all cases in point. But the weakness of the suggestion becomes apparent when the following question is asked: Are the psychological facts about the agent, together with a description of the situation, plus relevant psychological laws, supposed to *entail* that the agent would respond as indicated? If the answer is yes, then the counterfactual may be *true* but it is not a counterfactual of *freedom;* the agent is not then free in the relevant (libertarian) sense.[9] If on the other hand the answer is no, then how can those psychological facts provide good grounds for the assertion that the agent *definitely would* (as opposed, say, to *very probably would)* respond in that way?

Probably the best line for the proponent of middle knowledge to take here is the one suggested by Suarez: When a counterfactual of freedom is true, it is simply an ultimate fact about the free agent in question that, if placed in the indicated circumstances, she would act as the counterfactual states; this fact requires no analysis or metaphysical grounding in terms of further, noncounterfactual states of affairs. (Or, if the agent in question does not actually exist, it is a fact about a particular *essence* that, if it were instantiated and its instantiation were placed in such circumstances, the instantiation would act as stated.) Adams, commenting on this, says, "I do not think I have any conception . . . of the sort of . . . property that Suarez ascribes to possible agents with respect to their acts under possible conditions. Nor do I think that I have any other primitive understanding of what it would be for the relevant subjunctive conditionals to be true." Nevertheless, he admits that Suarez's view on this is of the "least clearly unsatisfactory type," because "It is very difficult to refute someone who claims to have a primitive understanding which I seem not to have."[10]

The Modern Theory

The modern theory of middle knowledge[11] differs from the classical version in virtue of the application to the counterfactuals of freedom of the powerful possible-worlds semantics for counterfactuals developed by Robert Stalnaker, David Lewis, and John L. Pollock.[12] The central idea of this semantics is that a counterfactual is true if some possible world in which the antecedent and the consequent are both true is more similar to the actual world than any in which the antecedent is true and the consequent false.[13] Thus (1) above is correctly analyzed as

> (5)   The actual world is more similar to some possible world in which David stays in Keilah and Saul besieges the city than to any possible world in which David stays in Keilah and Saul does not besiege the city.[14]

At this point it will be well to get a bit clearer about the exact positions both of the advocate and of the opponent of middle knowledge. First of all, it may be noted that the term "counterfactual," though customary and convenient, is not strictly accurate as a designation of the propositions in question. In some cases (namely, those whose antecedents God decides to actualize) both the antecedent and the consequent of the conditionals will be true, and so not counterfactual at all. A better term, therefore, would be, as Adams suggests, "deliberative conditionals." Having said that, however, we shall continue to refer to them as "counterfactuals of freedom."

But just what kind of conditionals are these? Both Lewis and Pollock distinguish "would" conditionals from "might" conditionals; the "might" conditional corresponding to (1) would be

(1m) If David stayed in Keilah, Saul *might* besiege the city.

But Pollock goes further and distinguishes three different kinds of "would" conditionals; these distinctions are not explicitly made by Lewis.[15] There are "simple subjunctives"; these are the conditionals most frequently, and most naturally, expressed by English sentences of the form "If it were the case that P, it would be the case that Q." Second, there are "even if" conditionals, of the form "Even if it were the case that P, it would (still) be the case that Q. "These are the conditionals Nelson Goodman calls "semi-factuals"; they are asserted when their consequents are believed to be true, whereas their antecedents may or may not be true, and their force is to deny that the truth of the antecedent would bring about the falsity of the consequent. Finally, there are "necessitation conditionals"; according to Pollock, "the notion of necessitation that I am trying to analyze here is that of the truth of one statement 'bringing it about' that another statement is true,"[16] so an appropriate formula might be "Its being the case that P would bring it about that Q"

Now, into which of these categories do we place the counterfactuals of freedom? Evidently they cannot be "might" conditionals. "Even if" conditionals are true only in (some of) those possible worlds in which their consequents are true, but the truth of the counterfactuals of freedom must be known to God quite independently of whether or not their consequents are true in the actual world. Pollock shows that a simple subjunctive is equivalent to the disjunction of a necessitation conditional and an "even if" conditional. If, then, we were to equate counterfactuals of freedom with simple subjunctives, it would follow that in those cases where the necessitation conditional is false the counterfactual of freedom would be equivalent to an "even if" conditional, which we have seen to be impossible. So if the counterfactuals of freedom are to be found among the varieties discussed by Pollock, they must be necessitation conditionals. As he says, "All counterfactual conditionals express necessitation."[17]

Now that we have clarified the nature of the counterfactuals of freedom, how exactly shall we characterize the view taken of such counterfactuals by the opponents of middle knowledge? There seem to be three alternatives: One may deny that such propositions exist at all; one may concede their existence but deny that they possess truth-values; or one may hold that all such propositions are false. The denial that there are such propositions as counterfactuals of freedom does not seem to have much to recommend it; as Plantinga says, he may conceivably be *wrong* in believing that if Adams were to invite him to climb Tahquitz Rock he would accept, but it would be passing strange to deny that *there is* such a proposition as the one he claims to believe. I think, in fact, that this view may best be understood as arising from an exigency; if one thinks (as the second view holds) that there is no way to assign truth-values to counterfactuals of freedom, and if one is also convinced that every proposition must be either true or false, then one is virtually forced to deny that there are such propositions—that is, one is forced to deny that the relevant sentences express any propositions at all.

The second view, according to which counterfactuals of freedom lack truth-values, probably arises from the reflection that there is no way to assign the truth-values because (where the consequent expresses a free choice to be made in hypothetical circumstances) there is in principle no way of knowing whether the consequent would be true if the antecedent were true. This, however, overlooks the possibility that we might be able to know whether the counterfactual is true *without* knowing this.

But how is this possible? The general relationship between counterfactuals and libertarian free will is something that still needs to be worked out. (Indeed, it is really the central theme of the present discussion.) But an extremely plausible view to take is the following: A situation in which an agent makes a libertarian free choice with respect to doing or not doing something is a situation in which the agent *might* do that thing but also might refrain from doing it. Suppose that A, if she found herself in circumstances C, would freely decide whether or not to do X. Then both of the following counterfactuals will be true:

(6)   If A were in C, she might do X.
(7)   If A were in C, she might refrain from doing X.

But if this is so, then there is no true counterfactual of freedom with respect to A's doing X in C. For (6) is inconsistent with

(8)   If A were in C, she would refrain from doing X.

Likewise, (7) is inconsistent with

(9)   If A were in C, she would do X.

If propositions like (6) and (7) properly characterize a situation of libertarian free choice, then all counterfactuals of freedom are false. In the ensuing discussion, this is the position which we shall assume the opponent of middle knowledge to be asserting and defending.

Objections to Middle Knowledge

Now that the opposition between proponents and opponents of middle knowledge has been delineated, how can we make progress on resolving the issue? As noted, proponents seem willing to rest their case on general considerations of plausibility, perhaps buttressed by allusions to the alleged theological necessity of the doctrine. Opponents can do the same, of course, and many do, but if the discussion is to be advanced, more substantial arguments are needed. And, in fact, such arguments are available. In this section three brief arguments against the theory will be spelled out, and in the next a somewhat more detailed argument will be developed.

The first objection to be considered is one we have already alluded to: What, if anything, is the *ground* of the truth of the counterfactuals of freedom? It is important to see that the question here is metaphysical, not epistemological. The question is not, How can we *know* that a counterfactualof freedom is true? It may be that we cannot know this, except perhaps in a very few cases, and although it is claimed that *God* knows them, it is not clear that the friend of counterfactuals (or any other theist, for that matter) is required to explain *how* it is that God knows what he knows. The question, rather, is What *makes* the counterfactuals true—what is the *ground* of their truth? As Adams says, "I do not understand what it would be for [counterfactuals of freedom] to be true."[18]

In replying to this Plantinga finds this notion of a requirement that there be something that "grounds" the truth of a proposition to be obscure. But insofar as the requirement does hold, he thinks the counterfactuals of freedom are no worse off with respect to it than are other propositions whose credentials are unimpeachable.

> Suppose, then, that yesterday I freely performed some action A. What was or is it that grounded or founded my doing so? I wasn't *caused* to do by anything else; nothing relevant *entails* that I did so. So what grounds the truth of the proposition in question? Perhaps you will say that what grounds its truth is just that in fact I did A. But this isn't much of an answer; and at any rate the same kind of answer is available in the case of Curley. For what grounds the truth of the counterfactual, we may say, is just that in fact Curley is such that if he had been offered a $35,000 bribe, he would have freely taken it.[19]

This answer of Plantinga's appears to be an endorsement of the view already attributed to Suarez: When a counterfactualof freedom is true, it is simply an ultimate fact about the free agent in question that, if placed in the indicated circumstances, she would act as the counterfactual states; this fact requires no analysis or "grounding" in terms of further, noncounterfactual states of affairs.[20]   It seems to me, however, that there is something seriously wrong about this answer. In order to bring this out, I want to try and formulate a certain intuition—an intuition that, I believe, underlies Adams's objection even though Adams does not explicitly formulate it. The intuition is this: In order for a (contingent) conditional state of affairs to obtain, its obtaining must be grounded in some categorical state of affairs. More colloquially, truths about "what *would be the case . . . if*" must be grounded in truths about what *is in fact* the case. This requirement seems clearly to be satisfied for the more familiar types of conditionals. The truth of a material conditional is grounded either in the truth of its consequent, or the falsity of its antecedent, or both.[21]   More interestingly, the truth of causal conditionals, and of their associated counterfactuals, are grounded in the natures, causal powers, inherent tendencies, and the like, of the natural entities described in them.[22]   The lack of anything like this as a basis for the counterfactuals of freedom seems to me to be a serious problem for the theory.[23]

Perhaps it is worthwhile to repeat here that the grounding *cannot* be found in the character, psychological tendencies, and the like of the agent. This point is, in effect, conceded by the defenders of middle knowledge; they recognize that such psychological facts are insufficient as a basis for the counterfactuals. And yet there is the following point: *In virtually every case where we seem to have plausible examples of true counterfactuals of Freedom, the plausibility is grounded precisely in such psychological facts as these.* (Again we recall Saul besieging Keilah, Plantinga climbing Tahquitz Rock, and Adams's butcher selling him a pound of hamburger.) And this, I think, ought to make us very suspicious of those examples. If the basis for the plausibility of the examples is in all cases found in something that has no tendency to show that the examples are correct—no tendency, that is, to show that the propositions in question really *are* true counterfactuals of freedom[24]—then the examples lose all force as support for the theory. And without the examples, there is very little in sight that even looks like supporting evidence.[25]

The second difficulty to be considered—one, so far as I know, not noticed in the literature to date—concerns the *modal status of counterfactuals of freedom*. To do the job required of them, these counterfactuals must be logically contingent—but I shall argue that, based on the assumptions of the theory of counterfactual logic, certain crucial counterfactuals should be regarded rather as necessary truths, if indeed they are true at all.[26]

The examples of counterfactuals considered so far (e.g., "If David stayed in Keilah, Saul would besiege the city") are in a certain way notoriously incomplete. The antecedent specifies a single crucial fact but leaves unstated many other facts about the situation which would undoubtedly be relevant to Saul's decision—facts about Saul's character and state of mind, but also facts about the strength and readiness of Saul's own military forces, about other threats to the kingdom, and so on. Now, it cannot seriously be supposed that the counterfactuals God considers in deciding about his own activity in creation and providence are incomplete in this way. Surely, the antecedents of the conditionals *he* considers must include *everything* that might conceivably be relevant to Saul's deciding one way or the other. In order to have some grasp on this sort of counterfactual, I suggest that we think in terms of *initial-segment counterfactuals,* in which the antecedent specifies a *complete initial segment of a possible world*[27] up to a given point in time, and the consequent an event that may or not take place at that time. (Of course, the antecedent will include any relevant causal laws that have held up until that time in that possible world.) If now we symbolize such counterfactuals using a capital letter followed by an asterisk to stand for the antecedent, then the initial-segment counterfactual corresponding to (1) would be:

(10) $A^* \rightarrow$ Saul besieges Keilah,

where 'A^*' represents a proposition specifying the entire initial segment of the possible world envisaged by God as the one in which Saul makes his decision. The contrary counterfactual then would be

(11) $A^* \rightarrow$ Saul does not besiege Keilah.

If, as we have been assuming all along, (1) is true, then (10) also will be true, and (11) false.

The interesting question, however, is whether (10) is a contingent or a *necessary* truth. Clearly, the theory of middle knowledge requires that it be contingent; if on the contrary it is necessary, then Saul's decision is *entailed* by a complete statement of antecedent conditions and his action is not free. (10), in fact, is to be evaluated in the same way as any other counterfactual proposition: To assert (10) is in effect to assert that some world in which "A^*" is true and Saul besieges Keilah is more similar to the actual world than any in which "A^*" is true and Saul does not do this. But, we may ask, if (10) is contingent, then under what possible circumstances would it be false? The answer is that (10) might be false if the actual world were different than it is; what is crucial is the similarity of envisaged possible worlds to the actual world, and so if the actual world were a different world (in ways we need not attempt to specify) than the one which is in fact actual, it might turn out that the world specified in (11) would be more similar to *that* world than is the world specified in (10), in which case (11) would be true and (10) false.

But this, I want to say, violates the fundamental idea that underlies the possible-worlds semantics for counterfactuals. For why exactly is it that counterfactuals are to be evaluated in terms of comparative similarity of possible worlds to the actual world? The answer to this is crucially related to the incompleteness, noted above, which attaches to the antecedents of the counterfactuals we use in everyday discourse. We simply do not have the resources to specify in the antecedents of our counterfactuals everything that might be relevant to the occurrence of the consequent, and even when we are clear in our own minds what the circumstances should be, we often do not take the trouble to state them. The notion of similarity to the actual world, then, removes what would otherwise be the ambiguity of our counterfactuals by specifying how the unstated conditions are to be understood: We are to think of the actual world as being modified *as little as possible* so as to accommodate the counterfactual antecedent. Thus, David Lewis states that the point of his "system of spheres representing comparative similarity of worlds" is "to rule out of consideration many of the various ways the antecedent could hold, especially the more bizarre ways."[28] He also says

A counterfactual $\phi \rightarrow \psi$ is true at world i if and only if ψ holds at certain ϕ-worlds; but certainly not all ϕ-worlds matter. *"If kangaroos had no tails, they would topple over"* is true (or false, as the case may be) at our world, quite without regard to those possible worlds where kangaroos walk around on crutches, and stay upright that way. Those worlds are too far away from ours. What is meant by the counterfactual is that, things being pretty much as they are—the scarcity of crutches for kangaroos being pretty much as it actually is, the kangaroos' inability to use crutches being pretty much as it actually is, and so on—if kangaroos had no tails they would topple over.[29]

So the point of the notion of comparative similarity between possible worlds is to place limits on the worlds that are relevant for the evaluation of a given counterfactual. But of course, (10) is already maximally limited in this way; it already includes *everything* about the envisaged world up until the time when Saul makes his decision. With regard to initial-segment counterfactuals, then, comparative similarity has no work left to do. Ask yourself this question: In evaluating (10), *why* should it make a difference whether the actual world is as it is, or is a world different in various ways from this one? After all, if A^* *were* actual, then *neither* "our" actual world nor that other one would *be* actual—so why should the truth of (10) depend in any way on which of those worlds is actual as things now stand? This contrasts sharply with the situation as regards Lewis's kangaroos: If, for instance, we lived in a world in which a large and active Animal Friendship League was assiduously providing prosthetic devices for "handicapped" animals, then we would "fill in" these conditions as we evaluate his counterfactual and would very likely judge it to be false. But with initial-segment counterfactuals there is just no room for this to happen; there are no spaces left to *be* filled in.

The situation, then, is as follows: The theory of middle knowledge is obliged to hold that some initial-segment counterfactuals are logically contingent. But in order to do this, the theory must apply to these counterfactuals the notion of comparative similarity to the actual world, and I have argued that this notion has no legitimate application here— which is to say, the notion is misapplied. The correct conclusion to be drawn from counterfactual logic, then, is that if initial-segment counterfactuals are true at all, they are true in *all* worlds and thus are *necessarily* true. But this conclusion is fatal to middle knowledge.

There is another, closely related point, one that connects this second argument with the first one given. Plantinga admits that "We can't look to similarity, among possible worlds, as *explaining* counterfactuality, or as *founding* or *grounding* it. (Indeed, any founding or grounding in the neighborhood goes in the opposite direction.)"[30] This means that (in some cases at least) of two worlds W and W', one is more similar to the actual

world *precisely because it shares counterfactuals* with the actual world—
it is *not* the case that, because one of those worlds is more similar to the
actual world *in other respects,* certain counterfactuals are true. But this, as
I have argued above, violates the reason for introducing the
comparative-similarity notion in the first place—that reason being, as
explained by Lewis, to secure that counterfactuals are evaluated in worlds
sufficiently similar to the actual world *in noncounterfactual respects.* How
can Plantinga justify relying on the principles of counterfactual logic when
at the same time he undercuts the rationale for accepting those same
principles?

The third (and final) objection of this group is one that was discovered
independently by Robert Adams and Anthony Kenny .[31] This difficulty
arises as we bring together the account given of the truth-conditions for
counterfactuals and the use God is said to make of them. As Kenny says, "If
it is to be possible for God to know which world he is actualizing, then his
middle knowledge must be logically prior to his decision to actualize;
whereas if middle knowledge is to have an object, the actualization must
already have taken place."[32]

Let's spell this out a bit more. We will suppose, contrary to the
argument in the preceding section, that some initial-segment
counterfactuals (namely, those whose consequents involve freely chosen
actions) are contingently true. Their truth, according to the theory,
depends on the similarity of various possible worlds to the actual world,
and thus it depends on which world *is* the actual world. But, which world
is actual depends, in part at least, on God's decision about what to create:
It is only by deciding to create that God settles which world is actual, and
therefore which counterfactuals are true. So rather than the
counterfactuals providing *guidance* for God's decision about what to create,
the fact is that their truth is determined only as a consequence of that very
decision!

Plantinga's answer to this is spelled out in his reply to Adams. In order
for the truth of the counterfactuals to be "available" to God as he makes
his creative decisions, it need not be already settled *in every respect*
which world is the actual world. What needs to be settled, in order for the
truth of a given counterfactual to be determinate and knowable, is only
that the actual world is a member of the *set of worlds* in which that
particular counterfactual is true. Now, why shouldn't this be the case,
even prior to God's decision about which particular world to actualize?
Why shouldn't it be the case, in other words, that *the same
counterfactuals of freedom are true in all the worlds God could actualize?*[33]
Why shouldn't the truth of the counterfactuals of freedom be
"counterfactually independent" of the various courses of action God could
have taken"?[34] If this is so, then the truth of the counterfactuals is settled
prior to God's decision about which world to actualize, and the
Adams-Kenny objection collapses.[35]

It must be acknowledged that this reply suffices as a formal answer to the objection, but I think it leaves us with a further, major problem. *How are we to explain* the alleged fact that the same counterfactuals of freedom are true in all the worlds God could actualize? These counterfactuals, according to the theory, are not necessary truths. Their truth, furthermore, is not due to *God's* decision; on the contrary, they constitute an *absolute limit* on which worlds God is able to actualize. For example: There are possible worlds, plenty of them, in which it is true that, if God had created Adam and placed him in Eden just as he did in the actual world, Adam would freely have refrained from sinning. (We will symbolize this initial-segment counterfactual as $"E^* \rightarrow \text{Adam}$ refrains from sinning.") Now, why didn't God actualize one of *those* worlds in preference to this one? The answer is, that *in fact* the true counterfactual, the one true in all the worlds God could actualize, is $"F^* \rightarrow$ Adam sins." But *why* is this counterfactual true? Not because of God's decision, and not because of any noncounterfactual truths about the creatures God has created. We will see in the next section that a very few of these counterfactuals are said to be true in virtue of the free choices made by created beings, but even if this answer proves tenable, it can account only for a tiny proportion of the whole. So we are confronted with this vast array of counterfactuals—probably, thousands or even millions for each actual or possible free creature—almost all of which simply *are true* without any explanation whatever of this fact being given. Is this not a deeply puzzling, even baffling state of affairs?

The three objections in this section have been developed independently, yet on close inspection they reveal a common theme. The first objection complained about the lack of a *ground* for the truth of counterfactuals in nonhypothetical, noncounterfactual reality. The reply is, that no such ground is needed. The second objection points out that if this is so, then the rationale is cut from under the principles of counterfactual logic on which the theory relies, thus making such reliance dubious at best. In the third objection, the groundlessness of counterfactuals reappears at a higher level, not concerned this time merely with individual counterfactuals but rather with the whole vast array of them, all allegedly true in all the worlds God could have actualized, and true without there being any ground for this either in the nature and actions of God, or in the natures of created beings, or (except for a tiny fraction) in the choices of created free agents. Without doubt, we are here confronted with something deeply mysterious—but is this the mystery of God's creation, or simply the mysteriousness of a misguided philosophical theory?[36]

A Refutation of Middle Knowledge

We turn now to a final, and slightly more complex, argument.[37] In this argument we shall not, as previously, argue directly against the counterfactuals of freedom. Instead, we shall concede, provisionally, that there are true counterfactuals of freedom and ask about them the question suggested in the last section: Who or what is it (if anything) that *brings it about*[38] that these propositions are true?

In order to give the discussion a touch of concreteness, imagine the following situation: Elizabeth, a doctoral student in anthropology, is in the concluding phase of her course work and is beginning to make plans for her dissertation field research. Her advisor has been asked to make a recommendation for a foundation grant to be awarded for observation of a recently discovered tribe in New Guinea. This assignment offers exciting prospects for new discoveries but would also involve considerable hardship and personal risk. The advisor asks himself whether Elizabeth would choose to undertake this study, or whether she would prefer to continue with her present plans to study a relatively placid group of South Sea islanders. He wonders, in other words, which of the following two counterfactuals of freedom is true:

(12) If Elizabeth were offered the grant, she would accept it (in symbols, $O \rightarrow A$).

(13) If Elizabeth were offered the grant, she would not accept it ($O \rightarrow \sim A$).

Now, Elizabeth's advisor may find himself unable to decide which counterfactual is true, or he may reach the wrong conclusion about this. But according to the theory of middle knowledge, one of the two counterfactuals is true, and God, if no one else, knows which one. For the sake of our discussion, we will assume it is (12) that is true rather than (13); we shall assume, moreover, that Elizabeth is in fact offered the grant and she accepts it. All this, however, is merely preparatory to raising the question already suggested: Who or what is it that *brings it about* that this proposition is true?

In the previous section we have considered the reasons why it cannot be *God* who brings it about that counterfactuals of freedom are true; we shall not rehearse those reasons here. The answer to this question that is in fact given by the friends of middle knowledge is that it is the *agent named in the counterfactual* who brings it about that the counterfactual is true. More precisely, it is the agent who brings this about *in those possible worlds in which the antecedent is true*.[39] It is this claim, then, that will be the principal subject of discussion throughout this section.

How might it be possible for the agent to bring it about that a given counterfactual of freedom is true? It would seem that the only possible way for the agent to do this is to perform the action specified in the consequent of the counterfactual under the conditions stated in the antecedent. That is to say: In the case of a genuinely free action, the only way to insure the action's being done is to do it. I believe the proponents of middle knowledge accept this, which is why they claim that the agent brings about the truth of the counterfactual *only in those possible worlds in which the antecedent is true.* It is in other words an accepted principle that

(14)　It is in an agent's power to bring it about that a given counterfactual of freedom is true, only if its truth would be brought about by the agent's performing the action specified in the consequent of the conditional under the conditions specified in the antecedent.

But is it possible for the agent to bring about the truth of a counterfactual of freedom in this way? What is required if it is to be the case that a particular event brings it about that a proposition is true? It seems initially plausible that

(15)　If E brings it about that "Q" is true, then "Q" would be true if E occurred and would be false if E did not occur ((E occurs) $\rightarrow Q$ and $\sim (E$ occurs) $\rightarrow \sim Q$).[40]

But this cannot be quite right, as is shown by the following examples: I knock on your door at ten o'clock, Sam knocks on your door at eleven o'clock, and no one else knocks on your door all day. It seems clear that my knocking on your door brings it about that "Someone knocks on your door today" is true, in spite of the fact that this would still be true even if I did not knock on your door. Or suppose we are bowling against each other, and you need a count of 5 or better on your last ball to win the game. If you roll a 9, your doing so brings about that you win the game, even though it need not be true that if you had not rolled a 9 you would not have won. (It may be that if you had not rolled a 9 you would have rolled a 7 or an 8.) In each case the problem arises because the event in question is a token of a type of event such that the occurrence of any event of that type (someone's knocking on the door, your rolling a 5 or better on your last ball) would bring about the truth of the proposition in question. With this in mind, we revise (15) as follows:

(16)　If E brings it about that "Q" is true, then E is a token of an event-type T such that (some token of T occurs) $\rightarrow Q$ and $\sim$(some token of T occurs) $\rightarrow \sim Q$, and E is the first token of T which occurs.

If then we add the simplifying assumption that if E were not to occur, no other token of T would occur, we get (15) as a special case. When, on the other hand, we have an event and a proposition such that the conditions specified in (15) and (16) are not satisfied, we will say that the truth of the proposition is independent of the event in question.

Applying this to our example, what we need to know is whether Elizabeth brings about the truth of the counterfactualof freedom "$O \rightarrow A$" by accepting the grant, or whether its truth is independent of her action, in the sense just specified. In order to determine this, we need to know whether the following propositions are true:

(17) If Elizabeth were to accept the grant, it would be true that $O \rightarrow A$ (i.e., $A \rightarrow (O \rightarrow A)$).

(18) If Elizabeth were not to accept the grant, it would be true that $O \rightarrow A$ (i.e., $\sim A \rightarrow (O \rightarrow A)$).

There can be no question about the truth of (17); if both "O" and "A" are true in the actual world, the counterfactual will be true. It might seem equally obvious that (18) is false: If Elizabeth does not accept the grant, how can it be true that, if offered it, she would accept it? This, however, is a mistake. If (18) seems to us to be obviously false, we are probably misreading (18) as

(19) If Elizabeth were to reject the grant, it would be true that $O \rightarrow A$ (i.e., $(O \And \sim A) \rightarrow (O \rightarrow A)$).

This is indeed obviously false, but it is not the same as (18); the antecedent of (18) says, not that Elizabeth rejects the offer, but merely that she does not accept it. It is consistent both with her rejecting the offer, and with the offer's never having been made. If she rejects it, then "$O \rightarrow A$" must be false, but if no offer is made, "$O \rightarrow A$" will still be true. So now we have to evaluate the counterfactuals

(20) If Elizabeth does not accept the offer it will be because she rejected it (i.e., $\sim A \rightarrow (O \And \sim A)$).[41]

(21) If Elizabeth does not accept the offer, it will be because the offer was not made (i.e., $\sim A \rightarrow (\sim O \And \sim A)$).

If (20) is true, (18) will be false, but if (21) is true, so is (18).

How shall we decide this question? According to our semantics for counterfactuals, the question about (20) and (21) comes down to this: Is a world in which Elizabeth received the offer and rejected it more or less similar to the actual world (in which the offer was accepted) than a world in which the offer was neither made nor accepted?

One's first thought might be that the world specified in (20), which differs from the actual world with respect to Elizabeth's acceptance of the offer, is more similar to the actual world than the world specified in (21), which differs with respect both to the making of the offer and to its acceptance. If so, however, then one's first thought (as is so often the case in matters counterfactual) would have overlooked important considerations. To see why, consider the following example: I have been hard at work making a poster announcing an upcoming event, and just as the poster is nearly completed I knock over my ink bottle, spilling ink on the poster and forcing me to start all over again. As I do this, I pause from cursing my clumsiness long enough to wonder what it would have been like not to have had my poster ruined in this way. Two possibilities occur to me: I might have refrained from knocking over the ink bottle in the first place, or, I might have knocked it over just as I did in the actual world, but instead of spilling any ink, the bottle spontaneously righted itself and come to rest again in its original position. I then wonder which of these scenarios would have occurred if I had not gotten the ink spilled on my poster. I am wondering, in other words, which of the following counterfactuals is true:

(22) If no ink had been spilled on my poster, it would have been because I did not knock over my ink bottle ($\sim S \to (\sim K \ \& \ \sim S)$).

(23) If no ink had been spilled on my poster, it would have been because I knocked over my ink bottle but no ink spilled ($\sim S \to (K \ \& \ \sim S)$).

I puzzle over this for a few moments, but my question is quickly answered along the same lines already suggested for (20) and (21). The (22)-world would have differed from the actual world with respect both to the bottle's being knocked over and the ink's spilling, whereas the (23)-world differs from it only in the latter respect. So the (23)-world is more similar to the actual world than the (22)-world; it is (23) that is true and not (22), and I realize that if my poster had not been ruined, the reason for this would have been, not that I was careful about my ink bottle, but that after I knocked over the bottle it miraculously righted itself without spilling any ink. And that makes me feel a little better about my clumsiness.

Of course this is absurd, but why is it absurd? What exactly is wrong with the reasoning that led me to conclude that (23) is true rather than (22)? The answer seems to be this: In the actual world certain counterfactuals are true, among them

(24) If I were to knock my ink-bottle in such-and-such a way, the bottle would fall over and spill ink on my poster.

This counterfactual is true in the actual world (as events have shown), and it is also true in the (22)-world, but not in the (23)-world. And in weighing the comparative similarity to the actual world of the (22)-world and the (23)-world, the truth in the (22)-world of the counterfactual (24) counts far more heavily than the slightly greater similarity of the (23)-world with

respect to factual content. So as we thought all along, it is (22) that is true
rather than (23).

But of course exactly similar considerations apply in the case of (20)
and (21). In the actual world, it is true that

(12)   If Elizabeth were offered the grant, she would accept it.

This counterfactual is true in the actual world, and also in the (21)-
world, but not in the (20)-world. And in a comparison of the latter two
worlds, the truth of the counterfactual (12) outweighs the slight
difference with respect to similarity in factual content, so that the
(21)-world is indeed more similar to the actual world than the (20)-world,
and it is (21) that is true rather than (20).

It might be suggested that the reason (24) is decisive with respect to
the decision between (22) and (23) is that (24) is backed by laws of nature;
counterfactuals of freedom such as (12) do not have such backing and are
therefore not decisive with regard to the choice (for example) between
(20) and (21). But this really will not do. For one thing, Plantinga himself
is pretty clearly committed to the view that, in deciding the comparative
similarity of possible worlds, counterfactuals outweigh differences in
matters of fact *whether or not* they are backed by laws of nature.[42] And
there are reasons that make it very difficult to justify weighting
counterfactuals of freedom less heavily than laws of nature. First, there is
the contention, noted in the last section, that the same counterfactuals of
freedom are true in all the worlds God can actualize and constitute
absolute limitations on God's power to bring about states of affairs. (Laws
of nature, clearly, do *not* limit God's power in this way; he could have
created a world in which different laws obtained.)

The proponent of middle knowledge, however, may object to this piece
of reasoning. He may point out that, although *God* cannot control which
counterfactuals of freedom are true, the *human beings* in question—the
agents named in the counterfactuals—*do* have control over this, since it is
they who, by making the choices that they do, bring about that those
counterfactuals are true. Now, of course, whether or not the agent brings
about the truth of the counterfactual is the very point at issue in the
present discussion. In view of this, one might tend to consider it
question-begging to introduce this point on *either* side at this stage of the
argument.[43] But the proponent of middle knowledge may feel this is unfair
to him. The claim that the agent brings about the truth of counterfactuals
of freedom is, he points out, an integral part of his position, one that he
should be permitted to appeal to until and unless it is refuted by his
opponent.[44] Suppose we concede this point and agree to evaluate the
immediate point in question—the question, that is, whether it is (20) or
(21) that is true—in the light of the claim that the agent decides which of

the counterfactuals about her actions are true. How will this affect the outcome of the discussion?

A natural view to take would seem to be that this point made by the proponent of middle knowledge tends to balance off, and thus to neutralize, the last point made in the previous paragraph. There it was pointed out that God has control over which laws of nature obtain, but not over which counterfactuals of freedom are true. The rejoinder is that human beings have control over some counterfactuals of freedom, but not over natural laws. If, as would seem to be the case, these considerations weight about equally on either side of the argument, the upshot would seem to be that we cannot decide, on the basis of these considerations alone, whether counterfactuals of freedom are more fundamental than laws of nature, or vice versa. If anything, what seems to be suggested is that the two are roughly at a parity. If we wish for a more definitive answer to our question, we must look further.

Now, what is at issue is whether it is counterfactuals backed by laws of nature or counterfactuals of freedom that have counterexamples in possible worlds "closer" to the actual world. It is relevant in this connection that we now know with virtual certainty that the fundamental laws of nature are probabilistic rather than strictly deterministic; thus, the counterfactuals backed by the laws of nature (such as [24]) are in fact *would-probably conditionals* rather than true necessitation conditionals. Surely, however, necessitation conditionals (such as the counterfactuals of freedom are supposed to be) have to be weighted *more* heavily than "would-probably" conditionals in determining the relative closeness of possible worlds. There is also the important point that God, according to Christian belief, can and does work miracles. If this is so, then some counterfactuals backed by laws of nature have counterexamples *in the actual world itself,* and therefore also in possible worlds as close to the actual world as you please. In view of all this, the counterfactuals of freedom seem to be considerably more fundamental, with respect to explaining why things are as they are, than the laws of nature; *a fortiori,* they are more fundamental than particular facts such as that Elizabeth is offered the grant.[45]

But if (21) is true, then so is (18), and (since [17] is also true) it follows that the truth of the counterfactual "$O \rightarrow A$" is independent of whether or not Elizabeth actually accepts the grant. (It is not true if she *rejects* the grant, but that is another matter.) And it also follows (by [16]) that Elizabeth's acceptance of the offer does *not* bring it about that the counterfactual "$O \rightarrow A$" is true. And in general, it is not true that the truth of a counterfactualof freedom is brought about by the agent.[46]

Does the conclusion we have reached constitute a serious problem for middle knowledge? Perhaps not. David Basinger has recently argued that the proponent of middle knowledge need not and should not hold that the truth of the counterfactualof freedom is brought about by the agent.[47] To be sure, the view that the truth of these counterfactuals is brought about by God must also be excluded, for the reasons already discussed. Rather, these counterfactuals simply *are true* without their truth having been brought about either by God or by anyone else. "Who is responsible for the truth of [the counterfactuals of freedom] in the actual world? The answer is that no one is responsible."[48]

This proposal, however, creates serious difficulties for middle knowledge. On the proposed view, Elizabeth is not responsible for the fact that, if she were offered the grant, she would accept it (i.e., for the truth of the counterfactual "$O \rightarrow A$"). Nor, we may assume, is she responsible for the truth of the antecedent—that is, for the fact that she is offered the grant. But if she is responsible for neither of these things, it is difficult to see how she can be responsible for accepting the grant—a conclusion that is entirely unwelcome to the proponents of middle knowledge.

But there is another, even more fundamental, difficulty. We have learned that Elizabeth does not bring it about that the counterfactual "$O \rightarrow A$" is true. What effect, if any, does this have on the question of what is in her power when the grant offer is made? In order to investigate this, we need what I call *power entailment principles,* principles that state that an agent's possessing the power to perform a certain kind of action entails that the agent also possesses the power to perform another kind of action. More will be said about power entailment principles in chapter 6, but a principle that will suffice for our present purposes is

(PEP)   If it is in A's power to bring it about that P, and "P" entails "Q" and "Q" is false, then it is in A's power to bring it about that Q.

A little thought will show this principle to be correct. If "P" entails "Q," it cannot be the case that P unless it is also the case that Q. If "Q" is already true, then the entailment presents no obstacle to A's being able to bring it about that P. (Since the sun is in fact rising, it is in your power to bring it about that you see the sunrise, even though you completely lack the power to bring about the sunrise itself.) But if "Q" is not true, it is not possible for you to bring it about that P unless it is also possible for you to bring it about that Q. (I approach your house with the intention of ringing your doorbell, only to discover that you do not have a doorbell. Unless it is in my power to bring it about that you have a doorbell—e.g., by installing one myself or having one installed—it is not in my power to ring your doorbell.)[49]

How does this principle apply to the matter in hand? In order to proceed we will make the assumption, which is sanctioned by the theory of middle knowledge, that of any pair of counterfactuals such as (12) and (13) one or the other is true; this implies that the disjunction of the two is necessarily true, true in all possible worlds. Given this assumption, we have the following as necessary truths:

(25) If Elizabeth is offered the grant and accepts it, it is true that $O \rightarrow A$ $((O \ \& \ A) \Rightarrow (O \rightarrow A))$.

(26) If Elizabeth is offered the grant and rejects it, it is true that $O \rightarrow \sim A$ $((O \ \& \ \sim A) \Rightarrow (O \rightarrow \sim A))$

That is to say, Elizabeth's acceptance or rejection of the grant *entails* the truth of the corresponding counterfactual of freedom.[50]

Now we are ready to consider what is in Elizabeth's power when the offer is made. First of all, is it in her power to accept the grant? One would suppose that it is, since in fact she actually does so. And (PEP) places no obstacle in the way of this conclusion. Her accepting the offer entails the truth of the counterfactual "$O \rightarrow A$," but that counterfactual is in fact true, and so the question of whether it is in her power to *bring about* its truth does not arise.

But now let us ask, does she have it in her power to *reject* the grant? Her rejecting the grant entails that the counterfactual "$O \rightarrow \sim A$" be true, but this counterfactual is in fact false. So—according to (PEP)—she can have the power to reject the grant only if it is in her power to bring it about that this counterfactual is true. If she does not have this power, then she lacks power to reject the grant.

And now the situation becomes serious. We have seen that it would be in Elizabeth's power to bring it about that the counterfactual "$O \rightarrow \sim A$" is true only if the truth of this counterfactual would be brought about by her rejecting the offer. But we have also seen that the truth of a counterfactual of freedom is *not* brought about in this way. It follows that Elizabeth does *not* have it in her power to bring it about that $O \rightarrow \sim A$, and lacking this, she also—by (PEP)—lacks the power to reject the offer.

It is time to summarize. In this section we are investigating the question, Who or what brings it about that the counterfactuals of freedom are true? We first considered the possibility that it is the agent named in the counterfactual who does this—in terms of our example, that Elizabeth by accepting the grant offer brings it about that $O \rightarrow A$. It turns out, however, that this counterfactual is true independently of whether or not she accepts the offer: It would be true if she were to accept the offer, and it would also be true were she not to accept the offer. To be sure, it would not be true if she were to *reject* the offer, but this turns out not to be relevant; if she did not accept the offer, this would be because the offer was never made and not because it was made and she rejected it. But since the counterfactual is true independently of whether or not she accepts the offer, it cannot be the case that she *brings about* the truth of the counterfactual by her acceptance of the grant.

We then went on to consider what Elizabeth has it in her power to do when the grant is offered to her. Clearly, she has it in her power to accept the grant, and she demonstrates this by doing so. But does she also have the power to reject the grant? Of particular importance here is the fact that (given the truth of the theory of middle knowledge) her rejection of the grant entails the truth of the counterfactual "$O \rightarrow \sim A$." But this counterfactual is not true, so it can be in her power to reject the grant only if it is also in her power to bring about the truth of this counterfactual. But we have already seen that this is impossible. She could have the power to bring about the truth of the counterfactual "$O \rightarrow \sim A$" only if its truth could be brought about by her rejection of the offer, but we have seen that the agent *cannot* in this way bring about the truth of a counterfactual of freedom. So it is not in her power to reject the grant.

The conclusion to be drawn from this is that the concession made earlier—that some counterfactuals of freedom are true—was unwarranted. It turns out from our consideration of the case of Elizabeth that insofar as such counterfactuals are *true*, they are not counterfactuals of *freedom*: If the counterfactual "$O \rightarrow A$" is true, it is not in Elizabeth's power to reject the offer, and she is not free in the required sense. And, on the other hand, insofar as an agent is genuinely free, there *are* no true counterfactuals stating what the agent would definitely do under various possible circumstances. And so the theory of middle knowledge is seen to be untenable: *There are no true counterfactuals of freedom.*

Endnotes

*Reprinted from William Hasker: *God, Time and Knowledge.* Copyright ©. 1989 by Cornell University. Used by permission of the publisher, Cornell University Press.

[1] This point, and also the uselessness of simple foreknowledge for the doctrine of providence, are argued in David Basinger, "Middle Knowledge and Classical Christian Thought," *Religious Studies* 22 (1986): 407-22. And see ch. 3 below.

[2] Plantinga developed his view independently; it was Anthony Kenny who pointed out to him the similarity between this view and the classical theory of middle knowledge. See Plantinga, "Self-Profile," in James E. Tomberlin and Peter van Inwagen, eds., *Alvin Plantinga, Profiles,* vol. 5 (Dordrecht: D. Riedel, 1985), p. 50.

[3] Molina, "De Scientia Dei," quoted by Anthony Kenny, *The God of the Philosophers* (Oxford: Oxford University Press, 1979), pp. 62-63.

[4] For my discussion of this passage I rely chiefly on R. M. Adams, "Middle Knowledge and the Problem of Evil," *American Philosophical Quarterly* 14 (1977): 109-117. See also Kenny, *The God of the Philosophers,* pp. 63-64.

[5] Kenny, *The God of the Philosophers,* p. 64.

[6] Adams, *"Middle Knowledge,"* p. 111.

[7] "Reply to Robert M. Adams," in Tomberlin and van Inwagen, eds., *Alvin Plantinga,* p. 373.

[8] Adams, "Middle Knowledge," p. 115.

9 There are complexities in our use of such expressions as "acting freely" that are not always sufficiently taken note of. For example, it may happen that an action is "psychologically inevitable" for a person, based on that person's character and dispositions, yet we say that the person acts "freely" *if the character and dispositions are thought to be the result of previous freely chosen actions of the person.* Thus, it is said of the redeemed in heaven both that they freely serve and worship God, and that they are not able to sin; this happy inability is the result of their own free choices and is not typically seen as a diminution of freedom. But acts of this sort are *not* free in the very strict sense required by libertarianism. If we are exacting in our *definition* of "free" but lax in *applying* the term, trouble is inevitable.

10 Adams, *"Middle Knowledge,"* p. 112.

11 The basic source for the modern theory of middle knowledge is Alvin Plantinga, *The Nature of Necessity* (Oxford: Oxford University Press, 1974), chap. 9.

12 See Robert Stalnaker, "A Theory of Conditionals," in N. Rescher, ed., *Studies in Logical Theory* (Oxford: Blackwell, 1968); David Lewis, *Counterfactuals* (Cambridge: Harvard University Press, 1973); and John L. Pollock, *Subjunctive Reasoning* (Dordrecht: D. Riedel, 1976). It should be noted, however that some contemporary adherents of middle knowledge have reservations about this semantics. Alfred J. Freddoso, for example, writes: "I repudiate the claim that the standard semantics applies to [counterfactuals of freedom] or to any other 'simple' conditionals that involve causal indeterminism" (personal communication).

13 Pollock argues that the relevant notion is not that of comparative similarity but rather that of a possible world "minimally changed" from the actual world so as to make the antecedent of the counterfactual true. (See *Subjunctive Reasoning*, pp. 17-23.) Pollock's argument seems to be correct, but the difference between the two formulations is not significant for present purposes, so we shall continue to employ the more familiar terminology.

14 Adams, *"Middle Knowledge,"* p. 112.

15 See Pollock, *Subjunctive Reasoning*, chap. 2, "Four Kinds of Conditionals."

16 Ibid., pp. 35-36. Pollock says, "Perhaps the term 'necessitation' is inappropriate for the notion I have in mind here, but I have been unable to find a better term" (p. 36). Pollock does not identify any single English locution that is customarily used in stating necessitation conditionals, though he thinks the force of such conditionals may be captured by the formula "If it were true that *P*, it would be true that *Q since* it was true that *P*" (p. 27).

17 Ibid., p. 34.

18 Adams, "Middle Knowledge," p. 110.

19 Reply to Robert M. Adams," p. 374. Plantinga here alludes to an example found in *The Nature of Necessity*, pp. 173-74.

20 That this is Plantinga's view is clearly implied by the argument given on pp. 177-79 of *The Nature of Necessity*.

21 Some would deny that these are genuinely *conditionals,* in the interesting sense of that term.

22 I am assuming that whereas these natures, causal powers, etc., may, because of our limitations, have to be *described* in terms of conditional statements, the *truth* of these conditionals is itself grounded in occurrent states of affairs—for example, in the microstructures of physical materials. It is noteworthy that Humeans, who deny the

existence of causal powers, natures, etc., have great difficulty in dealing with counterfactuals generally.

23 Freddoso points out that middle knowledge "cuts against the spirit, if not the letter, of the standard possible worlds semantics for subjunctive conditionals. For it is usually assumed that the similarities among possible worlds invoked in such semantics are conceptually prior to the acquisition of truth-values by the subjunctive conditionals themselves. . . . On the Molinist view the dependence runs in just the opposite direction when the conditionals in question are conditional future contingents . . . . If the standard possible worlds semantics for subjunctive conditionals presupposes otherwise, then Molinists will have to modify it or propose an alternative capable of sustaining realism with respect to conditional future contingents" (Introduction to Luis de Molina, *On Divine Foreknowledge (Part IV of the Concordia)*, trans. Alfred J. Freddoso [Ithaca, N.Y.: Cornell University Press, 1988, sec. 5.6).

24 Note, however, that such psychological facts might very well provide grounding for conditionals such as (3) and (4), asserting that under given conditions the agents would *probably* act in a certain way.

25 Plantinga says, "Surely there are many actions and many creatures such that God knows what he would have done if one of the latter had taken one of the former. There seem to be true counterfactuals of freedom about God; but what would ground the truth of such a counterfactual of freedom?" ("Reply to Robert M. Adams," p. 375) The answer to this, however, is obvious: The truth of such a counterfactual about God's action is grounded in God's *conditional intention* to act in a certain way. But humans, for the most part, have no such conditional intentions about choices they might be called upon to make—or, when they do have them, the intentions at best ground "*would probably*" counterfactuals.

26 Jonathan Kvanvig actually holds that the counterfactuals of freedom are contained in the *essence* of the free creature, (see Jonathan L. Kvanvig, *The Possibility of an All-Knowing God* [New York: St. Martin's, 1986], pp. 124-25). But this is fatal to the theory: No individual chooses, or is responsible for, what is contained in that individual's essence.

27 In order fully to explicate the notion of an "initial segment" of a possible world, we need the distinction between hard facts and soft facts about the past; for this distinction see chapter 5.

28 Lewis, *Counterfactuals*, p. 66.

29 Ibid., pp. 8-9.

30 "Reply to Robert M. Adams," p. 378.

31 See Adams, "Middle Knowledge," pp. 113-14; Kenny, *The God of the Philosophers*, pp. 70-71.

32 *The God of the Philosophers*, p. 71.

33 Plantinga seems to say that an even weaker requirement than this will suffice to enable the theory to work. He says:

It isn't at all clear that if (8) ["If God created Adam and Eve, there would be more moral good than moral evil in the history of the world"] could be God's reason for creating Adam and Eve, then there was nothing he could do to make it the case that (8) is false. For suppose (8) would have been false if God had created no free creatures. We can still imagine God reasoning as follows: "If I were to create no free creatures there would not, of course, be more moral good than moral evil; and it would be better to have more moral good than moral evil. But if I were to create free creatures, (8) would be true, in which case if I were to create Adam and Eve, there would be more moral good than moral evil. So I shall create Adam and Eve." Thus even if God could bring it about that (8) was false, (8) could perfectly well serve as his reason, or part of his reason, for creating Adam and Eve. ("Reply to Robert M. Adams," p. 377)

I believe this suggestion to be incoherent. For consider the following supposition, which on Plantinga's principles ought to be possible: Suppose, as Plantinga hypothesizes, (8) would be true if God created free creatures but false if he did not create free creatures. Suppose, furthermore, that God decided not to create free creatures. (Possibly he is more repelled by the prospect of moral evil than attracted by the prospect of moral good.) Then God, looking back on his decision to create a world that lacks free creatures, can truthfully say, "I'm glad I decided not to create Adam and Eve, for if I had created them there would have been more moral evil than moral good." But this contradicts the supposition of the example, which is that if God were to create free creatures, (8) would have been true. So the example is incoherent, and the correct requirement for the theory of middle knowledge is the one slated in the text: the same counterfactuals of freedom must be true in all the worlds God can actualize.

34 Ibid., p. 376.

35 It should be pointed out that Adams anticipated the possibility of a reply along these lines but rejected it because it seemed implausible to him that (for example) a world in which there are no free creatures at all would be "more like a world in which most free creaturely decisions are good ones than like a world in which most free creaturely decisions are bad ones" ("Middle Knowledge," p. 114). Plantinga, however, is unmoved by this—as we have already noted, he sees no reason why the similarities between worlds that are relevant for the truth of counterfactuals must have anything to do with similarities in noncounterfactual characteristics of those worlds.

36 It is evident that many (though not all) of these difficulties result from the applications to counterfactuals of freedom of the possible-worlds semantics. Thus, the proponent of middle knowledge may be tempted to dispense with the semantics, perhaps agreeing with Freddoso that "we might wonder why it wasn't perfectly obvious from the start that comparative similarity wouldn't help us if the conditionals in question involve genuine causal indeterminism" (personal communication). It is true that getting rid of the semantics makes the theory somewhat harder to attack, but it also eliminates a good deal of the theory's philosophical substance. Those philosophers (their name is legion) who are disposed in any case to be suspicious of counterfactuals can only have their suspicions confirmed if we are deprived of any systematic account of their semantics.

37 See William Hasker, "A Refutation of Middle Knowledge," Noûs 20 (1986): 545-57.

38 The concept of *bringing about* employed here and elsewhere throughout the book will be discussed in detail in chapter 6. For the present, suffice it to say that the concept is of an asymmetrical relation of dependence of what is brought about on the action or event that brings it about; the dependence in question may be, but is not necessarily, causal.

39 This is a view I have heard stated in discussion by Plantinga; I know of no written source. In any case, the attribution is not crucial, since we shall also be discussing the consequences for middle knowledge if this claim is *not* made.

[40] I speak both of an *event* as bringing about the truth of a proposition, and of a *person* as doing so. Thomas Flint ("Hasker's 'Refutation' of Middle Knowledge," unpublished, n. 12) correctly points out that there is a need for a principle to connect these two uses. The required principle is as follows: A person brings it about that a proposition is true just in case that person's performance of some action brings it about.

[41] The verbal formulations in (20) through (23) represent my attempts to express in natural-sounding ways some propositions that under normal circumstances we would seldom if ever have any occasion to state. No special emphasis is to be laid on the "because" language; the logically relevant content of the propositions is what is contained in the symbolic formulations.

[42] I take this to be the upshot of the argument given in *The Nature of Necessity*, pp. 177-78.

[43] Flint accuses me of begging the question (in my "Refutation of Middle Knowledge") by assuming that "since *God* has no control over which counterfactuals of creaturely freedom are true, neither do *we*" ("Hasker's 'Refutation' of Middle Knowledge," p. 20). But this is just false. I do not *assume* this; I *argue* for it, and the reader will search in vain to find this proposition, or anything equivalent to it, among the premises of my argument. What is true, however, is that I fail to consider this point (viz., the proponent's claim that agents control the truth of the counterfactuals of freedom) in my discussion of whether counterfactuals of freedom outweigh laws of nature, or vice versa.

[44] The position then would be similar to the one that obtains in discussions of the problem of evil, where the burden of proof is assumed by the nontheist and the theist is entitled to invoke all of her theistic beliefs unless and until the nontheist has refuted them.

[45] Freddoso, commenting on the version of this argument given in the article "A Refutation of Middle Knowledge," claims that the argument is "seriously flawed" because of my claim that "the proponents of middle knowledge hold, or should hold, that the truth of a counterfactual of freedom is as fixed in the worlds closest to the actual world as is the truth of a law of nature" (*Introduction to Molina, On Divine Foreknowledge*, sec. 5.7 and n. 96).

Now, since I do not think any counterfactuals of freedom are true *at all*, I have no views of my own concerning *when* they are true; I must therefore rely on inferences from principles that are or should be accepted by the proponents of middle knowledge. If the particular conclusion criticized by Freddoso turned out to be stronger than warranted, this would not create serious difficulties for my overall argument. What is required for my argument is only the much weaker claim that, in determining the relative similarity of possible worlds, counterfactuals of freedom outweigh particular facts such as that Elizabeth is offered the grant. Plantinga's argument cited in note 42 above seems to commit him to holding that they do, and in view of this the difficulty here does not seem especially serious.

But I am by no means convinced that the conclusion I have drawn is too strong. I believe that the arguments given in the text provide cogent reason for holding that, if there are true counterfactuals of freedom, they outweigh laws of nature in determining the relative similarity of possible worlds. If the friends of counterfactuals disagree with this, they are invited to present (at least) equally cogent arguments for the contrary conclusion.

[46] I am indebted to Alvin Plantinga for an extremely interesting objection to this argument. He suggests that the argument cannot be general in its force, because it will not work if we change the original supposition slightly. Suppose that in the actual world it is true that (14) $O \rightarrow \sim A$, rather than that (13) $O \rightarrow A$, and suppose furthermore that Elizabeth is offered the grant, and she rejects it. We then ask what it would have been like had she *accepted* the grant. And here, it may seem, the only reasonable answer is that, if she had accepted the grant, it would have been true that $O \rightarrow A$, and from this it is but a short step to say that she would *bring about* the truth of "$O \rightarrow A$" by accepting the grant. If we do not say that, what can we say? Surely not, that she accepted the grant because she was not offered it!

No, we can't say *that!* Rather, we proceed as follows: Starting with the assumption that "$O \rightarrow \sim A$" is true, and she in fact rejects the grant, we ask ourselves this question: What is the minimal change that would be needed in the actual world, such that if things were different in that way, Elizabeth would accept the grant? It may not be obvious what the answer is, but surely there must *be* an answer. Possibly the minimal change would be that all her other opportunities for field research have fallen through, so that if she does not accept the grant, her research, and the granting of her degree, will be postponed indefinitely. (If we represent the proposition saying that she is offered the grant under those modified circumstances as '$O\#$', then it follows from what has been said that "$O\# \rightarrow A$" is true even though "$O \rightarrow A$" is false.) Supposing this to be the case, we then ask, If Elizabeth were to accept the grant, would it be because "$O\#$" was true rather than "O," or because "$O \rightarrow A$" was true? And for the reasons already discussed, the correct answer will be that if she were to accept it this would be because the circumstances were different than they are in the actual world (in which she rejects it), and not because the counterfactual "$O \rightarrow A$" would be true. So it still is not true that Elizabeth brings about the truth of a counterfactual of freedom. The beauty of Plantinga's objection is that it brings out the generality of the argument in a way in which the original example does not.

[47] "Divine Omniscience and Human Freedom: A Middle Knowledge Perspective," *Faith and Philosophy* I (1984): 291-302.

[48] Ibid., p. 300.

[49] Freddoso (*Introduction to Molina, On Divine Foreknowledge*, sec. 5.7) rejects this principle, and with it the conclusion of the present argument. For his objection to (PEP), see chapter 6.

[50] If the inference-rule

(A) $P \& Q$; therefore, $P \rightarrow Q$

is accepted as valid, (25) and (26) can be derived without recourse to the assumption made in the text. But (A) may occasion some discomfort. Lewis admits that "it would seem very odd to pick two completely unrelated truths ϕ and ψ and, on the strength of their truth . . . to assert the counterfactual $\phi \square \rightarrow \psi$" (*Counterfactuals*, p. 28). Lewis suggests a semantics on which (A) would not hold, but in his own, "official" theory (A) is accepted.

I believe the right solution here is to be found in the distinctions made by Pollock between various kinds of subjunctive conditionals. (A) is valid for simple subjunctives, and also for "even if" conditionals. But as we have seen, the counterfactuals of freedom are necessitation conditionals, and for these conditionals (A) is invalid. (See

Pollock, *Subjunctive Reasoning*, chap. 2.) (A), then, is not valid for the counterfactuals of freedom.

Study Questions

1.   What is middle knowledge?

2.   How is middle knowledge to be differentiated from foreknowledge?

3.   What are the chief characteristics of the Classical Theory?

4.   What are the main objections to Middle Knowledge?

5.   What is a counterfactual conditional of freedom. Give an example of one. Why does Hasker think that God does not know them?

28

Divine Foreknowledge and Alternative Conceptions of Human Freedom

William Alston

William P. Alston is professor of philosophy at Syracuse University, is author of *Philosophy of Language; Epistemic Justification: Essays in the Theory of Knowledge; Perceiving God; Divine Nature and Human Language;* is editor of *Religious and Philosophical Thought;* and is co-editor of *The Problems of Philosophy,* and *Readings in Twentieth-Century Philosophy.*

The moral of his paper is, if we consider attempts to show that it is within no one's power to do other than what one does, we had better attend to the variant possibilities for understanding "within one's power"; and we had better make explicit how it is being understood in a particular context.*

Nelson Pike's important 1965 paper, "Divine Omniscience and Voluntary Action,"[1] presents an interestingly novel version of the old argument from divine foreknowledge to our inability to do (choose) other than what we in fact do.

1. "God existed at T_1" entails "If Jones did X at T_2, God believed at T_1 that Jones would do X at T_2."
2. "God believes X" entails " 'X' is true."
3. It is not within one's power at a given time to do something having a description that is logically contradictory.
4. It is not within one's power at a given time to do something that would bring it about that someone who held a certain belief at a time prior to the time in question did not hold that belief at the time prior to the time in question.

519

5. It is not within one's power at a given time to do something that would bring it about that a person who existed at an earlier time did not exist at that earlier time.

6. If God existed at T_1 and if God believed at T_1 that Jones would do X at T_2, then if it was within Jones's power at T_2 to refrain from doing X, then (1) it was within Jones's power at T_2 to do something that would have brought it about that God held a false belief at T_1, or (2) it was within Jones's power at T_2 to do something which would have brought it about that God did not hold the belief He held at T_1, or (3) it was within Jones's power at T_2 to do something that would have brought it about that any person who believed at T_1 that Jones would do X at T_2 (one of whom was, by hypothesis, God) held a false belief and thus was not God—that is, that God (who by hypothesis existed at T_1) did not exist at T_1.

7. Alternative 1 in the consequent of item 6 is false (from 2 and 3).

8. Alternative 2 in the consequent of item 6 is false (from 4).

9. Alternative 3 in the consequent of item 6 is false (from 5).

10. Therefore, if God existed at T_1 and if God believed at T_1 that Jones would do X at T_2, then it was not within Jones's power at T_2 to refrain from doing X (from 6 through 9).

11. Therefore, if God existed at T_1, and if Jones did X at T_2, it was not within Jones's power at T_2 to refrain from doing X (from 1 and 10).[2]

This argument has stimulated a flurry of discussion that shows no signs of abating.[3] But in this literature there is little attempt to spell out the intended sense of such crucial terms as "power", "ability", "could have done otherwise", "free", and "voluntary". And even where some attention is given to these terms there is no recognition that they might be used differently by different parties to the discussion. This is all the more surprising since, in another part of the forest, one finds elaborate analyses of competing senses of these terms. I refer, of course, to the extensive literature on free will. It is high time the fruits of this latter activity were brought to bear on Pike's argument, which, after all, is concerned to show that human actions are not free in some sense, that human beings lack the power, in some sense, to do other than what they do. I will be asking (1) what concepts of power, etc., Pike and other participants in the controversy mean to be using, and (2) how such concepts will have to be construed if their arguments are to be successful, or as successful as possible.

Rather than attempt to follow all the twists and turns in the free will literature, I will focus on the crucial distinction between a "libertarian" and a "compatibilist" understanding of terms like "within one's power". I will not attempt a full characterization of either interpretation. Instead I will focus on one basic respect in which they differ, viz., on whether its being within one's power to do A at t requires that it be "really possible" that one do A at t. What is *really possible* at t is what is "left open" by what has happened up to t; it is that the nonoccurrence of which is not necessitated by what has happened up to t. Now there are various ways in which previous states of the world can necessitate, prevent, or leave open a state of affairs. It is the causal way that has dominated the free will discussion. A previous state of affairs, F, *causally* necessitates E at t if the necessitation is by virtue of causal laws.

I.   E is causally necessitated by a previous state of affairs, F = $_{df}$. E is entailed by the function of F and some causal laws, and E is not entailed by either conjunct alone.[4]

And to say that E is *causally possible* is to say that not-E is not causally necessitated by any previous states of affairs.

II.   E is causally possible at t = $_{df}$. There is no state of affairs prior to t, F, such that not-E is entailed by the conjunction of F and some causal laws without being entailed by either conjunct alone.

Being causally ruled out by the past is not the only threat to real possibility. Contemporary thinkers who suppose that God's foreknowledge rules out human free choice do not typically suppose that divine knowledge causes us to act as we do.[5] They think, rather, that since God is necessarily infallible the fact that God believes at t_1 that Jones will do X at t_2 *by itself* logically entails that Jones will do X at t_2, and hence is, by itself, logically incompatible with Jones's refraining from doing X at t_2. Let's say that a state of affairs is "situationally logically necessitated" when it is entailed by a previous state of affairs alone.

III.   E is situationally logically necessitated by a previous state of affairs, F, = $_{df}$. E is entailed by F alone.

And let's say that a state of affairs is "situationally logically possible" ("S-logically possible") when its nonoccurrence is not entailed by past facts alone.

IV.   E is S-logically possible at T = $_{df}$. There is no state of affairs prior to t, F, such that not-E is entailed by F.

We may think of an event as "really possible" when it is both causally and S-logically possible.

V.   E is really possible at t = $_{df}$. There is no state of affairs prior to t, F, such that either (a) not-E is entailed by the conjunction of F and some causal laws without being entailed by either conjunct alone, or (b) not-E is entailed by F alone.

This formulation can be simplified. Clearly if not-E is entailed by the conjunction of F and some causal laws, this covers both the case in which both conjuncts are needed for the entailment and the case in which not-E is entailed by F alone. Hence the following is logically equivalent to V.

VI. E is really possible at $t =$ df. There is no state of affairs prior to t, F, such that not-E is entailed by the conjunction of F and some causal laws.

However, IV is more perspicuous in that it brings out the way in which a really possible event escapes being ruled out by the past in both of two ways.

Since the basic claim of the libertarian is that I am not really free to do X at t if doing X is ruled out by what has already happened, she will want to use the broader notion of real possibility for a necessary condition of freedom. She will want to make it a necessary condition of being free to do E (having it within one's power to do E) that E is neither causally nor S-logically necessitated by past events.

Recently, under the influence of William of Ockham, a distinction between "hard" and "soft" facts has been injected into the discussion of these and related issues.[6] Roughly, a dated fact is a "hard" fact about the time in question if it is wholly about that time, if it is completely over and done with when that time is over. Otherwise it is a "soft" fact about that time. Thus the fact that I was offered the job at t is a hard fact about t; it embodies only what was going on then and is fully constituted by the state of the world at t. On the other hand, the fact that I was offered the job two weeks before declining it is not a hard fact about t, even if t is when I was offered the job. That fact is not fully constituted until two weeks past t. This distinction is relevant to our account of real possibility in the following way. A soft past fact can entail the occurrence of non-E without thereby preventing E from being really possible. The fact that I was offered the job two weeks before declining it at t entails that I did not accept it at t; but this obviously fails to show that it was not really possible for me to accept the job at t. Of course my not accepting the job at t is entailed by any fact that includes my declining it as a conjunct; but that has no bearing on whether accepting it was a real possibility for me at the moment of choice. Thus III-VI must be understood as restricted to states of affairs that have completely obtained before t, i.e., to *hard* facts about times prior to t.

Some recent thinkers, again following Ockham, have sought to draw the teeth of arguments like Pike's by claiming that a divine belief at t is not a hard fact about t; and hence that the fact that "God believes at t_1 that Jones will do X at t_2" entails "Jones will do X at t_2" does not show that Jones's refraining from doing X is not a real possibility for Jones at t_2.[7] If that contention is accepted, Pike's argument never gets out of the starting gate, and the question of the kind of freedom it shows to be impossible does not arise. Since the issue is controversial, I feel free to preserve my problem by simply assuming, for purposes of this discussion, that a divine belief at t_1 is a hard fact about t_1. Setting aside this additional complication will enable us to focus on the differential bearing of the argument on different conceptions of freedom.

Returning to our two senses of "within one's power", the "compatibilist" interpretation of "within one's power" was specifically devised to ensure a compatibility of free will and determinism. It does this by adopting the following account of what it is for something to be within an agent's power.

> V11. It is within S's power at t to do A = $_{df}$. If S were to will (choose, decide, ...) at t to do A, S would do A.

In other words, its being within S's power to do A at t is simply a matter of S's being so constituted, and his situation's being such, that choosing to do A at t would have led to A's actually being done at t. As far as A is concerned, S's will would have been effective. To have been able to do other than what one actually did, in this sense, is obviously compatible with causal determinism. Even if my choice and action were causally necessitated by antecedent factors, it could be true even if it were causally impossible for me to choose or to do anything else. This is all quite analogous to the following physical analogue. Where only Ball A hit ball C at t, it could still be true that *if* ball B had hit ball C at t instead, C would have moved differently from the way it in fact moved; and this can be true even if all these motions are causally determined.

Thus in the compatibilist's sense of "A is within one's power" the causal possibility of A is not a necessary condition. And, by the same token, the S-logical possibility of A isn't either. Even if Jones's mowing his lawn logically follows from God's antecedent beliefs, that would seem to be compatible with the claim that *if* Jones *had* decided not to mow his lawn nothing would have prevented that decision from being implemented.[8] Hence we may say that neither form of real possibility is a necessary condition of A's being within one's power in a compatibilist sense of the term.

II

Turning now to the application of this distinction to the debate over foreknowledge and free will, I first want to ask what concept of "within one's power" Pike was employing. He is not very forthcoming about this. In the original article his focal term was "voluntary", and about this he says, "Although I do not have an analysis of what it is for an action to be *voluntary*, it seems to me that a situation in which it would be wrong to assign Jones the *ability* or *power* to do *other* than he did would be a situation in which it would also be wrong to speak of his action as voluntary.[9] This makes "voluntary" depend on "within one's power", but it gives no hint as to the understanding of the latter. Nor does Pike offer any further clues in his responses to critics.

Faced with this situation we should perhaps follow Wittgenstein's dictum: "If you want to know *what* is proved, look at the proof."[10] In that spirit, let's ask: in what sense of "within one's power" does Pike's argument show that divine foreknowledge is incompatible with its being in anyone's power to do anything other than what one does? Or, not to take sides between Pike and his critics, in what sense of "in one's power" is Pike's argument the strongest?

There would seem to be a clear answer to this question. We have distinguished the two concepts in terms of whether its being within one's power to do A requires that one's doing A is really possible. But Pike's argument is naturally read as being designed to show that, given God's forebelief that Jones mows his lawn at t_2, it is *not* really possible that Jones refrain from mowing his lawn at t_2. Underneath all its complexities Pike's argument essentially depends on the thesis that *God's believing at t_1 that Jones will do X at t_2* entails that *Jones will do X at t_2*, and hence that Jones not doing X at t_2 is not really possible. It is because of this entailment that in order for Jones to have the power at t_2 to refrain from doing X he would have to have the power to bring it about that the entailing fact did not occur, either because God did not exist at t_1 ((3) of Pike's step 6) or did not believe at t_1 that Jones would do X at t_2 ((2) of step 6), or would have to have the power to bring it about that the entailment does not hold ((1) of step 6). But if this entailment is the heart of the matter, the argument can be construed as an attempt to show that Jones's refraining at t_2 is not really possible, from which we conclude that it is not within his power to refrain. But we get this last conclusion only on a conception of *within one's power* that, like the libertarian conception, takes real possibility as a necessary condition. On the compatibilist conception the real impossibility of Jones's refraining cuts no ice. Thus it seems that Pike's argument shows, at most, that it is not within Jones' power to refrain from mowing his lawn in a libertarian sense of that term.

This may be contested. It may be claimed that the argument shows that Jones can't refrain even in a compatibilist sense. For if a necessarily infallible deity believes in advance that Jones mows his lawn at t_2, then Jones would do that even if he did decide to refrain. A mere momentary human decision surely wouldn't override eternal divine foreknowledge in the determination of what will happen. Hence if God believes in advance that Jones will do X at t_2,then even if Jones were to decide not to do X he would still do it. And so Pike's argument shows that it is not within Jones's power to refrain, even in a compatibilist sense.[11]

Thus we have plausible-looking arguments on both sides. This is not an unusual situation with counterfactuals, which are notoriously slippery customers. If Jones had made a decision different from the one he in fact made, what would have ensued depends on what else would have been different from the actual world. It is clear that there can't be a world different from the actual world only in that Jones decided at t_2 to refrain from doing X. For the actual decision will have resulted from certain causes and will in turn contribute to the causation of subsequent events.[12] Hence if Jones had decided at t_2 to refrain from X the causal influences on his decision-making would have been different; otherwise that decision to refrain would not have been forthcoming. And, in turn, the consequences of the decision to refrain from X will be different from the consequences of a decision to do X. The only alternative to this would be a change in causal laws that would permit this decision to refrain to be inserted into precisely the actual causal context. Hence a world in which Jones decides at t_2 to refrain from doing X will be different in *some* other respects from the actual world. And whether the counterfactual, "If Jones had decided to refrain from X, he would have refrained from X", is true depends on just what additional differences from the actual world are being presupposed, implied, or allowed for. If we hang onto the actual causal laws and keep the causal context as similar as possible, then the decision to refrain would lead to refraining, and God's forebelief that Jones does X at t_2 would have to be different.[13] On the other hand, if we keep God's actual beliefs unaltered so far as possible then Jones will still do X at t_2, which implies that either some further causal influences on his behavior are different, or that causal laws are not as they are in the actual world. So which is it to be?

I believe that it can be shown fairly easily that as the compatibilist understands his counterfactual, and as causal counterfactuals like this are commonly understood, the question of whether the proposition is true *is* the question of what would be the case if causal laws and causal factors were as much like the actual world as possible. When we wonder what Jones would have done had he decided differently, or whether that match would have lit if it had been struck, or whether Smith would have fallen from the ledge had the fireman not rescued him, we want to know what further difference this difference would have made, given our actual causal laws, and given the actual situation so far as it is logically compatible with this difference. If we are told that Jones still would have done X, despite the decision to refrain, if his behavior had been under radio control from Mars and the Martians in question had decided that Jones should do X, or if Jones's brain were organized in a quite different way, or if causal laws were quite different, that is all irrelevant to what we are asking. And it is equally clear that this is the way in which the compatibilist understands the counterfactual. For when the compatibilist maintains that, even given causal determinism, Jones *could* have refrained, in the sense that if he *had* decided to refrain he would have done so, what she is concerned to insist on is the point that the actual situation in which Jones found himself is such that a contrary decision, inserted into *that situation*, would give rise to a contrary action. Hence, as the compatibilist understands "in one's power", divine forebelief that Jones does X at t_2 has no tendency to imply that it is not within Jones's power to refrain from doing X at t_2. The crucial counterfactual will still be true, even though in the counterfactual situation God's belief as to what Jones does at t_2, as well as God's belief as to what Jones decides at t_2, will be different.

It may be useful to look at the matter from another angle. It is often held that when we wonder whether Y would have happened if X had happened, what we want to know is whether Y happens in a situation in which X happens and which is otherwise as similar as possible to the actual situation. In a recently popular possible-worlds formulation, the question is as to whether Y is the case in all the X-worlds (worlds containing X) that are "closest" to the actual world. (For purposes of this highly compressed discussion let's understand "closeness" as "similarity".) Now it may look as if there is a real contest on this point between those who think Pike's argument does apply to freedom in the compatibilist sense (extremists) and those who think that it does not (moderates). For the moderate will say that a Jones-decides-to-refrain world in which causal laws are the same and the causally relevant surroundings of Jones's decision are as much like the actual world as possible (but where God's belief about what Jones does at t_2 is different) is closer to the actual world than a Jones-decides-to-refrain world in which God's belief that Jones does X at t_2 is the same, but there are differences in causal laws or causally relevant factors. And the extremist will make the opposite judgment. This looks like a thorny issue as to which makes the *larger* difference from the actual world: (a) differences in causal laws or causal factors, or (b) differences in God's beliefs. And how do we decide a question like that?

But this appearance of a deep impasse is deceptive. There is really no contest. This can be seen once we set out the differences from the actual world that obtain in the worlds claimed by each side to be closest. The worlds favored by the extremist as closest we will call "Set I" and the worlds favored by the moderate as closest we will call "Set II". Let's begin by enumerating the differences apart from God's beliefs.

Differences from the actual world[14]

Set I	Both	Set II
Some additional causallyrelevant features of Jones's situation, or some causal laws, to block the implementation of the decision	Jones's decision to refrain at t_2, together with whatever changes in the past are required to produce this decision, and some differences that result from the decision.	Jones refrains from doing X at t_2

Intuitively it looks as if Set I worlds are further from the actual world than Set II worlds. But, says the extremist, it only looks that way until we realize that Set II, but not Set I, worlds will also differ from the actual world by the fact that God believes that Jones refrains from doing X at t_2. Hence, at the very least, is not clear that Set II worlds are closer to the actual world. However, a moment's reflection should assure us that this observation cuts no ice. Just as we have to add to the differences specified above for Set II the additional difference that God believes that Jones refrains from doing X at t_2, so we have to add to the differences specified above for Set I the additional difference that God believes that all these differences obtain. Thus bringing in differences in God's beliefs *could not* affect a previously existing difference in closeness. If world A is closer to the actual world than world B on all counts other than god's beliefs, then it can't be further away with God's beliefs taken into account. For since the beliefs of an omniscient and infallible deity will exactly mirror what is the case, the differences introduced by God's beliefs will exactly mirror differences in other respects. And so if Set II worlds have the edge in closeness with God's beliefs left out, they will necessarily retain that edge with God's beliefs taken into account.

III

On the basis of all this I will take it that Pike's argument is designed to show that it is not within anyone's power to do otherwise in a libertarian sense of that term. In what sense of the term are his critics contesting this?

The earliest published criticism of Pike's 1965 article was John Turk Saunders' "Of God and Freedom."[15] In considering the three alternatives embedded in step 6 of Pike's argument, Saunders concedes that Jones cannot have the first power, but he finds no bar to attributing the second or third. However, he first reformulates these powers, since he takes Pike to have been construing them as powers to causally influence the past.

. . . it is contradictory to speak of a later situation causing an earlier situation, and consequently, it is contradictory to speak of its being in Jones's power to do something at t_2 which causes God not to exist, or not to have a certain belief, at t_1. But, while such powers are contradictory, there is no good reason to think that Jones must possess such powers if he has the power to refrain from X at t_2. The power to refrain from X at t_2 is, indeed, the power so to act at t_2 that either God does not exist at t_1 or else God does not at t_1 believe that Jones will do X at t_2. But Jones's so acting at t_2 would not bring it about that God does not exist at t_1, or that God does not hold a certain belief at t_1, any more than Jones's doing X at t_2 brings it about that God believes, at t_1, that Jones will do X at t_2. Jones's power so to act at t_2 is simply his power to perform an act such that if that act were performed, then certain earlier situations would be different from what in fact they are.[16]

Backwards causation turns out to be a nonissue however, since in his reply to Saunders Pike disavows any causal interpretation of "bring it about" and acknowledges that Saunders' formulations might well do a better job of expressing his intent.[17]

Thus, it looks as if there is a head-on confrontation between Pike and Saunders with respect to the possibility that Jones has the second and third powers mentioned in step 6. But this is so only if they are using "within one's power" in the same sense. And this is definitely not the case, for it is clear from Saunders' article that he understands such terms in a compatibilist way.

. . . suppose that at t_1 I decide to skip at t_2 rather than run at t_2, that conditions are "normal" at t_1 and t_2 (I have not been hypnotized, drugged, threatened, manhandled, and so forth), and that I have the ability (knowhow) both to skip and to run. Suppose, too, that the world happens to be governed by empirical laws such that if ever a man in my particular circumstances were to make a decision of this kind, then he would not change his mind and do something else but would follow through upon his decision: suppose, that is, that, under the circumstances which prevail at t_1, my decision is empirically sufficient for my skipping at t_2. Clearly, it is in my power to run at t_2, since I know how to do so and the conditions for the exercise of this ability are normal. If I were to exercise this power then I would not, at t_1, have decided to skip at t_2, or else the circumstances at t_1 would have been different.[18]

. . . although it (logically) cannot be both that my decision, under the circumstances, is empirically sufficient for my doing what I decide to do and also that I change my mind and do not do it, it does not follow that it is not in my power to change my mind and run instead. It follows only that I do not change my mind and run instead: for the fact that I know how to run, together with the fact that it is my own decision, under normal conditions, which leads me to persevere in my decision and to skip rather than to run, logically guarantees that I skip of my own free will and, accordingly, that it is in my power to change my mind and run. To maintain the contrary would be to suppose that some sort of indeterminism is essential to human freedom, on grounds that if ever, under normal conditions, my own decision is empirically sufficient for my doing what I do, then my own decision compels me to do what I do.[19]

Saunders plainly does not take the real possibility of S's doing A at t to be a necessary condition of its being within S's power to do A at t. He insists that even if antecedent events are causally sufficient for my doing B at t it could still be within my power to do A at t instead, and, indeed, that this will be within my power, provided I know how to do A, conditions are normal, and nothing is preventing whatever choice I make between A and B from issuing in action. This is obviously compatibilism; we even have the standard compatibilist line that to require indeterminism for freedom is to confuse causation with compulsion.

Thus Saunders and Pike are arguing past each other. The conclusion of Pike's argument is to be construed, as we have seen, as the claim that it is not within Jones's power at t_2 to refrain from doing X in a libertarian sense of "within one's power". Whereas Saunders holds that it is often within our power to do other than what we actually do in a compatibilist sense of "within one's power". They are simply not making incompatible claims.

IV

The other exchange I wish to examine is that between Pike and Alvin Plantinga. In *God, Freedom, and Evil*[20] Plantinga contends, like Saunders, that the powers Jones must have in order to be able to refrain are not, when properly understood, impossible at all. From now on let's concentrate on Pike's (2), the power, as Pike originally put it, to bring it about that God did not hold the belief He held at t_1.[21] In working toward his own version of this power Plantinga does not, like Saunders, first set aside a backwards causation interpretation. Instead he first considers the following version.

It was within Jones' power, at T_2, to do something such that if he had done it, then at T_1 God would have held a certain belief and also *not* held that belief.[22]

Quite sensibly rejecting the supposition that Jones has any such power as this, Plantinga proposes instead the following as quite sufficient for Jones's having the power at t_2 to refrain from doing X.

> It was within Jones' power at T_2 to do something such that if he had done it, then God would not have held a belief that in fact he did hold.[23]

Let's call the power so specified, "P". The attribution of P, Plantinga says, would be "perfectly innocent." Note that this is substantially equivalent to Saunders' formulation.

We have seen that Saunders is a card-carrying compatibilist. This enables us to understand how he can regard P as "innocent". For, as we have seen, even if a necessary infallible God believed at t_1 that Jones would do X at t_2, it could still be true that Jones could have refrained from doing X at t_2, in the sense that *if* he had decided to refrain nothing would have prevented the implementation of that decision. Hence in *that* sense he could, given God's antecedent infallible belief that he would do X, have the power so to act that one of God's antecedent beliefs would have been other than it was in fact. But how can Plantinga regard the attribution as innocent? It can't be for the same reason. Plantinga has made it abundantly clear that he takes what I have been calling the "real possibility" of S's doing A to be a necessary condition of its being within S's power to do A, and the real possibility of both doing A and refraining from doing A to be a necessary condition of S's freely doing A, or freely refraining from doing A.

> If a person is free with respect to a given action, then he is free to perform that action and free to refrain from performing it; no antecedent conditions and/or causal laws determine that he will perform the action, or that he won't. It is within his power, at the time in question, to take or perform the action and within his power to refrain from it.[24]

But if Jones's having a power to do A at t_2 requires that "no antecedent conditions and/or causal laws" determine that Jones does not do A at t_2, how can Jones have power P? For clearly *God believes that p at t_1* entails *Jones does not do something at t_2 such that if he had done it God would not have believed that p at t_1*. And so if divine beliefs are "antecedent conditions" in the relevant sense, i.e., hard facts about the time at which a given such belief is held,[25] then Plantinga's condition for something's being within a person's power is not met by Jones and power P. Hence Plantinga, and anyone else who takes real possibility as a necessary condition for something's being within one's power, cannot regard the attribution of P to Jones as "innocent", at least not without denying that divine beliefs are "hard facts".

To support this verdict I will look at the way Plantinga defends his "innocence" claim. As a preliminary, let's specify the proposition Plantinga numbers (51).

(51) God existed at T_1, and God believed at T_1 that Jones would do X at T_2, and it was within Jones' power to refrain from doing X at T_2.[26]

Now the defense:

For suppose again that (51) is true, and consider a world W in which Jones refrains from doing X. If God is essentially omniscient, then in this world W He is omniscient and hence does not believe at T_1 that Jones will do X at T_2. So what follows from (51) is the harmless assertion that it was within Jones' power to do something such that if he had done it, then God would not have held a belief that in fact (in the actual world) He did hold.[27]

We can see that there is something wrong with a libertarian's taking this line when we reflect that just the same case could be made for holding that its being within Jones's power to refrain from doing X at t_2 is compatible with *Jones's doing X at t_2* being causally determined. Here is that parallel case. Instead of (51) we will have its analogue for causal determinism.

(51A) Causal factors obtained prior to t_2 that determined Jones to do X at t_2, and it was within Jones's power to refrain from doing X at t_2.

Suppose that (51A) is true, and consider a world W in which Jones refrains from doing X. If causal determinism holds in this world W then either causal laws in W are different from what they are in the actual world or some of the causal factors that affect what Jones does at t_2 are different from what we have in the actual world. So what follows from (51A) is the harmless assertion that it was within Jones's power to do something such that if he had done it then (assuming causal determinism still holds) either causal laws or causal factors would have been different from what they are in the actual world.

This is at least as strong as the case for the compatibility of divine foreknowledge of Jones's doing X, and Jones's power to refrain. If Jones can have it within his power to do something such that if he had done it then what God believed prior to that time would have been somewhat different, then surely Jones can have it within his power to do something such that if he had done it causal factors or causal laws would have been somewhat different.[28] Thus if Plantinga were in a position to argue as he does for the compatibility of *Jones's being able to do otherwise* with divine foreknowledge, he would equally be in a position to argue for the compatibility of *Jones's being able to do otherwise* with causal determinism. And that is just to say, once more, that Plantinga's argument goes through only on a compatibilist conception of "within one's power". It is not surprising, then, that in "On Ockham's Way Out" Plantinga finds a different way to oppose Pike's argument—by arguing that the beliefs of a necessarily infallible being at *t* are not hard facts about *t*.

V

The moral of all this is a simple but important one. If we are to consider attempts to show that it is within no one's power to do other than what one does, we had better attend to the variant possibilities for understanding "within one's power", and we had better make explicit how it is being understood in a particular context. Else we run the risk of arguing to no purpose.[29]

Endnotes

*Reprinted from *International Journal for Philosophy of Religion*, 18, No. 1 (1985), 19-32. Copyright © 1956 by Martinus Nijhoff Publishers. Reprinted by permission of Kluwer Academic Publishers.

[1] *Philosophical Review*, 74 (1965), 27-46.

[2] Ibid., pp. 33-34.

[3] In addition to the contributions that will be discussed in this paper, see Marilyn Adams, "Is the Existence of God a Hard Fact?," *Philosophical Review*, 76 (1967), 209-16; Joshua Hoffman, "Pike on Possible Worlds, Divine Foreknowledge, and Human Freedom," *Philosophical Review*, 88 (1979), 433-42; and the latest entry, so far as I know, John Martin Fischer, "Freedom and Foreknowledge," *Philosophical Review*, 92 (1983), 67-79. At a recent Pacific Regional meeting of the Society of Christian Philosophers, Pike presented a discussion of Fischer's paper, which was responded to by Marilyn Adams and Fischer, so that the conferees were treated to hearing Adams on Pike on Fischer on Adams on Pike, and Fischer on Pike on Fischer on Adams on Pike. "Enough!", you may well cry. And yet the beat goes on.

[4] This last requirement is designed to prevent causal necessitation from ranging over logical necessitation, in which a previous state of affairs alone entails E.

[5] Some classical theologians, e.g., St. Thomas Aquinas (*Summa Theologiae*, I, Q. 14, art. 8) hold that divine knowledge causes what is known. But Aquinas never had the opportunity of discussing Pike's argument.

[6] See, e.g., Marilyn Adams, "Is the Existence of God a Hard Fact?"; John Fischer, "Freedom and Foreknowledge"; Joshua Hoffman and Gary Rosenkrantz, "Hard and Soft Facts," *Philosophical Review*, 93 (1984).

[7] Alfred J. Freddoso, "Accidental Necessity and Logical Determinism," *Journal of Philosophy*, 890 (May 1983), 257-78; Alvin Plantinga, "On Ockham's Way Out," *Faith and Philosophy*, 2 (July 1986), 235-69.

[8] This may be contested. See the next section.

[9] "Divine Omniscience and Voluntary Action," p. 33.

[10] Ludwig Wittgenstein, *Philosophical Grammar* (Berkeley: University of California Press, 1974), p. 369.

[11] I am indebted to Pike for suggesting this line of argument, though he should not be taken as committed to it.

[12] Since the compatibilist typically assumes causal determinism, we are conducting this discussion on that assumption. If decisions, actions, and so on, are not strictly causally determined, similar points will hold, though the discussion would, perforce, be more complicated.

[13] I am assuming that the actual situation is such that there is nothing to prevent either a decision to do X or a decision to refrain from doing X from being carried out. This is a situation in which human beings often find themselves. If divine foreknowledge were to rule out the power to do other than what one in fact does, it would have to rule it out in this kind of situation.

[14] This is oversimplified a bit. For example, there may well be other differences in Set II that intervene between decision and execution. Moreover, each of the differences specified will ramify causally both backwards and forwards in time.

[15] *Philosophical Review*, 75 (1966), 219-25.

[16] Ibid., p. 220.

[17] "Of God and Freedom: A Rejoinder," *Philosophical Review*, 75 (1966), 371.

[18] "Of God and Freedom," p. 221.

[19] "Of God and Freedom," p. 222.

[20] Grand Rapids, MI: Eerdmans, 1974.

[21] I do so partly for the sake of greater focus in the discussion, and partly because more recent controversy over Pike's argument has centered around this part of the problem.

[22] *God, Freedom, and Evil*, p. 71.

[23] Ibid.

[24] Ibid., p. 29.

[25] Plantinga does not question the "hardness" of divine beliefs in *God, Freedom, and Evil*.

[26] Ibid., p. 69.

[27] Ibid., p. 71.

[28] There are two significant differences between the two cases. First, Plantinga takes it that God necessarily exists; the nonexistence of God in W does not constitute a possible difference between W and the actual world. Hence the nonexistence of God is not one of the ways in which W could accommodate Jones's refraining from X at t_2. Whereas since causal determinism fails to hold in every possible world, its absence in W is one of the ways in which W could accommodate Jones's refraining from X at t_2. Second, even if determinism holds in W, the causal laws that hold there might be different in such a way as to permit Jones's refraining from X in the face of the same causal factors. But the theological analogue to the specific content of causal laws, viz., the infallibility of God, is taken to be necessary and so not to vary across possible worlds. Note that these two differences do nothing to shake the point that if Jones has the power to refrain from what is entailed by past facts he also has the power to refrain from what is causally necessitated by past facts. On the contrary, the two differences mean that there is even more room for variations across possible

worlds in what *causally* determines what actually happens than there is with respect to what *theologically* determines what actually happens.

[29] I have greatly profited from discussing the issues of this paper with Jonathan Bennett, Nelson Pike, Alvin Plantinga, and Peter van Inwagen.

Study Questions

1.   What sort of variant of "within one's power" does William Alston think Pike employed?

2.   Why does Alston think that Pike and Saunders are "arguing past each other"?

3.   Why does Alston think that Saunders is a "card-carrying compatibilist"?

4.   Why does Alston think that Plantinga is a compatibilist?

5.   What is the moral of the discussion?

29

Eternity

Eleonore Stump and Norman Kretzmann

Eleonore Stump is professor of philosophy at Saint Louis University and author of *Dialectic and Its Place in the Development of Medieval Logic*, and is co-editor of *Reasoned Faith, Hermes and Athena: Biblical Exegesis and Philosophical Theology; The Cambridge Companion to Aquinas;* and *The Cambridge Translations of Medieval Philosophical Texts.*

Norman Kretzmann is professor of philosophy at Cornell University and co-editor of *Reasoned Faith, Hermes and Athena: Biblical Exegesis and Philosophical Theology,* and *The Cambridge Translations of Medieval Philosophical Texts.*

In this paper* Stump and Kretzmann expound the concept defended by Boethius of God's atemporal eternity, analyze implications of the concept, examine reasons for considering it incoherent, and sample the results of bringing it to bear on issues in the philosophy of religion.

The concept of eternity makes a significant difference in the consideration of a variety of issues in the philosophy of religion, including, for instance, the apparent incompatibility of divine omniscience with human freedom, of divine immutability with the efficacy of petitionary prayer, and of divine omniscience with divine immutability; but, because it has been misunderstood or cursorily dismissed as incoherent, it has not received the attention it deserves from contemporary philosophers of religion.[1] In this paper we expound the concept as it is presented by Boethius (whose definition of eternity was the locus classicus for medieval discussions of the concept), analyse implications of the concept, examine reasons for considering it incoherent, and sample the results of bringing it to bear on issues in the philosophy of religion.

Eternality—the condition of having eternity as one's mode of existence—is misunderstood most often in either of two ways. Sometimes it is confused with limitless duration in time—semipiternality—and sometimes it is construed simply as atemporality, eternity being understood in that case as roughly analogous to an isolated, static instance. The second misunderstanding of eternality is not so far off the mark as the first; but a consideration of the views of the philosophers who contributed most to the development of the concept shows that atemporality alone does not exhaust eternality as they conceived of it, and that the picture of eternity as a frozen instant is a radical distortion of the classic concept.

I. Boethius's Definition

Boethius discusses eternity in two places: *The Consolation of Philosophy*, book 5, prose 6, and *De Trinitate*, chapter 4.[2] The immediately relevant passages are these:

CP:
That God is eternal, then, is the common judgment of all who live by reason. Let us therefore consider what eternity is, for this makes plain to us both the divine nature and knowledge. Eternity, then, is the complete possession all at once of illimitable life. This becomes clearer by comparison with temporal things. For whatever lives in time proceeds as something present from the past into the future, and there is nothing placed in time that can embrace the whole extent of its life equally. Indeed, on the contrary, it does not yet grasp tomorrow but yesterday it has already lost; and even in the life of today you live no more fully than in a mobile, transitory moment.... Therefore, whatever includes and possesses the whole fullness of illimitable life at once and is such that nothing future is absent from it and nothing past has flowed away, this is rightly judged to be eternal, and of this it is necessary both that being in full possession of itself it be always present to itself and that it have the infinity of mobile time present [to it]. (*CP*, 422.5-424.31)

DT:
What is said of God, [namely, that] he is always, indeed signifies a unity, as if he had been in all the past, is in all the present—however that might be—[and] will be in all the future. That can be said, according to the philosophers, of the heaven and of the imperishable bodies; but it cannot be said of God in the same way. For he is always in that for him *always* has to do with present time. And there is this great difference between the present of our affairs, which is *now*, and that of the divine: our now makes time and sempiternity, as if it were running along; but the divine now, remaining, and not moving, and standing still, makes eternity. If you add *'semper'* to 'eternity', you get sempiternity, the perpetual running resulting from the flowing, tireless now. (*DT*, 20.64-22.77)[3]

The definition Boethius presents and explains in *CP* and elucidates in the earlier *DT* is not original with him,[4] nor does he argue for it in those passages.[5] Similarly, we mean to do no more in this section of our paper than to present and explain a concept that has been important in Christian and pre-Christian theology and metaphysics. We will not argue here, for instance, that there is an eternal entity, or even that God must be eternal if he exists. It is a matter of fact that many ancient and medieval philosophers and theologians were committed to the doctrine of God's eternality in the form in which Boethius presents it, and our purpose in this section of the paper is simply to elucidate the doctrine they held.

Boethius's definition is this: *Eternity is the complete possession all at once of illimitable life.*[6]

We want to call attention to four ingredients in this definition. It is clear, first of all, that anything that is eternal has life. In this sense of 'eternal', then, it will not do to say that a number, a truth, or the world is eternal, although one might want to say of the first two that they are atemporal and of the third that it is semiternal—that it has beginningless, endless temporal existence.[7]

The second and equally explicit element in the definition is illimitability: the life of an eternal being cannot be limited; it is impossible that there be a beginning or an end to it. The natural understanding of such a claim is that the existence in question is infinite duration, unlimited in either 'direction'. But there is another interpretation that must be considered in this context despite its apparent unnaturalness. Conceivably, the existence of an eternal entity is said to be illimitable in the way in which a point or an instant may he said to be illimitable: what cannot be extended cannot be limited in its extent. There are passages that can be read as suggesting that this second interpretation is what Boethius intends. In *CP* eternal existence is expressly contrasted with temporal existence described as extending from the past through the present into the future, and what is eternal is described contrastingly as possessing its entire life *at once*. Boethius's insistence in *DT* that the eternal now is unlike the temporal now in being fixed and unchanging strengthens that hint with the suggestion that the eternal present is to be understood in terms of the present instant 'standing still'. Nevertheless, there are good reasons, in these passages themselves and in the history of the concept of eternity before and after Boethius, for rejecting this less natural interpretation. In the first place, some of the terminology Boethius uses would be inappropriate to eternity if eternity were to be conceived as illimitable in virtue of being unextended. He speaks in *CP* more than once of the *fullness* of eternal life. In *DT*, and in *The Consolation of Philosophy* immediately following our passage *CP*, he speaks of the eternal present or an eternal entity as *remaining* and *enduring*.[8] And he claims in *DT* that it is correct to say of God that he is *always*, explaining the use of 'always' in reference to God in such a way that he can scarcely have had in mind a life illimitable in virtue of being essentially durationless. The more natural reading of 'illimitable', then, also provides the more natural reading of these texts. In the second place, the weight of tradition both before and after Boethius strongly favours interpreting illimitable life as involving infinite duration, beginningless as well as endless. Boethius throughout the *Consolation*, and especially in passage *CP*, is plainly working in the Platonic tradition, and both Plato and Plotinus understand eternal existence in that sense.[9]   Medieval philosophers after Boethius, who depend on him for their conception of eternity, also clearly understand 'illimitable' in this way.[10]   So, for both these sets of reasons, we understand this part of Boethius's definition to mean that the life of an eternal entity is characterized by beginningless, endless, infinite duration.

The concept of duration that emerges in the interpretation of 'illimitable life' is the third ingredient we mean to call attention to. Illimitable life entails duration of a special sort, as we have just seen, but it would be reasonable to think that any mode of existence that could be called a life must involve duration, and so there may seem to be no point in explicitly listing duration as an ingredient in Boethius's concept of eternality. We call attention to it here, however, because of its importance as part of the background against which the fourth ingredient must be viewed. The fourth ingredient is presented in the only phrase of the definition still to be considered: 'The complete possession all at once'. As Boethius's explanation of the definition in *CP* makes clear, he conceives of an eternal entity as atemporal, and he thinks of its atemporality as conveyed by just that phrase in the definition. What he says shows that something like the following line of thought leads to his use of those words. A living temporal entity may be said to possess a life, but, since the events constituting the life of any temporal entity occur sequentially, some later than others, it cannot be said to possess all its life *at once*. And since everything in the life of a temporal entity that is not present is either past and so no longer in its possession or future and so not yet in its possession, it cannot be said to have the *complete* possession of its life.[11] So whatever has the complete possession of all its life at once cannot be temporal. The life that is the mode of an eternal entity's existence is thus characterized not only by duration but also by atemporality.

With the possible exception of Parmenides, none of the ancients or medievals who accepted eternity as a real, atemporal mode of existence meant thereby to deny the reality of time or to suggest that all temporal experiences are illusory. In introducing the concept of eternity, such philosophers, and Boethius in particular, were proposing two separate modes of real existence. Eternity is a mode of existence that is, on Boethius's view, neither reducible to time nor incompatible with the reality of time.

In the next two sections of this paper, we will investigate the apparent incoherence of this concept of eternity. We will begin with a consideration of the meaning of atemporality in this connection, including an examination of the relationship between eternity and time; and we will go on to consider the apparent incoherence generated by combining atemporality with duration and with life.

II. The Atemporality of an Eternal Entity: Presentness and Simultaneity

Because an eternal entity is atemporal, there is no past or future, no earlier or later, *within* its life; that is, the events constituting its life cannot be ordered sequentially from the standpoint of eternity. But, in addition, no temporal entity or event can be earlier or later than or past or future with respect to the whole life of an eternal entity, because otherwise such an eternal life or entity would itself be part of a temporal series. Here it should be evident that, although the stipulation that an eternal entity completely possesses its life all at once entails that it is not part of any sequence, it does not rule out the attribution of presentness or simultaneity to the life and relationships of such an entity, nor should it. In so far as an entity is, or *has* life, completely or otherwise, it is appropriate to say that it has present existence in some sense of 'present'; and unless its life consists in only one event or it is impossible to relate an event in its life to any temporal entity or event, we need to be able to consider an eternal entity or event as one of the *relata* in a simultaneity relationship. We will consider briefly the applicability of presentness to something eternal and then consider in some detail the applicability of simultaneity.

If anything exists eternally, it exists. But the existing of an eternal entity is a duration without succession, and, because eternity excludes succession, no eternal entity has existed or will exist; it *only* exists. It is in this sense that an eternal entity is said to have present existence. But since that present is not flanked by past and future, it is obviously not the temporal present. And, furthermore, the eternal, pastless, futureless present is not instantaneous but extended, because eternity entails duration. The temporal present is a durationless instant, a present that cannot be extended conceptually without falling apart entirely into past and future intervals. The eternal present, on the other hand, is by definition an infinitely extended, pastless, futureless duration.

Simultaneity is of course generally and unreflectively taken to mean existence or occurrence at one and the same time. But to attribute to an eternal entity or event simultaneity with anything we need a coherent characterization of simultaneity that does not make it altogether temporal. It is easy to provide a coherent characterization of a simultaneity relationship that is not temporal in case both the *relata* are eternal entities or events. Suppose we designate the ordinary understanding of temporal simultaneity *T-simultaneity*:

(T)   T-simultaneity = existence or occurrence at one and the same
       time.

Then we can easily enough construct a second species of simultaneity, a
relationship obtaining between two eternal entities or events:

(E)   E-simultaneity = existence or occurrence at one and the same
       eternal present.

What really interests us among species of simultaneity, however, and
what we need for our present purposes, is not E-simultaneity so much as a
simultaneity relationship between two *relata* of which one is eternal and
the other temporal. We have to be able to characterize such a
relationship coherently if we are to be able to claim that there is any
connection between an eternal and a temporal entity or event. An eternal
entity or event cannot be earlier or later than, or past or future with respect
to, any temporal entity or event. If there is to be any relationship between
what is eternal and what is temporal, then, it must be some species of
simultaneity.

    Now in forming the species T-simultaneity and E-simultaneity, we
have in effect been taking the genus of those species to be something like
this:

(G)   Simultaneity = existence or occurrence at once (i.e., together).

And we have formed those two species by giving specific content to the
broad expression 'at once'. In each case, we have spelled out 'at once' as
meaning at one and the same *something*—time, in the case of T-
simultaneity; eternal present, in the case of E-simultaneity. In other
words, the *relata* for T-simultaneity occur together at the same time, and
the *relata* for E-simultaneity occur together at the same eternal present.
What we want now is a species of simultaneity—call it *ET-simultaneity*
(for eternal-temporal simultaneity) that can obtain between what is
eternal and what is temporal. It is only natural to try to construct a
definition for ET-simultaneity as we did for the two preceding species of
simultaneity, by making the broad 'at once' in (G) more precise. Doing so
requires starting with the phrase 'at one and the same _____' and
filling in the blank appropriately. To fill in that blank appropriately,
however, would be to specify a single mode of existence in which the two
relata exist or occur together, as the *relata* for T-simultaneity coexist (or
co-occur) in time and the *relata* for E-simultaneity coexist (or co-occur) in
eternity.[12] But, on the view we are explaining and defending, it is
theoretically impossible to specify a single mode of existence for two
relata of which one is eternal and the other temporal. To do so would be to

reduce what is temporal to what is eternal (thus making time illusory), or what is eternal to what is temporal (thus making eternity illusory), or both what is temporal and what is eternal to some *third* mode of existence; and all three of these alternatives are ruled out. The medieval adherents of the concept of eternity held that both time and eternity are real and that there is no mode of existence besides those two.[13]

Against this background, then, it is not conceptually possible to construct a definition for ET-simultaneity analogous to the definitions for the other two species of simultaneity, by spelling out 'at once' as 'at one and the same _____' and filling in the blank appropriately. What is temporal and what is eternal can coexist, on the view we are adopting and defending, but not within the same mode of existence; and there is no single mode of existence that can be referred to in filling in the blank in such a definition of ET-simultaneity.

The significance of this difficulty and its implications for a working definition of ET-simultaneity can be better appreciated by returning to the definition of T-simultaneity for a closer look. Philosophers of physics, explaining the special theory of relativity, have taught us to be cautious even about the notion of temporal simultaneity; in fact, the claim that temporal simultaneity is relative rather than absolute is fundamental to the special theory of relativity.

For all ordinary practical purposes, and also for our theoretical purposes in this paper, time can be thought of as absolute, along Newtonian lines. But, simply in order to set the stage for our characterization of ET-simultaneity, it will be helpful to look at a standard philosophical presentation of temporal simultaneity along Einsteinian lines.[14] Imagine a train travelling *very* fast, at six-tenths the speed of light. One observer (the 'ground observer') is stationed on the embankment beside the track; another observer (the 'train observer') is stationed on the train. Suppose that two lightning bolts strike the train, one at each end, and suppose that the ground observer sees those two lightning bolts simultaneously. The train observer also sees the two lightning bolts, but, since he is travelling toward the light ray emanating from the bolt that strikes the front of the train and away from the bolt that strikes the rear of the train, he will see the lightning bolt strike the front of the train before he sees the other strike the rear of the train. 'This, then, is the fundamental result events occurring at different places which are simultaneous in one frame of reference will not be simultaneous in another frame of reference which is moving with respect to the first. This is known as *the relativity of simultaneity*'.[15]

We want to leave to one side the philosophical issues raised by this example and simply accept it for our present purposes as a standard example illustrating Einstein's notion of the relativity of temporal simultaneity. According to this example, the very same two lightning flashes are simultaneous (with respect to the reference frame of the ground observer) and not simultaneous (with respect to the reference frame of the train observer). If we interpret 'simultaneous' here in accordance with our definition of T-simultaneity, we will have to say that the same two lightning flashes occur at the same time and do not occur at the same time; that is, it will be both true and false that these two lightning flashes occur at the same time. The incoherence of this result is generated by filling in the blank for the definition of T-simultaneity with a reference to one and the same time, where time is understood as one single uniform mode of existence. The special theory of relativity takes time itself to be relative and so calls for a more complicated definition of temporal simultaneity than the common, unreflective definition given in (T), such as this relativized version of temporal simultaneity:

(RT)   RT-simultaneity = existence or occurrence at the same time within the reference frame of a given observer.

This relativizing of time to the reference frame of a given observer resolves the apparent incoherence in saying that the same two lightning flashes occur and do not occur at one and the same time. They occur at the same time in the reference frame of one observer and do not occur at the same time in the reference frame of a different observer.[16]

Once this is understood, we can see that, if we persist in asking whether or not the two lightning bolts are *really* simultaneous, we are asking an incoherent question, one that cannot be answered. The question is asked about what is assumed to be a feature of reality, although in fact there is no such feature of reality; such a question is on a par with 'Is Uris Library *really* to the left of Morrill Hall?' There is no absolute state of being temporally simultaneous with, any more than there is an absolute state of being to the left of. We determine the obtaining of the one relationship as we determine the obtaining of the other, by reference to an observer and the observer's point of view. The two lightning flashes, then, are RT-simultaneous in virtue of occurring at the same time within the reference frame of the ground observer and not RT-simultaneous in virtue of occurring at different times within the reference frame of the train observer. And, Einstein's theory argues, there is no privileged observer (or reference frame) such that with respect to it we can determine whether the two events are *really* simultaneous; simultaneity is irreducibly relative to observers and their reference frames, and so is time itself. Consequently, it would be a mistake to think that there is one single uniform mode of existence that can be referred to in specifying 'at once' in (G) in order to derive a definition of temporal simultaneity.

These difficulties in spelling out even a very crude acceptable definition for temporal simultaneity in the light of relativity theory foreshadow and are analogous to the difficulties in spelling out an acceptable definition of ET-simultaneity. More significantly, they demonstrate that the difficulties defenders of the concept of eternity encounter in formulating such a definition are by no means unique to their undertaking, and cannot be assumed to be difficulties in the concepts of ET-simultaneity or of eternity themselves. Finally, and most importantly, the way in which we cope with such difficulties in working out a definition for RT-simultaneity suggests the sort of definition needed for ET-simultaneity. Because one of the *relata* for ET-simultaneity is eternal, the definition for this relationship, like that for E-simultaneity, must refer to one and the same present rather than to one and the same time. And because in ET-simultaneity we are dealing with two equally real modes of existence, neither of which is reducible to any other mode of existence, the definition must be constructed in terms of *two* reference frames and *two* observers. So we can characterize ET-simultaneity in this way. Let 'x' and 'y' range over entities and events. Then:

(ET)   for every x and for every y, x and y are ET-simultaneous iff

- (i)   either x is eternal and y is temporal, or vice versa; and

- (ii)   for some observer, A, in the unique eternal reference frame, x and y are both present—i.e., either x is eternally present and y is observed as temporally present, or vice versa; and

- (iii)   for some observer, B, in one of the infinitely many temporal reference frames, x and y are both present—i.e., either x is observed as eternally present and y is temporally present, or vice versa.

Given the concept of eternity, condition (ii) provides that a temporal entity or event observed as temporally present by some eternal observer A is ET-simultaneous with every eternal entity or event and condition (iii) provides that an eternal entity or event observed as eternally present (or simply as eternal) by some temporal observer B is ET-simultaneous with every temporal entity or event.

On our definition, if x and y are ET-simultaneous, then x is neither earlier nor later than, neither past nor future with respect to, y—a feature essential to any relationship that can be considered a species of simultaneity. Further, if x and y are ET-simultaneous, x and y are not temporally simultaneous; since either x or y must be eternal, it cannot be the case that x and y both exist at one and the same time within a given observer's reference frame. ET-simultaneity is symmetric, of course; but, since no temporal or eternal entity or event is ET-simultaneous with itself, the relationship is not reflexive; and the fact that there are different domains for its *relata* means that it is not transitive. The propositions

(1) x is ET-simultaneous with y.

and

(2) y is ET-simultaneous with z.

do not entail

(3) x is ET-simultaneous with z.

And even if we conjoin with (1) and (2)

(4) x and z are temporal.

(1), (2), and (4) together do not entail

(5) x and z are temporally simultaneous.

(RT) and the Einsteinian conception of time as relative have served the only purpose we have for them in this paper, now that they have provided an introductory analogue for our characterization of ET-simultaneity, and we can now revert to a Newtonian conception of time, which will simplify the discussion without involving any relevant loss of precision. In the first place, at least one of the theological issues we are going to be discussing—the problem of omniscience and immutability—depends on the concept of an absolute present, a concept that is often thought to be dependent on a Newtonian conception of absolute time. But the concept of an absolute present which is essential to our discussion is not discredited by relativity theory.[17] Every conscious temporal observer has an undeniable, indispensable sense of the absolute present, *now*, and that thoroughly pervasive feature of temporal consciousness is all we need. We do not need and we will not try to provide a philosophical justification for the concept of an absolute present; we will simply assume it for our present purposes. And if it must be said that the absolute present is absolute only within a given observer's reference frame, that will not affect our use of the concept here. In the second place, in ordinary human circumstances, all human observers may be said—*should* be said—to share one and the same reference frame, and distinguishing individual reference frames for our discussion of time in the rest of this paper would be as inappropriate as taking an Einsteinian view of time in a discussion of historical chronology.

III. Implications of ET-Simultaneity

If x and z are temporal entities, they coexist if and only if there is some time during which both x and z exist. But if anything exists eternally, its existence, although infinitely extended, is fully realized, all present at once. Thus the entire life of any eternal entity is coexistent with any temporal entity at any time at which that temporal entity exists.[18] From a temporal standpoint, the present is ET-simultaneous with the whole infinite extent of an eternal entity's life. From the standpoint of eternity, every time is present, co-occurrent with the whole of infinite atemporal duration.[19]

We can show the implications of this account of ET-simultaneity by considering the relationship between an eternal entity and a future contingent event. Suppose that Richard Nixon will die at noon on 9 August 1990, precisely sixteen years after he resigned the Presidency. Nixon's death some years from now *will be* present to those who will be at his death-bed, but it *is* present to an eternal entity. It cannot be that an eternal entity has a vision of Nixon's death before it occurs; in that case an eternal event would be earlier than a temporal event. Instead, the actual occasion of Nixon's dying is present to an eternal entity. It is not that the future pre-exists somehow, so that it can be inspected by an entity that is outside time, but rather that an eternal entity that is wholly ET-simultaneous with 9 August 1974, and with today, is wholly ET-simultaneous with 9 August 1990, as well. It is *now* true to say 'The whole of eternity is ET-simultaneous with the present'; and of course it was true to say just the same at noon of 9 August 1974, and it will be true to say it at noon of 9 August 1990. But since it is one and the same eternal present that is ET-simultaneous with each of those times, there is a sense in which it is now true to say that Nixon at the hour of his death is present to an eternal entity; and in that same sense it is now true to say that Nixon's resigning of the Presidency is present to an eternal entity. If we are considering an eternal entity that is omniscient, it is true to say that that entity is *at once* aware of Nixon resigning the Presidency and of Nixon on his death-bed (although of course an omniscient entity understands that those events occur sequentially and knows the sequence and the dating of them); and it is true to say also that for such an entity both those events are present at once.[20]

Such an account of ET-simultaneity suggests at least a radical epistemological or even metaphysical relativism, and perhaps plain incoherence. We *know* that Nixon is now alive. An omniscient eternal entity *knows* that Nixon is now dead. Still worse, an omniscient eternal entity also *knows* that Nixon is now alive, and so Nixon is apparently both alive and dead at once in the eternal present.

These absurdities appear to be entailed partly because the full implications of the concept of eternity have not been taken into account.

We have said enough to induce caution regarding 'present' and 'simultaneous', but it is not difficult to overlook the concomitant ambiguity in such expressions as 'now' and 'at once'. To say that we know that Nixon is now alive although an eternal entity knows that Nixon is now dead does not mean that an eternal entity knows the opposite of what we know. What we know is that:

(6)   Nixon is alive in the temporal present.

What an eternal entity knows is that

(7)   Nixon is dead in the eternal present.

and (6) is not incompatible with (7). Still, this simple observation does nothing to dispel the appearance of incompatibility between (7) and

(8)   Nixon is alive in the eternal present.

and, on the basis of what has been said so far, both (7) and (8) are true. But Nixon is temporal, not eternal, and so are his life and death. The conjunction of (7) and (8), then, cannot be taken to mean that the temporal entity Nixon exists in eternity, where he is simultaneously alive and dead, but rather something more nearly like this. One and the same eternal present is ET-simultaneous with Nixon's being alive and is also ET-simultaneous with Nixon's dying; so Nixon's life is ET-simultaneous with and hence present to an eternal entity, and Nixon's death is ET-simultaneous with and hence present to an eternal entity, although Nixon's life and Nixon's death are themselves neither eternal nor simultaneous.

These considerations also explain the appearance of metaphysical relativism inherent in the claim that Nixon's death is really future for us and really present for an eternal entity. It is not that there are two objective realities, in one of which Nixon's death is really future and in the other of which Nixon's death and life are really present; that *would* be incoherent. What the concept of eternity implies instead is that there is one objective reality that contains two modes of real existence in which two different sorts of duration are measured by two irreducibly different sorts of measure: time and eternity. Given the relations between time and eternity spelled out in section II of this paper, Nixon's death is really future or not depending on which sort of entity, temporal or eternal, it is being related to. An eternal entity's mode of existence is such that its whole life is ET-simultaneous with each and every temporal entity or event, and so Nixon's death, like every other event involving Nixon, is really ET-simultaneous with the life of an eternal entity. But when Nixon's death is being related to *us*, today, then, given our location in the temporal continuum, Nixon's death is not simultaneous (temporally or in any other way) with respect to us, but really future.[21]

IV. Atemporal Duration and Atemporal Life

With this understanding of the atemporality of an eternal entity's existence, we want to consider now the apparent incoherence generated by combining atemporality with duration and with life in the definition of eternity.

The notion of atemporal duration is the heart of the concept of eternity and, in our view, the original motivation for its development. The most efficient way in which to dispel the apparent incoherence of the notion of atemporal duration is to consider, even if only very briefly, the development of the concept of eternity. The concept can be found in Parmenides, we think,[22] but it finds its first detailed formulation in Plato, who makes use of it in working out the distinction between the realms of being and becoming; and it receives its fullest exposition in pagan antiquity in the work of Plotinus.[23] The thought that originally stimulated this Greek development of the concept of eternity was apparently something like this. Our *experience* of temporal duration gives us an impression of permanence and persistence which an analysis of time convinces us is an illusion or at least a distortion. Reflection shows us that, contrary to our familiar but superficial impression, temporal duration is only apparent duration, just what one would expect to find in the realm of becoming. The existence of a typical existent temporal entity, such as a human being, is spread over years of the past, through the present, and into years of the future; but the past is not, the future is not, and the present must be understood as no time at all, a durationless instant, a mere point at which the past is continuous with the future.[24] Such radically evanescent existence cannot be the foundation of existence. Being, the persistent, permanent, utterly immutable actuality that seems required as the bedrock underlying the evanescence of becoming, must be characterized by genuine duration, of which temporal duration is only the flickering image. Genuine duration is fully realized duration—not only extended existence (even *that* is theoretically impossible in time) but also existence *none* of which is already gone and *none* of which is yet to come—and such fully realized duration must be atemporal duration. Whatever has atemporal duration as its mode of existence is 'such that nothing future is absent from it and nothing past has flowed away', whereas of everything that has temporal duration it may be said that from it *everything* future is absent and *everything* past has flowed away. What has temporal duration 'does not yet grasp tomorrow but yesterday it has already lost'; even today it exists only 'in a mobile, transitory moment', the present instant. To say of something that it is future is to say that it is not (yet), and to say of something that it is past is to say that it is not (any longer). Atemporal duration is duration none of which is not—none of which is absent (and hence future) or flowed away (and hence past). Eternity, not time, is the mode of existence that admits of fully realized duration.

The ancient Greek philosophers who developed the concept of eternity were using the word 'aion', which corresponds in its original sense to our word 'duration', in a way that departed from ordinary usage in order to introduce a notion which, however counter-intuitive it may be, can reasonably be said to preserve and even to enhance the original sense of the word. It would not be out of keeping with the tradition that runs through Parmenides, Plato, and Plotinus into Augustine, Boethius, and Aquinas to claim that it is only the discovery of eternity that enables us to make genuinely literal use of words for duration, words such as 'permanence' and 'persistence', which in their ordinary, temporal application turn out to have been unintended metaphors. 'Atemporal duration', like the ancient technical use of 'aion' itself, violates established usage; but an attempt to convey a new philosophical or scientific concept by adapting familiar expressions is not to be rejected on the basis of its violation of ordinary usage. The apparent incoherence in the concept is primarily a consequence of continuing to think of duration only as 'persistence *through time*'.

Since a life is a kind of duration, some of the apparent incoherence in the notion of an atemporal life may be dispelled in rendering the notion of atemporal duration less readily dismissible. But life is in addition ordinarily associated with processes of various sorts, and processes are essentially temporal, and so the notion of an atemporal entity that has life seems incoherent.[25] Now what Aquinas, for example, is thinking of when he attributes life to eternal God is the doctrine that God is a mind. (Obviously what is atemporal cannot consist of physical matter; we assume for the sake of the argument that there is nothing incoherent in the notion of a wholly immaterial, independently existent mind.) Since God is atemporal, the mind that is God must be different in important ways from a temporal, human mind. Considered as an atemporal mind, God cannot deliberate, anticipate, remember, or plan ahead, for instance; all these mental activities essentially involve time, either in taking time to be performed (like deliberation) or in requiring a temporal viewpoint as a prerequisite to performance (like remembering). But it is clear that there are other mental activities that do not require a temporal interval or viewpoint. Knowing seems to be the paradigm case; learning, reasoning, inferring take time, as knowing does not. In reply to the question 'What have you been doing for the past two hours?' it makes sense to say 'Studying logic' or 'Proving theorems', but not 'Knowing logic'. Similarly, it makes sense to say 'I'm learning logic', but not 'I'm knowing logic'. And knowing is not the only mental activity requiring neither a temporal interval nor a temporal viewpoint. Willing, for example, unlike wishing or desiring seems to be another. Perceiving is impossible in any literal sense for a mind that is disembodied, but nothing in the nature of incorporeality or atemporality seems to rule out the possibility of awareness. And though *feeling* angry is impossible for an atemporal entity—if feelings of anger are essentially associated, as they seem to be, with bodily states—we do not see that anything prevents such an entity from *being* angry, a state the components of which might be, for instance, being aware of an injustice, disapproving of it, and willing its punishment. It seems, then, that the notion of an atemporal mind is not incoherent, but that, on the contrary, it is possible that such a mind might have a variety of faculties or activities. Our informal, incomplete consideration of that possibility is not even the beginning of an argument for such a conclusion, but it is enough for our purposes here to suggest the line along which such an argument might develop. The notion of an atemporal mind is not *prima facie* absurd, and so neither is the notion of an atemporal life absurd; for any entity that has or is a mind must be considered to be *ipso facto* alive, whatever characteristics of other living beings it may lack.

V. The Notion of an Eternal Entity's Acting in Time

The difficulties we have considered so far are difficulties in the concept of eternity itself. We have by no means dealt explicitly with all the objections to the concept which have been raised in contemporary discussions; but many of those objections involve difficulties over simultaneity, and such objections can, we think, be dealt with adequately in the light of our previous discussion of ET-simultaneity. We hope, for instance, to have revealed the misunderstanding underlying such attempted reductions of the concept to absurdity as this one:

> But, on St Thomas' view, my typing of this paper is simultaneous with the whole of eternity. Again, on his view, the great fire of Rome is simultaneous with the whole of eternity. Therefore, while I type these very words, Nero fiddles heartlessly on.[26]

We want now to turn to fundamental difficulties in theological applications of the concept, particularly those which arise in considering the possibility of interaction between eternal and temporal entities.

There are several reasons for thinking that an eternal entity, as we have characterized it, could not affect or respond to temporal entities, events, or state of affairs. Just as an eternal entity cannot exist in time, so, we might suppose, (I) an eternal entity cannot act in time. It might seem, furthermore, that (II) the nature of a temporal action is such that the agent itself must be temporal. Nelson Pike provides the following case in point:

Let us suppose that yesterday a mountain, 17,000 feet high, came into existence on the flatlands of Illinois. One of the local theists explains this occurrence by reference to divine creative action. He claims that God produced (created, brought about) the mountain. Of course, if God is timeless,

> He could not have produced the mountain *yesterday*. This would require that God's creative-activity and thus the individual whose activity it is have position in time. The theist's claim is that God *timelessly* brought it about that yesterday, a 17,000 feet high mountain came into existence on the flatlands of Illinois.... [But] The claim that God *timelessly* produced a temporal object (such as the mountain) is absurd.[27]

On this basis Pike denies that God, considered as atemporal, could produce or create anything; whatever is produced or created begins to exist and so has a position in time. And it might be argued along similar lines that (III) an atemporal entity could not preserve anything temporal in existence because to do so would require temporal duration on the part of the preserver.

If God is taken to be eternal, considerations I, II, and III are incompatible with some doctrines central to most versions of theism, such as the divine creation and preservation of the world, and divine response to petitionary prayer More specifically, they militate against the central doctrine of Christianity, since the Incarnation of Christ entails that the second person of the Trinity has a temporal nature and performs temporal actions during a certain period of time.

We think all three of these considerations are confused. In connection with consideration I, a distinction must be drawn between (*a*) acting in such a way that the action itself can be located in time and (*b*) acting in such a way that the effect of the action can be located in time. For temporal agents the distinction between (*a*) and (*b*) is generally nugatory; for an atemporal entity, however, (*a*) is impossible. An agent's action is an event in the agent's life, and there can be no temporal event in the atemporal life of God. But such an observation does not tell against (*b*). If an eternal God is also omnipotent, he can do anything it is not logically impossible for him to do. Even though his actions cannot be located in time, he can bring about effects in time unless doing so is logically impossible for him.

Considerations II and III may be construed as providing reasons for thinking that it is indeed logically impossible for an atemporal entity to produce temporal effects. Pike's version of consideration II, however, involves a confusion like the confusion just sorted out for consideration I. He says:

(9)   '[I]f God is timeless, He could not have produced the mountain *yesterday.*'
(10)   'The claim that God *timelessly* produced a temporal object (such as the mountain) is absurd.'

Both these propositions are ambiguous because of the possibility of assigning different scopes to 'yesterday' and to 'timelessly' (or 'atemporally'), and the ambiguities can be sorted out in this way:

(9)(*a*)   If God is atemporal, he cannot yesterday have brought it about that a temporal object came into existence.
(9)(*b*)   If God is atemporal, he cannot (atemporally) bring it about that a temporal object came into existence yesterday.
(10)(*a*)   It is absurd to claim that God atemporally brings it about that a temporal object came into existence.
(10)(*b*)   It is absurd to claim that God brings it about that a temporal object came into existence atemporally.[28]

Apparently without taking account of the ambiguity of propositions (9) and (10), Pike understands them as (9)(*a*) and (10)(*b*) respectively. Propositions (9)(*a*) and (10)(*b*) are indeed true, but they do not support Pike's inference that an atemporal God cannot produce a temporal object. In drawing that inference, Pike seems to be relying on an assumption about a temporal relationship that must hold between an action and its effect. The assumption is not entirely clear; in some passages of his *God and Timelessness* it looks as if Pike thinks that an action and its effect must be simultaneous, an assumption that is plainly false in general regarding actions and their effects as ordinarily conceived of. But if we do adopt co-occurrence as a theoretically justifiable condition on causal connection between an action and its effect, we can point out that any and every action of an eternal entity is ET-simultaneous with any temporal effect ascribed to it. And, since it would simply beg the question to insist that only *temporal* simultaneity between an action and its effect can satisfy this necessary condition of causal connection, we see no reason for denying of an eternal, omnipotent entity that its atemporal act of willing could bring it about that a mountain came into existence on [yesterday's date]. Consequently, we can see no reason for thinking it absurd to claim that a divine action resulting in the existence of a temporal entity is an atemporal action. In other words, we think that propositions (9)(*b*) and (10)(*a*) are false, although they are legitimate senses of the ambiguous propositions (9) and (10). And so we reject consideration II as well as I.

Our reasons for rejecting these first two considerations apply as well, *mutatis mutandis*, to consideration III. If it is not impossible for an omnipotent, eternal entity to act in eternity (by atemporally willing) in such a way as to bring it about that a temporal entity begins to exist at a particular time, it is not impossible for an omnipotent, eternal entity to act in eternity (by atemporally willing) in such a way that that temporal entity continues to exist during a particular temporal interval.

A different sort of difficulty arises in connection with answering prayers or punishing injustice, for instance, since in such cases it seems necessary that the eternal action occur later than the temporal action; and so our reasons for rejecting considerations I, II, and III, based on the ET-simultaneity of eternal actions with temporal events, seem inapplicable. The problem of answering prayers is typical of difficulties of this sort. An answer to a prayer must be later than the prayer, it seems, just because

> (11) Something constitutes an answer to a prayer only if it is done because of the prayer.

and

> (12) Something is done because of a prayer only if it is done later than the praying of the prayer.

We think that (11) is true; (12), on the other hand, seems doubtful even as applied to temporal entities. If at 3 o'clock a mother prepares a snack for her little boy because she believes that when he gets home at 3.30 he will ask for one, it does not seem unreasonable to describe her as preparing the food because of the child's request, even though in this case the response is earlier than the request. Whatever may be true regarding temporal entities, however, if (12) is true, it obviously rules out the possibility of an eternal entity's responding to prayers. But consider the case of Hannah's praying on a certain day to have a child and her conceiving several days afterward.[29] Both the day of her prayer and the day of her conceiving are ET-simultaneous with the life of an eternal entity. If such an entity atemporally wills that Hannah conceive on a certain day after the day of her prayer, then such an entity's bringing it about that Hannah conceives on that day is clearly a response to her prayer, even though the willing is ET-simultaneous with the prayer rather than later than it. If ET-simultaneity is a sufficient condition for the possibility of a causal connection in the case of God's bringing about the existence of temporal entity, it is likewise sufficient for the possibility of his acting because of a prayer prayed at a particular time.[30]

The principal difficulty in the doctrine of the Incarnation seems intractable to considerations of the sort with which we have been trying to alleviate difficulties associated with an eternal entity's willing to bring about a temporal event, because according to the doctrine of the Incarnation an eternal entity itself entered time. If we take the essence of the doctrine to be expressed in

(13)   'When the fulness of the time was come, God sent forth his Son, born of a woman' (Galatians 4:4).

it is not difficult to see, in the light of our discussion so far, how to provide an interpretation that shows that, as regards God's sending his Son, the doctrine is compatible with God's eternality:

(13')   God atemporally wills that his Son be born of a woman at the appointed time.

But the possibility of making sense of an eternal action with a temporal effect does not settle this issue, because the principal difficulty here does not lie in the nature of the relationship between an eternal agent and a temporal effect. The difficulty here is rather that an eternal entity is also a *component* of the temporal effect—an effect which is, to put it simplistically, an eternal entity's having become temporal without having ceased (*per impossibile*) to exist eternally. Formulating the difficulty in the doctrine of the Incarnation simplistically, however, simply exacerbates it. And whereas this formulation of it may present an insuperable difficulty for one or more of the heresies of the Patristic period that took the person of Christ to be only divine or only human, it is ineffective against the orthodox doctrines of the Trinity and the dual nature of Christ. A full treatment of those philosophically intricate doctrines lies outside the scope of this paper, but we will consider them very briefly on the basis of our limited understanding of them in order to suggest some reasons for supposing that the doctrine of the Incarnation is not incompatible with the doctrine of God's eternality.

The doctrine of the Trinity maintains that God, although one substance, consists in three persons, the second of which is God the Son. The doctrine of the dual nature maintains that the second person of the Trinity has not merely one essence or nature, like every other person divine or human, but two: one the divine nature common to all the persons of the Trinity, the other the human nature of the Incarnation. One of the explicitly intended consequences of the doctrine of the dual nature is that any statement predicating something of Christ is ambiguous unless it contains a phrase specifying one or the other or both of his two natures. That is, the proposition

(14)   Christ died.

is ambiguous among these three readings:

(14)(*a*)   Christ with respect to his divine nature (or *qua* God) died.
(14)(*b*)   Christ with respect to his human nature (or *qua* man) died.

(14)(*c*)　Christ with respect to his divine and human natures (or *qua* both God and man) died.

From the standpoint of orthodox Christianity (14)(*a*) and (14)(*c*) are false, and (14)(*b*) is true. (14)(*b*) is not to be interpreted as denying that God died, however—such a denial forms the basis of at least one Christian heresy—but to deny that God, the second person of the Trinity, died with respect to his divine nature. Such an account is loaded with at least apparent paradox, and it is not part of our purpose here even to sketch an analysis of it; but, whatever its internal difficulties may be, the doctrine of the dual nature provides *prima facie* grounds for denying the incompatibility of God's eternality and God's becoming man.

A Boethian account of the compatibility of divine eternality and the Incarnation might be developed along these lines, we think.[31] The divine nature of the second person of the Trinity, like the divine nature of either of the other persons of the Trinity, cannot become temporal; nor could the second person at some time acquire a human nature he does not eternally have. Instead, the second person eternally has two natures; and at some temporal instants, all of which are ET-simultaneous with both these natures in their entirety, the human nature of the second person has been temporally actual. At those times and only in that nature the second person directly participates in temporal events. We need no theologian to tell us how rudimentary this outline is, and no other philosopher to tell us how paradoxical it looks; but we are not now willing or able or required by our main purpose in this paper to undertake an analysis or defence of the role of the doctrine of the dual nature in establishing the compatibility of divine eternality and the Incarnation. We hope simply to have pointed out that the doctrine of the Incarnation cannot be reduced to the belief that God became temporal and that, if it is understood as including the doctrine of the dual nature, it can be seen to have been constructed in just such a way as to avoid being reduced to that simple belief. And those observations are all we need for now in order to allay the suspicion that eternality must be incompatible with the central doctrine of orthodox Christianity.

It seems to us, then, that the concept of eternity is coherent and that there is no logical impossibility in the notion of an eternal being's acting in time, provided that acting in time is understood as we have explained it here.

Endnotes

*Reprinted from *The Journal of Philosophy*, Vol. LXXVIII, 8 (August 1981), pp. 429-53. Reprinted by permission of the authors and *The Journal of Philosophy*.

[1] At least one contemporary philosopher of religion has recently turned his attention to the concept of divine eternality in order to reject it as incompatible with biblical theology and, in particular, with the doctrine of divine redemption. 'God the

Redeemer cannot be a God eternal. This is so because God the Redeemer is a God who changes' (Nicholas Wolterstorff, 'God Everlasting', in Clifton J. Orlebeke and Lewis B. Smedes (eds.), *God and the Good* (Grand Rapids, Mich., 1975), pp. 181-203, p. 182). (We are grateful to Kenneth Konyndyk for having supplied us with copies of this article, which is obviously highly relevant to our purposes in this paper. The work we are presenting here was substantially complete by the time we had access to Professor Wolterstorff's work.) Although it is no part of our purposes here to discuss Wolterstorff's arguments, it will become clear that we think he is mistaken in his assessment of the logical relationship between the doctrine of divine eternality and other doctrines of orthodox Christianity, including the doctrine of redemption, even in their Biblical formulations. Passages that have been or might be offered in evidence of a Biblical conception of divine eternality include Malachi 3:6; John 8:58; James 1:17.

2 Ed. E. K. Rand, in H. E. Stewart, E. K. Rand, and S. J. Tester, *Boethius: The Theological Tractates and The Consolation of Philosophy* (London and Cambridge, Mass., 1973).

3 There are at least two misleading features of this passage. In the first place, Boethius says that God's eternality *always* has to do with present *time*. In the second place, Boethius's etymology of 'sempiternity' is mistaken. '*Sempiternitas*' is an abstract noun constructed directly on '*semper*,' somewhat as we might construct 'alwaysness'. His etymology is not only false but misleading, associating 'sempiternity' with 'eternity' in a context in which he has been distinguishing between sempiternity and eternity.

4 Its elements stem from Parmenides via Plato, and Plotinus had already framed a definition of eternity on which Boethius's seems to have been based. See note 6 below. Cf. Romano Amerio, 'Probabile fonte della nozione boeziana di eternità', *Filosofia* 1 (1950), pp. 365-73.

5 The argument that is concluded in the last sentence of passage *CP* is based on premisses about God's eternality and omniscience, and is not an argument in support of the definition.

6 *Aeternitas igitur est interminabilis vitae tota simul et perfecta possesio'*, *De Trinitate*, p. 422.9-11. This definition closely parallels the definition developed by Plotinus in *Enneads* iii 7: 'The life, then, which belongs to that which exists and is in being, all together and full, completely without-extension-or-interval, is what we are looking for, eternity' (A. H. Armstrong (ed.), *Plotinus* (London and Cambridge, Mass., 1967), vol. 3, p. 304.37-39). The way in which Boethius introduces eternity suggests that he considers himself to be presenting a familiar philosophical concept associated with a recognized definition. The parallel between the Plotinian and Boethian definitions is closest in their middle elements: '*zoe homou pasa kai pleres'/'vitae tota simul et perfecta'*. Plotinus describes the possessor of this life, and Boethius does not; but, in view of the fact that Boethius is talking about God, he, too, would surely describe the possessor of eternity as 'that which exists and is in being'. The most interesting difference between the two definitions is that the Plotinian has 'completely without-extension-or-interval' and the Boethian has 'illimitable', which suggests that Boethius takes eternity to include duration but Plotinus does not. In the rest of *Enneads* iii 7, however, Plotinus goes on to derive duration from his definition and to stress its importance in the concept. For an excellent presentation and discussion of

Plotinus on eternity and time, see Werner Beierwaltes, *Plotin über Ewigkeit und Zeit* (*Enneade* iii 7) (Frankfurt am Main, 1967).

7 The many medieval discussions of the possibility that the world is 'eternal' really concern the possibility that it is sempiternal, and most often their concern is only with the possibility that the world had no beginning in time. Thomas Aquinas provides an important summary and critique of such discussions in *Summa Contra Gentiles*, bk. ii, chs. 32-8.

8 See, e.g., p. 424.51-56.

9 See Plato, *Timaeus* 37D-38C; Plotinus, *Enneads* iii 7 (and cf. note 6 above).

10 See, e.g., Thomas Aquinas, *Summa Theologiae*, pt. i, q. 10. Augustine, who is an earlier and in general an even more important source for medieval philosophy and theology than Boethius and who is even more clearly in the Platonist tradition, understands and uses this classic concept of eternity (see, e.g., *Confessions*, bk. xi, ch. 11; *The City of God*, bk. xi, ch. 21); but his influence on the medieval discussion of eternity seems not to have been so direct or important as Boethius's.

11 Notice that these characteristics of a temporal entity's possession of its life apply not just to finite temporal lives but even to a temporal life of beginningless, endless duration—a sempiternal life.

12 In the interest of simplicity and brevity, we will for the most part speak only of coexistence in what follows, taking it as covering co-occurrence too.

13 The medieval concept of the *aevum* or of *aeviternitas* seems to us to be not the concept of a third mode of existence, on a par with time and eternity. See, e.g., Thomas Aquinas, *Summa Theologiae*, pt. i, q. 10, arts. 5 and 6.

14 Our adaptation of this example is a simplified version of Wesley C. Salmon's presentation of it in his *Space, Time, and Motion* (Encino, Cal., 1975), pp. 73-81. We mean to do little more here than cite the example. An understanding of its significance for relativity theory requires a consideration of a presentation as full (and clear) as Salmon's.

15 Salmon, *Space, Time, and Motion*, p. 76.

16 It is important to understand that by 'observer' we mean only that thing, animate or inanimate, with respect to which the reference frame is picked out and with respect to which the simultaneity of events within the reference frame is determined. In the train example we have two human observers, but the example could have been set up just as well if the observers had been nothing more than devices, primitive or sophisticated, for recording flashes of light.

17 On this issue see William Godfrey Smith, 'Special Relativity and the Present', *Philosophical Studies*, 36(3) (Oct. 1979), pp. 233-44.

18 Since no eternal entity or event can itself be an element in a temporal series, no temporal entity or event can be earlier or later than the whole life or than any part of the life of an eternal entity. It is not clear that it makes sense to think in terms of parts of atemporal duration (cf. Aquinas, *Summa Theologiae*, pt. i, q. 10, art. 1, ad. 3); but even if it does, it cannot make sense to think of any such part as earlier or later than anything temporal. If the Battle of Waterloo were earlier than some part of atemporal duration, it would be uniquely simultaneous with one other part of atemporal duration, in which case one part of atemporal duration would be earlier than another, which is impossible.

19 In the development of the classic concept of eternity, geometric models were sometimes introduced in an attempt to clarify the relationship we are calling ET-

simultaneity. There is a passage in Boethius, for instance (*Consolation*, bk. iv, prose 6; *De trinitate*, pp. 364.78-366.82), which suggests that he took the relationship between time and eternity to be analogous to that between the circumference and the centre of a circle. Aquinas developed this sort of analogy in connection with an account of an eternal entity's apprehension of temporal events: 'Furthermore, God's understanding, just like his being, does not have succession; it is, therefore, always enduring all at once, which belongs to the nature of eternity. The duration of time, on the other hand, is extended in the succession of before and after. Thus the relationship of eternity to the whole duration of time is like the relationship of an indivisible to a continuum— not indeed of an indivisible that is a limit of the continuum, which is not present to each part of the continuum (an instant of time bears a likeness to that), but of the indivisible that is outside the continuum and nevertheless coexists with each part of the continuum or with a designated point in the continuum. For, since time does not extend beyond change, eternity, which is entirely beyond change, is nothing belonging to time; on the other hand, since the being of what is eternal is never lacking, eternity in its presentness is present to each time or instant of time. A sort of example of this can be seen in a circle. For a designated point on the circumference, although it is an indivisible, does not coexist together with another point as regards position since it is the order of position that produces the continuity of the circumference. But the centre, which is outside the circumference, is directly opposite any designated point on the circumference. In this way, whatever is in any part of time coexists with what is eternal as being present to it even though past or future with respect to another part of time. But nothing can coexist with what is eternal in its presentness except as a whole, for it does not have the duration of succession. And so in its eternity the divine understanding perceives as present whatever takes place during the whole course of time. It is not the case, however, that what takes place in a certain part of time has been existent always. It remains, therefore, that God has knowledge of those things that, as regards the course of time, are not yet' (*Summa Contra Gentiles*, bk. i, ch. 66).

20 In *The Consolation of Philosophy* Boethius introduces and develops the concept of eternity primarily in order to argue that divine omniscience is compatible with human freedom, and he does so by demonstrating that omniscience on the part of an eternal entity need not, cannot, involve *fore*knowledge. See also section VI below.

21 The claim that Nixon's death is really future rests on the assumption around which we all organize our lives, the view that the temporal present is absolute, that the expressions 'the present', 'the past', and 'the future' are uniquely (and differently) referring expressions on each occasion of their use, that 'now' is an essential indexical. On the notion of an essential indexical see John Perry, 'The Problem of the Essential Indexical', *Noûs* 13(1) (March 1979), pp. 3-21. We are grateful to Marilyn Adams for letting us see some of her unpublished work which brings out the importance of the notion of the absolute present in discussions of this sort particularly in the discussion we will take up in section VI below, and for calling our attention to Perry's article.

22 Most clearly in fr. 8, as we read it. For excellent examples of both sides of the controversy over the presence of the concept of eternity in Parmenides, see G. E. L. Owen, 'Plato and Parmenides on the Timeless Present', *Monist* L (3) (July 1966), pp. 317-340; and Malcolm Schofield, 'Did Parmenides Discover Eternity?'. *Archiv für Geschichte der Philosophie* 52 (1970), pp. 113-35.

23 See notes 6 and 9 above.

[24] For some discussion of this analysis of time in Aristotle and Augustine, see Fred Miller, Aristotle on the Reality of Time', *Archiv für Geschichte der Philosophie* 61 (1974), pp. 132-55; and Norman Kretzmann, 'Time Exists—But Hardly, or Obscurely (Physics iv, 10; 217b29-218a33)', *Aristotelian Society Supplementary Volume* I (1976), pp. 91-114.

[25] William Kneale has taken this notion to be genuinely incoherent and among the most important reasons for rejecting the classic concept of eternity. See his 'Time and Eternity in Theology', *Proceedings of the Aristotelian Society* 61 (1960), pp. 87-108; also his article 'Eternity' in Paul Edwards (ed.), *The Encyclopedia of Philosophy* (New York, 1967), vol 3, pp. 63-6. Cf. Martha Kneal, 'Eternity and Sempiternity', *Proceedings of the Aristotelian Society*, 69 (1968-9), pp. 223-38.

[26] Anthony Kenny, 'Divine Foreknowledge and Human Freedom', in Kenny (ed.), *Aquinas: A Collection of Critical Essays* (Garden City, NY, 1969), pp. 255-70, 264.

[27] Nelson Pike, *God and Timelessness* (London, 1970), pp. 104-5.

[28] These ambiguities, like the two interpretations provided for consideration I above, are of the sort extensively investigated by medieval logicians under their distinction between the compounded and divided senses of propositions. Thus (9)(*a*) and (10)(*a*) present the compounded senses of propositions (9) and (10), whereas (9)(*b*) and (10)(*b*) present their divided senses.

[29] 1 Samuel l:9-20.

[30] For a discussion of other philosophical problems associated with petitionary prayer see Eleonore Stump, 'Petitionary Prayer', *American Philosophical Quarterly*, 16(1) (Jan. 1979), pp. 81-91.

[31] Although Boethius treats of the Incarnation and the dual nature of Christ in his theological tractates, especially in his *Contra Eutychen et Nestorium* (in Stewart, Rand, and Testor, 1973), he does not apply his concept of eternity in those discussions as we think it ought to be applied.

Study Questions

1. How does Eleonore Stump and Norman Kretzmann characterize Boethius' notion of God's "atemporal eternity"?

2. How do the notions of "presentness""and "simultaneity" come to be defined?

3. What is "E-simultaneity"? What is "T-simultaneity"? What is "RT-simultaneity"? What is "ET-simultaneity"?

4. How does the Einsteinian conception of time figure in Stump and Kretzmann's discussion of ET-simultaneity?

5. How do Stump and Kretzmann develop the atemporal notion of eternity in giving account of the Trinity?

30

A New Doctrine of Eternity

Alan Padgett

Alan Padgett is professor of theology and philosophy of science at Azusa Pacific University, is author of *God, Eternity and the Nature of Time*, and *The Mission of the Church in Methodist Perspective*; and is editor of *Reason and the Christian Religion* (Fetschrift to Richard Swinburne).

In this chapter* of his book, Alan Padgett defends the notion that God is relatively timeless, considers objections to this view, and defends the idea that God is the Lord of time.

In this essay I wish to defend the intuition that God transcends time, of which he is the Creator. To do this, I will develop a new understanding of the term 'timeless eternity' as it applies to God. This assumes the inadequacy of the traditional notion of divine eternity, as it is found in Boethius, Anselm and Aquinas. Very briefly, the reasons for this inadequacy are as follows. God sustains the universe, which means in part that he is responsible for the fundamental ontological status of things. Because the universe is an ever-changing reality, things do change in their fundamental ontological status at different times—a change we must ascribe to God, and cannot ascribe to the objects themselves, since this has to do with their very existence. God himself, therefore, does different things at different times. This implies change in God. Whenever a change occurs, a duration occurs. Therefore, God is in time. But I do not think it is proper to say that God is in our time. God transcends time, and he is the Creator of our space-time. It is theologically more proper to say that we are in God's time, and I will adopt this language here.[1]

Time is notoriously difficult to define. Augustine's well-known lament is usually cited: 'What, then, is time? if no one asks me, I know: but if I wish to explain it to no one who asks, I know not.'[2] Richard Gale may well be correct, that it cannot adequately be defined.[3] In a very general way, one can think of time as a series of durations. A duration, in turn, is a series of related moments. I leave the notion of a 'moment' undefined, understood as some small part of a duration. Two things are clearly in the same time, then, if moments of their life are related (i.e. simultaneous, before, or after each other). 'Our time' will thus be any set of moments related to our 'now'. Of course these moves do not define time so much as plot out the interrelationships between the different words used concerning it.

With respect to eternity, there are a variety of ways in which this term cannot be unrelated in this way to our time, if God sustains our universe. For sustaining is a causal relation. If both cause and effect are temporal, a cause must be either before or simultaneous with its effect (those who believe in retrocausation may add 'after'; it does not affect the argument). Since both God and the world are temporal, and since God effects the world, the world must be in the same time as God. We are in God's time.

God is in himself temporal in some ways, because his relationship with the world. Further, because of this causal relationship, human beings are in God's time, and God is in the same time as humans. Does this mean, then, that God cannot be timeless? This depends upon what one means by 'timeless'. God cannot, to be sure, be absolutely timeless. But one would still think that, as the infinite Creator of all things, including time itself, God would in some way transcend time. I will argue that this is in fact the case. God is relatively timeless, and eternal in a revised sense of the term.

God experiences real change in relationship with the world. Therefore, God must in some way be temporal. For whenever a change occurs the subject of the change goes through some interval of time. Therefore, God is not absolutely timeless, and the traditional doctrine of eternity must be abandoned.

Yet this answer does not fully satisfied us at some deeper theological level. As the infinite Creator of all things, including time itself, God should in some way transcend time. Transcendence, of course, is a metaphor like so much of our talk about God. In this chapter I will unpack the idea of God "transcending" time more fully. I hope to show three aspects of this transcendence: God's life is the ground of time; God is the Lord of time, who is unchanged by time and lives forever and ever; and God is relatively timeless.

God as the Ground of Time

A timeless world is not an impossible world. This much, at least, has been argued well and at length by defenders of the traditional doctrine of divine eternity. Duns Scotus and his modern followers have shown us the ways in which something could be "alive" in an absolutely timeless world. Since an absolutely timeless world is possible, and God could live in such a world, it follows that the actual world could have been timeless. This means, further, that God has chosen eternally to live the kind of life he does and has chosen eternally to have a temporal universe in which to live. This choice is an eternal one, in that it must have always been made. There is not time before which this choice was made.

God's choice, then, to live a certain kind of life—to be dynamic, active, changing—is the ground of the temporality of the universe. I have suggested that we understand time to be the dimension of the possibility of change. This dimension, like space, is a creation of God's. The world could have been different. God's choice (eternally) to live a certain kind of life, a temporal and changing life, is the ground of time. Time need not have been in God's creation. This is one way in which God transcends time.

God Is the Lord of Time

To speak of God as the "Lord" of time is just another sort of metaphor, of course. What are the implications of this metaphor? First of all, it signifies that God has a design or plan which he is enacting in history. God is the Lord of heaven and earth, of time and eternity. Any changes that happen on earth do so because of the will and power of God, which sustain all changing things in their being. Even free and random events take place within the parameters established by God, and the things which undergo these random or free changes exist only because God causes their continued existence. Thus nothing happens outside the will of God, even though God does not will every event which takes place to happen in exactly the way it does. God sets the parameters within which all events take place, even those free events whose exact outcomes are not willed by God (i.e. are undetermined).

To say that God is the Lord of time would include the fact that he is not limited by any amount of time, either in the actions he can perform or the length of his life. While humans can fear the passage of time, because it brings them closer to the end of their life, God is everliving. He cannot die, and has nothing to fear from the future. Moreover, for God time does not press. Because of his infinite wisdom and power God is not limited in the amount of things he can accomplish, or problems he can work through, in a limited period of time. Nothing happens outside of his will, knowledge and power. In this way God's relationship to time is radically different from our human experience of time as a limitation upon us. John Lucas wrote in this regard (*Treaties on Time and Space*, 306):

> To understand eternity therefore we should not think of it as timeless or changeless, but as free from all those imperfections that make the passage of time for us a matter of regret. God is the master of events, not their prisoner; time passes, but does not press.

For the Lord of time and eternity, time is a servant and not a master.

Related to the idea that God is Lord of time is the fact that he is a necessary being, unchanged by time, who lives forever and ever. In traditional language, God is *a se*, necessary and immutable. God cannot die, and does not change in his fundamental nature. The aseity of God, as I understand it, means that God does not owe his existence to any other being(s) or states of affairs outside himself. God's existence does not have a causal explanation outside of himself, nor does it depend upon anything or anyone else.[4]

As well as being *a se*, I understand God to be "metaphysically necessary." By this I mean that he is the cause or he is a cause of every logically contingent "fact," or state of affairs, at any time and at any place (cf. Penelhum, "Divine Necessity"). If any state of affairs obtains, then God must exist either at that time, or earlier, in order to cause it. Finally, I understand God to be immutable, in that he cannot change in his nature, character, or perfections.

The fact that something was not changed by time, for Aristotle, was an important part of its being "timeless." The understanding of divine eternity developed in this book implies the falsity of the old, absolute notion of the immutability of God which has always been associated with his eternity. But this does not mean that God is not immutable, when the latter doctrine is properly understood. God is immutable in his character, nature and perfections. Such is the way that I. A. Dorner understood the doctrine of immutability, in what is arguably the single most important discussion of this doctrine in modern times.[5] We are fortunate that such excellent work on the doctrine of immutability has gone before us, and further that this modern understanding of immutability dovetails well the doctrine of eternity I am developing here.

On this view, God changes, indeed, but only in relationship to a changing reality of which he is the creator and Lord. God does not change in his basic nature, in his character, or in his perfections. The necessary existence of God, on the one hand, is immutable and eternal, since it is not affected or effected by anything else. But with respect to his power, for example, God's activity changes in relation to the changing world he sustains: but the fact that God is omnipotent does not change. God is immutable, therefore, but he is not absolutely immutable in the Augustinian-Thomistic sense. Paul Helm (*Eternal God*, 86) helpfully distinguishes between accidental and necessary immutability, and between immutability of all predicates and immutability of a particular set of predicates. In my view, then, God is necessarily or essentially immutable with respect to a limited set of predicates, which are his character and perfections.

From the properties of aseity, metaphysical necessity and immutability, it follows that God exists forever. As Lord of time, God cannot cease to exist, since he is immutable and his being is not caused by any other beings or states of affairs. Since God exists, he can never fail to exist, being immutable and *a se*. Thus God will always exist, and always has existed. This is a further aspect of his being the Lord of time.

The fact that God is the Lord of time I have understood to mean that he has a plan or design for human history, and nothing takes place outside of his will; that he is not limited or changed in any fundamental way by the passage of time; and that he is a necessary being (*a se* and metaphysically necessary) who lives forever and ever. These are further aspects of his transcendence of time.

God as Relatively Timeless

Is the "Lord of time" in time? Is he timeless or not? These are questions that need careful attention. Is some duration in God's life ever simultaneous, before or after some duration of our time? If so, it will follow that God is in our time, since we have defined a time as the sum of related moments.

Now it is hard to see how two temporal things, even if they are in different spaces, can lack temporal relations if they are causally connected. Consider the following logical necessity:

(33) When both cause and effect are temporal, a cause must be temporally related to its effect.

Consider the case where V causes W, and both are both in time. V will normally (or always) be before W in time. Perhaps, if one holds to simultaneous causation, V and W may be simultaneous. If one holds to retrocausation, then W may be before V. These different positions exhaust the logical possibilities. The gravamen is the same in any case: if V causes W, and both are temporal, then some temporal relation must (logically must) hold between V and W. If, as I have argued is the case with God, no duration occurs between direct divine act and immediate effect, then the divine cause will be Zero Time Related to the created effect. Since God is temporal in himself, and he sustains the world which is a causal relationship, there must be some temporal relationship between eternity and time.[6]

I have spoken previously of God being in our time. Yet the gravamen of this chapter will be to argue that, in fact, God transcends our time. Since this is the case, it is far more appropriate to say that we are in God's time, than that God is in our time. Since God is the ground of time, this is another reason to speak of us being in God's time, rather than God being in our time. The latter expression, though philosophically acceptable, is theologically backwards. It is not the Creator that is bound by and included in the creation; rather, the creation is bounded by the Creator. It is the Infinite that bounds the finite, not *vice versa*. Therefore it is best to speak of creation being "in" God's time or eternity.

God is in himself temporal in some ways: does this mean he cannot be timeless? This depends upon what one means by "timeless." Aristotle thought that something was timeless if (*i*) it was not measured by time, and (*ii*) it was not affected by time or "contained" by time. In a similar way, I have suggested that God is in fact both temporal and "relatively" timeless.

This revised doctrine of eternity is fully in harmony with the biblical witness about God and his eternity, as well as some of the early Greek philosophers. In fact, Scripture declares that "a thousand years in Your eyes are like yesterday when it passes, or a watch in the night" (Ps. 90:4); and "with the Lord one day is like a thousand years, and a thousand years like one day" (2 Pet. 3:8). Does this not appear to be something like our notion of God's relative timelessness? Some traditional foundation, then, can be given to the revised doctrine of eternity I am developing.

It is my purpose to argue, then, that God is "timeless" in the sense that his time is immeasurable, meaning that he is not in any Measured Time. Measured Time Words, therefore, would not truly apply in eternity. It could be possible, of course, for God to simply decree that a certain Measured Time would apply to his eternity. Perhaps he might do this to ease communication with his creatures. But this would be a wholly arbitrary convention, and would apply to the whole of eternity only because of the power of the divine decree, and not by anything in the nature of God's time.

The laws of nature, or better the law-like regularities of nature, are essential to the measurement of time. It is the laws of nature, among other things, that allow for the periodic processes that underlie isochronic clocks. Is God in any Measured Time? If not, does our Measured Time measure the eternity of God? I will argue that God is not in any Measured Time, and is not measured by our time, based on two considerations: (*i*) God is not subject to the laws of nature, as anything in Measured Time must be; and (*ii*) any Measured Time is relative to a particular frame of reference, which need not apply to God's time.

God is not subject to any of the law-like regularities of the natural order. As the Creator of all things including the natural order itself, God is of course not subject to any laws of nature. While the actions of God are not arbitrary, and thus not "random" in one sense, from the point of view of a Measured Time God's acts are "random." He does not conform to any order of nature that would cause him to repeat the same process over and over again in a uniform manner, as an isochronic clock is supposed to do. Further, any laws of nature that may obtain are contingent, and can be altered by God. How, then, can God be limited or contained by them, or by any measured Time dependent upon them? Since any Measured Time must depend upon the natural order, of which God is creator and Lord, God is not in any of himself in any Measured Time. There is nothing in eternity that could act as a kind of "intrinsic metric" for the time of God.[7] It would seem, then, that God is not in any Measured Time.

In and of himself, God cannot be subject to the laws of nature, as anything in Measured Time must be. Therefore he is not in any Measured Time. I also rejected, earlier, the notion of a Newtonian, "absolute time" against which God's life might be measured. There is no absolute "flow" of temporal measure which would act as an absolute guide by which any time, including God's, would correctly be measured.

But, an objector might urge, cannot the cosmic time of our universe itself act as a kind of "clock" in order to measure the duration of God's time?[8] After all, clocks can measure things that are fairly random and chaotic in themselves. It would thus seem that even if God is not subject to the order of nature, the universe might act as a kind of clock to measure some duration in eternity.

To develop this objection, suppose that God sustains two episodes of some object, $E1$ and $E2$. Say further that there is exactly one "Stund" between $E1$ and $E2$, a stund being a measure of cosmic time based upon the flow of fundamental particles. God changes in his power-to-act at moments of eternity Zero Time Related to the times of $E1$ and $E2$. Doesn't this mean that the term "one Stund" has meaning for God as he is in himself? The fact that God acts in our time, and his life is sometimes simultaneous with our time, the objection will go, means that the universe itself could act as a sort of clock to measure the duration of God's being. Since God must exist in order for $E1$ and $E2$ to exist, and since they are one Stund apart, doesn't it follow that God lived for one Stund? But if this is so, then God cannot be timeless, even in a relative sense.

The problem with this argument is, assumptions are made about how God is in himself based upon how God seems from a limited temporal perspective (i.e. a particular frame of reference). For while the temporal measure between $E1$ and $E2$ in the cosmic time of our universe is one Stund, it does not follow that $E1$-to-$E2$ is one Stund in some absolute sense which would apply outside our universe and its Measured Time system. $E1$-to-$E2$ does not have to be one Stund in God's time. In fact I would argue that the word "one Stund" does not have any meaning in a language which refers to things outside our universe, such as God, or angels, or some other universe God may have created. From the fact that $E1$ is before $E2$ we can only infer that the act which sustained $E1$ came before the act which sustained $E2$, in God's time. But it does not follow that $E1$-to-$E2$ is one Stund in God's time.

In fact, it does not even follow for some other created observers, moving non-linearly with us at velocities near the speed of light relative to their basic frames, that $E1$-to-$E2$ is one Stund long. The fact that $E1$ is one Stund before $E2$ is a contingent fact. Indeed, even cosmic time is a contingent matter, which holds for any actual, but not every possible, proper frame of reference. We know that $E1$ is in the light cone of $E2$: since they are episodes of the same object, there is a causal link between them which established a conical order. But because of the well known fact of time dilation, an observer moving at a velocity near c relative to her basic frame *will not* measure the duration between E1 and E2 as one Stund. If, then, for different observers in our own space-time the difference between E1 and E2 is not always one Stund, how can we insist (as the argument above does) that the duration between E1 and E2 will be one Stund *in God's time*? Such a conclusion absolutizes our cosmos, as though God could not create a thousand such universes, all with different times. A "cosmic time" is not the same thing as an absolute, Newtonian time. Cosmic time is contingent, and applies to our universe alone, and to a limited and particular frame of reference. We cannot conclude that it applies to anything beyond or outside our universe, unless some method of synchronization is set up (as it might be between different spaces in the same Measured Time). Since God is not of himself limited by any law-like regularity of nature (there is no intrinsic metric in eternity), no synchronization can be established. Thus the argument above fails, and we can conclude that, indeed, God transcends any Measured Time, and is thus relatively timeless.

If God is indeed relatively timeless, does this mean that any language about God using Measured Time Words is false or meaningless? Not at all. Dates, for example, are our way of pointing to certain moments. So the sentence "God created the world in 4004 BC" is true if God created the world during the time picked out by our dating system as 4004 BC. Likewise, "God has been sustaining the world for one hour" is true if God has been sustaining the world for the duration picked out by our Measured Time as one hour. We must insist, however, that such a convention is simply our human way of thinking and it does not mean that hours, seconds and minutes have any application to eternity apart from this convention. It is also true to say that God has always existed in eternity. But what we cannot give is a definite measure to how long that is. For that would be to give a measure to the divine Being, which is immeasurable and infinite. Thus God is not in any Measured Time, and therefore not in the same Measured Time as we are. In this sense, God is timeless.

In arguing that God is relatively timeless, I have stressed that fact that he is "outside" of our universe. Let's explore this idea further. What does it mean to say that God is "outside" our universe? Doesn't he act all the time "in" our history, and "on" our world? While God does act in our history and in our universe, he is not contained within it. God is spaceless, that is, he does not have any spatial location or extension. This is what I understand by God being "outside" our space-time universe. He is free, in himself, to ground our universe, without entering into it as a member of it.

Granted that God does transcend space and time, must God, of logical necessity, transcend both space and time? Another way to ask this is, couldn't God have a body? A body gives an agent some particular spatial and temporal location. A body is a limited mode of action and knowledge acquisition, through a particular lump of matter. Agents normally regularly act and know through their body, if they have one. Couldn't God have a "body" in this sense? Here I think we must trade on our fundamental intuitions about God. Would such a limited being really be God? We must ask ourselves the question, is the being we call God essentially (*de re*) omniscient and omnipotent? Are these properties incompatible with having a body? I frankly find nothing logically impossible in the person we call God having a body, being measured by our time, and having a particular spatial location as opposed to some other. I do not find this incompatible with the properties of omnipotence or omniscience. However, as Swinburne has persuasively argued, the universe as a whole does not function as God's body. And I do not think that, as a matter of fact, in the actual world God does have a body in this technical sense. The Christian doctrine of incarnation, to be sure, does not teach that God as a whole is fully embodied. So God does in fact transcend time and space—but he does not have to. Further discussion of this point would take us beyond the scope of our present topic.[9]

God, then, can enter into our space or Measured Time at will, but is not contained within it of necessity. And this is as one might expect, since God is the Creator of space and time. It is he that calls the universe into existence, and thus he cannot be limited by that which is wholly dependent upon him. God transcends both time and space. I have argued that he transcends time in that his life is the ground of time, he is the Lord of time, and he is relatively timeless.

Objections Considered

Having developed a new concept of eternity, it seems right to consider objections to it, since they will not doubt be raised in any case! It might be objected, first of all, that this revised understanding of eternity is not really a doctrine of time-*less* eternity, since it allows that God is in our time. If God is in some way temporal, how can we then assert that he is "timeless?" Against this objection, consider what the word "time" means in ordinary language. Expressions like "what time is it?" or "a long time ago" or "how time flies!" are examples of ordinary usage of the word in English. Some reflection upon the use of "time" in normal everyday discourse indicates that in normal usage "time" refers to Measured Time, to our history, and to physical processes. In the loose and popular sense, "time" does not mean an ontological category but the specifically human time of our history and our universe: the time of seconds, days, and centuries; the time of our space-time. When "time" is used in this popular sense, then, *God is timeless*. Although we are in God's time (and thus God is in our time, too) God transcends our time. I have tried to capture these insights by saying that God is (relatively) timeless. It is only when "time" is used in a very strict and narrow sense—when it refers to any sort of temporality—that the revised doctrine of eternity affirms that God is temporal.

Our basic question concerns divine eternity, not immutability, simplicity and perfection. But our partners in dialogue make some discussion of these last three divine attributes necessary. Thus each objection will be considered in turn, briefly looking at these three attributes as well. This will help to flesh out the revised doctrine of eternity which we are advocating. But a full and complete discussion of all these divine attributes would take us too far from our main subject.

I have already discussed the divine immutability. I understand God to be immutable, in the sense that his fundamental attributes, perfections and character—those attributes which he has eternally—cannot change or pass away. This, of course, is different from the traditional view of immutability, which states that God does not change in any way whatsoever. While acknowledging this difference, I deny that the traditional view is the only proper one.

The second objection arising from traditional theology concerns the divine perfection. If we allow that in eternity, God lives his life in stages, then God cannot be a perfect being as traditionally understood. As Aquinas wrote,

> anything in change acquires something through its change, attaining something previously not attained. Now God, being limitless and embracing within himself the whole fullness of perfection of all existence, cannot acquire anything, nor can he move out towards something previously not attained. So one cannot in any way associate him with change (ST, Ia, q.9, a.1).

According to the revised doctrine of eternity, God does change. It would thus seem that he cannot be perfect. If anything changes, it either diminishes in perfection or it grows in perfection, "attaining something previously not attained." Since God changes, one of these two options must be true. But if God diminishes, then he is no longer a perfect being. On the other hand, if God grows in perfection, he was not a perfect being in the past. Either way, God is not essentially perfect.

Granted that this is a valid argument, is it a sound one? Just because something changes, it need not diminish or grow in perfection. This is the point in the above argument that we can and should call into question. A thing can change in response to a variety of changing circumstances, without itself growing better or worse. And changes in God, remember, are a result of his decision to create a changing world and to be really related to it. Therefore God can change in some ways, and still be immutable and perfect. An example can clarify this point.

Say that "Milton" is the name of an essentially perfect poet. After writing a perfect poem on the beauty of nature, Milton then writes another poem on the pathos of human life. It too is a perfect poem. Let us stipulate that in writing these poems, the character of Milton does not change. He is the same in writing each poem, in this sense. Yet clearly Milton has changed in one sense, in writing the two poems. He changed from writing about and considering beauty, to writing about and considering human fate, suffering and death. And surely this is a real change in Milton—but it is not a change for the better or the worse. In both cases, Milton is still the perfect poet, and his poems are the perfect poems about their subjects. But the subjects of the poems are different. Now this example (which is not about historical Milton!) is coherent. And since it is coherent, something can change without either growing or diminishing in perfection. Thus it follows that the argument above is valid, but the conclusion is false: God can be perfect, and yet change in some ways. God can change in what he does, without changing who he is. God can be a perfect, immutable and timeless being, as I define these terms, even though he changes in relation to a changing world.

Traditional theologians will ague that God, as the source of all movement in other things, is himself unmoved. Nothing can affect, move or change God, since in order to affect God it would have to be stronger than God: which is impossible. What such an argument fails to consider is the idea that God might want to change himself, in order to be in relationship with a changing world (see further Ware, "Reexamination.") Now it was a principle of Aristotelian philosophy that nothing can move or change itself: but I see no reason to accept this principle, especially in the case of an omnipotent being. The ultimate explanation for why God changes can be found in himself alone, and in his will to be in relationship with his creatures. This fact is not true of created things. The answer to the third objection lies in this difference.

Traditional theologians will argue that a changing God cannot be the explanation of the world. For a changing thing requires an explanation of why it changes; the inference is, only an unchanging thing can be the ultimate explanation of all changes. Now on our understanding of his aseity and immutability, God is the ultimate explanation of change, including changes in himself. God is the ultimate origin of all changes, including changes that he himself undergoes in order to be really related to the world. The will of God, therefore, is the ultimate explanation of all change, including changes in God. Thus God does not require any explanation outside of himself, and this is certainly not true of changing things as we know of them in our world. The aseity of God means that he owes his existence to no other thing. Because of his aseity, God is not in the class of things that owe their existence or changes, ultimately, to things outside of themselves.

One might agree that things in the class of objects that owe their existence and changes to something outside of themselves, do as a class need some explanation. Let us agree, for the sake of the argument, that an infinite regress of causes in this class is inadequate as a complete explanation of the reality of the class as a whole. But this will only mean that God is not an element of the class of every changing thing which owes its changes to something outside of itself. It does not follow that God cannot change in some ways, namely in relation to a changing world. Further, since God is not a member of this class, he can be the ultimate explanation for the existence of the elements of this class, and the changes they undergo, without violating the insights of the traditionalist regarding the problems of an infinite regress of causes. Even given the point about an infinite causal regress being impossible (which could be questioned) God's will could still be the ultimate explanation for every event.

Anselm (*Monologion*, ch. 22) objected further to the idea that God changed himself, since a cause must precede its effect. This would mean that, if God changes, there was some aspect of the life of God that precedes another aspect; and further, that the prior aspect no longer exists, since it is replaced by the next stage in the life of God. Now on the doctrine of eternity we are developing it does follow that there will be stages in the life of God. Thus some stages in the life of God have ceased to exist in eternity. But Anselm objected to the idea that some stage in the life of God no longer exists, since this undermines the divine simplicity. So we now turn to this objection.

Traditionally, the divine simplicity has been defined as God being identical to all of his properties. This was made clear in my analysis of Aquinas , for example. None of God's actions can cease to exist, since the actions of God are identical with the essence of God, which necessarily exists. As Stump and Kretzmann put this Thomistic point, "the one thing that is God and is atemporally actual has a variety of effects in time . . . [These effects] are to be understood as various temporal effects of the single eternal act indentical [*sic*] with God" ("Absolute Simplicity," 356. If we follow the revised doctrine of divine timelessness, and the doctrine of immutability in the tradition of Dorner which it implies, this conception of divine simplicity must be abandoned. But this doctrine seems more at home in a Neoplatonic theology, such a Plotinus's, than in the Biblical theology of a dynamic God passionately involved in history.

I have responded to the four arguments which arise from traditional theology, with its emphasis on God as the ultimate origin of things, and on his simplicity, immutability and perfection. One other traditional attribute of God is usually linked to his eternity, and that is his foreknowledge. We owe the emphasis on this link to Boethius. But space does not permit further discussion of this divine attribute, since it is so involved with a number of other philosophical and theological difficulties. The doctrine of divine timelessness is theologically distinct from the discussion of divine foreknowledge. One may first examine the problem of what eternity is, and then turn to the problems associated with foreknowledge. This, at least, is the order I have followed.

Having dealt with problems arising from traditional theology, other possible objections to the revised doctrine of eternity come from two recent books: David Braine, *The Reality of Time and the Existence of God* and Paul Helm, *Eternal God*. Braine's stimulating and interesting work takes up the task of proving the existence of God from the reality of temporal order. Most of what Braine discuses will not concern us here. But Braine's concept of God as "incomposite" is at odds with the revised doctrine of eternity. And like the present work, Braine bases his conclusions about God on the fact that God sustains the world of changing things. Thus some response is in order, if only because of the similarity of topics.

With Braine I agree that God is "intrinsically underivative," or as I have expressed it, God has the properties of metaphysical necessity and aseity. God is not the effect of anything or anyone else. But Braine also insists that God is "incomposite," by which he means to contrast temporal things, which are "composite." Braine explains the term "composite":

> Temporal things, and anything whose existence is caused or contingent, are (we may say) 'composite,' defining compositeness in these rather abstract terms: a thing (or, we shall equivalently say, a thing's existence) is composite if and only if the distinction between a thing and its existence is positively pertinent to the efficient causal explanation of the thing's existence (p. 148).

What this seems to mean is, that every "substance" in an Aristotelian sense has a "nature" and an "existence." The "nature" of a thing,

> as a quasi-abstract object in the case of what has a cause is part of the formal specification of the causal background to the thing *qua* external or prior ground of its possibility, and in this way has its quasi-abstract existence prior to the actual existence of the thing (p. 166).

Thus the "nature" of an effected substance is the set of properties of a substance which it must have in virtue of those causes which bring it into being. God on the other hand, is "incomposite," in that he has no prior "nature" which is in any way different from his active existence. Since anything which is temporal must be composite, argues Braine, God is timeless.

Braine explains that "if the central indispensable realization of God's life and existence is not successive, then despite the tensedness of our statements about God, it will be false to describe the reality or nature they indicate as in itself temporal" (p. 132). Here we have to disagree with

Braine. God may not change on his account, and may not have any succession. But this does not affect the judgment that God is in our time (or as I prefer to say, we are in God's time). As long as God's life can be measured by our Measured Time, or is temporally related to our time, then God is in our time. And Braine explicitly rejects the idea that God is "in eternity" and only God's effects are "in time."

> [I]t is vital to maintain the dependence of the tensing of existential statements about substances on the tensing of predications of their actions—and vital that the time of God's actions is the time of its 'effects' (p. 131).

It seems then, from this quotation, that Braine ought to think that God himself is in our time, since his effects are in our time. Now the principle just cited, upon which Braine makes this conclusion, is wrong in our view. God can be in eternity, and his effects can indeed be in our time, without God himself being in our time. But if one accepts Braine's point, then one ought to maintain that God is everlasting in our time, and not timeless. On our own understanding of what it means to be in Measured Time, Braine's view of God ought to be that he is in our Measured Time, and not timeless even in a relative sense. This ought to be, since for him God's "substance" is certainly datable by the date of its effects, and thus God should be in Measured Time.

One further point should be made. While I am willing to grant that God is not "composite" in Braine's sense I cannot conclude from this fact alone that God is simple in the Thomistic sense, as Braine does (e.g., pp. 161, 223). In fact, Braine sets up a false dichotomy between temporal, mundane things as "composite," and God as the "incomposite" as he interprets it (viz. simple in the Thomistic sense). In his own terminology, I question the timelessness of the composite. In fact, I have demonstrated above that if God does sustain the world of time, then he must change in some ways, and cannot be incomposite as Braine has it.

In his recent book, *Eternal God*, Paul Helm objects to arguments for God's temporality, on the ground that, *mutatis mutandis*, such arguments lead to the conclusion that God must be located in space (ch. 3). Since I affirm both that God is not necessarily embodied, and that he is not absolutely timeless, Helm's indirect proof could have force against the position I am developing. So consider in brief the following argument for God's being temporal.

(34) God directly causes different effects at different times.
(35) Agents can only directly cause different effects at different times if they change their action.
(36) God changes his action.
(37) Anything that undergoes real change is temporal.

(38)　Changing one's action is a real change.

(39)　God is temporal.

If Helm's criticism is correct, then the above argument should lead to the conclusion that God must be in space, if terms for time are replaced by terms for space. These changes yield the following revised argument:

(34′)　God directly causes different effects at different places.

(35′)　Agents can only directly cause different effects at different places if they change their action.

(36)　God changes his action.

(37′)　Anything that undergoes real change is spatial.

(38)　changing one's action is a real change.

(39′)　God is spatial.

While the first argument is sound, the second Helmian modified argument is not. (37) in the first argument is true, for example, while (37′) is not. The difference between time and space ensures the absurdity of the second argument. god can spacelessly act directly upon two different places simultaneously, because two different places can coexist at the same time. But God cannot timelessly act directly upon things at two different *instants*, because two different instants cannot coexist (that is, cannot be simultaneous) at the same place. So Helm's criticism fails, and one can coherently hold that God is both not essentially embodied and not absolutely timeless.

I have considered objections to the revised doctrine of divine eternity, and found none of them convincing. Further criticisms may be forthcoming, but for now we can conclude that the concept is internally coherent, and congruent with other Christian doctrines (which the traditional view is not). In its essence, the revised doctrine of eternity rests upon the basic intuition that God transcends time, as its infinite Creator. God, then, exists in a "timeless time" which we call eternity.

Endnotes

*A version of this paper was presented to the XVIIIth World Congress of Philosophy, Brighton, 24 August 1988. The author wishes to express his gratitude to the Society of Christian Philosophers, and especially to Professor Konyndyk, for this opportunity. Reprinted from *God, Eternity and the Nature of Time*, New York: St. Martin's Press, 1992, and The Macmillan Press Ltd, London. © Alan G. Padgett 1992.

1 This paragraph is a brief presentation of conclusions argued for at length in my Oxford thesis, "Divine Eternity and the Nature of Time."

2 *Confessions*, 11.14.

3 *The Language of Time* (London: Routledge & Kegan Paul, 1968), p .5

4 I exclude from this, of course, "states of affairs" which are themselves entailed by "God exists" (see Swinburne, *Coherence*, 250, 266).

5 Dorner, "*Unveränderlichkeit Gottes.*" Ware, "Evangelical Reexamination of the Doctrine of the Immutability of God" is a significant thesis which develops Dorner's view in dialogue with process theology. My understanding of immutability is in debt to Dorner and Ware.

6 This consideration answers the problem raised by H. J. Nelson, "Time(s), Eternity, and Duration," 9. He argues that "God's time" cannot contain a trans-universal present which contains in one "now" the quite different presents of two different universes which by definition do not have the temporal relations of simultaneity, before or after. But since God must create both universes in order for them to exist at all, and since creating and sustaining are causal processes, from God's perspective at least there will be temporal relations between the two universes, given principle (33) above. Either God will create one and then the other after that one; or else the histories of the two will overlap and some instants will be simultaneous with some instant in God's time. Since simultaneity is a transitive relation, the two worlds will either sometimes be simultaneous, or one will be wholly before the other. In both cases temporal relations will exist between the two worlds. Therefore, Nelson was wrong in the beginning to stipulate that two universes, both created by God,cannot have any temporal relations between them.

7 I argue this in my article, "Can History Measure Eternity?" which is a reply to William Lane Craig, "God and Real Time."

8 This is the main point of W.L. Craig, "God and Real Time," a reply to an earlier article of mine, "God and Time."

9 For further discussion, see Grace M. Jantzen, *God's World, God's Body*, and T. F. Tracy, *God, Action and Embodiment*. Cf. R. G. Swinburne, *The Coherence of Theism*, 99-125.

Study Questions

1.   What does Alan Padgett mean by the phrase, "God is the Lord of time"?

2.   Padgett speaks of God as ""elatively timeless."" What does he mean?

3.   For Padgett, could God have a body?

4.   What is "measured time"?

5.   In what sorts of ways is Padgett's view of God's eternity different from Stump's and Kretzmann's?

For Further Reading

Anselm, St. 1903. *Proslogium Monologuum, An Appendix on Behalf of the Fool of Gaunilon, and Cur Deus Homo.* Trans. S.N. Dean. Chicago: Open Court.

Aquinas, Thomas. 1964-1981. *Summa Theologiae*. 61 vols. Eds. T. Bilby, *et al*. London: Eyre and Spottiswoode.

Augustine, St. 1961. *Confessions*. Trans. R. S. Pine-coffin. Harmondsworth: Penguin.

Braine, David, 1988. *The Reality of Time and the Existence of God*. Oxford: Oxford University Press.

Craig, William Lane. 1978. "God and Real Time." *Religious Studies*. 26: 335-347.

Dorner, I.A. 2883. "Uber die richtige Fassung des dogmatischen Unveränderlichkeit Gottes." *Gessamelte Schriften*, pp. 188-377. Berlin: W. Hertz.

Gale, Richard. 1968. *The Language of Time*. London: Routledge

Helm, Paul. 1988. *Eternal God: A Study of God Without Time*. Oxford: Oxford University Press.

Jantzen, Grace. 1984. *God's World, God's Body*. London: Darton, Longman and Todd.

Lucas, J.R. 1973. *A Treatise on Time and Space*. London: Methuen.

Nelson, Herbert J. 1987. "Time(s), Eternity, and Duration." *International Journal for Philosophy of Religion* 22: 3-19.

Padgett, Alan G. 1991. "Can History Measure Eternity? A Reply to William Craig." *Religious Studies* 27: 333-335.

Penelhum, Terrence. 1960. "Divine Necessity." *Mind*. 69: 175-186.

Pike, Nelson. 1970. *God and Timelessness*. London: Routledge.

Stump, Eleanore and Norman Kretzmann. 1985. "Absolute Simplicity." *Faith and Philosophy* 2: 353-382.

Swinburne, Richard. 1977. *The Coherence of Theism*. Oxford: Oxford University Press.

Tracy, T.F. 1984. *God, Action and Embodiment*. Grand Rapids: Eerdmans.

Ware, Bruce. 1984. "An Evangelical Reexamination of the Doctrine of the Immutability of God." Ph.D. thesis. Fuller Theological Seminary. Partial published in the following essays:

_____. 1985. "An Exposition and Critique of the Process Doctrines of Divine Mutability and Immutability." *Westminster Theological Journal* 47: 175-196.

_____. 1986. "An Evangelical Reformulation of the Doctrine of the Immutability of God." *Journal of the Evangelical Theological Society* 29: 431-446.

PART V

MIRACLES

31

The Argument From Miracles

Michael Martin

Michael Martin is professor of philosophy at Boston University, and is author of *Atheism: A Philosophical Justification*.

In *Atheism: A Philosophical Justification*, chapter 7, he considers the argument from miracles for the existence of God.* He acknowledges that there is no *a priori* reason for there not to be miracles, but there are difficult *a posteriori* obstacles to surmount before one can claim that miracles have occurred in either a direct or indirect sense. Furthermore, even if there were good reasons to suppose that miracles existed in either sense, this would not necessarily mean that the existence of miracles provides inductive support for theism.

The Argument in General

The literature of religious traditions is filled with stories of strange and mysterious events. Christian literature is abundantly supplied with such stories. According to the Bible, Jesus was born of a virgin, turned water to wine, walked on water, healed the sick, raised the dead, and was resurrected.[1] Moreover, within the Christian tradition, accounts of these sorts of events have continued down through the centuries. There have been stories of wondrous cures, of bleeding religious statues, of stigmata, and of visitations of the Virgin Mary.[2] For example, in Zeitoun, Egypt, from 1968 to 1970, thousands of people observed what seemed to be a luminous figure of the Virgin Mary walking on the central dome of the Coptic church known as St. Mary's Church of Zeitoun and occasionally hovering above it.[3] In Lourdes, France, many unexplained cures have been reported. After having been investigated by the Catholic Church, some of them have been declared to be miraculous. Strange and mysterious events have also been reported in the context of other religious traditions, such as the levitation of Hindu yogis.[4]

It seems that these reports, if accepted as accurate, cannot be explained in either commonsense or scientific terms. For example, there appears to be no ordinary way of explaining how Jesus raised the dead or turned water into wine, no scientific explanation of the luminous figure on the dome of St. Mary's Church of Zeitoun or of the cures at Lourdes, no known ordinary way to account for the levitation of yogis.

An argument for the existence of God that is based on evidence of such unexplained events proceeds as follows. Since these events cannot be explained in ordinary terms, they are miracles. Miracles by definition can only be explained in terms of some supernatural power. The most plausible supernatural explanation of miracles is that God caused them to occur. Hence it is probable that God exists.

Some form of the argument from miracles has been used by philosophers and theologians down through the ages either to prove the existence of God or more commonly to support the truth of some particular religion. For example, both Augustine and Aquinas[5] in the Christian tradition, Philo Judaeus[6] in the Jewish tradition, and Avicenna[7] in the Islamic tradition appealed to miracles. Indeed, the belief that the truth of the Christian religion can be proved on the basis of miracles has been a dogma of the Catholic Church since the third session of the First Vatican Council in 1870.[8] Although belief in the existence of miracles has been deemphasized in recent years by sophisticated Christian theologians,[9] even today most Christian theologians have not given up the belief that Jesus was miraculously resurrected.[10] Further, there are still philosophers of religion who believe that the argument provides some support for theism. Thus Richard Swinburne in *The Existence of God*[11] maintains that it provides support for the hypothesis that God exists, and Richard Purtill in *Thinking About Religion: A Philosophical Introduction to Religion* argues for a limited use of the argument.[12]

The Concept of Miracles

Before we attempt to evaluate the argument from miracles, it is important to be clear on what a miracle is and what it is not. A miracle is not simply an unusual event. There are many unusual events that are not considered miracles; for example, snow flurries in July in Boston and a newborn baby weighing more than 11 pounds. Nor is a miracle just an event that cannot be explained by currently known scientific laws. After all, among the many such events that are not considered miracles are the occurrences of cancer and birth defects.

What then is a miracle? Traditionally it is defined as a violation of a law of nature.[13] However, this traditional account has a serious problem that precludes its being adopted here. Consider a possible world where a god brings about some event, such as a cure of someone's cancer, that cannot be explained by any law yet known to science. However, suppose that in this world the god's action is governed by a law that governs the powers of gods. We could say that in this world a miracle had occurred but there was no violation of any law in that the god's actions are themselves governed by laws.

It is for this reason that I provisionally define a miracle as an event brought about by the exercise of a supernatural power.[14] This definition is compatible with a miracle violating no law. But what is a supernatural power? It is one that is markedly superior to those powers possessed by humans. Supernatural powers are possessed by supernatural beings: gods, angels, Superman, devils.[15] If supernatural beings exist, the powers they possess need not be in violation of the laws of nature. Indeed, one could imagine these abilities being governed by causal laws. As philosophers of science have commonly understood such laws, they are true universal statements that support counterfactual inferences and perhaps meet other technical requirements such as substitutivity. There is no reason why there could not be true generalities about supernatural beings and their powers that fulfill these conditions.

One can think of the situation in this way.[16] Nature in its broadest sense, $nature_b$, includes all entities (supernatural and natural) and their activities (determined by natural and supernatural powers). Thus $nature_b$ comprises the sum total of entities and their causal interactions. The only things not included in $nature_b$ are entities that are incapable of any causal interaction, such as numbers or sets. All entities and their causal interactions in $nature_b$ are governed by causal laws.

Nature in a narrow sense, $nature_n$, consists of the realm of human and subhuman entities and their powers. $Nature_n$ is part of $nature_b$ and, if there are no supernatural entities or powers, is identical with it. Miracles, on this view, do not go beyond $nature_b$; they go beyond $nature_n$. Or, to put it in a different way, miracles cannot be explained by laws governing $nature_n$; they might be explained by laws governing $nature_b$. If there are laws governing $nature_b$ that go beyond $nature_n$, these laws are not investigated by science.

Now, it may be objected that if supernatural beings such as a theistic God exist, their powers are not governed by causal laws. If this were so, our definition would not be affected. We could still say that it is not part of the *meaning* of "miracle," that it is a violation of a law of nature. After all, there could be supernatural beings who perform miracles whose actions are governed by causal laws. If God's actions are not governed by laws, then miracles would violate laws of $nature_n$, and $nature_b$ would not be governed by causal laws. But this would not mean that by definition miracles were violations of natural laws.

On the traditional view, miracles are nonrepeatable as well as being violations of natural law,[17] but I reject this characterization too. On my definition there is no *a priori* reason why a miracle cannot be repeated numerous times.[18] For example, it is not logically impossible for a miracle worker to being many people back to life. Indeed, so-called faith healers such as W. V. Grant and Oral Roberts have allegedly brought about numerous miracles of the same type. One might question the truth of these claims,[19] but there is nothing incoherent in the stories. One cannot say that the stories are false simply because the "miracles" was repeated. But if nonrepeatability is part of the definition of a miracles, one could.

The Probability that God Exists, Given the Existence of Miracles

We are now ready to begin an evaluation of the argument from miracles. The first thing to be considered is whether the existence of miracles would in fact support the hypothesis that God exists. Let us suppose that miracles in the sense defined above—that is, events brought about by the exercise of a supernatural power—do occur. Would this be good evidence for the existence of God? To state my answer briefly, it would not be, since miracles might be the result of the actions of other supernatural beings besides God.

The question must be considered more carefully, however. By "evidence for the existence of God" is meant inductive evidence in the sense that was characterized earlier. Let us consider whether H_1 (= God exists) is inductively supported by E (= Miracles have occurred). Following Swinburne,[20] let us distinguish two types of inductive arguments for miracles: C-inductive arguments and P-inductive arguments. In a good C-inductive argument,

(1) $P(H_1/E\&K) > P(H_1/K)$

where K is the background knowledge and $P(p/q)$ means that p is probable relative to q. In a good P-inductive argument,

(2) $P(H_1/E\&K) > P(\sim H_1/E\&K)$.

Now, (1) is true if and only if

(3) $P(E/H\&K) > P(E/K)$

so long as $P(H/K) \neq 0$. In turn, (3) is equivalent to

(4) $P(E/H_1\&K) > P(E/\sim H_1\&K)$.

One can immediately see a problem with (4). It is completely unclear why one should suppose that (4) is true. After all, $\sim H_1$ can be interpreted as a disjunction of hypotheses consisting of H_1's rivals. Included in this disjunction would be hypotheses that postulate finite but very powerful beings that have as their basic motive the desire to work miracles. The probability of E relative to these hypotheses about finite miracle workers would be one. The probability of E relative to other members of this disjunction would vary from zero to near one. There's no *a priori* reason to suppose that the probability of E relative to the entire disjunction would be less than the probability of E relative to H_1. It is important to see that:

$$P(E/H_1\&K) \neq 1.$$

That is, the hypothesis of theism does not entail the existence of miracles. Swinburne, for example, maintains only that miracles are probable given God's existence—how probable is unclear. The crucial question is whether miracles are more probable if theism is false. In his analysis Swinburne wrongly seems to suppose that the only rival to theism is naturalism. But there are numerous rival supernatural hypotheses that would explain the existence of miracles.[21]

Furthermore, some of the miracles that are reported in the Christian tradition seem to be better explained by non-Christian supernatural hypotheses. Some of the miracles performed by Christ, such as driving the demons into the Gadarene swine and cursing the fig tree, seem difficult to reconcile with belief in a kind and merciful God.[22] Moreover, a miracle by definition cannot be explained by any law governing nature$_n$. As such, the existence of miracles cannot be explained by science and indeed is an impediment to a scientific understanding of the world. Furthermore, there are great difficulties and controversies in identifying miracles. Thus whatever good effects miracles might have, they also impede, mislead, and confuse. A benevolent and all-powerful God would seemingly be able to achieve His purposes in ways that do not have these unfortunate effects. Moreover, some miracles seem to happen capriciously (for example, some people are cured and some are not), while other miracles seem trivial and unimportant (for example, bleeding statues and stigmata). They are not what one would have antecedently expected from a completely just and all-powerful being.[23]

So even if the existence of miracles is taken for granted, a good C-inductive argument for H_1 remains uncertain.[24] Thus even if one assumes that miracles exist, it is unclear whether this would support the hypothesis that God exists more than its negation.

Naturalism Versus Supernaturalism and the Existence of Miracles

Is there any reason to suppose that miracles do exist? And can we answer this question without a prior commitment to a general metaphysical position? C. S. Lewis, a well known Christian writer, maintains in

Miracles that in order to assess whether miracles exist, it is first necessary to decide between naturalism and supernaturalism. He argues:

> It by no means follows from Supernaturalism that Miracles of any sort do in fact occur. God (the primary thing) may never in fact interfere with the natural system He has created. . . . If we decide that Nature is not the only thing there is, then we cannot say in advance whether she is safe from miracles or not. . . . But if Naturalism is true, then we know in advance that miracles are impossible: nothing can come into Nature from the outside because there is nothing outside to come in, Nature being everything. . . . Our first choice, therefore, must be between Naturalism and Supernaturalism.[25]

His argument can perhaps be constructed as follows. Appeal to neither historical evidence nor personal experience will prove that miracles exist if we have already decided that miracles are *a priori* impossible or unlikely. One can decide that they are *a priori* impossible or unlikely only if one has decided that naturalism is correct. On the other hand, if one maintains that miracles are *a priori* possible or at least not *a priori* improbable, one has accepted supernaturalism.

If Lewis is correct, then the evidence of miracles could not provide any independent support for supernaturalism, since in order to establish the existence of miracles one would already have to assume supernaturalism. Lewis's position, if accepted, would perhaps do more to undermine the argument from miracles than any naturalistic critique of this argument. But should it be accepted?

Lewis is certainly right to suppose that in considering the question of whether miracles exist there is a danger that one will appeal to *a priori* arguments and assumptions. But the solution to this problem is not to decide on naturalism or supernaturalism beforehand. Rather, one must attempt to reject the *a priori* arguments and instead base one's position on inductive considerations. Lewis has not shown that this is impossible. Thus he has not shown that one must choose between naturalism and supernaturalism before investigating the possibility of miracles.

Moreover, when Lewis attempts to provide reasons for choosing supernaturalism over naturalism (N) he fails miserably. He defines N as the view that all events occurring in space and time are caused by earlier events, and this causal process is "going on, *of its own accord*";[26] that is, there is nothing outside this causal system or whole that intervenes or interrupts the causal process.[27] N is incompatible with both rational reasoning[28] and ethical ideals and judgments, he maintains.[29] If N is true, no one could argue for its truth and no naturalist has any business advocating ethical principles. Thus N is self-refuting, and naturalists are inconsistent.

However, Lewis's arguments for these remarkable theses are either very weak or non-existent. His argument for the first claim can be reconstructed in this way:[30]

(1) If N is true, all our thinking must be explicated in terms of cause and effect.
(2) If all our thinking must be explicated in terms of cause and effect, then N can give no account of rational inference.
(3) If N can give no account of rational inference, then a naturalist cannot know that N is true.
(4) If a naturalist cannot know that N is true, there can be no justification for believing N.

---

(5) Therefore, if N is true, there can be no justification for believing N.

The crucial premise is (1), and it is difficult to understand why Lewis holds it. For some reason Lewis seems to suppose that naturalists must distinguish different kinds of thinking (for example, rational and irrational) in *completely* causal terms. But they do. There is no reason why naturalists cannot use terms such as truth, validity, and probability to explicate rational thinking. Indeed, this is precisely what recent naturalists have done.[31]

The argument for the second claim follows similar lines and is really a special case of the first argument.

(1′) If N is true, then all moral judgments are unjustified.
(2′) If all moral judgments are unjustified, good and evil are illusions.
(3′) If good and evil are illusions, then naturalists are inconsistent when they advocate the good of humanity as an ethical idea.

(4′) Therefore, if N is true, then naturalists are inconsistent when they advocate the good of humanity as an ethical ideal.

Here again the problem is premise (1′), for there is no reason to suppose that it is true. It seems to rest either on the first argument that N cannot give an account of reason (hence naturalists can give no account of moral reasoning) and/or on a mistaken view of what ethical naturalists hold. Most ethical naturalists simply do not believe the view that there is no such thing as right or wrong, as Lewis seems to claim.[32] It is significant that Lewis does not cite *one* naturalist who holds the view he attributes to N.

I conclude that it is not necessary to choose between naturalism and supernaturalism prior to answering the question as to whether miracles exist. Moreover, supposing it is necessary, Lewis's arguments for rejecting naturalism are unsound.

The Difficulty of Showing the Existence of Miracles

Having considered the question of whether God's existence is inductively supported by the existence of miracles, I remain skeptical. Furthermore, Lewis's argument that one must decide between supernaturalism and naturalism before one can decide whether miracles exist is not compelling. The question remains, however, whether there is any reason to suppose that miracles do in fact exist.

David Hume gave a general argument against the existence of miracles in "Of Miracles."[33] According to one standard interpretation, Hume does not attempt to show that miracles are *a priori* impossible but rather that it is *a priori* impossible to have strong evidence for their existence. What does Hume mean by a miracle? On his view a miracle is a violation of a law of nature. Consequently, someone who argues that event E is a miracle has two burdens that are impossible to meet simultaneously[34]: to show that E has taken place *and* that E violates a law of nature. Consider the assumed law of nature L*:

(L*)   No person has been brought back to life.

(L*) has been confirmed by the deaths of billions of people; the evidence is overwhelming. Now consider the hypothesis (H*):

(H*)   Some people have been brought back to life.

If we had good evidence for (H*), this would disconfirm (L*). But we cannot have such evidence. The evidence that could support (H*) is based on human testimony, but even at its best it is subject to error. Thus there is no uniform relation in our experience between human testimony that something is so and its being so. However, our evidence for (L*) must be stronger than this. Since (L*) is a law of nature, there is a uniform relation in our experience between a person's dying and this person's not returning to life. Consequently, in terms of our experience the probability of (L*) must be greater than the probability of (H*). The low probability of (H*) relative to (L*) may be argued for in another way. On some interpretations of Hume, this violation is by definition nonrepeatable.[35] If miracles are nonrepeatable, there could at most be one confirmatory instance of (H*). However, there are billions of confirmatory instances of (L*). Again, the probability of (L*) must be higher than the probability of (H*).

There is much that is wrong with this argument. It assumes that our evidence for the laws of nature is based not on testimony but on personal experience. But it is not. For example, our knowledge of the truth of (L*) rests in large part on the testimony of others. Indeed, most of us have little direct experience of dead people. Our limited direct experience is supplemented and expanded by fallible human testimony. However, if we understand experience to include not just an individual's direct experience of no dead person's coming back to life but the combined experience of civilization that is based in part on testimony, then the argument seems to beg the question against (H*). After all, there have been a few reports of people coming back to life. How can we know *a priori* that their probability is low?

Moreover, if Hume's argument assumes the nonrepeatability of miracles, then the argument is further weakened. There is no reason why (H*) could not be confirmed by many instances. However, there is no reason why (H*) must be confirmed by many instances for (H*) to be probable. One confirmatory instance is enough. Suppose there were reports of Gandhi's being brought back to life (E). If the evidence for E was extremely good, there would be excellent grounds for thinking that (H*) was true and (L*) was false. For example, if the witnesses to E were extremely numerous, independent, and reliable, if there was excellent physical evidence of Gandhi's being brought back to life—video pictures, EEG records that brain death had actually occurred, and so on—this might be enough to reject (L*) as a law of nature.[36]

This Humean argument fails to show that there is any *a priori* reason to suppose that it is impossible to have strong evidence for the existence of miracles. But there are excellent *a posteriori* reasons, suggested by Hume and others,[37] to suppose that the evidence is not good.[38] Indeed, anyone who would argue for the existence of miracles must overcome at least three *a posteriori* obstacles.

The believer in miracles must give reasons to suppose that the event E, the alleged miracle, will probably not be explained by any unknown scientific laws that govern $nature_n$. Since presumably not all the laws that govern $nature_n$ have been discovered, this seems difficult to do. The advocates of the miracle hypothesis must argue the probability that E will not be explained by future science, utilizing heretofore undiscovered laws that govern $nature_n$. Given the scientific progress of the last two centuries, such a prediction seems rash and unjustified.[39] In medicine, for example, diseases that were considered mysterious are now understood without appeal to supernatural powers. Further progress seems extremely likely; indeed, many so-called miracle cures of the past may one day be understood, as some have already been, in terms of psychosomatic medicine. Whether other mysterious phenomena will be explained by future scientific investigation is less certain, but the possibility cannot be ruled out. The luminous figure on the dome of St. Mary's Church of Zeitoun may be explained in the future by parapsychology. For example, Dr. Scott Rogo has suggested that the luminous figure can be explained in terms of the psychic energy generated by the Zeitounians' expectation of the visitation of the Virgin Mary.[40] At the present time Rogo's theory is pure speculation, and there are no known laws connected with the manifestations of psychic energy. But the believer in miracles must suppose that probably no laws about psychic energy *or any other laws* of nature$_n$ will be discovered that could explain the luminous figure.

Believers in miracles may argue that some events not only are unexplained in terms of laws governing nature$_n$ but are in conflict with them. Someone who walks on water has done something that not only is not explained by the laws governing nature$_n$ but is in conflict with those laws. But then, in order to explain the event, it is necessary to appeal to the laws governing nature$_b$. The ability to walk on water indicates the causal influences of a supernatural power that goes beyond the working of nature$_n$.

The difficulty here is to know whether the conflict is genuine or is merely apparent. This is the second great obstacle for believers in miracles. They must argue that the conflict is more probably genuine than apparent, but this is difficult to argue, for there are many ways that appearances can mislead and deceive in cases of this sort.

One way in which an apparent conflict can arise is by means of deception, fraud, or trickery. The difficulties of ruling out hoax, fraud, or deception are legend. We have excellent reason today to believe that some contemporary faith healers use fraud and deceit to make it seem that they have paranormal powers and are getting miracle cures.[41] These men have little trouble in duping a public that is surely no less sophisticated than that of biblical times. Even in modern parapsychology, where laboratory controls are used, there is great difficulty in ruling out explanations of the results in terms of fraud. By various tricks, trained experimenters in ESP research have been deceived into thinking that genuine paranormal events have occurred.[42] Parapsychologists themselves have resorted to fraud— so-called experimenter fraud—to manufacture evidence favorable to the reality of ESP. It takes the most stringent controls, the use of experts such as magicians trained in detecting fakery, and inconsistence on independent investigators in order to have confidence that the positive results in ESP research are not based upon deceit. Thus when eyewitnesses report that they have seen yogis levitating, even when these reports are accompanied by photographs, they must be treated with skepticism unless there is excellent reason to rule out the possibility of fraud and hoax on the part of the yogi as well as of the witness to the event.

If it takes control and precaution today in scientific laboratories in order to eliminate fraud and deceit, what credence should we give to reports of miracles made in biblical times by less than educated and less sophisticated people without systematic controls against fraud?[43] The plausible reply would be: "Very little." One surely must ask: Did Jesus really walk on water or only appear to because he was walking on rocks below the surface?[44] Did Jesus turn the water into wine, or did he only appear to because he had substituted wine for water by some clever trick? The hypothesis that Jesus was a magician has been seriously considered by some biblical scholars.[45] The success of some contemporary faith healers and psychic wonders in convincing the public by the use of deception and fraud indicates that it was possible for Jesus, if he was a magician, to do the same.

Further, alleged miracles may not be due to some trick or fraud but to a misperception based on religious bias. People full of religious zeal may see what they want to see, not what is really there. We know from empirical studies that people's beliefs and prejudices influence what they see and report.[46] It would not then be surprising that religious people who report seeing a miraculous event have projected their biases onto the actual event. Did Jesus still the storm (Matt. 8.23-27), or did the storm by coincidence happen to stop when "he rose and rebuked the wind and the sea"? And did witnesses in their religious zeal "see" him stilling the storm?

In addition, religious attitudes often foster uncritical belief and acceptance. Indeed, in a religious context uncritical belief is often thought to be a value, doubt and skepticism a vice. Thus a belief arising in a religious context and held at first with only modest conviction may tend to reinforce itself and develop into an unshakable conviction. It would hardly be surprising, then, if in this context some ordinary natural event were seen as a miracle.

For another thing, an event that is not a miracle may appear like one if the observer has incomplete knowledge of the law governing nature$_n$ that appears to be violated. A scientific law holds only in a known range of conditions, not in all conditions. Thus Boyle's law holds only for gases in a specific temperature range; Newton's laws only correctly predict the mass of a body at accelerations not close to the speed of light. Often the range of application of a law becomes known with precision only years after the law itself is first formulated. Thus consider some physiological and psychological laws governing sight that seem to conflict with the apparent miracle of a faith healer's restoring someone's sight. This law may hold only in a fixed range of applications, and in special circumstances other laws governing nature$_n$ that explain the restoration of sight may hold. Both sorts of laws may be derivable from a comprehensive, but as yet unknown, theory. The advocates of miracles must maintain that an explanation of the event in terms of such a theory is less likely than an explanation by some supernatural power.

However, even if one shows it is more likely than not that some event is in conflict with deterministic scientific laws governing nature$_n$, this would not mean it is more likely than not that the event is a miracle. In other words, it would not show that the event could only be explained by the laws governing nature$_b$.

This brings us to the third great obstacle: What we thought were strictly deterministic laws may in fact be statistical laws. Since statistical laws are compatible with rare occurrences of uncaused events, the events designated as miracles may be wrongly designated since they may be uncaused—that is, they may be neither naturally nor supernaturally determined. Advocates of the miracle hypothesis, then, must show that the existence of miracles is more probable than the existence of uncaused events.

In sum, the advocates of the hypothesis that event E is a miracle (H_m) must show that H_m is more probable than the following:

(H_s) Event E will be explained by future scientific progress when more laws governing nature$_n$ are discovered.
(H_g) Event E seems compatible with laws that govern nature$_n$ but it is not.
(H_u) Event E is uncaused.

There is no easy way to assess the comparative probabilities that are involved. However, as we have already seen, the progress of science, the history of deception and fraud connected with miracles and the paranormal, and the history of gullibility and misperception all strongly suggest that (H_s) and (H_g) are better supported than (H_m).

It is less clear what one should say about the comparative probability of (H_m) and (H_u). Both seem unlikely in the light of the evidence. But it is certainly not clear that (H_u) is less likely than (H_m). Both seem unlikely in the light of the evidence. But it is certainly not clear that (H_u) is less likely than (H_m). On the one hand, science already allows indeterminacy on the micro level—for example, in quantum theory. On the other hand, macro indeterminacy, the sort of indeterminacy that would be relevant to explaining miracles, is not less incompatible with the present scientific world view than it is with (H_m). At the very least one can say that there is no reason to prefer (H_m) over (H_n) on probabilistic grounds.

Evidence of Miracles in One Religion as Evidence Against Contrary Religions

In a well-known passage in the *Inquiry*, David Hume says:

> Let us consider, that, in matters of religion, whatever is different is contrary; and that it is impossible the religions of ancient Rome, of Turkey, of Siam, and of China should, all of them, be established on any solid foundation. Every miracle, therefore, pretended to have

been wrought in any of these religions (and all of them abound in miracles), as its direct scope is to establish the particular system to which it is attributed, so has it the same force, though more indirectly, to overthrow every other system. In destroying a rival system, it likewise destroys the credit of those miracles, on which that system is established; so that all the prodigies of different religions are to be regarded as contrary facts, and the evidence of these prodigies, whether strong or weak, as opposite to each other.[47]

Hume has been interpreted as claiming in this argument that every alleged miracle whose occurrence would be evidence in favor of a given religion is such that its occurrence would be evidence against any religion contrary to the first. He has also been interpreted as arguing that the evidence in favor of the existence of a miracle (which would constitute evidence for one religion) would be evidence against the occurrence of any miracle (which would constitute evidence in favor of a contrary religion).

Put more formally, it has been argued that Hume is maintaining the validity of two arguments.[48] The first argument is as follows:

(1) E_1 increases the probability of H_1 more than H_2.
(2) H_1 and H_2 are contraries.

---

(3)   Therefore, E_1 decreases the probability of H_2.

The second argument is as follows:

(1′) E_1 is evidence for H_1 and against H_2.
(2′) E_2 is evidence for H_2 and against H_1.
(3′) H_1 and H_2 are contraries.

(4′)   Therefore, E_1 is evidence against E_2 and conversely.

However, both of these arguments are invalid.

Consider the following counterexample to the first argument form. Suppose that the fact that a .45 caliber gun was used to murder Smith (E) is evidence that Evans is the murderer (H_1). (We suppose Evans is suspect and always uses a .45 caliber gun.) Suppose further that H_2 (Jones is the murderer) is a contrary to H_1. Evidence E may still support H_2 although not as strongly. (We know that Jones uses a .45 caliber only 80 percent of the time.)

Consider the following counterexample to the second argument form. Let H_1 and H_2 represent what they did in the preceding example. Evans's fingerprints on the gun are evidence for H_2 and against H_1. Jones's footprints at the scene of the crime are evidence for H_2 and against H_1. But the one piece of evidence is not evidence against the other piece of evidence.

In the religious context, Jesus' walking on water (E_1) may be evidence for the truth of Christianity (H_1) but also for the truth of Hinduism (H_2), since Hindus might consider Jesus a manifestation of the absolute, not an incarnation of a personal God. A Baal priest curing a blind man (E_2), itself evidence for the hypothesis (H_3) that Baal is the supreme god, may support the fact that a priest of Zeus could cure a blind man, since we now have evidence that priests sometimes cure blind men. This in turn would be indirect evidence that the report that a priest of Zeus cured a blind man was true (E_3), which in turn would be evidence that Zeus was the supreme god (H_4).

When it is interpreted in the above way, Hume's two-part argument is invalid, but according to a different interpretation at least the first part of the argument is valid.[49] In the passage cited above, Hume's words suggest not just that the miracles of one religion make that religion more probable than it was before the occurrence of the miracles, but that the miracles make the religion more probable than not. Recall that he says it is impossible that rival religions should be "established on any solid foundation" by the evidence from miracles. Construed in this way, his argument becomes:

(1) Miracles $M_1, M_2, \ldots M_n$ occurring in the context of religion R_1 provide evidence that R_1 is more probable than not. $[P(R_1, M_1, M_2, \ldots M_n) > 0.5]$

(2) Religion R_1 and religion R_2 are contraries

---

(3) Therefore, R_2 is less probable than not. $[P(R_2, M_1, M_2, \ldots M_n) < 0.5]$

However, a similar argument could be used to show that R_1 is less probable than not by citing other miracles that occur within the context of R_2. Hume was therefore correct to suppose that the miracles of one system can "destroy" rival systems. Of course, one could escape from Hume's argument by maintaining that the evidence of the miracles of one religion does not make it more probable than not but only more probable than it was without this evidence. However, Hume was no doubt correct to suppose that at least in his day the existence of the miracles of one religion was often supposed to make that religion more probable than not—that is, to use his words, to establish that religion on a solid foundation. What advocates of this way of arguing overlooked was that it could also be used to establish rival systems and thus indirectly "destroy" their own system.

What about the second part of Hume's argument: that the evidence of the miracles of one religion destroys the credibility of the evidence of miracles in another religion? Here Hume was clearly wrong, and I know no way of revising Hume's argument that is in keeping with its spirit. This is not to say that one cannot argue from the problematic nature of miracles in the context of one religion to the problematic nature in another. But what Hume was apparently trying to do was to argue thus: If evidence E_1 in religion R_1 allows us to show that R_1 is more probable than not, and if evidence E_1 in religion R_2 allows us to show that R_2 is more probable than not, then E_1 makes E_2 improbable and E_2 makes E_1 improbable. This inference is wrong. But it would not be wrong to argue that since the evidence of alleged miracles associated with, say, the Christian religion is weak, then probably the evidence for miracles in other religions is also weak. This would be a straightforward inductive argument, and its strength would be a function of the representative nature of evidence for Christian miracles. If such evidence is not atypical of miracles in other religions and the evidence is weak, then one is justified in making such an inference. Unfortunately, in the above-quoted passage Hume does not seem to be giving this completely sound argument.

Miracles at Lourdes

So far we have considered in a general way the difficulty in determining whether an event is a miracle. It would be useful now to relate the problems just outlined to a concrete case. In modern times the most famous occurrences of alleged miracles have been at Lourdes in France. These are probably the best documented and most carefully considered in history. If these alleged miracles are suspect, we would have good ground for maintaining that other claims of miracles—in more distant times, when superstition prevailed and objective documentation was either nonexistent or at least much less in evidence—should not be taken seriously.

It all began in February 1858, when a 14-year-old uneducated girl named Bernadette Soubirous, while collecting wood near the grotto of Massabielle in Lourdes, allegedly saw a beautiful lady wearing a white dress with a blue sash, with a yellow rose on each foot and a yellow rosary. Bernadette allegedly saw the Lady of the Grotto 18 times. Speaking the local patois, the Lady told Bernadette to pray for sinners and to tell the priest to have a chapel built. She also said that she wished people to come to the grotto in procession. It was claimed by those in attendance that during one session with the Lady of the Grotto, spring water miraculously came from the ground when Bernadette touched it. In another incident Bernadette knelt before the Lady of the Grotto with her hand cupped around the flame of a candle. Those in attendance claimed that the candle slipped out of place, "causing the flames to dance between Bernadette's fingers for a good ten minutes."[50] Bernadette never flinched, it was said, and the fire did not burn her. On another occasion Bernadette claimed that the Lady said, "I am the Immaculate Conception."

Naturally, Bernadette's claims caused a great stir at the time. She was denounced by skeptics as a fraud, yet many people flocked to the grotto to see her transfixed by her own vision. After a four-year inquiry the Roman Catholic Church declared that Bernadette's vision was the Virgin Mary. Pilgrims, mostly from the surrounding area, began to visit the shrine that had been built there eight years after Bernadette's vision. By 1947 more than a million people were coming from all parts of France. In 1979, the centennial year of Bernadette's death, about 4.5 million people visited Lourdes—only one-third of them from France. Although the Lady of the Grotto never said to Bernadette that people would be cured at Lourdes, several cures were reported at the very beginning of the pilgrimages to Lourdes: A stone mason with one blind eye applied earth moistened from the spring to his eye, and his sight was restored a few days later; a mother dipped her paralyzed son into the spring and he was instantly cured.

Lourdes is unique among Catholic shrines where miracles are supposed to occur, for only at Lourdes is there a definite procedure for investigating and recognizing miracles. The procedure is this:[51]

(1) A person whose health is dramatically altered by a trip to Lourdes may come before the medical bureau at Lourdes. The bureau has one full-time physician, who is joined in examining and interrogating the pilgrims by other doctors who happen to be visiting Lourdes at the time.

(2) If a dossier (an official medical file) is to be started, the person alleged to be cured must have a "complete" medical record confirming the nature of the illness and dates of recent treatments. In order to rule out the possibility that the alleged cure was brought about by ordinary medical treatment the pilgrim has undergone, the effectiveness of the treatment must be known.

(3) Special criteria of recovery must be met. The illness must be life-threatening and must be a distinct organic disorder. The recovery must be sudden and unforeseen, and it must occur "without convalescence." There must be "objective evidence"—X-rays, blood tests, biopsies—that the pilgrim had the disease before becoming cured. No disease for which there is effective treatment is considered as a possible miracle. Further, the pilgrim must stay cured and is therefore required to return several times for reexamination.

(4) Cures that meet all these tests are submitted to an international medical committee, appointed by the bishop of the adjacent towns of Tarbes and Lourdes, that meets annually in Paris. The committee votes on one issue: Is the cure medically inexplicable?

(5) If the majority of the committee decides that the cure is inexplicable, the patient's dossier is given to the canonical commission headed by the bishop of the diocese in which the allegedly cured person lives. Only the church can make the final decision as to whether the event

is a miracle—that is, whether God has intervened in the natural course of events.

Before we consider the application of this procedure in actual practice, a few points should be noted in the light of previous discussion. First, it is difficult to see how the international committee that meets annually in Paris has the competence to decide if a cure is scientifically inexplicable in any absolute way—that is, in terms of $nature_n$. At best this committee would only have the competence to decide if the cure is scientifically explicable in terms of current knowledge of $nature_n$. This committee does not know what the future development of medical science will be; thus any judgment it makes about the absolute inexplicability of a cure in terms of $nature_n$ can and should have no particular authority.

In order to judge whether the cure is a miracle, one must be justified in believing that it will never and can never be explained in scientific terms—that is, in terms of $nature_n$. But would the committee have the competence to predict that, in the light of the evidence, probably no cure will ever be found? Given the rapid advances in medical knowledge, it is difficult to see that they would. Thus this committee's judgments exceed its scientific competence; indeed, a judgment of a committee *must* exceed its competence in order for it to be relevant to assessing whether a particular cure is a miracle.

Second, even if the international committee's judgment were justified that a particular cure was scientifically inexplicable in some absolute sense, the church seems to have no rational basis for making the final judgment that (a) the cure was a miracle and (b) the miracle was caused by God. As we have already seen, the cure could be uncaused. If so, it would be inexplicable in principle but not a miracle. Further, even if it was caused by some supernatural force or forces, this need not be the Christian God. Church officials who make the final decision about whether a cure is a miracle and, if so, is caused by God apparently ignore these alternatives. As a result, the final decision that the cure is a miracle explained by God's intervention is more like a leap of faith than a rational decision.

So far we have argued that although the doctors on the international committee do not have the competence to decide that a cure is inexplicable in terms of the law of $nature_n$ in some absolute way, they do have the competence to decide if a cure is inexplicable in terms of present scientific knowledge of $nature_n$. However, although they have this competence *in principle*, things may in fact be quite different. The doctors of the international committee may not have adequately applied the procedures specified.

One case in point is that of Serge Perrin, a French accountant, who in 1970 while at Lourdes experienced a sudden recovery from a long illness. After investigation the international committee said that Perrin was suffering from "a case of recurring organic hemiplegia [paralysis of one side of the body] with ocular lesions, due to cerebral circulatory defects.[52]

They attempted to substantiate their findings in a 39-page document complete with a medical history of Perrin and his family, a review of the events leading up to his recovery, a detailed discussion of the symptoms of his illness, and supporting evidence including visual field diagrams and X-ray pictures. On the basis of its diagnosis and report, the international committee declared his recovery scientifically inexplicable; the church finally declared Perrin's cure to be a miracle, the 64th and latest official miracle in the history of Lourdes.

But was Perrin's cure inexplicable in terms of current scientific knowledge, let alone inexplicable in some absolute sense? In light of recent evidence this seems dubious. A small sample of specialists in the United States who independently examined the document produced by the international committee of doctors found the cure of Perrin very suspicious, the data in the document highly problematic, the document obscure and filled with technical verbiage. For example, Donald H. Harter, professor and chairman of the department of neurology at Northwestern University Medical School in Chicago, found "an absence of *objective* neurological abnormalities." Drummond Rennie, associate professor of medicine at Harvard Medical School, maintained that the document presented by the international committee of doctors "was unscientific and totally unconvincing." Robert A. Levine, assistant clinical professor of ophthalmology at the University of Illinois, argued that the visual field diagrams presented in the documented are mislabeled and inconsistent with the text of the document. He called the description as a whole "a lot of mumbo jumbo."[53]

The doctors who reviewed the document found a variety of problems. For example, although crucial laboratory tests such as a spinal tap and radioactive brain scan were standard in most hospitals for diagnosing the illness Perrin was said to have, they were not performed. The reviewers also considered the diagnosis of hemiplegia implausible; because he had right leg weakness *and* left visual and motor symptoms, more than one side of Perrin's brain had to be involved. In addition, symptoms of generalized constriction of his visual field and various sensorimotor disturbances suggested hysteria rather than an organic illness. Moreover, the American specialists who reviewed the document maintained that if there was an organic illness at all, multiple sclerosis was the most likely explanation of Perrin's symptoms. However, it is well known that multiple sclerosis has fleeting symptoms with periodic severe flare-ups followed by remissions that are sometimes complete.

There are also problems accepting the 63rd and penultimate official miracle in the history of Lourdes.[54] In this 1963 case, while at Lourdes a 22-year-old Italian, Vittorio Micheli, experienced a sudden recovery from a sarcoma type of tumor on his hip that had destroyed part of the pelvis, iliac, and surrounding muscles. The Lourdes medical bureau said X-rays confirmed that a bone reconstruction had taken place that was unknown in the annals of medicine. In 1976 the church official recognized Micheli's recovery as a miracle.

However, as James Randi has pointed out in his investigation of this case, spontaneous regression of malignant tumors of the hip are not unknown in the annals of medicine.[55] To be sure, if Micheli's hip had been completely regenerated, this would indeed be unprecedented. But in order to verify that complete regeneration of the bone had taken place, exploratory surgery would have been necessary. X-rays cannot distinguish between a genuine regeneration and a regrowth known as a pseudo-arthrosis, which is not unknown in the annals of medicine. But there is no record of any surgical procedure being done to validate Micheli's complete regeneration. Indeed, Randi notes that a case virtually identical to Micheli's was reported in 1978 in the *Acta Orthopaedica Scandivanica*.[56] In both instances no medical treatment was reported, the recovery took place in the same way, and the results were the same. However, in this latter case no claim was made that a miracle had occurred.

Medical authorities to whom Randi submitted Micheli's dossier for examination were incredulous at the medical treatment Micheli is reported to have received. For example, according to the dossier the hospital waited 36 days before it took an X-ray and 43 days before it performed a biopsy. Moreover, according to the dossier Micheli lived in a military hospital for ten months before he went to Lourdes, during which time he received no medical treatment of any kind except painkillers, tranquilizers, and vitamins. On the other hand, there are hints in the dossier that he did receive drugs and radiation. All this is extremely puzzling and surely casts doubt on the accuracy of the dossier.

The problems with the 1963 Micheli case and the 1970 Perrin case suggest that there is something badly amiss in the application of the procedures used by the Catholic Church for officially declaring something a miracle cure at Lourdes. An apparently questionable diagnosis of Perrin and an unsubstantiated judgment about Micheli's cure were accepted by the Lourdes medical bureau and the international committee.

Furthermore, there is a general problem connected with the procedures at Lourdes that I have not yet mentioned: the expertise of the doctors who first examine a pilgrim at Lourdes who claims to have recovered from an illness. The only qualification needed for a person to join the full-time medical bureau doctor in examining an allegedly cured pilgrim is the person be a doctor and be visiting the shrine. But one might well question the objectivity of doctors who accompany the sick to Lourdes or who visit Lourdes for other reasons. For one thing, doctors who visit Lourdes may well get caught up in the awe and the excitement of the pilgrimage. For another, doctors who want to visit Lourdes may be initially disposed to accept miracle cures.

Every doctor has of course seen cures and remissions of diseases for which there is no explanation. Some of these diseases are self-limiting;

others, like multiple sclerosis, have periods of flare-ups and remissions; still others have hysterical origins. It is difficult to separate hysterical symptoms from organic ones. The problem is made more difficult by the fact that hysterical symptoms may follow and take the place of organic ones. Moreover, in some illnesses, among them multiple sclerosis, physical and hysterical symptoms can exist at the same time. As we have seen, doctors in the United States who reviewed the report of the international committee suggested that Perrin suffered from hysteria or multiple sclerosis; it is conceivable that he had both types of symptoms.

If the alleged miracle cures at Lourdes are merely remissions or are cures based on natural processes that are not understood by the examining physicians at Lourdes then one would expect that the number of inexplicable cures accepted by the Lourdes medical bureau would decline over the years as medical knowledge and sophistication increased. Indeed, this is precisely what has happened. From 1883 to 1947 nearly 5,000 cures were accepted as inexplicable by the physicians at the Lourdes medical bureau. This is approximately 78 per year. But from 1947 to 1980 only 28 cures were accepted as inexplicable, less than one per year.[57] And we may well expect that there will be further decreases in the "inexplicable" cures as medical knowledge increases. Such evidence surely casts doubt on the 64 official declared miracles at Lourdes, especially the earlier ones. If the doctors at the Lourdes medical bureau had had the expertise of contemporary doctors, it is doubtful that many of the alleged miracles that occurred before 1947 would have made it through the first screening.

Since the cures at Lourdes are perhaps the best documented of all the so-called miracle cures, and their evidential value seems dubious, one may well have grave doubts about other claims of miracle cures that are less well documented.

Indirect Miracles

Earlier in this chapter I provisionally defined a miracle as an event brought about by the exercise of a supernatural power. However, there is a modern view of miracles that is not captured by this definition,[58] namely that God set up the world in such a way that an unusual event would occur to serve as a sign or message to human beings. Suppose, for example, that God set up the world so that at a certain time in history the Red Sea would part. The parting would be governed by the laws of nature$_n$—for instance, a freak wind might part the sea. Given the circumstances surrounding the event, this parting would convey a message to religious believers. Although no direct intervention of God would be involved, God would be behind the scenes, setting up the particular working of nature$_n$ so that the Red Sea parted at the exact time needed to save his chosen people.

This view of miracles has become popular in modern philosophy, although it can be traced back at least to Maimonides. To accommodate this sort of case, my provisional definition is revised in the following way: A miracle is an event brought about by the direct or not necessarily direct exercise of a supernatural power to serve as a sign or communicate a message.[59] The second disjunct of the definition is necessary to account for miracles on the modern view (*indirect miracles* let us call them), and the first disjunct accounts for ones on the traditional view (let us call them *direct miracles*).

The difficulties with indirect miracles are apparent. Why believe that an event is a miracle in this indirect sense? Why not suppose that it is merely a coincidence? Moreover, even if one has good reason to suppose that something is an indirect miracle, there is no good reason to believe that God, rather than some other supernatural force, indirectly brought it about.

There is an additional problem. One wonders how much free will is left to humans on this view of miracles. Consider the parting of the Red Sea. If the event had occurred an hour earlier, it would have been of no help; if the event had occurred an hour later, it would have been too late to help the Israelites. This seems to entail that the Israelites, in order to be at the right place at the right time, could not have chosen any differently than they did. For example, if they had decided to rest a little longer along the way, God's plan would have been upset; the sea would have parted before they arrived.

This seems to conflict with the commonly held religious belief that humans have free will and that even God cannot know what they will decide, in that, given the notion of an indirect miracle, it is essential to know what human beings will decide so that the miracle will occur at the right time.[60]

Conclusion

I must conclude that there is no *a priori* reason for there not to be miracles—no reason even for there not to be good evidence for miracles. However, there are difficult *a posteriori* obstacles to surmount before one can claim that miracles have occurred in either the direct or the indirect sense. Furthermore, even if there were good reasons to suppose that miracles existed in either sense, this would not necessarily mean that the existence of miracles provides inductive support for theism. As we have seen, the existence of miracles provides inductive support for theism only in the existence of a miracle is more probable relative to theism and background information than it is relative to the negation of theism and background information. But it is not at all clear that it is. Thus the argument from miracles fails.

Endnotes

*Reprinted from Chapter 7 of Michael Martin, *Atheism: A Philosophical Justification*. Philadelphia: Temple University Press, 1990. © 1990 by Temple University. All rights reserved.

1 See Alan Richardson, *The Miracle-Stories of the Gospels* (New York: Harper & Brothers, 1941).

2 See D. Scott Rogo, *Miracles* (New York: Dial Press, 1982).

3 Ibid., pp. 250-257.

4 Ibid., pp. 33-34.

5 As we saw in Chapter 4, Aquinas appealed to miracles occurring within the Christian tradition to justify the reliance on Christian revelations.

6 See Harry A. Wolfson, "Philo Judaeus," *The Encyclopedia of Philosophy*, ed. Paul Edwards (New York and London: Macmillan and Free Press, 1967), vol. 6, p. 152.

7 Fazlur Rahman, "Islamic Philosophy," *Encyclopedia of Philosophy*, vol. 4, p. 222

8 The canon runs as follows: "If anyone shall say that miracles cannot happen. . . or that the divine origin of the Christian religion cannot properly be proved by them: let them be anathema." See H. Denzinger, *Enchiridion Symbolorum*, 29th rev. ed. (Freiburg im Breisgau: Herder, 1953), sec. 1813. Quoted in Antony Flew, *God: A Critical Enquiry*, 2d ed. (La Salle, Ind.: Open Court, 1984), p. 136.

9 For an analysis of some recent views on miracles, see Ernst and Marie-Luise Keller, *Miracles in Dispute* (Philadelphia: Fortress Press, 1969).

10 Flew, *God: A Critical Enquiry*, p. 136.

11 Richard Swinburne, *The Existence of God* (Oxford: Clarendon Press, 1979), chap. 12.

12 Richard S. Purtill, *Thinking About Religion: A Philosophical Introduction to Religion* (Englewood Cliffs, N.J.: Prentice Hall, 1978), pp. 124-134. Reprinted in Louis P. Pojman, *Philosophy of Religion* (Belmont, Calif.: Wadsworth, 1987), pp. 287-289.

13 See, for example, Antony Flew, "Miracles," *Encyclopedia of Philosophy*, vol. 5, p. 346.

14 I am indebted here to Paul Fitzgerald, "Miracles," *Philosophical Forum*, 18, 1985, pp. 48-64. The definition adopted here is compatible with the view that every event is brought about by some supernatural power. It is also compatible with the view that the world would not exist without the conserving power of some supernatural being. See Alvin Plantinga, "Is Theism Really a Miracle?" *Faith and Philosophy*, 3, 1986, p. 111. Our definition should be compared with Richard Swinburne's in *The Concept of Miracle* (London: Macmillan, 1970), p. 1. Swinburne gives a general definition of a miracle as an event of an extraordinary kind brought about by a god and of religious significance. However, he argues that the word is sometimes used in a narrower or wider sense.

15 Is it logically possible for a human being to have supernatural powers? It may be argued that it is logically possible for humans to have powers of ESP and psycho-kinesis. These are often called paranormal powers, but the difference between a paranormal and supernatural power is not completely clear. See Fitzgerald, "Miracles," pp. 5051; see also Stephen E. Braude, *ESP and Psychokinesis* (Philadelphia: Temple University Press, 1979), pp. 242-263.

[16] Fitzgerald, "Miracles" pp. 58-62.

[17] See, for example, Swinburne, *Existence of God*, pp. 228-230; see also Swinburne, *Concept of Miracle*, pp. 26-27.

[18] For a similar argument, see Andrew Rein, "Repeatable Miracles?" *Analysis*, 46, 1986, pp. 109-112.

[19] See the special issue of *Free Inquiry*, 6, Spring 1986, on faith healing.

[20] Swinburne, *Existence of God*, chap. 1.

[21] See Swinburne, *Concept of Miracle*, chap. 6.

[22] Criticisms similar to this were raised by eighteenth-century deists Thomas Woolston and Thomas Chubb. See R. M. Burns, *The Great Debate on Miracles* (Lewisburg, Penna.: Bucknell University Press, 1981), pp. 77-79.

[23] This argument from miracles against the existence of God has obvious similarities to the argument from evil against the existence of God, which I consider in Part II. See Christine Overall, "Miracles as Evidence Against the Existence of God," *Southern Journal of Philosophy*, 13, 1985, pp. 347-353.

[24] C. S. Lewis, *Miracles* (New York: Macmillian, 1978), chaps. 12-16. Lewis argues at some length that belief in the Christian God is compatible with miracles. This does not seem very controversial. The crucial question is whether the existence of miracles gives more support to theism than to other supernatural theories. Lewis does not address this question.

[25] Ibid., pp. 10-11.

[26] Ibid., p. 6.

[27] It seems clear that Lewis is referring to what above we call nature.

[28] Lewis, *Miracles*, chap. 2.

[29] Ibid., chap. 5.

[30] Ibid., p. 18.

[31] See, for example, D. M. Armstrong, *Belief, Truth, and Knowledge* (London: Cambridge University Press, 1974), chap. 6.

[32] Lewis, *Miracles*, p. 36. For example, see Richard Brandt, *Ethical Theory* (Englewood Cliffs, N.J.: Prentice Hall, 1959), chap. 7.

[33] See David Hume, *An Inquiry Concerning Human Understanding* (New York: Liberal Arts Press, 1955), sec. 10. Reprinted under the title "Against Miracles," in Pojman, *Philosophy of Religion*, pp. 264-273.

[34] Cf. J. L. Mackie, *The Miracle of Theism* (Oxford: Clarendon Press, 1982), pp. 26-29, and Fitzgerald, "Miracles," p. 56.

[35] For example, Fitzgerald in "Miracles" clearly interprets Hume in this way. Whether Richard Swinburne "Miracles," *Philosophical Quarterly*, 18, 1986; reprinted under the title "For the Possibility of Miracles," in Pojman, *Philosophy of Religion*, pp. 273-279 so interprets Hume is less clear. Whether Hume actually held that miracles by definition are nonrepeatable is uncertain.

[36] Cf. Gary Colwell, "On Defining Away Miracles," *Philosophy*, 57, 1982, pp. 327-336. Notice, however, that this evidence would not be enough to suppose that E was not governed by a law of nature. Consequently, it would not be enough to suppose that E was a miracle.

[37] As Burns has shown, Hume was not the first to propose the sort of *a posteriori* arguments found in "Of Miracles" against the existence of miracles. See Burns, *Great Debate on Miracles*, chaps. 3 and 4.

[38] See Mackie, *Miracle of Theism*, pp. 14-16, for a lucid exposition of these arguments.

[39] John B. Gill, "Miracles with Method," *Sophia*, 16, 1977, pp. 19-26. Gill has argued that miracle claims are compatible with scientific progress, since such claims may be only tentatively held and are compatible with reconsidering the claims in the light of new evidence. Although it may well be true that such openmindedness is logically compatible with miracle claims, one wonders if it in fact works this way. Historically it seems clear that belief in miracles has been detrimental to scientific progress; and given the psychology of typical believers, it is likely to remain so. Moreover, even if such claims are put forth tentatively, the question is whether they are justified in the light of the rapid increases in knowledge in such fields as medical science. As we show later, in discussing the cures at Lourdes, as medical knowledge has increased the number of inexplicable cures has decreased. This evidence suggests that miracle claims in the area of medical science, even if tentatively held, may be unjustified in terms of the progress of medicine.

[40] Rogo, *Miracles*, p. 256. Oddly enough, Rogo does not even consider the possibility that the luminous figure may have been the result of fraud and deception. The technical capacity to create such a luminous figure certainly existed in the late 1960s, yet Rogo provides no evidence of any attempt to rule out fraud.

[41] See James Randi, "'Be Healed in the Name of God!' An Exposé of the Reverend W. V. Grant," *Free Inquiry*, 6, 1986, pp. 8-19. See also James Randi, *The Faith Healers* (Buffalo, N.Y.: Prometheus Books, 1987)

[42] See James Randi, "The Project Alpha Experiment: Part I, The First Two Years," *Skeptical Inquirer*, 7, Summer 1983, pp. 24-33; "Part 2, Beyond the Laboratory," *Skeptical Inquirer*, 8, Fall 1983, pp. 36-45.

[43] Cf. Gary Colwell, "Miracles and History," *Sophia*, 22, 1983, pp. 9-14. Colwell argues that in the Bible in Lk. 24:1-11 and Jn. 20:24-29 one finds examples of skeptical humanity among Jesus' followers who were forced to accept his miracles from love of truth. But it is unclear why Colwell accepts these biblical stories as true, since there are many inconsistencies in the story of the resurrection, where the examples of skeptical humanity are supposed to be found. Furthermore, Colwell ignores the independent evidence we have from contemporary faith healers, indicating the difficulty of being skeptical when one is deeply involved in a religious movement. See Paul Kurtz, *The Transcendental Temptation* (Buffalo, N.Y.: Prometheus Books, 1986), pp. 153-160, for an analysis of these inconsistencies; and see Randi, *Faith Healers*, for the lack of skepticism in the context of faith healing.

[44] Carl Friedrich Bahrdt, a German theologian of the Enlightenment, suggested that Jesus walked on floating pieces of timber. For a discussion of Bahrdt's views see Ernst and Marie-Luise Keller, *Miracles in Dispute*, pp. 69-70. The Kellers raise two objections to Bahrdt's explanation. They argue that according to Scripture the boat was not near the shore, and that in any case Jesus' disciples would have noticed the timber. However, it is uncertain whether Scripture is correct about the location of the boat. In any case, if we substitute rocks for timber, the location of the boat according to Scripture can be accepted. Rocks below the surface of the water may extend for many furlongs out to sea. The Kellers mention Bahrdt's not-implausible explanation of the failure of the disciples to notice. "They were 'held prisoner' by the prejudices of their own miracle-believing age—with constantly inflamed imaginations—always saw more in the phenomena than was there in reality" (p. 71).

45 See Morton Smith, *Jesus the Magician* (New York: Harper & Row, 1978).

46 See, for example, A. Daniel Yarmey, *The Psychology of Eyewitness Testimony* (New York: Free Press, 1979).

47 Hume, *Inquiry Concerning Human Understanding*, pp. 129-130.

48 See Bruce Langtry, "Hume on Miracles and Contrary Religions," *Sophia*, 14, 1975, pp. 29-34.

49 Cf. David A. Conway, "Miracles, Evidence and Contrary Religion," *Sophia*, 22, 1983, pp. 3-14; Bruce Langtry, "Miracles and Rival Systems of Religion," *Sophia*, 24, 1985, pp. 21-31.

50 Ellen Bernstein, "Lourdes," *Encyclopedia Britannica*, Medical and Health Annual, 1982, p.130.

51 Ibid., pp. 131-133.

52 Ibid., p. 134.

53 Ibid.

54 See Patrick Marnharm, *Lourdes: A Modern Pilgrimage* (New York: Coward, McCann and Geoghegan, 1981).

55 Randi, *Faith Healers*, pp. 27-29.

56 *Acta Orthopaedica Scandinavica*, 49, 1978, pp. 49-53. Cited in Randi, *Faith Healers*, pp. 28-29.

57 Bernstein, "Lourdes," p. 139.

58 See Fitzgerald, "Miracles," p. 61.

59 Ibid.

60 As we shall see in Chapter 15 on the free will defense, some philosophers have argued that free will in the contracausal sense, in which human decisions are uncaused, is compatible with God's knowing how human beings will decide and how they would decide under certain hypothetical circumstances. However, as I argue, this view is difficult to make sense of.

Study Questions

1. What are the essentials of a miracle on Michael Martin's account?

2. Why does Martin think that there is no *a priori* reason why a miracle could not be repeated many times?

3. Why does Martin conclude that one does not have to choose between naturalism and supernaturalism prior to answering the question whether miracles have occurred?

4. What is the difficulty in "showing the existence of miracles"?

5. What is Martin's final verdict on miracles?

32

For the Possibility of Miracles

Richard G. Swinburne

One of the most vigorous critics of Hume has been Richard Swinburne, professor of philosophy of religion at Oxford University, who in our second reading takes issue with him. Swinburne first inquires whether there could be evidence that a law of nature had been violated and, second, whether there could be evidence that the violation was due to a god. To satisfy the first inquiry, we would have to have good reason to believe that an event has occurred contrary to the predictions of a law that we had good reason to believe to be a law of nature; and furthermore we would have to have good reason to believe that events similar to the event would not occur in circumstances similar to those of the original occurrence. For if the event were repeatable, we would have to account for both events through the formulation of a law. Swinburne's example is levitation, a person's rising into the air and remaining there.

But to be a miracle the violation of a natural law would have to be the work of a god, who is not a material object. What kind of evidence would we have to have to believe that a divine being had intervened in our world? Here Swinburne distinguishes between situations in which we do and in which we do not have sufficient circumstantial evidence to warrant our attributing the anomalous event to the work of an invisible deity. The circumstantial evidence must be strong before we are justified in believing that the event is a genuine miracle. An answer to a prayer, for example, fulfills the necessary conditions.*

In this article I wish to investigate whether there could be strong historical evidence for the occurrence of miracles, and contrary to much writing which has derived from Hume's celebrated chapter "Of Miracles," I shall argue that there could be. I understand by a miracle a violation of a law of Nature by a god, that is, a very powerful rational being who is not a material object (viz., is invisible and intangible). My definition of a miracle is thus approximately the same as Hume's: "a transgression of a law of nature by a particular volition of the Deity or by the interposition of some invisible agent."[1] It has been questioned by many biblical scholars whether this is what the biblical writers understood by the terms translated into English 'miracle'. I do not propose to enter into this controversy. Suffice it to say that many subsequent Christian theologians have understood by 'miracle' roughly what I understand by the term and that much medieval and modern apologetic which appeals to purported miracles as evidence of the truth of the Christian revelation has had a similar understanding of miracle to mine.

I shall take the question in two parts. I shall enquire first whether there could be evidence that a law of nature has been violated, and secondly, if there can be such evidence, whether there could be evidence that the violation was due to a god.

First, then, can there be evidence that a law of nature has been violated? It seems natural to understand, as Ninian Smart[2] does, by a violation of a law of nature, an occurrence of a non-repeatable counter-instance to a law of nature. Clearly, as Hume admitted, events contrary to predictions of formulae which we had good reason to believe to be laws of nature often occur. But if we have good reason to believe that they have occurred and good reason to believe that similar events would occur in similar circumstances, then we have good reason to believe that the formulae which we previously believed to be the laws of nature were not in fact such laws. Repeatable counter-instances do not violate laws of nature, they just show propositions purporting to state laws of nature to be false. But if we have good reason to believe that an event E has occurred contrary to predictions of a formula L which we have good reason to believe to be a law of nature, and we have good reason to believe that events similar to E would not occur in circumstances as similar as we like in any respect to those of the original occurrence, then we do not have reason to believe that L is not a law of nature. For any modified formula which allowed us to predict E would allow us to predict similar events in similar circumstances and hence, we have good reason to believe, would give false predictions. Whereas if we leave the formula L unmodified, it will, we have good reason to believe, give correct predictions in all other conceivable circumstances. Hence if we are to say that any law of nature is operative in the field in question we must say that it is L. This seems a natural thing to say rather than to say that no law of nature operates in the field. Yet E is contrary to the predictions of L. Hence, for want of a better expression, we say that E has violated the law of nature L. If the use of the word 'violated' suggests too close an analogy between laws of nature and civil or moral laws, that is unfortunate. Once we have explained, as above, what is meant by a violation of a law of nature, no subsequent confusion need arise.

The crucial question, not adequately discussed by Smart, however, is what would be good reason for believing that an event E, if it occurred, was a non-repeatable as opposed to a repeatable counter-instance to a formula L which we have on all other evidence good reason to believe to be a law of nature. The evidence that E is a repeatable counter-instance would be that a new formula L^1 fairly well confirmed by the data as a law of nature can be set up. A formula is confirmed by data, if the data obtained so far are predicted by the formula, if new predictions are successful and if the formula is a simple and coherent one relative to the collection of data.

Compatible with any finite set of data, there will always be an infinite number of possible formulae from which the data can be predicted. We can rule out many by further tests, but however many tests we make we shall still have only a finite number of data and hence an infinite number of formulae compatible with them.

But some of these formulae will be highly complex relative to the data, so that no scientist would consider that the data were evidence that those formulae were true laws of nature. Others are very simple formulae such that the data can be said to provide evidence that they are true laws of nature. Thus suppose the scientist's task is to find a formula accounting for marks on a graph, observed at (1, 1), (2, 2), (3, 3), and (4, 4), the first number of each pair being the x co-ordinate and the second the y co-ordinate. One formula which would predict these marks is x = y. Another one is $(x - 1) (x - 2) (x - 3) (x - 4) + x = y$. But clearly we would not regard the data as supporting the second formula. It is too clumsy a formula to explain four observations. Among simple formulae supported by the data, the simplest is the best supported and regarded, provisionally, as correct. If the formula survives further tests, that increases the evidence in its favour as a true law.

Now if for E and for all other relevant data we can construct a formula L^1 from which the data can be derived and which either makes successful predictions in other circumstances where L makes bad predictions, or is a fairly simple formula, so that from the fact that it can predict E, and L cannot, we have reason to believe that its predictions, if tested, would be better than those of L in other circumstances, then we have good reason to believe that L^1 is the true law in the field. The formula will indicate under what circumstances divergences from L similar to E will occur. The evidence thus indicates that they will occur under these circumstances and hence that E is a repeatable counter-instance to the original formula L.

Suppose, however, that for E and all the other data of the field we can construct no new formula L^1 which yields more successful predictions than L in other examined circumstances, nor one which is fairly simple relative to the data; but for all the other data except E the simple formula L does yield good predictions. And suppose that as the data continue to accumulate, L remains a completely successful predictor and there remains no reason to suppose that a simple formula L^1 from which all the other data and E can be derived can be constructed. The evidence then indicates that the divergence from L will not be repeated and hence that E is a non-repeatable counter-instance to a law of nature L.

Here is an example. Suppose E to be the levitation (viz., rising into the air and remaining floating on it) of a certain holy person. E is a counter-instance to otherwise well substantiated laws of mechanics L. We could show E to be a repeatable counter-instance if we could construct a formula L^1 which predicted E and also successfully predicted other divergences from L, as well as all other tested predictions of L; or if we could construct L^1 which was comparatively simple relative to the data and predicted E and all the other tested predictions of L, but predicted divergences from L which had not yet been tested. L^1 might differ from L in that, according to it, under certain circumstances bodies exercise a gravitational repulsion on each other, and the circumstance in which E occurred was one of those circumstances. If L^1 satisfied either of the above two conditions, we would adopt it, and we would then say that under certain circumstances people do levitate and so E was not a counter-instance to a law of nature. However, it might be that any modification which we made to the laws of mechanics to allow them to predict E might not yield any more successful predictions than L and they be so clumsy that there was no reason to believe that their predictions not yet tested would be successful. Under these circumstances we would have good reasons to believe that the levitation of the holy person violated the laws of nature.

If the laws of nature are statistical and not deterministic, it is not in all cases so clear what counts as a counter-instance to them. How improbable does an event have to be to constitute a counter-instance to a statistical law? But this problem is a general one in the philosophy of science and does not raise any issues peculiar to the topic of miracles.

It is clear that all claims about what does or does not violate the laws of nature are corrigible. New scientific knowledge may force us to revise any such claims. But all claims to knowledge about matters of fact are corrigible, and we must reach provisional conclusions about them on the evidence available to us. We have to some extent good evidence about what are the laws of nature, and some of them are so well established and account for so many data that any modifications to them which we could suggest to account for the odd counter-instance would be so clumsy and ad hoc as to upset the whole structure of science. In such cases the evidence is strong that if the purported counter-instance occurred it was a violation of the laws of nature. There is good reason to believe that the following events, if they occurred, would be violations of the laws of nature: levitation; resurrection from the dead in full health of a man whose heart has not been beating for twenty-four hours and who was, by other criteria also, dead; water turning into wine without the assistance of chemical apparatus or catalysts; a man getting better from polio in a minute.

So then we could have the evidence that an event E if it occurred was a non-repeatable counter-instance to a true law of nature L. But Hume's argument here runs as follows. The evidence, which *ex hypothesi* is good evidence, that L is a true law of nature is evidence that E did not occur. We have certain other evidence that E did occur. In such circumstances, writes Hume, the wise man "weighs the opposite experiments. He considers which side is supported by the greater number of experiments."[3] Since he supposes that the evidence that E occurred would be that of testimony, Hume concludes "that no testimony is sufficient to establish a miracle, unless the testimony be of such a kind, that its falsehood would be more miraculous, than the fact which it endeavours to establish."[4] He considers that this condition is not in fact satisfied by any purported miracle, though he seems at times to allow that it is logically possible that it might be.

One wonders here at Hume's scale of evidence. Suppose two hundred witnesses claiming to have observed some event E, an event which, if it occurred, would be a non-repeatable counterinstance to a law of nature. Suppose these to be witnesses able and anxious to show that E did not occur if there were grounds for doing so. Would not their combined evidence give us good reason to believe that E occurred? Hume's answer which we can see from his discussion of two apparently equally well authenticated miracles is–No. But then, one is inclined to say, is not Hume just being bigoted, refusing to face facts? It would be virtually impossible to draw up a table showing how many witnesses and of what kind we need to establish the occurrence of an event which, if it occurred, would be a non-repeatable counter-instance to a law of nature. Each purported instance has to be considered on its merits. But certainly one feels that Hume's standards of evidence are too high. What, one wonders, would Hume himself say if he saw such an event?

But behind Hume's excessively stringent demands on evidence there may be a philosophical point which he has not fully brought out. This is a point made by Flew in justification of Hume's standards of evidence: "The justification for giving the 'scientific' this ultimate precedence here over the 'historical' lies in the nature of the propositions concerned and in the evidence which can be displayed to sustain them . . . the candidate historical proposition will be particular, often singular, and in the past tense . . . . But just by reason of this very pastness and particularity it is no longer possible for anyone to examine the subject directly for himself . . . the law of nature will, unlike the candidate historical proposition, be a general nomological. It can thus in theory, though obviously not always in practice, be tested at any time by any person."[5]

Flew's contrast is, however, mistaken. Particular experiments on particular occasions only give a certain and far from conclusive support to claims that a purported scientific law is true. Any person can test for the truth of a purported scientific law but a positive result to one test will only give limited support to the claim. Exactly the same holds for purported historical truths. Anyone can examine the evidence, but a particular piece of evidence only gives limited support to the claim that the historical proposition is true. But in the historical as in the scientific case, there is no limit to the amount of evidence. We can go on and on testing for the truth of historical as well as scientific propositions. We can look for more and more data which can only be explained as effects of some specified past event, and data incompatible with its occurrence, just as we can look for more and more data for or against the truth of some physical law. Hence the truth of the historical proposition can also "be tested at any time by any person."

What Hume seems to suppose is that the only evidence about whether an event E happened is the written or verbal testimony of those who would have been in a position to witness it, had it occurred. And as there will be only a finite number of such pieces of testimony, the evidence about whether or not E happened would be finite. But this is not the only testimony which is relevant—we need testimony about the character and competence of the original witnesses. Nor is testimony the only type of evidence. All effects of what happened at the time of the alleged occurrence of E are also relevant. Far more than in Hume's day we are today often in a position to assess what occurred by studying the physical traces of the event. Hume had never met Sherlock Holmes with his ability to assess what happened in the room from the way in which the furniture lay, or where the witness was yesterday from the mud on his boot. As the effects of what happened at the time of the occurrence of E are always with us in some form, we can always go on examining them yet more carefully. Further, we need to investigate whether E, if it did occur, would in fact have brought about the present effects, and whether any other cause could have brought about just these effects to investigate these issues involves investigating which scientific laws operate (other than the law L of which it is claimed that E was a violation), and this involves doing experiments ad lib. Hence there is no end to the amount of new evidence which can be had. The evidence that the event E occurred can go on mounting up in the way that evidence that L is a law of nature can do. The wise man in these circumstances will surely say that he has good reason to believe that E occurred, but also that L is a true law of nature and so that E was a violation of it.

So we could have good reason to believe that a law of nature has been violated. But for a violation of a law of nature to be a miracle, it has to be caused by a god, that is, a very powerful rational being who is not a material object. What could be evidence that it was?

To explain an event as brought about by a rational agent with intentions and purposes is to give an entirely different kind of explanation of its occurrence from an explanation by scientific laws acting on precedent causes. Our normal grounds for attributing an event to the agency of an embodied rational agent A is that we or others perceived A bringing it about or that it is the sort of event that A typically brings about and that A, and no one else of whom we have knowledge, was in a position to bring it about. The second kind of ground is only applicable when we have prior knowledge of the existence of A. in considering evidence for a violation E of a law of nature being due to the agency of a god, I will distinguish two cases, one where we have good reason on grounds other than the occurrence of violations of laws of nature to believe that there exists at least one god, and one where we do not.

Let us take the second case first. Suppose we have no other good reason for believing that a god exists, but an event E then occurs which, our evidence indicates, is a non-repeatable counter-instance to a true law of nature. Now we cannot attribute E to the agency of a god by seeing the god's body bring E about, for gods do not have bodies. But suppose that E occurs in ways and circumstances C strongly analogous to those in which occur events brought about by human agents, and that other violations occur in such circumstances. We would then be justified in claiming that E and other such violations are, like effects of human actions, brought about by agents, but ones unlike men in not being material objects. This inference would be justified because, if an analogy between effects is strong enough, we are always justified in postulating slight difference in causes to account for slight difference in effects. Thus if because of its other observable behaviour we say that light is a disturbance in a medium, then the fact that the medium, if it exists, does not, like other media, slow down material bodies passing through it, is not by itself (viz., if there are no other disanalogies) a reason for saying that the light is not a disturbance in a medium, but only for saying that the medium in which light is a disturbance has the peculiar property of not resisting the passage of material bodies. So if, because of very strong similarity between the ways and circumstances of the occurrence of E and other violations of laws of nature to the ways and circumstances in which effects are produced by human agents, we postulate a similar cause—a rational agent, the fact that there are certain disanalogies (viz., we cannot point to the agent, say where his body is) does not mean that our explanation is wrong. It only means that the agent is unlike humans in not having a body. But this move is only justified if the similarities are otherwise strong. Nineteenth-century scientists eventually concluded that for light the similarities were not strong enough to outweigh the dissimilarities and justify postulating the medium with the peculiar property.

Now what similarities in the ways and circumstances C of their occurrence could there be between E (and other violations of laws of nature) and the effects of human actions to justify the postulation of similar causes? Suppose that E occurred in answer to a request. Thus E might be an explosion in my room, totally inexplicable by the laws of nature, when at the time of its occurrence there were in a room on the other side of the corridor men in turbans chanting "O God of the Sikhs, may there be an explosion in Swinburne's room." Suppose, too, that when E occurs a voice, but not the voice of an embodied agent, is heard giving reasonable reasons for granting the request. When the explosion occurs in my room, a voice emanating from no man or animal or man-made machine is heard saying "Your request is granted. He deserves a lesson." Would not all this be good reason for postulating a rational agent other than a material object who brought about E and the other violations, an agent powerful enough to change instantaneously by intervention the properties of things, viz., a god? Clearly if the analogy were strong enough between the ways and circumstances in which violations of laws of nature and effects of human action occur, it would be. If furthermore the prayers which were answered by miracles were prayers for certain kinds of events (e.g., relief of suffering, punishment of ill-doers) and those which were not answered by miracles were for events of different kinds, then this would show something about the character of the god. Normally, of course, the evidence adduced by theists for the occurrence of miracles is not as strong as I have indicated that very strong evidence would be. Violations are often reported as occurring subsequent to prayer for them to occur, and seldom otherwise; but voices giving reason for answering such a request are rare indeed. Whether in cases where voices are not heard but the occurrence of a violation E and of prayer for its occurrence were both well confirmed, we would be justified in concluding that the existence of a god who brought E about is a matter of whether the analogy is strong enough as it stands. The question of exactly when an analogy is strong enough to justify an inference based on it is a difficult one. But my only point here is that if the analogy were strong enough, the inference would be justified.

Suppose now that we have other evidence for the existence of a god. Then if E occurs in the circumstances C, previously described, that E is due to the activity of a god is more adequately substantiated, and the occurrence of E gives further support to the evidence for the existence of a god. But if we already have reason to believe in the existence of a god, the occurrence of E not under circumstances as similar as C to those under which human agents often bring about results, could nevertheless sometimes be justifiably attributed to his activity. Thus, if the occurrence of E is the sort of thing that the only god of whose existence we have evidence would wish to bring about if he has the character suggested by the other evidence for his existence, we can reasonably hold him responsible for the occurrence of E which would otherwise be unexplained. The healing of a faithful blind Christian contrary to the laws of nature could reasonably be attributed to the God of the Christians, if there were other evidence for his existence, whether or not the blind man or other Christians had ever prayed for that result.

For these reasons I conclude that we can have good reason to believe that a violation of a law of nature was caused by a god, and so was a miracle.

I would like to make two final points, one to tidy up the argument and the other to meet a further argument put forward by Hume which I have not previously discussed.

Entia non sunt multiplicanda praeter necessitatem.—Unless we have good reason to do so we ought not to postulate the existence of more than one god, but to suppose that the same being answers all prayers. But there could be good reason to postulate the existence of more than one god, and evidence to this effect could be provided by miracles. One way in which this could happen is that prayers for a certain kind of result, for example, shipwreck, which began "O, Neptune" were often answered, and also prayers for a different kind of result, for example, success in love, which began "O, Venus" were also often answered, but prayers for a result of the first kind beginning "O, Venus," and for a result of the second kind beginning "O, Neptune" were never answered. Evidence for the existence of one god would in general support, not oppose, evidence for the existence of a second one since, by suggesting that there is one rational being other than those whom we can see, it makes more reasonable the postulation of another one.

The second point is that there is no reason at all to suppose that Hume is in general right to claim that "every miracle . . . pretended to have been wrought in any . . . (religion) . . . as its direct scope is to establish the particular system to which it is attributed; so has it the same force, though more indirectly, to overthrow every other system. In destroying a rival system it likewise destroys the credit of those miracles on which that system was established."[6] If Hume were right to claim that evidence for the miracles of one religion was evidence against the miracles of any other, then indeed evidence for miracles in each would be poor. But in fact evidence for a miracle "wrought in one religion" is only evidence against the occurrence of a miracle "wrought in another religion" if the two miracles, if they occurred, would be evidence for propositions of the two religious systems incompatible with each other. It is hard to think of pairs of alleged miracles of this type. If there were evidence for a Roman Catholic miracle which was evidence for the doctrine of transubstantiation and evidence for a Protestant miracle which was evidence against it, here we would have a case of the conflict of evidence which, Hume claims, occurs generally with alleged miracles. But it is enough to give this example to see that most alleged miracles do not give rise to conflicts of this kind. Most alleged miracles, if they occurred, would only show the power of god or gods and their concern for the needs of men, and little else.

My main conclusion, to repeat it, is that there are no logical difficulties in supposing that there could be strong historical evidence for the occurrence of miracles. Whether there is such evidence is, of course, another matter.

Endnotes

*Reprinted from Richard Swinburne, "Miracles," *Philosophical Quarterly* 18 (1968), by permission of the publisher, Basil Blackwell.

[1] David Hume, *An Enquiry Concerning Human Understanding*, ed. L. A. Selby-Bigge (Oxford, 2nd ed., 1902), p. 115, footnote.

[2] Ninian Smart, *Philosophers and Religious Truth* (London, 1964), Ch. 11.

[3] Op. cit., p. 111.

[4] Op. cit., p. 116.

[5] Antony Flew, *Hume's Philosophy of Belief* (London, 1961), pp. 207ff.

[6] Op. cit., pp. 121ff.

Study Questions

1.   Does Swinburne think that there could be evidence that a law of nature had been violated?

2.   What is Anthony Flew's contrast, and why does Swinburne think it is mistaken?

3.   What, in addition to verbal or written testimony, is evidence overlooked by Hume?

4.   Does Swinburne think that the agent of a violation of a law of nature has to be material or non-material?

5.   Swinburne makes two points at the end. What are they?

33

Miracles: What If They Happen?

Richard L. Purtill

Richard Purtill is professor of philosophy at Western Washington University, and is author of *Logic, Argument, Refutation, and Proof*.

In this selection he continues the critique initially begun by Swinburne, and presents a two-stage case for miracles.* He argues first for the general possibility of miracles, and then for their actuality. The laws of nature are compared to national laws., and he argues that a miracle is analogous to a violation of a national code. As to whether miracles have ever taken place, he sets forth limiting criteria: 1) miracles are not "fairy-tale" like; 2) "the miraculous [must be] interwoven with the primary story (of the religion);" 3) there must be independent evidence for the religion in question.

"It's a miracle," said Mrs. Kennedy, sitting up in her bed, and even as Dr. Buchan put out a cautioning hand, he knew that yesterday she wouldn't have had the strength to sit up that far. "We call it a spontaneous remission," he replied, trying to make his voice as calm as possible. "They happen sometimes, we don't know why."

But Sarah Kennedy was sure she knew why and wasn't shy about saying so. "It's the power of prayer, Doctor," she said earnestly, "the prayers of my family and Father O'Sullivan and the good Sisters. . . ."

Despite himself, Buchan was drawn into arguing with her. "I presume that other people in the hospital are being prayed for just as hard, but they haven't had recoveries like yours," he snapped.

There were tears in Mrs. Kennedy's eyes now. "Ah, Doctor, it's a mystery of God," she said. "The Lord knows that I prayed as hard for my husband Michael, and for the daughter that died young, as anyone ever prayed. But prayer is just asking and sometimes God says no. It's no virtue of mine that He's spared me this time–maybe He has a job for me to do yet."

Buchan smiled a little coldly. "Very convenient," he said. "If you get well it's the power of prayer; if you don't it's the will of God. So whatever happens, you win."

He wondered if he'd gone too far, but he was reassured when he saw a trace of Mrs. Kennedy's old spirit in her grin. "Well, Doctor, tell me now," she said, "can you explain with all your great medical knowledge why a week ago I was at death's door and today I'm here taking the Mickey out of you?"

"No, I can't," he admitted, "but that isn't to say that we might not understand some day why things like this happen. The mind and body are related in ways we're only just beginning to understand."

But Mrs. Kennedy was not going to let him off so easily. "So it's faith healing, is it Doctor? But it's a funny kind of faith healing that can work on a person when she knows about as much of what's going on around her as a mackerel on ice."

Buchan got up from the edge of the bed where he had been, very unprofessionally, sitting. "No, Sarah, your case isn't faith healing and I'll admit that I don't know what it is. But these spontaneous remissions happen to people who don't pray as often as they occur to people that do, so you're not going to convert me to religion by getting up and dancing a jig. Don't overdo, and remember these things can get worse again as suddenly as they got better."

Mrs. Kennedy lay back. "Ah, you're a terrible old heathen, Doctor, but you've been a good friend to me and mine. Go off to your pills and your laboratory tests, but you won't find any explanation in them for what's happened to me." And as Dr. Buchan slipped out the door wearing an indulgent smile, she muttered to herself, "And I'll pray for your conversion too, you old devil. Though that would be a bigger miracle than this one."

Some religious believers think that miracles continue to occur; others believe that they have occurred only at specific places and times, where extraordinary needs brought forth extraordinary help from God. But even if events which cannot be explained by science do occur in some religious contexts, what do such events prove?

One traditional way of providing a rational basis for religious belief begins with arguments for the existence of God and goes on to argue that a certain body of religious beliefs can be known to be a revelation from God because miracles have been worked in support of those religious beliefs. For example, a Christian of one traditional sort, when challenged as to the basis of one of his beliefs—say the Second Coming of Christ—would cite certain words said by Christ. When asked why we should believe these words of Christ, he would cite the miracles done by Christ, and especially His Resurrection, as evidence that Christ's words were backed up or authenticated by God. And when asked why he believed that those miracles had indeed occurred, the traditional Christian would argue that if God exists miracles cannot be ruled out, and that miracle is the best or only explanation for certain events recorded by history. If challenged as to the existence of God, he would try to give arguments based on reason and experience for God's existence.

Thus, this kind of traditional Christian, whom we might call a rationalistic believer, nowhere appeals to blind faith or personal experiences not shared by unbelievers, but bases his assent to particular doctrines on authority, his acceptance of authority on the evidence of miracles, and his acceptance of miracles on philosophical arguments for God and historical arguments for the actual occurrence of miracles.

Nowadays not only most nonbelievers but many people who would call themselves religious believers would challenge this way of providing a basis for religious belief. They would argue that accounts of miracles are not historically reliable and that a faith based on such accounts is open to historical and scientific objections. The traditional believer understands such objections from non-believers in God, but finds them puzzling from people calling themselves believers in God. For if God is the Creator and Ruler of the universe, then surely miracles are possible. Of course, if miracles were impossible, then any historical account which tells of the occurrence of miracles, as the Old and New Testaments plainly do, must be rejected as unhistorical. If miracles are tremendously improbable, then we must reject any account of them unless we get evidence of a kind which, in the nature of the case, history almost never gives us. But if God exists, miracles are not impossible, and unless we have some argument to show that they are improbable, then we cannot assume that they are. This undercuts most of the "historical" objections to miracles, for if we have no metaphysical objections, then we will have to examine the historical evidence on its merits. And if we do this we may find, as many reasonable and hardheaded men have found, that miracle is the best explanation for certain recorded events.

There may, of course, be historical objections to certain accounts of miracles—for example, one account may seem to be a mere imitation of another, or other historical evidence may render that particular supposed miracle improbable, and so on. But the general objection to miracles is not based on anything peculiar to history as such, but on philosophical grounds.

Another objection to miracles is the supposed objection from experience. Most versions of this objection trace back more or less indirectly to a famous objection by David Hume, which goes as follows:

A miracle is a violation of the laws of nature; and as a firm and unalterable experience has established these laws, the proof against a miracle, from the very nature of the fact, is as entire as any argument from experience can possibly be imagined. . . . Nothing is esteemed a miracle, if it ever happens in the common course of nature. It is no miracle that a man, seemingly in good health, should die of a sudden;

because such a kind of death, though more unusual than any other, has yet been frequently observed to happen. But it is a miracle that a dead man should come to life; because that has never been observed in any age or country. There must, therefore, be a uniform experience against every miraculous event, otherwise the event would not merit the appellation. And as a uniform experience amounts to a proof, there is here a direct and full proof, from the nature of the fact, against the existence of any miracle; nor can such a proof be destroyed, or the miracle rendered credible, but by an opposite proof, which is superior.[1]

Now obviously we must interpret Hume's objection in such a way that it is not an objection to any unique event. After all, up to a certain date, there was "uniform experience" against a man setting foot on the moon. It must, therefore, be a certain *class* or *kind* of events we are eliminating. But what class? Miracles? But this begs the whole question. As an "argument" against the statement that miracles occur, we have the assertion that there is uniform experience against miracles—in other words, the unsupported assertion that miracles don't happen!

Put in this way the point may seem obvious, but both in Hume's original account and in modern restatements of views like Hume's the point is often concealed. Instead of saying boldly that experience shows that miracles do not occur, which is obviously question-begging in the context of this argument, the class of events which "experience proves don't happen" is described in some other way—as events which "exhibit causal irregularity" or as events which "neither obey known scientific laws nor are taken as refuting alleged scientific laws," or some similar description. But looked at carefully, all such descriptions turn out to be indirect ways of describing miracles. And to argue for the conclusion that miracles do not happen by assuming that miracles, under whatever description, don't happen is just to argue in a circle or beg the question.

This is not to deny that there could be some argument which concludes that miracles don't happen. But whatever that argument is, it must not have as one of its premises an assertion which amounts to saying that miracles don't happen, because that would be assuming what is supposed to be being proved.

Of course defenders of a Humean position would deny that they are arguing in a circle in this way. But to avoid the charge of circularity they must show that the class of events they are claiming experience rules out is not just an indirect description of the class of miracles. So far as I can see neither Hume's own argument or any neo-Humean argument can meet the challenge.

I think that the only respectable way of interpreting what Hume says here is to take him as arguing that past experience gives us some kind of assurance that laws of nature cannot be suspended. (If it merely alleges that they have never been suspended, it is just "miracles don't happen" in a new guise.) We interpret Hume, then, as saying that experience proves that natural laws are "unsuspendable." But how could experience show any such thing? Any such theory must be a philosophical interpretation of experience, not the direct result of experience. So before coming to any decision on this matter, we must look at the philosophical, as well as the historical, pros and cons with regard to the question of miracles. We can distinguish two separable arguments which need to be looked at in turn: the argument for (the possibility of) miracles, and the argument from miracles (for religious belief).

The argument for miracles consists of two stages—an argument for the general possibility of miracles, and an argument for the historical actuality of certain miracles. The first stage is philosophical and can be developed fairly completely within the limits of this chapter. The second stage is historical and we can only indicate the main lines of the argument. The argument from miracles for religious belief also has two stages—the first stage a philosophical consideration of the evidential value of miracles, and the second stage a historical consideration of what specific beliefs the evidence of miracles supports. Again, we will try to cover the philosophical stage as completely as we can and only indicate the general lines of the historical argument.

Let us begin, then, with a definition of miracle. By a miracle we will mean an exception to the natural order of things caused by the power of God. By this we will mean very much what people mean when they define miracle as a suspension or violation of natural law, but for reasons that will become clear "exception" is preferable to the terms "suspension" or "violation," and "natural order of things" is preferable to the term "natural law." Notice that by this definition no event which occurs as part of the natural order of things, no matter how improbable or how faith-inspiring, will count as a miracle. There may be a wider and looser sense of miracle in which striking coincidences which inspire religious belief are called "miracles," but they are not miracles in the stricter and narrower sense in which we are now using that term.

Before we can speak of exceptions to the natural order of things we must believe that there *is* a natural order of things. If anyone holds that there is no natural order, that the universe is chaotic, that the apparent order and understandability of the universe is an illusion, then that person can give no meaning to the idea of miracle, for that idea depends on contrast. Before there can be exceptions there must be rules or patterns for them to be exceptions to. The progress of science gives us an enormously strong argument against the idea that the universe is chaotic and without order and pattern, and we will assume in what follows that we can speak of the universe as genuinely orderly and intelligible. But if anyone really wished to challenge this, we would have to settle that issue before going on to any argument with him either for or from miracles.

Given that the universe is orderly and understandable, however, we can ask whether this order can have exceptions and whether such exceptions could be due to the power of God. The answer to this question depends on the answer to another question. How can we account for the order and understandability of the universe? Ultimately there are only two possible answers to this question. We can account for the order of the universe by saying that the universe was made by a person, by a Being with knowledge and will, by someone who knows what he is doing and what he intends—in other words by God. And we can account for the understandability of the universe by saying that we are made in the image and likeness of the God who made the universe; our minds resemble His, however remotely. Or we can account for the order of the universe by saying that there is some inherent principle of order in the fundamental stuff of the universe, and account for our understanding that order by saying that our minds are the outcome of the unfolding of this inherent principle of order.

Either theory, if accepted, would have consequences. If we really accepted the idea that our minds were the accidental result of the workings of mindless forces, we should be haunted by doubts as to whether our apparent understanding of the universe is illusory. Dogmatic confidence of any kind, including dogmatic confidence that certain sorts of events "can't happen" is not what we should logically expect from a Universe Ultimate view. (Of course, insofar as dogmatism is often the outcome of a feeling of uncertainty, we might explain the dogmatism psychologically.) The consequences of the God theory are rather different. Our confidence in the understanding of the universe given to us by science would be considerable, but it would not be absolute. If the natural order is the result of God's action, then sometimes God might act in such a way as to make exceptions to the natural order.

In this view an exception to the natural order would be like the exceptions we sometimes make to established rules and procedures—for example, allowing an exceptionally gifted child to skip grades or enter college without graduating from high school, or declaring a holiday on a day that would normally be a working day. We can often see that not making exceptions to rules would be unreasonable or unkind. Exceptions must, of course, be rare if rules are to be generally relied upon, but we can live perfectly well with a system of rules or procedures which have occasional exceptions. We may or may not think President Ford's pardon of ex-President Nixon wise or fair, but occasional exceptions to legal procedures, such as presidential pardon, do not make our legal system chaotic or unreliable.

Furthermore, provided that God wished to give us strong evidence that a given message has His authority behind it, there would seem to be no better way than a miracle. If I claim to have authority in a certain organization, strong evidence of my authority would be an ability to suspend the rules or make exceptions to usual procedures. You might meditate on the problem of how a God who never interfered with the working of the universe could establish a message from Himself as authoritative.

The scientist, of course, as a scientist, ignores the possibility of miracles, just as the lawyer, as a lawyer, must ignore the possibility of a presidential pardon for his client, since there is nothing he can do as a *lawyer* which will ensure a presidential pardon. A pardon is a free action by the President, which cannot be guaranteed by any legal maneuver; a miracle is a free act by God which the scientist cannot bring within *his* procedures.

A presidential pardon is like a miracle in that though the *origin* of the pardon is outside ordinary legal procedures, a pardon once granted has legal consequences. A miracle, once it has occurred, has consequences which fit into the kind of patterns scientists study: Drinking too much of the wine Christ made from water at Cana in Galilee would make a wedding guest drunk, and if a scientist had been there with his instruments he could verify, though not explain, the change and measure the alcoholic content of the wine made from water.

It is important to note that a presidential pardon is not *il*legal: It does not violate any laws. Furthermore, it does not suspend the laws in the sense that at a given time or place some laws cease to operate in all cases— as if, for example, the laws of libel were suspended in Hannibal, Missouri on the first Sunday in March, so that no libels in that place or time were punishable. Rather, an individual exception is made to the law, so that of two men convicted of the same crime at the same time, one may be pardoned and the other not. Similarly, a miracle does not *violate* the laws of nature, nor suspend them for all events at a given time or place: The water in one jar might be changed to wine and that in an adjacent jar be unchanged. Lazarus may be raised and a man in an adjacent tomb who died at the same time may remain dead.

A presidential pardon cannot be compelled by any legal means; it can only be asked for. It is a free act of the President. Similarly, a miracle cannot be brought about by scientific means; it can only be prayed for. It is a free act of God. A presidential pardon cannot be predicted from the legal facts and it does not create a precedent: A pardon may be granted in one case, and in precisely similar circumstances another request may be denied. Similarly, a miracle cannot be predicted by scientific means and it gives no scientific grounds for prediction once it has occurred: The miracle at Cana in Galilee does not increase the probability that water will change to wine in similar circumstances.

To sum up: We can imagine a different legal system in which there were no pardons and so no exceptions to the rule of law. However, our system is not such a system but rather one in which certain exceptions to the legal order, called presidential pardons, sometimes occur. Lawyers as such have no concern with presidential pardons, for they cannot predict them, bring them about, or draw any precedents for them. A presidential pardon is, you might say, supralegal and therefore of no legal interest. Similarly, it could be that our universe was one in which there were no exceptions to the natural order, but if traditional religious believers are right, our universe is not such a universe, but one in which certain exceptions to the natural order, called miracles, sometimes occur. Scientists, as such, have no concern with miracles, for they cannot predict them, bring them about, or draw any conclusions about the future course of nature from them. A miracle is supernatural, and therefore of no scientific interest.

We could not settle whether presidential pardons are possible by looking at the day-to-day business of the courts; rather, we must ask what kind of legal system we live under. We cannot settle whether miracles occur by looking at the ordinary course of nature; we must ask what kind of universe we live in. This is a philosophical, not a scientific, question, and one very relevant philosophical consideration is that a universe made by God leaves room for confidence in human reason, whereas a universe of natural necessity does not.

If we come to the conclusion that miracles are possible, then we must consider miracle as one possible explanation of certain events recorded in history. Again, because most readers of this book will have been influenced to some extent by Christianity, we will consider Christian claims with regard to miracles. Early Christians claimed that the tomb of Christ was empty and that Christ had risen from the dead. The Roman and Jewish authorities did not refute this claim by producing the body, as they would certainly have done had *they* removed it from the tomb. The Apostles suffered persecution, hardship, and martyrdom to proclaim the message of Christ risen from the dead, which they surely would not have done if *they* had removed and hidden Christ's body. Christians claim that no naturalistic explanation which tries to explain the disappearance of the body and the confidence of the early Christians comes anywhere near accounting for all the facts.

If miracles were impossible, we should have to try to account for the data in some other way; but there is no good argument which shows that miracles are impossible. If miracles were tremendously improbable, many times more improbable than the most farfetched naturalistic explanation of the data, then it might be reasonable to accept an otherwise very implausible naturalistic explanation. But there seems to be no argument to show that miracles are tremendously improbable. It is not enough to say that they are rare and unusual—an event may be rare and unusual but still to be expected in given circumstances. It is rare to have world records in athletic events broken, but it is to be expected at the Olympic Games. President Ford's pardon of ex-President Nixon was a rare and unusual event, but not unexpected in the very unusual circumstances which then prevailed. The Resurrection of Christ was a rare and unusual event, but in the context of His life and teaching, was it unexpected?

It is even possible to give some general idea of the circumstances in which miracles are to be expected. The first is extraordinary goodness or holiness on the part of the miracle worker. As the man born blind said to the Jews, "We know for certain that God does not answer the prayers of sinners." The second circumstance is the need to back up or authenticate a message from God. Christ was as good and holy the year before He began his public ministry as He was after He began it, but He did not begin to work miracles until He began to preach. There is, I think, a third condition: an openness and willingness to learn on the part of the audience. In some places Christ worked few miracles because of the hardness of heart of those in that place. Christ worked no miracles at Herod's request; He cast none of His pearls before that swine.

Let me pause here and make a parenthetical remark which is not directly relevant to my main theme, but has a connection with it. I have been mentioning as examples various miracles attributed to Christ in the Gospels, including the Fourth Gospel. This may seem to some to fly in the face of much recent biblical scholarship, which has argued that the miracles attributed to Christ are additions to the record of His life made by later generations of Christian believers rather than accounts of what actually happened at the time given by eyewitnesses. Now in some cases there may be reasons for doubting on purely textual grounds whether a certain part of the New Testament as we now have it was part of the original record, for example, in the debated case of the "long ending" of Mark's Gospel. But a careful examination of a good deal of "higher" criticism (as opposed to textual criticism) of the New Testament shows that it is not the case that the miraculous element is rejected because the text is doubtful, but rather that the text is regarded as doubtful because of a prior rejection of any miraculous element.

Insofar, then, as we can show by philosophical argument that neither science nor reason requires us to reject the possibility of miracles, we undermine the kind of doubt as to the reliability of our texts which is based on hostility to a miraculous or supernatural element in Scripture. We must entertain the possibility that Luke recounts the Virgin birth of Christ because it actually happened and not because the later Christian community borrowed elements from pagan mythology to enhance the importance of the founder of Christianity. To the unbiased eye the first hypothesis might seem much more plausible than the second. We might even be daring enough to entertain the hypothesis that the Fourth Gospel, which is full of eyewitness detail and local knowledge, was actually written by the Apostle John, and that its theological depth as compared to the other Gospels is due to the fact that John understood his Master better than some of the other disciples, rather than due to later interpretations by second-generation Christians. Plato's picture of Socrates is more

profound than Xenophon's, at least partly because Plato was better fitted
to understand Socrates than Xenophon was.

Do historical arguments based on the New Testament record, which
argue that miracle is the only or best explanation of certain well-attested
events amount to a *proof* that miracles have occurred? So long as we
understand that the term "proof" means something different in historical
studies than it does in mathematics or science or philosophy, it may well
be that we do have adequate historical proof of miracles. But to show this
in detail would involve getting down to the historical nitty-gritty, and I
cannot do that here.

Let me turn, then, to the related question of what miracles prove. If it
is granted, at least for the sake of argument, that God exists, that miracles
are possible, and that we have good historical evidence that miracles
marked the beginning of Christianity, does this prove the Christian claim
to the truth of the revelation given to us by Christ? Before we can decide
this, we will have to examine three apparent difficulties.

The first difficulty is what we might call the problem of contradictory
miracles. If it were the case that genuine miracles were worked in support
of contradictory religious revelations, we would not know what to think. It
would be like a witness whose integrity we were absolutely sure of giving
contradictory testimony for both sides of a dispute. Something would have
to give. We would have to conceive that the witness was not really honest,
or deny that he actually gave the testimony on both sides, or find some
way of showing that the contradiction was only apparent.

Similarly, if it were claimed that miracles are worked in support of
contradictory religious revelations, we would have to give up the idea of
miracles as proving a system of religion, unless we could show that the
contradiction was only apparent, or that one set of opposed miracles was
not genuine.

In some cases perhaps we can show that there is no genuine conflict.
Many religious believers accept both Old Testament and New Testament
miracles, and deny the claim (which has been made) that Old Testament
miracles worked in the name of the One God of Judaism are in some ways
incompatible with New Testament miracles worked in the name of God
the Father, God the Son, and God the Holy Spirit. (This is, of course,
because they would deny, on theological grounds, that Christian belief in
the Trinity amounts to belief in three Gods.)

Many Christian religious believers would not even deny the
possibility that God might have worked miracles for the "virtuous
pagans" before Christ, to encourage them to emphasize those parts of their
religion closest to the truth. If, for instance, God had worked a miracle for
the Egyptian Pharaoh Amenhotep in support of his efforts to establish
monotheism and overthrow the dark gods of old Egypt, they would find in
this no challenge to Christianity, even though Amenhotep's monotheism
might have been very crude and contained elements of untruth.

What would threaten the argument from miracles for the truth of Christianity would be genuine miracles worked in opposition to Christian claims or in support of incompatible claims. If, for instance, a Moslem holy man raised a man from the dead in order to persuade Christians that Mohammed's revelation had superseded that of Christ, this would be a case of genuine incompatibility. However, so far from any case of this kind being established, it is hard to show that any case of this kind has even been claimed. General statements are often made by opponents of Christianity that miracles are claimed by all religions, but leading cases of these alleged claims are hard to come by.

Certainly fairy-tale-like legends sometimes grow up around a figure like Buddha or Mohammed, but these have certain common characteristics. Such tales arise centuries after the time of their alleged occurrence. They contain strong elements of the fantastic (e.g., Mohammed riding his horse to the moon) and in their manner of telling they reveal their kinship to legend and myth. Compare any of these accounts with the accounts we find in the Gospels and the difference in atmosphere is at once apparent. Either the Gospel accounts are eyewitness accounts of real events occurring in genuine places, or the four writers we call Matthew, Mark, Luke, and John independently invented, out of the clear blue sky, a sort of realistic fantasy or science fiction which has no antecedents and no parallels in ancient literature. Those who have no metaphysical objections to miracles may find the hypothesis that the events really happened as they are related immensely more plausible than the other hypothesis.

It may be worthwhile to take a quick look, for purposes of comparison, at the closest thing we have around the time of the Gospels to an attempt at a realistic fantasy. This is the story of Appollonius of Tyana, written about A.D. 220 by Flavius Philostratus, which is sometimes referred to by controversialists as if it were a serious rival to the Gospel accounts of Christ's ministry and miracles. Penguin Classics publishes an excellent little paper back edition of this story, to which you may go for details, but let me note a few points in passing.

The story concerns a wandering sage who allegedly lived from the early years of the first century until about A.D. 96 or 98. Philostratus mentions some earlier sources for his work but at least some of these sources are probably his own invention. For one thing, Philostratus's account contains serious historical inaccuracies about things like dates of rulers, which seem to rule out reliance on any early source. The work was later used as anti-Christian propaganda, to discredit the uniqueness of Christ's miracles by setting up a rival miracle worker, as Socrates was sometimes set up as a rival to Christ as a martyr and teacher of virtue.

Still, there is some evidence that a neo-Pythagorean sage named Apollonius may really have lived, and thus Philostratus's work is a real example of what some have thought the Gospels to be: a fictionalized account of the life of a real sage and teacher, introducing miraculous events to build up the prestige of the central figure. It thus gives us a good look at what a real example of a fictionalized biography would look like, written at a time and place not too far removed from those in which the Gospels were written.

The first thing we notice is the fairy-tale atmosphere. There is a rather nice little vampire story, which inspired a minor poem by Keats, entitled Lamia. There are animal stories about, for instance, snakes in India big enough to drag off and eat an elephant. The sage wanders from country to country and wherever he goes he is likely to be entertained by the king or emperor, who holds long conversations with him and sends him on his way with camels and precious stones.

Interspersed with picturesque adventures there are occasional accounts of miracles, often involving prophecy or mind reading. A ruffian threatens to cut Apollonius's head off and the sage laughs and shouts out the name of a day three days hence; on that day the ruffian is executed for treason. Here is a typical passage about healing miracles:

> There came a man about thirty who was an expert lion-hunter but had been attacked by a lion and dislocated his hip, and so was lame in one leg. But the Wise Man massaged his hip and this restored the man to an upright walk. Someone else who had gone blind went away with his sight fully restored, and another man with a paralysed arm left strong again. A woman too, who had had seven miscarriages was cured through the prayers of her husband as follows. The Wise Man told the husband, when his wife was in labor, to bring a live rabbit under his cloak to the place where she was, walk around her and immediately release the hare: for she would lose her womb as well as the baby if the hare was not immediately driven away (Bk. 3, Sec. 39).

Now the point is not that Appollonius is no serious rival to Christ; no one ever thought he was except perhaps a few anti-Christian polemicists about the time of some of the early persecutions of the Church. The point is that this is what you get when imagination goes to work on a historical figure in classical antiquity; you get miracle stories a little like those in the Gospels, but also snakes big enough to eat elephants, kings and emperors as supporting cast, travelers' tales, ghosts, and vampires. Once the boundaries of fact are crossed we wander into fairyland. And very nice, too, for amusement or recreation. But the Gospels are set firmly in the real Palestine of the first century, and the little details are not picturesque inventions but the real details that only an eyewitness or a skilled realistic novelist can give.

As against this, those who wish to eliminate miracles from the Gospels have not textual evidence, but theories. We do not have any trace of early sober narratives of the life of Christ without miracles and later versions in which miracles are added. What we have is a story with miracles woven into its very texture. Someone once made a shrewd point about this. Christ, say the Gospels, "went about doing good." Fine. But what good did He do? Did He clothe the naked, visit prisoners, counsel people on personal problems? No. He went about making the extravagant claim to forgive sins and backing this up by working miracles, mostly miracles of healing. Eliminate this element and, setting aside His preaching, what good did He go about doing?

The point is that the miraculous is interwoven with the primary story of Christianity in a way in which the miraculous is not interwoven with the primary story of Buddhism or Mohammedanism. Again, however, this is a matter for detailed inquiry into comparative religion and the history of religions.

The second major difficulty as to the evidential value of miracles which we will consider is the objection that what seems to us to be an exception to the natural order may just be the operation of some natural regularities which we do not yet understand. Perhaps, says this objection, Jesus was merely a rare type of charismatic personality who could arouse a faith response in people such that their minds acted on their bodies in a way that freed them from illness. After all, the relation of the mind and body in illness is a mysterious one, and some studies suggest that mental attitude has a great deal to do with illness. Thus we may someday understand scientifically, and even be able to reproduce, some of Christ's apparently miraculous cures.

The first comment to make on this line of objection is that, like any argument which depends on what science may be able to discover in the future, it is extremely weak. But we can also ask what range of illnesses and cures this theory is supposed to account for. For example, Christ might have cured a paralytic because the paralysis was hysterical and subject to psychosomatic healing. But what about the cure of leprosy? What about the cure of the man blind from birth? And it is no use saying that psychosomatic illnesses cured by the impact of a charismatic personality account for some of Christ's cures and that the rest are fictional, for this would be to pick and choose among the evidence in a blatant way. If I am allowed to pick which of the evidence I will explain and reject the rest, I can make almost any theory look plausible.

But, of course, the cases which are decisive against any theory of psychosomatic cures are the raisings from the dead reported in all four Gospels. A last-ditch attempt to explain these "naturally" might be to allege that the seemingly dead persons were only in a cataleptic state, but cases of this kind are so rare that to allege this as an explanation of the raising of the daughter of the Jairus, *and* of the son of the widow of Nain, and Lazarus, brings in coincidence to a fantastic degree. Each of these accounts is highly circumstantial, and none can be plausibly treated as a variation on one of the others.

In other words, the proponent of the view that Christ's cures were psychosomatic—"faith healing" in a limiting sense—must make up his mind whether or not he accepts the written records as factual or fictional, or whether he holds them to be a mixture of fact and fiction. If the records are fictional, no explanation of the cures is necessary. If the account is factual, all of the reported miracles must be accounted for, not just those which can be plausibly accounted for on naturalistic grounds. If it is alleged that there is a mixture of fact and fiction, there must be an independent standard of what is factual in the record and what is fictional. We cannot in logic allow the principle of choice: "What I can explain is fact, the rest is fiction." (Think what ex-President Nixon could have done to the Watergate story using that principle!)

If the proponent of an explanation by so far unknown laws of nature goes so far as to say that even raisings from the dead can be accounted for by these laws, he must again explain a tremendous implausibility: either that these laws operated coincidentally in the neighborhood of Jesus, or that an obscure provincial carpenter somehow was able to discover and make use of natural powers and possibilities that none of the wise sages or deep researchers had ever been able to master or control.

A final difficulty about the evidential value of miracles rests on the fear that some supernatural power less than that of God might account for the wonders worked by Christ—that Jesus did His works, if not by the powers of Beelzebub, then at least by the power of some spiritual being less than God. To say what power this might be, of course, would be in some sense to give a theological account of what powers greater than human there might be, and how they are related to one another.

Consider, however, a line of argument sometimes heard from people influenced by certain sorts of Eastern religions, which goes something like this: Yes, of course Jesus was able to do apparently miraculous things; He was a Master, or Adept, and they can all do things of this sort. Jesus, living at the time and place that He did, tried to teach the Palestinian people a simple religion of love, put in terms of their own religious concepts, and this message has reached us in a distorted form. His real power lay in spiritual enlightenment, which you can learn by practicing Yoga (or going to Tibet, or studying with Mahatma X, or the like).

Again, there is a large blank check, drawn this time not on science, but on some sort of mystical religion. A friend of mine, arguing religion with opponents who seemed dogmatically sure of what God could or could not create, would challenge them, if they knew so much about creation, to create just one small rabbit—"to establish confidence." A similar challenge might be put to the exponents of "Eastern Wisdom" to duplicate even the least of Christ's miracles, to establish their claims. If they admit their own lack of power but claim others have performed some feats as great as Christ's, the problem simply reduces to one of the evidence for rival miracles discussed earlier.

In addition, there is a theological question as to whether a wise and loving God would allow people to be misled by permitting some lesser being to work apparent miracles. Real raising from the dead, creation of food or wine which is genuine and not illusory—such miracles seem by their nature to be the province of God only. But even in such things as the reading of thoughts or the manipulation of matter in scientifically inexplicable ways were possible to powers less than God, would God permit such occurrences in a context which gave rise to a false belief in men of good will, or seriously challenged the true beliefs of those already on the right path? *A priori*, it would seem not; and again, it does not seem that there is any reliable record of any such occurrences. (This is not to say that God may not sometimes permit "wonders" of this sort to be worked in order to refute them by His own power—for example, the story in Acts of the girl with the "prophetic Spirit.")

The preceding comments, necessarily brief, give some indication of the lines along which the evidential value of miracles must be assessed. Are there indeed rival miracles? Can miracles be explained as due to powers less than God? If the answer to all these questions is no, then we are forced to grant that miracles give a strong argument for the existence of God.

Endnotes

*Reprinted from Richard L. Purtill, *Thinking About Religion: A Philosophical Introduction to Religion,* Copyright 1978, pp. 123-34. Reprinted by permission of Prentice Hall, Inc., Englewood Cliffs, NJ, Nonexclusive world rights in all languages.

1 David Hume, *Enquiries*, ed. L.A. Selby-Bigge (Oxford: Oxford University Press, 1955), pp. 114-15.

Study Questions

1.   What are the two stages to the argument for miracles?

2.   How does Richard Purtill define "miracle"?

3.   According to Purtill, how is a presidential pardon like a miracle?

4.   What is the problem of "contradictory miracles"?

5.   What are the "limiting criteria" for miracles?

34

Miracles and the Laws of Nature

George I. Mavrodes

George Mavrodes is emeritus professor of philosophy at the University of Michigan, is author of *Belief in God, A Study in the Epistemology of Religion, Revelation and Religious Belief;* and is co-editor of *Problems and Perspectives in the Philosophy of Religion,* and *Rationality and Religious Belief.*

    Construing miracles as "violations," I argue that a law of nature must specify some kind of possibility. But we must have here a sense of possibility for which the ancient rule of logic—*ab esse ad posse valet consequentia*—does not hold. We already have one example associated with the concept of statute law, a law which specifies what is legally possible but which is not destroyed by a violation. If laws of nature are construed as specifying some analogous sense of what is naturally possible, then they need not be invalidated by a (rare) violation, and Humean miracles remain a genuine possibility.*

Some people, as you know, claim that miracles have actually occurred, they are a real part of the history of the world, just like the more ordinary wars, marriages, and inventions which figure in our history books. Christians, for example, characteristically claim that Jesus was a real historical man, and that he actually did some miracles. These claims generate a considerable range of philosophical questions and puzzles.

    On one hand, there are the questions which are primarily *epistemological.* For example, what would be a satisfactory sort of evidence that a miracle had actually occurred? What sort of evidence do we have in fact for the reality of miracles? And, going in the other epistemological direction, what would a miracle be evidence *for*? What sort of religious position or doctrine could be established or supported by reference to a miracle? And so on. For the most part I will ignore questions of this epistemological variety in this paper.

    There are also questions, however, which call directly for an analysis or clarification of the concept of a miracle. Just what are Christians claiming, for example, when they say that Jesus performed miracles?

Were all of his acts miracles? If not, how are the allegedly miraculous acts supposed to differ from the others? And what must the world be like if an act or event of that sort is to be possible? These questions appear to combine a metaphysical concern with a desire for a better understanding of a suggestive and problematic concept. In this paper I try to follow out one such line of questioning.

More specifically, I want to explore to some degree the ways in which the concepts of the *miraculous* and of a *law of nature* react on one another. And I will also be speculating about what sorts of laws of nature the world must have if miracles are to be a genuine possibility in it.

Our inquiry can begin with David Hume's famous discussion which has generated so many responses and continuations. In that discussion Hume put forward what is probably the most influential philosophical definition of "miracle" ever given:

> A miracle may be accurately defined, a transgression of a law of nature by a particular volition of the Deity, or by the interposition of some invisible agent.[1]

This definition has two parts. On the one hand, it specifies the relation of the miraculous act or event to the laws of nature. On the other hand, it specifies the relation of that event to a divine or supernatural agent. It seems to me that both of these elements reflect aspects of the pre-philosophical way in which miracles are construed, at least in Christian contexts.

One of these pre-philosophical elements is that the miracle is something which would not have happened—indeed, which *could not* have happened—in the ordinary course of events. It strikes the observer, the observer who recognizes it as a miracle, as being somehow a break in the structure of the world. It need not, of course, be an unwelcome break. It may well be recognized, as C.S. Lewis suggests, as a break which is *fitting*, appropriate to the situation in which it occurs.[2] But it is seen as something which does not "naturally" belong to that situation.

In one of the Gospels, for example, it is said that Jesus was a guest at a wedding party in which the supply of wine was unexpectedly exhausted. He asked the servants to fill several jugs with water, and then immediately had them serve a sample of this drink to the master of the feast. That worthy gentleman found it to be wine of a better quality than had been originally provided.[3] Apparently the water had been converted, more or less instantaneously, into wine. Regardless of whether we believe this story to be true most of us, I think, will recognize it as belonging to a different genre than a story about someone who sends a servant out to buy some more wine from the local supplier.

One way of trying to formulate this difference—but it is only an initial approximation—is to say that this act, like the healings, the raising of

Lazarus from the dead, and so on, is *hard*. Not everyone could do it. There is, as it were, a resistance in things against events of this sort, and it requires a special power to accomplish them. No doubt this power is sometimes construed simply as a force which coerces things into a course which they would not otherwise follow. But sometimes in the Gospels there seems to me to be a different suggestion, a construal of the requisite power not as a force but as an authority. This distinction, however, is not one we can follow out here.

That the miraculous act is hard to do is, of course, not exactly the right thing to say. It apparently is not hard in just the same way in which it is hard to run a mile in four minutes, and it does not require special powers in the same way as breaking an Olympic record requires unusual strength, endurance, and skill. We are tempted to say that it is even harder than that. But of course that is not quite right either. Maybe Hume's way of putting it, in terms of laws of nature, is more illuminating. At any rate, once we have the concept of a law of nature—once it seems to us that we can say something penetrating and revealing about the world by using that notion—then it also seems natural to try to explain the special character of the miraculous in those terms. That is the project which I want to explore in this paper.

Whether we can illuminate the idea of the miraculous, however, by means of the concept of the laws of nature will presumably depend on what the content of that latter concept is. It may be that the idea of a law of nature was first introduced in the West by thinkers operating more or less within a Christian framework of thought. But for several hundred years now that idea has been developed and applied in a largely secular way, without much concern for its religious connections. Does it still connect usefully with the religious concept of the miraculous?

Before we get into that, however, let us return to the pre-philosophical context for a moment to notice that the second element in it, that of the miracle's being the act of a special agent, is closely connected there with the first. We may try to get across a sense of the special character of the miraculous act by saying, as I did above, that not everyone could do it—it must take a very special sort of person to convert water into wine, to calm a storm by speaking to it, to call the dead from the grave, and so on. But of course we might also try to convey a sense of the special character of the person by reference (in part) to the miraculous acts which he did. Jesus, that is, must be a very special sort of man because he could, and did, raise the dead, etc. At the pre-philosophical stage, then, the two elements which appear in Hume's analysis are closely inter-twined. Perhaps we wish (is it for the sake of clarity?) that they could be separated.

In Hume's analysis itself, it seems to me, they *are* separated. Hume conjoins these elements, of course. Nothing will count as a Humean miracle unless it is *both* a violation of a law of nature and the action of a divine agent. But, so far as I can see, Hume leaves this conjunction as possibly purely external. He suggests no internal connection between these concepts. If we take his analysis seriously, therefore, we can ask whether it is possible that there is an event which satisfies one-half of the analysis but not the other. Could there be, for example, an event which was a violation of a law of nature, but which was not (in any special way, at least) an act of God? Such an event would not, of course, be a Humean miracle. But could such an event occur? Do such events occur? Do we have a special name for them? And on the other hand, could there be an act of God—in a sense, that is, in which not everything is an act of God—which was not a violation of a law of nature?

Though I mention these questions here, I will have only a little to say about them in this paper. Like most of the discussions growing out of Hume's analysis—indeed, like Hume's own discussion—mine here will focus mainly on the first element in his definition, the relation of the miraculous to the laws of nature. And I begin with what seems to me to be a powerful objection to the reality of Humean miracles.

The objection of which I am thinking is put by Alastair McKinnon, for example, in this way:

> The idea of a suspension of natural law is self-contradictory. This follows from the meaning of the term... [Natural laws] are simply highly generalized shorthand descriptions of how things do in fact happen.... Hence there can be no suspensions of natural law rightly understood.... Once we understand natural law in this proper sense we see that such a law, as distinct from our conception of it, is inherently inviolable. Hence anything which happens, even an apparent miracle, happens according to law.... This contradiction may stand out more clearly if for *natural law* we substitute the expression *the actual course of events. Miracle* would then be defined as "an event involving the suspension of the actual course of events." And someone who insisted upon describing an event as a miracle would be in the rather odd position of claiming that its occurrence was contrary to the actual course of events.[4]

McKinnon, as we see, holds that it is not logically possible that an event satisfy the first part of Hume's analysis—i.e., it is not logically possible that there be an event which is a violation of a law of nature. And why would miracles be logically impossible? It is because a law of nature does not allow—that is, it *logically* does not allow—of any violations.

I said earlier that miracles may be thought of as being hard to do, and as requiring special powers. The objection we are now considering does not proceed, however, by construing the laws of nature themselves as being so resistant as to surpass any counter-vailing power. McKinnon, in fact, says explicitly that laws of nature "exert no opposition or resistance to anything, not even to the odd or exceptional."[5] No, it is simply that the laws of nature are being construed either as invariant regularities in the natural world or else as the statements which express, or assert the occurrence of, such regularities. As McKinnon puts it, they are just generalized descriptions of the actual course of events, no matter what those events happen to be.

If we construe a law of nature in this way, then the proposition which corresponds to a law of nature will have the form of a universal generalization. The alleged violation, on the other hand, will presumably be a particular event—something like the conversion of the water into wine or the raising of Lazarus from the dead. The corresponding proposition will be either a singular proposition or an existential generalization. And now what is the logical relation of this proposition to the universal generalization which corresponds to the law of nature?

Well, if these two propositions are logically compatible then evidently the particular event is compatible with the invariant regularity. But in that case it is not a violation of that regularity, and hence it is not a Humean miracle. If, on the other hand, the two propositions are logically incompatible, then it is not logically possible that they should both be true. If it is the proposition asserting the occurrence of the particular event which is false, then that event did not occur. There has therefore been (so far, at least) no miracle. If, on the other hand, it is the universal generalization which is false, then the world does not in fact contain the corresponding invariant regularity. But (on this view) that amounts to saying that the world does not contain that law of nature after all. It was at best merely an *apparent* law of nature, what was *thought* to be a law of nature, or some such thing. But since the regularity was not in fact invariant it did not constitute a genuine law. Hence there has been no violation of a genuine law, and so again there has been no genuine Humean miracle.

Every possibility, therefore, seems to lead to the same result. No Humean miracle has occurred. And therefore, it would seem, no such miracle is possible. Put somewhat picturesquely, this view of things claims that either the alleged event can co-exist peacefully with the regularity or else it must kill the regularity, showing it to be a sham. In neither case is there a genuine violation of a genuine regularity, and therefore in neither case is there a genuine miracle.

As I said, this seems to me to involve a powerful and significant objection, but in the way in which it has been put here it invites an easy reply. We can begin by observing that the conclusion which we have attributed to the objector need not be greatly disturbing to any religious person or any "friend of miracles." Nothing that the objector has said tends to show at all, or to make it in any way probable, that Jesus did not turn water into wine, that he did not calm a storm with a word or raise Lazarus from the dead, and so on. Nor does it tend to show that these events did not have a profound religious significance. It does not even tend to show that these things, if they happened, were not miracles. At most (for better or worse) it tends to show that they are not *Humean* miracles. That is, if the objector is right in this argument, then the friend of miracles cannot use Hume's analysis to elucidate the concept of a miracle. Either he must leave that concept in its somewhat inchoate pre-philosophical condition, or he must find some illuminating alternative to Hume's suggestion. The concept of natural law which is adopted by McKinnon, then, is not helpful to the friend of miracles, but neither is it damaging to him. It simply turns out to be pretty much irrelevant to the topic of miracles.

We need not, it seems to me, think that it must be a great tragedy if the concept of natural law turns out not to be very useful in explaining the concept of a miracle. After all, we have lots of concepts which are not closely connected with the miraculous. And we might well be able to find some other useful way of analyzing and explaining what a miracle is. In this paper, however, I am continuing to explore what we can do with laws of nature in this connection.

As I say, we can observe that McKinnon's claim here need not be disturbing to the friend of miracles. Perhaps more fruitful, however, would be the observation that this objection itself relies on an unsatisfactory conception of a law of nature, or at least one which is widely thought to be unsatisfactory. If a law of nature is simply an invariant regularity then we do not provide for a distinction in this connection between those regularities which are *accidental* and those which are somehow more deeply rooted in the nature of things. Put in the more formal mode of speech, it is often pointed out that some universal generalizations seem to entail a corresponding set of counter-factual hypotheticals, while other generalizations do not. It may be true, for example, that everyone here today is a U.S. citizen. But even if this is true it does not seem to imply that if Margaret Thatcher were here today then she would be a U.S. citizen. If it is true, however, that all masses attract each other according to Newton's formula, then that *would* seem to imply that if I were wearing a massive helmet right now then it would be attracted by the earth. Generalizations of the latter sort are often called *nomological* or *law-like*, and the other sort are the accidentals. And it is rather commonly held that it is only the nomological generalizations which represent, or correspond to, laws of nature. And if that is correct, then McKinnon's account here is defective.

We may note in passing, however, that ignoring this distinction, as McKinnon appears to do, makes much more plausible something else that McKinnon holds. He says that scientists "assume that all events are law-like (whatever that really means) or, at least, that they must be treated as such. They assume that every event can be shown to be an instance of some generalization, whether simple or statistical. This is why the scientist holds that there are no suspensions of natural law."[6]

Now, it is a fact that if we place no restriction on the type of generalization which is allowable, then every event, no matter how bizarre and anomalous it may be, will be subsumable under some generalization. This is like the fact that no matter how randomly a set of points may be distributed on a graph, there is some line which can be drawn through them. Given, then, what appears to be McKinnon's version of a law of nature, what is here ascribed to the scientist as an "assumption" turns out to be a necessary truth.

If, however, we restrict the relevant generalizations to those which are nomological, and perhaps also (as Richard Swinburne does) to those which are relatively simple, then it is not at all clear that all events are subsumable in this way.[7] And if some scientists do *assume* that this is the case, as McKinnon says, then we might well ask them what has led them to this curious assumption.

Returning now to our main line of inquiry, I will proceed on the supposition that the nomological/accidental distinction is an important one for our concept of a law of nature. The notion of a nomological is, of course, not perfectly clear itself. I don't have much that is illuminating to say about it right here, though I will have one further suggestion later on. For the time being let me just observe that I find a suggestion of R. F. Holland attractive in this connection. Objecting to the view that a law of nature is just a description, Holland says that "the law tells us, defines for us, what is and is not *possible*. . ."[8] And he goes on to say that a law of nature, like a legal law, "stipulates" something. And this suggests that the formal representation of such a law will be a universal generalization with the modality of necessity.

Adopting this suggestion however, as I propose to do, seems to re-instate McKinnon's objection, perhaps now in a less vulnerable form. For the singular statement, "This A is not B" seems to be incompatible with "Necessarily, every A is B" just as it is with the unmodalized "Every A is B." And so must it not again be the case that every actual event which apparently violates a law of nature really only shows that this was not a genuine law after all, since the modalized generalization is shown to be false by the counter-example to it?

Holland's own solution to this difficulty is to propose that we reject "that time-honored logical principle," *ab esse ad possee valet consequentia*.[9] And this is equivalent to rejecting a stock theorem of modal logic to the effect that *Necessary p* entails *p*.

That proposal does seem to solve the difficulty. If "Necessarily, every A is B" does not entail "Every A is B," then "this A is not B" does not seem to be incompatible with the modalized statement. And consequently, it would seem, both the law-like "Necessarily, every A is B" and the anomalous singular statement "This A is not B" may be true together. And so, if we can swallow Holland's proposal, we need not take the violation to invalidate the putative law.

What, however, becomes of the idea of violation here? If the singular statement is not incompatible with the law-like, modalized, generalization, then how does the singular statement represent a *violation* of the corresponding law? I think that we can answer this question. We can introduce the expression, "the *formal content* of P," where P is a modalized proposition, to refer to whatever proposition follows the (first) modal operator in P. Thus, the formal content of "Necessarily, every A is B" will be simply "Every A is B." The "time-honored principle" which Holland proposes to reject says that every necessary proposition entails its own formal content. But even if we follow Holland in rejecting this entailment, we can still recognize that the formal content of a necessary proposition bears a special and intimate relation to that proposition. We can therefore say that, where L represents a law of nature and P represents an event, then P represents a *violation* of L IFF P is logically incompatible with the formal content of L.

Well, this would seem to give us a usable notion of a violation of a law of nature, but perhaps the price seems too high. If we must reject a standard theorem of modal logic in order to retain the idea of a violation would it not be better to give up on that idea, give up on Hume's definition, and look for some other way of explaining what a miracle is? After all, if "necessarily, p" does not entail "p," then what will be left of modal logic at all?

Well, I think that there is something to this reaction, alright, but it need not be conclusive. We do need to recognize, I think, that Holland's way of putting the thing is unnecessarily paradoxical. He speaks of rejecting the time-honored principle. (Curiously, he also speaks of accepting "a contradiction in our experience."[10] But the effect of rejecting the time-honored principle is precisely to prevent the miracle from being contradictory to the law.) But nothing in the situation requires us to reject that principle in general. The most that we need along this line is to find *some* sort of necessity for which the principle does not hold. If we could ascribe that sort of necessity to the laws of nature, then we would be in a position to recognize violations of those laws. But we would not need to deny that the time-honored principle of logic still held for other sorts of necessity, for example for logical necessity.

Now, it is a curious and significant fact that we seem *already* to have at hand, and in common use, a sense of necessity which has just this feature. It is a sort of necessity for which the time-honored principle does *not* hold, one in which the fact that something is necessary does not entail that the thing actually happens. And where do we find this sort of necessity? Well, one place is in the law—not a law of nature now, but the sort of law that legislatures enact and which courts enforce, what I will call *legal* law. In that sort of law there is a necessity for which "necessarily, p" does not entail "p."

One common way to express a legal law is simply as a universal generalization, something like "Every resident having an annual income over $1,000 shall file a return by April 15. . . ." etc. Of course, there must be something in the context that indicates that the generalization is to be taken as a law. The fact that the generalization was adopted by a state legislature, for example, would perform that function. Given that context, however, the universal generalization expresses a legal law.

Now, this legal law seems to invite just the sort of observations which Holland makes about the laws of nature. The legal law is not simply a description of actual regularities in human behavior. Rather, it defines or stipulates a certain sort of possibility—it tells us what is *legally* possible and impossible. And, of course, the law admits of violations. That is, it provides a context or background against which the idea of a violation makes sense and furthermore, the actuality of a violation does not invalidate the law. Though the violation is a *violation* precisely in virtue of its contrariety to the law, nevertheless both the law and its violation can co-exist.

We can, of course, imagine someone's making the analogue of McKinnon's objection. Observing that someone has not filed a return, he would point out that this fact is logically incompatible with the truth of the universal generalization. The generalization must therefore be false. And how, he may ask, could a false generalization express a true and valid law?

In the case of the legal law, however, we recognize this objection to be misdirected. A person who makes such an objection to the propriety of the alleged law betrays his misunderstanding of what a legal law amounts to.

Though legal laws are often expressed simply as categorical generalizations sometimes the modal element in them is made more explicit by the inclusion in them of some modal expression. "All residents *must* file a return. . . ." Here the necessity seems to be open, on the surface of the expression. But it is a necessity for which the time-honored principle does not hold. A McKinnon-type objection to the validity of this law would again be misdirected.

Perhaps this point should be made more carefully. We can begin by observing that there is a sense in which expressions like

(1)   Mr. N, a resident, etc., did not file a return.

can be taken as representing or reporting a fact about the world, an actual event, etc. And there is a sense in which

(2)   All residents, etc., will file a return.

can be understood as a generalization which is logically incompatible with (1). (2), for example, might be a prediction made by a fortune teller or a political scientist. In that case, (1), if true, would show (2) to be false.

If legislature, however, were to adopt a sentence identical with the one which appears in (2) (doing so in the prescribed way, etc.) then it would not be asserting the proposition asserted in (2). The legislature would not be committing itself to something which was logically incompatible with (1). We could say that the legislature was adopting a *nomic* generalization.

(2N) All residents, etc., will file a return.

And this nomic generalization, though it uses the same sentence as (2), is not logically incompatible with (1). That is why a McKinnon-type objection fails. It confuses (2N) with (2).

In a similar way we need to distinguish

(3)   Necessarily, all residents will file . . .

from its nomic analogue, (3N), which might be expressed using the same sentence or a similar one. There are some sorts of necessity—logical necessity, for example,—for which (3) entails (2), and for which, therefore, (3) is logically incompatible with (1). In order to understand the law we do not need to deny that there are such types of necessity, nor need we entertain any doubt about that entailment. (3N), however, does not involve that sort of necessity. Perhaps (3N) entails (2N) (though I suspect that they are identical), but it does not entail (2). And therefore it is not logically incompatible with (1).

Earlier, I defined the expression, "the formal content of P," where P was a modalized expression. We should now revise this definition. The formal content of (3N) should not be taken to be (2N). It is, rather, simply (2). I.e., the formal content of a modalized proposition is the *non-nomic* analogue of the proposition which follows the (first) modal operator. We can then explain the notion of a violation just as before. Since (1) is logically incompatible with (2), the formal content of (3N), it is a violation of (3N).

Legal laws are not logically incompatible with their violations, and are not invalidated by their violations. It does not follow, of course, that legal laws have no bearing on human behavior. In some societies at least, the fact that something was legally necessary would be a good reason for expecting the thing to happen, and the fact that an alleged event was legally impossible would be a good reason for suspecting that the event did not really happen. And we could also go in the other direction. If we could not discover the legal laws of that society "directly," e.g., by reading the law books, then we might attempt to determine them inductively, by generalizing from observed behavior. If we noticed a lot of people rushing to the post office to file tax returns on April 15, for example, we might form the hypothesis that this date was specified by a law. We might go on to test this hypothesis further, coming to think, perhaps, that it was not exactly accurate, refining it to include a provision for automatic extension, and so on, until we came to some formulation as our best guess, subject, of course, to future correction, of one of the laws underlying the behavior of that society.

Well, we have had a long excursion into the law, the legal law, that is. Can we return to the laws of nature? I know that it is often said that the laws of nature are not at all like legal laws, that it is an anthropomorphic fallacy to think that they are similar, and so on. This is repeated so often, it seems to me, that perhaps we should take it to be the currently received doctrine on the subject. Must we therefore also take it to be *true*? I guess that I am not now ready to do so. For one thing, despite this alleged complete dissimilarity it has apparently been natural for hundreds of years, right down to the present, to use the very same word, "law," for both of these cases. That strikes me as significant, suggesting that there has been a long and persistent recognition of important structural similarities. Nor need we be completely vague about what those similarities are. We have just been noticing some of them, at least, in the last few minutes. I suspect that our long practice in the West of using the same terminology for legal laws and laws of nature has a substantial foundation in the nature of the phenomena which are being discussed.

At any rate, we do not seem to be at a loss for a sense of necessity, already in hand, which allows for violations. If we were to construe the laws of nature as having that sort of necessity, or some similar sort, then it would seem possible for there to be events which satisfy the first part of Hume's definition. That concept of a law of nature seems to promise some utility in explaining what a miracle is.

Well, I suppose that we can have one concept or another. Is that all there is to it? One feels like saying that there must be more. What idea of the laws of nature actually fits the world? What sort of laws are there, "out there"? I don't know that I can say much that is illuminating about this. Let me close, however, with one observation. Much contemporary discussion of this sort of topic by contemporary philosophers of science leaves us, I think, in an unsatisfactory position. I mentioned, early on in this paper, the distinction between accidental and nomological generalizations. Well and good; there does seem to be such a distinction. Some of these propositions support the corresponding counter-factuals and others do not. But why is that? It doesn't seem as though it could be due to a difference in the surface grammar of these statements, since at that level they are the same, simply universal generalizations. Maybe, however, it can be said that these propositions are to be understood in different ways. One of them is to be taken "simply" as a generalization, entailing only those instantiations which fall under it in the actual world. The other, however, is intended to be taken as a *law*. I.e., it is intended to be understood as entailing not only its actual instantiations but also the counter-factuals. So it covers not only the actual world but also a range of possible worlds. And I, at least, suppose that some account like this is probably true.

What happens, however, if we insist on understanding the so-called accidental as if it were a nomological? I.e., we understand it to entail the corresponding counter-factuals, or at least to support them. Well, presumably what happens in that case is that it just turns out to be false. Understood as nomological, the statement "Everyone here is a citizen of the U.S." is just false. There is simply no such law of nature. But what is it that makes this proposition, interpreted nomically, false? Well, perhaps it is the fact that it entails a proposition such as "If Margaret Thatcher were here today she would be a U.S. citizen." And that counter-factual proposition is false.

Well, perhaps that is why the generalization, interpreted nomically, is false. But that, of course, invites us to ask why this counter-factual is false, while the counter-factual which asserts that if I were wearing a helmet it would be attracted by the earth it true. One is tempted to say that one of these is true and the other is false because there is a law of nature which governs the attraction of the helmet and the earth, while there is no law of nature connecting presence in this hall with U.S. citizenship. That, no doubt, is true. But we began this series of questions by trying to understand the difference between the propositions which express laws of nature and those which express universal, but accidental, generalizations. If the present claim, therefore, that there is a law of nature concerning the attraction of the helmet to the earth is to be illuminating in this connection the reference here to a law of nature can't be understood to be simply a reference to some proposition. It must rather be taken as a reference to some element of the actual world. We must be asserting that some propositions, understood nomically, actually connect with some feature or aspect of reality, while others, if they are taken in the nomic sense, do not. That is what makes some of them true and others false. The laws of nature, then, will be actual features of the real world. We cannot generate or produce a law of nature simply by formulating the corresponding proposition, nor by understanding it in the nomological way. For if we do understand, for example, the proposition about U.S. citizenship in this way, then we do not make it into a law of nature. We simply convert it into a falsehood.

Now, we may of course still be somewhat puzzled to know exactly what sort of features of the world a law of nature is. It does not appear to be a physical object. Perhaps it is more like a relation. But it is apparently not a spatial relation, not a temporal relation, and so on. Nor can it be the relation (if any) which is expressed by an ordinary universal generalization. For if it were then every such true generalization would express a law of nature. At least one striking oddity about it is that if it is a relation, then it relates non-existent things just as well as existent things. In order to generate the counter-factuals it has to govern the non-existent helmet which I might be wearing but am not, just as well as it governs the existing shoes which I am actually wearing.

Now, some of the things which David Hume says in connection with the idea of causality might be interpreted as maintaining that this alleged relation is not a perceptual object.[11] We have no sense impression of it. Consequently, the alleged concept of this relation does not refer to any such impression or to the residue of any impression. Consequently, there is no genuine idea there. The words which we use in this connection are *merely* words—empty sounds. We cannot, therefore, have any genuine assertions or denials involving it. If we do interpret Hume in this way then either the common distinction between accidental and nomological generalizations is vacuous, or else Humean theory itself is mistaken. And if it is mistaken, then either we do have an impression of this relation after all, or else it is possible to have a genuine concept without having the corresponding impression. I am strongly inclined to think that the accidental/nomological distinction is valid and important, and consequently I think that the theory which I have tentatively attributed to Hume is mistaken. But I do not right now have any strong leaning toward locating the mistake in one rather than the other of its two possible locations.

We might still feel, of course, that we don't yet have a full idea of just what relation this is. I don't know that I can now go much further with this. I'm inclined to try one further step, using the ideas of a "power." I'm not fully confident of it. You can try it yourself and see whether you come up with something better. I'm somewhat attracted by the idea that the laws of nature reflect powers which are somehow embedded in reality, powers which run along certain lines, we might say, and not along others. There is perhaps a power which "seizes," so to speak, upon objects which are close to one another, and which then, impels them toward one another. If there is such a power, then it would be what the law of gravity amounts to. There is, on the other hand, no deep power in nature which seizes upon people who enter this hall, and impels them into U.S. citizenship. The absence of such a power, then, would explain why the fact that everyone here is a U.S. citizen, if it is a fact, is an accidental rather than a nomological fact.

Well, whatever the fate of this idea of powers may be, it seems as though if we take up a realistic notion of the laws of nature as being features of reality, features which tend to produce certain effects, then we can also think of something which may over-ride such a feature or negate its effect. It appears, then, that a realistic construal of the laws of nature provides both a distinction which is apparently important to the understanding of science and also an attractive way of explaining at least part of the concept of the miraculous.

University of Michigan

Endnotes

*Reprinted from *Faith and Philosophy*, Vol. 2, No. 4, October 1985. All rights reserved.

[1] David Hume, *Enquiry Concerning Human Understanding,* Sec. x, Part i.

[2] C. S. Lewis, *Miracles: A Preliminary Study* (London: The Centenary Press, 1947. 220 pp.), pp. 115-20 (ch. xii).

[3] John, ch. 2,vs. 1-11.

[4] Alastair McKinnon, " 'Miracle' and 'Paradox,' " *American Philosophical Quarterly*, Vol. 4, No. 4 (Oct. 1967) p. 309.

[5] Ibid.

[6] Ibid.

[7] Richard Swinburne, *The Concept of Miracle* (London: Macmillan and Co., 1970. 76pp.), pp. 23ff.

[8] R. F. Holland, "The Miraculous," *American Philosophical Quarterly, Vol . 2,* No. I (Jan. 1965), p, 46.

[9] Ibid., p. 49.

[10] Ibid., p. 51.

[11] David Hume, *A Treatise of Human Nature,* Book 1: Part i, Sec. i, and Part iii, Sec. ii.

Study Questions

1. What two conditions are necessary for a Humean miracle?

2. Alastair McKinnon thinks that one of the conditions in the answer to question (l) cannot be satisfied. Which one is it and why?

3. What are "nomological generalizations"?

4. Mavrodes finds a sense of "necessity" required for a "law of nature" in what area?

5. What sort of "feature (or features) of the world" is a law of nature?

35

Bayes, Hume, and Miracles

John Earman

John Earman is professor of philosophy at the University of Pittsburgh.

Recent attempts to cast Hume's argument against miracles in a Bayesian form are examined.* It is shown how the Bayesian apparatus does serve to clarify the structure and substance of Hume's argument. But the apparatus does not underwrite Hume's various claims, such as that no testimony serves to establish the credibility of a miracle; indeed, the Bayesian analysis reveals various conditions under which it would be reasonable to reject the more interesting of Hume's claims.

Recent articles by Dawid and Gillies (1989), Gillies (1991), Owen (1987), and Sobel (1987, 1991) have applied the machinery of modern Bayesianism to Hume's argument against miracles. There are some historical grounds for a Bayes-Hume connection, albeit of a somewhat tenuous kind. The current dating of Bayes' essay supports the conjecture that Bayes had read and was in part reacting to Hume's skeptical attack on induction.[1] In the other direction, Richard Price, who arranged for the posthumous publication of Bayes' essay, produced a work entitled *Four Dissertations*, the fourth of which cited Bayes' essay as part of an attack on Hume's argument.[2] Hume acknowledged Price's work in a cordial letter,[3] and Price returned the compliment by praising Hume in the second edition of *Four Dissertations* as "a writer whose genius and abilities are so distinguished, as to be above any of *my* commendations" (1768, p. 382). Nevertheless, the application to Hume of what we now call Bayesianism is anachronistic. For example, Bayes' theorem, so-called, is not to be found in either Price's work or in Bayes' original essay.[4]

Despite its anachronistic character, I agree with Dawid, Gillies, et al. that modern Bayesianism does serve to clarify the structure and substance of Hume's argument. I differ with the authors of these excellent articles on details of the interpretation of Hume and, more importantly, on what the analysis shows about the force of Hume's argument vs. what it shows about Bayesianism. While I am under no illusion that I can bring closure to this complex and endlessly fascinating topic, I hope to identify more accurately the points which a resolution of the problems involved must address.

1. Hume's Maxim on Establishing a Miracle

In Section X ("Of Miracles") of the *Enquiry Concerning Human Under-standing*[5] Hume offered the following Maxim:

> That no testimony is sufficient to establish a miracle, unless the testimony be of such a kind that its falsehood would be more miraculous, than the fact, which it endeavors to establish; and even in that case there is a mutual destruction of arguments, and the superior only gives us an assurance suitable to that degree of force, which remains, after deducting the inferior. (pp. 115-116)

In offering a Bayesian explication of the first part of Hume's Maxim, I will adopt Dawid and Gillies (1989) notation, where A is the proposition asserting the occurrence of the miraculous event in question, a is the proposition that a witness W has testified to the occurrence of the event, and K is the background knowledge. Since we are in a context where we know that W has testified, we should according to one standard Bayesian line conditionalize on a.[6] So the relevant probability of the falsehood of the testimony is the conditional probability $Pr(\neg A/a \& K)$, and the relevant probability of the fact which the testimony endeavors to establish is the conditional probability $Pr(A/a \& K)$. And since for one thing to be more miraculous than another is for the former to be less probable than the latter, the unless clause of Hume's Maxim is rendered

$$Pr(A/a \& K) > Pr(\neg A/a \& K). \tag{1}$$

On this reading the first part of Hume's Maxim is surely correct. For the testimony to establish the credibility of a miracle in the sense of making the miracle probable, a must combine with K so that

$$Pr(A/a \& K) > .5, \tag{1'}$$

and (1) is necessary and sufficient for (1'). It could be objected to my reading that it makes the first part of Hume's Maxim a platitude of Bayes-speak. On the contrary, I take this consequence to be a virtue especially since Hume says that he is offering a "general maxim."

Gillies (1991) and Sobel (1991) propose to interpret the unless clause of Hume's Maxim as asserting that

$$Pr(A/K) > Pr(a \& \neg A/K). \tag{2}$$

It has to be admitted that (2) fits better than (1) with Hume's declaration that the argumentation of Part I of his essay is based on the assumption that the "falsehood of the testimony [to the miracle] would be a real prodigy" (p. 116); for if the prodigy consists of a low value for $Pr(\neg A/a \& K)$ rather than for $Pr(a \& \neg A/K)$, then (1) and (1') automatically hold. But perhaps Hume's declaration was only meant to signal that in Part I he was not addressing the credibility problems that attach to testimonial evidence for miracles deemed to have religious significance. Moreover, immediately after stating the Maxim, Hume gives the following illustration:

> When anyone tells me, that he saw a dead man restored to life, I immediately consider with myself, whether it be more probable, that this person should either deceive or be deceived, or that the fact, which he relates, should really have happened. I weigh the one miracle against the other; and according to the superiority, which I discover, I pronounce my decision, and always reject the greater miracle. (p. 116)

The most straightforward reading of the probabilities involved is in terms of the conditional probabilities in (1).

Of course, if K contains a then (2) coincides with (1) (since $Pr(a \& \neg A/a \& X) = Pr(\neg A/a \& X)$).[7] But if not, then (2) does not coincide with (1); in particular, (2) is not sufficient for (1) or (1'), which is awkward since Hume sometimes talks as if the fulfillment of the unless clause of his Maxim is sufficient to establish a miracle, as when he writes that "If the falsehood of his testimony would be more miraculous, than the event which he relates; then, and not till then, can he pretend to command my belief or opinion" (p. 116).[8]

In any case, Gillies and Sobel are correct in noting that, assuming $Pr(a/K) > 0$, (2) is a necessary condition for (1). Applying Bayes' theorem to both sides of (1) and performing a couple of elementary operations leads to

$$Pr(A/K) > \frac{Pr(a \& \neg A/K)}{Pr(a/A \& K)}. \tag{3}$$

Since $Pr(a/A \& K) \leq 1$, (3) can hold only if (2) holds.

Since Hume himself did not use probability notation and was evidently not familiar with the probability calculus, it is hardly surprising that his Maxim is ambiguous as viewed through the lens of probability. Various ambiguities were pointed out as early as 1838 by Charles Babbage in his *Ninth Bridgewater Treatise*. One of Babbage's readings is in line with (1), my preferred interpretation. Babbage also suggests reading the unless clause of the Maxim as requiring that $\Pr(A/K)$ > $\Pr(a/\neg A \& K)$, which is less useful since it is neither necessary nor sufficient for (1).[9]

Whatever Hume's intentions, it is (1) that counts for deciding whether the testimony has established the credibility of a miracle. Thus, in what follows I will use (1) as the Bayesian reading of the unless clause of Hume's Maxim. A little further manipulation of the equivalent (3) of (1) produces another and, for Hume's purposes, more useful necessary and sufficient condition for (1):

$$\Pr(A/K) > \Pr(a/\neg A \& K) \times [(1 - \Pr(A/K))/\Pr(a/A \& K)]. \tag{4}$$

I will have occasion below to use (4) in assessing the strength of Hume's argument.

2. Hume's Goal: Strong Form

Any assessment of Hume's argument against miracles must, of course, start from the goals he was trying to reach. As a first rough cut we can say that Hume had two goals, corresponding to his division of "Of Miracles" into two parts. Part I purports to supply a *"proof* ... against the existence of any miracle" (p. 115), and this is so even on the assumption that the falsehood of the testimony, upon which the miracle is to be founded, "would be a real prodigy" (p. 116). Part II provides, as it were, a fall back position, by arguing for a pair of more modest claims. The first is that the assumption in question is unwarranted in all actual historical cases, with the upshot that no testimony has ever established the probability of a miracle. The second claim is that when we take into account the special features attending alleged religious miracles, the assumption in question always fails, with the upshot that no testimony can ever have the force to establish a miracle as "a just foundation of religion" (p. 127). In fact, however, the division is not so neat. Part II repeats some of the sentiments of Part I. And in the editions of the *Enquiry* prior to 1768, Part II contained the assertion that "... it appears that no testimony for any kind of miracle can ever possibly amount to a probability, much less a proof."[10] I will not attempt to resolve this and other puzzles of organization to be remarked on below, but instead I turn to a critical examination of Hume's claims.

When Hume claims in Part I to offer a *"proof* ... against the existence of any miracle," I take him at his word: he means his argument to apply to any miracle, not just miracles that are supposed to have religious significance. This literal reading seems to be belied by a footnote. After first defining a miracle as "a violation of the laws of nature" (p. 114), Hume adds the qualification that "A miracle may be accurately defined, *a transgression of a law of nature by a particular volition of the Deity, or by the interposition of some invisible agent"* (p. 115, n. 1). I regard this note as an organizational aberration, but whether or not I am correct, the key point here is that nothing in Hume's argument for his strong claim in Part I rests on a presumed supernatural cause of the violation of the law. Hume's note is, however, relevant to a kind of last-ditch position which will be examined below in section 4.

Hume's "proof" is admirably brief. The challenge here is to find a plausible Bayesian reading of it. "A miracle," according to Hume "is a violation of a law of nature; and as a firm and unalterable experience has established these laws, the proof against miracles, from the very nature of the fact, is as entire as any argument from experience can possibly be imagined" (p. 114). A little later Hume argues that because the miraculous type event has never been observed in any age or country

> There must, therefore, be a uniform experience against every miraculous event, otherwise the event would not merit that appellation. And as uniform experience amounts to a proof, there is here a direct and *full* proof, from the nature of the fact, against the existence of any miracle . . . (p. 115)

Perhaps in Bayesian terms this should be taken to mean that if A is a counterinstance to a well confirmed (putative) law of nature L, and if K summarizes "firm and unalterable experience," then $Pr(A/K) = 0$ and, consequently $Pr(A/a\&K) = 0$, which in turn means that (1) fails.[11] If L can be thought of as an infinite conjunction of a countable number of instances in the sense that $Pr(L) = \lim_{n \to \infty} Pr(\neg A(1)\&\neg A(2)\&...\&\neg A(n))$, then setting $Pr(A(i)/K) = 0$ for each $i = 1, 2, ...$ entails that $Pr(L/K) = 1$, which grates against both common sense and actual scientific practice. Scientists not uncommonly spend many hours and many dollars searching for events of a type that past experience tells us never have occurred (e.g., proton decay). Such practice is hard to understand if the probability of such an event is flatly zero and the probability of the putative law asserting the non-occurrence of this type of event is unity. Richard Price (1768) argued as much.

> It must, however, be remembered, that the greatest uniformity and frequency of experience will not afford a proper proof, that an event will happen in a future trial, or even render it so much as probable, that it will always happen in all future trials. . . [L]et us suppose a solid which, for ought we know, may be constituted in any one of an infinity of different ways, and that we can judge of it only from experiments made in throwing it ... But though we knew, that it had turned the same face in every trial a million of times, there would be

no certainty that it would turn this face again in any particular future trial, nor even the least probability, that it would never turn any other face (pp. 392-393). These observations are applicable, in the exactest manner, to what passes in the course of nature, as far as experience is our guide. Upon observing, that any natural event has happened often or invariably, we have only reason to expect that it will happen again, with an assurance proportioned to the frequency of our observations. But, we have no absolute proof that it will happen again in any particular future trial; nor the least reason to believe that it will always happen. (p. 395).

It is ironic indeed that Hume's strong claim against miracles makes him out to be much less of an inductive skeptic than his opponent Price.[12]

Hume also held that "the evidence, resulting from the testimony, admits of diminution, greater or less in proportion as the fact is more or less unusual" (p. 113).[13] He might then have reasoned that since a miraculous event is not merely an unusual one but an extremely unlikely one, the testimony is so diminished that it cannot possibly establish a miracle in the sense of (1). If so, he was mistaken. Take the strength of the evidence resulting from the testimony to be measured by $Pr(A/a\&K)$. Then Bayes' theorem shows that Hume was correct to the extent that this strength is directly proportional to $Pr(A/K)$. So if the unusualness of the event is reflected in the assignment of a low prior probability, then the unusualness of the event does, other things equal, diminish the strength of the testimony. But other things need not be equal. And Bayes' theorem shows how and under what circumstances testimonial evidence can make A more probable than not as long as we set—as I argued above we should—$Pr(A/K) > 0$.

There is a sense in which we did not need to go through this exercise of first searching the text of "Of Miracles" to find possible motivations for Hume's strong claim against miracles, and then rejecting each in turn; for one knows in advance that this claim cannot stand. Every student of "Of Miracles" knows the dilemma that faces Hume's definition of miracles as a violation of laws of nature. In the Bayesianized setting, this dilemma takes the following form. If a law of nature is defined as true general proposition and, therefore, one without exceptions, then there cannot—logically cannot—be a miracle, and no Bayesianizing is required to show it. On the other hand, if by a law Hume meant a putative law—that is, a proposition lawlike in form (here fill in your favorite account of law likeness), which has no known counter instances and many known positive instances—then we certainly do not want to be committed to the position that no amount of testimonial evidence can ever make us reasonably sure (in the sense of a posterior probability greater than .5) that the proposition fails. If Bayesianism entailed such a position—and no extant form of it does—then Bayesianism would be suspect.

How could Hume have gone so wrong? The answer lies in Hume's crude view about how probability considerations are to be applied. Roughly, his idea was that when we are dealing with a type of event which, in the appropriate circumstances, sometimes occurs and sometimes not, then the probability calculus is to be brought into play in forming estimates of the chances that the event will occur in some future trial; but if the event has invariably occurred in the appropriate circumstances, then on Hume's view probability considerations are irrelevant since we have a full "proof."[14]

3. Hume's Goal: Modest Forms

In Part II Hume reviews a number of historical cases and concludes—in editions after 1768—that "Upon the whole, then, it appears that no testimony for any kind of miracle ever has amounted to a probability, much less a proof" (p. 127). Later in the same paragraph Hume makes a stronger and more interesting in-principle claim that "no human testimony can have such a force as to prove a miracle, and make it a just foundation for any such [i.e. any popular] religion." On one plausible reading this latter claim is to be understood as the assertion that no testimony can establish the violation of a (putative) law when the violation is deemed to have religious significance. The type of example Hume has in mind here is a resurrection, a walking on water, and the like. In the following section I will consider a weaker reading of the in-principle claim.

Hume's argument for the in-principle claim is based on the notion that "if the spirit of religion join itself to the love of wonder, there is an end of common sense; all human testimony, in these circumstances, loses all pretensions to authority" (p. 117). The argument offered refers back to the second half of the Maxim, which suggests a kind of subtraction procedure. The subtraction procedure becomes more explicit in Part II:

> It is experience only, which gives authority to human testimony; and it is the same experience, which assures us of the laws of nature. When, therefore, these two kinds of experience are contrary, we have nothing to do but subtract the one from the other, and embrace the opinion, either on one side or the other, with that assurance which arises from the remainder. But according to the principle here explained, this subtraction, with regard to all popular religions, amounts to an entire annihilation; and therefore we may establish it as a maxim, that no human testimony can have such force as to prove a miracle, and make it a just foundation for any such system of religion. (p. 127)

This subtraction procedure may seem to involve an illicit double counting. If $\Pr(A/a\&K) > .5$, then that's the way it is; the dangers of self-deception and deceit in cases where the alleged miracle is deemed to have religious significance have already been taken into account. But there is a more plausible version of Hume's argument that can be rendered by using formula (4). From the definition of miracle we can agree that the left hand side of (4) has a tiny but non-zero value. For sake of illustration let us set $Pr(A/K) = 10^{-8}$. The witnesses who testify to miraculous events deemed to have religious significance tend to be religious believers or those predisposed to religious belief. It is then fair to assume that such a witness will almost surely report a miraculous event of alleged religious significance if she observes it. Thus, $Pr(a/A\&K)$ is very near 1, though perhaps not as near as $1 - Pr(A/K) = 1 \, 10^{-8}$, with the upshot that the square bracketed term on the right hand side of (4) has a value of 1 or somewhat greater than 1. So for (4), and consequently for (1), to obtain, it is necessary that $Pr(A/K) > Pr(a/\neg A\&K)$. But surely (the Bayesianized Hume may argue) the probability that the witness will offer a testimonial on an occasion when the miraculous event does not occur far exceeds 10^{-8}. For witnesses who are already religious believers or who are predisposed to religious belief are vulnerable to self-deception and to the deception of others, and the converted are not above using deceit to win over the unconverted.

It is worth emphasizing that this version of Hume's argument does not rest on the contentious principle that the evidence of testimony is diminished in direct proportion to the improbability of the event testified to. Price countered that "improbabilities as such do not lessen the capacity of testimony to report the truth" (1768, p. 413). As an example, he noted that our inclination to believe a newspaper report that, say, ticket #11,423 was drawn in the lottery is not diminished in proportion as the number of lottery tickets is increased and, consequently, as the improbability of the event is increased.[15] However, Price conceded that in some circumstances the improbabilities may "affect the credit of testimony, or cause us to question its veracity" (1768, p. 417). Further, "The chief reason of the effect of improbabilities on our regard to testimony is, their tendency to influence the principles of deceit in the human mind" (1768, p. 420). Thus, it is not the improbability *per se* of a miraculous event that tends to diminish the value of the testimony but the fact that miracles are the kind of events that engage the passions of religion and the love of wonder and surprise. This concession is all that is needed for the above Bayesianized argument against miracles.

There is an appealing common sense core to this Bayesianized version of Hume's argument for his in-principle claim against religious miracles, and those who subscribe to the cautionary tale I sketched may be tempted to say that in this case Bayesianism is just common sense writ quantitatively. Giving in to that temptation would be a mistake, for there is nothing in Bayesianism per se that proves the in-principle claim. Those readers who know the dirty but by now fairly public secrets of

Bayesianism will already know why this is so. Convincing those not already in the know is complicated only because the tent flying the banner "Bayesianism" has all manner of campers under its canvas, and each of the many sub-groups needs to be treated separately. Since a detailed examination of this matter would take me too far afield, I will restrict myself here to a classification which, though crude, is sufficient to illustrate the main points.[16]

Perhaps the largest group of campers call themselves personalists. For them, epistemology is conducted in terms of personal or subjective degrees of belief. These degrees of belief are, of course, required to satisfy the axioms of probability. Some but not all personalists also require (as assumed above) that when a person has a learning experience, the content of which is captured by a proposition, then her degrees of belief after the experience ought to equal her previous degrees of belief conditionalized on the learned proposition.[17] It should be evident without much argument that this personalist wing of Bayesianism allows for a wide latitude in degrees of belief, so wide in fact that some of the campers in this wing will agree with Hume's in-principle claim while others will have degrees of belief that satisfy (4) and, therefore, (1) for some miracles deemed to have religious significance.

Thomas Bayes himself was not a pure personalist. His goal was to explicate the notion of reasonable or rational inductive inference, which he thought to require constraints on the assignment of prior probabilities. An examination of Bayes' proposed constraints reveals a sophisticated though problematic theory.[18] But even supposing Bayes' method of imposing constraints were unproblematic, it would be unavailing in the present context. Bayes was concerned with the event or state of affairs of an objective chance parameter taking a certain value p. Assuming that p is known, the probabilities of outcomes of running the chance experiment a specified number of times can be calculated.[19] As a result, the posterior probability that p lies in a specified interval is fixed once the prior distribution over p is given. By contrast, the Bayesianized Hume who is trying to combat belief in miracles is concerned with a case where not only the prior probability $\Pr(A/K)$ but also the likelihoods $\Pr(a/A\&K)$ and $\Pr(a/\neg A\&K)$ are up for grabs.

Those Bayesians who count themselves as objectivists would use frequency data to guide assignment of values to these factors. We have already seen that in the case of $\Pr(A/K)$ the guidance cannot take the simple minded form of using the value of the frequency of A-type event in past experience. That frequency may be flatly zero, but it seems unwise to set $\Pr(A/K) = 0$. For one thing, this leads to a probability measure that is not "strictly coherent." If probability is used as a guide to betting behavior, the agent whose degrees of belief are represented by such a measure can be induced to take a bet with the property that in no possible case can she win anything while in some possible case she will suffer a loss. As for the factors $\Pr(a/A\&K)$ and $\Pr(a/\neg A\&K)$ it is in principle possible to get relevant frequency data. But in the actual cases of alleged miracles of religious significance there is not enough undisputed data to give reliable estimates of the relevant frequencies. To overcome this difficulty one can try to reason by analogy with cases where the witnesses in question or ones like them testify as to the occurrence of a type of event that allows us to get undisputed and reliable frequency data. But there are no accepted rules for such analogical reasoning; and in keeping with the spirit of Bayesianism, such rules as we do fashion will be of a probabilistic form, involving priors and likelihoods about which the campers may differ. The chances of ending the regress that has started so that all would-be objectivists arrive at the same numbers seems dim at best.

The upshot is that every wing of the big tent of Bayesianism contains campers who meet all of the rationality constraints demanded by their brand of Bayesianism and yet who do not subscribe to Hume's in-principle claim that human testimony cannot have such a force as to establish a religious miracle.

This is hardly a surprising or unwanted conclusion. As any number of commentators have remarked, information about the probity of a particular witness or the weight of testimony from a number of independent witnesses may overcome initial doubts stemming from concerns about deception and deceit.[20] Bayes' theorem offers a simple explanation for the effect of independent witnessing coupled with minimal probity. Let a^n stand for the proposition that n witnesses have testified to the occurrence of the event. And for simplicity assume that each witness is as likely as any other to testify truly (i.e. $\Pr(a/A\&K) = p$ for each) and is equally likely as any other to testify falsely (i.e. $\Pr(a/\neg A\&K) = q$ for each). If we take independence to mean that $\Pr(a^n/A\&K) = p^n$ and $\Pr(a^n/\neg A\&K) = q^n$, Bayes' theorem yields

$$\Pr(A/a^n\&K) = \cfrac{1}{1 + \left[\dfrac{\Pr(\neg A/K)}{\Pr(A/K)} \left(\dfrac{q}{p}\right)^n \right]}$$

Minimal probity means that $p > q$, with the result that (assuming $\Pr(A/K) > 0$) as $n \to \infty$ a, $(q/p)^n \to 0$ and, hence, $\Pr(A/a^n\&K) \to 1$. The higher the probity ratio p/q, the faster certainty is reached. Or, to put the point in the manner of Charles Babbage (1838), no matter how small $\Pr(A/K)$ is as long as it is non-zero, it is possible to choose the number n of independent witnesses such that $\Pr(A/a\&K) > .5$.[21]

Turning from in-principle considerations to actual cases, what is disconcerting to common sense is that Bayesianism doesn't underwrite Hume's minimalist claim that no actual testimony for a religious miracle has ever amounted to a probability. My personal probabilities are in line with this claim. But the alignment is not dictated by the personalist form of Bayesianism or by any other workable form of Bayesianism of which I am aware. For those who find this negative result disconcerting, much worse is to follow.

4. A Retreat That Becomes a Rout?

Given the discussion of the preceding section we may assume that there are Bayesian agents and an A such that (1) holds, where A asserts the occurrence of an event which violates a well-confirmed (putative) law and which is of the type deemed to have religious significance. Having gotten this far we might as well simplify the subsequent discussion by further assuming that $Pr(A/a\&K)$ is so near one as makes no odds. Hume might have responded that even though a miracle has been proved, it "can never be proved so as to be a foundation of a system of religion." I am suggesting that the quoted phrase now be interpreted to mean that whatever religious significance the adherents of a religion want to attribute to the violation of the (putative) law, there are always alternative explanations of the violation that do not involve a divine being or similar notions at the core of the religion in question; and such alternatives can never be ruled out with certainty.

As already remarked above, Hume added a footnote in which he says that "A miracle may be accurately defined, *a transgression of a law of nature by a particular volition of the Deity, or by the interposition of some invisible agent*" (p. 115, n. 1). The charitable interpretation of this note is that Hume is anticipating the last ditch stand just sketched.[22] Without the charity, much of "Of Miracles" makes little sense. Part II discusses several examples of attested miracles from profane history, such as Tacitus' report of Vespasian who supposedly cured a blind man with spittle (p. 122), and Hume's hypothetical example of reports that Elizabeth I died on January 1, 1600 and that after being interred for a month, she reappeared and resumed the throne (p. 128). In such cases the testimony is only to the occurrence of the alleged event and not to any divine origin. But nevertheless Hume thought that all of his strictures apply. About the Queen Elizabeth case he says that "I should only assert that it [her death] to have been pretended, and that it neither was, nor possibly could be real" (p. 128). He does go on to add that should this alleged miracle be ascribed to a new system of religion, "this very circumstance would be full proof of a cheat" (p. 129). But that is because

As the violations of truth are more common in the testimony concerning religious miracles, than in that concerning any other matter of fact; this must diminish the authority of the former testimony, and make us form a general resolution, never to lend any attention to it ... (p. 129)

What then are we to say about the last ditch argument sketched above? Hume himself might have wished to use this argument, but a Bayesianized Hume cannot. To repeat, for a Bayesian, epistemology is not a matter of certainties but of greater and lesser probabilities.

The question now becomes whether the hypotheses at the core of a religion—for example the hypothesis D that there exists a divine being with specified characteristics—can be probabilified by the testimonial evidence to miracles. Since we have assumed that $\Pr(A/a\&K) = 1$, the question devolves onto the conditional probability $\Pr(D/A\&K)$. The first sub question is whether A confirms or supports D in the sense that

$$\Pr(D/A\&K) > \Pr(D/K). \tag{6}$$

Bayes' theorem gives as separately necessary and jointly sufficient conditions for (6): (i) $\Pr(D/K) > 0$ and (ii) $\Pr(A/D\&K) > \Pr(A/K)$ or, equivalently, (ii') $\Pr(A/D\&K) > \Pr(A/\neg D\&K)$. Needless to say, the adherents of the religion will be eager to affirm (i). And for a miracle of the appropriate type they will surely think that A is more likely under the assumption that the divine being exists than it would be if He did not exist (see, for example, Swinburne 1979). For these adherents, (6) holds. Furthermore, there is no reason in principle why the accumulation of a series of miracles of the appropriate types cannot boost the probability of D above .5.

At least all of this is consistent with being a good Bayesian personalist. It may be uncongenial to those Bayesians who want all terms in Bayes' theorem to be grounded in objective frequencies. But such scruples would disqualify not only the probabilification of D but many of the non-statistical theoretical hypotheses of the advanced sciences.

The logical positivists and their fellow travelers thought that they had a different way of disqualifying D; namely, they labelled it as "cognitively meaningless." Initially they took verifiability, or falsifiability, or some combination of the two as the touchstone of the meaningful. But under pressure of various counter examples they were forced to abandon this tack.[23] Reichenbach opted for a confirmability criterion by which a cognitively meaningful hypothesis is one which can have its probability raised or lowered by the evidence of observation. Reichenbach chose this criterion in part for its "overreaching" chara-cter.[24] He wanted to be a realist about the unobservables talked about in modern physics, and the Bayesian framework provides the means by which observation and experiment can generate degrees of belief in hypotheses about such entities. What I am suggesting is that the overreaching character of the method stretches much further than Reichenbach might have wanted and, indeed, it stretches into the religious realm. Reichenbach no doubt would have tried to draw the line using his frequency theory of probability. But nowhere does he give a workable frequency interpretation of the various terms of Bayes' theorem as applied to the theoretical hypotheses of modern science. Thus, Reichenbach's views on probability do not provide a way to block the reach of Bayesian inference to religious hypotheses that does not also block the reach to hypotheses of theoretical physics.

For those who want to be Bayesians and anti-religious at the same time, the situation I am pointing to can perhaps be partly defused by appealing to a Carnapian relativism.[25] There are (the story goes) a wide variety of linguistic/conceptual systems. It is the syntactical and semantic rules of a system that determine whether or not an expression is meaningful in that system. In some systems D and its like are well-formed and meaningful. And in these systems the Bayesian machinery can be used to discuss the confirmation of D by the testimony to miracles and by other evidence. In other systems D and its like will be ill-formed, either syntactically or semantically. For these systems the Bayesian machinery never gets into gear. The question, "Are we entitled to believe D?" must now be divided. It could be taken as an internal question, a question asked within a specified system. The answer is then as it is. If the system is one in which D is ill-formed, the answer is no because belief (or disbelief) does not properly attach to D. If the system is one in which D is well-formed, the answer is supplied for any person by cranking her version of the Bayesian machinery for the total available evidence. On the other hand, the question can be construed as an external question, a question asked from without all the systems. As such it can only be given sense as a query about which of the various systems one ought to use. Here the spirit of Carnap would reply that this query points to a pragmatic decision whose outcome will vary with the uses to which one chooses to put the system.[26]

I suspect that many religionists and anti-religionists alike would be unhappy with such a reading of their dispute. Certainly Price and Hume thought that they were engaged in a well-defined and heads-on cognitive dispute, not some relativist shuffle or a hassle over pragmatic factors. But I also think that this is the best anti-religionist Bayesians can do if they do not want their machinery turned against them.

To inject a personal note, my own Carnapian decision is in favor of a system within which religious hypotheses are counted as meaningful. And I agree with Swinburne (1979) that within such a system Bayesianism can be used to marshal inductive arguments in favor of these hypotheses. But my personal probabilities are not in line with Sunburns ultimate conclusion that, all evidence considered, the balance of probability is in favor of the existence of the Christian deity. Of course, such disagreements arise for scientific as well as religious matters. What is striking about modern science is the objectivity of scientific belief in the sense of a tight consensus of degrees of beliefs regarding core scientific hypotheses. I would contend, however, that there is no distinctively Bayesian explanation of this consensus and that one must look elsewhere, such as to evolutionary or sociological factors, for an explanation.[27]

5. Conclusion

Commentators on Hume's miracle argument tie themselves in knots trying to craft a definition of 'miracle'. I suspect that there is no single, simple definition that answers to all of the demands that are put on this concept. But we do not have to settle on any one definition to see the holes in Hume's argumentation.

1) If the argumentation of Part I of Hume's essay works, then it works against a miracle defined as a violation of a well confirmed and here-to-fore unviolated lawlike regularity. Only a crude view of induction and probability could have led to such a result. The more sophisticated view of inductive reasoning developed by the Rev. Thomas Bayes is an antidote, but since Bayes' essay was not published until 1763, Hume could not have availed himself of this approach.

2) Whatever the niceties of the definition of 'miracle', it is abundantly clear that for Hume a resurrection counted as a clear case of a miracle. It would be surprising if it were otherwise since the 18th century debate over miracles as a basis for the Christian revelation focused on this case. Moreover, Hume's concentration on testimonial evidence is explained by the fact that the belief in the resurrection of Christ depended on the testimony of the Apostles. Several claims can be made about such a miracle. (a) Because of man's love of wonder and the passions of religion, one should be cautious about accepting testimony to the occurrence of such a miracle. (b) No testimony in the actual historical record establishes the credibility of such a miracle. (c) It is not possible in principle to establish the credibility of such a miracle by means of testimonial evidence. (d) Evidence for such a miracle (testimonial or otherwise) cannot serve to establish the credibility of doctrines at the core of popular religions. Claim (a) is a platitude that does not require the support of any philosophical argumentation, Bayesian or otherwise. Claim (c) is a non-starter, at least by Bayesian lights. Claim (b) is not vindicated by Bayesianism. Bayesianism can be used to show how to argue for (b); but it can also be used to show how to argue against (b).[28] A similar point holds for (d), but this point deserves a more detailed discussion.

3) Some commentators want to define a miracle as an event which defies any natural explanation and which, therefore, demands a religious or at least a supernatural explanation. Hume seems to presuppose such a view when he states his contrary miracles argument. Suppose that the proposition M_i, i = 1, 2, ..., asserting the occurrence of a miracle of type i, is evidence for religious doctrine D_i in the strong sense that M_i could only be true if D_i is true. Then if the D_i are pairwise incompatible (as will be the case if they belong to competing religions), then no two of the miracles could have occurred and, consequently, any evidence for M_j tends to cancel evidence for M_k when j ≠ k. As Hume puts it, if a miracle has the force to establish a particular system of religion, "so it has the same force, though

more indirectly, to overthrow every other system . . ." (p. 121). From the Bayesian perspective this argumentation presupposes a crude view of the evidential role of miracles since it fails to allow that miracles can serve as evidence for a religion in the sense of raising the probability of the truth of its doctrines without serving as proof positive. Of course, one now has to face the problem that on the more sophisticated conception of the evidential import of miracles, evidence for the resurrection of Jesus of Nazareth will not serve as unequivocal evidence for the Christian religion. But an exactly similar situation obtains in the sciences where there are often many competing theories and where the evidence of observation and experiment rarely accords with only one of the theories. In both situations, the evidence has to be assessed in terms of degrees of belief, not in terms of "proofs." Here a Hume who has donned the mantle of Bayesianism might maintain that there is nevertheless an important in-principle distinction between the two cases: that whereas in science the accumulating evidence can lead to a firm consensus about which of the competing theories is probably true, the evidence for miracles is incapable of engendering a rational consensus about which religion is probably true. Such a scepticism about the theological doctrines of competing religions is compatible with Hume's declaration that considerations of design make it reasonable to believe in the existence of *a* deity. Of course, some argument for this more sophisticated form of religious skepticism is needed. The argument, if it could be made, would be more interesting than anything found in "Of Miracles."[29]

University of Pittsburgh

Endnotes

[1] Bayes' essay was published in 1763 under the title "An Essay Towards Solving a Problem of the Doctrine of Chances," *Philosophical Transactions of the Royal Society (London)* 53: 370-418. It is reprinted in *Biometrika* 45 (1958): 296-315. For the dating of Bayes' essay, see Dale (1986).

[2] Price gives a reference to Bayes' essay but does not mention Bayes by name; see Price (1768, p. 395).

[3] See Klibansky and Mosser (1954, p. 234).

[4] There are many different versions of "Bayes' theorem." The one used here states that

$$Pr(H/E\&K) = \frac{Pr(H/K) \times Pr(E/H\&K)}{Pr(E/K)}$$

Sometimes the principle of total probability is used to rewrite the denominator on the right hand side as $Pr(E/H\&K) \times Pr(H/K) + Pr(E/\neg H\&K) \times Pr(\neg H/K)$. The reader is invited to think of H as a hypothesis at issue; K as the background knowledge; and E as the additional evidence. $Pr(H/E\&K)$ is called the posterior probability of H.

$Pr(H/K)$ and $Pr(E/H\&K)$ are respectively called the prior probability of H and the (posterior) likelihood of E.

[5] All page references are to the Selby-Bigge/Nidditch edition of the 1777 posthumous edition of the Enquiry.

[6] See the discussion in section 3 below.

[7] Sobel (1987) points out that the problem of "old evidence" rears its ugly head in this context. I will ignore the problem here although I think that it poses one of the most difficult challenges facing Bayesian confirmation theory; see my 1989.

[8] Price paraphrased Hume's Maxim as asserting that "no testimony should engage our belief, except the improbability of the falsehood of it is greater than that in the event it attests." (1768, p. 405) Price explicitly states that (in our notation) the improbability of the event means $Pr(\neg A/K)$. His subsequent discussion leaves in doubt his interpretation of the improbability the falsehood of the testimony. One reading suggested by his examples is that he took this term to mean $Pr(\neg A/a\&K)$. This turns Hume's Maxim into an absurdity since the unless clause comes to the condition that $Pr(\neg A/K) < Pr(\neg A/a\&K)$ or, equivalently, that $Pr(A/K) > Pr(A/a\&K)$, which says that the testimony disconfirms A.

[9] A superficial reading of Babbage might suggest that he is putting forward the Gillies-Sobel condition that $Pr(A/K) > Pr(a\&\neg A/K)$. However, his formulas do not make sense unless interpreted in terms of the conditional probabilities $Pr(a/A\&K)$ and $Pr(a/\neg A\&K)$. See Babbage (1838, pp. 196-197).

[10] See Hendel (1955, p. 137, n. 11).

[11] Sobel (1987) considers the possibility that $Pr(A/K)$ be given a non-zero but infinitesimal value. On this suggestion, see Owen (1987) and Dawid and Gillies (1989).

[12] Using Bayes's suggested prior probability distribution, it follows that if n trials are run and the type of event in question occurs in each of them, then the probability that the event will occur in the next trial is $(n + 1)/(n + 2)$. Bayes's prior makes the probability of the hypothesis that the event will occur for all (countably infinite) future trials flatly 0, which strikes some as being overly skeptical.

[13] This contention is challenged directly by Price; see the following section.

[14] In modern parlance, Hume subscribed to Reichenbach's "straight rule" of induction which violates strict coherence; see section 4 below.

[15] It is instructive for the reader to apply formula (4) to this case, taking A to be the proposition that ticket #11,423 was drawn in the lottery and a as the proposition that a report to this effect appeared in the newspaper. Dawid and Gillies (1989) analyze the crucial term $Pr(a/\neg A\&K)$ on the assumption that if the newspaper makes a mistake and prints an incorrect number, it is no more likely to print one number than another. The reader may also want to consider the, perhaps, more plausible assumption that if the newspaper prints an incorrect number, the most likely scenario is that it has reversed two digits or mistranscribed one of the digits.

[16] More details can be found in my 1992.

[17] As an example of someone who rejects conditionalization, see van Fraassen (1989).

[18] For details, see my 1990 and 1992.

[19] The calculation assumes what David Lewis (1980) calls the "Principal Principle." Very roughly the idea is that if I know for sure that, say, the objective probability of heads on a flip of a coin is p, then my subjective probability that the

next flip ought to be heads is p, regardless of what else I know about the number of heads in past flips.

[20] Hume himself says as much in discussing the case of an eclipse which contravenes Newtonian laws (see Selby-Bigge 1975, pp. 127-128). But immediately thereafter in discussing the hypothetical case of a resurrection of Queen Elizabeth, he says in effect that no amount of testimony would convince him that "so signal a violation of the laws of nature" had taken place. Hume gives no principled way to distinguish the cases. But presumably he thinks that in the latter case the witnesses cannot be as independent as in the eclipse case. And presumably the quasi-religious nature of the latter miracles raises a greater suspicion of "knavery and folly."

[21] Babbage's calculation suffers from the fact that he assumes that q = 1 - p (see Note E, pp. 186-203 of his 1838). Babbage does not refer to Bayes but instead relies on the work of Laplace, Poisson, and Demorgan. I am grateful to Sandy Zabell for calling Babbage's work to my attention.

[22] Here I part company with Flew's interpretation; see Flew (1985, pp. 4-7).

[23] The story is too well known to need repetition here; for a retelling, see Hempel (1965).

[24] In Experience and Prediction Reichenbach wrote that "The probability theory of meaning ... allows us to maintain propositions as meaningful which concern facts outside the domain of immediately given verifiable facts; it allows us to pass beyond the domain of given facts. This overreaching character of probability inferences is the basic method of the knowledge of nature." (1961, p. 127). Religionists may claim that it is also the basic method of the knowledge of God.

[25] I have in mind Carnap's (1934) and (1952).

[26] I do not know whether Carnap himself would have wanted to apply the internal/external question apparatus to questions about the status of religious beliefs. But I note that he did apply it to questions about physicalism and mind-body identity; see Carnap (1963).

[27] See Ch. 6 of my 1992. Powerful merger of opinion results can be proven within the Bayesian framework. However since these results refer to an infinite limit, they fail to explain the actual consensus beliefs that arise in the medium and short runs. Moreover, these results are unavailable when the hypotheses at issue are under determined by the possible evidence.

[28] Some will rejoice in such a conclusion. Others will brood that Bayesianism cannot be the whole story of ampliative inference. Banner (1990) tries to overcome some of the perceived weaknesses of Bayesianism through a methodology based around inference to the best explanation. He then argues that religious beliefs can be justified using this methodology. I share van Fraassen's (1989) misgivings about inference to the best explanation.

[29] Thanks are due to Donald Gillies, Howard Sobel, and Sandy Zabell for helpful comments on an earlier draft of this paper.

Study Questions

1. John Earman focuses on David Hume's Maxim for establishing a miracle. What is it?

2.   What is Hume's goal?

3.   What, in your own words, is the Bayesian account of the Humean argument?

4.   Why does Earman think that one does not need to have a final definition of "miracle" to answer Hume?

5.   The Bayesian analysis adds a new dimension to the discussion of miracles for Earman. What is it?

For Further Reading

Babbage, C. 1838. *The Ninth Bridgewater Treatise*, 2d ed. (London: Frank Cass and Co., 1967).

Banner, M.C.. 1990. *The Justification of Science and the Rationality of Religious Belief* (Oxford: Clarendon Press).

Carnap, R. 1934. *Logische Syntax der Sprache* (Wein: Julius Springer).

Carnap, R. 1952. "Empiricism, Semantics, and Ontology," in L. Linsky (ed.), *Semantics and the Philosophy of Language* (Urbana: University of Illinois Press).

Carnap, R. 1963. "Herbert Feigl on Physicalism," in P.A. Schilpp (ed.), *The Philosophy of Rudolf Carnap* (La Salle: Open Court).

Dale, A.I. 1986. "A Newly Discovered Result of Thomas Bayes'," *Archive for the History of the Exact Sciences 35*: 101-113.

Dawid, P. and Gillies, D. 1989. "A Bayesian Analysis of Hume's Argument Concerning Miracles," *Philosophical Quarterly 39*: 57-63.

Earman, J. 1989. "Old Evidence, New Theories: Two Unsolved Problems of Bayesian Confirmation Theory," *Pacific Philosophical Quarterly 70*: 323-340.

Earman, J. 1990. "Bayes' Bayesianism," *Studies in the History and Philosophy of Science 21*: 351-370.

Earman, J. 1992. *Bayes or Bust? A Critical Examination of Bayesian Confirmation Theory* (Cambridge: MIT Press/Bradford Books).

Flew, A. (ed.) 1985. Of Miracles (La Salle: Open Court).

Gillies, D. 1991. "A Bayesian Proof of a Humean Principle," *British Journal for the Philosophy of Science 42*: 255-256.

Hempel, C.G. 1965. "Empiricist Criteria of Cognitive Significance: Problems and Changes," in *Aspects of Scientific Explanation* (New York: Free Press).

Hendel, C.W. (ed.) 1955. *An Enquiry Concerning Human Understanding* (Indianapolis: Bobbs-Merrill).

Klibansky, R. and Mosser, E.C. (eds.) 1954. *New Letters of David Hume* (Oxford: Clarendon Press).

Owen, D. 1987. "Hume versus Price on Miracles and Prior Probabilities: Testimony and the Bayesian Calculation," *Philosophical Quarterly 37*: 187-202.

Price, R. 1768. *Four Dissertations* 2d ed. (London: A. Millar and T. Caddel).

Reichenbach, H. 1961. *Experience and Prediction* (Chicago: University of Chicago Press).

Selby-Bigge, L.A. and Nidditch, P.H. (eds.) 1975. *Enquiries Concerning Human Understanding and Concerning the Principles of Morals* (Oxford: Clarendon Press).

Sobel, J.H. 1987. "On the Evidence of Testimony for Miracles: A Bayesian Interpretation of David Hume's Analysis," *Philosophical Quarterly* 37: 166-186.

Sobel, J.H. 1991. "Hume's Theorem on Testimony Sufficient to Establish a Miracle," *Philosophical Quarterly* 41: 229-237.

Swinburne, R. 1979. *The Existence of God* (Oxford: Clarendon Press).

van Fraassen, B.C. 1989. *Laws and Symmetry* (Oxford: Clarendon Press).

PART VI

DEATH AND IMMORTALITY

36

The Finality of Death

Bertrand Russell

Eminent British philosopher, Bertrand Russell, and author of numerous books, contends that life after death is not possible because it requires certain bodily states that are absent at death. He argues that it is not reasonable therefore to believe in life after death, and that the inclination to such belief is generated by emotional factors.*

Before we can profitably discuss whether we shall continue to exist after death, it is well to be clear as to the sense in which a man is the same person as he was yesterday. Philosophers used to think that there were definite substances, the soul and the body, that each lasted on from day to day, that a soul, once created, continued to exist throughout all future time, whereas a body ceased temporarily from death till the resurrection of the body.

The part of this doctrine which concerns the present life is pretty certainly false. The matter of the body is continually changing by processes of nutriment and wastage. Even if it were not, atoms in physics are no longer supposed to have continuous existence; there is no sense in saying: this is the same atom as the one that existed a few minutes ago. The continuity of a human body is a matter of appearance and behavior, not of substance.

The same thing applies to the mind. We think and feel and act, but there is not, in addition to thoughts and feelings and actions, a bare entity, the mind or the soul, which does or suffers these occurrences. The mental continuity of a person is a continuity of habit and memory: there was yesterday one person whose feelings I can remember, and that person I regard as myself of yesterday; but, in fact, myself of yesterday was only certain mental occurrences which are now remembered and are regarded as part of the person who now recollects them. All that constitutes a person is a series of experiences connected by memory and by certain similarities of the sort we call habit.

If, therefore, we are to believe that a person survives death, we must believe that the memories and habits which constitute the person will continue to be exhibited in a new set of occurrences.

No one can prove that this will not happen. But it is easy to see that it is very unlikely. Our memories and habits are bound up with the structure of the brain, in much the same way in which a river is connected with the riverbed. The water in the river is always changing, but it keeps to the same course because previous rains have worn a channel. In like manner, previous events have worn a channel in the brain, and our thoughts flow along this channel. This is the cause of memory and mental habits. But the brain, as a structure, is dissolved at death, and memory therefore may be expected to be also dissolved. There is no more reason to think otherwise than to expect a river to persist in its old course after an earthquake has raised a mountain where a valley used to be.

All memory, and therefore (one may say) all minds, depend upon a property which is very noticeable in certain kinds of material structures but exists little if at all in other kinds. This is the property of forming habits as a result of frequent similar occurrences. For example: a bright light makes the pupils of the eyes contract; and if you repeatedly flash a light in a man's eyes and beat a gong at the same time, the gong alone will, in the end, cause his pupils to contract. This is a fact about the brain and nervous system—that is to say, about a certain material structure. It will be found that exactly similar facts explain our response to language and our use of it, our memories and the emotions they arouse, our moral or immoral habits of behavior, and indeed everything that constitutes our mental personality, except the part determined by heredity. The part determined by heredity is handed on to our posterity but cannot, in the individual, survive the disintegration of the body. Thus both the hereditary and the acquired parts of a personality are, so far as our experience goes, bound up with the characteristics of certain bodily structures. We all know that memory may be obliterated by an injury to the brain, that a virtuous person may be rendered vicious by encephalitis lethargica, and, that a clever child can be turned into an idiot by lack of iodine. In view of such familiar facts, it seems scarcely probable that the mind survives the total destruction of brain structure which occurs at death.

It is not rational arguments but emotions that cause belief in a future life.

The most important of these emotions is fear of death, which is instinctive and biologically useful. If we genuinely and wholeheartedly believed in the future life, we should cease completely to fear death. The effects would be curious, and probably such as most of us would deplore. But our human and subhuman ancestors have fought and exterminated their enemies throughout many geological ages and have profited by courage; it is therefore an advantage to the victors in the struggle for life to be able, on occasion, to overcome the natural fear of death. Among animals and savages, instinctive pugnacity suffices for this purpose; but at a certain stage of development, as the ;Mohammedans first proved, belief in Paradise has considerable military value as reinforcing natural pugnacity. We should therefore admit that militarists are wise in encouraging the belief in immortality, always supposing that this belief does not become so profound as to produce indifference to the affairs of the world.

Another emotion which encourages the belief in survival is admiration of the excellence of man. As the Bishop of Birmingham says, "His mind is a far finer instrument than anything that had appeared earlier—he knows right and wrong. He can build Westminster Abbey. He can make an airplane. He can calculate the distance of the sun.... Shall, then, man at death perish utterly? Does that incomparable instrument, his mind, vanish when life ceases?"

The Bishop proceeds to argue that "the universe has been shaped and is governed by an intelligent purpose," and that it would have been unintelligent, having made man, to let him perish.

To this argument there are many answers. In the first place, it has been found, in the scientific investigation of nature, that the intrusion of moral or aesthetic values has always been an obstacle to discovery. It used to be thought that the heavenly bodies must move in circles because the circle is the most perfect curve, that species must be immutable because God would only create what was perfect and what therefore stood in no need of improvement, that it was useless to combat epidemics except by repentance because they were sent as a punishment for sin, and so on. It has been found, however, that, so far as we can discover, nature is indifferent to our values and can only be understood by ignoring our notions of good and bad. The Universe may have a purpose, but nothing that we know suggests that, if so, this purpose has any similarity to ours.

Nor is there in this anything surprising. Dr. Barnes tells us that man "knows right and wrong." But, in fact, as anthropology shows, men's views of right and wrong have varied to such an extent that no single item has been permanent. We cannot say, therefore, that man knows right and wrong, but only that some men do. Which men? Nietzsche argued in favor of an ethic profoundly different from Christ's, and some powerful governments have accepted his teaching. If knowledge of right and wrong is to be an argument for immortality, we must first settle whether to believe Christ or Nietzsche, and then argue that Christians are immortal, but Hitler and Mussolini are not, or vice versa. The decision will obviously be made on the battlefield, not in the study. Those who have the best poison gas will have the ethic of the future and will therefore be the immortal ones.

Our feelings and beliefs on the subject of good and evil are, like everything else about us, natural facts, developed in the struggle for existence and not having any divine or supernatural origin. In one of Aesop's fables, a lion is shown pictures of huntsmen catching lions and remarks that, if he had painted them, they would have shown lions catching huntsmen. Man, says Dr. Barnes, is a fine fellow because he can make airplanes. A little while ago there was a popular song about the cleverness of flies in walking upside down on the ceiling, with the chorus: "Could Lloyd George do it? Could Mr. Baldwin do it? Could Ramsay Mac do it? Why, NO." On this basis a very telling argument could be constructed by a theologically-minded fly, which no doubt the other flies would find most convincing.

Moreover, it is only when we think abstractly that we have such a high opinion of man. Of men in the concrete, most of us think the vast majority very bad. Civilized states spend more than half their revenue on killing each other's citizens. Consider the long history of the activities inspired by moral fervor: human sacrifices, persecutions of heretics, witch-hunts, pogroms leading up to wholesale extermination by poison gases, which one at least of Dr. Barnes's episcopal colleagues must be supposed to favor, since he holds pacifism to be un-Christian. Are these abominations, and the ethical doctrines by which they are prompted, really evidence of an intelligent Creator? And can we really wish that the men who practiced them should live forever? The world in which we live can be understood as a result of muddle and accident; but if it is the outcome of deliberate purpose, the purpose must have been that of a fiend. For my part, I find accident a less painful and more plausible hypothesis.

Endnote

Study Questions

1.   What is the central point to Bertrand Russell's contention that it is not reasonable to believe that persons survive death?

2.   Russell thinks that memory depends upon a property which is observable in certain "material structures." What is it?

3.   What, according to Russell, gives rise to the belief in life after death?

4.   What is the most important emotion?

5.   There is another emotion that gives rise to the belief in survival. What is it?

37

Monism and Immortality

Bruce Reichenbach

Bruce Reichenbach is professor of philosophy at Augsburg College, is author of *The Cosmological Argument: A Reassessment, Is Man the Phoenix?, Evil and a Good God, The Law of Karma: A Philosophical Study;* and is co-author of *Reason and Religious Belief.*

In chapter five of his book, *Is Man the Phoenix? A Study of Immortality,* he offers an analysis of dualism and concludes that there are no compelling arguments for dualism, and opts for monism, and acknowledges that though survival is not possible at death, life after death is possible through a recreation of the person.*

At this point it might be helpful to pause briefly to review what we have accomplished thus far. We have defined immortality as the actual existence of the individual human person for an indefinite period subsequent to his death, with that which makes for his own personal identity and the awareness of this self-identity essentially intact. Further, we have suggested that the problem of human immortality is in reality two problems. First, "What must man be like in order for there to be the possibility that he could live subsequent to his death?" and secondly, "What good reasons can be given for maintaining a belief in life after death?" In order to answer the first question, it was necessary to explore various views of the nature of man. These contending views were grouped under two classifications: dualism (or pluralism), in which the individual is composed of elements of different kinds, including an immaterial part called the mind or soul; and monism, in which the individual is a psycho-physical unity.

In the third chapter we undertook to explore the dualistic view and what it means to say that man has a soul. On the basis of our study of the nature of the soul, we concluded that man, understood in this fashion, was capable of being immortal. When the individual "died," his physical body died; but since his true person—his soul—was non-physical, it was not subject to death and hence could continue to exist. However, in chapter four we noted that there are serious difficulties confronting this position. Its denial of the death of the real person contradicts our ordinary way of speaking about death; it seems to conflict with science's conclusion that the body is a necessary condition for the existence of mental processes; it fails to inform us how the mind and body can and do interact with and influence each other; its language about the soul appears to involve the appeal to the philosophically untenable theory of private language.

The weight of these difficulties has been such as to suggest to some that we must abandon a pluralistic analysis of man and instead understand man as being a psycho-physical unity. But what does it mean to say that man is a psycho-physical unity? And how does this view account for and interpret human mental processes? Is immortality possible if one adopts this position? It is the answers to these questions which will occupy our attention in this chapter.

Behaviorism

The view of man which stands opposed to the dualistic thesis is usually termed monism. Those who maintain this position reject the supposed existence of a spiritual soul or mind which, though functioning within a body structured and operated according to natural laws, cannot be described in terms of the concepts employed by physical scientists. Man is a physical organism, such that all of his functions and operations—mental as well as bodily—are ultimately physiological events or behavioral acts.

The monistic theory has appeared in a number of guises throughout the course of Western thought. In the present century, two interpretations have had wide appeal. One of these, Behaviorism, was originally developed by the psychologist J. B. Watson. Traditional psychology considered itself to be a science of consciousness or of the mind. Accordingly, the bodily or physical aspect of man was largely neglected in its studies. As a science of mind, psychology proceeded by introspection. The psychologist or philosopher reflectively observed the contents of his own consciousness, presumably in a detached, critical, objective manner, so as to understand the nature of mental processes. Behaviorism, however, rejected these arm-chair, introspective procedures on the grounds that they introduced a subjective element into psychology. The phenomena so reported could not be observed and confirmed by independent observers, as was the case in other natural sciences. The obvious consequence of this lack of objective checking procedures was the great variety of introspective accounts and interpretations of human mental processes. To be a science, all subjectivity had to be rigorously excluded. Since Behaviorism desired to develop a scientific account of man, it replaced the methodology of an introspective account of consciousness with an objective account of human and animal behavior.

Behaviorism, however, went beyond mere methodological concerns to proffer a view of man himself. It claimed that mentalistic concepts such as "mind," "thinking," and "consciousness" had no place in an objective, scientific account, for they presupposed an outmoded and unscientific mentalistic philosophy. How then were mental phenomena to be understood? Since there is no soul but only the physical organism, mental concepts were to be redefined or analyzed in terms of objectively observable behavior. As such, what was once considered to be distinctively mental was now reduced to or seen to be nothing but behavioral responses of the organism as it interacted with its physical environment.

For example, thinking and imagery are not internal, subjective mental processes; they are not activities of a spiritual mind or soul. They are human behavioral activities. Watson equated them with faint reinstatements of certain muscular responses originally involved in speech and other motor behavior. Thinking is thus a muscular response of the organism to its environment, most frequently located in the larynx. Similarly, emotions and feelings are behavioral patterns or physical responses, predominantly of the visceral and glandular systems.

But what about mental and emotional processes which seem to occur when there are no behavioral manifestations? It seems to make sense to say that John is angry even though he is so controlling himself that he is not manifesting the kind of overt behavior which is commonly character-istic of individuals whom we term angry. Also there is evidence in terms of subsequent reports or actions to show that individuals do in fact think, even though we cannot measure any movement of their larynx. Watson's response to this was to define mental and emotional processes in terms of implicit (unobservable or minutely visible) as well as explicit behavior. In all cases of thinking, he argued, even when we cannot observe movement, there are minute or implicit movements of the laryngeal muscles. Similarly with the emotions, they are implicit as well as explicit movements of the visceral and glandular systems. What is needed are more delicate and sophisticated instruments to detect these faint movements.

Some who have attempted to improve the Behaviorist model have suggested that instead of appealing to implicit or covert behavior (which is in effect an appeal to ignorance), we should introduce the notion of disposition to account for the statement, for example, that someone is angry, though he is not manifesting anger-behavior. On this view, mental processes are to be analyzed either in terms of behavioral acts of the organism, or else in terms of dispositions of the individual to behave in a certain way should certain circumstances obtain. For example, when we say that a glass vase is brittle, brittleness is to be understood as a dispositional property. It is to assert a conditional proposition about the vase: if we dropped it from a normal height on a hard surface, or if the vase were struck by a hard object, it would not dissolve or evaporate, but would shatter into many fragments. The glass vase might never be dropped or struck; it might never manifest this brittleness. Yet we can say it is brittle because it would shatter given certain circumstances. Similarly, if I am said to be envious, it means that I am disposed to act in a certain way should certain circumstances obtain. If I had enough money, I would purchase objects similar to those possessed by the one whom I envy, I would try to outdo him by lavish spending; I would attempt to wean his friends or admirers from him to myself.

However, "dispositional statements are neither reports of observed or observable states of affairs, nor yet reports of unobserved or unobservable states of affairs. They narrate no incidents."[1] "To possess a dispositional property is not to be in a particular state or to undergo a particular change; it is to be bound or liable to be in a particular state, or to undergo a particular change, when a particular condition is realised."[2] Dispositional properties are logical constructions out of behavior. Thus, the Behaviorist thesis is maintained: "When we describe people as exercising qualities of mind, we are not referring to occult episodes of which their overt acts and utterances are effects, we are referring to those overt acts and utterances themselves[3]."

The Identity Theory

Subsequent philosophers have felt that more is needed to fully explain human conscious processes. For one thing, it is not enough to leave the analysis of mental processes simply on the level of behavior or dispositions, for explanations of this behavior or of these dispositional properties can be suggested. Just as one might explain the dispositional property of brittleness in the glass vase by noting its molecular composition and the strength of the bond between the particles (that is, by noting its physical properties), so too one might explain the behavior or disposition to behave by appeal to certain physical properties. The dispositional property of brittleness is explained by the physical state of the glass; likewise the disposition to behave in a certain way can be explained by the physical state of the organism. It is this state which causes or brings about the behavioral manifestations of the disposition. As such, an analysis of man in terms of behavior and dispositions to behave does not go far enough.

"Secondly, related to what we have just said, the mental appears to have a genuinely causal explanatory role. We might say that John acted the way he did at the party *because* he was envious. But an analysis in terms of dispositions eliminates this apparently causal explanatory aspect of the mental, for if envy as a disposition is a mere logical construction out of envy-behavior, we cannot rightly say that it caused an action.

Thirdly, the reports of mental processes going on inside me, of which I am immediately aware, appear to be *genuine* reports of real processes.

> When I think, but my thoughts do not issue in any action, it seems obvious as anything is obvious that something is going on inside me which constitutes my thought. It is not simply that I would speak or act if some conditions were to be fulfilled. Something is going on, in the strongest and most literal sense of "going on," and this something is my thought. Rylean Behaviorism denies this, and so it is unsatisfactory as a theory of mind.[4]

My behavior is not identical with my thought, as Behaviorism claims but is rather the expression of my thought.

Rejecting Behaviorism as a not completely satisfactory theory, while at the same time refusing to opt for a dualist view of man, recent monists have developed what is termed the Identity or Central-State Materialist Theory of the mind. The Identity Theory contends that insofar as a statement about a mental state or sensation is a report of something, that something is in fact a brain process, brain state, or a process within the central nervous system.[5]

This must not be understood to mean that "thought" means the same as "brain process of a certain sort." Statements about thoughts and sensations cannot be translated into nor are synonymous with statements about brain processes. Neither does it mean that statements about sensations and thoughts can be reduced to or analyzed into statements about states of the brain. It is *not* a theory about the meaning of mental terms or concepts at all, but rather about a logical identification which, if true, can ultimately be subject to empirical verification.

Neither do the proponents of the Identity Theory deny the existence or reality of mental or psychical states such as perceiving, conceiving, remembering, and imagining; mental states are as real as those physical processes which can be objectively observed. However, the event which the mental language reports is ultimately the same as or identical with the event which would be reported by the neurologist. What they deny is that states of consciousness are irreducibly psychical. Using thinking as an example, the event is one and physiological—an electro-chemical transference in the brain—though the perspectives from which the event is reported (as a mental state or as a process of the central nervous system) and the language used to report these perspectives (language about minds, thinking, and concepts, and language about brain waves, synapses, and electrochemical discharges) are two. Reports based on both of the perspectives are genuine; both of the languages used are legitimate; but both refer to one and only one physical event, for thinking is a brain process.

Perhaps one of their favorite illustrations will be of help.[6] The event of lightning can be reported from two different perspectives, using different language games or systems. The physicist reports a concentrated electrical discharge occurring at a particular time and place in the atmosphere; the ordinary observer reports a bright flash of light, jaggedly etched across the stormy sky. Both of these reports are genuine and use different and non-interchangeable language; but the event they report is one and the same. Similarly, the neurologist reports electro-chemical processes within the brain, whereas the individual states that at that time he was thinking about last winter's vacation in Peru. Both of these report real events. The one uses language about synapses, neurons, and electro-chemical discharges in the brain, the other uses language about minds, ideas, concepts, and memories. Further, these two languages are logically independent, containing non-interchangeable elements. However, the events reported by these two language systems are not two different events; they both report the same event.

In short, on this view man is *in toto* a physical organism: he possesses no non-physical entity. Man does have mental experiences, but his reports of them do not refer to separate and unique events, over and above certain physical processes of the organism.

Why should one opt for this view? Those who do so readily admit their materialistic bias. But it is not a bias without support. Recent advances in neurophysiology (developing plausible electro-chemical accounts of the workings of the brain) and in molecular biology (discovering the physical and chemical mechanisms which lie at the basis of all life) provide good reasons for opting for this view of man. But not only does this metaphysical view grow out of scientific advances, it also has the advantage of potentially being empirically verifiable. If and once we establish what the logical criteria are for "deciding whether two sets of correlated observations refer to the same event or to two separate but causally related events,"[7] then it becomes a matter of empirical and scientific research to discover whether or not there is a physiological process which satisfies these logical criteria. It is this consonance with the methods and results of science, and the possibility of empirical verification which it allows, which makes this metaphysical view of man philosophically attractive.

The Question of Immortality

But if we understand man's nature in this fashion, is human immortality possible? Traditionally, those who have maintained this view of man have held that it is not possible. Man is a physical organism who dies when his body ceases to function in certain significant ways. Nothing remains in or of man which would allow him to witness his own funeral.

Moreover, it is this view of the nature of man which is most frequently presupposed by critics of the doctrine of personal life after death. Arguing from this perspective, they contend that arguments for immortality are useless because life after death is impossible.

However, this position can be challenged; even if one grants a monistic view of the nature of human beings, I think it can be shown that personal immortality is possible. It is true that, since the individual is identical with that physiological organism which ceases to function at death, he likewise ceases to exist. However, life after death is possible because, first of all, it is not self-contradictory that an individual could be physically re-created or reconstructed to possess all of the physical characteristics of the deceased, such that he would look identical to the person who died. And since consciousness is a brain process, his brain could be so re-created and programmed as to have neural and chemical components and structures identical to the deceased, such that he would have the same memories, ideas, perspectives, and personality traits as the individual who died. In short, a person precisely identical to the deceased could be re-created, with the result that the person re-created would be the same person as the one who died; he would begin again to live where the deceased left off.

This is possible, secondly, because God is omnipotent; that is, he can perform any action which does not entail a self-contradiction. Since the re-creation of the same individual is not self-contradictory, he can re-create the very same individual to begin to live at the point where death brought an end to his experience, at a time and place of God's own choosing.

In short, life after death is possible for man, even if he be interpreted in a monistic fashion. Since man is viewed as being ultimately a physiological entity, such that all his behavior can be traced back to physiological events, it is perfectly possible, and not self-contradictory, for him to be re-created physiologically identical to his past constitution and to be reprogrammed to precisely the same level of experience and intellect that he had at his death or even prior to his death. In this fashion the one who died can now live again, by the creative power of an omnipotent God.

Objections

Several objections might be raised at this point. First, it might be objected that this must mean that the deceased will be in a state of unconsciousness for a certain period of time. The answer to this must be negative. In order for an individual to be unconscious, there must exist a person who can be unconscious. But after death and prior to re-creation, there is no such person. Thus, the individual who dies will not be unconscious for a period of time (or to put it in more theological terms, there is no soul-sleep involved, for there is no sleeper). The next moment of consciousness for the person who dies will occur at the time of his re-creation and reprogramming.

But would not the deceased be aware of a time lapse between death and re-creation? Here again, the answer must be no. As in the case of non-dreaming sleep, where we are not conscious of time passing, so here too, where there is no consciousness during the intervening time between death and re-creation, there can be no consciousness of a time lapse. Re-creation, to the person re-created, will appear to take place at the next moment after death, though speaking in terms of objective measurement of time, it might be any number of years or eons later.

The point just made rests on a distinction which we frequently make, that is, between subjective time and objective time. Suppose that you are sitting in an idling car in a "No Parking or Standing" zone, waiting for your son to come out of the post office after mailing a package. You sweat a little, maintain constant alertness for a prowling police car, and glance anxiously at the post office door. It seems like it is taking forever for him to mail the package. When he finally comes out and gets into the car, you inquire, "What took you so long?" Puzzled, he turns and says, "What do you mean? It only took three minutes." The point of contrast is between two kinds of time: objective time as measured by standard reference to certain celestial movements, and subjective time as measured in terms of an individual's subjective experience.

Applying this to the time of re-creation, measured in terms of objective time, the temporal gap between an individual's death and his re-creation might be thousands, even millions, of years. However, measured in terms of subjective time, that is, in terms of the individual's own experience, the re-creation will seem to occur at the very next moment after death. The reason for this is that the deceased has had no experiences between the experiences of dying and those immediately following re-creation. The latter will seem to follow immediately upon the former. Thus, in speaking about the time of re-creation, one should make clear whether one is referring to objective time or subjective time.

Finally, and undoubtedly the most significant objection: How can the individual who is re-created be the same person as the individual who died? The person re-created will possess entirely different physical elements and will begin again to exist at a time significantly later than his death. Because he has a different composition and lacks spatio-temporal continuity, is it not nonsense to suppose that the re-created person could be identical with the deceased? To answer this objection, we must consider whether these two features are necessary conditions for all cases of personal identity.

Personal Identity

One thing we apparently do not mean by "same person" is that the individual is composed of the same material elements now as he was previously. For example, between cooking my supper last evening and frying my eggs this morning, my wife has undergone significant change. Her body cells have produced millions of new cells, and old cells which have died were washed away by her morning shower or eliminated through body waste. Indeed, if I say that she is the same person as the person I married eleven years ago, more than likely her entire physical constitution in terms of her organic cell structure has changed. One might respond that, in any case, during the time which transpired there has been a significant proportion of elements carried over from one time to the next. But this simply shows that any plausibility which this purported criterion might have initially had really derived from an application of the criterion of spatio-temporal continuity. That is, it is the continuity, not the composition, which is important.

Thus, a more likely interpretation of "same person" is in terms of continuous, spatio-temporal physical existence. My wife now is the same person that I married, either wholly or in part because it is in principle possible to trace her continuous physical existence from that wedding day until this present moment.

But is bodily continuity a necessary and/or sufficient condition for personal identity? Many have maintained that it constitutes a sufficient condition; we have tried to show in the previous chapter that this is not the case. However, the determination of whether or not it is sufficient is irrelevant to the re-creationist's case, for his view entails the absence of this condition with respect to personal life after death. That which poses a problem for him is whether spatio-temporal continuity constitutes a necessary condition for all cases of personal identity for, on his scenario, the re-created person lacks bodily continuity with the deceased. If someone cannot be identical with an individual existing at some prior time without being spatio-temporally continuous with that person, then the re-creationist's position is nonsense; the presence of a space-time gap precludes any identification.

What grounds can be adduced for the truth of the claim that bodily continuity is a necessary condition for, is part of the meaning of, personal identity? On the one hand, it would not seem to follow analytically from the concept of personal identity. Indeed, merely to stipulate this as a condition for personal identity would do little but beg the very question at issue. Further, it might be reasonably contended that re-creationism presents a relevant counter-example providing reason why this condition should not be incorporated into the definition of "personal identity."

On the other hand, ground for this might be sought in experience. But if experience be the ground, the requisite universality is absent. This is particularly the case with respect to the re-creationist's thesis, for we have had no (or relatively few) experiences with recreated individuals and therefore possess no experiential grounds from which to argue that the re-created person, though spatio-temporally discontinuous with the deceased, is not the same person. It remains possible that the re-created person provides a unique (and despoiling) case where the condition of spatio-temporal continuity does not apply.

But we need not rest our case simply on an appeal to ignorance. Our position will be strengthened if we can supply cases where we know the criterion in question to be absent, and yet continue (or would continue) to identify the person as identical with the previously encountered one. If we are successful in this, we will have shown that experience likewise fails to establish this as a criterion covering all cases.

Before considering a case involving personal identity in particular, let us first consider the identity of something which is not a person. Take, for example, a deck of cards. Generally speaking, we might agree that to predicate of this deck of cards that it is identical with a deck existing at a prior time requires that it have been spatio-temporally continuous between these times. However, let us consider the deck in the context of a *genuine* act of magic. The magician places the deck of cards into a hat, waves his magic wand, and then tilts it to the viewer, showing that the cards have disappeared. Another wave of the wand and, presto! they have returned. Note that we do not say that the deck of cards now in his hat is a new deck; rather, we affirm that it is the same deck that disappeared and was magically returned to the hat. In saying that the deck of cards *disappeared* and was magically *restored*, we indicate that neither we nor the magician nor anyone else could have traced its spatio-temporal existence between the first wave of the wand and the second. It simply disappeared. If we believed that we or he could trace its existence, or if we believed that the deck of cards now in the hat was a different deck from the first, he would not be a genuine or authentic magician but someone who was skilled in sleight of hand. Indeed, in this case it is the fact of their actual disappearance which distinguishes genuine magic from sleight of hand. In short, for this to be an instance of true magic, the restored deck must be the same deck as the original; hence spatio-temporal continuity is not a necessary condition for all cases of identity.

Two objections might be raised. First, it might be argued that this is a case involving merely an object and therefore is not relevant to personal identity. However, we could substitute Howard Cosell for the deck of cards in the above example, with identical results. The second objection is that such a case is not possible because there can be no real magic, only sleight of hand. Indeed, the necessity of spatio-temporal continuity for constituting identity is proof enough of this. Thus, to mitigate this objection we need to turn to a clearer case, one which involves *personal* identity and avoids appealing to the assumed possibility of magical acts.

For a half hour each weekday afternoon, *As the World Turns* features Bob Hughes, Lisa Coleman, and a number of other individuals. During this time they discourse on events occurring at the hospital, who of their acquaintances is having marital problems, and of the various and sundry affairs of their friends. Following the final soap commercials they disappear until the following afternoon, when they take up living at a point in time and space related in varying degrees to that when and where the previous show ended. Their existence is one of installments encompassing numerous gaps. In this case there is no possibility of tracing their existence between yesterday and today; they did not exist during that time span. (One should be careful here not to confuse the actor—Don Hastings—who plays Bob with Bob; Don Hastings might exist between times, but not Bob Hughes.) Yet on their next appearance, we recognize and identify them as the same individuals we watched yesterday, despite their lack of spatio-temporal continuity. In such cases, bodily continuity does not appear to be a necessary condition for personal identity.

This example might be developed even further. Suppose that Don Hastings dies or takes another job, and is replaced on the production set. When the replacement appears on the screen, we are at first hesitant about acknowledging that this "new" individual is really Bob Hughes; his different physical appearance clearly indicates that he is spatio-temporally discontinuous with Bob as he appeared on Tuesday. Yet, in most cases we eventually would in fact identify the "newcomer" as Bob. And we would make this identification on the grounds that he remembers doing things that Bob previously remembered and we watched him do, manifests similar character traits, and treats other individuals and is treated by them in the same manner as the previously embodied individual. Indeed, we can clearly differentiate the case of Bob appearing with a new body from the appearance of an entirely new character, Fred.

If bodily continuity were a necessary condition of personal identity, none of this would be possible. Characters in television serials and stage plays would be different individuals after their daily or weekly gaps or fifteen minute intermissions; they could not change bodies and yet remain the same person. That these space-time gaps are possible and do in fact occur in the serials and plays shows that bodily continuity is not a necessary condition for personal identity in all cases.

It might be objected that these are not real individuals, but merely fictions created for or by us. And since they are not real individuals, they do not constitute a counter-example to the space-time continuity criterion. However, that they are not real in the sense that they do not inhabit our world—one would not expect to meet Bob Hughes in the department store or the hospital emergency ward —does not mean that they have no reality. Reality is contextual. For those reading this, individuals in television serials and theatrical productions are not real but fictitious individuals. But within the context of the television or theater production, the characters are real people, as distinguished from, say, a character in Lisa's dreams or Bob's fictitious cousin. Further, that they do not inhabit our particular reality seems quite irrelevant to whether or not they can be spoken of as having personal identity. Within their own particular context, there can be little doubt that Bob and Lisa each has a unique personal identity.

Indeed, the very reaction of the public to soap operas is an indicator of this. The characters (not the actors) are flooded with thousands of letters yearly, warning that so-and-so is out to get them, or that they should not marry so-and-so. It might be interesting to pursue what this widespread, mistaken view of the nature of their reality entails (e.g., that they are conceived to have personal identity on the level of the letter-writer), but this would take us afield. What is significant for us is the common belief that gap-inclusive people possess personal identity.

In sum, what examples of this sort show is that the absence of spatio-temporal continuity does not necessarily constitute a falsifying condition of personal identity. Of course, we have not established, nor are we trying to establish, the thesis that there is no conceivable situation in which bodily identity would be necessary. All we are asserting is that "at least one case can be consistently constructed in which bodily identity fails."[8] Thus, the re-creationist's claim that individuals can be gap-inclusive is far from nonsense.

If bodily continuity is not a condition for personal identity with respect to gap-inclusive people, what then are the conditions which determine personal identity in such cases? The re-creationist responds that, where bodily continuity is absent, physical similarity, internal states of consciousness (including conceptual categories and memories), and personality traits or patterns become highly determinative. It is true that this is still very ambiguous; we are left in the dark as to *which* physical features are necessary, *what* personality traits must be identical, *how many* memories must correspond with the deceased. However, I do not believe that it is necessary that the re-creationist solve the problem of personal identity. All he need do is to trace out the problem sufficiently so as to enable one to decide whether there are reasonable grounds for deciding whether the recreated individual is the same person as the deceased. We do not need, at this point, to determine the specifics with respect to these general features because we are not inquiring about what ways the re-created individual can be changed and still be the same person, for we have supposed that he is the same in all these respects to the deceased.

On the other hand, our task of showing re-creationism to be a reasonable and coherent doctrine is not yet complete, for the introduction of internal states of consciousness, and in particular memory, provides the basis for two other objections to the re-creationist's thesis. The first objection seeks to return to bodily continuity as a necessary condition for personal identity by contending that the appeal to memory claims presupposes this very condition, whereas the second goes further to claim that neither bodily continuity, physical similarity, nor internal states of consciousness are sufficient to establish personal identity. The decision to call someone identical with rather than merely similar to another is purely conventional. Let me consider these in turn.

Regarding the first, it is argued that one cannot affirm memory but deny bodily continuity as a necessary condition for personal identity. Use of memory claims presupposes bodily continuity of the individual both at some previous point of existence and at the present moment. Memory claims are fallible. Thus, we need some way of distinguishing between mere claims to remember past performances and the actual remembering of these performances (which is infallible). But verification of memory claims presupposes (1) previous physical (embodied) existence, and (2) continuous contemporary physical existence. Only if the person now exists physically continuous for a time can we test whether he can correctly use the term "remember," that is, whether he understands memory language. And only if the person existed for a length of time embodied can we check out claims to remember. But if this is the case, the objection proceeds, memory is not an independent standard of personal identity; it presupposes and is dependent upon bodily continuity.[9]

That the appeal to memory is *previous*[10] continued bodily existence is, I believe, indisputable. To use an illustration from B.A.O. Williams, suppose that a man went

> to a crowded party, where he sees a girl who is like all the other girls at the party except that she has red hair. This girl sings various songs and quarrels with the band; she is easily identified on each occasion by the colour of the hair. The man later meets a platinum blonde who recalls singing songs at a party and quarreling with the band. He can identify her as the red-haired girl at the party, even though she has changed the colour of her hair in the meantime. . . . [However] if the girl had remarkably changed the colour of her hair between songs and before the quarrel, identifying her at the various stages of the party would have been more difficult, but not impossible; but if [she] had changed bodies frequently, identification would become not just difficult but impossible.[11]

In such a case, the recollection by the platinum blonde encountered later of being the singer at the party would be difficult or impossible to verify, because there was no continuously existent, embodied singer to be identified with.

However, that some sort of bodily continuity during the event remembered is required by the criterion of memory (to enable witnesses to identify the person who performed such and such a token act), does not entail that there *always* had to be bodily continuity. That is, it does not entail that the platinum blonde necessarily had continuous existence between the party and the later encounter. She might have ceased to exist immediately after the party, and was re-created prior to the second encounter. In such a case it would be (theoretically) possible both to check out her memory claims about the past, and also to now test whether she can correctly use "remember." Thus, though memory as a criterion for personal identity presupposes that at some time or other (that is, during the events which are purportedly remembered) there was or is bodily continuity on the part of the individual, this does not entail the stronger thesis that memory is dependent upon unbroken bodily continuity. Or to put it another way, this point about memory refutes the thesis which asserts that there is no conceivable situation in which bodily continuity would be necessary, though it does not refute the thesis that such continuity need not occur in every case or all the time.

The second objection is that merely to have memory claims about being the person who performed such and such actions at a previous time does not *compel* us to assert the identity of the individual who makes the memory claims with the individual whose actions are purportedly recalled. The reason for this is that "it is not logically impossible that two different persons should *claim* to remember being this man, and this is the most we can get."[12] Again taking an example suggested by Williams, suppose that two individuals, Charles and Robert, come into existence or undergo changes, and that they both claim that they remember performing actions which Guy Fawkes performed. If we grant that one individual cannot be in two places at the same time, then we cannot claim that they both are identical with Guy Fawkes. Neither can we say that one is he but the other is only like him, for we have no way of determining which is which.

> So it would be best, if anything, to say that both had mysteriously become like Guy Fawkes, clairvoyantly know about him, or something like this. If this would be the best description of each of the two, why would it not be the best description of Charles if Charles alone were changed?[13]

Thus, it is concluded, memory claims are not sufficient to force us to conclude that the re-created individual is identical with rather than merely similar to the deceased. Only if there were determinable bodily continuity could we guarantee that Charles and not Robert is Guy.

This argument, of course, does not show or prove that Charles is not and cannot be Guy Fawkes. That he is Guy certainly still is logically possible. What it does seem to indicate is that there is no necessity for concluding that he really is Guy rather than that he is merely like him (similar to him in the above-described respects). We can opt for identity; but it is not logically requisite that we do so. Thus, whether or not such a person was the same is a matter of linguistic decision: it depends on whether we choose to call him the same person. This conventionality is purportedly fatal to the recreationist's position, for he has failed to provide a criterion to ensure that the person in the after-life is identical with the deceased and not merely similar to him.[14]

In reply, it might be granted that the investigator cannot discover any specific evidence which would compel us to say that Charles is identical with rather than merely similar to Guy. There seems to be nothing contradictory involved in denying that, even with identical physical features, personality traits, and memory claims, Charles is not Guy. Thus, one might agree that what is required here is a decision on the part of the individual himself or an observer that Charles is Guy. However, to say that it is a matter of decision is not to say that the decision is an arbitrary one. The decision that he is the same person as Guy can be made on the ground that, not only is there no good reason not to identify him with Guy (in the case where there is only one such claimant), but there is good reason to thus identify him. Of course two people could look alike, have the same character and skills, personality and memory claims, and still be merely similar. There is no way of deducing identity from these features (though of course the greater the extent of these similarities, the greater the likelihood there is that we are dealing with the same individual and not merely a similar one). However, two people cannot have the same memories (true memory claims) about deeds performed only by one agent and still not be the same. Identity appears to be deducible from true memories. Accordingly, if one holds, as I think it is reasonable to hold, that seriously proffered memory claims about past actions are frequently (though by no means always) right, this would then give good reason to say that Charles was Guy, not merely similar to him. This, of course, does not enable us to decide the reliability of any one particular memory claim. However, where there is a large bank of claims which could be verified, it does provide good reason for claiming identity.

It is true that if there were more than one claimant with identical features, we would have no good reason to say that one rather than another is identical with the deceased, for we could not decide whose memory claims were true and whose were false. However, the recreationist's supposition is that there will be one and only one recreated individual per deceased, and that each claimant would make memory claims concerning the solo-performance acts of each deceased respectively on a one-to-one basis. In such a situation, it would appear reasonable to claim that memory claims, in conjunction with the other features specified above, would provide good grounds for identity claims.

Application to Immortality

We can now respond to the objection that the re-creationist's thesis cannot be held to be a rationally coherent doctrine—that the recreated individual could not be the same as the deceased person. So long as the re-created person has the same or substantially similar physical, mental, and personality traits and memories to the deceased, it would seem most reasonable to conclude that he can be and probably is identical with the deceased. Further, lack of bodily continuity would not be sufficient to falsify his claim to personal identity with the deceased. Thus, even on a monistic view of the nature of man, life after death is possible.[15]

One might wonder, however, whether immortality after this fashion really is desirable. In particular, would I want to be precisely identical to the way I was at the time of my death? If I died in old age, would a future life lived in a state of decrepitude or senility be meaningful or desirable? Or if I died, afflicted with a disease accompanied by tormenting pain and irreversible debilitation, would I want to be re-created at a point where this would continue? Given these and similar considerations, would I indeed want to begin living at the point where I died?

The re-creationist, however, is not committed to a position which requires exact similarity of the re-created to the deceased in every detail. Above we noted that all that is required is that the features instantiated be substantially similar to those of the deceased. That is, the re-created person can be different in ways which do not essentially affect that person's personal identity; slight modifications of features—physical, mental, personality—do not constitute a falsifying condition of his personal identity with the deceased. For example, if my father, between the time I last saw him and the next time I see him, loses an appreciable amount of hair, gains visible inches at the belt line, or even loses one of his limbs, I could still identify him as the same individual whom I once called my father. Similarly with personality and mental traits: if he has become more forgetful or has changed his opinion about certain matters, he could still be identified by me as my father.

How much one can alter specific physical, mental, and personality traits before one loses one's personal identity is a difficult and perhaps ultimately unresolvable problem. The very quest for a critical threshold might itself be a meaningless one. What can be affirmed, however, is that some changes can occur in the re-created person without a change in personal identity occurring.

To what extent this observation allows St. Paul's affirmation in I Corinthians that the re-created body will be a spiritual, not a physical, body remains to be determined. In particular, it depends upon two things: what a "spiritual" body is, and the extent to which features can be altered before personal identity is lost. A hint as to the former is provided by the accounts of the post-resurrection appearances of Jesus. On the one hand, it is clear that he possessed new abilities and powers: he could appear and disappear at will or pass through walls unharmed. On the other hand, these new powers which he acquired apparently were not sufficient to make him a different individual from the one who was crucified. At the very least it is clear that he was physically recognizable to his disciples. Unfortunately, however, we are told next to nothing about the status of this recreated body.

The point I wish to make, despite the uncertainty surrounding these two factors, is that re-creation conceivably can result in slightly different characteristics. However, for the re-created individual to be the same person as the deceased, the former characteristics cannot be so altered that they affect one's personal identity.

Finally, one should be careful to distinguish what is possible under monism from that which is possible under a dualistic schema. Under the form of dualism discussed in chapter three, death of the person is not possible; immortality is provided for by the persistence of a soul-entity which is myself and does not die. Under monism (and the form of dualism where the complex of body and soul, not merely the soul, is the person) survival is not possible; the individual does die. What is possible is *life after death*. Thus, if one adopts a monistic view of man, one must be careful to distinguish life after death from survival (or "immortality" narrowly defined as "not-dying"), only the former is possible under this view. Hence, the monist should be guarded about his language, taking care to use "immortality" in the broad sense of "life after death."

Endnotes

*Reprinted by permission of the author from Chapter Five of *Is Man the Phoenix? A Study of Immortality*. (Washington DC: Christian University Press, a subsidiary of the Christian College Consortium, 1978).

1 Gilbert Ryle, *The Concept of Mind* (New York: Barnes and Noble, 1949), p. 125.

2 Ibid., p. 43.

3 Ibid., p. 25

4 D.M. Armstrong, "The Nature of Mind," *The Mind-Brain Identity Theory*, ed. C.V. Borst (New Y.ork St. Martin's Press, 1970), p. 72.

5 J.J.C. Smart, "Sensations and Brain Processes," *The Philosophical Review*, LXVIII (1959); reprinted in Borst, ibid., p. 56.

6 U.T. Place, "Is Consciousness a Brain Process?" *The British Journal of Psychology*, XLVII (1956); reprinted in Borst, ibid., pp. 47f.

7 U.T. Place, "Materialism as a Scientific Hypothesis," *The Philosophical Review*, LXIX (1960); reprinted in Borst, ibid., p. 84.

8 B.A.O. Williams, "Personal Identity and Individuation," *Proceedings of the Aristotelean Society*, LVII (1956-57), 229.

9 Terence Penelhum, *Survival and Disembodied Existence* (London: Routledge & Kegan Paul, 1970), p. 56.

[10] That it is dependent upon *present* bodily existence is more disputable. That I now have a true memory claim is not dependent upon someone else being able to check whether I use "remember" properly or consistently, unless one contends that I cannot know for myself when I am correctly using such. Fortunately we can avoid this problem by granting the above claim, since we are not arguing for disembodied, but rather embodied, future existence.

[11] Williams, *op. cit.*, p. 242.

[12] Ibid., p. 238.

[13] Ibid., p. 239.

[14] C. B. Martin, *Religious Belief* (Ithaca, N.Y.: Cornell University Press, 1959), pp. 106-107.

[15] It should be noted that this same reasoning can be applied to show that personal immortality is possible where man is conceived dualistically as having, rather than as being, a soul — i.e., where the soul is not held to be the locus of personal identity and the body is a necessary condition for both personal identity and the existence of the person.

Study Questions

1.   Does Reichenbach favor Behaviourism or the Identity Theory?

2.   Reichenbach responds to several objections to his Identity Theory. What are they?

3.   What does Reichenbach mean by "recreationism"?

4.   How does Reichenbach handle the matter of a continuing identity?

5.   Which position seems more compatible with the Christian data, Reichenbach's materialism or dualism?

38

The Possibility of Resurrection

Peter van Inwagen

Peter van Inwagen is professor of philosophy at Syracuse University, and author of
An Essay on Free Will and *Material Beings.*

   In this essay he argues that the Christian doctrine of the resurrection is
possible.* He rejects what he calls the "Aristotelian" view that bodies are
reconstituted, and offers instead a recreationist account that allows for continuity
and personal recognition in the resurrection state.

The real philosophical problem facing the doctrine of resurrection does not
seem to me to be that there is no criterion that the men of the new age could
apply to determine whether someone then alive was the same man as some
man who had died before the Last Day; the problem seems to me to be that
there *is* such a criterion and (given certain facts about the present age) it
would, of necessity, yield the result that many men who have died in our
own lifetime and earlier will not be found among those who live *after* the
Last Day.

   Let us consider an analogy. Suppose a certain monastery claims to have
in its possession a manuscript written in St. Augustine's own hand. And
suppose the monks of this monastery further claim that this manuscript
was burned by Arians in the year 457. It would immediately occur to me to
ask how *this* manuscript, the one I can touch, could be the very manuscript
that was burned in 457. Suppose their answer to this question is that God
miraculously recreated Augustine's manuscript in 458. I should respond to
this answer as follows: the deed it describes seems quite impossible, even
as an accomplishment of omnipotence. God certainly might have created a
perfect duplicate of the original manuscript, but it would not be *that* one;
its earliest moment of existence would have been after Augustine's death;
it would never have known the impress of his hand; it would not have been
a part of the furniture of the world when he was alive; and so on.

Now suppose our monks were to reply by simply asserting that the manuscript now in their possession *did* know the impress of Augustine's hand; that it *was* a part of the furniture of the world when the Saint was alive; that when God recreated or restored it, He (as an indispensable component of accomplishing this task) saw to it that the object He produced had all these properties.

I confess I should not know what to make of this. I should have to tell the monks that I did not see how what they believed could *possibly* be true. They might of course reply that their belief is a mystery, that God had *some* way of restoring the lost manuscript, but that the procedure surpasses human understanding. Now I am sometimes willing to accept such answers; for example, in the case of the doctrine of the Trinity. But there are cases in which I would never accept such an answer. For example, if there were a religion that claimed that God had created two adjacent mountains without thereby bringing into existence an intermediate valley, I should regard any attempt to defend this doctrine as a "mystery" as so much whistle-talk. After all, I can hardly expect to be able to understand the Divine Nature; but I do understand mountains and valleys. And I understand manuscripts, too. I understand them sufficiently well to be quite confident that the monks' story is impossible. Still, I wish to be reasonable. I admit that one can be mistaken about conceptual truth and falsehood. I know from experience that a proposition that *seems* to force itself irresistibly upon the mind as a conceptual truth can turn out to be false. (If I had been alive in 1890, I should doubtless have regarded the Galilean Law of the Addition of Velocities and the Unrestricted Comprehension Principle in set theory as obvious conceptual truths.) Being reasonable, therefore, I am willing to listen to any *argument* the monks might have for the conclusion that what they believe is possible. Most arguments for the conclusion that a certain proposition is possible true take the form of a story that (the arguer hopes) the person to whom the argument is addressed will accept as possible, and which (the arguer attempts to show) entails the proposition whose modal status is in question.

Can such a story be told about the manuscript of Augustine? Suppose one of the monks is, in a very loose sense, an Aristotelian. He tells the following story (a version of a very popular tale): "Augustine's manuscript consisted of a certain 'parcel' of matter upon which a certain form had been impressed. It ceased to exist when this parcel of matter was radically deformed. To recreate it, God needed only to collect the matter (in modern terms, the atoms) that once composed it and reimpress that form upon it (in modern terms, cause these atoms to stand to one another in the same spatial and chemical relationships they previously stood in)."

This story is defective. The manuscript God creates in the story is not the manuscript that was destroyed, since the various atoms that compose the tracings of ink on its surface occupy their present positions not as a result of Augustine's activity but of God's. Thus what we have is not a manuscript in Augustine's hand. (Strictly speaking, it is not even a *manuscript*.) (Compare the following conversation: "Is that the house of blocks your daughter built this morning?" "No, I built this one after I accidentally knocked hers down. I put all the blocks just where she did, though. Don't tell her.")

I think the philosophical problems that arise in connection with the buried manuscript of St. Augustine are very like the problems that arise in connection with the doctrine of the Resurrection. If a man should be totally destroyed, then it is very hard to see how any man who comes into existence thereafter could be the *same* man. And I say this not because I have no criterion of identity I can employ in such cases, but because I have a criterion of identity for men and it is, or *seems* to be, violated. And the popular quasi-Aristotelian story which is often supposed to establish the conceptual possibility of God's restoring to existence a man who has been totally destroyed does not lead me to think that I have got the wrong criterion or that I am misapplying the right one. The popular story, of course, is the story according to which God collects the atoms that once composed a certain man and restores them to the positions they occupied relative to one another when that man was alive; thereby (the story-teller contends) God restores the man himself. But this story, it seems to me, does not "work." The atoms of which I am composed occupy at each instant the positions they do because of the operations of certain processes within me (those processes that, taken collectively, constitute my being alive). Even when I become a corpse—provided I decay slowly and am not, say, cremated—the atoms that compose me will occupy the positions relative to one another that they do occupy *largely* because of the processes of life that *used* to go on within me: or this will be the case for at least some short period. Thus a former corpse in which the processes of life have been "started up again" may well be the very man who was once before alive, provided the processes of dissolution did not progress too far while he was a corpse. But if a man does not simply die but is totally destroyed (as in the case of cremation) then *he* can never be reconstituted, for the causal chain has been irrevocably broken. If God collects the atoms that used to constitute that man and "reassembles" them, they will occupy the positions relative to one another they occupy because of God's miracle and not because of the operation of the natural processes that, taken collectively, were the life of that man. (I should also be willing to defend the following theses: the thing such an action of God's would produce would not be a member of our species and would not speak a language or have memories of any sort, though, of course, he—or *it*—would *appear* to have these features.)

This much is analogous to the case of the burned manuscript. Possibly no one will find what I have said very convincing unless he thinks very much like me. Let me offer three arguments against an "Aristotelian" account of the Resurrection that have no analogues in the case of the manuscript, and which will perhaps be more convincing to the generality of philosophers. Arguments (a) and (b) are *ad homines*, directed against Christians who might be inclined towards the "Aristotelian" theory. Argument (c) attempts to show that the "Artistotelian" theory has an impossible consequence.

a. The atoms of which I am composed cannot be destroyed by burning or the natural processes of decay; but they *can* be destroyed, as can atomic nuclei and even subatomic particles. (Or so it would seem: the principles for identity through time for subatomic particles are very hazy; physical theory has little if anything to say on the subject.) If, in order to raise a man on the Day of Judgment, God had to collect the "building blocks"—atoms, neutrons, or what have you—of which that man had once been composed, then a wicked man could hope to escape God's wrath by seeing to it that all his "buildings blocks" were destroyed. But according to Christian theology, such a hope is senseless. Thus, unless the nature of the ultimate constituents of matter is different from what it appears to be, the "Aristotelian" theory is inimical to a central point of Christian theology.

b. The atoms (or what have you) of which I am composed may very well have been parts of other people at some time in the past. Thus, if the "Aristotelian" theory is true, there could be a problem on the day of resurrection about *who* is resurrected. In fact, if that theory were true, a wicked man who had read his Aquinas might hope to escape punishment in the age to come by becoming a lifelong cannibal. But again, the possibility of such a hope cannot be admitted by any Christian.

c. It is possible that none of the atoms that are now parts of me were parts of me when I was ten years old. It is therefore possible that God could collect all the atoms that were parts of me when I was ten, without destroying me, and restore them to the positions they occupied relative to one another in 1952. If the "Aristotelian" theory were correct, this action would be sufficient for the creation of a boy who could truly say, "I am Peter van Inwagen." In fact, he and I could stand facing one another and each say truly to the other, "I am you." But this is conceptually impossible, and therefore, the "Aristotelian" theory is *not* correct.

No story other than our "Aristotelian" story about how it might be that a man who was totally destroyed could live again seems even superficially plausible. I conclude that my initial judgment is correct and that it is absolutely impossible, even as an accomplishment of God, that a man who has been burned to ashes or been eaten by worms should ever live again. What follows from this about the Christian hope of resurrection?

Very little of any interest, I think. All that follows is that if Christianity is true, then what I earlier called "certain facts about the present age" are *not* facts.

It is part of the Christian faith that all men who share in the sin of Adam must die. What does it mean to say that I must die? Just this: that one day I shall be composed entirely of non-living matter; that is, I shall be a corpse. It is not part of the Christian faith that I must at any time be totally annihilated or disintegrate. (One might note that Christ, whose story is supposed to provide the archetype for the story of each man's resurrection, became a corpse but did not, even in His human nature, cease to exist.) It is of course true that men apparently cease to exist: those who are cremated, for example. But it contradicts nothing in the creeds to suppose that this is not what really happens, and that God preserves our corpses contrary to all appearance. . . . Perhaps at the moment of each man's death, God removes his corpse and replaces it with a simulacrum which is what is burned or rots. Or perhaps God is not quite so wholesale as this: perhaps He removes for "safekeeping" only the "core person"—the brain and central nervous system—or even some special part of it. These are details.

I take it that this story shows that the resurrection is a feat an almighty being *could* accomplish. I think this is the *only* way such a being could accomplish it. Perhaps I'm wrong, but that's of little importance. What *is* important is that God can accomplish it this way or some other. Of course one might wonder *why* God would go such lengths to make it look as if most people not only die but pass into complete nothingness. This is a difficult question. I think it can be given a plausible answer, but not apart from a discussion of the nature of religious belief. I will say just this. If corpses inexplicably disappeared no matter how carefully they were guarded, or inexplicably refused to decay and were miraculously resistant to the most persistent and ingenious attempts to destroy them, then we should be living in a world in which observable events that were *obviously* miraculous, *obviously* due to the intervention of a power beyond Nature, happened with monotonous regularity. In such a world we should all believe in the supernatural: its existence would be the best explanation for the observed phenomena. If Christianity is true, God wants us to believe in the supernatural. But experience shows us that, if there is a God, He does not do what He very well *could* do: provide us with a ceaseless torrent of public, undeniable evidence of a power outside the natural order. And perhaps it is not hard to think of good reasons for such a policy.

Endnote

*Reprinted from "The Possibility of Resurrection." *International Journal for Philosophy of Religion,* vol. 9 (1978). Reprinted by permission of Kluwer Academic Publishers.

Study Questions

1.   Peter van Inwagen sees a philosophical problem facing the doctrine of the resurrection. What is it?

2.   How is the case of the buried manuscript analogous to resurrection of the body?

3.   What is the "impossible consequence" of the Aristotelian theory?

4.   According to van Inwagen, what does it mean to say, "I must die"?

5.   What does van Inwagen think happens in the resurrection?

39

The Future of the Soul

Richard Swinburne

Richard G. Swinburne is Nolloth Professor of the Philosophy of the Christian Religion at Oxford University, and is author of *Revelation, The Concept of Miracle*; (co-author) *Personal Identity, Space and Time, An Introduction to Confirmation Theory*; (editor) *The Justification of Induction, The Existence of God, Faith and Reason, The Coherence of Theism, The Evolution of the Soul*, and *The Christian God*.

In Chapter 15, the final chapter of his book, *The Evolution of the Soul*, Professor Swinburne argues that the soul will function if it is plugged into a functioning brain, but if the brain is not functioning, then neither will the soul. But the soul can be revived and made to function again by reassembling the brain, which is a task involving no contradiction and is an achievable task at some future time by an omnipotent God.*

Four thousand million years of evolution produced man, a body and soul in continuing interaction. A human soul is more dependent for its development on its own states than is an animal soul, for it has complex beliefs and desires kept in place and changing in accord with other beliefs and desires. Other animals having only much simpler beliefs and desires are much more dependent for their continuing beliefs and desires directly on their bodily states. Can this complex evolved human soul survive on its own apart from the body which sustains it? I have argued so far that the functioning of the human soul (i.e., its having conscious episodes) is guaranteed by the functioning of the brain currently connected with it (connected, in that the soul's acquisition of beliefs about its surroundings and action upon those surroundings is mediated by that brain). I considered in Chapter 10 what it is for a man or his soul to exist unconscious, and I argued that that was a matter which required to be settled by definition. The definition which I suggested was that a soul exists if normal bodily processes or available artificial techniques can bring the man to be conscious, i.e. his soul to function again.

When the body dies and the brain ceases to function, the evidence of the kind considered in Chapter 10 suggests that the soul will cease to function also. For that evidence suggests that the soul functions only when the brain has rhythms of certain kinds, and at death the brain ceases to function altogether. If the soul does not function before there is a functioning brain, or during deep sleep, when the brain is not functioning at a certain level, surely it will not function after there ceases to be a functioning brain? However, there are arguments and evidence of less usual kinds which purport to show that things are different after death from what they are before birth.

Before we face the question of whether the soul can function without the functioning of the brain currently connected with it, we must consider the question of whether, after death, the brain which ceases to function at death can be made to function again and whether thereby the soul can be revived.

Can the Brain Be Reactivated?

A crucial problem is that we do not know how much of the brain that was yours has to be reassembled and within what time interval in order that we may have *your* brain and so your soul function again. We saw this earlier in the split brain cases. If both half-brains are transplanted into empty skulls and the transplants take, both subsequent persons will satisfy to some extent the criterion of apparent memory (as well as the brain criterion) for being the original person. One subsequent person might satisfy the criterion better than the other, and that would be evidence that he was the original person; but the evidence could be misleading. The situation is equally unclear with possible developments at death.

Suppose you die of a brain haemorrhage which today's doctors cannot cure, but your relatives take your corpse and put it straight into a very deep freeze in California. Fifty years later your descendents take it out of the freeze; medical technology has improved and the doctors are able quickly to mend your brain, and your body is then warmed up. The body becomes what is clearly the body of a living person, and one with your apparent memory and character. Is it you? Although we might be mistaken, the satisfaction of the criterion of apparent memory (together with the—at any rate partial—satisfaction of the criterion of brain continuity) would suggest that we ought to say 'Yes'. So long as the same brain is revived, the same functioning soul would be connected with it—whatever the time interval. But what if the brain is cut up into a million pieces and then frozen? Does the same hold? Why should there be any difference? Suppose that the brain is reduced to its component atoms; and then these are reassembled either by chance or because they have been labelled radioactively. Again, if the subsequent person makes your memory claims, surely we ought to say that it is you. But how many of the original atoms do we need in the original locations? That we do not know. So long as the subsequent person had many similar atoms in similar locations in his brain, he would claim to have been you. So, the criterion of apparent memory will be satisfied. Total non-satisfaction of the brain criterion would defeat the claims of apparent memory (in the absence of any general failure of coincidence in results between these criteria). But it remains unclear and indeed insoluble exactly how much of the original brain is needed to provide satisfaction of the brain criterion .

This problem of how much of the original body is physically necessary when other matter is added to it so as to make a fully functioning body, in order that the original soul may be present and function, is a problem which concerned the thinkers of the early Christian centuries and of the Middle Ages. They considered the imaginary case of the cannibal who eats nothing but human flesh. Given that both the cannibal and his victims are to be brought to life in the General Resurrection, to whom will be flesh of the cannibal belong? Aquinas[1] begins his answer by saying that 'if something was materially present in many men, it will rise in him to whose perfection it belonged', i.e. that that part of the body which is necessary for a man being the person he is will belong to him in the General Resurrection. But what part is that, and what guarantee is there that the matter of that part cannot come to form the essential part of a different man who cannot therefore he reconstituted at the same time as the original man (given the operation of normal processes)? Aquinas goes on to produce an argument that the 'radical seed' (i.e., the sperm, which according to Aristotle formed the original matter of the embryo) forms the minimum essential bodily core around which a man could be rebuilt. But we know now, as Aquinas did not, that the sperm does not remain as a unit within the organism, and there seems to me no reason why all the atoms which originally formed it should not be lost from the body, and indeed come to form parts of original cells of many subsequent men. The atoms of the original cell are not therefore the most plausible candidate for being the part of the body physically necessary for human personal identity. Aquinas's problem remains without modern solution.

Nevertheless, although neurophysiology cannot tell us which part of his brain is physically necessary for the embodiment of a given man, it does tell us, as I argued earlier, that some of the brain is thus necessary. For the functioning of a given human soul, there has to be a man whose brain contains certain of the matter of his original brain (but which matter we do not know), similarly arranged. A certain amount of the original brain matter has to be reassembled in a similar arrangement and reactivated by being joined to other brain matter and a body if the soul is to function again. And how likely is it that physical processes will bring about such a reassembly? As the time since death increases, and brain cells and then brain molecules are broken up, burnt by fire, or eaten by worms—it becomes very, very unlikely indeed that chance will reassemble them; or even that human agents can do so for they will not be able to re-identify the atoms involved. (One must, however, be careful here about the possibilities for technology in the twenty-second century. Maybe a brain map could be constructed and a process of labelling constituent atoms devised, which would make possible a reassembly after many years. But the possible development of such a technology seems to me very unlikely.) When the original atoms are reduced to packets of energy, then since these perhaps cannot be individuated, reassembly finally becomes not merely physically very, very improbable, but totally impossible physically. (But the word is 'perhaps'; it is a difficult question in the philosophy of physics whether bursts of energy can be individuated.) I conclude that it is very, very unlikely (and with increasing time virtually impossible) that after death souls will again have reassembled the brain basis which we know makes them function.

Is there any good reason to suppose that the soul continues to function without the brain functioning? Arguments to show that the soul continues to function without the brain functioning may be divided into three groups, involving different amounts of theoretical structure, to reach their conclusions. First, we may consider arguments which purport to show that certain men have survived death, in the sense that their souls have functioned without their brains functioning, directly—i.e. without needing first to establish anything about the nature of the soul or any more systematic metaphysical structure. Arguments of this kind may be called parapsychological arguments.

Arguments From Parapsychology

First, there is the alleged evidence of reincarnation, that souls function in new bodies with new brains on Earth. There are Indian children who claim to remember having lived a certain past life, and whose memory claims coincide with the events of some real past life about which—allegedly—they could not have learnt by what they were told or had read.[2] Now, it is of course open to serious question whether perhaps those Indian children had read or were told or learnt in some other perfectly normal way the details of those past lives. But even if for a few Indian children there was this coincidence between their memory claims and the events of a certain past person's life, without there being any normal cause of the accuracy of their memory claims that would not be enough evidence to show their identity with those persons. For, as I argued in Chapter 9, given the general coincidence of sameness of memory with continuity of brain, we must take continuity of brain as a criterion of identity; and the nonsatisfaction of that in the case of the few Indian children (who do not have the same brain matter as the cited past persons), must remain substantial evidence against the supposition that they are those persons.

Next, there is the alleged evidence of spiritualism, that souls function without bodies or with new bodies and brains in another world. Mediums purport to have telepathic communication with dead persons. The evidence that they do is allegedly provided by the knowledge of the details of the dead person's life on Earth (not obtainable by the medium by normal means) which the medium's reports of the telepathic communications reveal. In the reincarnation case there is no doubt that there exists in the present a living conscious person; the debatable question concerns his identity with the past person. In the spiritualism case the crucial issue concerns whether there is a conscious person with whom the medium is in communication.

A serious issue in medium cases, like the similar issue in the supposed reincarnation cases, concerns the source of the mysterious knowledge. Perhaps the medium gets her knowledge from some spy who has done research on the dead person's life. But even if investigation showed clearly that the mediums had gained their knowledge of the past lives of dead person by no normal route, the evidence would still, I suggest, not support the hypothesis of telepathic communication with the dead. For also compatible with the evidence would be the hypothesis that the mediums have clairvoyance—they see directly into the past and acquire their knowledge thus. (Adopting the latter hypothesis would involve supposing either that the mediums were deceiving us about the kind of experiences they were having (apparent two-way traffic with a living person), or that they were deceiving themselves, or that their experiences were illusory.) On the choice between the two hypotheses there seem to me to be two important reasons for preferring the clairvoyance hypothesis. First, there are no cross-checks between mediums about the alleged present experiences of the dead in the afterlife. Mediums never give independently verifiable reports on this. Secondly, their reports about the present alleged experiences of the dead are themselves very banal. Yet one would expect because of the total lack of dependence of the dead on their past bodies, that they would live in a very different world, and that this would emerge in their reports on that world.[3]

Finally, there is the interesting and recently published alleged evidence that souls function while their bodies are out of action. There has been careful analysis of the experiences of those who clinically were as good as dead and then recovered. Such experiences are often called 'near-death experiences'.[4] Fifteen per cent of subjects resuscitated after being in such a condition report strange experiences of one of two kinds. Many of them report the following 'transcendental experiences':

> an initial period of distress followed by profound calm and joy; out-of-the-body experiences with the sense of watching resuscitation

events from a distance; the sensation of moving rapidly down a tunnel or along a road, accompanied by a loud buzzing or ringing noise or hearing beautiful music; recognising friends and relatives who have died previously; a rapid review of pleasant incidents from throughout the life as a panoramic playback (in perhaps twelve per cent of cases); a sense of approaching a border or frontier and being sent back; and being annoyed or disappointed at having to return from such a pleasant experience—"I tried not to come back", in one patient's words. Some describe frank transcendent experiences and many state that they will never fear death again. Similar stories have been reported from the victims of accidents, falls, drowning, anaphylaxis, and cardiac or respiratory arrest.[5]

Resuscitated patients other than those who had transcendental experiences have undergone 'a wide variety of vivid dreams, hallucinations, nightmares and delusions', but some of those who had transcendental experiences also experienced these and sharply distinguished between the two kinds of experience. The 'dreams' were regarded as dreams, and were quickly forgotten; the 'supposed glimpses of a future life' were regarded as real and permanently remembered. These glimpses were reported as having occurred at moments when 'breathing had ceased, the heart had stopped beating, and the patients showed no visible signs of life'. The principle of credulity might suggest that we ought to take such apparent memories seriously, especially in view of the considerable coincidences between them, as evidence that what subjects thought they experienced, they really did. But although the subjects referred these experiences to moments at which the heart had stopped beating, etc., I do not know of any evidence that at these moments their brains had ceased to function. And if the brain was still functioning then, what the evidence would show is not that the soul may function when the brain does not, but only that its perceptual experiences (i.e. sensations and acquisitions of belief about far away places) are not dependent on normal sensory input.

The same conclusion will follow with respect to the considerable but not overwhelming evidence of those resuscitated patients who had experiences of the other strange kind, 'out-of-body-experiences', i.e. being able to view their own bodies and events in the operating theatre from a distance, obtaining thereby information which they would not have been able to obtain by normal means (e.g. having visual experiences of events which they would not have got from use of their eyes, such as views of parts of the theatre hidden from their eyes).[6] This again suggests that the subject's acquisition of information is dependent on some factor quite other than normal sensory input to the brain. But again I know of no evidence that these experiences occurred while the brain was not functioning; and so the available evidence does not support the suggestion that the soul can function without the brain functioning.

My conclusion on parapsychology is that it provides no good evidence that the soul continues to function without the brain to which it is currently connected, functioning.

Arguments for Natural Survival

The second class of arguments purporting to show that the soul survives death purport to show from a consideration of what the soul is like when it functions normally that its nature is such that the failure of the brain to function would make no difference to the operation of the soul. Such arguments verge from very general arguments of what the soul must be like to be conscious at all to arguments which appeal to particular empirical data.

Dualist philosophers of the past have usually affirmed the natural immortality of the soul—that the soul has such a nature, or the laws of nature are such, that (barring suspension of natural laws) it will continue to function forever. There have been a variety of general arguments for the natural immortality of the soul. Each argument has, in my view, its own fallacies; and the fallacies being fairly evident today, there is no need for any extensive discussion of such arguments. (Expositions of the arguments do, incidentally, usually suffer from confusing the existence of the soul with its functioning; wrongly supposing that when it exists, necessarily it will function.)

To illustrate the fallacies of such arguments, I take just one famous argument, put forward by Plato.[7] Plato argues that the soul being an immaterial thing is unextended, and so does not have parts; but the destruction of a thing consists in separating from each other its parts; whence it follows that souls cannot be destroyed and must continue to exist forever.

Now certainly the normal way by which most material objects cease to exist is that they are broken up into parts. The normal end of a table is to be broken up; likewise for chairs, houses, and pens. But this need not be the way in which a material object ceases to exist. Things cease to exist when they lose their essential properties. The essential properties of a table include being solid. If a table was suddenly liquified, then, even if its constituent molecules remained arranged in the shape of a table by being contained in a table-shaped mould, the table would have ceased to exist. So if even material objects can cease to exist without being broken up into parts, souls surely can cease to exist by some other route than by being broken up into parts.

Nor are the more empirically based arguments of traditional dualists any more successful at showing that the soul has a nature such as to survive death. In *The Analogy of Religion*, Joseph Butler pointed out that many men die of disease, when in full possession of powers of thought; and this, he considered, suggested that weakening of powers of body has no effect at all on many powers of soul:

> as it is evident our present powers and capacities of reason, memory, and affection do not depend upon our gross body in the manner in which perception by our organs of sense does; so they do not appear to depend upon it at all in any such manner as to give ground to think that the dissolution of this body will be the destruction of these our present powers of reflection, as it will of our powers of sensation; or to give ground to conclude, even that it will be so much as a suspension of the former.[8]

But, although it is true that weakening of certain bodily faculties does not affect powers of thought, the evidence is manifest that other bodily damage or disease or mere sleep does affect powers of thought. Drugs and alcohol affect clarity of thought, and, as we saw in Chapter 10, there is no reason to suppose that any conscious events occur during periods of deep sleep.

The failure of the above arguments is, I suggest, typical of the failure of dualist arguments to show that the soul has an immortal nature or at any rate a nature such that it is able to go on functioning 'under its own steam'. We need a form of dualism which brings out that the soul does not have a *nature* so as to function on its own.[9]

Is the Soul Naturally Embodied?

If it cannot be shown that the soul has a nature so as to survive death without its connected brain functioning, can it be shown that the soul has a nature such that its functioning is dependent on that of the brain with which it is connected? Can we show that there is a natural law which (i) connects consciousness of a soul with the functioning of some material system, and (ii) connects the consciousness of each soul with the functioning of a particular material system; so that of natural necessity a soul can only function if the brain or other complex system with which it is at some time connected continues to function?

The answer given in Chapter 10 is that this cannot be shown. It has not been shown and probably never can be shown that there is any naturally necessary connection of these kinds between soul and body. All we are ever likely to get is correlations—between this kind of brain-event and that kind of mental event. And in the absence of a theory which explains why a material system of this kind is needed to produce a soul, how this sort of physical change will produce this kind of mental state, how just so much of the brain and no more is needed for the continuity of a certain soul (as opposed to the mere functioning of a soul with similar apparent memories), we have no grounds for saying that souls *cannot* survive the death of their brains. We do not know and are not likely to find out what if any natural necessity governs the functioning of souls.

The situation is simply that the fairly direct kinds of evidence considered so far give no grounds for supposing that anyone has survived death, but we know of no reason to suppose that it is not possible for anyone to survive death. The situation is thus similar to that in many areas of enquiry when no one has yet found a so-and-so but no one has shown that so-and-sos do not exist. Maybe there are living persons on other planets, naturally occurring elements with atomic numbers of over 1,000, or magnetic monopoles; but as yet no one has found them. Someone may argue that failure to find something when you have looked for it is evidence that it does not exist. But that is so only if you would recognize the object when you found it, and if there is a limited region within which the object can exist and you have explored quite a lot of the region. Failure to find oil in the English Channel after you have drilled in most parts of it, or to find the Abominable Snowman if you have explored most of the Himalayas, is indeed evidence that the thing does not exist. But that is hardly the case with souls whose brains have ceased to function. Maybe they are reincarnate in new bodies and brains on Earth but, as they have lost their memories, the evidence of their identity has gone. Or maybe they are where we cannot at present look. They may still function without being embodied (I argued for the coherence of this supposition in Chapter 8) and so there be no place which they occupy. Or if they are re-embodied in another body with another brain, they may be anywhere in this universe or some other. Failure to find souls who have survived death shows no more than that if they do exist, they are not in the very few places where we have looked for them or that if they are, the marks of their identity (e.g. apparent memories of past lives) have been removed. In the absence of any further evidence as to whether souls do survive death we can only remain agnostic and wait until further evidence does turn up.

Evidence of Survival Via Metaphysical Theory

There is however a third kind of evidence about whether men survive death which we have not yet considered. This is evidence of a wide ranging character which is most simply explained by a very general metaphysical theory of the world, which has as its consequence that human souls survive death as a result of their nature or as a result of the predictable action of some agent who has the power to bring them to life.

One such theory is the Hindu-Buddhist metaphysic of karma, a deep law of retribution in nature whereby an agent who lives a life thereafter lives another in which he gets the deserts (reward or punishment) for the previous life. (The establishment of such a system would have the consequence that, despite the lack of evidence for this on which I commented in Chapter 10, souls exist before birth; in order to be reborn they must then normally lose much of the character which, I have argued, comes to characterize the soul by the time of death.)

Another such theory is of course Christian theism. The theist has first to argue for the existence of God, a person (in a wide sense) of infinite power, wisdom, goodness, and freedom. He may argue that the existence of God provides the simplest explanation of the existence of the universe, the virtual total regularity of its behaviour in its conformity to natural laws, and various more particular phenomena within the universe. It would then follow that God, being omnipotent, would have the power to give to souls life after death (and if there is no natural law which ties the functioning of a soul to the operation of a brain, God would not need to suspend natural laws in order to do this). The Christian theist will need further to show that God intends to bring souls to function after death. He could show this either by showing that it was an obligation on an omnipotent being to do such a thing, and so that, being good, God would do it; or by showing that God had announced his intention of doing this (e.g. by doing something which God alone could do such as suspending a law of nature, in connection with the work of a prophet as a sign that the prophet who had said that God so intended was to be trusted.)[10]

It will be evident that any argument via metaphysical theory to the survival of death by human souls will have a lengthy and complicated structure. But of course those who produce such arguments are equally concerned about most of the other things which need to be proved on the way. Few people are interested in the existence of God solely for its value in proving life after death. And if I am right in- my claim that we cannot show that the soul has a nature such that it survives 'under its own steam', and that we cannot show that it has a nature such that it cannot survive without its sustaining brain, the only kind of argument that can be given is an argument which goes beyond nature, i.e., that shows there is something beyond the natural order embodied in laws of nature, and that the operation of that something is to some extent predictable.

If God did give to souls life after death in a new body or without a body, he would not in any way be violating natural laws—for, if I am right, there are no natural laws which dictate what will happen to the soul after death. The soul doesn't have a nature which has consequences for what will happen to it subsequent to the dissolution of its links to the body.

In the last chapter I argued that the human soul at death had a structure, a system of beliefs and desires which might be expected to be there to some degree in the soul if that soul were to be revived. If a man does survive death, he will take his most central desires and beliefs with him, which is the kind of survival for which, I suspect, most men hope. In hoping to survive death, a man hopes not only that subsequent to his death, he will have experiences and perform actions. He hopes also to take with him a certain attitude to the world. That attitude certainly does not always include all aspects of a man's present character. Much, no doubt, many a man would be happy to dispense with. But it does include some of his character, and that part just because it is the part which he desires should continue, is the most central part.

Note that if there does occur a general resurrection of souls with new bodies in some other world, yet with apparent memories of their past lives (or a general reincarnation on Earth with such memories), they would have grounds for reidentifying each other correctly. For then the general failure of the results of the criterion of bodily continuity to coincide with those of apparent memory would by the arguments of Chapter 9 justifiably lead us to abandon the former criterion and rely entirely on the latter. Not merely is a general resurrection logically possible but it would be known by the subjects to have occurred.

Conclusion

The view of the evolved human soul which I have been advocating may be elucidated by the following analogy. The soul is like a light bulb and the brain is like an electric light socket. If you plug the bulb into the socket and turn the current on, the light will shine. If the socket is damaged or the current turned off, the light will not shine. So, too, the soul will function (have a mental life) if it is plugged into a functioning brain. Destroy the brain or cut off the nutriment supplied by the blood, and the soul will cease to function, remaining inert. But it can be revived and made to function again by repairing or reassembling the brain—just as the light can be made to shine again by repairing the socket or turning on the current. But now, my analogy breaks down slightly (as all analogies do—else they would not be analogies). Humans can repair light sockets. But there is a practical limit to the ability of humans to repair brains; the bits get lost. Humans can move light bulbs and put them into entirely different sockets. But no human knows how to move a soul from one body and plug it into another; nor does any known natural force do this. Yet the task is one involving no contradiction and an omnipotent God could achieve it; or maybe there are other processes which will do so. And just as light bulbs do not have to be plugged into sockets in order to shine (loose wires can be attached to them), maybe there are other ways of getting souls to function than by plugging them into brains. But investigation into the nature of the soul does not reveal those ways. And humans cannot discover what else is needed to get souls to function again, unless they can discover the ultimate force behind nature itself.

Endnotes

* Reprinted by permission of Kluwer Academic Publishers © Richard Swinburne 1986. Reprinted from *The Evolution of the Soul* by Richard Swinburne (1986) by permission of Oxford University Press.

1 *Summa Contra Gentiles*, 4. 81. 12 and 13. (Book IV, translated under the title *On the Truth of the Catholic Faith*, Book IV, by C. J. O'Neill, Image Books, New York, 1957.)

2 For references to the literature, see John Hick, *Death and Eternal Life*, Collins, London, 1976, pp. 373-8.

3 On the alleged evidence of spiritualism, see John Hick, op cit., ch. 7.

4 There is a brief and well-balanced survey of this evidence in Paul and Linda Badham, *Immortality or Extinction?*, Macmillan, London, 1982, ch. 5. My summary of the evidence is based on this chapter, but I also make use of a very careful and balanced account of a new programme of investigations by Michael B. Sabom, *Recollections of Death*, Harper and Row, New York, 1982.

5 *Lancet*, 24 June 1978, quoted in Badham, op. cit.

6 On this, see Sabom, op. cit., chs. 3, 6, 7, and 8.

7 *Phaedo*, 78b-80e. See also, for example, Berkeley: 'We have shown that the soul is indivisible, incorporeal, unextended, and it is consequently incorruptible'—G. Berkeley, *Principles of Human Knowledge*, § 141.

8 *The Analogy of Religion*, 1. 1. 3.

9 Although Aquinas like most other dualists taught that the soul has a natural immortality (see *Summa Theologiae*, la. 7s. 6), he did claim the powers which its nature gave to a bodiless soul are less than those which it has when embodied, and less even than those which Butler ascribed to it—although understanding and will remain, Aquinas claimed, memory does not. (See *Summa Contra Gentiles,* 2. 81. 11 and 14, translated as *On the Truth of the Catholic Faith*, Book II, *Creation*, by James F. Anderson, Image Books, New York, 1956.)

10 I have argued for the existence of God in my *The Existence of God*, Clarendon Press, Oxford, 1979; and I have analysed the structure of an argument to show that God has revealed something through a certain source in my *Faith and Reason*, Clarendon Press, Oxford 1981. ch. 7. (That chapter elucidates the 'in connection with' of the sentence in the text.)

Study Questions

1. For Swinburne, what does it mean for the soul to be naturally embodied?

2. What sorts of arguments from parapsychology does Swinburne discuss?

3. What is Swinburne's conclusion regarding arguments from parapsychology?

4. How does he provide evidence for survival *via* metaphysical theory?

5. How would you compare and contrast the views of Reichenbach, van Inwagen and Swinburne?

PART VII

RELIGIOUS PLURALISM

40

Religious Pluralism and Salvation

John Hick

John Hick is emeritus professor of philosophy at Claremont Graduate School, and formerly professor at the University of Birmingham, England; and is author of *Evil and the God of Love, Faith and Knowledge, Philosophy of Religion, Death and Eternal Life*, and other major works of modern theology.

Let us approach the problems of religious pluralism through the claims of the different traditions to offer salvation—generically, the transformation of human existence from self-centeredness to Reality-centeredness. This approach leads to a recognition of the great world faiths as spheres of salvation; and so far as we can tell, more or less equally so. Their different truth-claims express (a) their differing perceptions, through different religio-cultural "lenses," of the one ultimate divine Reality: (b) their different answers to the boundary questions of origin and destiny, which questions do not require true answers for salvation; and (c) their different historical memories.*

I

The fact that there is a plurality of religious traditions, each with its own distinctive beliefs, spiritual practices, ethical outlook, art forms and cultural ethos, creates an obvious problem for those of us who see them, not simply as human phenomena, but as responses to the Divine. For each presents itself, implicitly or explicitly, as in some important sense absolute and unsurpassable and as rightly claiming a total allegiance. The problem of the relationship between these different streams of religious life has often been posed in terms of their divergent belief-systems. For whilst there are various overlaps between their teachings there are also radical differences: is the divine reality (let us refer to it as the Real) personal or non-personal; if personal, is it unitary or triune; is the universe created, or emanated, or itself eternal; do we live only once on this earth or are we repeatedly reborn? and so on and so on. When the problem of understanding religious plurality is approached through these rival truth-claims it appears particularly intractable.

I want to suggest, however, that it may more profitably be approached from a different direction, in terms of the claims of the various traditions to provide, or to be effective contexts of, salvation. 'Salvation' is primarily a Christian term, though I shall use it here to include its functional analogues in the other major world traditions. In this broader sense we can say that both Christianity and these other faiths are paths of salvation. For whereas pre-axial religion was (and is) centrally concerned to keep life going on an even keel, the post-axial traditions, originating or rooted in the 'axial age' of the first millennium B.C.E.—principally Hinduism, Judaism, Buddhism, Christianity, Islam—are centrally concerned with a radical transformation of the human situation.

It is of course possible, in an alternative approach, to define salvation in such a way that it becomes a necessary truth that only one particular tradition can provide it. If, for example, from within Christianity we define salvation as being forgiven by God because of Jesus' atoning death, and so becoming part of God's redeemed community, the church, then salvation is by definition Christian salvation. If on the other hand, from within Mahayana Buddhism, we define it as the attainment of *satori* or awakening, and so becoming an ego-free manifestation of the eternal Dharmakaya, then salvation is by definition Buddhist liberation. And so on. But if we stand back from these different conceptions to compare them we can, I think, very naturally and properly see them as different forms of the more fundamental conception of a radical change from a profoundly unsatisfactory state to one that is limitlessly better because rightly related to the Real. Each tradition conceptualizes in its own way the wrongness of ordinary human existence—as a state of fallenness from paradisal virtue and happiness, or as a condition of moral weakness and alienation from God, or as the fragmentation of the infinite One into false individualities, or as a self-centeredness which pervasively poisons our involvement in the world process, making it to us an experience of anxious, unhappy unfulfillment. But each at the same time proclaims a limitlessly better possibility, again conceptualized in different ways—as the joy of conforming one's life to God's law; as giving oneself to God in Christ, so that 'it is no longer I who live, but Christ who lives in me' (Galatians 2:20), leading to eternal life in God's presence; as a complete surrender (*islam*) to God, and hence peace with God, leading to the bliss of paradise; as transcending the ego and realizing oneness with the limitless being-consciousness-bliss (*satchitananda*) of Brahman; as overcoming the ego point of view and entering into the serene selflessness of nirvana. I suggest that these different conceptions of salvation are specifications of what, in a generic formula, is the transformation of human existence from self-centeredness to a new orientation, centered in the divine Reality. And in each case the good news that is proclaimed is that this limitlessly better possibility is actually available and can be entered upon, or begin to be entered upon, here and now. Each tradition sets forth the way to attain this great good: faithfulness to the Torah, discipleship to Jesus, obedient living out of the Qur'anic way of life, the Eightfold Path of the Buddhist dharma, or the three great Hindu *margas* of mystical insight, activity in the world, and self-giving devotion to God.

II

The great world religions, then, are ways of salvation. Each claims to constitute an effective context within which the transformation of human existence can and does take place from self-centeredness to Reality-centeredness. How are we to judge such claims? We cannot directly observe the inner spiritual quality of a human relationship to the Real; but we can observe how that relationship, as one's deepest and most pervasive orientation, affects the moral and spiritual quality of a human personality and of a man's or woman's relationship to others. It would seem, then, that we can only assess these salvation-projects insofar as we are able to observe their fruits in human life. The inquiry has to be, in a broad sense, empirical. For the issue is one of fact, even though hard to define and difficult to measure fact, rather than being settleable by *a priori* stipulation.

The word 'spiritual' which occurs above is notoriously vague; but I am using it to refer to a quality or, better, an orientation which we can discern in those individuals whom we call saints—a Christian term which I use here to cover such analogues as arahat, bodhisattva, jivanmukti, mahatma. In these cases the human self is variously described as becoming part of the life of God, being 'to the Eternal Goodness what his own hand is to a man'; or being permeated from within by the infinite reality of Brahman; or becoming one with the eternal Buddha nature. There is a change in their deepest orientation from centeredness in the ego to a new centering in the Real as manifested in their own tradition. One is conscious in the presence of such a person that he or she is, to a startling extent, open to the transcendent, so as to be largely free from self-centered concerns and anxieties and empowered to live as an instrument of God/Truth/Reality.

It is to be noted that there are two main patterns of such a transformation. There are saints who withdraw from the world into prayer or meditation and saints who seek to change the world—in the medieval period a contemplative Julian of Norwich and a political Joan of Arc, or in our own century a mystical Sri Aurobindo and a political Mahatma Gandhi. In our present age of sociological consciousness, when we are aware that our inherited political and economic structures can be analyzed and purposefully changed, saintliness is more likely than in earlier times to take social and political forms. But, of whichever type, the saints are not a different species from the rest of us; they are simply much more advanced in the salvific transformation.

The ethical aspect of this salvific transformation consists in observable modes of behavior. But how do we identify the kind of behavior which, to the degree that it characterizes a life, reflects a corresponding degree of reorientation to the divine Reality? Should we use Christian ethical criteria, or Buddhist, or Muslim . . . ? The answer, I suggest, is that at the level of their most basic moral insights the great traditions use a common criterion. For they agree in giving a central and normative role to the unselfish regard for others that we call love or compassion. This is commonly expressed in the principle of valuing others as we value ourselves, and treating them accordingly. Thus in the ancient Hindu *Mahabharata* we read that 'One should never do to another that which one would regard as injurious to oneself. This, in brief, is the rule of Righteousness' (*Anushana parva*, 113:7). Again, 'He who . . . benefits persons of all orders, who is always devoted to the good of all beings, who does not feel aversion to anybody . . . succeeds in ascending to Heaven' (*Anushana parva*, 145:24). In the Buddhist *Sutta Nipata* we read, 'As a mother cares for her son, all her days, so towards all living things a man's mind should be all-embracing' (149). In the Jain scriptures we are told that one should go about 'treating all creatures in the world as he himself would be treated' (*Kitanga Sutra*, 1.ii.33). Confucus, expounding humaneness (*jen*), said, 'Do not do to others what you would not like yourself (*Analects*, xxi, 2). In a Taoist scripture we read that the good man will 'regard [others'] gains as if they were his own, and their losses in the same way' (*Thai Shang*, 3). The Zoroastrian scriptures declare, 'That nature only is good when it shall not do unto another whatever is not good for its own self (*Dadistan-i-dinik*, 94:5). We are all familiar with Jesus' teaching, 'As ye would that men should do to you, do ye also to them likewise' (Luke 6:31). In the Jewish Talmud we read 'What is hateful to yourself do not do to your fellow man. That is the whole of the Torah' (*Babylonian Talmud*, Shabbath 31 a). And in the Hadith of Islam we read Muhammad's words, 'No man is a true believer unless he desires for his brother that which he desires for himself' (*Ibn Madja*, Intro. 9). Clearly, if everyone acted on this basic principle, taught by all the major faiths, there would be no injustice, no avoidable suffering, and the human family would everywhere live in peace.

When we turn from this general principle of love/compassion to the actual behavior of people within the different traditions, wondering to what extent they live in this way, we realize how little research has been done on so important a question. We do not have much more to go on than general impressions, supplemented by travellers' tales and anecdotal reports. We observe among our neighbors within our own community a great deal of practical loving-kindness; and we are told, for example, that a remarkable degree of self-giving love is to be found among the Hindu fishing families in the mud huts along the Madras shore; and we hear various other similar accounts from other lands. We read biographies, social histories and novels of Muslim village life in Africa, Buddhist life in Thailand, Hindu life in India, Jewish life in New York, as well as Christian life around the world, both in the past and today, and we get the impression that the personal virtues (as well as vices) are basically much the same within these very different religio-cultural settings and that in all of them unselfish concern for others occurs and is highly valued. And, needless to say, as well as love and compassion we also see all-too-abundantly, and apparently spread more or less equally in every society, cruelty, greed, hatred, selfishness and malice.

All this constitutes a haphazard and impressionistic body of data. Indeed I want to stress, not how easy it is, but on the contrary how difficult it is, to make responsible judgments in this area. For not only do we lack full information, but the fragmentary information that we have has to be interpreted in the light of the varying natural conditions of human life in different periods of history and in different economic and political circumstances. And I suggest that all that we can presently arrive at is the cautious and negative conclusion that we have no good reason to believe that any one of the great religious traditions has proved itself to be more productive of love/compassion than another.

The same is true when we turn to the large-scale social outworkings of the different salvation-projects. Here the units are not individual human lives, spanning a period of decades, but religious cultures spanning many centuries. For we can no more judge a civilization than a human life by confining our attention to a single temporal cross-section. Each of the great streams of religious life has had its times of flourishing and its times of deterioration. Each has produced its own distinctive kinds of good and its own distinctive kinds of evil. But to assess either the goods or the evils cross-culturally is difficult to say the least. How do we weigh, for example, the lack of economic progress, and consequent widespread poverty, in traditional Hindu and Buddhist cultures against the endemic violence and racism of Christian civilization, culminating in the twentieth century Holocaust? How do we weigh what the west regards as the hollowness of arranged marriages against what the east regards as the hollowness of a marriage system that leads to such a high proportion of divorces and broken families? From within each culture one can see clearly enough the defects of the others. But an objective ethical comparison of such vast and complex totalities is at present an unattainable ideal. And the result is that we are not in a position to claim an over-all moral superiority for any one of the great living religious traditions.

Let us now see where we have arrived. I have suggested that if we identify the central claim of each of the great religious traditions as the claim to provide, or to be an effective context of, salvation; and if we see

salvation as an actual change in human beings from self-centeredness to a
new orientation centered in the ultimate divine Reality; and if this new
orientation has both a more elusive 'spiritual' character and a more
readily observable moral aspect—then we arrive at the modest and
largely negative conclusion that, so far as we can tell, no one of the great
world religions is salvifically superior to the rest.

III

If this is so, what are we to make of the often contradictory doctrines of
the different traditions? In order to make progress at this point, we must
distinguish various kinds and levels of doctrinal conflict.

There are, first, conceptions of the ultimate as Jahweh, or the Holy
Trinity, or Allah, or Shiva, or Vishnu, or as Brahman, or the
Dharmakaya, the Tao, and so on.

If salvation is taking place, and taking place to about the same extent,
within the religious systems presided over by these various deities and
absolutes, this suggests that they are different manifestations to
humanity of a yet more ultimate ground of all salvific transformation. Let
us then consider the possibility that an infinite transcendent divine
reality is being differently conceived, and therefore differently
experienced, and therefore differently responded to from within our
different religio-cultural ways of being human. This hypothesis makes
sense of the fact that the salvific transformation seems to have been
occurring in all the great traditions. Such a conception is, further, readily
open to philosophical support. For we are familiar today with the ways
in which human experience is partly formed by the conceptual and
linguistic frameworks within which it occurs. The basically Kantian
insight that the mind is active in perception, and that we are always
aware of our environment as it appears to a consciousness operating with
our particular conceptual resources and habits, has been amply confirmed
by work in cognitive psychology and the sociology of knowledge and can
now be extended with some confidence to the analysis of religious
awareness. If, then, we proceed inductively from the phenomenon of
religious experience around the world, adopting a religious as
distinguished from a naturalistic interpretation of it, we are likely to find
ourselves making two moves. The first is to postulate an ultimate
transcendent divine reality (which I have been referring to as the Real)
which, being beyond the scope of our human concepts, cannot be directly
experienced by us as it is in itself but only as it appears through our various
human thought-forms. And the second is to identify the thought-and-
experienced deities and absolutes as different manifestations of the Real
within different historical forms of human consciousness. In Kantian terms,
the divine noumenon, the Real *an sich,* is experienced through different

human receptivities as a range of divine phenomena, in the formation of which religious concepts have played an essential part.

These different 'receptivities' consist of conceptual schemas within which various personal, communal and historical factors have produced yet further variations. The most basic concepts in terms of which the Real is humanly thought-and-experienced are those of (personal) deity and of the (non-personal) absolute. But the Real is not actually experienced either as deity in general or as the absolute in general. Each basic concept becomes (in Kantian terminology) schematized in more concrete form. It is at this point that individual and cultural factors enter the process. The religious tradition of which we are a part, with its history and ethos and its great exemplars, its scriptures feeding our thoughts and emotions, and perhaps above all its devotional or meditative practices, constitutes an uniquely shaped and coloured 'lens' through which we are concretely aware of the Real specifically as the personal Adonai, or as the Heavenly Father, or as Allah, or Vishnu,, or Shiva, . . . or again as the non-personal Brahman, or Dharmakaya, or the Void or the Ground . . . Thus, one who uses the forms of Christian prayer and sacrament is thereby led to experience the Real as the divine Thou, whereas one who practices advaitic yoga or Buddhist zazen is thereby brought to experience the Real as the infinite being-consciousness-bliss of Brahman, or as the limitless emptiness of sunyata which is at the same time the infinite fullness of immediate reality as 'wondrous being.'

Three explanatory comments at this point before turning to the next level of doctrinal disagreement. First, to suppose that the experienced deities and absolutes which are the intentional objects of worship or content of religious meditation, are appearances or manifestations of the Real, rather than each being itself the Real *an sich,* is not to suppose that they are illusions—any more than the varying ways in which a mountain may appear to a plurality of differently placed observers are illusory. That the same reality may be variously experienced and described is true even of physical objects. But in the case of the infinite, transcendent divine reality there may well be much greater scope for the use of varying human conceptual schemas producing varying modes of phenomenal experience. Whereas the concepts in terms of which we are aware of mountains and rivers and houses are largely (though by no means entirely) standard throughout the human race, the religious concepts in terms of which we become aware of the Real have developed in widely different ways within the different cultures of the earth.

As a second comment, to say that the Real is beyond the range of our human concepts is not intended to mean that it is beyond the scope of purely formal, logically generated concepts—such as the concept of being beyond the range of (other than purely formal) concepts. We would not be able to refer at all to that which cannot be conceptualized in any way, not even by the concept of being unconceptualizable! But the other than purely formal concepts by which our experience is structured must be presumed not to apply to its noumenal ground. The characteristics mapped in thought and language are those that are constitutive of human experience. We have no warrant to apply them to the noumenal ground of the phenomenal, i.e., experienced, realm. We should therefore not think of the Real *an sich* as singular or plural, substance or process, personal or non-personal, good or bad, purposive or non-purpose. This has long been a basic theme of religious thought. For example, within Christianity, Gregory of Nyssa declared that:

> The simplicity of the True Faith assumes God to be that which He is, namely, incapable of being grasped by any term, or any idea, or any other device of our apprehension, remaining beyond the reach not only of the human but of the angelic and all supramundane intelligence, unthinkable, unutterable, above all expression in words, having but one name that can represent His proper nature, the single name being "Above Every Name" (*Against Eunomius*, I, 42).

Augustine, continuing this tradition, said that 'God transcends even the mind' *(True Religion,* 36:67), and Aquinas that 'by its immensity, the divine substance surpasses every form that our intellect reaches' *(Contra Gentiles,* I, 14, 3). In Islam the Qur'an affirms that God is 'beyond what they describe' (6:101). The Upanishads declare of Brahman, 'There the eye goes not, speech goes not, nor the mind' *(Kena Up.,* 1, 3), and Shankara wrote that Brahman is that 'before which words recoil, and to which no understanding has ever attained' (Otto, *Mysticism East and West,* E. T. 1932, p. 28).

But, third, we might well ask, why postulate an ineffable and unobservable divine-reality-in-itself? If we can say virtually nothing about it, why affirm its existence? The answer is that the reality or non-reality of the postulated noumenal ground of the experienced religious phenomena constitutes the difference between a religious and a naturalistic interpretation of religion. If there is no such transcendent ground, the various forms of religious experience have to be categorized as purely human projections. If on the other hand there is such a transcendent ground, then these phenomena may be joint products of the universal presence of the Real and of the varying sets of concepts and images that have crystallized within the religious traditions of the earth. To affirm the transcendent is thus to affirm that religious experience is not solely a construction of the human imagination but is a response—though always culturally conditioned—to the Real.

Those doctrinal conflicts, then, that embody different conceptions of the ultimate arise, according to the hypothesis I am presenting, from the variations between different sets of human conceptual schema and spiritual practice. And it seems that each of these varying ways of thinking-and-experiencing the Real has been able to mediate its transforming presence to human life. For the different major concepts of the ultimate do not seem—so far as we can tell—to result in one religious totality being soteriologically more effective than another.

IV

The second level of doctrinal difference consists of metaphysical beliefs which cohere with although they are not exclusively linked to a particular conception of the ultimate. These are beliefs about the relation of the material universe to the Real: creation *ex nihilo*, emanation, an eternal universe, an unknown form of dependency . . . ? And about human destiny: reincarnation or a single life, eternal identity or transcendence of the self . . . ? Again, there are questions about the existence of heavens and hells and purgatories and angels and devils and many other subsidiary states and entities. Out of this mass of disputed religious issues let me pick two major examples: is the universe created ex *nihilo,* and do human beings reincarnate?

I suggest that we would do well to apply to such questions a principle that was taught by the Buddha two and a half millennia ago. He listed a series of 'undetermined questions' *(avyakata)*—whether the universe is eternal, whether it is spatially infinite, whether (putting it in modern terms) mind and brain are identical, and what the state is of a completed project of human existence (a Tathagata) after bodily death. He refused to answer these questions, saying that we do not need to have knowledge of these things in order to attain liberation or awakening (nirvana); and indeed that to regard such information as soteriologically essential would only divert us from the single-minded quest for liberation. I think that we can at this point profitable learn from the Buddha, even extending his conception of the undetermined questions further than he did—for together with almost everyone else in his own culture he regarded one of our examples, reincarnation, as a matter of assured knowledge. Let us, then, accept that we do not *know* whether, e.g., the universe was created *ex nihilo,* nor whether human beings are reincarnated; and, further, that it is not necessary for salvation to hold a correct opinion on either matter.

I am not suggesting that such issues are unimportant. On their own level they are extremely important, being both of great interest to us and also having widely ramifying implications within our belief-systems and hence for our lives. The thought of being created out of nothing can nourish a salutary sense of absolute dependence. (But other conceptions can also nurture that sense.) The idea of reincarnation can offer the hope of future spiritual progress; though, combined with the principle of karma, it can also serve to validate the present inequalities of human circumstances. (But other eschatologies also have their problems, both theoretical and practical). Thus these—and other—disputed issues do have a genuine importance. Further, it is possible that some of them may one day be settled by empirical evidence. It might become established, for example, that the 'big bang' of some fifteen billion years ago was an absolute beginning, thus ruling out the possibility that the universe is eternal. And again, it might become established, by an accumulation of evidence, that reincarnation does indeed occur in either some or all cases. On the other hand it is possible that we shall never achieve agreed knowledge in these areas. Certainly, at the present time, whilst we have theories, preferences, hunches, inherited convictions, we cannot honestly claim to have secure knowledge. And the same is true, I suggest, of the entire range of metaphysical issues about which the religions dispute. They are of intense interest, properly the subject of continuing research and discussion, but are not matters concerning which absolute dogmas are appropriate. Still less is it appropriate to maintain that salvation depends upon accepting some one particular opinion or dogma. We have seen that the transformation of human existence from self-centeredness to Reality-centeredness seems to be taking place within each of the great traditions despite their very different answers to these debated questions. It follows that a correct opinion concerning them is not required for salvation.

V

The third level of doctrinal disagreement concerns historical questions. Each of the great traditions includes a larger or smaller body of historical beliefs. In the case of Judaism these include at least the main features of the history described in the Hebrew scriptures; in the case of Christianity, these plus the main features of the life, death and resurrection of Jesus as described in the New Testament; in the case of Islam, the main features of the history described in the Qur'an; in the case of Vaishnavite Hinduism, the historicity of Krishna; in the case of Buddhism, the historicity of Guatama; and his enlightenment at Bodh Gaya; and so on. But although each tradition thus has its own records of the past, there are rather few instances of direct disagreement between these. For the strands of history that are cherished in these different historical memories do not generally overlap; and where they do overlap they do not generally involve significant differences. The overlaps are mainly within the thread of ancient near eastern history that is common to the Jewish, Christian and Muslim scriptures; and within this I can only locate two points of direct disagreement—the Torah's statement that Abraham nearly sacrificed his son Isaac at Mount Moriah (Genesis 22) versus the Muslim interpretation of the Qur'anic version (in Sura 37) that it was his other son Ishmael; and the New Testament witness that Jesus died on the cross versus the Qur'anic teaching that 'they did not slay him, neither crucified him, only a likeness of that was shown them' (Sura 4:156). (This latter however would seem to be a conflict between an historical report, in the New Testament, and a theological inference—that God would not allow so great a prophet to be killed—in the Qur'an.)

All that one can say in general about such disagreements, whether between two traditions or between any one of them and the secular historians, is that they could only properly be settled by the weight of historical evidence. However, the events in question are usually so remote in time, and the evidence so slight or so uncertain, that the question cannot be definitively settled. We have to be content with different communal memories, enriched as they are by the mythic halo that surrounds all long-lived human memories of events of transcendent significance. Once again, then, I suggest that differences of historical judgment, although having their own proper importance, do not prevent the different traditions from being effective, and so far as we can tell equally effective, contexts of salvation. It is evidently not necessary for salvation to have correct historical information. (It is likewise not necessary for salvation, we may add, to have correct scientific information.)

VI

Putting all this together, the picture that I am suggesting can be outlined as follows: our human religious experience, variously shaped as it is by our sets of religious concepts, is a cognitive response to the universal presence of the ultimate divine Reality that, in itself, exceeds human conceptuality. This Reality is however manifested to us in ways formed by a variety of human concepts, as the range of divine personae and metaphysical impersonae witnessed to in the history of religions. Each major tradition, built around its own distinctive way of thinking-and-experiencing the Real, has developed its own answers to the perennial questions of our origin and destiny, constituting more or less comprehensive and coherent cosmologies and eschatologies. These are human creations which have, by their association with living streams of religious experience, become invested with a sacred authority. However they cannot all be wholly true; quite possibly none is wholly true; perhaps all are partly true. But since the salvific process has been going on through the centuries despite this unknown distribution of truth and falsity in our cosmologies and eschatologies, it follows that it is not necessary for salvation to adopt any one of them. We would therefore do well to learn to tolerate unresolved, and at present unresolvable, differences concerning these ultimate mysteries.

One element, however, to be found in the belief-systems of most of the traditions raises a special problem, namely that which asserts the sole salvific efficacy of that tradition. I shall discuss this problem in terms of Christianity because it is particularly acute for those of us who are Christians. We are all familiar with such New Testament texts as 'There is salvation in no one else [than Jesus Christ], for there is no other name under heaven given among men by which we must be saved (Acts 4:12), and with the Catholic dogma *Extra ecclesiam nulla salus* (No salvation outside the church) and its Protestant equivalent—never formulated as an official dogma but nevertheless implicit within the 18th and 19th century Protestant missionary expansion,—no salvation outside Christianity. Such a dogma differs from other elements of Christian belief in that it is not only a statement about the potential relationship of Christians to God but at the same time about the actual relationship of non-Christians to God. It says that the latter, in virtue of being non-Christians, lack salvation. Clearly such a dogma is incompatible with the insight that the salvific transformation of human existence is going on, and so far as we can tell going on to a more or less equal extent, within all the great traditions. Insofar, then, as we accept that salvation is not confined to Christianity we must reject the old exclusivist dogma.

This has in fact now been done by most thinking Christians, though exceptions remain, mostly within the extreme Protestant fundamentalist constituencies. The *Extra ecclesiam* dogma, although not explicitly repealed, has been outflanked by the work of such influential Catholic theologians as Karl Rahner, whose new approach was in effect endorsed by Vatican II. Rahner expressed his more inclusivist outlook by suggesting that devout people of other faiths are 'anonymous Christians,' within the invisible church even without knowing it, and thus within the sphere of salvation. The present Pope, in his Encyclical *Redemptor Hominis* (1979) has expressed this thought even more comprehensively by saying that 'every man without exception has been redeemed by Christ' and 'with every man without any exception whatever Christ is in a way united, even when man in unaware of it' (para. 14). And a number of Protestant theologians have advocated a comparable position.

The feature that particularly commends this kind of inclusivism to many Christians today is that it recognizes the spiritual values of other religions, and the occurrence of salvation within them, and yet at the same time preserves their conviction of the ultimate superiority of their own religion over all others. For it maintains that salvation, wherever it occurs, is Christian salvation; and Christians are accordingly those who alone know and preach the source of salvation, namely in the atoning death of Christ.

This again, like the old exclusivism, is a statement not only about the ground of salvation for Christians but also for Jews, Muslims, Hindus, Buddhists and everyone else. But we have seen that it has to be acknowledged that the immediate ground of their transformation is the particular spiritual path along which they move. It is by living in accordance with the Torah or with the Qur'anic revelation that Jews and Muslims find a transforming peace with God; it is by one or other of their great *margas* that Hindus attain to *moksha;* it is by the Eightfold Path that Theravada Buddhists come to *nirvana;* it is by *zazen* that Zen Buddhists attain to *satori;* and so on. The Christian inclusivist is, then, by implication, declaring that these various spiritual paths are efficacious, and constitute authentic contexts of salvation, because Jesus died on the cross; and, by further implication, that if he had not died on the cross they would not be efficacious.

This is a novel and somewhat astonishing doctrine. How are we to make sense of the idea that the salvific power of the dharma taught five hundred years earlier by the Buddha is a consequence of the death of Jesus in approximately 30 C.E.? Such an apparently bizarre conception should only be affirmed for some very good reason. It was certainly not taught by Jesus or his apostles. It has emerged only in the thought of twentieth century Christians who have come to recognize that Jews are being salvifically transformed through the spirituality of Judaism, Muslims through that of Islam, Hindus and Buddhists through the paths mapped out by their respective traditions, and so on, but who nevertheless wish to retain their inherited sense of the unique superiority of Christianity. The only outlet left for this sense, when one has acknowledged the salvific efficacy of the various great spiritual ways, is the arbitrary and contrived notion of their metaphysical dependency upon the death of Christ. But the theologian who undertakes to spell out this invisible causality is not to be envied. The problem is not one of logical possibility—it only requires logical agility to cope with that—but one of religious or spiritual plausibility. It would be a better use of theological time and energy, in my opinion, to develop forms of trinitarian, christological and soteriological doctrine which are compatible with our awareness of the independent salvific authenticity of the other great world faiths. Such forms are already available in principle in conceptions of the Trinity, not as ontologically three but as three ways in which the one God is humanly thought and experienced; conceptions of Christ as a man so fully open to and inspired by God as to be, in the ancient Hebrew metaphor, a 'son of God'; and conceptions of salvation as an actual human transformation which has been powerfully elicited and shaped, among his disciples, by the influence of Jesus.

There may indeed well be a variety of ways in which Christian thought can develop in response to our acute late twentieth century awareness of the other world religions, as there were of responding to the nineteenth century awareness of the evolution of the forms of life and the historical character of the holy scriptures. And likewise there will no doubt be a variety of ways in which each of the other great traditions can rethink its inherited assumption of its own unique superiority. But it is not for us to tell people of other traditions how to do their own business. Rather, we should attend to our own.

The Claremont Graduate School

This paper as originally delivered as the second Kegley Lecture at California State University, Bakersfield, on February 10th, 1988. For a fuller account of its proposals the reader is invited to see my *An Interpretation of Religion* (New Haven: Yale University Press and London: Macmillan, 1988).

Endnote

Study Questions

1.   What does John Hick mean when he says that "salvation" has "functional analogies in other religions"?

2.   What other term does he discuss in Section II that has "functional analogies in other religions"?

3.   Hick provides a general account of the picture of religious experience. What are its chief characteristics?

4.   How does Hick characterize exclusivism? Inclusivism? Where does Hick go with the discussion and why?

5.   On Hick's account, is there anything unique about Christianity? What, if anything?

41

Plantinga, Pluralism and Justified Religious Belief

David Basinger

David Basinger is professor of philosophy at Roberts Wesleyan College, and is co-author of *Reason and Religious Belief*.

In this paper* Basinger shows that Plantinga is a nonevidentialist in the sense that he thinks that we need not search for propositional evidence to support our formed beliefs or the reliability of our own belief-forming faculties. He contends that, given the pluralistic challenge, the knowledgeable theist is required to look for such propositional evidence although she can justifiably continue to consider her formed beliefs properly basic even if none is found.

According to Alvin Plantinga, it has been widely held since the enlightenment that if theistic beliefs are to be considered rational, they must be based on propositional evidence. It is not enough for the theist just to refute objections. The theist "must also have something like an argument for [such a] belief, or some positive reason to think that the belief is true."[1] But this is incorrect, Plantinga argues. Basic beliefs are beliefs not based on propositional evidence; such beliefs are "properly basic in a set of circumstances" if they can be so affirmed in those circumstances "without either violating an epistemic duty or displaying some kind of noetic defect."[2] And, according to Plantinga, theistic beliefs can be properly basic. For example, he argues that "under widely realized conditions it is perfectly rational, reasonable, intellectually respectable and acceptable to believe there is such a person as God without believing it on the basis of evidence—propositional evidence vs. the kind instanced by 'the evidence of the senses'."[3]

But can a properly basic belief such as this have any epistemic credibility (warrant) if it is not conferred by other propositions whose epistemic status is not in question? Yes, Plantinga replies. There are two significantly different ways in which a proposition can acquire warrant.

There is propositional warrant—warrant conferred by an evidential line of reasoning from other beliefs. However, there is also nonpropositional warrant.

> [We have] cognitive faculties designed to enable us to achieve true beliefs with respect to a wide variety of propositions—propositions about our immediate environment, about our interior lives, about the thoughts and experiences of other persons, about our universe at large, about right and wrong, about the whole realm of abstracta—numbers, properties, propositions, states of affairs, possible worlds and their like, about modality—what is necessary and possible—and about [ourselves]. These faculties work in such a way that under the appropriate circumstances we form the appropriate belief. More exactly, the appropriate belief is formed in us; in the typical case we do not decide to hold or form the belief in question, but simply find ourselves with it. Upon considering an instance of modus ponens, I find myself believing its corresponding conditional; upon being appeared to in the familiar way, I find myself holding the belief that there is a large tree before me; upon being asked what I had for breakfast, I reflect for a moment and then find myself with the belief that what I had was eggs on toast. In these and other cases I do not decide what to believe; I don't total up the evidence (I'm being appeared to redly; on most occasions when thus appeared to I am in the presence of something red; so most probably in this case I am) and make a decision as to what seems best supported; I simply find myself believing.[4]

And from a theistic point of view, Plantinga continues, the same is true in the religious realm. Just as it is true that when our senses or memory is functioning properly, "appropriate belief is formed in us," so it is that God has also created us with faculties which will, "when they are working in the way they were designed to work by the being who designed and created us and them," produce true theistic beliefs.[5] Moreover, if these faculties are functioning properly, a basic theistic belief thus formed "has positive epistemic status to the degree [the individual in question finds herself] inclined to accept it."[6]

But what of the alleged counterevidence to theistic beliefs? What, for example, of all the arguments which conclude that the theist has no justifiable basis for believing in God? Can they all be dismissed as irrelevant? Not immediately, answers Plantinga. We must seriously consider alleged defeaters of our basic beliefs. We must, for instance, seriously consider the claim that religious belief is mere wish fulfillment and the claim that God's existence is incompatible with (or at least improbable given) the amount of evil in the world. But to undercut such defeaters, we need not engage in positive apologetics: produce propositional evidence for mere beliefs. Only "negative apologetics"—the refutation of such arguments—"is required to defeat...defeaters."[7]

Moreover, it is Plantinga's conviction that such defeater defeaters do normally exist. With respect to belief in God's existence, for example, he maintains that "the nonpropositional warrant enjoyed by [a person's] belief in God [seems] itself sufficient to turn back the challenge offered by some alleged defeaters"— e.g., the claim that theistic belief is mere wish fulfillment. And other defeaters such as the "problem of evil," he adds, can be undercut by identifying validity or soundness problems or even by appealing to the fact that experts think it is unsound, or that the experts are evenly divided as in its soundness."[8] Thus, even considering all the seeming evidence against God's existence and other theistic beliefs, Plantinga is still inclined to believe that at least some such beliefs are properly basic for most theists—even intellectually sophisticated adult theists."[9]

There is much that Plantinga says with which I agree. His contention that many individuals simply discover theistic beliefs formed in them seems to me to be correct. Philosophers and theologians have for millennia discussed the 'evidence' for and against various theistic beliefs. But it is doubtful that many theists initially acquire theistic beliefs on the basis of such evidential discussions. Many, if not most, appear to have just found themselves with the inclination to affirm such beliefs.

And his contention that such beliefs are generated by divinely created religious belief-forming faculties which produce beliefs in a manner analogous to our visual and moral belief-forming faculties also seems acceptable. Of course, those who believe there is no God will not believe that any of our belief-forming faculties are divinely created. But Plantinga only claims that this is what he and other theists believe to be the case. Thus, in a day when a 'convincing' refutation of God's existence seems less likely than ever, Plantinga's qualified contention appears safe.

In fact, if we drop consideration of the origin of the faculties in question, Plantinga seems to be offering us a very plausible description of how certain theistic beliefs *are* in fact initially formed in many theists. Few deny that we have 'visual faculties' which receive external data— e.g., light reflected off a tree—process such data, produce in us visual images expressible by propositions such as "I am being appeared to treely," and then incline us to believe certain things—e.g., that there actually is a tree in front of us. And, analogously, it seems quite plausible to believe that many humans possess 'faculties' (whether or not they are held to be 'mental' and/or 'physical' and whether or not they are held to be divinely and/or naturally created) which receive external data—for example, encounter the starry heavens—process such data, and then produce both the religious concepts expressible by propositions such as "God exists" or "God has spoken to me" and the inclination to believe these propositions to be true.

However, I shall argue that the undeniable existence of pervasive religious pluralism places knowledgeable theists under a prima facie obligation to do more than engage in negative apologetics. It requires such theists to *attempt* to produce positive evidence for their religious beliefs. And I shall then discuss the implications of this for for Plantinga's claim that some theistic beliefs are properly basic for most theists—even intellectually sophisticated adult theists."

I

It seems to me that the essence of Plantinga's model of belief justification can be captured in what I shall label his Negative Apologetical Thesis (NAT).

> *NAT:* For a theist to be in a position to maintain justifiably that the basic religious beliefs formed by her religious faculties are properly basic—i.e., to be in a position to maintain justifiably that her basic formed beliefs are true even though she has no "positive reason" to think they are true—she is only obligated to defend herself against the claim that her religious faculties are not functioning properly— i.e., are not functioning as they are intended to function or are not producing true beliefs.

Or, to be even more explicit about those aspects of NAT with which this paper will be concerned, it seems to me that Plantinga is making two related, but distinct, claims about negative apologetics. He is claiming that a theist is not obligated to produce independent evidence for the beliefs that her faculties have formed. And he appears to be claiming that she is also not obligated to establish the reliability of her own religious faculties—i.e., he is claiming that she can assume the reliability of her own religious faculties until they are proven faulty.

But why accept NAT? Specifically, why should a theist assume her religious faculties are reliable until proven unreliable rather than assume such faculties are unreliable until proven reliable? The most popular argument for this aspect of NAT—and one to which Plantinga seems at times at least implicitly to be appealing—can be called the General Reliability Argument (GRA). We as humans, it is held, are naturally endowed with a considerable number of belief-forming faculties. As a result, many of us simply find ourselves believing we are 'seeing' a tree or believing that we had eggs yesterday or believing we have a headache or believing that from the conjunction of (a then b) and (a), (b) follows or believing God exists. Now, in general, we cannot prove that such formed beliefs are true and, thus, on this basis, that our faculties are reliable. Some of the greatest philosophical minds—e.g., Descartes and Hume—

have tried but with a notable lack of success. But the onus is not on us to furnish such proof. We all rely on these faculties daily, and in general they serve us quite well. In fact the assumed reliability of such faculties serves as the basis for some of our most noncontroversial examples of 'knowledge'. So our basic stance toward such faculties—including our 'religious' faculties—should be to assume they are 'innocent until proven guilty'.

In short, the argument is that since we as humans can justifiably assume, without proof, that religious faculties in general are reliable, an individual theist can justifiably assume, without proof, that her own religious faculties are reliable until proven otherwise.

Now with respect to most of our human faculties—e.g., our visual faculties—GRA seems noncontroversially true. But can our 'religious faculties' be considered appropriately analogous to our other faculties in this context? Or, to put the question in its more useful form, is there any reason not to assume that religious faculties are as reliable as visual or auditory or inferential faculties?

When considering the formed beliefs of many individuals in specific, homogeneous cultural contexts, the answer to this latter question would appear to be no. For, in these contexts, all of the faculties in question appear to function in an analogous manner: they all produce consensus. That is, it is not only the case that most individuals in such cultural contexts find the same basic visual and inferential and auditory beliefs being formed in them; they also find the same basic religious beliefs being formed in them. Thus, such individuals quite justifiably assume that their religious faculties are as reliable as the others.

However, when we survey the 'world scene', a major difficulty arises. The problem, of course, is that on a world-wide scale, religious faculties consistently and pervasively produce a myriad of different, often incompatible, basic religious beliefs.

For instance, such faculties produce no common conception of God. Most theists conceive of God as a 'supreme being' in some sense. But there is little consensus on such a being's essential characteristics. While some find themselves believing in the existence of a being who is 'personal', others do not. Rather, they find themselves believing either that God is some sort of impersonal force or that God is simply the sum total of all there is. And while some find themselves believing that God is the sole, unilateral creator and controller of all, others find themselves believing that God can unilaterally create or control nothing. All reality, they maintain, is always co-creative. In fact the 'religious' faculties of some individuals produce disbelief in the existence of any sort of 'supreme being'.

Now, of course, such divergence can be explained in part by the fact that many individuals have never observed human activity outside of their own culture or have not been exposed to alternative theistic and nontheistic perspectives or have not seriously analyzed them. However, even among those knowledgeable individuals who have considered roughly the same data, nothing close to a basic consensus has emerged. Their visual faculties generally produce similar visual beliefs in similar settings. Their memories draw forth similar beliefs in similar settings. And their introspective and inferential faculties frequently produce similar beliefs in similar contexts. But their religions faculties simply do not.

In short, pervasive religious pluralism brings into serious question whether we ought to consider religious faculties to be analogous to other belief-forming faculties in the way GRA suggests. The existence of such pluralism gives us no reason to deny that religious faculties *produce* beliefs in us in a manner analogous to the way visual or auditory faculties produce beliefs. But since the reason we do not question the reliability of most of our faculties is that such faculties consistently generate similar beliefs in most individuals, the fact that religious faculties do not, in general, produce similar beliefs in similar contexts does make it much more difficult to assume they possess the same sort of reliability status. That is, this lack of consensus in the religious realm makes it difficult to assume that religious faculties, in general, produce true beliefs. And if this is so, then, of course, GRA is greatly weakened (I personally believe defeated) as a justification for affirming NAT—or, more specifically, is greatly weakened as a basis for assuming that we need only defend our religious belief-forming faculties against the claim that they are unreliable.

It will not help here, it must be explicitly noted, to move to the religious version of GRA in which Plantinga explicitly appeals: our human faculties—including our religious faculties—can be assumed innocent until proven guilty because they "have been designed, no doubt, with reliability in mind" by an all-powerful, all knowing creator.[10] This changes the 'origin' of the alleged reliability. But the same problem remains. How can religious faculties justifiably be assumed to possess the same degree of reliability as that granted other belief-forming faculties when religious faculties do not produce consensus in a manner analogous to the others?

If I am correct, where does this leave the proponent of NAT? If she is no longer in a position to assume that *her own* religious belief-forming faculties are reliable because religious faculties, in general, can justifiably be assumed to be so, must she now abandon this aspect of Plantinga's negative thesis? She might conclude that she must. That is, she might conclude that, in the absence of some helpful version of GRA, she must now do more than simply defend herself against attacks on the reliability of her own religious faculties, which is all that NAT requires. She might decide that each theist must now independently *establish* the reliability of her own religious faculties—independently identify positive reasons for believing her own faculties are reliable—before she can justifiably claim that the religious beliefs they form are properly basic.

However, in Plantinga's own words, to believe one must have "some positive reason to think" a belief is true is to be an evidentialist. Thus, although to abandon NAT in this manner is not to become an evidentialist with respect to the beliefs one's religious faculties have formed, it is to become an evidentialist with respect to the other aspect of Plantinga's negative apologetical thesis: the reliability status on one's own religious faculties.

This is not to say, it must be explicitly emphasized, that Plantinga ought not, himself, be viewed as an evidentialist in *any* sense. He does appear to view GRA (in its religious and/or natural version) as a form of evidence—as a positive reason—for holding certain opinions about our formed beliefs. Specifically he seems to see GRA as a basis for claiming that a theist can assume her religious beliefs to be 'innocent until proven guilty'—i.e., as a reason for believing each theist need not independently establish the reliability of her religious faculties. But the proponent of the line of reasoning in question, on the other hand, sees the inadequacy of GRA as a reason to believe each theist does need to establish independently the reliability of her religious faculties. Thus, this theist has now become an evidentialist in the exact sense Plantinga claims in NAT she need not.

It might be argued, however, that the proponent of NAT ought not give up so easily. The existence of pervasive religious pluralism does seriously challenge any version of GRA as a justification for the affirmation of NAT. But the burden of proof still lies with the critic. We may not have good reasons for holding that religious faculties are in general reliable. But it is still the case for any given theist that, unless it can be established that her specific religious faculties are in fact unreliable, she remains wholly justified in maintaining that her formed beliefs are properly basic—can be affirmed without positive evidence. In short, it might be argued that a theist can still justifiably affirm Plantinga's negative apologetical thesis, even if she can no longer justifiably appeal to some version of GRA.

It seems to me, though, that this line of reasoning is unacceptable. The existence of pervasive pluralism does challenge, and I think defeat, any version of GRA designed to allow us to assume the general reliability of religious faculties. But I believe that such pluralism *also* functions as a *direct* challenge to the affirmation of NAT itself—as a direct challenge to the claim that to defend the proper basicality of our formed religious beliefs, we need only *defend* ourselves against attacks on such beliefs and the faculties which have produced them. An illustration related to another type of belief-forming faculty may be helpful. Let us assume that Tom and Bill, both students in the same Introduction to Philosophy class, are discussing a forthcoming exam. What soon emerges is that, while Tom believes the exam is on Friday, Bill believes it is on the following Monday. Before their discussion neither had any reason to doubt he was correct. Both had been in class the day the exam date was announced, and neither had previously had any reason to believe his auditory faculties or memory was not functioning properly.

But what is the proper epistemological response now that a conflict has arisen? An improper response, obviously, would be for either Bill or Tom to assume immediately that his faculties had, in fact, not functioned in a reliable manner and, thus, that his formed belief ought no longer be considered true. And the same, I believe, holds in the religious realm. It is undeniably the case, for instance, that Christians or Hindus or Buddhists often find the religious beliefs formed in them to be incompatible with the religious beliefs formed in the members of other religious groups. But this fact alone is not a justifiable reason for a proponent of any given religious perspective to assume immediately that her religious faculties are, in fact, unreliable and thus that the beliefs formed by such faculties ought no longer be affirmed.[11]

Does this mean, accordingly, that the knowledgeable theist who becomes aware of the pervasively pluralistic nature of religious beliefs is under no greater epistemic obligation than before? Can it be argued that since the existence of religious pluralism is not a sound reason for giving up any specific theistic belief, the theist can justifiably dismiss further consideration of this phenomenon and simply continue to assume her religious faculties are producing beliefs which are properly basic—i.e., can justifiably continue to maintain that her formed beliefs can be affirmed without positive evidence.

I do not think so. Conflicts between beliefs produced by other faculties, we all know from experience, *sometimes* occur because one of the faculties was not functioning properly. For example, two students have sometimes 'heard' different test dates because one had an ear infection or wax in his ear or was taking a prescription drug which had affected his hearing and/or memory. Moreover, we also know from experience that such conflicts can *at times* be resolved by further investigation. For example, students can usually resolve a conflict of the type under discussion simply by calling the instructor. Accordingly, *if the goal is to maximize 'truth' and minimizing 'error'*, then all parties are, I believe, under a *prima facie* obligation to attempt to resolve such conflicts.

Now, of course, students may not always be interested in determining exactly when an exam is to be given. Perhaps they have already studied or plan not to study. But most theists (and nontheists) do claim to be interested in affirming 'truth' and avoiding 'error'. Thus, the existence of pervasive pluralism—the fact that seemingly reliable religious faculties continually produce incompatible religious beliefs—does, I believe place the knowledgeable theist under the type of *prima facie* epistemic obligation in question.

It must be emphasized, of course, that such an obligation is *prima facie*. There may be many legitimate reasons why it cannot in fact immediately or ever be discharged. A theist, for instance, may not have the time or resources to investigate further. Moreover, I do not believe that the mere existence of this obligation need have any immediate bearing on the epistemic status of a theist's formed beliefs.[12] This is not to any, of course, that a theist who becomes aware of religious pluralism may not, in fact, find herself less inclined to affirm certain formed beliefs. And information uncovered during an attempt to resolve the conflict in question may well lead a theist to believe she is now more or less justified in affirming her formed religious beliefs than she was initially. However, the mere recognition of the existence of the obligation in question does not itself require her to modify her epistemic attitude toward her formed beliefs.

But I *am* arguing that once the theist becomes aware of the pluralistic challenge, she can no longer justifiably choose to retain a purely defensive posture. Or stated differently, *I am arguing* that the knowledgeable theist cannot justifiably claim that because the existence of pervasive pluralism does not require her to abandon her formed beliefs, she is under no obligation to consider the matter further. If she desires to determine the 'truth' of the matter to the extent possible, she is obligated, in principle, to engage in further investigation. The arena of positive apologetics must at least be entered. The game of 'negative apologetics' will no longer be enough.

Or, to put all this more explicitly into the language of NAT, the existence of pervasive pluralism is not a sufficient reason for believing that any given theist's formed beliefs are false or that her belief forming faculties are unreliable. Nor, as we shall see, is the existence of such pluralism a sufficient reason in every case to deny that our formed religious beliefs can ultimately be considered properly basic. But religious pluralism does challenge the assumption that a theist need only defend her formed beliefs and the reliability of the faculties which have produced them to preserve the proper basicality of such beliefs. The knowledgeable theist, I am arguing, is obligated to attempt to resolve the pluralistic conflict—enter the arena of positive apologetics—*before* any 'final' decision concerning the epistemic status of her formed religious beliefs can be made.

What if someone refuses to attempt to meet this obligation? This, of course, is not relevant to the question of whether formed beliefs can or cannot, in principle, be considered properly basic. But for a given theist to purposely violate the duty in question does mean, I believe, that she has forfeited her right to claim that her formed beliefs are properly basic. For, as Plantinga himself has told us, basic beliefs can only be considered properly basic if they can be affirmed without "violating an epistemic duty." And the theist in question has in essence chosen not to attempt to maximize truth and minimize error and has, thus, violated one of the basic criteria for epistemically rational behavior.[13]

II

Let us assume that I am correct. This raises two distinct, but related questions. Can the pluralistic challenge be resolved? That is, can we determine which set of formed religious beliefs is true or most worthy of affirmation? And either way, can a theist justifiably continue to maintain that her formed beliefs are properly basic—i.e., can she justifiably continue to affirm such beliefs without possessing positive reasons for believing they are true?

We will consider potential modes of resolution first. In what ways might the theist attempt to resolve the problem posed by religious pluralism? That is, in what ways might a theist attempt to improve her epistemic position in the debate? Further exploration of our student scenario may be helpful in this respect. If Tom and Bill really do desire to determine which, if either, has correctly remembered the day of the next exam, there are two basic approaches available.

The first is to turn their attention directly to the formed beliefs in question. The most promising possibility along these lines would be to check with the instructor directly or at least see if the instructor has listed the test dates in the course syllabus. But this approach will obviously be of little value in attempting to resolve the challenge of religious pluralism. What makes this method of conflict resolution so promising in our student scenario is the fact that Tom and Bill agree on the identity of their instructor, agree that the syllabus in question was produced by this person and agree that they will be able to arrive at a mutually acceptable interpretation of what the syllabus indicates concerning this matter. However, the very basis for the problem of religious pluralism under consideration is, at least in part, the fact that we as humans cannot seem to agree on the 'identity' of the being who can justifiably be labeled 'God' (or even agree that any such being exists). Moreover, even among those who do 'believe in God', there is no agreement on which set of writings, if any, can justifiably be considered an authoritative communication from this being. And finally, even among those who affirm the same divinely inspired, written revelation, there is often little agreement on what is actually said on important issues.

There remains, however, other means by which Tom and Bill can attempt to assess their conflicting beliefs. If Tom and Bill aren't able to contact the instructor or find a syllabus, they might contact other students who had attended class on the day the date for the exam in question was announced. If all those contacted are in agreement with either Tom or Bill, then the issue will for all practical purposes be settled. But, of course, this method will also be of little value in the religious context since the pluralistic challenge only exists, at least in part, because no consensus of the requisite type has emerged.

Finally, if Tom and Bill are also not able to contact a sufficient number of class members, they might attempt to construct some sort of evidential argument intended to establish directly the correct date. For example, they might attempt to discover if all the previous exams have been given on a certain day of the week and use this as an objective evidential standard for resolving the conflict.

Now, of course, this approach has in fact often been employed in discussions of religious pluralism. Many have given serious consideration to those independent arguments for or against the 'formed' beliefs in question—e.g., those arguments for or against the existence of the Judeo-Christian God or the claim that we as humans can communicate with such a being. And this approach has, in principle, the greatest potential for objectively resolving the conflict in question. In fact historically, many theists have thought the pluralistic conflict can in this manner be resolved. That is, they have firmly believed that sound arguments do establish that the beliefs formed by the faculties of one set of religious individuals are alone true. Even today, many philosophers and theologians believe that the consideration of such arguments can help us clarify issues and possibly 'weed out' certain religious beliefs which are inconsistent or in other ways defective. However, few philosophers and theologians—especially those such as Plantinga in the analytic tradition—now believe that there exists any argument supporting a given set of specific theistic beliefs which obligates all who consider it to accept its conclusion.

However, might there not at least be some way in which a theist can justifiably establish the truth of her formed beliefs for herself? That is, might it not be the case that, although she cannot produce arguments which obligate all individuals to acknowledge that the religious beliefs which have been formed in her are more worthy of affirmation that those incompatible beliefs produced by the faculties of others, she can at least establish that *she* is justified in believing her own formed beliefs are most worthy of affirmation? One possibility along this line presents itself.

Many theists, someone might argue, believe that God has produced an external epistemic standard by which we can judge our formed beliefs. Many Judeo-Christians, for instance, believe the Bible to be the ultimate epistemic standard in relation to which believers not only can, but must, assess the 'accuracy' of their formed beliefs. Now, of course, such an evaluation tool cannot be used to resolve the pluralistic challenge in an objective, 'public' sense. But it can be used justifiably by a theist to resolve the pluralistic challenge in a personal, 'private' sense. That is, a theist who accepts the epistemic authority of this external standard can justifiably cite consistency with this standard as a basis for believing that only those formed beliefs consistent with her own are true. In one sense, this line of reasoning seems quite plausible. If we grant a theist her independent grounds for believing not only that her God exists and has created her with religious belief-forming faculties but also that this being has produced an authoritative written and/or natural epistemic standard, then there appears to be little reason, in principle, not to grant that she could justifiably use such a standard to attempt to resolve the pluralistic challenge for herself.

But this line of reasoning generates a negative response to the other question with which we are presently concerned: the question of whether, in the face of religious pluralism, a theist's formed religious beliefs can still be considered properly basic. For if the consideration of the pluralistic challenge has led a theist to believe that she must assess her 'formed beliefs' by an independent epistemic standard before she can justifiably accept them as true, then, of course, such beliefs can no longer be considered basic. Whatever positive epistemic status such beliefs *now* possess is based primarily on the theist's independent grounds for the acceptance of the assessment standard in question. In short, such a theist has now clearly become an evidentialist.

But there are, as mentioned earlier, *two* basic approaches available to those attempting to resolve epistemic conflicts of the type under consideration. One can, as we have seen, attempt to establish directly that one set of formed beliefs is true. But one can also turn one's attention to the reliability of the faculties in question. That is, one can attempt to find reasons for supposing that one's belief forming faculties are working better than one's rivals. For example, Bill and Tom might try to assess the reliability of their belief forming faculties by attempting to determine whether either had stayed up too late the night before the relevant class or had been taking some form of medication or had been talking to another student when the announcement was made.

This approach, of course, has also often been employed by those attempting to resolve the challenge of religious pluralism. Many theists have argued, for instance, that their opponents have faculties which have been damaged by 'the fall' or are under the control of some evil force or have been desensitized by too much interaction with 'worldly' concerns. But, not surprisingly, those criticized in this manner do not agree. In fact, they criticize the reliability of their opponents' faculties on exactly the same grounds. And I can see no objective, nonquestion-begging basis for determining which, if any, of the parties in this debate is correct.

But cannot the theist at least use this approach to attempt to resolve the pluralistic challenge for herself? It will, of course, not help her in this context to make any sort of appeal to the reliability of religious belief-forming faculties in general. It won't help her, for example, to argue with Plantinga that she as a theist can trust her own faculties because she has good reasons to believe they "have been designed, no doubt, with reliability in mind" by an all-powerful, all-knowing creator.[14] Such reliability, if established, only exacerbates the pluralistic challenge. For the better the reasons we have for assuming that religious faculties are, in general, reliable, the harder it becomes to make sense of the fact that such faculties generate such a wide variety of often incompatible beliefs.

But what if a theist maintains that she has what she considers to be adequate reasons for believing that the religious faculties of only a small subset of individuals (herself included) function reliably? What if she maintains, for example, that she has good reasons to believe that the 'fall' tainted the religious faculties of all but a select few (herself included), whose faculties God has chosen to reinfuse with reliability. As stated earlier, she will certainly not be able to establish this fact in an objective, public sense. But if we grant her this contention, can't she then justifiably argue that the problem of pluralism has been resolved for her personally? And, more importantly, can't she also justifiably contend that her formed religious beliefs retain their proper basicality?

I believe the answer to both questions is yes. If we grant a theist the exclusivity thesis in question, then I see no reason to deny she has justifiably resolved the pluralistic challenge for herself. And she has done so without appealing to arguments whose conclusions are the formed beliefs in question. She has done so rather by establishing the epistemic superiority of the belief-forming faculties from which the beliefs in question have come. Thus, I believe such formed beliefs can justifiably be considered *basic*—i.e., not themselves based on propositional evidence. And since she has met her obligation to attempt to resolve the pluralistic challenge, I believe these basic beliefs can be considered properly basic.

However, by approaching the pluralistic challenge in this manner, our theist has in a very important, anti-Plantingan sense again become an evidentialist. The proponent of NAT, remember, does not believe she is obligated to produce propositional evidence for her formed beliefs. Nor, more importantly, does she feel obligated to establish the reliability of her own belief-forming faculties—i.e., she believes she can justifiably assume her own religious faculties are innocent until proven guilty. But the theist in question acknowledges that the pluralistic challenge obligates her to do more than simply defend her own religious faculties. She believes she must establish the 'epistemic superiority' of her faculties. Moreover, she believes she has identified positive reasons for doing so— i.e., for maintaining that her belief-forming faculties are superior to those of her opponents. Thus, since to be an evidentialist in this context, remember, is to be someone who thinks we must have "some positive reason to think" a belief is true, our theist has again entered the evidentialist camp in a sense incompatible with one aspect of Plantinga's negative apologetic thesis.

Where, then, does all this leave the knowledgeable theist who has discovered no compelling 'public' or 'private' evidential basis for resolving the pluralistic challenge? That is, where does this leave the theist who can find no compelling public or private evidential basis for holding either that her specific beliefs alone are true or that her faculties are superior? Is there any nonevidential manner in which she can resolve the pluralistic challenge for herself while continuing to maintain justifiably that her formed beliefs are properly basic?

I believe the answer to this question is yes. If a theist who has comparatively analyzed the various competing sets of religious (and nonreligious) truth claims in an attempt to resolve the pluralistic challenge has not uncovered any compelling evidential basis for affirming hers, then I believe she is justified in resolving the conflict in her favor by an appeal to personal preference—a feeling (itself a basic, formed belief) that the set of basic religious truth claims she has found formed in her better organizes and explains the relevant components of reality than any other. Moreover, since she has met the relevant epistemic obligations by comparatively analyzing the competing sets of truth claims, I believe she is justified in claiming that her formed beliefs remain properly basic.

However, it is important in closing to distinguish once again between this model of 'nonevidential' religious belief justification and that proposed by Plantinga. Plantinga is a nonevidentialist in the sense that he thinks that we *need not* search for propositional evidence to support our formed beliefs' or the reliability of our own belief-forming faculties. On the other hand, it is my contention that, given the pluralistic challenge, the knowledgeable theist is required to look for such propositional evidence although she can justifiably continue to consider her formed beliefs properly basic even if none is found.

Moreover, I believe this distinction is important. If leading analytic philosophers of religion such as Plantinga were to use their considerable skills not only to defend religious beliefs but also to evaluate comparatively the 'content' of such beliefs, we could, I believe, begin to address seriously many of the theoretical and practical conflicts which differing religious perspectives generate.[15]

Roberts Wesleyan College

Endnotes

*Reprinted from *Faith and Philosophy*, Vol. 8, No. 1, January 1991. All rights reserved.

1 Alvin Plantinga, "The Foundations of Theism: A Reply," *Faith and Philosophy* 3 (July, 1986): 307.

2 Ibid, p. 300.

3 Alvin Plantinga, "On Taking Belief in God as Basic," Wheaton College Philosophy Conference (October 23-25, 1986), Lecture I handout, p. 1.

4 Plantinga "Justification and Theism," *Faith and Philosophy* 4 (October, 1987):405, 406.

5 *Ibid*, p. 411.

6 Ibid., p. 410.

7 Plantinga, "The Foundations of Theism," p. 313, n. 11.

8 Ibid., p. 312.

9 Ibid.

10 Plantinga, *Justification and Theism*, p. 413.

11 To draw such analogies is not affected by the fact that we cannot consider our religious and other belief-forming faculties to be analogous in the context of GRA. In that context, the issue is whether all can be assumed to be equally reliable. The issue here is how we ought to respond to conflicts between formed beliefs, which can (and do) arise in relation to all our belief-forming faculties.

12 Since the phrase 'epistemic status' has various meanings, it is important to state explicitly that in those instances in which I inquire about the epistemic status

of a theist's formed beliefs, I will be concerned with the question of whether she is within her rights in affirming the belief.

13 See, for example, David Basinger, "The Rationality of Belief in God: Some Clarification," *The New Scholasticism* 5 (Spring, 1986), pp. 163-85.

14 Plantinga, ibid, p. 413.

15 I would like to thank William Alston and William Hasker for helpful comments made on earlier drafts of this paper.

Study Questions

1.   How does David Basinger show that Alvin Plantinga is a nonevidentialist?

2.   What are the specifics of Plantinga's model of belief justification?

3.   What are the two basic approaches available to those who are interested in resolving epistemic conflicts?

4.   Does Basinger think that there is a nonevidentialist route open to the theist who wants to resolve the pluralistic challenge? If so, what is it?

5.   According to Basinger, why can the theist continue to think that her formed beliefs are properly basic even if no propositional evidence is available?

42

Thinking About
Theocentric Christology

S. Mark Heim

S. Mark Heim* is professor of philosophy of religion at Andover Newton Theological School, and author of *Is Christ the Only Way?*, and is co-editor of *Spirit of Truth: Ecumenical Perspectives on the Holy Spirit*.

Paul Knitter's recent book, *No Other Name?*, is a careful argument for the movement in contemporary theology toward "theocentric Christology." In such an approach, the focus shifts from Christ as the guide to God, to God as the key for theological interpretation of Christ. The "exclusivist" character of Christian faith—its Christocentrism—can then be overcome, without diminishing its authenticity or power. This article** analyzes and critiques Knitter's exposition of theocentrism in Christology, under two main headings. First, questions are raised about the coherence and meaning of "theocentrism" in theology. In particular, what are the character and provenance of that knowledge of God to which we may refer in relativizing other religious norms? Second, Knitter's argument that "theocentric Christology" has a solid basis in scripture and Christian tradition is examined and argued to be convincing.

I

Christology is a particularly yeasty field today. The challenges raised in philosophical and biblical studies continue to be debated. However, despite occasional furors like that over *The Myth of God Incarnate*, these fields no longer seem to generate the greatest interest. The discussion is more prominently focused in two areas. One of these is a *praxis* imperative applied to Christology primarily by feminist and liberation theology: the criteria for contemporary Christology are evolved both from the argued past effects of traditional Christology and the foreseen personal and social effects of new views. The second area of ferment comes out of consideration of Christology in an interfaith perspective. Here the questions of Christology are addressed with interreligious dialogue in mind and a change in Christianity's attitude toward other religions at heart.

In a world of many faiths, Christianity is increasingly exhorted not to evaluate its theology only according to "internal norms." It is also called to consider how its doctrines shape the possibilities of cooperation and community in a pluralistic world, including the attitudes of "Christian" nations toward those not predominantly so. In its continued relation to its parent faith, Judaism, Christianity is faced with the necessity to articulate its belief in Jesus Christ with reference to terms and history that belong rightfully as well to a people who do not share that belief. In the face of the political and social struggles for liberation and identity, Christianity is faced with an increasingly acute *praxis* test for its doctrine: what is the "cash value" of various theological perspectives, and which serves most effectively to further the work of God? In all these areas there are concrete histories which give added point to the concerns: colonialism, Anti-semitism, sexism, and oppression.

Those who work in these various streams of theological reflection tend to find their concerns converging in Christology. Some, at least, find broad agreement on the direction theological reconstruction in this area ought to take. The term "theocentric Christology" is sometimes used to indicate such agreement. An "exclusive" Christology is one which sees salvation as limited to those in direct and conscious relation to Jesus Christ, while an "inclusive" Christology would say that, by virtue of God's act in Christ, salvation is open to those beyond the arena where the name is named.[1] Obviously, any theology which believes Paul to be correct when he tells us Abraham was saved by faith is to some extent "inclusive." Much recent Christian theology has been broadening and systematizing the character of this inclusivity, along the lines of Karl Rahner's "anonymous" Christianity.

"Theocentric Christology" is not a synonym for inclusive Christology. Indeed, it would criticize inclusive Christologies as halfway houses, still founded on an "exclusivist" view of Christ's role and significance, while spreading the christological "benefits" about in a more universal and inclusive manner. If we might borrow a phrase from economics, inclusive Christianity is faulted because it is a "trickle-down" Christology: God's saving grace to humanity—even though it be supposed to be everywhere available and not necessarily bound to confession of Christ—nevertheless passes decisively, uniquely, and normatively *through* Christ. It is this notion to which theocentric Christology places itself in opposition.

For the purposes of this discussion I will deal specifically with the recent book by Paul Knitter, *No Other Name?*[2] Knitter is not the inventor of the substance or the title of theocentric Christianity, but he provides one of the most careful and thorough presentations of its character. His is a book to be reckoned with by those interested in this discussion. To gain the advantages of specificity and to avoid the dangers of straw persons, I will deal with Knitter's views. He reminds us, however, that these views are largely if not totally congruent with those of a number of other theologians: most notably John Hick, Stanley Samartha, Rosemary Ruether, Tom Driver, and Raimundo Panikkar, to name a few. With them, Knitter sees himself as a part of a broad front in theological reformation.

Knitter's book has three parts. The first is a consideration of three popular approaches to the fact of various religious faiths in the world: "They are all relative," "They are all essentially the same," "They all have a common psychological origin." The first three chapters critically examine these pieces of conventional wisdom, taking Troeltsch, Toynbee, and Jung as representative, if sophisticated, spokespersons for them. The second part of the book treats major models of Christian theological response to the fact of religious pluralism. A chapter each is given to the conservative evangelical, the Roman Catholic, the mainline Protestant, and the developing theocentric models. In the final section of the book, Knitter offers his own version of theocentric Christology and a prospect of the way this Christology would condition interfaith dialogue.

Theocentric Christology represents what Knitter calls a "Copernican revolution" or paradigm shift in Christian understanding of other religions and of Christ. Yet, it is a shift which he sees as part of a long evolutionary process in Christian consciousness. A recent crucial step in this process was a shift from ecclesiocentrism to Christocentrism in theology. The ecumenical movement and the Second Vatican Council moved toward the admission that no single church captured the full reality of Jesus Christ, that even the church universal was not to be identified with the realm of God, and that there was salvation outside the church. Christ, not the church, was the center. Further, Christ might be at work "incognito" outside the church, which meant also within other religions. As this tendency developed in the Christian ecumenical environment, another evolutionary shift began within the context of interfaith relationships. As narrow understandings of the church had been an obstacle to ecumenical dialogue, some began to see that narrow understandings of Christ were barriers to interfaith dialogue. Above all, the insistence upon the finality and normativity of Christ was such a barrier. Thus, the evolution at hand is from Christocentrism to theocentrism.

Those who led in the journey from ecclesiocentrism to Christocentrism performed a great service. But, as is often the case in evolutionary process, it is precisely the norm or lever which they used to move from one state to the next which must be relativized now in order to go further. As it was well to subordinate the church to Christ, it is logical now that we take seriously the subordination of Christ to God. The various theocentric theologians whom Knitter reviews are, he says, trying to place God and not the church or Christ at the center of things. They advance different types of arguments, some stressing the "myth of incarnation," some expanding upon a *logos* Christology, some departing from a prior "theology of religions." Knitter does not endorse all of these in equal measure—indeed, some are incompatible—but he is certain that they move in the right direction.

One of the notable aspects of Knitter's own argument is his attempt to meet the objections of theocentric Christology on their own ground. He recognizes that his proposal might appear to violate the New Testament understanding of Christ and to undercut both personal commitment to Christ and a distinctly Christian contribution to the world's pluralism. His intention is to show that this is not the case. In other words, theocentric Christology is not only the key to amicable and fruitful interfaith relations, but it is also authentically Christian and can be validated as such from scripture and tradition. He recognizes that it cannot be a precondition of dialogue that any faith, including Christianity, be required to give up its essential identity. Therefore, it is crucial that theocentric Christology be sustained by reference to Christian norms.

On this point Knitter is commendably clear, and this clarity undergirds his criticism of simplistic conventional solutions to the problem of religious pluralism, as well as his reservations about some aspects of others' theocentric Christology. His book presents theocentric Christology in a careful and nuanced way. It would seem that critical reflection upon it would prove to be of broader application as well. Accordingly, I should like to explore two types of questions which arise from the exposition. The first type has to do with the positive meaning of theocentric Christology, which still remains rather cloudy, given that Knitter deals more extensively with the "why" than the "what" of this view. The second type has to do with the Christian warrants which Knitter adduces for it.

II

The power of Knitter's argument can be summarized in a few sentences. Christ divides, being the unique object of faith of one tradition. God unites, being the supposed common object of worship of all faiths. Given that for Christians Jesus Christ is the Son and Word of *God*, the servant and herald of the reign of *God*, the revealer and image and incarnation of *God*, would it not be both faithful to Christian belief and fruitful in present circumstances to shift the focus from Christ to God? God is inclusive, Christ exclusive. By getting the priorities right—and surely this means putting God first—the inclusiveness comes uppermost. The exclusiveness is seen to be secondary and functional.

For *Christians*, Christ is exclusive. That is, they do not divide their loyalty and love for Christ by apportioning them in graduated measure to other objects of faith, any more than a husband or wife portions out equal measures of commitment to many spouses. However, they simply ought to recognize that this exclusivity is not normative, not founded on objective fact. Or, to add an important nuance in Knitter's presentation, they ought to recognize this *provisionally*. It is just conceivable that Christ is the "norm above all other norms." If this is so, there must be reasons for its being so which are universally and equally available to all people.[3] Only in interfaith dialogue could this be discovered, for only there would universal reasons for Christ's finality become apparent.

Theocentric Christology presents itself as the way to surmount several nasty problems and yet to allow Christians to remain as warmly fervent as ever in their personal devotion to Christ. It has all the marks of an irresistible proposal: no visible drawbacks. Yet, there is some puzzlement about the coherence of the notion itself.

As Knitter expounds the paradigm shift from ecclesiocentrism to Christocentrism to theocentrism, it is assumed that the meaning of theocentrism is made clear as the extension of a long-term process whose character is constant. The meaning is given by analogy: theocentrism is to Christocentrism what Christocentrism was to ecclesiocentrism. This is a definition which obscures more than it reveals. If we cut one foot off a piece of lumber, and then cut off another foot, we are continuing the same process. It is not obvious, however, that we have now made it twice as likely to fit its intended use. We may have passed the point where it can serve at all for that use. In one sense, we have continued in the same direction; in another, we have not.

Christocentrism in theology represents a change of focus, as Knitter says. In this shift, the new focus serves to define the old. The church is seen to exist to serve and to proclaim Christ. Where it fails in this task, Christ is the norm by which it is found wanting and by which forces or groups other than the church may be affirmed. The church exists with Christ as its head, for the sake of the reign of God. The church, with its institutional practices, teachings, and traditions, is not to be the norm for Christ and so for theology. Instead, Christ, known through scripture, Spirit, and experience (all undeniably shaped by the church), is the norm for the church and so for theology. If this was a step in the right direction, Knitter says, theocentrism takes us further in the right direction. This is arithmetic and linear logic, of the sort illustrated in the lumber analogy. The question is whether it is appropriate to the case.

Both ecclesiocentrism and Christocentrism provide norms for theological work. In both cases we have clear resources and standards which we may use in our effort to build a church- or Christ-centered theology. What does Knitter propose as the touchstone by which we may seek to be God-centered? Instead of the church being judged by reference to Christ, Christ is now to be judged by reference to God. If this is so, there must be some firm knowledge about God available somewhere. What is the source of this knowledge about God which must be so much more precise and certain than that claimed by Christians—or indeed by any faith? An answer to this question would seem to be a prerequisite to any meaningful talk of theocentric Christology.

At the risk of belaboring the obvious, Christocentrism is a *form* of theocentrism, not a substitute for it. That is the only rationale for being christocentric. The definition and normative status attached to Christ reflects a *way* of being theocentric. Quite so, Knitter might respond: *one* way among others. This is true. What is not clear is where, short of the adoption of some other way, a standard would be found to which this one (Christ) could be subordinated. Christians affirm that to know and follow God most adequately one should follow Christ. This may be wrong, radically wrong. If so, there must be another way of being theocentric, of knowing and relating to God, which can serve as a norm and corrective. Where does it come from?

If we intend to be "centric" in any respect, we must locate a center. In ecclesiocentrism or Christocentrism we have some idea of what that location might be. Therefore they seem to be both workable and corrigible—though not necessarily correct—theological norms. In the ecumenical discussion among churches to which Knitter refers there is an ostensible norm which also has practical content: shared scripture and tradition. In the discussion which he proposes as analogous among religions he suggests an ostensible norm (theocentrism) without providing any practical content. Christocentric theology asserts that Christ is its norm for defining and understanding God, the guide for locating the center such that God is there. Theocentric Christology asserts that God is its norm for understanding Christ. The problem is that for there to be a theocentric Christology there must certainly first be a theocentric theology. In it, presumably, *theos* will be the norm for defining ... *theos*. What does or can this mean?

It may be proposed that meaning can be given to *theos* as a norm if we use and sift *all* religious faiths and data, producing from them an inclusive picture of God. However, unless the data be shamelessly skewed from the start—practicing exclusivism in method and selection rather than in confession—this is surely an impossible project. Knitter asks how it is possible for a Christian theology of religions to use religious data honestly,[4] to which it only remains to add that the same question would seem to carry equal weight for any project which seeks to derive a norm from all religions. We cannot build an inclusive picture of God from the total field of religious data without practicing some selectivity, without excluding, for instance, those options which do not recognize or which reject the idea of *theos* or the idea of "center."

It will be necessary to sift the data with some principle in mind. For those traditions which intend to be "theocentric," each has some norm which guides the effort. For Christians this is Christ. What is the principle which will take that place in theocentric Christology? If it is borrowed from some other tradition, why is that tradition's norm to be accepted as universal? If it is formulated by admixture from many traditions, why is this formulation given a status different from that of the individual norms, many of which also purport to be a kind of admixture? Why is this synthesized norm not simply another one way, among many?

Presumably, there is or ought to be a theocentric understanding of the Qur'an in Islam and of the Torah in Judaism. Neither ought to be considered by its adherents the decisive and normative revelation of God, relevant to all people. If, then, they are to be understood as partial aspects of a true theocentric norm, it would seem that those in these traditions are entitled to know what this inclusive characterization of God is and where it comes from. Knitter adumbrates several possible responses to this question. One answer would be to propose an ethical norm as the key to theocentric theology. Knitter states clearly that he does not want a norm so broad that it would validate *every* kind of religious expression, even if all kinds are the proper field from which to derive the norm.[5] Some standard is required. It is not entirely clear what this standard is to be for Knitter. The closest thing to such a standard appears to be "social betterment" and individual wholeness.[6] This ethical, if somewhat cloudy, principle would become the norm in theocentric theology.

This is certainly intelligible and would be functional, given a quantum improvement in the detailed description of social betterment and individual wholeness. The very vague nature of the universal *"tao"* which is sometimes argued to exist across religions is not very helpful, since the terms in which it is expressed are themselves understood by various groups in heavily religion-dependent ways. In other words, the more general the *"tao,"* as in the notions of social betterment and personal wholeness, the more plausible is its universality. The more concrete its definition, so as to be able to serve in some meaningful way as a norm, the less universal it looks. This will then lead to the question of why an affirmation of a "once for all" revelation of God is presumed to be so problematic and pernicious, while a "once for all" ethical norm of this sort (which certainly is not recognized everywhere) is exempt from such presumption.

There is another possibility latent in Knitter's exposition. Perhaps what I have said so far represents a misunderstanding of his project. It may be that theocentrism has no normative principle and desires none. It is precisely the open-endedness of theocentric Christology which is its virtue. No special separate insight into the nature of God, different from that of individual religious traditions, is presupposed. What is presupposed is that normlessness is, at least provisionally, normative.

We do not have a way of locating God which can serve as a norm above all the various religious faiths. *Theos* remains a center without location.

The meaning of theocentrism is that each particular norm for *theos* must be held as non-absolute. To be theocentric is to be centerless, to refuse to fill the center, out of piety. It is the commandment against idolatry, or the "Protestant principle," on a world religious scale. We should be open to the possibility that to be truly theocentric would be to hold open a center which is at some remove—as yet undefined—from each of the religious norms. To be theocentric would be to refuse to "locate" God definitively as personal and equally to refuse to "locate" God as impersonal, and so on. We do not know that this is the correct course to take, but somehow each of us in our own faith and thinking ought to take it into account. *How* ought we to do so? Certainly one of the fundamental ways Knitter has in mind would be to adopt the presuppositions of interfaith dialogue which he proposes. These are three in number. First, dialogue must be based on personal religious experience and firm truth claims. Second, it must be based on recognition of the possible truth in all religions, grounded in the hypothesis of a common ground and goal for all religions. Third, dialogue must be based on openness to genuine change and conversion.[7]

The second proposition is significant. Knitter says that, although religions may have a common interest in the unity of humankind and in warding off world destruction, this goal cannot really be achieved unless their efforts are rooted in a deeper common ground, which allows them to be talking, in different ways, about the same reality. The deepest level of dialogue, he says, *cannot* (emphasis mine) be a matter of "apples and oranges." If we are not talking about the same God, then ultimately humanity itself is apples and oranges. "Division, the fertilizer of discord and destruction, will have the final word."[8] Though it is called a hypothesis, this appears to be a fundamental tenet of theocentrism as Knitter understands it. He speaks of its verification in dialogue, for instance, but not of its possible lack of verification. It would seem, then, that theocentrism cannot simply be a conviction that all religious norms are to be regarded, at least provisionally, as penultimate. It proposes a principle for locating *theos*, and, broad though the principle may be, it would appear that it must be universally normative, or else the theocentric project as Knitter conceives it collapses. The caution of theocentrism is not that some or all religious norms may be imperfect or simply wrong: Quite the contrary! Its caution is that they all must be regarded as true. The real question is: what is that about which they can all be telling the truth?

Theocentrism does not intend to be skeptical but deeply credulous. This would rule out the option which we have just considered—that theocentrism is a principled normative normlessness. God can be located in one absolute sense as that identical reality with which all "phenomenal" religions have to do. This is a positive and normative statement. It is a view favored by many sociologists and some philosophers of religion, but as a universal norm for *theos* it will have to be defended with other arguments than those used in favor of a provisional relativizing of all definitions of God. If it is itself relativized, then the kind of dialogue which Knitter commends is only one among many and has no claim to be *the* form of dialogue.

Perhaps the theocentric norm is to be defended by reference to the ethical norm mentioned above: being the only way to make religion function to overcome the nuclear danger, say, such an approach is necessarily normative for all religions. The cogency of this will rest on two considerations. The first will have to do with the status of the ethical norm, as discussed above. The second and related consideration would be whether or not it is empirically true that the theological conviction advanced by Knitter is the one and only doctrine which would serve the desired ethical end. Are those who believe that the object of their faith is not the same as the object of all other people's faith simply heretics on ethical grounds? Or is it possible that they, too, may have a crucial contribution to make toward securing peace among people who assuredly have and will continue to have different political, social, and personal beliefs?

In Knitter's approach, which he calls "unitive pluralism," pluralism itself is accorded only a curiously superficial reality. Though the distinctions it represents are not to be done away with, it is to be presumed, as the basis of dialogue, that they are distinctions of one basic thing, rooted in common apprehension of a single reality. True polytheists are not welcome in this world of pluralism, yet there is no reason to rule out a further reach of pluralism, in which we find not that under surface differences we have to do with the same thing but that under surface differences we are truly different. This possibility is not in view here, save as a pernicious doctrine to be anathematized. Why this is so—besides a deep conviction that pluralism must serve us as a solution rather than in any way as a problem (we have so many!)—is not plain.

To raise one final question in this area: why ought we to assume that theocentrism is the last term in this series? Is it not necessary to go beyond the imperialism of *theos,* to escape the dangers and sins of "theofascism" as well as of "Christofascism?"[9] Why make normative a theology which is centered on a reality denied or simply ignored by important groups, including some Buddhists and most humanists? Should we not, on Knitter's grounds, look toward a further and yet more adequate paradigm shift which might take us perhaps to a numinocentric theology? John Hick speaks of "one spirit" or "one divine reality" or "one *logos*" and carefully does not use the word "God." Knitter is less cautious, but he does not address the question of whether a more thoroughgoing paradigm shift is mandated by his own logic.

As the ante is upped—church, Christ, God—we would appear to be moving increasingly toward a more transcendent, more universal, and less limited perspective, but at some point in such a progression it may be we begin to do exactly the opposite. When we reach a concept so transcendent that it is said we have *no* comprehensible or tangible criteria for it, we have not attained universality but parochialism. Since there is no common set of reference points for understanding "God," the appeal to God—as in theocentrism—can represent less of a curb on our narrow outlooks, not more. It does not mean that we are necessarily forced to define God in a broader, wider, more universalistic way than that given in an individual tradition (which likely encompasses many centuries and many different cultural settings). It does mean that we are free to define God in line with a limited contemporary cross-section of various traditions and experiences, construed within present dominant modes of thought. Interfaith dialogue is the apparent antidote for this difficulty, in Knitter's view, for it ought to overcome the limitations of any single tradition. What then of the conditions which Knitter wishes to place upon this dialogue, by making theocentrism its norm? Is this not simply a different kind of limitation?

As long as the norm for *theos* is as indistinct as it seems to be in theocentric theology, that norm will be interpreted—in effect supplied—by the predilections of the practitioners. Christians are often criticized by reference to the norms they have themselves professed. These norms seem to be sufficiently concrete for Christians to have them turned against themselves and to acknowledge on occasion the validity of the process. In theocentric theology one would hope this capacity would be heightened, not diminished.

These comments are all simply to indicate that it seems to me that there is some difficulty, even with the assistance of Knitter's impressive exposition, in knowing what theocentric Christology actually means. It seems such Christology relies heavily upon intuitive "picture" concepts to make its case. It is presented largely as though there were a basic block, "God," upon which some people put a second block, "Christ," while others put instead a block "Qur'an," and so on. Many people readily think in this way, but the fact that they do so is not necessarily the result of wide and deep experience of pluralism. It may be exactly the opposite.

The notion of a common or root concept of God is one that comes readily to those of us who have been immersed within a monotheistic tradition. If some within this cultural context deny the specific particulars of such a tradition (a "Christian" God or a personal God), it may be that they still vehemently affirm as universal a generalized form of that particular (not monotheism, but theocentrism). What we learn of various cultures and faiths, however, brings home to us the manner in which ideas of God (where there are such ideas) are particular, "down to the ground" so to speak. It is not a matter of a simple, common foundation, with many various superstructures. This is why interfaith dialogue is the fascinating and perplexing experience that it is: the other's life and belief cannot be grasped finally in pieces but only all at once. It is this very "all-at-onceness" of the various faiths, which Knitter values and is in one sense the occasion of his work, that makes his theocentric Christology problematic.

III

I have tried to indicate some puzzlements about the *meaning* of theocentric Christology. In conjunction with his exposition of this Christology, Knitter advances several clear arguments for it on the basis of Christian norms. It is to these arguments that I now turn. As I have already indicated, Knitter addresses himself directly to the grounding of theocentric Christology in scripture, using three main arguments. The first is that Jesus was theocentric. The second is that there is a diversity of christological trajectories within the New Testament. The third is that the "one and only" language about Jesus in scripture was a function of the cultural medium, not the true message of Christian faith.

Knitter also stresses a fourth point: that Christian christological interpretation itself developed out of dialogue with a pluralism of other religions and cultures. This is a significant observation, and it would seem to conflict with Knitter's earlier statement about pluralism's posing questions which "religious persons of the past, secure in their own isolated religious camps, never had to face."[10] When coming to the New Testament material, Knitter implicitly acknowledges that such a bald statement is indefensible. The early Christians indeed had to face pluralism. Knitter argues in fact that their minority status was one of the things that led them to their "accidental" forms of exclusive language with respect to Christ. He also argues that, because the church's confession was to some extent shaped by encounter with other religions, there is a mandate for us to shape our confession today in response to modern pluralism.

The argument that Jesus was theocentric is surely sound. Knitter's treatment of the New Testament is notable for his familiarity with the broad outlines of recent scholarship. Both implicitly and explicitly he distances himself from Hick's attempt to maintain an unreconstructed unilinear view of christological development. He recognizes that it is not possible to divide the New Testament data into earlier "low" views of Jesus and later "high" views. Instead, we find trajectories, each of which has preferred categories for understanding Jesus, each of which has very early roots, and each of which represents from the beginning its own version of a "high" view of Jesus.

The transition of Jesus from proclaimer to the one proclaimed is an intrinsically valid transition, in that Jesus understood himself in some way as a final eschatological prophet, God's "last word" to humanity. The fact that some or all of the christological titles are applied to Jesus by the church is, Knitter acknowledges, in no way as decisive as earlier liberal scholars had thought or as Hick continues to assume. Thus, for instance, Knitter recognizes that the theory that Christian views of Christ were determined by conformity to a prior gnostic redeemer myth has not proved to be tenable. It is probable that Christian thought influenced the development of such myths themselves, the most that Knitter can add being that such influence was (perhaps) mutual. He also acknowledges that none of the images and titles used for Jesus were a perfect fit for that which Christians experienced in Jesus.

This is notable, for it forecloses the wide and simplistic path to theocentric Christology. Knitter faces it squarely. He summarizes this history, in carefully chosen words, as "an evolution from a predominantly functional, eschatological understanding of Jesus as Son of God to an incarnational, even ontological, proclamation of his divinity."[11] Both Jesus and the church saw Jesus as unique and special in representing God. Much of New Testament language about Jesus is exclusive and/or normative. To close one's eyes to this, says Knitter, is dishonest. When the early Christians used "one and only" language about Jesus they did not understand it as "mythic conditioning" or as "love language" in Krister Stendahl's sense.[12] They meant it. However, if Christology is evolutionary, Knitter wonders whether such "final" language really belongs to the main content of what the church believed and what Jesus actually was, or to the "accident" of the language in which he was described. He argues that the latter was the case.

Given the cultural context in which these experiences took place, it was natural—"even necessary"—that they were described in terms of finality and exclusivity. There was "no other way, no other language" for them to talk about it. Living in a classicist culture that took it for granted that truth was one and certain, when they encountered the overwhelming truth of Jesus, they would *have* to describe it as the only or the final truth."[13] Expecting the end of history, they naturally did not even consider the possibility of further revelations.

As the intensive use of imperative and exclusive language on Knitter's part indicates, this is the point where the argument comes to rest. Living, as fish in water, in a culture with a mistaken view of truth, Christians inevitably and helplessly expressed the very real truth of Jesus in a medium—in fact a whole variety of mediums—which was incidental or actually inimical to it. Now, however, Knitter argues, there has been a genuinely new evolution in the texture of human experience that makes our context different from that of the New Testament. Not to understand Jesus anew in this texture "is to run the risk of confining the past in an idolatrous 'deposit of faith,' "[14] and the way to understand Jesus anew is to see him as indeed universally relevant, but not universally decisive or normative.

Knitter starts out to show that theocentric Christology is in keeping with scripture. His conscientious survey indicates that in fact it is not, if we take that evidence on its own terms. He then argues that it *is* in keeping with scripture if we subtract the "accidental" medium of culture.

Since we live in a radically different culture, it is imperative for us to understand Jesus according to our context. Several things may be said about this approach. The first is that it seems to be a peculiarly modern way to attempt to escape the constraints of critical-historical method (which are part of our context for understanding Jesus). Having examined scripture with the question of "what it meant then" in mind, Knitter finds the answer largely uncongenial to the tack he would like to take in terms of "what it means now." Instead of pressing on with this sticky problem of drawing present meaning and past meaning into coherent relation, Knitter appeals instead to the expansion of the interpretive horizon of the text: as "human experience evolves from the tribal to the global, there *must* be new interpretations of the text."[15] Surely there must be. The question is whether the text in its original context exercises any control over the variety and validity of these interpretations.

It does seem to me valid to say that the way a text uses its own sources, its own authorities, can be taken to some extent as authorization for analogous use of the text itself. Thus, Knitter appeals to the fact that reflection on Christology seems to have developed internally in the New Testament out of encounter and dialogue with other religions and cultural forces. He takes this as a scriptural mandate to do christological reflection today in the midst of such dialogue. I think this is sound. However, as he notes, on the different trajectories of this scriptural development the decisiveness and normativeness of Christ is retained, even though categories of expression change. It would seem then that here we find a similar internal scriptural norm: that in the interplay of many different cultures and forms of expression the decisiveness of Christ shall continue to be expressed. At this point, however, Knitter turns to the assertion that a common culture, transcending all the religious and cultural pluralism which affected the New Testament, locked in an accidental affirmation of Christ's normativeness.

This aspect of the argument turns largely on Knitter's philosophical view of an ontological or "classicist," as opposed to a "processive-relational," view of reality. In a view which regards creation as a stable and hierarchical order of being, the classicist view of truth is natural. Knitter further suggests that it is from this ontology that the "one and only" or normative view of Christ flows. However, our new context teaches us that reality is instead properly understood more as becoming than as being, more in terms of a nexus of relations than in terms of individual interactions. Knitter does not provide a great deal of explication of this, other than some references to Teilhard, to Darwin, to physicist David Bohm, and (more extensively) to process thought. It appears at the very least questionable whether this distinction can be sustained in the categorically historical way Knitter puts it.

Whitehead, at any rate, was much more hesitant to suggest the "processive" view of reality as a uniquely modern discovery. He suggested the Psalms as being a rich illustration of at least a poetic apprehension not only of the flux of reality but also of the reality of flux.[16] If this new view of reality comes to regard persons much less as atomistic individual existents and more as centers of relation, it would seem that it was to some extent anticipated by Hebrew views, views which were the soil for interpretation by and of Jesus. In short, more argument is required if Knitter intends to enforce this hermetic seal around early thought about Christ, so that, since no notion of relational reality could even come within its horizon, its view of Christ as normative may be discounted. Nor does Knitter address himself to the sticky question of how we might recognize a valid claim to normativeness which might be made within a cultural situation where, apparently, all claims would accidentally be cast in this form.

Even if it were the case that early Christians were victims of a cultural necessity to think that truth is one, certain, and unchanging, it is patently obvious that they were under no such compulsion to think that there could be only one decisive and normative *form* of this one truth. Readily apparent around them were approaches to religious pluralism which took just this tack. That one and the same God should be called by different names or take a slightly different form in different cultures was not only supposed by the educated but also accepted in practice by many ordinary people. On Knitter's assumption—that the normativeness of Christ was no part of the essential Christian message but only of its determined cultural form—we should expect that amidst the variety of christological interpretation in the New Testament there would be some which availed itself of this option, present in the cultural environment. In other words, there would be trajectories which identify Christ with Apollo or with Mithras. Some may argue that such "heterodox" notions existed but were kept out of the New Testament canon. Where this so, however, it would only reinforce the point at issue here: the early church *knew* of such options and rejected them. It may have been wrong, but the church definitely had the *chance* to be at least partially right, in Knitter's terms. Knitter cannot rectify the choice now by maintaining that it never really existed.

When they encountered an overwhelming truth in Jesus, gentile Christians, at least, would find no cultural taboo on supposing this one truth was present under other forms. Indeed, there was significant cultural compulsion for them to go in precisely this direction. These early Christians *did* identify Jesus with some of the greatest figures of Israel's tradition and, at the same time, within the earliest strata, with that tradition's God. In other words, they did say that the one truth known in Jesus was in fact known, at least to some extent, under another "form"—the revelations of Yahweh to Israel. They made this identification within a Jewish context where there was certainly hostility to the extreme (incarnational) of such identification. Yet, in the midst of other cultures, which were in principle much more receptive to such notions, they rejected the idea that Jesus could be identified with existing deities.

This certainly does not forget the way in which the apologists, for example, were willing to argue that philosophy had reached in a parallel and anticipatory way some knowledge of Christian truth. The point is not that early Christians believed Christ to be the exclusive *exhaustive* truth. The point is a more limited one. It has to do with the question of Christ as a singular and decisive norm and of whether the early church was somehow incapacitated, unable even to conceive of any alternative to a "once for all" norm. While the cultural alphabet of the early Christians may have been limited, it appears that it was not so impoverished that it could not spell a rather decided negative on Knitter's hypothesis about the accidental character of Christ's normativeness.

Just as Knitter assumes that ideas of normativeness or finality are necessary accidental attendants of an ontological view of reality, he seems to assume that they are necessary casualities of a "processive-relational" one. This latter point seems, if anything, even more questionable. Knitter seems to presume as a matter of course that the idea of Christ as normative and decisive rests upon incarnational and ontological forms of interpretation of Christ. If the latter are only forms within which the reality is interpreted, then the former is likewise a dispensable interpretive form. Nevertheless, on the basis of his own exposition of the New Testament evidence, this hardly seems to be the case. In other words, Knitter acknowledges that the very earliest strata of Christian witness view Christ in extraordinary high functional terms. This is so even apart from any use of the ontological language of divine being, yet Knitter goes on to claim that it is interpretation of Christ in terms of a certain "level" of being which itself actually entails the normative claim.

Strictly speaking, normativity is independent of this debate over ontology. In a processive-relational reality there may still be persons, moments, decisions, relations which are decisive and normative, even universally so. Otherwise, Knitter, in arguing for a process-relational view of reality, would be arguing necessarily for normlessness. He clearly is not doing this. Conversely, even in the "classicist" worldview he paints, to have a certain level of being is not automatically to be exclusively normative, unless one can know in fact that there is no other who shares the level of being. There is no *a priori* reason that Christians could not have viewed Christ as God fully incarnate, the divine bodily present among them, *and* also as not exclusively normative, for this same event could have been thought to take place on other occasions.

The first Christians professed that they had functionally (savingly) encountered in Christ unparalleled normative truth, power, and love. To Knitter's mind, this *means* that, since what they encountered was a relational reality for them, it could not be normative, and their expression could not have been intended as normative. However, the question will not admit of being resolved in such an imperious way. What they encountered might have been transforming in an unparalleled manner for them and not regarded as normative, *or* so transforming and also regarded as normative. The evidence seems to favor the latter case. The "high" early Christology which Knitter acknowledges need not have been "high" only on the believers' end (that is, this is so very important *to us*) simply because it was often expressed in functional terms.

To put it plainly, Knitter seems to think that, if one could move the focus away from incarnation (ontological being) and toward salvation (processive becoming), then Christ would necessarily become less normative. However, as Kenneth Surin has persuasively argueed, as long as one wants to keep some contact with the New Testament (as Knitter does), the idea that a focus on salvation obviates Christocentrism is profoundly mistaken.[17] If anything, the opposite is true. Even if we grant Knitter both the philosophical dichotomy of "classicist" and "processive" worldviews and the hard historical periodization which would make the former the blanket reality of the past and the latter the unique discovery of recent modernity, it does not seem that these can decide the question.

IV

I have explored a few questions about the meaning of theocentric Christology and suggested that, despite the urgency with which its necessity is argued, the positive features of such a Christology remain somewhat unclear. This may be a natural stage for a view which, originating as a criticism of traditional approaches to pluralism, is only now beginning to find its own constructive formulation. It may, alternatively, indicate defects in the whole line of approach. I have also argued that the warrants which Knitter advances for theocentric Christology on Christian grounds are not persuasive. This would appear to raise a theology like Knitter's which is so commendably scrupulous about dealing with religious traditions on their own terms.

I have not been able to deal with all the aspects of Knitter's significant book. In particular, I have not dealt adequately with the form and conditions of interfaith dialogue which Knitter sees as correlative to theocentric Christology. Since Knitter and others suggest that such stated conditions of interfaith dialogue should increasingly become internal norms in the work of Christian theology, this question is one that deserves further attention in its own right. I hope to return to it in a future discussion.

The issues which Knitter has so carefully raised are crucial ones for us all. Those who wish to pursue them can hardly do better than to start with his work. I trust it will not be taken amiss if I hope that they do not stop there.

Endnotes

* S. Mark Heim has been an Assistant Professor of Christian Theology at the Andover Newton Theological School since 1982. He had an Association of Theological Schools Award for Theological Scholarship and Research for 1986-87, spending six months in 1986 on sabbatical in South India and Thailand, including serving as a visiting professor at United Theological College in Bangalore.

**Reprinted from "Thinking About Theocentric Christology," in *Journal of Ecumenical Studies*, Vol. 24, No. 1 (Winter, 1987) by S. Mark Heim. Used by permission.

[1] The categories of exclusivism, inclusivism, and pluralism (Knitter's "theocentrism") are taken from Alan Race, *Christians and Religious Pluralism: Patterns in the Christian Theology of Religions* (Maryknoll, NY: Orbis, 1985).

[2] Paul F. Knitter, *No Other Name?* (Maryknoll, NY: Orbis, 1985).

[3] Ibid., p. 143.

[4] Ibid., p. 115.

[5] Ibid, p. 53.

[6] Ibid., p. 70.

[7] Ibid., pp. 207-212.

[8] Ibid., p. 209.

[9] See ibid., p. 164.

[10] Ibid., p. 1.

[11] Ibid., p. 180.

[12] Ibid., p. 185.

[13] Ibid., p. 183.

[14] Ibid., p. 173.

[15] Ibid., pp. 172-173.

[16] A.N. Whitehead, *Process and Reality* (New York: Macmillan, 1929), p. 317.

[17] Kenneth Surin, "Revelation, Salvation, the Uniqueness of Christ, and Other Religions," *Religious Studies* 19 (September, 1983): 323-343.

Study Questions

1. How does Mark Heim think that the theist can overcome the "exclusivist" character of the Christian faith?

2. What is "theocentric Christology"? Why is it important to Heim's discussion?

3. What does Paul Knitter mean when he says that Theos "remains a center without location"?

4.   What is "unitive pluralism"?

5.   What is Heim's verdict regarding Knitter's work?

Glossary

a fortiori , an asyllogistic mediate inference of the form that, if B is greater than C, and A is greater than B, then A is greater than C.

a priori, for Kant, it meant universal and necessary conditions for knowledge, or generally it means knowledge that comes through reason alone, apart from the senses, or it means by definition.

a posteriori, is knowledge that is derived from experience, an *a posteriori* argument is one that is based on experience.

actualization, "strong_," what God alone causes or brings about, "weak_," what God and created agents cause or bring about.

agnosticism, the view that the evidence does not clearly point to the existence or non-existence of a supreme being, hence one is unsure.

Allah, the Islamic name for God.

amightiness, for Geach, God's power over all things.

analogia entis, (analogy of being) Thomas Aquinas attempts to provide a rational explanation of the universe in terms of the analogy of being, because the intellect's first glance considers the being of a thing. On this level, one sees that being belongs to all things in proportion to their nature.

analogia fidei, (analogy of faith) instead of working with *analogia entis*, Karl Barth works with the analogy of faith according to Romans 12:6, where human knowledge of God is converted into humans being known by God.

analogy, of attribution, when two analogues do not have a sameness of quality, but both are ascribed the property; of proportionality, when two analogues have a sameness of quality, but there may be difference in the degree to which it is possessed.

analytic, a statement or proposition is analytic if the predicate term is included in the subject term.

angel, a created being having only a spiritual nature, but at times capable of taking on human form.

anthropomorphism, an expression in human form of a being that is not human, usually of God, such as, "the eyes of God."

apologetics, the attempt to defend a set of beliefs, commonly associated with religious beliefs.

aseity, having a nature that is not derived, or that is not-dependent.

atemporal eternity, the view that eternity completely transcends time.

atheism, the view that God does not exist, or that there is strong evidence that he does not exist.

atonement, as a theological term, to make payment for sin.

Bayes' Theorem , the formula for conditional probabilities, where the probabilities of the antecedent are the prior probabilities, and those on the right (the consequent of the conditional) are conditional probabilities.

behaviorism, philosophical, the view that persons are reducible to behavior.

belief, to be in a positive psychological state relative to a proposition or statement such that the proposition or statement is thought to be true.

best-of-all-possible worlds, the idea that there is a best world of all the possible worlds facing God when he contemplated bringing a world into existence.

blik, the idea of R. M. Hare, that religious beliefs are not truth claims, but rather, ways of looking at the world.

Brahma, in the Hindu religion, the supreme soul or essence of the universe.

Christian Empiricism (exemplified in Thomas Reid), the view that knowledge comes from experience, and the sensory knowing apparatus is trustworthy because God created it.

Christology, the doctrine or theory of Christ, the Second Person of the Christian Trinity.

compatibilism, respecting free will and determinism, it is the belief that both can be given a sense such that both can be taken as true.

Confucianism, the eastern religion initiated by the Chinese thinker, Confucius (about 600 B.C.)

consistency strategy, to attempt to show two alleged contradictory propositions are really logically compatible because both are compatible with a third proposition.

contemplation, to attend to, meditate upon or concentrate upon, as with intellectual or spiritual matters.

Cosmological argument, to argue from factual premises about the world to the existence of a supreme being.

counterbalancing good, a good which on balance equally counterweighs an evil.

counterfactual conditionals of freedom , conditional propositions that pertain to human free choice, where the antecedent (the prior term) is false, and in some sense necessitates the consequent, such that, were the antecedent true, the consequent would be true.

de dicto **necessity,** propositional necessity, for example, 2 + 2 = 4.

de re **necessity**, necessity with regard to being, such as a necessary being, an attribute theists commonly ascribe to God.

decree, the eternal will of God often expressed as the divine decree(s).

defeater, a line of reasoning or argument which discounts or destroys another.

deism, the view that God is the creator of the world, but that he no longer has anything to do with it.

deontological, having to do with duty or obligation, rather than consequences.

Design argument, to argue from alleged intelligence and purpose in the universe, to a supernatural universe maker.

dharma, in Hinduism, a religious law or conformity to it, or an ancient sage.

desire, to long for, want or wish for.

divine command theory, the view that the term "good" means "what God commands," such is the view presented and defended by Robert Merrihew Adams.

doxastic assurance, having a positive conviction relative to a belief, that it is true.

dualism, regarding the question, What is a person?, it is the position that persons are made up of two distinct and independent substances, mind and body.

duty, to have a moral obligation to render some action or service to another.

dysteological suffering, suffering that appears to have no reason or justification.

epistemic dilemma , the idea that there is a problem regarding beliefs held by a person, because the beliefs either appear to be contradictory, or really are. The former are soft epistemic dilemmas, the latter are hard epistemic dilemmas.

epistemic distance, pertaining to the creature and the Creator, God is viewed as not intending to transparently reveal himself to the creature.

epistemic probability, the probable truth of propositions or statements.

epistemology, having to do with theory of knowledge.

eschatology, the doctrine of last things.

essence, the basic reality of an entity.

ET-simultaneity, the contemporary occurrence of events in God's eternity, with "contemporary" having a special meaning.

eternal, having no beginning or ending.

evidentialism, the view that one ought to proportion one's belief to the evidence.

evil, surd, evil that appears to be without reason or justification.

ex nihilo, as in creation, creation is viewed as not coming from some preexistent stuff or matter.

explanans , the explanation in the task of definition.

explanandum, what is to be explained in the definitional task.

facts, hard, soft,, "hard_," a dated fact, such as, "I was offered a job at time t," whereas if I was offered a job two weeks before, but not at t, we have a "soft_" about t."

faith, a concept with many different meanings, with one standard definition that analyzes the term into three parts, "knowledge" (*notitia*), "conviction" (*assensus*), "trust" (*fiducia*).

fall, as in the Fall, the moral corruption that entered the human family historically, as held by Augustine; others take the term as symbolizing the moral corruption universal to the human family.

falsification, to provide evidence that a proposition or statement under consideration is false.

family resemblance, the idea in the "later Wittgenstein," that certain terms may not be definable in terms of necessary and sufficient conditions, but rather bear a similarity to each other only with regard to certain features.

fideism, the view that religious belief rests on faith alone, not on evidence or facts.

finite-infinite distinction, an entity is finite if it has boundaries or limits, and infinite, if it has no boundaries or limits.

foreknowledge, to know in advance what will happen.

foundationalism, the view in theory of knowledge, that there are basic beliefs which can be known and are certain, the truth of which does not depend on prior beliefs.

free knowledge, knowledge of what is actual.

free will, libertarian, the view that an agent can make choices that are not necessitated by antecedent causes and conditions.

free will defense, the arguments of Augustine and Plantinga, that evil exists and is to be explained in terms of morally bad choices of free agents, or the possibility of such choices.

frequency theory of probability, the view of probability that focuses on the relative frequencies of events (Hans Reichenbach, Wesley Salmon).

God, a supernatural being, the God of Christianity.

goods, means or ends which have positive value.

gratuitous evil, an evil which appears to have no reason or justification.

greater-good defense, the idea that for every evil, there is a counterbalancing good which logically requires it, or some evil like it, and some evils have overbalancing goods which logically require these evils, or some evils at least as negative.

Haecceitism, that quality in terms of which a thing becomes a definite individual.

hermeneutics, the science of the principles of interpretation.

hiddenness of God, God so orders the universe he created that there is little evidence of His existence.

heuristic, a device that stimulates interest or furthers the investigation of an inquiry.

Hinduism, an eastern religion of India (with beginnings about 1700 B.C..).

identity theory, the view that the mind is identical with the brain.

image of God, elements of the creature resemble in some way features of the divine nature, such as in respect to knowledge, holiness, and knowledge of the truth.

imitatio dei, in imitation of God.

immutability, the property of changelessness, commonly ascribed to God.

imputed righteousness, righteousness that is transferred.

incarnation, an entity that assumes a human nature or form.

incomprehensibility, the attribute of not being fully understood because the being in question is transcendent in respect to knowledge, for some it is so radical as to include a difference as to mode of knowing, the content of knowledge, and the object of knowledge.

inconsistency strategy, to attempt to show a set of beliefs is untenable because it is contradictory.

incontinence, to fail to show moral control over one's appetites and wants.

indexed propositions, propositions which are so particularized that they pick out certain specifics of states of affairs, such as a specific time (*It is now 10* A.M..), or a first first-person reference as in a first-person report, for example, *I sense that I am in pain.*

inductive probability, the probability of an inference from premises to a conclusion, such as, *if b, then-probably c.*

infallibility, the attribute of being without error in respect to knowledge.

Islam, the religion that worships Allah (with beginnings about 600 A.D.).

immortality, to live after death, the view of ancients like Plato, who held that the soul lives on after death because it is not capable of being destroyed.

Judaism, the O.T. religion that worships the Old Testament deity, Jahweh (with beginnings about 2000 B.C.)

Karma, the principle that individuals reap what they sow, and that this happens without fail through the workings of nature.

kenotic Christology, the idea that Christ, the Second person of the Trinity, in the incarnation, emptied himself of the attributes of omnipresence, omniscience and omnipotence.

kerygma, the basic kernel of the Gospel, the preaching of religious truth.

law, natural, principles in nature which admit of no exception. In ethics, the view that there are universally valid ethical principles known by reason alone, and so they are accessible to all persons.

lemma, a theorem proved in the course of, and for the sake of another theorem.

libertarian freedom, freedom which involves choices that are not necessitated by antecedent causes and conditions.

Logos, the Second Person of the Trinity (Christianity).

metaphor, a figure of speech, in which a word or expression meaning one thing is analogously used to depict something else (*She was a light to others.*)

metaphysics, theory of reality, or of what is real.

meticulous providence, guidance of God that extends to every detail and event of the world so that nothing happens by accident.

middle knowledge, knowledge of counterfactual conditionals of freedom (see Molinist).

miracle, according to Hume, a violation of a law of nature; others take a moderate line such that it is viewed as a special convergence of laws of nature brought about by God or by powers he bestows upon creatures.

modal, *de dicto* (see *de dicto*) having to do with the affirmation of possibility, impossibility, necessity, or contingency of a proposition, or in cases of *de re* (see *de re*) the same modes are applied to entities.

model, a way of looking at things.

Molinist, one who like Molina, denies the Boethian way of solving God's claim to knowledge of what free persons would do, and contends that God has middle knowledge, that is, knowledge of counterfactual conditionals of freedom.

monotheism, the belief that there is one God.

Mysterium tremendum, the idea of Rudolph Otto, that there is a feature of reality that brings forth awe and fear in the creature.

mystical, not having rational explanation or account.

mystical experience, an encounter that defies rational explanation. According to William James, they are either of an internal sort, or external in nature. The former involve interior states while the latter involves a sense of oneness with the external world.

mysticism, the tradition that gives central attention to mystical experiences.

natural theology, that branch of theology which focuses on God's self-revelation in nature. It's what can be known about God by the natural light of reason without special revelation (the Bible).

naturalism, that view which claims that there is nothing beyond the realm of the physical universe.

necessary being, a being which could not not exist.

Numinous, the idea of Rudolph Otto, that there is something beyond the sensory world.

omnibenevolence, the property or attribute of being all-good or of having a disposition to maximize the good for all creatures.

omnifiscence, the property or attribute of all-creating.

omnipotence, that being is omnipotent who can bring about any logically possible states of affairs also consistent with the nature of the agent in question.

omnipresence, that property of being everywhere present, or the ability to act everywhere and manifest a presence everywhere.

omniscience, the property of having knowledge of all true propositions.

Ontological argument, to argue from the nature of a being defined in such a way to his existence.

orison, a process of meditation and spiritual discipline whereby a person draws close to God.

paradox, there are two senses, the first says there is an actual contradiction, the other says that there appears to be a contradiction, but a resolution of the conflict is possible.

perfectly free, an agent is perfectly free if he can do only morally perfect actions.

pluralism, religious, the position that all religious orientations have a legitimacy, and that no one set of religious beliefs has exclusive claims to truth.

possibilism, universal possibilism, one reading of Descartes which sees him as affirming the view that there are no necessary truths, and limited possibilism, which views Descartes as saying that there are necessary truths but God has given them that status.

praiseworthy, the attribute ascribed to a being because of earned merit of some sort.

predestination, the doctrine that events are ordered to happen in a certain way in advance; the view entertained by John Calvin (1509-1564).

prima facie, at first glance, or upon first inspection.

principle of sufficient reason, the principle that things do not happen without a cause adequate to bring them about.

process theology, that theological tradition which has its roots in the process philosophy of Alfred North Whitehead, who held that the world is in process, and that God is incorporated into that process.

proof, something that is person-relative, or relative to a person holding beliefs which serve as premises to an argument, and the person in question holds the premises to be true, and the argument as not begging the question.

RT-simultaneity, is the occurrence at the same time within the reference frame of a given observer.

ratio evidens, evidence of reason.

rationalism, in the religious realm, the view that religious belief must rest on reason, not physical evidence.

rationality, the property of having a coherent account according to the dictates of reason.

recreationism, the view of Bruce Reichenbach, that persons are physical beings, and that this is the promise of the resurrection spoken of in the New Testament.

redemption, the doctrine that sin requires some sort of payment.

reincarnation, the doctrine that persons pass from one body to another at death, and that the series is endless.

relata, two or more things in relation.

resurrection, the doctrine that humans live on in a new body after death.

sacraments, certain elements and ceremonies in worship which are a means of grace (as in the Roman Catholic Church).

satori, a level of achievement, usually brought about by means of a puzzle that is not capable of resolution by rational means.

self-transcendence, willing to be myself, and letting God be God.

sign, a mark or device having some special meaning.

significantly free, an agent that is free in the sense that he/she can do good or evil.

simpliciter, without qualifiers or further qualifications.

sin, a moral failure or fault for which an agent is morally responsible and so blameworthy.

simple foreknowledge, knowledge of all actual free choices of created agents, including those yet to be made, but not those choices that might have been but never are actualized.

states of affairs, what is the case.

sufficient reason (see Principle of Sufficient Reason)

supernaturalism, the view of the universe which allows that there are entities such as angels and God over and above the physical cosmos.

symbol, something that stands for something else.

Taoism, a system of religious belief founded upon the doctrine of the ancient Chinese philosopher, Laotsze (about 550 B.C), and ranks with Confucianism and Buddhism as one of the three main religions of China.

Teleological argument, the argument for God's existence based on premises that draw attention to design and purpose in the universe.

temporal eternity, that view of eternity which holds that temporal terms like 'before" and "after" apply, have meaning and application, and does not claim that eternity is "outside" of time.

theodicy, to offer a complete account of all of the reasons God has for all the evils that exist in the world. Defense is a more modest posture, and involves offering a reason or reasons that might account for some evils.

transworld depravity (Plantinga), a morally defective essence that has existence in more than one possible world.

transworld identity, an entity that enjoys existence in more than one possible world.

Trinity, the doctrine of Christianity which says that God is a trinity of persons, Father, Son, and Holy Spirit, and that each is divine.

Verification Principle, the central principle of Logical Positivism, which says that a statement or proposition (an empirical or fact claim, not an analytic statement) is meaningful only if it can be verified by observation.

Via negativa, an approach to definition or explanation which resorts to description or definition by way of negation (e.g., God as spirit is not body).

world, according to Ludwig Wittgenstein, is all that is the case.

Yoga, in Hindu religious philosophy, Union with the Supreme Being.

Zen, that branch of Mahayana Buddhism that claims lineage back to Gautama.

Zoroastrianism, that system of thought begun by Zoroaster.

Bibliography

I. FAITH AND REASON

CLARK, KELLY JAMES. *Return to Reason.* Grand Rapids: William B. Eerdmans, 1990.

DELANEY, C. P., editor. *Rationality and Religious Belief.* Notre Dame: University of Notre Dame Press, 1979.

EVANS, C. STEPHEN, WESTPHAL, MEROLD, editors. *Christian Perspectives on Religious Knowledge.* Grand Rapids: William B. Eerdmans, 1993.

EVANS, C. STEPHEN. *Philosophy of Religion, Thinking About Faith.* Downers Grove: InterVarsity Press, 1985.

EVANS, C. STEPHEN. *Subjectivity & Religious Belief.* Grand Rapids: Christian University Press, 1978.

FLINT, THOMAS P., editor. *Christian Philosophy.* Notre Dame: University of Notre Dame Press, 1990.

HICK, JOHN. *Faith and Knowledge,* 2nd ed. Ithaca: Cornell University Press, 1978.

MILLER, ED. L. *God and Reason,* 2nd ed. Englewood Cliffs: Prentice-Hall, 1995.

O'HEAR, ANTHONY. *Experience, Explanation and Faith.* London: Routledge & Kegan Paul, 1984.

PADGETT, ALAN, editor. *Reason and the Christian Religion.* Oxford: Clarendon Press, 1994.

PETERSON, MICHAEL, HASKER, WILLIAM, REICHENBACH, BRUCE, BASINGER, DAVID. *Reason & Religious Belief.* Oxford: Oxford University Press, 1991.

PHILLIPS, D. Z. *Faith After Foundationalism.* London: Routledge, 1988.

PLANTINGA, ALVIN, editor. *Faith and Philosophy.* Grand Rapids: William B. Eerdmans, 1964.

PLANTINGA, ALVIN, WOLTERSTORFF, NICHOLAS, editors. *Faith and Rationality:* Notre Dame, University of Notre Dame Press, 1983.

SWINBURNE, RICHARD. *Faith and Reason.* Oxford: Clarendon Press, 1981.

STUMP, ELEONORE, editor. *Reasoned Faith.* Ithaca: Cornell University Press, 1993.

YANDELL, KEITH. *Christianity and Philosophy.* Grand Rapids: William B. Eerdmans Publishing Company, 1984.

WOLTERSTORFF, NICHOLAS. *Reason within the Bounds of Religion,* 2nd ed. Grand Rapids: William B. Eerdmans Publishing, 1984.

II. ARGUMENTS FOR THE EXISTENCE OF GOD

ALSTON, WILLIAM. *Perceiving God.* Ithaca: Cornell University Press, 1991.

DAVIS, STEPHEN. *Logic and the Nature of God.* London: Macmillan, 1983.

FLEW, ANTONY & MACINTYRE, ALASDAIRE. *New Essays in Philosophical Theology.* London, SCM Press, 1955.

GUTTING, GARY. *Religious Belief and Religious Skepticism.* Notre Dame: University of Notre Dame Press, 1982.

HICK, JOHN, editor. *The Existence of God.* New York: Macmillan, 1964.

HICK, JOHN. *Philosophy of Religion,* 3rd ed. Englewood Cliffs: Prentice-Hall, 1983.

KATZ, STEVEN T., editor. *Mysticism and Philosophical Analysis.* Oxford: Oxford University Press, 1978.

KÜNG, HANS. *Does God Exist?* Random House, New York, 1981.
MATSON, WALLACE I. *The Existence of God.* Ithaca: Cornell University Press, 1965.
MAVRODES, GEORGE. *Belief in God.* New York: Random House, 1970.
PLANTINGA, ALVIN. *God, Freedom and Evil.* New York: Harper & Row, 1974.
PLANTINGA, ALVIN. *God and Other Minds.* Ithaca: Cornell University Press, 1974.
PROUDFOOT, WAYNE. *Religious Experience.* Berkeley: University of California Press, 1985.
REICHENBACH, BRUCE R. *The Cosmological Argument: A Reassessment.* Springfield: Thomas, 1972.
ROSS, JAMES F. *Philosophical Theology.* Indianapolis: Bobbs-Merrill, 1969.
SWINBURNE, RICHARD. *The Existence of God.* Oxford: Clarendon Press, 1979.
UNDERHILL, EVELYN. *Mysticism.* Cleveland: Meridian Books, 1955.
YANDELL, KEITH. *The Epistemology of Religious Experience.* Cambridge: Cambridge University Press, 1993.

III. PROBLEMS OF EVIL AND STRATEGIES OF DEFENSE*

AHERN, M. B. *The Problem of Evil.* London: Routledge & Kegan Paul, 1971.
BERTOCCI, PETER. *The Goodness of God.* Washington: University Press of America, 1981.
GEACH, PETER. *Providence and Evil.* Cambridge: Cambridge University Press, 1977.
GRIFFIN, DAVID RAY. *God, Power and Evil: A Process Theology.* Philadelphia: The Westminster Press, 1976.
HICK, JOHN. *Evil and the God of Love,* 2nd ed. New York: Harper & Row, 1977.
HUME, DAVID. *Dialogues Concerning Natural Religion,* Norman Kemp Smith, editor. New York: The Bobbs-Merrill Co., 1947.
KENNY, ANTHONY. *The God of the Philosophers.* Oxford: Clarendon Press, 1979.
LEIBNIZ, G. W. *Theodicy,* Austin Farrer, editor, E. M. Huggard, trans. New Haven: Yale University Press, 1952.
MADDEN, EDWARD H. and HARE, PETER H. *Evil and the Concept of God.* Springfield: Charles C. Thomas Publishers, 1968.
McCLOSKEY, H. J. *God and Evil.* The Hague: Martinus Nijhoff, 1974.
PETERSON, MICHAEL. *Evil and the Christian God.* Grand Rapids: Baker Book House, 1982.
PIKE, NELSON. *God and Evil.* Englewood Cliffs: Prentice-Hall, 1964.
PLANTINGA, ALVIN. *The Nature of Necessity.* Oxford: Oxford University Press, 1974.
REICHENBACH, BRUCE. *Evil and a Good God.* New York: Fordham University Press, 1982.
ROWE, WILLIAM. *Philosophy of Religion.* Encino: Dickenson Pub., 1978.
STEWART, MELVILLE Y. *The Greater-Good Defence, An Essay on the Rationality of Faith.* London: Macmillan; New York: St. Martin's Press, 1993.
YANDELL, KEITH., editor. *God, Man and Religion.* New York: McGraw-Hill, 1973.

---

*See the bibliography at the end of William Alston's selection.

IV. THE ATTRIBUTES OF GOD**

ALSTON, WILLIAM. *Divine Nature and Human Language.* Ithaca: Cornell University Press, 1989.

CRAIG, WILLIAM LANE. *The Only Wise God: The Compatibility of Divine Foreknowledge and Human Freedom.* Grand Rapids: Baker Book House, 1987.

FERRÉ, FREDERICK. *Language, Logic and God.* London: Harper & Row, 1961.

FISCHER, JOHN MARTIN, editor. *God, Foreknowledge, and Freedom.* Stanford: Stanford University Press, 1989.

FREDOSSO, ALFRED J., translator. *Luis De Molina, On Divine Foreknowledge* (Part IV of the *Concordia*). Ithaca: Cornell University Press, 1988.

HARTSHORNE, CHARLES. *The Divine Relativity.* New Haven: Yale University Press, 1948.

HASKER, WILLIAM. *God, Time, and Knowledge.* Ithaca: Cornell University Press, 1989.

LUCAS, J. R. *The Future.* Oxford: Basil Blackwell, 1989.

MORRIS, THOMAS V., editor. *Divine and Human Action.* Notre Dame: University of Notre Dame Press, 1989.

NASH, RONALD H. *The Concept of God.* Grand Rapids: Zondervan Publishing House, 1983.

ORLEBEKE, CLIFTON J., and SMEDES, LEWIS B., editors. *God and the Good.* Grand Rapids: William B. Eerdmans, 1975.

PADGETT, ALAN. *God, Eternity, and the Nature of Time.* London: Macmillan; New York: St. Martin's Press, 1993.

PIKE, NELSON. *God and Timelessness.* London: RKP, 1970.

PLANTINGA, ALVIN. *Does God Have a Nature?* Milwaukee: Marquette University Press, 1980.

SWINBURNE, RICHARD. *The Christian God.* Oxford: Clarendon Press, 1994.

SWINBURNE, RICHARD. *The Coherence of Theism.* Oxford: Clarendon Press, 1993.

URBAN, LINWOOD, WALTON, DOUGLAS N., editors. *The Power of God.* New York: Oxford University Press, 1978.

WIERENGA, EDWARD. *The Nature of God.* Ithaca: Cornell University Press, 1989.

ZAGZEBSKI, LINDA. *The Dilemma of Freedom and Foreknowledge.* Oxford: Oxford University Press, 1991.

V. MIRACLES***

FLEW, ANTHONY. "Miracles," *Encyclopedia of Philosophy*, Vol. 5.

FLEW, ANTHONY, editor. *Of Miracles.* La Salle: Open Court, 1985.

KELLER, ERNEST, KELLER, MARIE-LUISE. *Miracles in Dispute.* Philadelphia: Fortress Press, 1969.

LEWIS, C. S. *Miracles.* New York: Macmillan, 1978.

MACKIE, J. L. *The Miracle of Theism.* Oxford: Clarendon Press, 1982.

**See the bibliography at the end of Alan Padgett's essay.

***See the bibliogaphy at the end of John Earman's essay.

MARTIN, MICHAEL. *Atheism: A Philosophical Justification*. Philadelphia: Temple University Press, 1990.
PURTILL, RICHARD L. *Thinking About Religion: A Philosophical Introduction to Religion*. Englewood Cliffs: Prentice-Hall, 1978.
ROGO, D. SCOTT. *Miracles*. New York: Dial Press, 1982.
SMART, NINIAN. *Philosophers and Religious Truth*. London:SCM, 1964.
SWINBURNE, RICHARD. *The Concept of Miracle*. London: Macmillan, 1970.

VI. DEATH AND IMMORTALITY

BADHAM, PAUL, BADHAM, LINDA. *Immortality or Extinction?* London: Macmillan, 1982.
COOPER, JOHN W. *Body, Soul, & Life Everlasting*. Grand Rapids: William B. Eerdmans, 1989.
HICK, JOHN. *Death and Eternal Life*. London: Collins, 1976.
PENELHUM, TERRENCE. *Survival and Disembodied Existence*. London: Routledge & Kegan Paul, 1970.
PHILIPS, D. Z. *Death and Immortality*. London: Macmillan; New York: St. Martin's, 1970.
REICHENBACH, BRUCE. *Is Man the Phoenix?* Washington: Christian University Press, 1978.
RUSSELL, BERTRAND. *Why I Am Not a Christian*. London: George Allen & Unwin, 1957.
RYLE, GILBERT. *The Concept of Mind*. New York: Barnes and Noble, 1949.
SABOM, MICHAEL L. *Recollections of Death*. New York: Harper & Row, 1982.
SHOEMAKER, SYDNEY, & SWINBURNE, RICHARD. *Personal Identity*. Oxford: Blackwell, 1984.
SWINBURNE, RICHARD. *The Evolution of the Soul*. Oxford: Clarendon Press, 1986.

VII. RELIGIOUS PLURALISM

ANDERSON, G. H., and STRANSKY, T. F., editors. *Christ's Lordship and Religious Pluralism*. Maryknoll: Orbis, 1981.
HESSELGRAVE, DAVID, editor. *Theology and Mission*. Grand Rapids: Baker, 1978.
HICK, JOHN. *God Has Many Names*. Philadelphia: Westminster, 1982.
HICK, JOHN, editor. *Truth and Dialogue in World Religions*. Philadelphia: Westminster Press, 1974.
HICK, JOHN, and HEBBLEWAITE, BRIAN, editors. *Christianity and Other Religions*. Philadelphia: Fortress, 1980.
KNITTER, PAUL F. *No Other Name?* Maryknoll: Orbis, 1985.
NETLUND, HAROLD. *Dissonant Voices: Religious Pluralism and the Question of Truth*. Grand Rapids: William B. Eerdmans, 1992.
TOYNBEE, ARNOLD. *Christianity Among the Religions of the World*. New York: Scribners, 1957.
TROELTSCH, ERNST. *The Absoluteness of Christianity and the History of Religions*. Richmond: John Knox, 1971.

Index